Dear Family

Dear Family

THE L'ABRI FAMILY LETTERS
1961–1986

Edith Schaeffer

A Ruth Graham Dienert Book

1817

HARPER & ROW, PUBLISHERS, SAN FRANCISCO

New York, Grand Rapids, Philadelphia, St. Louis
London, Singapore, Sydney, Tokyo

Library of Congress Cataloging-in-Publication Data
Schaeffer, Edith.
  Dear Family

  "A Ruth Graham Dienert book."
  1. Schaeffer, Edith—Correspondence. 2. Schaeffer, Edith—Family. 3. Schaeffer family 4. L'Abri (Organization) 5. Christian life. 6. Christian biography.
I. Title.
BR1725.S354A4   1989   267'.13'0924 [B]   88-45683
ISBN 0-06-067096-7

FIRST EDITION

89   90   91   92   93   HC   10 9 8 7 6 5 4 3 2 1

To my four children and their spouses four!!!!
and
My fifteen grandchildren plus spouses four!!!
and
My five great-grandchildren (the fourth generation)

– Priscilla Schaeffer & John Sandri (Mr. & Mrs.) –
Lisby Sandri & Greg Laughery (Mr. & Mrs.)
Vincent Laughery
Rebecca Sandri & Rodman Miller (Mr. & Mrs.)
Kimberly Miller
Thomas Miller
Giandy Sandri
– Susan Schaeffer & Ranald Macaulay (Mr. & Mrs.) –
Margaret Macaulay & Doug Curry (Mr. & Mrs.)
Gordon Curry
Elizabeth Curry
Kirsteen Macaulay
Fiona Macaulay
Ranald John Macaulay
Fostered by Macaulays
Philip Hodder
Abigail Hodder
– Deborah Schaeffer & Udo Middelmann (Mr. & Mrs.) –
Natasha Middelmann & Jean Francois Veu (Mr. & Mrs.)
Samantha Middelmann
Naomi Middelmann
Hannah Middelmann
Isaac Middelmann
– Francis A. Schaeffer V & Genie Walsh (Mr. & Mrs.) –
Jessica Schaeffer
Francis A. Schaeffer VI
John L. Schaeffer

CONTENTS

Dear Family

FOREWORD

A Letter to You from the Author

Dear Reader:

You have read the first volume, and perhaps you *feel* those twelve years from 1948 to 1960 as if you had lived through them with us. How astounding it is that words can bring to us sights, smells, sounds, feelings, hopes, fears, excitement, and sorrow as if we were living in another part of the world, or in another period of history. What a truly exciting, as well as basic thing it is that we are "verbalizing creatures"! If we could not relate happenings, tell stories, describe mountains and seas, snow storms and battles, quiet waters and green pastures, we would be limited to the immediate surroundings, and to the people our eyes could see. Spoken words are so important to our expressing what is inside our heads and to hearing what is going on in someones else's head. However, written words make it possible not only to know what someone was thinking long before we were born, but also to read accounts of what took place . . . many years ago . . . as well as thousands of miles away!

What a wave of thankfulness comes over me as I think of books! What would life be without books? Books to read in a hammock swinging on a wide porch, books to read on a beach, or in the woods, books to read in a room high up in a city block of apartments with a bird in a cage for company, books to read snuggled in bed on a cold night with just enough pillows. Books—so essential to being transported into another place, another time, with another group of people. Books are the "door" to diversity and "transportation" to another part of the world, even to reliving pieces of past history. Books are the most rapid way to get away from a place or a situation, to have a change of atmosphere. Although life is too short to explore all our interests, how great that books can multiply the possibilities for discovery!

Dear reader, you followed us through twelve years of life in volume one, *With Love, Edith*. Now prepare to walk through twenty-six years.

This continued series of Family Letters follows along regularly through the years. Each letter was written without knowing what the next would contain. I never dreamt that my typewriter would be moving to a house near St. Mary's Hospital in Rochester, Minnesota, and that the last chapter of Fran's life would be the content of one of my Family Letters! This typewriter faithfully wrote for me in Switzerland, then went on responding to my fingers and pouring out words on empty paper here in Minnesota.

Many details have been carefully recorded . . . life, death, birth, marriages, illnesses, accidents, answered prayers, disappointments. However this volume two has had to be cut even more than volume one. A portion of *each* letter is in the book, but 80 to 85 percent of each letter has been *cut* out. It was an agony to slash for Elsa Van Buskirk (my sister), for Mary Lou Sather (a friend here in Rochester), and for my editor Christine Anderson. I often felt physical pain when I had to cut out one more story of the Lord's amazing work in lives, or the description of what was taking place in L'Abri or in the families of Workers.

I even hated to leave out lists of names, let alone stories of those same people. I can imagine someone grabbing the book and saying, "I was there in 1973 . . . let me find that part . . . Oh . . . there is nothing in about the week I was there" or "my name isn't even mentioned."

All I can say is, when your name is entered into the Lamb's Book of Life no one can ever edit it out. That book never gets too long . . . and the One who records our names knows the very number of hairs on our heads and doesn't forget the details, let alone where we belong in history!

What you have here is only a part of what was written in the first place, and that was only a part of what happened in lives. We have an eternity to "read" or "discover" the way it all fits together.

With much love,

EDITH

1961

(Back Home!)
Chalet les Mélèzes
Huemoz sur Ollon, Switzerland

Dear Family:

It seems to me that the heart of Satan's battle with the Christian is that if he can upset our trust or cause our firm belief to waver in *practice*, he has gained a victory. He attacked Eve at this point. . . . "Ye shall not surely die." Whom did she believe? He attacked Job in the area of trusting the Lord in the midst of all the troubles and difficulties. Satan is not very original and you'll find him following the same pattern in his attacks upon you. At least I do find this in my life. How thankful we can be for the pattern the Lord gives us in "overcoming him"—not once, or twice, but over and over again. . . .

Our opportunities here, in this realm, have been many since writing the last letter. The frustrations we experienced as we returned from America were many: the emotional struggle of leaving families behind; the frustration of finding a coal-dust-coated Franky the first morning "out" (taking hours to clean up as the freighter *Corvaglia* moved out to sea); the heavy responsibility of Workers at the chalet handling both physical and spiritual work connected with having *112 different* guests, some for as long as three weeks, some for several recurrent visits during the months of July and August and the first of September; the short-lived joy of the newly hooked up stove to replace the one the electricians had spoiled . . . only to find it also had been hooked up to receive too

---

*After the first book of L'Abri Family Letters, *With Love, Edith,* was finished and ready for press, another letter was discovered that should have been included. Although this second book says 1961–1986, you will see that the first letter here was written in 1960. Since I can't send a copy of this to all of you to help bridge the gap, I'll slip it in as your first letter in this book, even though the date doesn't match what is on the cover. You can excuse me and thank me at the same time, because the history is more complete with it.

many volts, plunging us back into the use of the gas stoves (already described); the lack of water for over 10 days; the discovery that our hoped-for and rejoiced-about new Worker scheduled to arrive in September (Mary Meester, Aly's sister) had been put to bed for an indefinite time by her doctor—verdict: jaundice!; the statement of our local doctor that he felt Trudy should go home to have her appendix out; the sudden announcement that Beau Site, rented as a part of L'Abri for three years and in constant use of young men over weekends as well as for Workers' living quarters is *for sale!*; the realization that the living room at the same time is becoming too small for the number coming to church, bringing the need of a chapel into more immediate reality; the provision for Debby of a fine arrangement for living with a Christian family and going to a Swiss girls' school in Lausanne, which brought with it the loss of Debby's help here with Franky and various other things; the increase in the number coming for weekends coming simultaneously with the decrease in Workers; the abscessed tooth Franky suffered for a week and sciatica added to my headaches time after time; Beau Site's leaking roof and the breaking of the grate in Chesalet's little furnace; the coming of 15 patients to Bellevue [rehabilitation center] with so many of them really helpless that it seems impossible for the Workers there to combat the fatigue of the needful long working hours to care for them adequately. . . .

Those were some of the small, and big, opportunities to trust Him, and at the same time, temptations to sink down in despair. These few "cut out bits" will help you to see what we saw as we returned: that this work is the work of the Spirit, and not of any one human being. And now that we are back again, we all feel that He is unfolding a *new* step.

The new step? Ran has felt led of the Lord to enroll in London University's course leading to a degree in theology, which can be studied "externally." Therefore, he will be studying here at L'Abri, and helping in the work as his "practical theology" as well as having discussions or "seminars" with Fran to go over various things which will arise in his studies. At the same time we received letters from Deirdre and her husband, Richard (a Christian pilot preparing to be a missionary pilot), asking if they could come here for six months of study and at the same time help in the work. We feel the Lord has given us a name for this special place of study and preparation and are calling it "Farel House." Farel was the Reformer who preached in Switzerland before Calvin, and who came to Huemoz to preach many years ago, being chased out at that time with rotten potatoes!! He preached in the church in Ollon at the foot of our mountain road, and this led to the Reformation in this part of Switzerland. Farel House will open in November with three students, in the sunroom of Beau Site, where five desks have been ordered to be made to special measurements by the carpenter M. Dubi, and where a "Branch Library of the Evangelical Library of London" will provide some of the needed books, as well as providing additional books for those coming to

L'Abri to read. We have no plans for enlarging Farel House, nor any desire to see a big thing, but we feel the Lord has opened this as simply a step more in the same direction as He has led in the past in bringing Workers for a year in the middle of their studies. "Answers" to atheists, Hindus, existentialists, etc., will not be learned academically, but in listening to the constant and very real discussions with the stream of people the Lord brings here.

Another new step the Lord seems to be opening up is in the direction of having a chapel on the land Betty bought below Chesalet last year. The Lord has sent in some money toward such a chapel, and Hansjorg, a Swiss student of architecture who will be graduating in January, and who was born again here a little more than a year ago, is drawing up lovely plans for such a building to be presented to the community for their approval and permission to build. . . .

One more news item: Mr. and Mrs. Francis A. Schaeffer have the pleasure of announcing the engagement of their daughter, Susan Jane, to Mr. Ranald Macaulay of Southern Rhodesia. Sue and Ran expect, Lord willing, to be married sometime next summer, the definite date needing to be fitted in to the time of his parents' coming, the work of L'Abri, and his exams at London University. We rejoice that the Lord has led them to help in L'Abri as Workers during the time of his preparation for whatever future work the Lord has in His plan for them. Ran, as you remember, is a graduate of Cambridge University in law, but felt called into the Lord's work sometime after his salvation in Cambridge over 3 years ago. Sue is taking her exams in anatomy, psychology, and so on, in Oxford at this present time, and then will return to teach in the mornings at Beau Soleil and help in the work of L'Abri the rest of the time.

Finally: David Woodson, L'Abri's youngest "Worker" is now a fine, healthy, six-month-old baby and has cut two teeth! He has completely charmed the writer of this letter, and I'm certain he is a great addition to the work in Italy!

With love in Him whose power is *great* and whose understanding is infinite,

EDITH

February 13, 1961   Cambridge, England

Dear Family:
. . . Just one year ago this week, Jane Stuart Smith came to L'Abri after having had her final talk with her manager, whom she told she was leaving opera. Since that time she has been a L'Abri Worker. You may remember that I told you in a previous letter how she felt the Lord spoke

to her to give up her costumes to Him, and how she did this in prayer, telling Him that if they were sold the money would go toward the building of a chapel on the field below Chalet le Chesalet. In a sense the sacrifice was made at that time, and the gorgeous costumes were no longer hers but the Lord's. However, they were still in trunks in Milan, and not in anyone else's possession. If anyone were to buy them, it would have to be someone who sang the same parts in the same operas for which the costumes were made, and it would have to be someone the same size—at least approximately. Humanly looking at it, this combination seemed unlikely, and the costumes sat there month after month. However, much prayer has continued through the months—and with God, all things are possible! This past week a climax came in this story, as a telegram arrived from a singer in Rome saying she would like to meet Jane and see the costumes—in Milan. The night before we left Switzerland to come here to England, Jane called from Milan, and I heard what the Lord had done. It is another instance of a supernatural answer to prayer. The singer, a Yugoslavian girl named Lucille, does sing all the same parts Jane did. She did not expect to be interested in the whole wardrobe as she has many of her own costumes already, but when she saw them— the beauty and the perfection of these silver embroidered velvets, brocades, handpainted silks and so on (designed especially for Jane), they simply took her breath away. She tried them all on, right down to the last glove and jewel and hat, and—they fit perfectly, even to her hands, feet, and head being the same size!! But the plan of the Lord did not stop there. Jane told Lucille the story of her conversion and of how the Lord led her out of opera, and into L'Abri work. Tears were shed before it was all over, and I would ask you to pray for Lucille's salvation—for the Lord's ways are beyond all imagination, and He is able to bring this whole matter to a more glorious conclusion than anyone could have expected.

It is not easy to fold up one's beloved possessions and to see them carried away to be used by someone else to dazzle the audiences one could have been standing before oneself. At such a moment Satan would like to turn the eyes of God's child toward the enormity of the sacrifice, and to whisper tempting thoughts of self-pity. This is the case for each of us and has been ever since Abraham toiled up the hill to tie Isaac his son and place him upon the wood on the altar. But He, who Himself folded away the glory of heaven to come down to that Bethlehem stable, suffered every temptation we can ever know and had victory over every one. He it is who died to make it possible for us to know victory in our own lives through the power of the Holy Spirit.

And the chapel? The amount being paid for the costumes is between two thousand five hundred and three thousand dollars. It would seem that this is the "sign" we have prayed for as that which would indicate that the chapel is to be begun this summer. I have pictured very vividly those costumes spread out on the flowery field below Chesalet—the

Jane Stuart Smith as Norma in
the opera Norma. *This is one of*
the costumes that I envision "turning into
chapel walls."

field which is now a gift of Betty Carlson's upon which to build a chapel. In my mind's eye those costumes change shape and rise up into wooden and fieldstone walls, with large glass windows making the mountain peaks form the fourth "wall." Now, I see another "picture" as these chapel walls in a very real way can be seen to be taking the place of the costumes about Jane's shoulders, giving a suitable background in this Alpine spot, where the Lord has placed her, to sing to His glory. Our prayer is that He may draw many to this spot, in His own amazing way, to hear His praises sung and preached, overlooking the magnificent mountain peaks which speak of the wonder of His creation, and that the Holy Spirit may open their eyes of understanding as they hear the message from His Word. Only the Lord knows the extent of the use of this new portion of the L'Abri work He has planned. . . .

You will remember that in the last Family Letter, written at the end of October, I listed a number of difficult and frustrating things that had been, and were, going on. Some of them continued (for instance, the new stove was not fixed and in working order until the end of January!), and added to these things we had a fair amount of illness, Jane was called away for four weeks, and we continued to feel the shortage of Workers. One who works as hard as anyone at L'Abri, quietly and so often in "unseen ways" (such as cleaning the stove and refrigerator when one might suppose she had gone to bed), is Trudy. During November she spent more time "filling in" in the kitchen and so on, than could be afforded from her work on the books. As a result the accounts got behind—so that it was mid-December before she got the final balances for October and November finished, and at 10 P.M. the night she got that far, a sickening fact showed up: for the first time in history, L'Abri had "overspent," for we had gone on spending normally, without realizing that money was low, and we should have been economizing drastically. Because there was money in the bank (designated for the chapel), no bills had been unpaid, but we had overspent in the two months a total sum of $686.00. The sudden news of this made it difficult to go quietly to sleep that night, and as we thought and prayed, a heaviness as to the possibility of finishing the year in this state settled over us. Christmas was just a few days off—and the year's end would come six days after that—would the year's books finish in the "red" this time, and could this be to the glory of the Lord? We had times of prayer together, and each one had special prayer for the need, but as mails came, and we rushed to see what was in them each day, very little arrived in the way of gifts, and a number of bills added to the dark picture.

On the 23rd of December Mr. Annex, the Zurich brother of the brothers who own Beau Site, came to talk to us to see whether we wanted to buy the house, or not. You can imagine how we shrank from talking to him at such a time. Not only had not enough come in designated for Beau Site to give us a sign as to what the Lord would have us do—but we had this heavy burden upon us. As Fran and I went down to talk with him in the living room, Franky got Debby and Susan and Linette together up in his room. "We've got to pray," he said. "Annex came, and we don't have money to buy Beau Site, so we've got to pray about it." As they prayed "around" the little circle sitting on Franky's bed, they weren't the only ones asking the Lord to show the way! Down in the living room we felt we saw the Lord's answer for that moment unfold in a miraculous way. For in a very short time we were telling this businessman the story of the work of L'Abri, and the fact that we live by prayer, and were frankly telling him we did not yet know what the Lord would have us do about Beau Site, although we need it for our work. He in turn told us the price he wants for it, but then surprisingly said, "Why don't you keep praying about it for two more months, and then we'll meet again. If God wants you to buy it, you will receive the money, and if not you may still rent it. However, I cannot see my way clear to make any repairs." In addition to this statement, he went on to show interest in spiritual things, and the conversation went on with Fran giving "answers" which turned it into that which sounded like a L'Abri Saturday night, instead of a business transaction! I came upstairs feeling I had seen the Lord working before my eyes, and needless to say everyone in the house was thrilled, including Franky. . . .

The next day found us all scurrying around making the usual preparations for going to Champéry for the Christmas Eve service. (We had considered before the Lord the expense for this service but in finding we had enough personal tithe money to cover it felt it the right thing to go on with plans.) Lunch must be early that day, and a dessert of tangerines and homemade cookies is eaten in the taxi on the way over. The morning bus brought Walter, an American student at the University of Lausanne whom the Christians in the Lausanne class had been praying for for some time . . . so for his benefit the L'Abri "story" was commenced as we whittled candles away with kitchen knives, at the back of the chapel, preparing them to poke into the logs, made now 12 years ago for the first Champéry Christmas Service, by an Englishwoman from Kenya! Deirdre (who made the posters announcing the services on the hotel bulletin boards . . . blue with silver snow flakes) was pointing out to her husband Richard the little room where she had heard the gospel preached for the first time *nine* years ago when she was a girl in finishing school. As the candles were being lit by Linette, Franky, Margaret (a Dutch girl from South America) and others, and more than 85 English people trooped in to take their places . . . that fearsome nagging feeling . . . that arose in connection with the financial need and the end of the year . . . kept creeping in beneath the rejoicing.

"Hello, hello," the call was from Montreux and it was Mr. Tchividjian asking a "favor." He explained that since his heart attack his doctor had forbidden him to come up to our altitude, and that therefore he and his family had very much been missing the church services. "Could I be selfish and ask that all of L'Abri come to me, after church tomorrow, for dinner and the afternoon? I will send the large taxi and a car and also see that you are driven back again. Mr. Schaeffer then could bring us a little message in the afternoon." This was the first time in history that all of L'Abri had been invited out to dinner! What a treat it would be not to have to do dishes and prepare dinner and tea. It also seemed the Lord was feeding us as with the "ravens," for now our provisions for the special Sunday dinner of the 25th could be saved for another meal! We drove down in the warm sunshine of a wonderfully crystal clear day, enjoying a restful view of the lake, and the unhurried feeling of no meal to prepare. We all remarked that it seemed like a fairy tale, as we sat in the large living room waiting to be served, instead of serving—and enjoying the sparkling blue of the lake below. After dinner Fran went to rest and pray before giving his message later in the afternoon. Then, just before the service was to begin, Mr. Tchividjian's eldest son and daughter lighted the many candles on their enormous pine tree whose branches were hung with oranges, and others carried in boxes and placed them on the floor by the tree. Franky excitedly sat with the rest of the children and received three lovely presents much to his delighted amazement. We were filled with the warmth of sharing this family occasion with the reality of being truly *one* family in the Lord. Then in the midst of the glow a thick white envelope was dropped into my lap by Mr. Tchividjian. I peeked at the beautiful Christmas card and its handwritten message, and then drew in my breath as I saw the figures written on an attached check; my eyes smarted with quick tears as I whispered to the Lord, "You have answered, the year is to finish once again with no deficit. How great is Thy faithfulness, and Oh Lord Thou art there! Thou art there!" I quickly slipped it to Fran who was sitting next to me, and I knew by his face that the same thoughts and worship were filling his mind. Never will we forget that afternoon and the Lord's over-and-above-answer that Christmas day, as the check of 5,000 Swiss francs (about $1,250.00) met the need in full, but the *way* it happened was gift in itself of deep assurance to both the givers, and those of us who received, that He had directed and planned. After the service, during which the young people sang together in front of the candle-lit tree, and Fran gave a long and thorough study on Bethlehem—The House of Bread—tracing its history and the spiritual significance from Old Testament times on through the Bible, we had a wonderful talk with Mr. Tchividjian in which he told us from their side what had led them to do this, and we told of our ten days of special prayer! He was as thrilled as we were. You see, a few days before, he had become burdened with a feeling that he should do something for L'Abri. Then he had gathered his family around him: his mother, wife, son, and eldest daughters (there are other younger children too), and they prayed together that the Lord would lead them as to what to give. After prayer, they each said they felt this specific amount should be given, and hence the decision was made. Now, to find that it exactly met the need, not only of the month, and the amount that had been overspent, but that it would make the year's books balance, was a joy to them all, for they *had not known* this before.

Can the God who rolled back the Red Sea also spread a table in the wilderness? Oh, for a more constant *trust* and a reality in looking directly to *Him*—that men may *know* that He is God, as we declare His wonders. If you had been in the station-wagon taxi that night as we drove under the stars, you would have heard us singing with "bursting throats" to *His* praise—who is *able*. . . .

By mid-November we had realized an English-Dutch trip was impossible, and that as the Lord was sending so many for the weekends, and the number of Workers was still low—it would seem that it was His will for us to remain and care for the work at hand. However, it did seem possible and right, to go to Holland between weekends, and then to pray about an English trip later on. Therefore November 28th to December 3rd found Fran and me in Holland, during days which seemed very much to have been planned by the Lord. We had discussion groups and personal conversations with individuals in both Amsterdam and Leiden as before, and then Fran was asked to speak to the student body of the Theological Seminary at Kampen, on reaching intellectuals with the gospel in the twentieth century. . . .

The second half of this trip is just taking place right now, as I write this letter in England. The Lord has given us a very full schedule, starting with a discussion group in Paris, then a solid series of discussions here in London. One continuous time consisted of people arriving at 4 P.M. and continuing to arrive and leave throughout eight hours—during which Fran never stopped answering questions, and I never stopped serving tea!—with many nationalities and types of people coming; two full days in Oxford; two very, very full days in Cambridge, then on the 17th we shall be in St. Andrews University in Scotland for three solidly "booked up" days, and then a day in Glasgow with the Hughes family, whom we shall be happy to see again, and during which Joyce Hughes has arranged to have a discussion group in the evening. A report of this present trip could fill up a whole six pages by itself. . . .

This is an announcement: Susan Jane Schaeffer and Ranald Corrigal Macaulay expect to be married on April 7th in the historic 12th-century church in Ollon where Farel commenced the Reformation in that section of Switzerland. Lord willing, they shall sail for South Africa on April 13th—where they will be visiting Ran's close relatives and old friends, and then will be driven to Rhodesia by his parents who expect to come to South Africa to get them. This trip is a wedding gift on the part of Ran's parents, who have found it impossible to come to the wedding and are bringing the young people to them instead. Do pray for them as they go, for there will be many "missionary opportunities" and they go desiring a work of the Holy Spirit through them. Lord willing, they will be back at L'Abri by early July to help in the work of the summer, and Ranald expects to continue his studies in Farel House for another year or two—looking unto the Lord for guidance as to the future. . . .

There isn't time to tell you of all the difficulties which seemed constantly to be Satan's attacks in attempt to discourage us completely this winter. A variety of flu hit us, which comes—seems to be better, and then returns full force again. All of the family has gone down with this—and most of the Workers too. The wonderful thing is that in spite of it all, the Lord has given victory, and the work has continued. Sometimes He has used the very illnesses to bring about contacts—such as Franky's complicated dental problem which took us to Geneva to a dental surgeon and enabled us to spend some time at the home of a psychologist who has recently become interested in coming to L'Abri, and in sending some of her contacts to us. Only the Lord can see the whole battle, and know the significance and importance of the small victories, and the small "deaths" that come "daily." . . .

Susan's examination marks arrived in January. Though they are taken in November, these examinations are countrywide, and marked at a central place, having nothing to do with the professors one has at one's school. As you know, Susan left school to come and work at L'Abri when Jane had to go home because of her father's death, and we were in America longer because of Franky's operation—so we were intensely interested to know the outcome of those examinations, taken after such an interrupted time, and after personal study rather than classroom lectures. Susan received the highest marks in her school and was one of the seven top ones in all who had taken these exams over England! You can imagine the squeals of joy that received this news!

German Udo* who is back at his law studies in the University of Berlin, having been born again at the chalet at the end of the summer, before we returned, writes in such a manner that we can follow his steady growth in the Lord. . . .

But now I must end these bits of news, leaving out many I'd like to mention, with this resolve—Lord willing, I shall write the next letter in two months, so that so much will not need to be skipped.

With love and grateful hearts for all of you whose prayers are being answered in the unfolding of this work,

EDITH

March 25, 1961 Cambridge, England

Dear Helen and Marian Duckworth, Doris de Hart, and Janey Mitchell†:
It is far, far too late for our seed order, and I just don't have proper excuses—or that is to say—it would take pages to tell you all the reasons why other things got done first!! Needless to say L'Abri is growing and it becomes harder all the time for me personally to keep up with all there is to do—and now—Sue's wedding, plus making the wardrobe for South Africa has taken out a few chunks of time too. I am sending duplicate copies of this list and letter to you three people, in the hope that perhaps you can telephone each other, and that Janey or Helen or Marian can get the seeds, and that Doris can bring them with her when she comes to Switzerland. I would be glad to pay "extra baggage weight" for them if she carried them with her, perhaps in an extra "Swiss air bag" or one of those canvas things. That would save my life! I really don't know what to do, as the "boys" (who? I don't yet know) must dig gardens right after the wedding, and I must plant.

Much much love to you each,

EDITH

*Here is the first appearance of Udo Middelmann, later to become our third son-in-law as Debby's husband.

†Members of our former congregation in Chester, Pennsylvania.

L'Abri Seed Order 1961

6672	SPECIAL (3 green pod bush beans, Burpee's Tender Pod, Burpee's Improved Tendergreen	½ lb each	$1.40
6171	Burpee's Brittle Wax Beans	½ lb	$ .55
6232	Burpee's Golden Beans	1 pkt	$ .20
6183	Burpee's Fordhook Green Beans	1 pkt	$ .25
6193	Burpee's Red Ball Beets	1 oz	$ .55
6196	Burpee's White Beets	1 pkt	$ .25
6203	Detroit Dark Red Short Top Beets	1 oz	$ .45
5123	Lutz Green Leaf Beets	1 pkt	$ .20
	Chinese Cabbage		
5236	Michihli	½ oz	$ .50
6067	Burpee's Hybrid	½ oz	$1.00
6267	Earliana Cabbage	1 pkt	$ .35
6017	Perfection Drumhead Cabbage	1 pkt	$ .25
6026	Burpeeana Cauliflower	1 pkt	$ .40
6255	Greenbud Broccoli	1 pkt	$ .40
6007	Calabrese Broccoli	½ oz	$ .50

If possible to be brought along, I'd love Asparagus roots.

6901	Mary Washington	25 roots	$1.50
6022	Burpee's Fordhook Celery	1 pkt	$ .35
6028	Giant Pascal Celery	1 pkt	$ .25
5126	White Midget Corn	2 pkts	$ .70
5156	Carmelcross Corn	1 pkt	$ .25
6023	Burpee's Hybrid Cucumber	2 pkts	$ .65
6274	Burpeeana Hybrid Cucumber	2 pkts	$ .95
6253	Burpeeana Lettuce	1 pkt	$ .35
6046	White Boston Lettuce	1 pkt	$ .25
6041	Burpee's Wayhead Lettuce	1 pkt	$ .25
6053	Great Lakes Lettuce	1 pkt	$ .25
6055	Imperial No. 44 Lettuce	1 pkt	$ .25
6057	Imperial 847 Lettuce	1 oz	$ .75
5035	Cos or Romaine Lettuce, Paris White	1 oz	$ .60
6058	Burpee Greenhart Lettuce	1 pkt	$ .30
6042	Salad Bowl Lettuce	1 oz	$ .85
6073	Extra Curled Dwarf Parsley	1 pkt	$ .25
6221	Thomas Laxton Peas	1 lb	$ .80
6222	Burpeeana Early Peas	1 lb	$ .95
6231	Fordhook Wonder Peas	1 lb	$ .95
5077	Hybrid No. 7 Spinach	1 pkt	$ .25
6093	Bloomsdale Long Standing Spinach	1 oz	$ .35
5052	Virginia Blight Resistant Spinach	1 pkt	$ .20
6096	Burpee's White Radish	1 oz	$ .60
6085	Cherry Belle Radish	¼ lb	$1.65

6097	Burpee's Red Giant Radish	1 pkt	$ .25
6236	Burpee's Hybrid Zucchini	1 pkt	$ .35
5074	Golden Ball Turnip	1 oz	$ .35
6126	Burpee's Purple-Top Yellow Rutabaga	1 oz	$ .35
9254	Legume Aid	2 pkts	$ .60

July 21, 1961   Huemoz sur Ollon, Switzerland

Dear Family:

Kung looked over his shoulder with a grin as his hands kept on busily washing dishes in the steaming hot soapy water. "Did you know, Mrs. Schaeffer, Chinese have fried noodles only for very special occasion? Very, very special, only one time a year maybe?" Kung's smile lighted up his Korean features with joy as he went on to tell how impressed his three Chinese friends were with our choice of fried noodles on the special birthday dinner for John Chang. "No, I didn't know that." It was no cleverness on my part but only another tiny instance of how the Lord tenderly fits details together to make people from so many different "tribes and nations," so many language groups and backgrounds, feel at home here at L'Abri. It is a tiny picture of the larger thing, of the fact that this whole work is the Lord's plan, not ours. The wee kitchen was full of people stacking plates, emptying water glasses, drying dishes, trying to avoid knocking elbows and stepping on each other's feet, while I was holding the beater so that it could whir a seven-minute icing into peaks to decorate the birthday cake. "We'll serve cake and tea after the Bible class, Kung, and I hope I can copy those Chinese characters so that John can recognize his name. It partly depends on whether the icing is stiff enough so that it won't run, making quite different characters!"

A few hours later as the candles glowed showing up the two lines of characters on the two oblong cakes, and we all sang "Happy birthday to you" heartily—John *did* recognize his name with surprised excitement. "How did you know the Chinese?" The joy was all far deeper than you can imagine, for we were celebrating more than John's birthday which had been Sunday, the day before; we were celebrating his "new birth" which had also taken place the day before during the church service. And as I looked at his beaming face bent over the pink Chinese characters, I wondered if this is how his name looks in the Book of Life where the angel had recorded it the day before. It will be interesting to find out when we get to Heaven, whether the Lamb's Book of Life records names in all the languages, or whether it is in the language of Heaven. Whichever it is, we know one thing, the One who died that those names might be written there knows each name and each face that belongs to each name—individually and personally. . . .

The Shepherd knows all His sheep by name! What a marvelously loving and personal Shepherd is leading us. Can we ever grasp the wonder of it all? But in our awe and worship, do we still live as though we thought we could plan our own lives more effectively than this One whose "ways are perfect" and whose wisdom is based on infinite knowledge and understanding?

It was the Shepherd's calling His own sheep by *name* that so filled us with wonder as the sermon Sunday morning took us through the unending vistas one may glimpse in John 10. The sermon took an hour and a half, and as I sat in the hall with our mailgirl Alice, and Franky, I could occasionally glance at the intent faces of at least 25 young men from many different countries. No one realized how long the service was lasting . . . the time seemed to go by like a passing wind . . . but it was a time so Spirit-filled that the "wind" left its effect.

Look around the room with me as the hymn is being sung and see who is there: Chinese Peter, an engineer from Shanghai formerly and Hong Kong now, who is a Christian (and who knows Lok, the Chinese boy at Depauw University for whom we all have been praying); Chinese David Chang, studying engineering in London, who became a Christian shortly after the last London trip when Fran spoke to a group of Orientals; David's brother John, a businessman from Hong Kong, who was so deeply moved during the service that by the time of the singing of the hymn, he had passed from death to life . . . though we were not to know it till later. Kyung, the Korean theological student who was here all last summer, is sitting beside Peter Pattison, the young doctor who brought all this group from London. On the front row are two olive-skinned Indian fellows, for Probal, an engineer from Calcutta, has brought his engineer friend from Bombay to hear the explanation of Biblical Christianity, which he has left Hinduism to embrace. Yes, Probal made a profession of faith in Christ, some weeks ago here at the chalet, having been brought here by John R., a South African electrical engineer!! Next to the Hindu sits Jim Hurley, the American boy from Aiglon College, who with his brother Morris has been coming regularly to the chalet. This is Jim and Morris's last Sunday. I am filled with emotion as well as prayer as I watch them taking part in this last service before they go off to their college years in America. "Oh Lord, hold them fast, and use them in Thy power during these years," I pray. A bit farther back in the room I look at Danielle, the French Jewish girl we met in Paris our last trip there, who is here for a short time in Farel House, looking forward to coming for longer study later on. Susan is sitting beside Jewish Cecille from Paris, translating the sermon phrase by phrase into French. The hour and a half of whispering leaves her hoarse, as it does Trudy, who is sitting facing the opposite direction so that the cerebral palsy young people in wheelchairs, who understand German, can hear her translation whispered directly to them. . . . Among the "25 men" are six Cambridge graduates: Chinese Peter; Jack, who has come to be a visiting student in Farel House for three weeks; Guy, an engineer, and Eric, a theological student who are Workers for the summer; our own Ran; and Jeremy Jackson who has been teaching at Beau Soleil this year, but who now has become a L'Abri Worker. (Sunday night two more Cambridge men arrived, so that we had 8 at one time from that university!) . . . Over by the door sits Marika, the Hungarian refugee girl who came six months ago to the chalet, refused to come back, but who is now close to a nervous breakdown and cannot work for a time. How we pray that the Spirit may open her understanding of the One who can truly help her. . . . Four Dutch young people are among those listening: Marry Meester, Rita, Friedus, Adri. We pray, as we see them, for the various young Dutch men who have written wanting to come later in the summer . . . Hansjorg, the Swiss architect who is now a Farel House student, is among the serious-faced ones, as is Joe Martin, our new Worker, Jane back at the piano, Linette taking copious notes, and Janet Waters, back for the first time in a year, coming from Holland where she has been working as a therapist in a hospital. There are workers from Bellevue, as well as the patients, but . . . look how much space it has taken just to try to make this small group *real* to you as *persons* with *names* and personalities, backgrounds and nationalities!! Yet *the Shepherd* knows all His sheep by name!

I could spend the whole six pages telling you about this past weekend, from explaining the feeding arrangements for so many—Sue and Ran fed six over there at Beau Site (eight counting themselves), while we had only 29 here (22 in the dining room, the rest outdoors)—to telling individual stories of the various ones who were here. But I must jump back across the months to give you a tiny "bird's-eye view," for those who want to follow the work in a more or less chronological order.

April had nine more days after the writing of my last letter. If you had been a bird looking down at the chalets, you would have seen Udo listening to the Romans' studies on tapes, taking notes hour after hour. The sound from the window would have made you think Fran was tirelessly teaching Romans without rest for days! We began to see in the three weeks Udo was with us what the tapes could mean to the various ones coming back for deeper Bible study, in giving them opportunity to go ahead at their own speed. . . . Jeremy Jackson has also moved in as a L'Abri Worker full time, taking over the copying of tapes which is proving an almost full-time job. The Lord put it on the hearts of two "L'Abri spiritual children" to sacrificially give gifts of tape recorders so that we now have four, almost always in use. Two are for making copies of tapes, two for playing them back.

*Sue and Ran (now Mr. and Mrs. Macaulay!) outside the Ollon
church after their wedding. Debby is the bridesmaid in the
background visiting with wedding guests. Notice the early
spring blossoms on the tree!*

During May we had fog and rain day after day, until the 14th of June, when suddenly the sun shone through and the mists cleared away. The rain was depressing enough when people expect lovely "May weather," but a succession of difficulties came at that same period, which seemed to us an attack of Satan in an attempt to discourage and spoil the work. The money came in *very* slowly and there was need for special prayer for the immediate needs of those weeks. The rain and fog made garden planting most difficult; a portion of the planting rotted in the ground and had to be redone. Debby became ill with rheumatic fever! She had had a strep throat before Susan's wedding, seemed to be well again, but simply "dragged" at school and in her home life in Lausanne. The Christian family with whom she lives said they felt there was something definitely wrong. Then when pains started in her joints, followed by swollen knees, she was kept home in bed, a stay which lengthened to two months, necessitating her dropping out of school—I was miserable during that time, in fact until toward the end of June I felt I must have come suddenly to the "end" of my "rope," though now as I look back, I know I had some sort of virus which hung on. At any rate, I was without energy, short of breath, miserable, working most inefficiently for weeks! Marry Meester, on a busy Saturday, rushed to the garden to pick lettuce (in the rain) and slipped on a grassy bank, hitting her head on a stone step. The doctor was coming anyway to see Franky and Debby (yes, Franky had been sick with a bad bronchitis), so he was there within a few minutes after Marry fell. He pronounced it a concussion; Marry was put to bed for three weeks. It was just at the time I was at my worst, looking so awful that the doctor sent me off for a rest to the latest addition to L'Abri, a small chalet on the back road which we have rented for additional space, Chalet Argentine. I did nothing for three days but read, pray, and sleep—mostly sleep. Meantime the misery at the chalet was added to by Alice's dislocating her toe by stubbing it as she was running across the front garden. You can imagine how we missed Sue and Ran in all this, how correspondence piled up, and the work of remodeling Beau Site loomed up as an impossibility. It seemed Satan was almost succeeding in putting a stop to the work for a time—yet in it all the Lord was working. . . .

June came along without being noticed as the rain continued, and the first weekend raincoated Italians walked to the village store for postcards of scenes they were *not* seeing (fog) to send back to Milan. It was the "big Italian weekend" when about eight or nine from Milan came from Thursday to Sunday for times of Bible study and discussion. Jane was able to teach them in Italian and had cozy times of Bible study with them in front of Chesalet's fireplace the afternoons when rain made the expected walks an impossibility. The discussions in Mélèzes went on long after dinner, and also turned into Bible studies. Both for the Christians who came and the unsaved, it seemed a most blessed weekend. Hurvey and Dorothy [Woodson] could not come with them because they had others at the L'Abri villa in the Italian mountains for the same sort of weekend. We were glad not only for what the Holy Spirit did among the Italian group that weekend, but for an opportunity to hear of all the wonderful things that have been going on among them in Milan.

It was in June that the first American family, traveling in Europe with a Volkswagen bus made into a sleeping and eating car, stopped at L'Abri for a couple of days. Several such families have visited us since then, coming to sleep, or staying in their bus for the night, but joining in on meals and conversations. Franky has been delighted because most of these families have had a boy about his age. One family had twin boys nine years old, so you can imagine the variety of things they did with the combination of vivid imaginations, even in the space of a short day!! . . .

In July off trotted Franky to the grocery store where he "persuaded" the lady to search out her last year's leftover 1st-of-August fireworks, to sell him for the 4th of July celebration. (Franky had to go back and apologize for his rather strong and insistent "persuasion," but all ended well!) Franky reminded us so much of Susan at the same age, as he arranged the fireworks and went next door inviting the whole of

Bellevue, workers and patients alike, then wrote notices on various spots of our flagstone walk—"THIS SPACE RESERVED FOR WHEEL-CHAIRS"—and then "put on the display" himself, with very little help from his father and some of the young men! We had a large group when we were all assembled in the dark at the front of the chalet, with several American visitors, two teachers, Madeline and Emmy Lou, who are friends of Betty Carlson's and Colonel Currie and Les, who were back again after having been working in Germany some time. The Colonel, you may remember, was completely paralyzed by polio some five years ago, and has to be in a wheelchair all the time, yet coura-geously lives a life that would "stagger" many a well man, keeping a schedule of business appointments to which he must be driven or flown from town to town in Germany or in Switzerland. He read about L'Abri last year in *Time* magazine and felt drawn to the work. It would seem that the Lord has brought him here for a special reason, both for his own study and spiritual growth, and for the work. He expects, Lord willing, to have his wife and children living in Switzerland within a year, and to be very close to the work of the little church here, and to L'Abri.

The 5th of July was another exciting day. Franky was up, preparing for it early. His preparations involved the donning of an old brown fur rug, pinned over one shoulder with a safety pin, the painting of his face, as well as the fixing of an old broom handle with a pointed stick tied on for a "spear end," and the slinging over his other shoulder of a "bow." He was ready to welcome Susan and Ranald home from Africa!! We didn't let him go out on the train platform that way, but when we got to the taxi, there was Franky waiting beside it, standing like an African warrior at attention!

You can imagine how difficult it was to say all that was on our hearts to say, yet listen at the same time, for we had much to tell them, and they had so much to tell us of how the Lord had blessed their time in South Africa and Rhodesia. There were many changes for them to see, but not as many as we had hoped there would be, for the workmen we had been calling almost daily to come and begin the plumbing, the electrical work, the putting up of three new ceilings, etc., at Beau Site, had finally arrived the *very day* of Sue and Ran's return, so that in addition to a house full of young men, they had the banging of workmen to greet them! Incidentally, the work is going slowly as all workmen are over-worked at present with the great number of new chalets being built, so even yet the new bathroom hasn't been started. With fourteen men waiting to shave, one bathroom presents quite a problem in the morn-ings! . . .

How can I possibly tell all there is left to tell you on this one page? There are so many changes going on—yet as the Lord unfolds the work of His planning, we feel no sudden jolt at changes and the "family atmo-sphere" seems to keep right on. So many still say, "I feel more at home

Coxe and Jane Stuart Smith organizing the Evangelical Library in the room next to the sunroom in Beau Site.

here then anywhere in the world." The only explanation is that the Lord has made it *be* a home, a real "shelter" for those who are seeking, and when they have found *Him* this becomes the place of their spiritual birth and so "home" in that sense too.

Farel House is set up in the sunroom at Beau Site, which has six large desks, now opening into the next room which Jane and Joe are rapidly filling with books, a branch of the Evangelical Library. New bookshelves stretch from ceiling to floor, but with almost 500 theological books, they are beginning to think of space for more shelves to hold a whole new shipment which will be on its way soon. Farel House students meet for prayer together in Farel House at 9 o'clock, and then they concentrate on their study until 1 P.M. when lunch is served. Workers and guests may be working in the garden together, talking, or guests may be listening to a tape of either a Romans study or a discussion. After lunch this day, you'd find the ones who had eaten at Beau Site coming over for the "every-other-day" report on Farel's life brought to us by Roger, so you'd have to move to make room for everyone to squeeze into the dining room—or we'd all move down to the living room. Each new chapter fills us with thankfulness for the name we have chosen, for it seems to us that Farel is the warmest and most understanding of all the Reformers. His letters and sermons cause us to exclaim with wonder!

L'Abri is changing and growing—but how can I bring to you the feeling of oneness there is, and the blending together of the parts of the work, so that weeding gardens, washing dishes, emptying trash, scrubbing floors, typing letters, keeping accounts, painting tables—all seem just as important and just as glorifying to the Lord as the Bible studies themselves? I think you almost have to *be* here to really feel the oneness and unity among us which gives that "enlarged Family" feeling, instead of institutional, to it all. . . .

Financial needs, spiritual needs, changed lives, wandering ones brought back, work unfolded and Workers blended together—all directly in answer to prayer alone. With Hudson Taylor we can say by experience that God *is able* to move man by prayer alone. What a glorious and all-powerful God we have—and One who makes and *keeps* promises. Let us study His promises more and search our hearts to see if we harbor any doubt in the place of trust.

Much love in Him in Whom we may have utter confidence,

EDITH

October 27, 1961   Huemoz sur Ollon, Switzerland

Dear Family:

. . . How hopeless I feel sitting in front of a piece of blank paper, the months of July, August, September, most of October spread out before me in calendar form, and spread out in my memory as a vast changing view, full of important details, emotions, facts, personalities, miracles of changing lives, of unanswered and answered prayer, of spiritual struggles, of glimpses of the reality of the Holy Spirit at work, of glimpses of our own complete nothingness and weakness and His wonderful strength, all mingled with the daily sights and sounds, joys and sorrows, fears and hopes. . . .

Our Debby has been spending months in bed with one attack after another of rheumatic fever, until the disappointing fresh attack toward the end of September meant not only that she had to miss the "family vacation" when Fran, Franky, and I went to Italy for ten days of rest, but that there would be no hope at all of going to school in Lausanne this fall and winter. Did the months in bed stretch out in dark frustration and sadness? No, the patience and quiet trust the Lord has been developing in Debby shine through these experiences of disappointment. You'd have to hear her "singing through the hymnbook," watch her knitting and chattering to visitors, laughing cheerily, helping others with their problems, to know of the reality of the joy the Lord has given her in the midst of this "dark time," to know that the joy has been real, not a "brave front" for others to see. Struggles? Yes, but obvious victories too. At this writing, Debby is getting better, but still in bed, getting up only a couple of hours a day. . . .

In the last letter I told you of numbers reaching 37 during June and July, but in August one weekend we had 46 altogether in the four chalets, and the number never went below 25 at any time. In fact, in the three months this letter covers, we had about 200 different people here—some staying longer lengths of time to study in Farel House, others for short periods of time. As you know, L'Abri feels part of its purpose is to show forth the reality of the existence of God—or to "demonstrate His existence"—and one way we believe the Lord has led us to do this is to simply pray for His provision of all our needs materially, as well as every other way. No one who comes to L'Abri as a guest pays for board and room. It is not a "conference," it is a place where doors are open, as a private home would be, to those whom the Lord sends with special spiritual needs. In telling of the past three months, it would not be fair *not* to tell you that, while so many were coming, the funds were low, and at the end of September we discovered that we needed to economize drastically. No one had been turned away from L'Abri because of not enough food, for the Lord had made it possible to care for all He sent, but you *must* see that the story is not always the same—that when the Lord is working in answer to prayer, sometimes the prayer is not answered as we would want or expect it to be. We have received large gifts in the past "in the nick of time"—which makes an exciting story, but this time the Lord chose to allow us to go through a period of extreme economy, and when some gifts came, they were designated "for vacation"! As we prayed about this matter in early October, everyone agreed vacations were needed by some and that the Lord had opened the way for them. Hence, Jane went to Italy for a couple of weeks, Trudy visited Italy for ten days (in Milan, a help to the L'Abri group there), and Fran, Franky, and I went to Italy for a ten-day rest. It was most interesting to see the very *clear* guidance come as to these vacations. The designated gifts came from such different parts of the earth—from the mid-part of the United States, from a northern point in Canada, from Switzerland. We could not have comfortably gone away and left the folks here carrying on with such extreme economy had the way not been made so clear. . . .

Let me ask you to pray that the Lord will show us clearly when we should next go to England. We had thought to be able to go in November to care for the many requests we have had to come—from London, Oxford, Cambridge, Bristol, Reading, and St. Andrews and Glasgow in Scotland. But as we prayed, the answer seemed to be "no" as the money for such a trip did *not* come. We feel that when one is praying for this sort of guidance, then "no" must be taken as from the Lord just as rapidly as "yes" and we must trust Him and thank Him for His wisdom in such leading.

As we look back on the summer, look with me at the village procession carrying lighted lanterns and winding its way to the Haute Crete for the First of August celebration, and note how many there are from

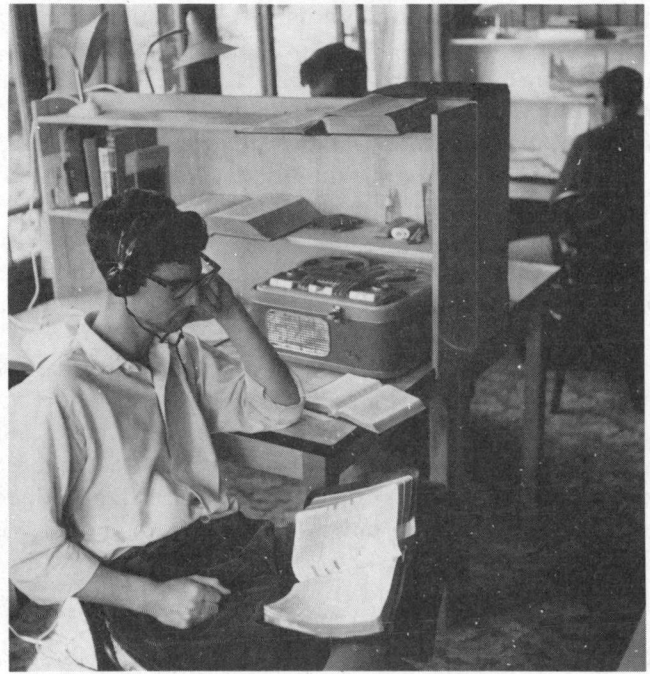

This is Farel House study time in the sunroom.
The carpenter's good design allows us to use a small
space for tape recorders and to study books in an
atmosphere of concentration.

L'Abri and from Bellevue, as the wheelchairs of the excited children join the rest of us there. Now it is a morning scene and two jeeps are waiting out front. "Who has the sandwiches? Is everyone ready?"—and off we go, literally stuffed into the jeeps (eleven in one and twelve in the other) to be taken up to about 7,000 feet, above the tree line, so that we can have a day of high mountain hiking. An article is taken along to read during the picnic lunch, as it is Farel House luncheon day, so really L'Abri is continuing during this day which is nevertheless a refreshment to each one who goes. There was Jane's birthday party which she combined with a celebration of Chalet Chesalet's 250th anniversary (it was a barn to begin with that long ago) for which Joe and Jane made a cake in the form of a chalet.

Almost any time of the day you could have found four tape recorders being used—often all in the same room, as people plug in earphones to listen without disturbing each other. We are impressed with the efficiency of having the L'Abri story on tape, as well as discussions, Bible studies, and sermons. Any beautiful afternoon found the gardens being cared for (watered, weeded, thinned, planted) by young people usually deep in some serious discussion, and the lawn being mowed by others. On Sundays at 5 o'clock you would find a group from L'Abri, headed by

Jane with her autoharp, singing hymns with the Bellevue children out-doors. At other times two or three L'Abri young men could be seen tear-ing over to Bellevue to help carry children up or down stairs, depending on the time of day!

There is always the beautiful walk to the garbage dump being taken by one or two young men, often trying to set a record for speed, pulling the *petit char,* which cart is getting sadly dilapidated! People shelling peas, peeling potatoes, peeling tomatoes for canning, or breaking off the ends of beans, are often clustered together in the sunshine of the balco-ny or terrace. There are goodbyes being said at the yellow bus, with all of us moving out into the road in a group to wave it "out of sight," and at times the goodbyes are to those who have been Workers and it means another change and closing of a period, even though short. One is al-ways being reminded of the reality of *time*—oh, that at times it would stand *still* until we accomplish more, or fulfill all we had expected to do within its "limits," but it rushes on and when we realize its fleetingness, we feel increasingly unable in our own strength to choose what to do with it. How could we possibly know what is "important," and what is not, unless we could see the end from the beginning, and know what part each little thing has to do with the "big things"? But He who prom-ises to guide us *does* know! Oh, that we might more sincerely *want* and *trust* His guidance! . . .

Out of darkness into *His* glorious light. What else is there to offer this poor dark world today as it shrinks from fear of the future! Oh, that more may hear His voice through the tumult of false voices, and see the *true* light amid the "lights that are darkness"! Please pray with us that *He* may fill us and use us to His glory before it is too late, while our lives speed by as the hours do with the chiming of the village clock.

Love in Him, Who *is the light,*

EDITH

1962

February 6, 1962 Huemoz sur Ollon, Switzerland

Dear Family:

Sheer poetry is the view framed in the wide, tall, grey-draped Dutch windows of this third-floor living room of the Rookmaakers'* home in Leiden, Holland.

Sea gulls swoop and whirl, wings arched, gliding in and out of the delicate pattern of leafless black tree twigs outlined against a grey sky. Wild ducks float effortlessly along the ripples of quickly flowing dark water of the Singel river, whose curved banks are carpeted with bright green grass even in February, while green benches, and masses of leafless bushes border hard earth paths running along this water. A wind blows the scarf of a bicycler, hurrying home with groceries securely in the basket tied on the back, as she passes another pedaling more slowly with a dignified briefcase as his "tied-on luggage" and his professor's attire unruffled by wind or spattering raindrops. . . .

Yes, I'm writing this during a "Dutch trip." Fran is in Kampen tonight, speaking to students of the Theological Seminary there, and others invited to his lecture, and tomorrow morning he'll be speaking to a Seminar, and answering students' questions. I have stayed at the Rookmaakers to talk and pray with Coxy and Anky Rookmaaker, and to write this. We've read verses aloud from their Dutch Bibles (Psalms 142 and 143) and have listened to them sing in Dutch as they had family prayers. How wonderful to see another family of children growing in the knowledge of the Lord in this home where L'Abri discussion groups and Bible classes are being held for students. I prayed silently, as they prayed in Dutch for the many L'Abri couples springing up in many different places, saved at L'Abri and making their homes a place where the Lord will be spoken about naturally, and where people will come with their

*Dutch art critic Hans Rookmaaker and his family.

25

*Susan instructs Franky in Calvert studies outside in
the sun at Chalet Beau Site. As you see, every bit of
space inside and out is being used in diverse ways
at different times.*

questions. Oh, what a work there *could* be in homes scattered through
the world, if the Holy Spirit would be given His place in the lives of
Christians unhindered by the terrible demands self makes when "self"
takes first place in hearts! . . .

The Dutch windows so impress me that my mind is visualizing things
through windows at this time! And in thinking back through the
months to report them to you, we'll "peek" through a few windows at
various moments of the months' history. It is the end of October and
Franky has begged for a Halloween party. As Franky's school consists of
going to Beau Site each morning and pursuing Calvert Course under
Susan's teaching (while she gets some mending, ironing, and other odd
jobs done in the "schoolroom" while he writes or reads to her), he
misses the usual school activities. An occasional "treat" makes up for
this, as do other things the Lord provides for him. After supper that
night everyone disappeared to "cook up" a costume with his or her ingenuity and whatever was at hand. The results made us wish we had
planned to take flash pictures! (But we hadn't so we can't let you see except by description.) Yes, the living room of Les Mélèzes was transformed by Udo, Roger, and Franky, working with cornstalks and orange
crepe paper, candles, and little scooped out turnips made into small jack-
o'-lanterns by Trudy. Into this transformed room you saw a number of
characters walk, gazing at each other trying to distinguish who is who.
Hungarian Marika was a perfect gypsy with a red skirt, peasant blouse,

spangles and bangles gathered from attic trunks, and Susan as a June bug with an old green "trainee suit" (a sort of gym sweat suit) that used to be Betty Carlson's back in Chalet Bijou, and an ingenious headdress of her own making. Next was Franky himself as a spaceman wearing boxes covered with silver foil, made by himself (with a little help) to look very like the pictures he has been seeing in *Newsweek*. Fran was the Wizard of Oz with a hat made by Debby and Franky (who also made a wand), Alice the Postmistress's big wool cape, borrowed for the evening, and his red-and-white-striped pajama trousers showing below. Debby didn't take the effort to dress up, as we felt coming down was in itself enough for her that evening, and she was ensconced on the couch. My nephew Jonathan looked for all the world as if he had stepped out of a Latin book, with a white blanket forming a Roman toga, and a scroll in his hands, his head of curly hair grown quite long and Roman-looking! Roger rustled in as a strangely pixie-looking little animal peering out of a cornshock. (He had made an animal head and face out of a white paper bag placed over his head and his sheet-swathed form was hidden behind a whole pile of cornstalks tied around his body with string so he had to stand up all evening!) Udo poled himself in, a Venetian gondolier in a striped jersey, a gondolier hat, and trousers, with Joe behind him, bringing a burst of laughter as Joe has a beard, you know, and he had dressed himself in a dress, hat, and high heels (which he couldn't manage without teetering) as the bearded lady. Jeremy was an amazing sight having covered himself with a thin layer of mud which had dried and clothed himself with old fur rugs, an ax in one hand—he was supposed to be a caveman, and he surely didn't need a mask, for the mud transformed his face! Dutch Bert was an astrologer with a tall peaked hat and a tablecloth for a cape. I had dug an old black long dinner dress out of a trunk, along with the high comb, mantilla, etc., to turn me into a Spanish señorita, and Trudy had found in the same trunk a long dress which she used as a base to make herself into a little 18th-century lady. We played a few simple games (charades, the telling of a story—each one adding his or her imagination, around the circle, etc.), had refreshments, and finished the evening with those who had been at elaborate worldly parties saying they had enjoyed themselves more in this simple impromptu evening of recreation than any of the high-powered things the world has to offer. "It has simply been more fun" was the thought. . . .

On the 6th of November Danielle arrived from Paris. Slim, dark-haired Danielle we had first met in Paris, though she had accepted the Lord as her Saviour during the year she was in London. French Jewish Danielle had been waiting for her 21st birthday to take the sober step of leaving her family (who had forbidden her to be baptized) and coming to the Chalet to be baptized, and to enter as a student in Farel House. It was a moment of joy, but also of sadness for her, as her family had made it as hard as possible and had brought as much emotional pressure to bear upon her departure as they could. How many of you have faced being put out of home and cut off without an inheritance because of your firm stand for the Lord? Perhaps few of us ever have that particular type of persecution to face, but not one of us can truly put the Lord first without facing the reality of some kind of suffering. There is a cost to be paid when we leave the cozy rut of doing what is expected of us—to ask the Lord what He would have us to do and to tell Him, "I really want Thy will—even at the cost of destroying my dearest plans and facing the disapproval of even Christian friends." Danielle is going on in her Farel House studies now, and already the Lord has given her an inkling of her next step—and she faces a period of placing a decision before the Lord in prayer, wanting His clear guidance before making it. . . .

A week after Thanksgiving Fran and I were in Paris sitting in Danielle B's living room! Danielle B. is the one who was born again here in Huemoz on the day of my mother's death. That I will never forget. We met this Danielle during the first London trip—and she introduced us to the second Danielle. . . . What a mass of international young people there are studying in Paris—and what sort of answers are most of them getting? Existentialist philosophy, confusion, blackness. . . . The taxi careened around a corner the next morning and we were driving along the Seine River looking at the picturesque curved bridges and talking of the need of the students. "I wonder what would happen if there was time to just sit on the bench by the river or at a café table and talk? I wonder—" It was Fran speaking, and I echoed his thought. "How impossible it is to know where to spend one's time, for how can we ever know what is the important thing to be doing with time, or the strategic place to be." Yes, over and over again we come to the same *absolute* truth—there is just *no* way for a human being to make choices that fit in with God's plan and for his life, except by his acknowledging that he has no wisdom, and asking for the Lord's wisdom and plan. This can't be just a doctrine we accept mentally while planning our lives in detail—we have to have an attitude of mind and heart, and a practical way of demonstrating to the Lord that shows *Him* we mean it, and gives *Him* an opportunity to lead us. . . .

Back at the chalet, during our time in Paris, the Workers had carried on: Ran, Jeremy, Joe, our daughter Sue, Jane, Trudy, with a "regular weekend." . . . There were 45 people in all to find places for at meals and beds for the nights! It worked out amazingly well, however, as we had made cooking preparations ahead of time, and Sunday dinner was served in three chalets—by Sue in Beau Site, Jane in Chesalet, and ourselves here at Mélèzes. The groups were selected prayerfully for "conversation"—asking the Lord to lead us in placing people in the right places, as the mealtime conversations can be more personal in dealing with individual questions, than the larger more general circle in the living room. Workers and students can talk with those who are sitting next to them, and conversations can be carried on in several languages. Joe was just remarking the other day that the first day he arrived (it was mealtime) and walked into the dining room, it confused him to hear German coming from one cluster of people, French from another, Italian somewhere else, and English from Fran's end of the table, all at one time and in a very small room! . . .

And then the 13th of January came, the day the Lord had arranged for the L'Abri Family to go away for a week of rest! What a happy surprise the Lord's answers to prayer sometimes are—that is, to the requests we wonder about as to whether we are selfish in asking. A winter holiday for a family of 16 people? What a request! But the Lord showed clearly it was His tender, loving answer when He sent in designated money in a number of unusual ways—which, when added together along with the regular food money, made exactly the amount needed for a week high above tree line where we could ski, read, and rest. The hotel gave a special price because it was an "off season" week, and we were such a large group. The most wonderful part about such a clear leading of the Lord is the reality of communication—He, the living God had answered in a way each one of the group could take as unto himself or herself. . . .

Dot and Hurvey [Woodson] have had a lovely little baby sister, Anne, for David to enjoy! Cynthia Stanton, an English girl, has come to be a Worker for some months. The Evangelical Library in London continues to send splendid books for the theological students here at Farel House, among these a Breeches Bible. Dear Trudy has finished the long job of preparing the financial books for the year, and taking them to be gone over by the Fiduciare in Lausanne, and all turned out well, with praise to the Lord for fully meeting another year's expenses. We shall be going to London, Purley, Oxford, Reading, Cambridge, Glasgow and St. Andrews, Scotland, February 26th to March 17th. Sue and Ran's baby is expected early in April. Debby is still having pains in joints and periods of fever. Jane arrived back safely from her singing tour to America. All these items should cause you to have a part in prayer, even though I haven't had space to tell you anything in detail. Oh, that the *windows of Heaven* might be opened by the Lord, so that a blessing would be *poured* out!

Much love in Him Who is able to open and shut "windows" as well as "doors" in His care and leading of His children,

EDITH

December 17, 1962   Huemoz sur Ollon, Switzerland

Dear Family:

Wild hurricane winds a hundred miles an hour shook the chalet, bent trees to the ground, tore tin roofs off and blew roof tiles around as though they had been autumn leaves. A half a forest was uprooted over in Champéry and many villagers filled with dismay as their cozy homes filled with wind through yawning gaps that appeared as roofs disappeared! On and on it blew throughout the long night of November 7th to 8th, filling some hearts with fear, others with awe and worship of the God of all power Who commands the wind and is said to "walk on the wings of the wind."* The results are still strikingly before us on every side as one walks through the woods. Our Christmas trees this year will be tops of fallen trees. So much timber has come down, the forester does not want to cut more. Today again the wind is coming in gusts to swirl the snow into little airborne whirlpools, to bang shutters, and to push the blue spruce, bent over by the November wind, back into place again! The mountains are transformed into something out of another world, as the wind blows wet snow against them so that even the steepest, sheerest rocks are entirely covered with white, a sight one seldom sees, not even a grey streak to mar what suddenly looks like a heavenly kind of carved marble. "Fire, and hail; snow, and vapours; stormy wind fulfilling his word:"—"He bringeth the wind out of his treasuries"—"He caused an east wind to blow in the heaven: and by his power he brought in the south wind."† Oh, how we cry out within ourselves in the face of such power, "What is man that thou art mindful of him?" What are we?—a speck in the universe?—an eggshell to be crushed?—a piece of fluff to be blown away in the gigantic whirl of the universe full of atoms and planets? How could it matter about *us*? Through the stormy swirls of snow some tiny bits of color just appeared, soft taupe-brown and rosy red, bright yellow with streaks of black and white and grey, a fluttery ball of grey-brown—yes, birds; tits, wood-hatches, sparrows, lighting on the balcony rail, pecking hungrily at seeds and crumbs scattered there. "Are not two sparrows sold for a farthing? and one of them shall not fall on the ground without your Father . . . Fear ye not therefore, ye are of more value than many sparrows."‡

Power—and tenderness, control of the gigantic stretches of space and forces beyond our imagination—and attention given to the tiniest details too small for us to see or know about—this is our God, the God who exists, who is really there. Infinite! And then suddenly we see something of the meaning when we look out in the face of a fierce blizzard knowing we can do nothing to stop it, and watch a tiny bird in the midst of it who is being *noticed, known, cared for*—by God. *Time* to care for every tiny detail in the universe, *able* to do endless numbers of things at once—this is our infinite God—our Father. This is the One who cares for us as His children when we are born into His family through Christ. This is the One who has said, "Be careful for *nothing*"; [be anxious for nothing, what does that leave out? what can we worry about?] "but in

---

*Psalm 104:3.
†Psalm 135:7, 78:26.
‡Matthew 10:29–31.

every thing by prayer and supplication with thanksgiving let your *requests* be made known unto God.* Every thing, what isn't covered by *every thing*?—Are some requests too small? Are some too big? Are some too "impossible"?. . .

Surely Gracie Holmes's story shows the Lord's tenderness. Gracie was staying as a helper with a village family, after having had a stroke and being unable to go on with her work in North Africa as child's nurse. A baby found in a London trash can, brought up in an orphan asylum, working in other people's families in strange lands, Gracie had no family and few friends. The Lord wonderfully brought her in touch with us at L'Abri. We kept her here until an arrangement was made for her in a pension by Swiss government authorities. There she is cared for, but we are now her family and she returns here for frequent weekends. She is a part of *the* family too, because she was born into the family of God here. I wish you could have been in the living room the Sunday morning she was baptized and joined our little church. Partially crippled by her stroke, unable to keep the tears back, she stood, a living proof of the Lord's tender seeking of lost lambs.

Bruce had come from a totally different background, but the Lord had just as definitely and carefully brought him through circumstances and experiences, across oceans and lands, to face the reality of *His* existence. Bruce is Roger's younger brother. He never got to L'Abri seven years ago when Roger first came from the school in Geneva. Bruce had entered art school in America after spending his army years in Korea as an interpreter, when suddenly he was recalled into the army and spent another year waiting impatiently to get "started in life" and thinking over some of life's deeper questions. In this year he decided to come and spend some time traveling with Roger. During their talks, Bruce promised to come and study a few weeks in Farel House, to see what it was Roger had studied here, more with the thought of refuting it than of believing it. The work of the Holy Spirit in Bruce's mind and heart those first six days he was here was a real demonstration of the Holy Spirit's existence and of the Lord's care in details. To see someone step from death to life, from darkness to light, from agnosticism to assurance of the existence of the God of the Bible, is exciting. I'm going to do something I rarely do. I'm going to let you read a small portion of Bruce's letter to his father, written two weeks after he, an artist with Bohemian outlook, became a Christian.

I discovered that Christianity does not mean insipid art—a field of great interest to me of course. That there is an abundance of insipid and miserable art being produced under the name of "Christian Art" I do not deny—how could I with so much of it around to repulse the eye? The fact is though that it need not be insipid—nowhere does the Bible say that art must be representational—Christian art is not insipid, rather it is the artists that produce it that must be the problem. I have had training in modern art and I appreciate and understand the forms

*Philippians 4:6.

used—there is no reason why I can't continue as a Christian artist yet as a contemporary artist also. Such is the case in any field of life—the idea that one becomes a Christian and a blob at the same time is quite wrong. . . .

Bruce came to Farel House as the first agnostic student and left as a born-again Christian! "But I thought Farel House was for theological students. How could someone *not* a Christian be a theological student?" "But I thought L'Abri was just a family, living on the side of a mountain, with an open house for people who want to ask questions?" Are these among your questions? Is it confusing to you? The last Family Letter told you something of how L'Abri is changing, so that rather than one family receiving guests with "questions" in their minds and hearts, it is now a small community of families ready to do the same thing, to share the work as one big family at the same time. In this letter I have been asked to give you a history of Farel House to complete the picture.

As L'Abri began we determined to *not* make plans, but to really pray that the Lord would send whom *He* would to L'Abri and unfold His plan as to the future of the work. We felt then that we were ready to have only two or three at a time, for quiet family discussion times around the table or fireplace—all our lives, if that were the Lord's will. But never make the mistake of thinking that *any* "resolve," "determination," "covenant" taken in the Christian life is a permanent thing, a "once-for-all" thing. Our salvation is once-for-all; our justification, to be exact, is once-for-all. Once we are born into the family of God, we cannot be unborn, but our growth, our Christian life, our sanctification, the desires we have for the fullness of the Spirit, our determination to live by prayer alone, these things must be renewed moment by moment. Our Christian life is to be lived in the power of the Spirit moment by moment as individuals, and the continuance of a work must be kept under the direction of the Lord moment by moment. The human "drift" is not in this direction naturally! By the grace of God then, attempting to never push ahead and make plans, how did such a thing as Farel House come about?

The second year of L'Abri Hurvey Woodson asked if he could come as a Worker; leaving his theological studies for a year he felt would be more valuable for all he could learn from discussions and so on. The following years two others did the same thing, Arnie Jantzen and John Boice. Several others asked to study here; then, it was while we were in Long Island during the summer of 1960, the year of Franky's operation and my mother's death, that two letters arrived in the same mail. One came from Ranald, Susan's fiancé at that time, suggesting the possibility of studying at L'Abri while being an external student of London University theological school; the other came from Richard and Deirdre Ducker of London asking if they could come to L'Abri to learn what they could from discussions, study the Bible, and help in the work. After prayer it seemed these requests pointed the way to having a place where young people could gain in understanding of the Scriptures by study and by lectures, not as guests or Workers, but as students. "Farel House" seemed an appropriate name. Farel is the Swiss Reformer who preceded Calvin, and who preached in this very area back in 1530; in fact he was chased out of Huemoz by irate women with their clothes-washing sticks, under a shower of stones and rotten potatoes! We felt his name should be honored here!

Upon our return to Huemoz, the sunroom at Beau Site seemed the most suitable place for a modest room to be called Farel House. Hence Mr. Dubi, the carpenter, was called, desks were designed and five of them built and fitted in within the next weeks. On November 1, 1960, Farel House officially began. The first winter was not easy. Beau Site needed much repair and the sunroom was freezing cold! However, the three students each gained much from the time and it did seem that the Lord had planned the year for their individual needs in which the difficulties blended as training. In the spring the Duckers left for their next step in preparing for missionary aviation; Ran and Sue were married and went to Africa for some months, but before they returned three new students had come to Farel House: Fritz, Swiss, preparing for the ministry; Hansjorg, Swiss, an architect who wished to become grounded in Christianity better to talk about it among laymen; Roger, American, whose coming by way of India you know about. After Ran's return, Danielle came from Paris. These five then comprised the second year's Farel House students. During the summer of 1962 there were fourteen students in Farel House counting Ran. . . .

Now, as to *study and tuition:* How does it work? Students are to meet in Farel House at 9 A.M. The first few minutes are spent in prayer, then each goes to his own studies for four solid hours. After lunch, time is given by students to work in the gardens or around the grounds and in the houses. At present John Sandri has charge of this work. Farel House is not a "school," specifically not a Bible School. Most of those who come have finished or are in the midst of university or college work. The studies follow assigned subjects, research, and reports, with Dr. Schaeffer acting as Senior Tutor. He gives lectures twice a week. These have covered roughly 30 different topics, e.g.: "Dr. Machen's Struggles with Liberalism," "The Roman Catholic Missal," "The Christian Philosophy of Science," "The Christian and Satan," "Wesley's Perfectionism," "The Intellectual Climate and the New Theology," "The Present Vatican Council." Lectures are about two hours each; some are a series of up to 20 individual lectures, all on tapes. Thus far there are two Farel House extension courses on tapes: (1) Fourteen Studies on Romans 1–8; and (2) Twenty-two Studies on the Principles of the Exegesis of Prophecy. These can be listened to with earphones and can be used even in a quiet library. Three other things fall under this heading of tuition and study:

1. *Seminars*—The attendance consists of students and two invited guests (though at times everyone is invited). Some of the papers delivered by students have been of sufficient value to be copied for the "Farel House Archives."

This photo captures a rare gathering of L'Abri Workers outside of Chalet le Chesalet. Standing are: Ran, Jane Stuart Smith, Hans and Anky Rookmaaker, and Linette. Crouching are: Susan, Olave, and Trudy.

2. *Outside Speakers*—Jane Stuart Smith has delivered three lectures on the music of Bach. Dr. Hans Rookmaaker of Holland has been here twice. Last summer he delivered a series of lectures on the "Philosophy of Herman Dooyeweerd."

3. *Sermons*—Under the direction of Dr. Schaeffer some of the men students have preached to the "community" on Sunday evenings after high tea. This has given a very real opportunity for homiletical training, in a "live situation" rather than in a more artificial classroom situation. Women have given devotional studies occasionally during these tea-time hours.

The financial basis of Farel House is as follows: Students pay nothing for room and tuition, but do pay two American dollars a day to meet food, household expenses, etc., as it was felt that such students should not burden L'Abri with extra expense. Seventy-five per cent of this money goes for food and household expenses, 25% for such things as desks, books, and so on. *Guests* come to L'Abri as true guests, and money is never charged—it is truly an "open home."

Library—A wonderful "sign" from the Lord of His plan and direction of Farel House was the establishment here of a branch of the Evangelical Library. Mr. Williams in London, the director of the Evangelical Library, kindly has sent most excellent books, so valuable to those studying here.

The Evangelical Library has branches scattered throughout the world, with the purpose of providing Christian books for reading and study, to help those who could not buy many. Jane is librarian for this library, and Joe Martin is her assistant.

Farel was a strong man, not a compromiser. He had courage to dare to stand for God and for God's will, no matter what man might do to him. Our prayer is that those who go from Farel House will be men and women of Farel's caliber, filled with courage and power such as the Holy Spirit gives to those who commit their lives fearlessly to Him—courage to *stand* no matter who is falling all around them, in an age of confusion and compromise when "words" need redefinition as they have been emptied of that which they used to mean, and so often have been given a meaning the very "opposite." Time—for study of the Word, consideration of problems and subtle trends, meditation and waiting upon God—this is what men and women of today need.

Small? Yes—a "detail"? Yes, a very small detail in the history of God's people is this Farel House—but we believe it is a detail of *His* plan, and therefore important in His plan. A mighty sweeping blizzard of blurred unbelief, doubts, Barthianism, neoorthodoxy and the "new theology" beyond it—can the tiny blown-about ones (Christians, even the theologically trained ones) remain "alive" through it all? Yes, because He whose eye is on the sparrow is able to care for His own in the midst of intellectual and spiritual storms, too, to keep alive that "life" He has a plan for, that "life" important in His whole connected plan.

Don't you see it? Infinite, powerful, able to do all things: the wild storms, stirred up or stilled; the waves beating high, and quieted; and through it all, the infinite power to care for the tiny birds, and the incidents of eternal value. Our God. Our Father. And He loves us. Oh, *do* we trust Him?—and *believe* Him in our lives, as well as our intellects?

You'll be in the New Year when you read this—oh, may it be a year committed to trusting Him *Who* loves you and Whose schedule is not crowded—never too crowded to have you bring Him every detail of every day!

Love in this Infinite One,

EDITH

1963

February 27, 1963   Huemoz sur Ollon, Switzerland

Dear Family:

Yesterday the workmen arrived. Sounds of shrill drills, thudding hammers, saws biting their way through wood, fill the air. Welcome sounds, which spell the end of a certain period of frustration and the beginning of a new one! What workmen? What frustration? You will remember that last *July* the swarm of workmen finally arrived to cut out the wall and commence the work of finishing the enlarged kitchen (the outside shell of which had been made in May and June). However, if you will remember, I wrote you in August and told of how the work had come to a standstill!! One reason or excuse followed another, the main one being sinks which were being made to order to fit were causing delay as the factory could not deliver them according to the original promise. In November the sinks arrived, and new, shiny, adequate sinks were placed across one side of the room. Splendid, except for the worm-eaten section of wood above them revealed by the torn out tiles, and the barn-like appearance of the rest of the kitchen: cement walls meeting the old flaked-off walls, cement floor meeting the old floor in the middle, old cabinets torn off the walls, orange crates holding provisions, bowls, and cooking utensils, ice forming on the windows and wet places growing "moss" as cold weather and the unfinished condition held hands during the winter! Ugh! What frustrated feelings were stirred up in all of us who worked in the kitchen.

November, if you remember, was the month of the windstorm. That storm, strangely enough, kept the workmen away! Why? Well, many roofs were torn off, and, "Madame, people need roofs more badly than you need the kitchen finished." Excuse followed excuse, and finally eleven days ago, we were told to take *everything* out of the kitchen as they would be there about seven in the morning and wanted to work immediately!! A new exodus of all the movable things in the kitchen took place. To be put where? In the dining room once again. Benches were moved in from the balcony eating nook, benches to hold more of the foodstuff, pots, pans, baking utensils, flour, sugar, salt, pepper, spices, etc. Dining room tables, sideboard, old bedside tables, all in the dining room holding kitchen things, with the dining room chairs removed to be used elsewhere! What a mess! But at least they are *coming!* Then, Monday morning dawned and *no* workmen! "An emergency has arisen; they'll be there tomorrow." Next day? Rain! "Madame, we could not bring the new unfinished wood through the rain, it would spoil it." And so the days went on. When they *did* come, it was to announce, "Oh, your walls are too wet, something has to be done about this. The cement balcony (roof of the new section of the kitchen) will have to covered with tin." More frustration! Now at last the work has commenced, seven months after it was left in "the middle"!! Now, for a period (the length of which we do not know) we shall have to cook in the tiny downstairs kitchen on a gas stove, and serve meals in the living room, trekking to the dining room (which means up and down stairs dozens of times) to get supplies. This will bring time-consuming hindrances for indefinite time and frustrations.

What is a frustration? To me it is a wall where I expected a door; a locked gate where I expected an open one; a barrier across a path; a dead end where I thought a street connected with another street; an unexpected dam forming a pool out of a free-running, happy stream in the forest; a dropped wind causing sails to go limp! And every frustration *should* have only one immediate result in the Christian's life. It should cause an immediate turning the heart and eyes to the Lord, with something like this on the lips, "Lord, is this from Satan, or from Thee? Is Satan trying to hinder Thy will in my life? If so, *Thine* is the victory, and I believe Thou canst do the impossible *now.* If, Lord, this thing is from Thee to cause me to pause, to walk with someone beside this wall until a door is found, to sit with someone beside this quiet pool before I race downstream, to pray with someone in this floating, drifting boat before the wind comes up, to change my course to another path which has no barrier, then show me Thy purpose for this moment of changed plans, and help me to do what Thou has for me to do." Not only should this be our reaction when the frustrating thing comes, but it should be that which we determine to do ahead of time as we read in Proverbs, "Boast not thyself of tomorrow; for thou knowest not what a day may bring forth."* . . .

Trudy worked away in January on the financial books for the yearly check up at the Fiduciare (Certified Accountant) in Lausanne. Even with Joe's help (as Acting Treasurer) this is a frustrating job and becomes triply so when one has to add columns over again, and search down a mistake. The books, by the way, showed the story of answered prayer once again, as the financial year finished with all bills paid, and even some left

*Proverbs 27:1.

over. We praised God for this eighth year of living by prayer, believing that *He is able* to hear and answer specific prayer for specific needs, materially as well as spiritually. But to go back to Trudy, "the books" do *not* comprise all of Trudy's work. Sleeping in a narrow little bedroom with a desk under the window which fills one end of the room, Trudy spends many hours of the day typing in here too, as this room doubles for her office. She takes dictation from Fran upstairs, but comes down to type the letters, to make stencils for two-page letters and prayer lists. At times her frustration, like that of the rest of us, comes from trying to decide what to do first: whether to stay in her wee room typing, or to come to the rescue of those in the kitchen preparing a meal, setting a table, washing some dishes, or pitching in to freshen up a room for an unexpected guest. The surface "seen" things of each of us are not the only frustrations. There are inward, private struggles, too, that find us alone on our knees. At times Trudy and I pray together in that space beside her bed which is so narrow our toes need to be curled under to fit in front of the long, thin bureau, and her cozy office-bedroom becomes a prayer room. . . .

I'll close with a word about the babies, Priscilla's Elizabeth and Susan's Margaret. The frustrations of the two families sharing one kitchen and serving guests with two lively babies to care for in one house and cramped quarters can be left to your imagination. The two babies have their own frustrations. Watch Margaret at nine months trying to walk. There she goes successfully making it around the couch and then venturing out for a few steps alone. Bravo! Ah—but the frustration she has when she watches Elizabeth at 16 months running across the room to hide behind a curtain! She finally has to give in and crawl to make speed. But Elizabeth is frustrated too. Her "baby" cousin whom she likes to pat lovingly and a bit condescendingly as she says, "Baby baby babeee" is now trying to *walk*, an accomplishment that she considers hers, *exclusively*, in this relationship! So when Margaret tries to walk alone, Elizabeth hurries over to push her down, to keep her crawling where she feels she belongs!! "Babeeeee"! Funny? Yes, to us, but I wonder how our dear Heavenly Father regards our big and little frustrations. Some of them are tragic sufferings, and His sympathy and understanding are perfect; some of them are because of our limited understanding as "babies" in some realm, compared to His perfect understanding, and what we need is *time* to see how premature and foolish our frustration was. However, *because* frustrations are present in your place of living, your work, your inward life, this does *not* prove that you are not in the Lord's place for you. The Lord can do two things for each of us: (1) Remove the cause by a miracle of answered prayer, or (2) give us strength in the midst of it. Often #2 comes first and then #1 is graciously given! Oh, let us "rest in the Lord, and wait patiently for Him" for "He satisfieth the longing soul."

With love in Him Who knows our every need,

EDITH

June 8, 1963   Huemoz sur Ollon, Switzerland

Dear Family:

Early the morning of June 6th I was running down the road to the village to get some cornflakes for Fran's breakfast. The sun was flooding the valley and making bright white the wisps of cloud hovering between us and the valley, the mountains were dazzling against the blue sky, and the variety of greens of the new leaves, new grasses, new tips on the pine branches made me want to count the hues, but I was already counting my steps to the village store, when suddenly, "Mom, oh Mom, will you stop by on your way back? I think today is going to be the day. . ." came floating down to me from the balcony of Chalet Tzi No. I stopped and looked up to see Priscilla waving from their new home (an old chalet which became suddenly available to rent, as a real answer to prayer for such a place to be provided before the new baby arrived), and I called back, "Have to take something home for breakfast, then I'll come back after that."

Sometime later I was having my second run down the back road, looking up at the inviting field and woods above, but keeping on the path regardless of the tempting songs of the birds, to read my Daily Light with Pris, instead of having a time alone to read and pray. This was the moment we had been waiting for, "The Day"—the day of the new baby's birth. A thousand years is as a day to the Lord, and a day is as a thousand years, I thought. He is infinite, and He understands time totally, but my, we *can* understand *something* of time in its very different effect upon us, and the seemingly elastic quality. Some days seem a week long—some months seem a year long, as we wait for the birth of a baby, or some event we are impatient to know about. Some days seem an hour long, some weeks a day long, when we are with someone, or doing something we love and have longed for and waited for. What a puzzling thing time is: a lifetime, a never-to-be-forgotten hour that is as tangible as a statue, yet never to be recaptured. Time and memory, time and expectancy, time and hope, past—present—future; how real, how important time and history are. Pris and I sat outside on the bench in the sunshine watching Elizabeth play around picking flowers and floating them in a pan of water. "Fifteen minutes—they seem to be coming fairly regularly. I think this is the real thing this time." A committee meeting composed of Jane, Joe, John, and Fran, were meeting around on the other side of the house. The day went on as usual with people coming and going, work needing to be done, but twenty-four hours later, I stood at the telephone in Tzi No's hall (where I had stayed all night to care for Elizabeth) talking to John in the hospital. "Mother, Rebecca Anne was born at 8:10 this morning. She weighs 7 lbs. 8 oz. and she looks a lot like Elizabeth. Pris is fine, though she had a hard half-hour at the end." Priscilla's time of waiting had come to an end, but Rebecca's time in the world—and eternity—had just begun!

39

Could it possibly have been over a *year* since we had sat in this pleasant grey and white book-lined room overlooking the Singel in Leiden, with its floating ducks and weeping willow trees? It had been February 1962 when we had our Dutch trip last year; now it was March 1963 and time seemed to have shrunk with the familiar faces, sights, and sounds surrounding us. You know the feeling, I'm sure: "Why, it seems no time at all since we were here before." Yet as the Rookmaakers and we talked over what had happened during the year, it seemed far longer than a year. That first evening in Leiden was a most vivid one of discussion as the room was filled with people from various professions, some students of Leiden University, and several bearded art students from the University of Delft. The questions of the unbelieving art students set the direction of the evening, and answers and the questions arising from them rounded out into a presentation of the intellectual reasonableness of the Christian system as taught in the whole Bible. Fran spoke in Kampen, in the theological seminary there, another night, and also had a time of questions and discussion with theological students. Another night he spoke in Groningen to theological students there, and the discussion time went on to 2 A.M.! We had a day in Amsterdam, during which I had a long talk with Marry Meester; Fran had a discussion group in Meester's home; we had a Chinese dinner and discussion with some fellows who had been at the chalet, and we visited Mr. VanderWeyden's lovely furniture store, Arti-home; but now the Lord had a different experience for us to share, a totally unexpected one for any of us a year before. We walked into the antiseptically white room in an enormous Amsterdam hospital with Friedus (VanderWeyden's son who was born again at the chalet some years ago) leading the way. Tall, slender, greyhaired, blue-eyed, handsome Mr. VanderWeyden looked like a wax figure of himself as he slowly raised one hand with effort to greet us. His cheeks sunken, wound healed but obviously recent—it seemed impossible that it had been only two weeks ago that we had sat in the Mélèzes dining room having tea, and that a short time after that Fran had bid the two of them goodbye as Mr. VanderWeyden flew home for an operation and Mrs. VanderWeyden went back by train to arrive a few hours later. A doctor in Lausanne had said there was a growth, not just sinus trouble as had been believed before, and now the operation had uncovered the real hidden trouble—not only a growth in the sinuses, but a tumor pressing against the brain—cancer! His lips barely moving, Mr. VanderWeyden whispered, "Always I everything could do myself; now I nothing can do." It seemed only "yesterday" he had been pulling up more chairs, seeing that everyone had a delightful little pottery cup of coffee and that his daughter had passed around enough tiny pastries, during the discussion group in his store, now—? What is important in life? *Using* our time as the Lord would have us use it in the *present*. There was the present moment in the hospital. "Yes, Mr. VanderWeyden, the wonderful thing about being a Christian is that even *now* you may be having your most important victory by simply loving God and praising Him in the midst of this. It can be that this moment is more important than any active thing you ever did in your Christian life." He nodded perceptibly. Fran read Psalm 23, Isaiah, Revelation, and we prayed. He communicated with us in English quite understandably, and some in Dutch which Friedus translated. He sent greetings to everyone by name in Huemoz, then waved goodbye as we left. Later we were told he never spoke so clearly again. It was not long after that that he went into a coma, and in six days he left his body to be "present with the Lord." His time on earth in this life over, his time in the presence of the Lord commenced. It is the *present* that is important! Preparation? Yes. Waiting? Yes. But while preparing for a future time, while waiting for a future event, the *present* is being used *or* wasted. We are to be full of hope, expectancy, faith for the answer to prayer to come, but we are to be doing the Lord's will this hour, this day, this week while we are waiting. The moment of birth ends the mother's waiting and brings joy and a beginning; the moment of death ends a lifetime on this earth and brings for the Christian also joy and a beginning! Both moments are unpredictable, but inevitable. Being *ready*, however, for changes, death, or the Lord's coming—involves using the *present time* to the Lord's glory, in His chosen way.

And while we were in Holland during March, what was going on at the chalet, in the same time? The work of L'Abri goes right on when we are away, as there are Ran and Sue, Joe and Linette, Pris and John, Jane, Trudy, and other Workers who continue to have the Bible class discussion groups, care for the chalets, write letters, and answer questions as guests come seeking help. . . .

Jane told us of an answered prayer Mr. Langascher, the Bee Man, had during this time. He was burning leaves and sticks in a field when a high wind whipped up the fire and it spread dangerously near the forest below. Another few moments and the fire would have caught the trees. What to do? Nothing could be done by one man in this "split second" of time—but yes, he thought of the *one* possible thing to do, and this powerfully built man of the woods and fields bowed his head simply to pray, "Oh God, save the forest; don't let this fire spread further." Almost before he lifted his head, Mr. Langescher felt the wind change—and discovered that it had shifted to an exact opposite direction!! No human help could have done anything effective in that moment of time. Oh yes, *time* in the *Lord's* hands is a different thing. He can do "the impossible"—and if we would only *truly* believe and base our lives on His promises, with a willingness first for His will, we would realize that *often* the very best use of our "waiting" time would be spent in real prayer. How thrilling it is to see people in many walks of life realize that this is applicable not just to Christian workers' lives, but to all Christians' lives.

April: I couldn't put emotions and struggles, realities of spiritual answers to prayer and just sheer hard work in hours and energy into this small space of paper—and if I did it without condensing, you'd be bored! Thirteen beds in Beau Site for Susan to wash sheets for as people come and go. Thirteen beds in Mélèzes that need the same! Six beds in Bethany for Linette to lug sheets up to Beau Site to wash, and now ten beds in Tzi No for Pris to care for, also using the Beau Site washer, which happily heats its own water and so can be used over and over again. That's just washing for beds. Add people and babies and the Farel students (*not* guests' clothing, however) and you can see that with houses to keep clean and food to cook, marketing to do, there is a lot of energy expended on *top* of everyone keeping their minds on the fact that letters must be answered, and people *talked* to. Schedules for classes are posted: Joe teaching at Villars, Joe and Linette together in Beau Soleil, John at Champéry, Ran at Montreux, Fran in Lausanne, Pris and Jane and Trudy at Bellevue. Schedules for Farel lectures; schedules for meals and division of people for meal discussions—yes, there is much that I can't write about but without which you miss the "feel" of what is going on. Oh, how to make it all *real* to you!!

April—going by with days full—and an English trip scheduled as indications seemed to be clear that the Lord would have Fran and me go, yet no money for the trip in sight! At the last minute all became certain, as a gift arrived in England which covered the expenses, and the Lord provided hospitality in other ways too.

We were twelve days in Cambridge, six in Glasgow, four in London, three in Oxford, then four in London and Surrey again. Doing what? In Cambridge there were evenings with theological students with Fran giving lectures and then having time for questions and answers; evenings with research scientists, and another with undergraduate scientists. There were times with individual students who had questions, and times when I told the L'Abri story to various ones. There was a day when Fran went from Cambridge to speak in the theological college near London in which Rupert Studd studies, and there was a day when I went from Cambridge to Purley to speak to a group Jennifer had gathered in her home to hear me. Jennifer became a Christian at the chalet during the first year of L'Abri, and now with her husband, Tim, and little boy, David, has returned several times. It is wonderful to see the reality of this home based on the Lord, in the "small" things such as little four-year-old David planting his garden and praying over the seeds as he pats them into the earth, and the "larger" things such as the courageous stand for the entire Bible among those who have discarded so much of it.

In Glasgow there was a morning message Fran gave at the Glasgow Bible Training Institute, and another morning message given to the Glasgow Presbytery of the Church of Scotland Free, as well as evenings in Audrey Carson's flat, arranged by Helen Sinclair. There was a blessed Sunday afternoon when among other guests for dinner at the apartment was David Aruldasan, the Indian Treasurer of Dohnavur, who had brought with him a tape recording of Dohnavur children beautifully singing some of Amy Carmichael's hymns! What a joy to have a foretaste of what I expect we shall have lots of time for in heaven, a personal talk with those who have prayed for us and for whom we have prayed for years without meeting!

In London the telephone rang—the doorbell—incessantly it seemed; and mornings, afternoons, and evenings were filled with conversations and discussions and times of question and answer. One day Fran spoke at All Nations Bible College to a group of men preparing for the mission field, and another day I spoke in a girls' school to girls from 12 to 18 years old—telling the L'Abri story and many instances of the Lord's leading, answered prayer, and the new birth of souls. One Sunday we were invited to the Queen's chapel for the morning church service at which John Stott was preaching, and then to have dinner at the home of one of the choristers (the father of Henry, who was a Farel House student and arranged our time in Cambridge). After a very concentrated conversation about Christianity during dinner and the early afternoon, Fran was taken to the heart of London to spend time at the Mayflower Settlement work, and I went back to the flat to give the L'Abri story and a Bible study to a group of young office girls.

In Oxford there was a debate between Fran and a humanist who was past-president of the Humanist Society and a defender of Humanism in his writings. The last weekend we spent in Reigate at the home of Franky's schoolteacher, where we had a group of people Saturday evening for tea, listening to an explanation of the rise of liberalism and its changes as it becomes "Neoorthodoxy," related to the changing philosophies and the consequent danger to Biblical Christianity in our day.

It would be totally incomplete as even a tiny *glimpse* of the English trip, to give this much without telling you that one book was spoken about in every conversation and discussion group and was on the tongue of "everyone" in England, so it seemed. We found this book on tables in students' rooms, as well as displayed in bookstore windows, and discussed in newspapers, and presented on television. Which book? A new book written by an English bishop, J.A.T. Robinson, called *Honest to God*. It is really Paul Tillich's theology carried a little bit further and brought to the ordinary public in a popular book that everyone is reading. He speaks about the problem of communication and needing "a new set of propositions" but he really does not have anything to communicate when it comes to the true Biblical God. It really is the communication of a new religion, not new words to make Biblical truth more real. The bishop is really pantheistic. It is frightening to see the speed with which television, newspapers, book distribution spreads such an undermining of Christianity, and it gives one a preview of how the anti-Christ will sweep the world with his teachings when his time comes. . . .

We returned from England on May 22nd, only two-and-a-half weeks ago (and *that* really doesn't seem possible in the light of all that has happened since). We found that the work had been going on full swing during our absence. Weekends were *full;* gardens had been dug and the manure turned in; Pris and John had moved to their rented chalet, Tzi No; Blanche (an American nurse) and Penny (a South African girl) had become Workers; and Franky had gotten on the soccer team of his school! These past two-and-a-half weeks have been unbelievably full. We have had our yearly Members' meeting, with Mr. Exhenry coming from Champéry and Hurvey from Milan to discuss the many things before us. There have been new Farel House students arriving. The weekends have become so full every bed is usually used and the countries represented sound like a league of nations. . . .

Births, deaths, new births, sudden illnesses, daily necessities of life, yet through it all the Lord's work to be done. *Time*—is there *ever* time enough? If Time is going to be used for the Lord, whether for prayer or active work, if money is going to be used for the Lord it must be with some measure of sacrifice in our present moment. A day may be a thousand years, but a thousand years is also as a day and in our own smaller measure, time suddenly runs out and we must say with Mr. Vander-Weyden, "Now, I nothing can do."

With love in Him Who can do with a brief word more than we can do in a lifetime, yet—Who hears us when we pray, answers us, and promises to give us *His* strength in the present!

EDITH

August 28, 1963 Huemoz sur Ollon, Switzerland

Dear Family:

. . . A shaft of sun comes through the clouds to lighten the field below Chesalet. There stands the Bee Man in his gardening hat, and in the background, fellows digging up the turf to make larger vegetable gardens. . . . You will remember that several years ago, in 1960, to be exact, some of us began praying about a chapel. Many were the disappointments as one month after another went by, and still no possibility of a real beginning to build seemed to be in sight. Then, the Bee Man accepted Christ as his Saviour, as Jane and Betty talked to him in two languages. Our rejoicing over that fact had no thought in it of how the Lord would use the Bee Man. A few months ago the Bee Man began to talk to Jane and Betty about a foundation he had built for a chalet on a steep property across the dirt "lower road" bordering the field below Chesalet. "I've been thinking and praying about the need of a larger place for our Sunday church service," said the Bee Man, "And it came to me that with some changes such as enlarging the foundations and size

Here is the Bee Man (M. Langascher)
working in the field beside the
Chesalet garden.

of the building, that chalet could be built for a chapel. I would do it with my heart in it as unto the Lord. I could not give all my time, but the total cost would be *much* less than if you built a chapel with a commercial company of builders. It would give me deep joy to do this." When some of us first heard this sentence, all sorts of bells began to ring in our thinking. "A Swiss" "village man" "born again at L'Abri" "careful carpenter who would work with love" "able to present plans to village council for their approval so much better than any of us" and so on and on. Yet it seemed that a certain amount of money should be on hand before giving a "go ahead." Now we feel that the Lord has led clearly that we should *begin* and even now the plans are almost ready to be presented to the village council. A Swiss bank said they will give a mortgage on the building, and other indications have come from the Lord. It is a step of faith and it will open up many new possibilities for the work. For instance, people in the ski resorts near here, as well as valley towns, hesitate coming to a house for a service, especially as often space is a problem. It would seem that a separate building for services would give freedom to come in for that hour. Then, too, the crowdedness of our house when every bed is full (as has been the case this past number of weeks) presents a problem expressed by Mrs. Stokes who was here for a few days, "It is so wonderful here, but in the noise and confusion of this morning, I have been struck with your need of a chapel, a place that would be like a House of Prayer, where one could go for Bible reading and prayer, on a rainy or cold day when voices deep in conversation, voices chattering away in the crowded kitchen, music in the living room, mingle together and sift through all the wooden walls, making a quiet time difficult. I am going to pray for a chapel for you." It was then I stopped to tell her the story you have just read! That prayer is still *needed*, as there will be many problems before the chapel becomes a reality, but it is in the process of being answered. The chapel also will have a room beneath the main room, against the side of the mountain with the window side looking out over the valley. This room will serve as a larger space for Farel House students to study. And it will be a place where the ceiling can be high enough and the space large enough to give the acoustics necessary for Jane to sing, and others too, to have music that will float out over the hills in praise of the Lord. It would seem that in this building the Lord is bringing into focus a number of things that have been on various people's hearts and minds for prayer, and that as yet we cannot *begin* to see *all* the details of what *He* is working out. Oh, how many times, I wonder, do we have to go through foggy, cloudy times only to suddenly see what wonders God was preparing "behind the curtain" with excitement and amazement at the extent of His *understanding* of our needs and desires, before we will be ready to *wait* with *patience* when the *next* "cloud" blots out our view!!!

The earliest rays of the rising sun, lighting up the sky and peaks first with a rosy glow as birds' songs fill the quiet air, suddenly streak through to hit Chalet Tzi No. It is 5 A.M. and John Sandri is up, glorying in the beauty of the early morning and in the hush that surrounds the one who is working while others still sleep, a special kind of hush that is the reward of such a one. What is he doing so early? Copying tapes. Why? Well, people in various parts of the world are waiting for copies of tapes to arrive, copies of the "Prophecy Tapes," of sermons, of Farel House lectures, of discussion, and they'll never get them if someone doesn't take the time to copy them. But why at such a time as this? Because first of all John has much to do throughout the days to sort out tapes for the people who want to listen to various topics here, and at the present time Farel House is having two shifts: morning and afternoon. Hence he has to be busy with students both sections of the day. Secondly, the tape recorders are limited; we haven't enough for the students, so they have to await their turn, as each one is usually listening to something different. Therefore, as two recorders are needed for copying purposes, the copying must be done when the students are not needing the recorders! Some of the students are already listening at 7 A.M. these days, with a cup of coffee beside them, though Farel House really commences at 9! If you kept watching Tzi No as the sun rose higher and the rays kept lighting it up, you'd see Pris feeding baby Rebecca, then Elizabeth, and starting her morning's work which includes preparing lunch for about eight or ten people these days. . . .

It's night now, and supper dishes are being done, and into the hall come three or four fellows. Several people in the kitchen move out into the hall to see who they might be. Debby darting out seeing a "new face" says cordially, "And are you John?" "Why yes," comes the reply, "But

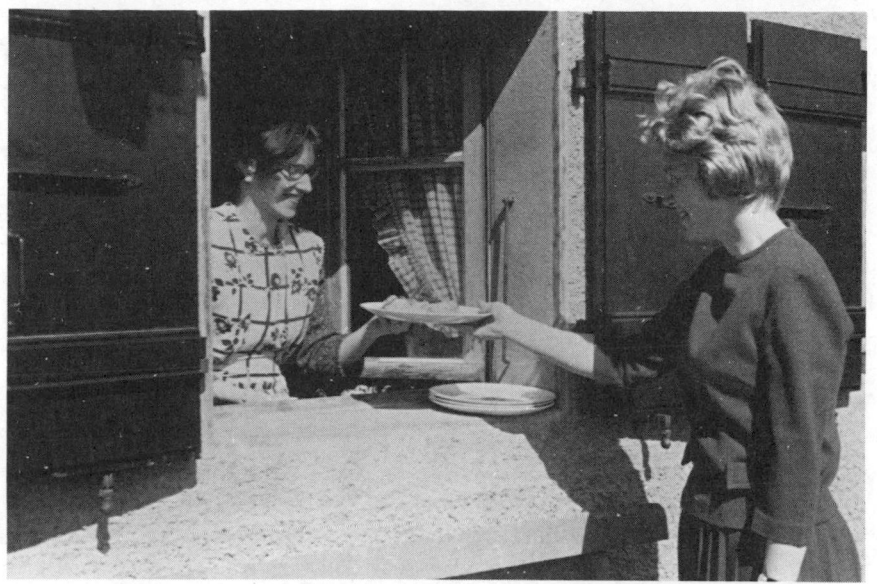

Priscilla passing plates of lunch out of Sandri's Chalet Tzi No window! This takes place on warm sunny days ... the kitchen is the only other place to eat.

how did you know?" "Oh," she says, laughing gaily. "We were expecting you." "You *were*," comes the astonished reply, "But how could that be?" "Why you're on the list—in fact, you've been on it for a few days, so you're late!" "I *am?*" says this fellow, absolutely incredulous by this time, "I'm a hitchhiker these fellows picked up—What list am I on?" You can imagine the shrieks of laughter which pealed forth as Debby blurted out, "Oh, you're the wrong John then!" From that moment on we distinguished this particular John from several other Johns by calling him "the wrong John." Since food had been left over that particular night, it was only a matter of moments until a full dinner was dished out, piping hot, and served to the newcomers on the dull green linen tablecloth with the special bark, moss, and flower arrangement that had been the centerpiece for dinner. "I feel as if I should say 'Dr. Livingston, I presume,' " says the wrong John as he views all this. "Why, it is just as astonishing as finding a man in the jungle, to come in out of the night, hitchhiking with a pack on my back, to find a dinner like this in a moment's time. It just isn't possible." "The wrong John" turned out to be a Cambridge University student, not a Christian, but one who is "seeking."

Now the sun is on a garden patch where Dorie and I are bent over a job of transplanting ... with a constant discussion going on, sticks and stones being used to substitute for pencil and paper, as sticks do well to make lines, and stones make circles in illustrating various points in Bible study and "bird's-eye views" of subjects. Dorie, who had never planted, weeded or picked vegetables before is fascinated at all the variety found in the garden, but she hasn't come to L'Abri to learn gardening . . . nor, in fact, to learn anything! She, like Deane, was only going to stay a short time . . . with the added remark to a friend before coming, "If I can stand it that long." Dorie, a dean in a girls' boarding school, among other degrees has a degree from a very liberal theological school and was horrified when I first made a remark that we actually believed the Bible *"literally"* . . . creation, Adam and Eve, and all! . . . One night Dorie made a decision in conversation with Fran and came to tell me—face glowing with more than sunburn! . . .

A particularly vivid day was the 30th of July—the annual day of prayer and fasting. Yes, we have a day of prayer once a week in which we take turns in the prayer room (the Mélèzes living room at this present time), each taking a half-hour or so of prayer so that someone is praying all through the day. But once a year we have a day of prayer and fasting which frees all the Workers for prayer and quiet meditation without any of the usual work. No one is required to fast. Bread, butter, fruit, cheese, and tomatoes are placed on a table, and the guests and anyone else who wants to may eat a simple meal without anyone taking the time to prepare it. We feel that fasting is an individual thing, between an individual and the Lord. Some do find it helpful to put aside the normal "good" things of life, such as eating and conversation, to concentrate for a whole day on not only prayer, but reading the Bible, that the communication between the Lord and the individual may be something very special that day. Fasting not only releases *time* for prayer, but also puts aside the distractions of mealtime for that one day. Fasting, to me, is also a kind of *underlining* or emphasis for prayer. I feel about it as I do about underlining verses in the Bible—it is an emphasis on the importance I feel prayer has so that I am saying to the Lord, "This matter for which I am praying is far more important to me than eating." Are there not other things in your life which at times take precedence over eating? Surely you have chosen at some time to skip a meal in order to do some other thing that seemed far more important. Well, fasting, among other reasons, is to me a realistic way of placing prayer in "first place" from time to time. It is a day that we all find refreshing, and I must say it is rather deeply moving to see people go off with Bibles and prayer lists: Blanche and Trudy in two different directions in the woods; Debby over at Beau Site in a sunny spot beyond the tree-sheltered bench; Nettie off in the direction of Chesiere; Ran with his Bible and things in a knapsack going "up" somewhere; Dutch Wim and Arie disappearing down the road. If one believes and understands even a tiny fraction of all that the Bible teaches concerning prayer, such a day has the potentialities of accomplishing so much more than a day of work that it would be impossible to do the "multiplication"! Oh, that the "light" of His Word given us in the Spirit's power would bring sharply and clearly to us the reality of prayer and all that He has given prayer to *be* and to *do* in our lives. . . .

The numbers of guests seemed to increase as summer went on. It has been a time during which most of us have had a feeling that the *Lord* is doing a work here which is as startling and "unbelievable" to live through, as it is to hear about. How do we stand the confusion and constancy of work and sharing our homes with a constant stream of people?—There is nothing in us to point to, and we are ashamed of the various emotions that need to be struggled against at times—but we do know that the Lord is *real* and that He has, and *is* answering prayer—and that He has, and is, and *will* be giving us the supply of our needs as we make them known to Him. Perhaps the greatest need to ask for is patience. . . .

With love in Him,

EDITH

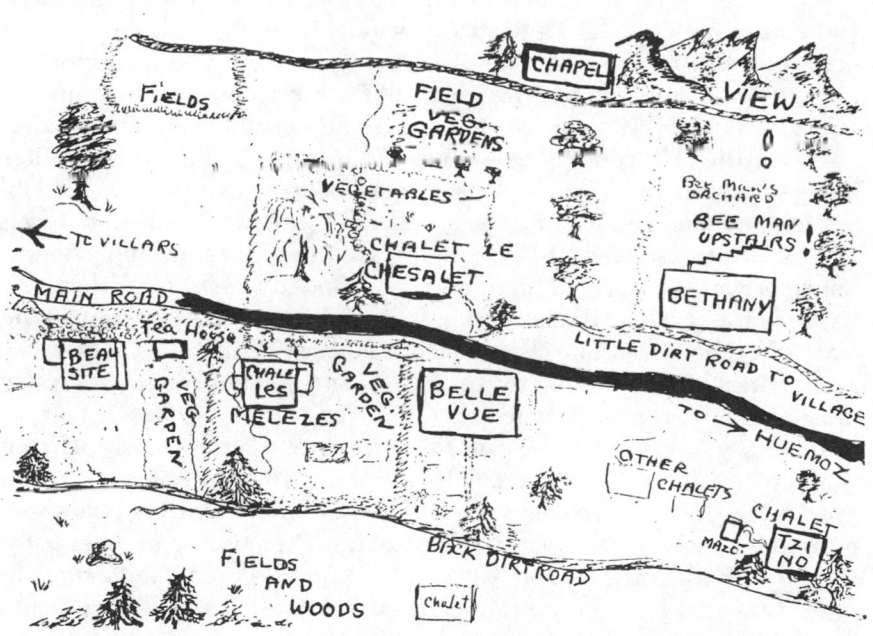

October 31, 1963   Huemoz sur Ollon, Switzerland

Dear Family:

The above sketch is *not* done to scale, nor is it supposed to give the right proportions in *any* way, or form. It is a kind of Winnie-the-Pooh sketch of "the forest where all the animals live"—so that anyone reading the story can have a vague idea of places and people and directions!! This, then, is our "forest" so to speak—where the L'Abri chalets are which you hear mentioned in the letters. They look a little squashed together in this "map," but at least you can have a basis for using your imagination when you picture us! In fact, that is what this letter is going to try to do—outline the chalets and territory and identify the people who live here. People who arrive with little or no knowledge of the place are confused for a time, until they get it sorted out, but you who read the letters and who have never been here in person, must feel even more confused at times.

Let's start with the lower left-hand corner of the sketch—though it is *higher* ground, looking down over the rest of the map. We can sit down together under the first pine tree which is way up at the top of the field. Perhaps you're a little out of puff—so you'll be glad to sit down and look over the view. For people who don't live in the mountains, it seems a bit steep, coming up the field, but it really isn't too bad. I've carried breakfast trays up there, with a hot drink, eggs, toast, and have found an almost-level spot to put it down and eat, read, and pray. . . .

Coming along a bit of the back dirt road, we go down steep dirt steps and a steep path to pass the Beau Site vegetable garden and arrive at the door leading into the Beau Site hall. The first door on your right is the kitchen door, leading into the small, narrow kitchen which is Susan's domain! As you pass a stairway leading up on the right, and one leading down on the left, you will come into the living/dining room, a rather large, square room with an old black "marble" fireplace in it, flanked by a piano and couches, making the living room end, and with an old oval table and antique sideboard forming the dining room end. Here Sue and Ran serve meals to six, eight, or at times a dozen guests. Here they also have tea for various village people, or friends from the Montreux Bible class, or other Swiss contacts; here Farel House Seminars are held, prayer meetings or discussion groups, as well as Sunday School on Sunday mornings for the smallest members of L'Abri. If you go up the stairs at the right, you can visit Sue and Ran's private quarters: a bed/sitting room, baby Margaret's room, and a bathroom. You can also peer in and see the five-bed bedroom and the two-bed bedroom which enables seven guests to stay in the upstairs of Beau Site. There is also another bathroom up there for guests. It is an old, old house, and the boards are creaky and rickety, and the stone and plaster walls are cold and damp, but it has improved a hundred per cent from the original "Beau Site" we first rented! Back in the downstairs hall you can come to the steps which bring you to the Farel House section. Very, very simple indeed: just a big old bedroom holding four beds which we use for men, with floor space for sleeping bags when necessary; a narrow book-lined library with a window, a couch, a desk, and a glass door opening out to the sun porch where seven desks and lamps give that many students places to study at one time, and to listen to tapes with earphones. Now turn on down the very old and crooked steps leading to an old brick-floored kitchen, which is now the laundry. A fine washing machine and double sinks are down here, but the place is usually a storm, because not only does Sue do her washing, the sheets for all those beds, and Farel House students wash here, but Pris used this for her washing for her family of four plus the guests who stay in Tzi No, and Linette used it for her washing for three, and the guests staying in Bethany, and others arrange to use it from time to time. It is a very busy washing machine!!! A doorway from the laundry leads into a dark room, under ground level, with only a tiny window. It is in the process of being "lightened" by having its ceiling and cupboards painted white, and drapes and curtains made to cover some of the dark, badly stained wood walls. This is the *tape room*—where people can listen to tapes and where the tape library is installed. . . .

Now we're on our way to Les Mélèzes, and we have to go on the narrow walk between the Tea House and the hedge. (The Tea House, by the way, is a fancy name for a very weather-beaten old garden house, with rough benches and log tables in it—half of which is partitioned off into a coal bin and a chicken coop!) We will enter the Les Mélèzes living room, on the ground floor at the front of the house, and see that long but rather narrow room which has been the scene of so many, many things. Here church is held on Sunday mornings, with part of the furniture moved out and the chairs put in in rows; here Saturday night hot dog roasts and discussions are held, as well as the more "dressed up" Sunday "high tea," after which there is a Bible study, a reading of some passage or sermon or missionary biography and a hymn sing. Here people read, listen to classical music, sing, or talk, around the fireplace, or at the piano end of the room! And here the day of prayer finds one at a time praying. A new idea has been put into practice recently, making the Les Mélèzes living room the "private" living room for the girl Workers living at Mélèzes, on Monday nights so that they can have *some* time away from "people" without retreating to their bedrooms.

On this ground floor are also Trudy's bedroom/office, a combined toilet and ski room, a combined tiny kitchen and washroom, a furnace room (where chairs for Sunday service are stored), a "cave" where fruit and vegetables and canned things are kept, and a "cave" where garden tools, boxes, tools, etc., are kept. (A "cave" in French means a dirt-floored room that is without heat.)

The next floor of Les Mélèzes has a small office and telephone room, *the* dining room which is *much* too small to hold the 23 people we *can* get into it!, and the enlarged kitchen (which is *really* finished at last and even the roof is at last waterproof for the winter!). There is also a double-decker bunk bedroom, and a tiny single end room for workers, a four-bed bedroom for female guests, and a bathroom.

Who lives in Mélèzes? Fran and I, Debby, Franky, and Trudy, our Swiss Worker; Coxe, our Dutch Worker; and Blanche, our American Worker. As you know, Trudy does the financial books, secretarial work,

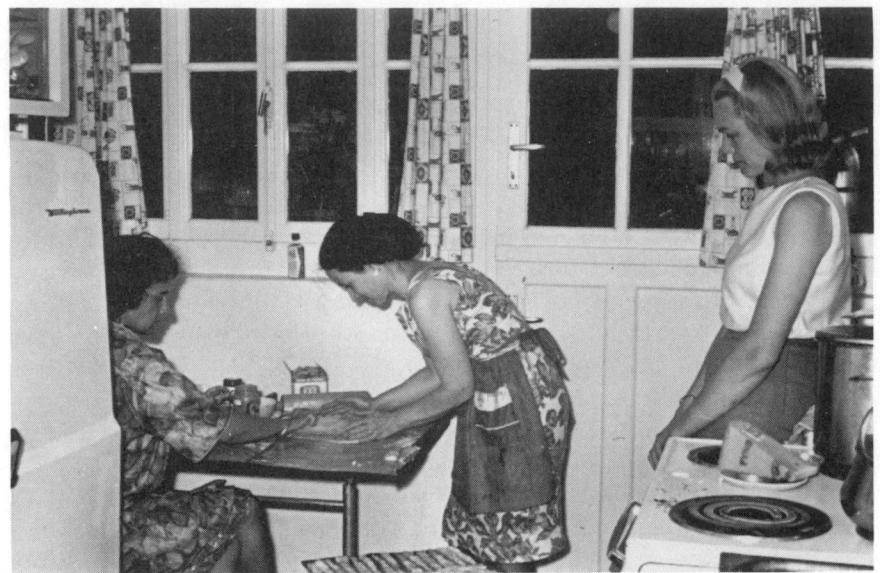

*Here I am preparing a meal in the finished enlarged Chalet
Mélèzes kitchen. Notice that we have a door now to the outside.
A wonderful improvement!*

and translates for German-speaking guests, teaches Sunday School in
German at Bellevue, plus a million other things as she pitches in to help
in the kitchen, clean the living room, or anywhere help is suddenly
needed. Blanche helps with the cooking, and takes over very well in my
absence in buying and planning. She also helps with laundry (which
keeps being mountainous!) and cleaning, talking to guests, and all the
variety of things which makes up L'Abri. Coxe is arriving this month, to
help first of all with typing up special lectures so that they can be printed, such as "The Intellectual Climate and the New Theology." She will
also help in general office work and in housework. We are *always* behind in some portion of the work. Recently, two Farel House students
have been living in Mélèzes, too, and they could underline the statement about our always being behind in some work, as they help in afternoons and have felt that they'd never come to the end of peeling apples
for making apple butter for the winter! Quarts of apple butter disappear
amazingly quickly. When L'Abri is "full-up" that means that Trudy has
someone in her upper bunk, all the beds are full in the four-bed bedroom and the other bunk room, *and* some are sleeping in the living room
on couches. You can imagine how amused we are when someone writes
(not knowing the nature of L'Abri, thinking it is some sort of summer
conference) and says, "I'd like a double room and bath" or something of
that sort!!

Now, are you still looking at the "map"? We'll go straight across the
Mélèzes path through the hedge opening, to Bellevue. Bellevue is the

rehabilitation home for cerebral palsy children. It is a big chalet, which once was a small hotel. When we first came to Mélèzes, it was owned by a Roman Catholic organization, but in an amazing way, during the time Anne and Mary (two American occupational therapists who had been commencing a school of occupational therapy in connection with a Swiss hospital) were with us as L'Abri Workers, praying for the next "step" in their lives to be shown to them. Bellevue was put up for sale and the girls were led to pray for clear signs as to whether they should buy it. God opened the way for Bellevue to be bought, added Rosemary as a third person to commence the work (Rosemary had been born again at L'Abri and is also an American occupational therapist) and God also opened up the way for the girls to have a medically accredited rehabilitation home. It was not long before they were filled up to capacity with 17 patients of all ages, from a few months to twenty years of age, and had nurses, a teacher, and other helpers to help them with this *full-time* nursing, giving therapy, being mothers, teachers, and missionaries to these children. Bellevue garden has blossomed in the years with a fine paved terrace, swings and play equipment, tables for eating outdoors and gay umbrellas, and the inside has also become gradually more and more "fixed up" to be both bright and attractive as well as efficient. Some Bellevue children come over for our church service in their wheelchairs; Jane Stuart Smith leads a hymn sing for the children on Sunday afternoons; and Trudy, Debby, and Susan have Sunday School for the children. Jane also teaches a class there regularly. Some of the Bellevue workers come over for the discussion Saturday nights, and other L'Abri events, and Jane's "choir practice" is attended by Bellevue Workers as well as Farel House students and some L'Abri Workers. So you see, although we are not "organizationally connected," so to speak, Bellevue is very much a part of our community, and a part of God's *plan* which He knew about before L'Abri ever started!

Let's come up the steps from Bellevue's back garden, up to the back dirt road and down this road to Tzi No where John and Pris live. It is a five-minute walk but I had to let it come in on the edge of the paper even though the proportionate distance is wrong. Tzi No is just past Argentine, for any of you who have been here, on the left side of the road, hidden by bushes and trees. The "upstairs" is what you come into if you come in the first door you see. The "downstairs" is level with the ground around at the other side of the house. "Upstairs" John and Pris have their bedroom and a bedroom for Elizabeth, aged two, and Rebecca, four months old, and there is a toilet on that floor. Come down a picturesque, ladder-like stairway, and you come right into a charming big old kitchen, white plaster walls hung with antique wrought iron and wooden things the owner has collected (it is a rented chalet). It is in this kitchen that Pris cooks and serves eight guests at a time. A door from the kitchen leads into a sort of bed/sitting room where John copies tapes and where one L'Abri guest sleeps. A door leads from that room into another small bedroom! So that means two girls, or two fellows may use these two rooms. Now next to Tzi No (look at the map), you'll see a tiny little place labeled "Mazot," which has one room downstairs, and one room upstairs. It is very rustic indeed and needs some more "fixing." But still, four people can sleep there and four have slept there many nights since this place was rented in May. There is a toilet there. But if anyone wants to wash in hot water, the only hot water there comes from a tap in the Tzi No's bathtub. (Yes the *only!* That means no hot water in the kitchen sink.) And guess where the bathtub is???? It is in a little hallway leading from the kitchen to the "cave" where Pris keeps her potatoes and fruits, etc. Inconvenient? Yes, but they manage somehow, and Pris can keep an eye on Elizabeth in the bathtub and still cook!! . . . John teaches the Champéry class in French, takes charge of the tape program, is "Senior Student" at Farel House, and like Ran, John teaches various ones who come to L'Abri, preaches at times, and so on. It really is difficult to sort out the work. In fact, right now I remember I have forgotten to tell you that Ran teaches a class in Montreux. But this identification letter as well as the identification picture is only a *partial* description, and *not* complete! . . .

Now come along the main road until in front of the *laiterie* (milk depot) there branches off a dirt road you'll see marked on the map. Climb along this uphill until you come to Bethany. Open a dark wooden gate, walk along between fruit trees trained to stretch their arms out flat to let you past and you'll be ready to knock at Joe and Linette's door. Little baby Keith, now three months old, is sleeping in his screened-off "room" in the hall. Now you can see where this is in relation to the rest of the houses. The Bee Man, whose picture was in the last letter, lives upstairs. In fact, this is his house! . . . Bethany* has a four-bed bedroom, too, for guests and is the scene of meals, conversations, and kitchen Bible classes held at all sorts of hours from early morning to late night, as Joe fits them in to what he feels to be the immediate need of people there. Joe is Treasurer of L'Abri.

We must go out to the dirt road again to push uphill a little more to Bethany's next door neighbor, Chalet le Chesalet, Betty Carlson's home. Betty has become a resident of Switzerland, Huemoz, and the L'Abri community, and has settled down to write in Chesalet until it becomes a bit too noisy and she runs off to seek a quieter spot to finish a book! Betty writes a newspaper column, but also Christian books, some of which you may have read. Sharing Chesalet with her is Jane Stuart Smith and four chickens! Betty is a private citizen of our community who gives time and energy to helping in in-between moments; Jane is a L'Abri Worker who answers much correspondence, writes "thank-you" letters, teaches Bible classes, leads the "choir" and prepares and practices for more "music" to be released when the chapel is ready—and gardens, talks to guests, cares for the Evangelical Library, and the bookstore, and

*Now called Bourdonette.

cooks when it is her turn to care for guests (Betty cooks too in turn!), and oh yes, the chickens lay eggs—white ones. Chesalet is a beautiful chalet and the living room is the warm scene of prayer meetings, teas, and so on, as it is used in many ways. Betty and Jane have been used, too, to contact various people in Villars and the village.

Now let's go down through the vegetable garden, along the loosely placed flagstones, through the gate in the corner of the fence, around the lower vegetable garden, and through the field to the lower road beyond. Here we find the foundations and walls of the chapel being worked on. The Bee Man, and his brother, and John could have been found there any October morning—pouring cement, and working "like mad"—early and late. Ran also joined them several days, and Udo helped dig when they needed help. The 5 o'clock A.M.—till 8:30 P.M. sort of "push" was needed as they raced against a possible change in the weather. They needed to get a certain amount finished before snow and frost would erase the work. October was a beautiful month and the necessary work *did* get finished in time. We thank God for the weather and for the willingness of the men to throw themselves into the hard physical work and for protection against accident. At one time a whole flow of cement threatened to cause a really serious accident, which was just averted in the nick of time. The Bee Man led in prayer each morning as they stood in the early morning light, heads bent, feet on rough ground, asking for just such protection. . . .

I shall be, Lord willing, writing the story of the way L'Abri began, into a book during the month of November. Hence, as you look over the map and think of the people in the chalets, you must subtract Fran and me from Mélèzes, see Franky in Beau Site being cared for by his sister Sue and brother Ran, and remember that the work must be carried on by the other three couples and the four single Workers. The weekend of November 1st to 4th will be a heavy "test" at the beginning as a large number is coming up from Milan, several from Paris, some from Zurich, and others from Lausanne, so everyone will be *more* than busy! But it is good for people to see (ourselves, as well as others) that L'Abri is *not* one, or two, or three, or four people, it is a plan of the Lord's and He is able to fill with His Spirit, and use whom He will, to meet the needs of the *people He sends in answer to prayer.* It is important to remember that people *don't* come because of advertising—they come, whether they know it or not—because people are *praying* that God will draw the ones of His choice, and will keep away all others. Do you believe it?

Do we really believe that God *has* done "the impossible" in the past, *is* doing "the impossible" now—*will do* "impossible" in answer to prayer? Or are we doubting Him in our emotions, attitudes, and deep inner responses while we "pay lip service" with our singing of hymns and spoken words. Oh, for growing faith and trust!

With love in Him,

EDITH

1964

February 26, 1964   Huemoz sur Ollon, Switzerland

Dear Family:

... Fran and I had run down through the fields yesterday afternoon to look at the chapel and discuss beams for the front wall and were amazed ourselves at the beauty of this simple chalet. It will be an enlarged living room for Sunday church services and larger discussion groups, and Farel House lectures, an enlarged room to hold those who will come to hear the Bible taught and preached, and to hear Bach trios with violin, organ, and Jane's voice, or the choir made up of Workers at Bellevue, Workers at L'Abri, and students give an evening of praise to the Lord in song. It seems so "just right"—a warm, rustic living room sort of room, yet with the proportions which will lend itself to being a good auditorium for 150 people tucked in the slope of a sharp mountainside, with the balcony like an overhanging cliff, yet safely railed in. The view can only carry one's thoughts to the Creator who made the mountains, and whose Word draws so many illustrations from that which we can sit and look at there. Yes, it seems almost like a dream, or an idea—rather than reality.

We came outside and slid down the loose dirt to the level below the main room. Here is room for another whole "floor" for very practical uses. One side, of course, will be windowless, as it is backed up against the hill; the other will look out below the balcony to the same view. Toilet, shower, and a small kitchen will take part of the space. The rest will give a new room for more Farel House desks and shelves for the Evangelical Library books. Every inch of space will be utilized.

Yesterday was February 25th. I have a notation in the margin of my Bible marked Feb. 25, 1955: "Cleave the rock for us, Lord, and let the water *gush*." It is in the margin beside Isaiah 48:21, and it was written and prayed to the Lord during the time of house-hunting when we had been put out of Switzerland. I remember that as I wrote it, it seemed *im-*

possible to find a house, impossible to be able to arrange to live in it when we had no permit to live in Switzerland, impossible to imagine the future in the light of the immediate problems. Then this verse hit me— "And they thirsted not when he led them through the deserts; he caused the waters to flow out of the rock for them; he clave the rock also, and the waters gushed out." And I prayed, for the house, for the unfolding of the Lord's plan for the future to be supernaturally given, by Him who did cause water to come out of a rock in the wilderness in a specific moment of history and who can do just as unique things for His children today in just as impossible circumstances, in answer to prayer. . . .

As I went up the steps of Mélèzes, my mind was full of all that had been done by the Lord during the past nine years and the fact that nine years ago that very day, I had been pleading for "water from the rock." Our circumstances had many rock-like aspects of hard impossibility. Not even a place to live in ourselves, nor an idea of where we might go, then the whole story of what had taken place, fresh in my mind from having written it recently, and the feel, smell, and sight of the fresh pine wood of the chapel making a reality of the latest development of the work and the community, I felt overcome with the realization of how very much more than I had imagined, the Lord had answered and had given to that plea, "Cleave the rock for us, Lord, and let the water *gush*." It isn't right to ask for great things, miraculous things, as the ten lepers did in asking for their healing, and then to forget to be thankful. So often it is easy to think of all the immediate problems that are *not* solved, rather than to remember all that the Lord *has* done, or to long for *un*fulfilled desires, rather than to marvel over what we have *already* been given, or saved from. . . .

In November Fran was invited to speak in a church in Willow Grove, Pennsylvania, for two weeks of meetings, morning and evening. The church cared for his travel expenses from here to America and back again. Other requests soon followed, when people knew he was coming, and six weeks were very tightly packed so that, for instance, an early morning flight from Boston to Chicago gave opportunity to speak in the morning chapel all the way out in Wheaton, Illinois! Meetings and discussion groups were held in University groups or churches in Philadelphia, Boston, Chicago, Wheaton, St. Louis, Pittsburgh and area, Nashville, and New Jersey.

Back in June of last year, Betty C. was praying one day when she felt certain that the Lord would have her give her monthly check to me for the writing of the L'Abri story into book form. Being a writer herself, she realized that this task would probably not be accomplished unless a month away from the work were taken for writing. After she told the Lord, "Yes I'll do that," she was beset by the usual "fears" that come when one has felt led to give sacrificially. "What about this expense, Lord, and that? How can I?" But she was so certain that it had been of the Lord, that she put aside the fears as Satan's niggling doubts and made the step a certain one. The certainty of her leading to give the gift for that particular purpose, plus the other circumstances making it possible for me to take November away from the chalet, seemed to be the Lord's leading for the use of November by me in "hibernating" to write. Franky came each weekend for 22 hours (Saturday evening until Sunday afternoon) but otherwise I pressed on day after day, with some all-night times of working, in a hotel room by the lake. It would take a whole letter to tell of that experience, which was both an agony of struggle (reading through material from 15 years of letters "home" made me feel "it is *impossible* to condense and write it into a readable story") and an exhilarated time of seeing it all take shape as if I were watching something take place rather than having a part in it. It was sort of like having a baby. One is a part of the work and agony of birth, and one has the exhilarated feeling of accomplishment, yet, the miracle is *not* of one's own cleverness and design. It leaves one with a feeling of awe—awe and worship of the One who put the atoms together in the patterns which produce creativity. Yes, the book was finished (in its first draft, with some needed corrections, etc.) within the last minute, literally, of the month! Now please pray that the time will be given to correct and prepare it for a publisher.

Meantime, the work at the chalets went on. There was one very big "Italian weekend" when a large group came up from Milan and had concentrated times of Bible study and discussion, and there were always guests arriving.

Having been away for a month in a hotel room, with concentrated writing and rarely a person to talk to, and buying food at a grocery to eat in the room alone, it was quite a contrast to come into the midst of a full L'Abri for 20 hours before leaving for England. It seemed impossible to stop talking—after such a long silence! There was much to hear in the way of news, as well as much to tell (about the book writing and the various people in the hotel with whom the Lord had given me conversation). Franky's greatest desire was that I would come to see the chapel, but 20 hours was too short a time to unpack from a month, pack for a trip away, go over stacks of mail, talk, and make any tour of inspection. Hence it was not until I was speeding down the mountain in a taxi, Trudy with me so that we could use the time talking, that I saw the impressive framework of the chapel, dominating the view. I gazed at it with wonder, as it had been only a cement foundation when I went away—then looked again with a squeal, "Why, there's *Franky* nailing boards on the open framework of the roof—I hope he doesn't fall!" I learned later that he was tied, to eliminate great danger (if he fell, he'd just dangle somewhere!) and that he was really helping in the push to get the roof on before the first snow came. Everyone was on the roof before it was all over, as tiles had to be placed, after the boards were all nailed firmly in place and it seemed to be a race with the weather. Never before had there been such a mild sunny November and December. On

December 11th the last tile was on, and village people expressed wonder, along with our own people, as snow fell on the 12th!! The whole winter has been mild, and February has brought spring birds and spring flowers at an unheard-of early date. The chapel building has continued without the expected hindrances of heavy snow.

I met Fran in England, as his flight back from America included a stop in London at no extra cost. We had a full week there, with discussion groups at the flat as usual, and some time also spent in the "country" at the home of Franky's former schoolteacher, Anne Spink. One night at the flat, Gilpie, from St. Louis, brought ten people, including a young fellow and his enormous, but beautiful and beautifully behaved dog! That gave us a new record in the tiny living room designed to hold six people comfortably: 24 people and one large dog!! . . .

At Sunday afternoon tea time, the evening meeting some miles away was being discussed, when the topic of conversation suddenly changed to Franky's education, and the problems connected with his always living at L'Abri surrounded by adults. It went from that to a description of the prep school that young John Spink goes to. "John is just Franky's age, and he loves it there—keeps saying that everything is 'super.' " "I wish you could see the school," said Anne. And Mr. Spink jumped up with, "I'll call the headmaster right now—perhaps we could stop on our way to the church. It wouldn't be many miles out of the way." He came back with a big smile. "Yes, he says he'd be glad to meet you. We can have a glimpse of John, too. He'll be surprised!" As we drove through the dark hedge-bordered English country roads, we were told of how splendid this school is; of the fine Christian headmaster and his wife who really love boys and also really love the Lord. We heard of the good scholastic program, but also of the outdoor life in the 280 acres of wooded land. We heard of the sports, but also of dam-building contests in the small river, and of the building done by the boys themselves, as well as the milking of cows. We heard of the overnight hikes, and cooking outdoors, and many other things which showed the imagination of the men caring for these boys to be full of ideas which really please boys as well as teaching something. Then we stopped in front of a building and stepped out into the night. A wide door let us into a big hall in which a large fireplace predominated. Clustered around the blazing log fire were grey-clad boys reading, doing puzzles, waiting for the tea bell to ring. Glimpses of murals on the stairway walls, painted by the boys themselves, and of a schoolroom full of interesting maps and all kinds of "collections" gave impressions as we then went into the big living room where evidences of boys having just left were all around—open Bibles in big chintz-covered chairs, notebooks and pencils scattered about, a huge dog stretching himself in front of an even bigger fireplace with even larger logs ablaze. A piano standing in a bay window had a cluster of music racks and small yellow leather stools around it, speaking silently of a boys' orchestra of some sort. We soon were talking with the headmaster and his wife, and I was inwardly struggling. I knew I liked it. In fact, I *knew* somehow that this *was* going to be Franky's school, and that someday soon he would be among the grey-clad boys. Yet, a sick feeling battled against this assurance. I didn't want to like it and I didn't want to be sure. I wanted to keep Franky with us! So often in life as one prays for the Lord's leading, for the Lord's solutions, for the unfolding of the Lord's plan, there is excitement, amazement, wonder at the perfection of the unfolding, of the meeting of needs, yet along with it comes fear and that "homesickness" of wanting things to remain as they are, of shrinking from change, or from the unknown. How thrilling, however, to be able to say, "Oh, Lord, I do trust Thee, I do want Thy will. Please let no mistake be made—" And to know that *He can* communicate His will and *He* can prevent mistakes being made, which would inevitably be made if we trusted our own judgment. Both Fran and I, as well as others, have been praying for the solution to Franky's need of further education. In giving this answer I feel certain the Lord is doing a combination of things. I am certain this *is* His will for Franky at present, but that also there will be other results coming out of it. I am certain that this is not just for Franky, but for other people with whom we are meant to have contact in L'Abri. I mustn't give you more detail, but let me just tell you that although the school is "full," a place is being made for Franky, and he will be entering, Lord willing, on April 27th. On April 20th Fran, Franky, and I will go to England and we shall have one of our "English trips" with all sorts of discussion groups in people's homes, as well as in University rooms, and at the same time we shall be preparing Franky's clothing and things in order to take him to the Great Walstead School. Openings are coming in new places this time. . . .

It was late in January that we were having a farewell supper for Margie, prior to her leaving Farel House to go back to the States. I was in the kitchen serving the plates, when I noticed Debby giggling, and pressed her as to why. Finally she burst out, "Haven't you noticed anything *new*?" I looked both Debby and Udo over carefully, and suddenly noticed the rings!!! They had been engaged for quite a few months, but had just bought their rings. According to German custom wedding rings are worn on the right hands to show engagement, and then transferred to the wedding fingers the day of the marriage. They had decided to just put theirs on and wait until we noticed them. I promised not to say anything to anyone at the table, but just before dessert was finished, I finally decided that no one was going to notice, so I announced that there was something new at the table and everyone looked around and guessed ridiculous things, until finally someone discovered the "announcement." Udo (accepted as a L'Abri Worker in January) expects to leave law and study theology, preparing himself for Christian work, and he and Debby are praying as to whether the Lord would have them in America or England for study. Meantime, Debby is working hard toward her Diplome in French. It is "impossible" for her to get it this July, but she is going to take the exams, and just between you and me, I think she may really do the "impossible"!

One other wonderful answer to prayer to squeeze in here at the end: For a long time we have been praying for the village of Huemoz, and asking the Lord to use us here in His own way. A few weeks ago the village pastor asked Claudie Halbritter and Susan to teach the village Sunday School. This means that every Sunday morning Priscilla gathers our own tiny tots (Claudie's Tim and Sue's Margaret, along with Craig Kramer, and her own Elizabeth) into her warm kitchen for Sunday School, freeing the two girls to go to the village and teach the village children. Susan has the younger ones, Claudie the older ones, and the opening time they have together. It means that all 30 of the village children are in one or the other of the two classes, and the Luke Lessons, which Fran and I wrote some years ago, are being taught to them, along with all the object lessons and verses to learn. The way of salvation is made clear, and week by week their knowledge of the Word is increasing. It is exciting to see how much the children like it, and to know that the attendance has doubled, as never before did *all* the children come.

No more space this time—but oh, there is so much to pray for, God is able to change hearts, to open eyes, and you can be at the other end of the triangle in effective intercession.

With love,

EDITH

April 14, 1964   Huemoz sur Ollon, Switzerland

Dear Family:

A brand new thing took place in March. At a little after 5 A.M. the alarm went off one March Monday morning, and by 5:30 breakfast was served. Suitcases were soon out and down by the road—and by 6 o'clock Cossandy's taxi-bus was on its way to catch the early express train to Italy, which doesn't stop at Aigle, so must be caught at Montreux. "Are the sandwiches in? Who has the bag of oranges? Have you counted the suitcases? Everyone must be responsible for his own." We were soon running behind a porter to find our reserved seats in a car near the front of the train—and we settled in to take roll call. Are we all here? There are—Fran and I, Coxe, Blanche, Frances Kramer (at present living in the community), Bryant (Farel House student from Florida), Hansjorg, and Hurvey Woodson (L'Abri Worker in Milan) were going to join us in Milan—when we changed trains at 1 o'clock.

Where were we all going?

We were on our way to Florence, Italy, for a new "twig" of L'Abri work. It had come about this way: After Fran spoke at the Missionary

Conference in Naples at New Year's, he was asked whether he could give some lectures tying up art and so on with the Christian message, and giving some ideas as to how to reach the 20th-century man with the gospel, to a gathering of missionaries from various boards, in Italy. After thought, and prayer, the "Florence trip" emerged. It turned out to be a very exciting medium for doing several things at a time. There were missionaries to Italy gathered from many different backgrounds, though most of them had never studied art nor had they been in museums in Italy. We were all booked to sleep in either the Salvation Army hostel, or in an orphans' home, and our first evening meal was together in a nearby restaurant. The plan of how the week would work out was very "open" and we all approached the week with much curiosity.

We began a round of art museums and churches, with Fran as our guide and lecturer. He gave lectures which bound together history of art, history of philosophy, and history of changing theology and history of the church, showing the changing thinking of man, and showing what we who believe the Bible face today in the way of speaking to the 20th-century man so that he can really understand what we are talking about. Mere words and phrases are not enough; an understanding of *his* problems is needed, and a careful use of words with enough definition to be sure they are not being taken in an entirely different connotation is also needed. Mornings and some afternoons were full with these guided, illustrated tour-lectures. Evenings brought forth summary, and further lectures, taking about two hours each time.*

Not only were the Farel House students, a few L'Abri Workers, missionaries, and some Italian Christians present, but also there were two junior-year-abroad students in the Florence University who didn't want to miss any of it and who had therefore canceled travel plans to stay through the week!! In addition to that, we found that in each art museum a few people gathered around the edges of our group, peering at the illustration we were standing in front of, and listening to whatever was being said. Some of these followed along with us for a couple of hours, and one Persian fellow studying in Florence came for an evening lecture too. We felt it was a very unique type of "street meeting" in which people were hearing at least bits of the Christian message.

The thrilling climax came after the last evening lecture, when people were standing around talking in little clusters, and commenting on how much they had learned, and how they hoped it might be done again in a different city. Just then someone called me to the telephone and it was one of the Florence University students at the other end. They had just left us shortly before.

"Oh, Mrs. Schaeffer," she said, a bit breathlessly, "I just had to call you right away. Guess what? Joan just accepted Christ as her Saviour this

---

*Thus began the lecture series that was to become the book and film *How Shall We Then Live?*

evening. She told me in the taxi on our way to the station. I'm so happy about it!"

You can imagine how we all felt! The lectures had not been intended to be evangelistic, but to set forth the problems of man philosophically and in other ways and to show how the truth of the Bible meets these problems. The last lecture had been very strong and had set forth the reality of separation from God in hell, as well as other things. This was no sentimental or fuzzy decision—it was one on the background of the clear teaching of taking a stand on the entire Word of God. Joan comes from a Unitarian family, a fine, closely knit family who stand together. She has no illusions that it will be easy to be a Christian, to stand firmly upon the truth and reality of her belief in the whole Trinity, and in the death of Jesus Christ, God's Son, for her. But she has in very fact bowed before the Triune God, and committed the future to Him, as she takes this step into the circle of life, and out of the circle of death. The news of Joan's decision affected each of the missionaries as they went off, each to their own place of study or work, knowing that the work of the Holy Spirit is *real*, and that there is no manner of explanation that can be finally effective without His work—but knowing by example that the "intellectual" answer does *not* exclude the warmth of spiritual result. . . .

Minna was seventeen when she came to the airport in Geneva to have a brief, but intense, conversation with the Schaeffers . . . as they waited to board the plane to England. She had been brought by another girl in the same boarding school, who felt Minna needed to "know the answers" too! The result was that a few months later, just before our next English trip, Minna arrived for a week's stay. A breakfast conversation lengthened out to take the whole morning . . . but the frantic ten-minute packing for the English trip was not too great a price for us to pay for the joy of having had that morning time end with Minna's decision to accept Christ as her Saviour. . . . For Minna there was struggle, dark moments, and some bright moments of answered prayer and reality of the Lord's help . . . but it was not easy for years. Any letters from L'Abri were burned or destroyed those first weeks. Then came college where the whole heavy cloud of "relativism" settled down upon her and crept into her attitudes and thoughts without her realization at times. She stood up for the truth in arguments presenting logically the system the Bible teaches . . . but at times the reality seemed to be slipping away . . . She received only scattered letters through the five-and-a-half years—this Family Letter and personal answers to her letters. The hidden link? Effectual prayer and intercession. Then at 21, Minna, herself, appeared at the door, having flown from New York to Geneva . . . and via train and bus to our doorstep. Five-and-a-half years is a long time to get caught up! "The thing that thrills me," she said after a few weeks, "is that you really don't have to separate your Christianity into a compartment by itself, and then think of art and music separately . . . But that *really* you can hold your head up unashamedly as a Christian and know

John's daily cello practice while tapes are copied (note the tape recorders) in the tiny one-room Mazot (very small chalet). This is a true picture of John who uses his time efficiently!

that it all fits together . . . and that there are logical and valid answers."

This has been a partial and very tiny glimpse of what happens to people who become Christians at L'Abri. But even in a partial and tiny "peek" one must remember the tapes. Hundreds of hours of tapes are now stacked up for listening purposes, so that those who get tape recorders and listen may be continuing with studies in Romans; Doctrines (following the outline of the Westminister Confession of Faith); The Christian Life or True Spirituality—and what this means with regard to psychological problems and communication in marriage and in the church, etc.; Principles of Exegesis of the Prophetic passages in the Bible; The Book of Revelation; The Intellectual Climate and the New Theology; Lectures on Art and Music (some by Fran, but some also by Jane and some by Dr. Rookmaaker); taped discussions, etc., etc. Some who have become Christians at L'Abri continue to learn what is being taught here. John Sandri is working long, hard hours on copying tapes, and there is need for prayer as to facilities which would make that copying more accurate professionally so that the tapes may be easier to listen to. . . .

Yes, the Lord alone can *really* see ahead in *any* of our lives: yours, and mine. What a comfort to be able to let *Him* plan today, and this next hour, in the light of that fact!!

Love in Him Who alone knows us, and the future,

EDITH

August 21, 1964   Huemoz Sur Ollon, Switzerland

Dear Family:

. . . Tuesday April 14th when I last wrote, my left leg was already hurting as if I had strained a muscle. By Thursday I thought perhaps the doctor ought to see it and rushed off to catch a ride with Joe, after our Members' meeting, as he was taking someone to Aigle. The doctor said, "Just a tight muscle" and said it was all right to go on doing what I would normally do. However the next night at 3 A.M. when we were getting ready for bed I looked down to find my left leg weirdly unlike the right; in fact it was swollen double its normal size. Even sleeping with it up on a pillow made no difference by morning, and as I tried to work around the kitchen clutching the table when sharp pains shot through it, I finally went over to seek comfort and advice from Ran and Sue. The result was another trip to the doctor that afternoon. This time he tightened his lips and shook his head. "This is different, it has changed—it is a phlebitis (or a blood clot in a vein)." He went on to say that there was nothing to do but to go to bed with my leg elevated and hot alcohol compresses on it, plus taking some medicine, and staying there with this sort of treatment for at least a week, not getting out for anything!

"But Dr. Laurent," I almost wailed, "We are leaving for England on Monday, we have many for the hot dog roast tonight; Sunday is always a very heavy day with so many at the chalet. There is packing to do, Franky is being taken to boarding school! I *can't* go to bed!" He looked sympathetic, but said even more firmly, "You are going to bed with your leg up. You are not going to England *this* Monday." The door had slammed shut in my face and there was just *no* possibility of pushing through this stone wall. I went home and cleared off my office bed with Sue's help, and soon had my leg propped up on a board which was resting on a suitcase, with thick, hot alcohol-and-water-soaked cotton wrapped around it, and plastic keeping the bandages from dripping.

It was difficult to stay put and realize that not only was Susan having the care of my leg added to all that she had to do (Pris and Debby and even Franky took turns changing the compresses) but that my work was having to be divided among the rest. However, the most difficult part for a few hours was the reflection over past weeks of guidance for this English trip, combined with taking Franky to England and preparing him for entrance into Great Walstead, a Christian prep school. Hadn't the Lord clearly led in all this? It became very rapidly clear to me that the Lord certainly *had* led, but that did not prove that I was the one to go at this time. He had led in the plans being made, but He also could have someone who He had planned to have take my part in this next week in London and a very important purpose in my being in that office in bed! If the Lord wanted the English trip to be exactly as planned except with someone else filling my place—and if He wanted me in that bed ready to talk to people and to write letters, wasn't His leading clear enough? I had time to pray in the next hours, as well as to prepare two notebooks. One was called "Edith's Brain," jokingly, because I realized that the whole schedule of the trip was in my head, as I had expected to be there to say, "Today we are scheduled to do this, etc., etc." That notebook was prepared so that anyone taking my place could not only help Fran with the scheduled meetings, etc., but could know exactly what to buy for Franky, when he was due at the school for an interview, and so forth. The second was a menu book with not only menus and shopping lists, but recipes to go with each day's menus, so that Coxe could immediately begin to take my place in the kitchen and carry on even if later I could go away.

In the next hours definite answers to prayer came as guidance as to who should take my place, and it became evident that Ran was the Lord's choice. Money was given by someone who did not know I was praying for money enough for Ran's flight ticket as one "sign," so that by early Monday morning everything was in readiness and off Ran went to do a fine job caring for Franky's shopping and preparation, and also to be present at meetings in Reigate, Burgess Hill, and Ealing, at which he met many people whom we are *sure* the Lord meant him to get to know before he and Sue commenced to live in England and do L'Abri work there. In England Ran and Fran were constantly amazed at the *clear* assurance that Ran was meant to be there, and in Huemoz there was a succession of clear reasons why my presence was needed at the chalet. That little office became the scene of a constant stream of people who often remarked, "It is so wonderful to know you are right here, and that we can find you to have a quiet time of talking and prayer with you." And in between visits, I was able to catch up on all the back correspondence. And not least of all, the whole complex of events was a tremendous help to those who were living in L'Abri as students or guests at the time, and everyone remarked that they felt there was a *reality* of trusting the Lord which they could not have learned, or been witness to, if they had never seen an example of living through a difficulty of illness, upset plans, and even danger (as the clot was thought to be dangerous for a time). The thrilling thing to me was the illustration of the *purpose* of difficulties and disappointments, and of course the seen purpose is only a partial thing, because there is so much we do *not* see, but which is even more important in the total purpose for the incident in our lives.

Part of the purpose of Ran's being in England seemed obvious—it gave him time to start house-hunting in preparation for his and Sue's move in midsummer. When at the end of the week the doctor gave me permission to travel, I joined Fran in Burgess Hill. We had a few days all together, during which Franky arrived at the emotional moment of entering boarding school and parting with his family for the first time in his life, and then Fran and I went off to commence our usual discussion groups and individual conversations at the flat, and on up to St. Andrews, Scotland. It was while we were in Scotland that Ran telephoned us with an excited voice and arranged to have us meet him at Victoria upon our return, from which place he would drive us to see the house he felt the Lord had led him to.

As we drove along Ran began to talk. "It was late in the afternoon and I was so discouraged. I had spent several days in fruitless search—everything was too small, too far from transportation, or too expensive, and I had come to the place of just driving around looking for "For Sale" signs, within a radius of underground stops. I really didn't know where I was when I went into that tearoom. As I was looking over a map which I had spread out on the table before me, a woman at the next table got up and stepped over. 'Are you lost?' she said. 'Are you looking for anything in particular?' I replied that I was looking for a house and in a short time she had exclaimed that she was trying to sell a house, asking if I would like to look at it as it was nearby. Well, we're nearly there now, and you can see it for yourselves. It has a big living room, opening out into a garden with French doors, and seems so suitable for L'Abri discussions and so on, as well as being near a heath for walks with Margaret." . . .

We looked at the house with a feeling that "This is it," and pictured Sue and Margaret in their day-by-day life in the various rooms and garden, and ourselves coming on the English trips. We met and talked with the owner and before we left for Oxford the next morning, it seemed that everything pointed toward God's leading us to that particular place, and the whole circumstance of His leading Ran there was an exciting reality of guidance. There didn't seem to be any "perhaps" about it. Our feeling was that we had arrived at *the* solution for both Ran and Sue and London L'Abri.

Before we left England, however, a shadow had fallen across the clear sunlight of certainty—there was a hint that this property was quite restricted. It was a leasehold property, which means that one buys it for only a certain number of years and that at the end of that time, it returns to the original land lease association. This is common in London, but the main difficulty is that the *land* is always owned by the association, and they have power to place restrictions upon the property, all the way from what you may do in the house, to what color you may paint the doors! Some property is more free than others. The owner who wanted to sell it to us assured us that no one pays any attention to the restrictions, but Fran felt that the lawyer ought to study the lease and let us know whether he felt the restrictions were normal ones, or whether they would really be extreme and hinder the freedom of L'Abri work. We came back home with a growing uneasiness about the possibility of having discussion groups and hymn sings, Sunday afternoon services, or Bible classes.

The day after we were back at the chalet we received word from the lawyer saying that he had felt that the land lease association needed to be asked point blank as to their interpretation of a clause in the lease, and they replied that it meant *no* religious meetings of *any* kind could be held in the house.

But hadn't the Lord led us there? Each of us individually prayed and we agreed unanimously that we must pursue the matter more thoroughly and not just give in too quickly, for certainly the circumstances of the Lord's leading were most outstanding. The decision that evening was to send me as a representative of L'Abri back to London to talk to the lawyer and to do whatever could be possible to "not leave a stone unturned." As I flew out on the plane the next afternoon, it was with the feeling of Alice in Wonderland dropping down the well. The flat was in the process of being sold. The furniture had been removed. Where was I going to sleep—let alone what was I going to do!! Yet the Lord had given the Members all an amazing certainty and oneness of mind in sending me, so surely He had a plan that would be unfolded. My verse that night, and through the next week, was "They shall not be ashamed that wait upon Thee." "Oh Lord," I prayed, "This is Thy work, I am waiting upon Thee for Thy direction. Many eyes are upon this step in London. Bring about a result to Thy glory."

As I waited to get my suitcase out of customs, I saw Cynthia Stanton peeking around the barrier and felt a huge wave of relief that I was being met and that there would be two of us to discuss my sleeping place that night! There was no discussion on that point needed, however, because Cynthia simply announced to me: "You're staying at the Spinks' in Burgess Hill where Franky is for mid-term break, then you can come up to London whenever you need to, from there." Seeing Franky was an unexpected treat sandwiched in during a time when he had gone home with a classmate after Sports Day. Now in addition to having a place to sleep, I had a face-to-face account of the events of Sports Day from a very happy and excited boy who kept saying, "I keep being afraid you are just a dream, Mother. I never expected to see you until summer vacation." Franky then accompanied me to London to visit the lawyer, to talk with the house owner, to visit neighbors in the neighborhood of the Golders Green house, quite content to sit through business conversations to have the chance to be with me. For a time it looked as though things might work out to take that house, then it became darker, and the only possibility left was the seeing of a representative of the land lease association. I was to have an appointment the next day and was to call the lawyer to find out at what time. But that night the phone rang after 11 o'clock. Who could be calling at such a time? "It's for you, Edith," said Mr. Spink, and I answered to find Cynthia speaking. "I went to sleep early this evening, and was awakened at 10 by a phone call. Suddenly I thought 'I *must* call Mrs. Gilbert-Smith tonight and ask her to pray about the matter of the L'Abri house.' " It was at Mrs. Gilbert-Smith's home in Ealing that a lecture and discussion time had been led by Fran when he and Ran were together during that former English trip. "Guess what she said when I spoke to her? She exclaimed, 'You don't mean that the Schaeffers are looking for a house for L'Abri? Why, I have Christian friends who are selling their home, and *praying* for Christians to buy it. It has always been used as an open home for the Lord, and they so very much want it to continue to be used for Him. It has a 34-foot living room which is just perfect for gatherings. Tell Mrs. Schaeffer she must see it, but it must be right away, as they have put it on the open market only two days ago (after waiting a month to see first if Christians would buy it) and a non-Christian man wants to sign papers to buy it in a day or two.' "

So it was that the next morning I got off the bus in front of 52 Cleveland Road to walk into a perfectly charming walled-in garden, through a wrought-iron gate, to enter an old Victorian house, with gables, bay windows, high ceilings, no central heating, but a most "lived in," homey place full of interesting nooks and corners. I met Mrs. Bird and had an exciting talk with her as we both grew to feel that the Lord had brought us together in order to answer both their prayers and ours. It was from this home that I telephoned the lawyer. And when he said, "I have a great disappointment for you, Mrs. Schaeffer," and proceeded to tell about the absolute refusal of the land lease commission to see me, I answered, "No, it's not really a disappointment because I have found another house which really is perfect for our needs." A decision had to be made in 24 hours because at that time if we were *not* expecting to buy it, a promise had to be kept to sell it to the other people who had asked for it. "If the Lord means this to be the L'Abri house, then 24 hours is long enough!!"

That night I got in touch with Fran in Milan where he was speaking, with the Members at Huemoz (they had a meeting together that evening), and by the next morning I had word that they were all in agreement. Mr. Spink and Mr. Malpas, who had been following the affair of the other house, were much more satisified with this new possibility, as it is a "freehold house" which means it is bought outright forever, not just for a certain number of years. The price was higher, but the property was in a much better condition, was larger as to rooms and space, and had both front and back gardens which are so well kept and are planned to give outdoor living space. There was no mistaking the fact that it is an amazing opening with tremendous "possibilities" for L'Abri discussion groups and Bible classes, and perhaps a room to be put aside for people wanting to listen to tapes. Of course, it will *not* be a place to keep overnight guests, although it will provide room for us when we come on English trips, but it will be L'Abri as the flat was, only with more space, and with a permanent couple living in it. The suddenness of this new turn of events was breathtakingly exciting. Money to buy it? Well, amounts came in to pay cash for about ⅗ of the total amount, and an interested Christian businessman is arranging a mortgage for the rest of the amount. Oh, I almost forgot, a thousand pounds is being loaned interest free for five years by the Birds themselves. The speed with which this suitable place was substituted for the "impossible house" startled the lawyer who had said one *must* count on a year to find a suitable place for such a use!!

But why had the Lord led Ran to Golders Green? . . . In answer, we began reviewing the things we ourselves could already "see" as reasons why we could be sure the Lord was leading, and that the Golders Green episode was a *part* of His leading, and a very *necessary* part to the present moment. *If* the Birds had announced the sale of their home that previous night, the answer Fran and Ran would have given then would have been "No" because the price was far beyond anything we had in mind. The preparation of fruitless house hunting, and the vivid illustration of possible problems that can hamper such an open home as L'Abri hopes to have in London, was necessary in order to appreciate what the Ealing house could mean in giving freedom to have a L'Abri. Then there was the fact that in all that had happened in connection with the Golders Green house, various people had been contacted and conversations had taken place which would otherwise never have taken place at all. . . .

But let's look at another quite different example of leading, through which we are all living right now, but in which Debby and Udo were most involved.

As we looked forward to the summer, it seemed an impossible time because of all that had to be included. There were Debby's big exams for her Diplome, and Sue and Ran's moving; there was Claudie and Allan's moving into Beau Site after Sue and Ran's departure, and Joe and Linette's trip to England to sell the flat, and then their moving into their new chalet, Bethany, with all the settling in and fixing up of rooms for a boys' dormitory—all with a new little sister or brother on its way to join Keith. There was the usual huge work in the ever-increasing gardens, and the long list of prospective Farel House students and others coming to L'Abri. There was Franky's expected arrival from school, and then there was a wedding to be fitted into all the rest. A wedding meant sewing—sewing for Debby's needed clothing for a trousseau, and sewing for the wedding itself. We all knew that the summer would mean three meals a day with spiritual conversation and care for the individual personalities, quite different from three meals a day served by a restaurant or hotel. How could it all possibly fit together and how could decisions be made as to the *timing* of the various events?

Ran and Sue felt strongly that they should leave in mid-July to visit Ran's relatives in Scotland, and to prepare for their autumn move into the Ealing house and Ran's entrance into London University to further study theology with the one sad factor that meant that they would *not* be here for Debby's wedding. . . . Debby passed her Diplome exams at Lausanne University with honors. Meantime people were coming—You can't imagine how little time is "left around the edges" when cooking and gardening, serving and conversing with 50 or more people is undertaken day after day.

In the midst of all this, Debby and Udo tried to select a date for their wedding that would fit. There was not just L'Abri to consider, but their own next steps. They prayed that the Lord would show them the timing of it all. *If* Debby had a teaching position offered her in St. Louis for the fall term, they felt the wedding must be as early as possible, in order to leave on an early freighter to cross the Atlantic in time. . . . Hence August 8th was chosen for the wedding, and all preparations were made for that date.

The wedding itself was a tremendous example of L'Abri. Not only did Madame Marclay of Champéry help in the sewing, but my back sewing room was used by a variety of seamstresses: American Jean; Swiss Trudy; Rosemary, a German girl; Gillian and Gwyneth (two English schoolteachers); myself, and at the last minute the final snaps and hooks were sewed on by a Bellevue worker "loaned" for a few hours. The bridesmaids, Kathie Kramer and Mary Leigh Smith (Jane's niece) and Jennifer Kramer (aged 10) also came in and out to help in whatever they could. When it came time for a general housecleaning, there was a whole army of "cleaners" with mops and pails and floor cloths and brushes under the command of Gillian who was General for the day! When it came time to get greens to trim the church, two cars filled with Farel House students and L'Abri helpers went off to a lush woodsy spot on the other side of Gryon and came back with masses of ferns to be planted in flower pots, sheets of moss, moss-covered logs, and long, trailing pieces of ivy. We trimmed the old 12th-century church with its fat stone columns and uneven stone floor and the afternoon of the 7th and during the early morning hours of the 8th. When it was finished it not only looked like a part of the woods, but smelled of moss, fern, and leaf. Pale yellow dahlias nodded their heads at the end of each pew, ivy outlined the aisles, and moss covered each pot so that the fern and dahlias had the appearance of growing from moss. Logs covered with moss gave the finishing touch of a natural deep woods setting. As I looked around after we finished, satisfied with the results, I was struck with the fact that it took Jean and her car, the others with their knives and energy, Larry's willingness to be buried in fern in the back of the car, to make the "idea" take shape.

At 12 o'clock noon the Ollon bells began to ring the traditional 15 minutes to announce a wedding, and Minna began to play. Then Jane and Frances came to the front, standing just behind the ferns, logs, and flowers, and "Jesu, Joy of Man's Desiring" came forth with organ notes blending with the sweet tones of the violin, and Jane's full voice brought the meaningful words. After a pause, clear trumpet notes burst forth, with organ and cello taking up the theme. It was Purcell's "Trumpet Tune and Voluntary." Minna was flanked by two young men, one playing the trumpet, and the other playing the cello. It really was a triumphant, joyous piece of music, and the trumpet made me think with great satisfaction of the coming day when the most glorious trumpet

*This picture will give you a glimpse of Debby and Udo Middel-
mann's wedding reception by the lake in Montreux. Left to right:
Debby and Udo, myself with Franky, Fran, Priscilla, Becky in
John's arms, and Elizabeth.*

music we have ever heard will announce some of the most stupendous
moments of the historic future!

First the men came in to take their places waiting at the front: Franky
as Junior Usher, then Bernd, and then Egon (Udo's brother) as Best Man,
then Udo himself. All three young men were tall and blond and
straight, in their dark suits, and all had given their lives to the Lord for
His use. Ran had been used to lead Udo to his acceptance of Christ as
Saviour five years ago. . . .

Now heads turned to watch the girls starting slowly up the aisle. First
little Jennifer, her blond hair hanging nearly to her waist in Alice-in-
Wonderland fashion, her slim waist emphasized by the full taffeta skirt;
then Kathie, her 15-year-old sister, in her slightly more sophisticated
dress also down to the floor, also with short sleeves, also carrying one
yellow dahlia with its pale lemon color blending with the yellow lights
in the dress; Mary Leigh followed her in an identical dress. These dresses were of yellow and green changeable taffeta looking like wheat fields
blowing in the wind on a sunny day, and the girls looked as fresh as a
spring morning in such a field! My eyes turned to look across the filled
pews of the church as I stood up when the bride and her father started
up the aisle. What a L'Abri gathering it was! . . . There were some of
Debby's French-speaking Sunday School children from the cerebral palsy rehabilitation home next door, people from Champéry, some from

Lausanne and Montreux. There were the sisters of one of Switzerland's rotating presidents, and the taxi driver and his wife. There were aunts, uncles, and cousins of Udo's from Germany, and his aristocratic, digni- fied grandmother. There were artists, writers, singers, musicians, stu- dents of all kinds, doctors, engineers, theological men, lawyers, pastors, and teachers. There were Swiss, Dutch, French, American, Canadian, English, South African, German, Danish, Italian, Austrian, Scottish, Norwegian. There were those with a host of different problems and struggles from alcoholism to psychological depressions, or broken pur- poses. There were strong Christians, strong atheists, agnostics, liberals, fuzzy, mixed-up ones, and newly converted ones. They all had one thing in common; the Lord had brought them to L'Abri at one time or another in the past, or had in the present for the first time, for a purpose of His own in their lives. All this I saw in a fleeting glance as my eyes went over the people and bits and pieces of their individual histories rushed through my mind causing me to feel a bit choked up about the reality of what the Lord has done here, and being allowed to have been a part of it all.

Jane sang in the middle of the service, "And Ruth said, thy people shall be my people, and thy God my God . . ." and it brought back the memory of the first time we ever were lifted to the heights by her voice as she sang that in Priscilla's wedding seven years ago, and of all that has happened in her life since that time! Allan Baldwin preached a splendid message on the need of forgiveness in the married life, bringing in the gospel clearly as he spoke. Then Fran took the ceremony itself. The sol- emn vows were clearly repeated, the trumpet, organ, and cello split the silence with the traditional recessional and it was over with a sigh as the bride and groom started out, and the attendants went out two by two.

My space is far too short to share the reception with you, or the events of the weekend as L'Abri went on in full force and the next day being Sunday, gave Les Mélèzes 35 to feed for Sunday dinner (even with every other chalet having guests), and 70 for high tea! The week went busily on with brief messages from Debby and Udo assuring us of their well- being as they "honeymooned" in Switzerland, waiting for their visas to go to Beirut to visit his parents. Until Saturday night, one week after the wedding, the telephone called me from preparing the hot dog roast to hear a tearful report from Debby of a motor scooter accident which had taken place a couple of hours before. "Udo has stitches above his eye and behind his ear, and I have cut my knee. We'll be taken to the Swiss bor- der by a French couple who picked us up; can you meet us there?" With blankets, aspirin, hot-water bottles, and orange juice, Jean Morris and I went off in her car to bring home the injured bride and groom.

This accident made it necessary to rest here for the time being, cancel- ing the Beirut trip. While in bed, Debby and Udo read together a letter from St. Louis offering her a position teaching French in a private school, "Come as soon as possible." A reversal? . . . All the "pieces" have not yet been arranged. So we are in the *middle* of this "illustration." I have told you because I feel the Lord has something for you in the "family" there, as well as for us here, in showing us how His leading is only one small step at a time, and we cannot say He is not leading when stepping stones lead in quite a different direction than we had imagined they would.

You have been asking, "What about Franky's school?" Naturally, he has missed L'Abri as well as home, but—let me quote a few snatches from one of his frequent letters—

Another thing, guess what! In science class we are doing real dissections, with the right kind of dissecting tools, and not homemade ones. We started with a frog and are working up to a more complicated thing, and bigger things like rabbits. Also it is so much fun in a real laboratory with a big microscope and all. You know something, somedays I just think, "Am I at Great Walstead? *Really* at Great Walstead? How wonderful!" and I can hardly believe it. Well, all I can say is I love it here and wouldn't go back to that other school if you tried to push me in with a bulldozer. Just think how fast time has gone. Also I have found I have a hidden talent at the high jump. I am one of the best high jumpers in the school and I am hoping to really do something on sports day with my high jumping. Even if I came in 5th it would be pretty good out of 115 boys in the school. In the running I don't think I will be able to do much, but still it will be fun. I wish that you could come on sports day, still I am happy that at least someone can come and see me, which will be Jennifer and Tim and David also. I wish I could see you, but I love it here and everyone is so nice. Also there is such a big difference in having Christian masters. Mr. Parke is always fair. . . .

Sorry this was so long—but really it is two letters!—in one envelope! . . .

Much love in Him in Whose plan our lives have somehow touched,

EDITH

November 28, 1964   Huemoz sur Ollon, Switzerland

Dear Family:

Thanksgiving Day has come and gone again. The very word for an American conjures up so many memories of family gatherings, tantalizing odors of roasting turkey or baking pies mingled with November's burning leaves or late chrysanthemums' special scent. For Christians, the word "thanksgiving" brings a flood of thankfulness for such a variety of things that the *un*fulfilled longings and present sufferings and struggles are buried under a sudden big wave of thankfulness for all that the Lord has done for us in big things and tiny details of the past, as well as giving us such a vivid reality of *hope* for the future. . . . Yet as I sat at the Thanksgiving dinner table in the living room and thought of some of my own "thankfulnesses" it seemed to me that *most* of the things for which we are thankful are preceded by fears and urgent needs in *some* area of life. . . .

As I listened to people relating something of their own struggles and difficulties as they told of things for which they were thankful, and of things in which they had had specific answers to prayer, it struck me that in each case there had been moments of fear, dismay, struggle, or urgent need which gave rise to the fervency of their prayers. I thought of my own thankfulness of the past few *hours* and of how it fit into that same pattern, and then I began to think of the things we had been thankful for in the last three months, since last writing to you. And as I thought of specific moments of overwhelming thankfulness, I realized that a true picture could not be given without telling the background. For instance, you could not understand the excitement and wonder with which we in the kitchen thanked Elfie as she presented us with a box one Sunday afternoon in October and said, "The father of one of the children (patients) next door brought a lot of croissants and braided white bread. It really is quite hard now, and we have far too much— could you do something with it?" How could we be so excited about stale bread? Only because the possibility of having a really nice Sunday tea seemed a bit dim that day because of a lowness of food supply. In no time at all we were dipping the dry croissants in melted margarine and heating them—sprinkling the bread with water and heating it encased in paper bags, and we had lovely fresh hot things spread out on trays— as if it had been planned that way! But how could you know the wonder of an answer to prayer for such a small thing, if you never were *without* such a small thing? If always every loaf of bread and every bit of meat were there to be eaten without any question, except limitations of hunger—or diet! . . .

Our finances themselves are an illustration of that as we pray, the Lord touches hearts to give, but the care of the finances as the Lord sends in the funds is very methodical and careful; it is not lax in any way. As money comes in, undesignated, it is put in a general fund—and at the *end* of the month, or a few days after the next month has commenced, the accounts are finished up, and we hear the "news" of what amounts are to be divided. The first things to be paid are the rents, medical insurances, electricity, gas, etc. Then if there is a "full" amount, there is a certain amount of money given to the housekeepers for food, based on so much per person for the people they have fed during the month *just finished*. So you see we are paid for the month past, not the one ahead, as far as food money goes, but we must buy during the month ahead. After food money is paid, then the "Workers' gifts" are given, which amount to about $25 for a Worker and about $36 for a Worker who has been here longer than three years. If there is money left over, it goes into the next month's account, unless there is some pressing need which we all agree upon, such as a fence to keep the children from going out on the road, or some such thing. Now when enough comes in to meet the full need, we can get along very nicely by careful planning of meals. When there is only half the amount, then food money is cut in half and it becomes more difficult to cook attractive meals. It *can* be done, but it takes more work!!!! When we say that in nine years we have never had an unpaid bill, we mean it, and we thank God that no one has ever been turned away because we did not want to share what we had with him, or her, or because there was nothing to share, *but* there have been very "low" times, which have been used as a spiritual blessing to us in many ways, and which have proved over and over to us who have been here for years, or have proved to new Workers, that the coming in of money is *not* automatic, but really *is* an answer to prayer.

Now to tell the story of the three months just behind us. During July, August, and September, the incoming money was increasingly low, so that each month finished with a smaller fraction to be given each one for food, and with nothing at all for "Workers' gifts." That meant that during August, September, and October, we were experiencing an increasingly difficult time in planning and preparing meals, and in meeting personal expenses such as toothpaste and stamps! All this gave the background and opportunity for very exciting personal answers to prayer in small things along the way as well as later for the "big answers" which did come. There was the time that a tube of toothpaste was found, left behind by some unknown person, half used to be sure, but gleefully received by one who had finished the last squeeze of toothpaste that morning, and marveled at the detail of the Lord's supply. There was the time when a box of cake mixes and Jellos and puddings arrived in time to make Saturday night and Sunday tea desserts when money for the ingredients was not there. There was the time when one of the couples received a personal and unexpected gift from some member of the family in a distant place which met a necessity in a wonderful way, though the giver thought it was being sent for some treat. The timing of this caused this couple to marvel. There was the time when at Mélèzes there was no money at all to get the weekend order, and a member of the community was visiting me for tea, when suddenly he pulled out fifty francs ($12) saying, "This is an unexpected rebate I got on some carpentry work. It came in the post this morning, and I stuffed it in my pocket. I think you might have a use for it." The "use" included some margarine, a can of salad oil, flour, sugar, rice, some hamburger meat, and frozen chickens and some dried beans. With the plentiful garden vegetables, and eggs from our own chickens, this made the basis for chili con carne for a crowd on Saturday night, and for a chicken dinner with rice and gravy and vegetables on Sunday.

Debby's wedding expenses were provided in answer to prayer in a variety of ways, and no one would have known that there had been *need* of urgent prayer about it, had they been only a wedding guest. Vacations were provided also in a variety of ways, so that in spite of the continued general need, specific needs were met by designated money arriving. It seemed strange somehow, that at a time when tiny expenses were a problem, there was a chapel being built; and when it came time to put in the electricity, there was *just* enough to pay for the wiring; and when it came time to lay the floor, there was *just* enough to pay for that. In this same period, the negotiations for buying the London house were being made, and as various official letters came and went—it again seemed strange that thousands of dollars of designated money were being discussed to buy that property, yet centimes were being counted to pay for postage! Yet—how else would there be such a satisfying assurance that the purchase of the house, the building of the chapel, were all things the *Lord* was doing as a part of His plan for L'Abri and for the individuals involved?

It was early in October that the continued state of finances, the continual arrival of mail without any checks that would change the picture, began to become a bit confusing as well as giving rise to tiny "fears" of one kind or another, to one person or another. "Is there something in me that is hindering?" some of us wondered, or "Have we not really been praying seriously enough?" "Is the Lord saying something to us that we are not understanding?" "Are we meant to curtail the work?" Fleeting thoughts sometimes, or persistent thoughts at other times. We spoke about calling a day of special fasting and prayer concerning the material needs, and this was done. For myself personally, I felt strongly led to make it three days, quietly and in between other work, I used parts of three days for prayer, and fasted as "unto the Lord" in this particular situation. With a sense of expectancy I came to the end of this time, one Thursday morning, and in mid-morning rushed upstairs to get a black sweater to stick on as Minna had called, "I'm ready to go to Migros*, are you coming, Mrs. Schaeffer?" I pulled open the bottom drawer of a big old chest in the back sewing/sitting room. I shook it out—unable to believe my eyes! "It's full of holes! How horrible— moths?" I was talking to myself, but I had to tell someone! "What about the short-sleeved black one?" I found that it looked as if a naughty child had cut it with scissors. Then I began pulling one out after another, a supply gathered through sixteen years of life in cold chalets where sweaters are worn most of the year, many of them gifts or bought on sales, and most of them "old," but good nonetheless. I found *all* of them had something, either a lot of holes like lace, or a few holes, or perhaps just a few bites out of the edges of the cuffs. "*Mice!*" I exclaimed. "Only *mice* could have done that much damage in so short a time!" And I ran downstairs to tell Minna and show her the awful evidence of what I was saying.

My immediate solution was to put on two sweaters in such a way that the holes wouldn't show, but that was temporary. Was *this* the ending of

---

*A large supermarket chain found across Switzerland.

three days of special prayer? I felt something of the whispers of Satan, and prayed for victory over his attempts, remembering Job. I bought mouse poison with money I preferred using for food!!!

The next incident happened within a day or two. We had ordered soup back *before* we realized that money was going to be low, several cartons of Knorr dried soups, which are Swiss, you know, and used here as much cheaper than canned soups. The bill had been coming repeatedly, but the soup had *not* arrived. We complained to the company and said we could not pay until it had been delivered. Finally, we discovered that it *had* come the day before Debby's wedding, and that three fellows had carried it up from the post office! But where could three large cardboard cartons weighing many pounds be *lost*??? We searched the fruit cellars, the attics, even the wood bins of all our L'Abri chalets, but nothing was found and the bill had to be paid! It seemed a tragedy to have to pay for something we did not have at a time when food and food money was so low. *And,* on top of being a difficult thing, it was one of the most *exasperating* things we had yet experienced. "It couldn't be *lost!*" we kept saying to each other, and the "lost soup" was often a topic of conversation, as well as of prayer.

Later I had another shock when in opening other drawers I found that the mice had eaten holes in gloves, in handkerchiefs, and in my store of "yard goods" kept on shelves for sewing for various ones (as it seems wise to buy remnants when they are a particularly good buy) and in my *desk* drawers I found that the mice had made confetti out of carbon copies of letters and had eaten through envelopes of letters still in their envelopes.

Day after day new losses turned up: The toaster broke, the record player broke, and other things went out of commission. The most frightening climax came when I ran down one Friday at lunch time to get a frozen vegetable out of the freezer, and I opened it to find beet juice running down all over everything, and realized with a sickening shock that it was *defrosting.* I'm afraid I got into a bit of a panic about that and I ran back up calling out, "Quick, someone, the freezer is defrosting, look at the fuses. Could anyone have pulled out the plug? I can't find it. It's behind the thing . . ." All our summer garden crop so carefully put away was in danger of being lost. When Joe said, "You'd better get it into a public freezing locker," I turned away from the suggestion, so *sure* that it must be just a matter of some carelessly pulled out plug or a fuse. It *must* start humming again soon!!! The Westinghouse man said he could not send anyone until Monday, and finally, after several calls, he suggested that we take everything out and put it in a public freezing locker. By that time, it was late afternoon, and I could find no one who could drive down to Ollon, and we ourselves have no car. I rushed over to Rosemary next door, and she very kindly rose to the emergency, gave her special "child" to someone else to put to bed, and drove us down. We had taken all the food out, put it in big cardboard cartons, and placed it in the back seat of their special Volkswagen bus built to take wheelchairs. And off we went: Fran, Rosie, and I to Ollon in the growing dusk to save the summer crop! It was a bit dramatic, for I had worn thin little flat-heeled black shoes and nylon stockings and had on a spring coat, plenty warm enough for the day, but *not for the freezer*. When the man told us there were a couple of empty lockers we could put them into, I had not realized that meant entering the below-freezing room (about 5 degrees below zero) and climbing up on an icy ladder, to put our cold plastic packages, one at a time, away!!! Fran handed them up to me for a while, then we ran out to warm up; then I handed them up to him! There was a tense moment when the man told us we were running a risk of freezing because the "blowers" had not been turned off, and they cause faster freezing! After that "clutched moment" we got through the rest of it, feeling as if we had had an Arctic expedition. But at least the vegetables were saved!

And guess what? When the Westinghouse repair man came on Monday, he found a *dead mouse* in the works! He said the mouse had electrocuted himself chewing through an important wire and had dropped down into the works, further complicating matters!!! One mouse less, but it was an expensive mousetrap!!!

You understand why we feel it has been a real "plague." We have had mice all through the years and have caught them in various ways. They have done bits of damage in the fruit cellar, but nothing has happened like this series before. When the oven of our American electric stove stopped working in the middle of baking rolls for Saturday night, we all wondered whether mice had been at work again, but Hugh John, the electrical engineer from South Africa who works in Zurich, came to fix the stove and could find nothing to connect the trouble with mice! So I hope that is the end of the negative part of this story!

One late October afternoon, I picked up the small handful of letters from the box in the downstairs office and began looking through them to see if there was anything "interesting." They were mostly bills, ads, and form letters. One long white envelope had the address of a bank in Pittsburgh on it. I flicked the flap open easily and slipped out a stiff white letter and two checks. Then I gasped, "Oh, the Lord has answered us such a *long* time 'before we called' yet, with such wonderful *timing*." The letter told of two codicils clipped to the will of Miss Marion Paden, one back in 1956 and one in 1960, both of which were for an amount of $500 for the work of L'Abri. Dear Cousin Marion, a faithful missionary in Egypt for over forty years, had felt led by the Lord to place these two amounts to be given immediately when her will should be cared for, to the work of L'Abri. She had never spoken about this, so she had not been thanked while she was on earth. It was only possible to thank the Lord, in this case! . . .

Trudy bent over "Karl's list" with me as we unfolded it a few days later, after November had commenced. This was the list for the last half of October and would tell us the final news as to whether the total for October would enable "full amounts" to be given out. (You see Karl Woodson* sends a list twice a month, along with a check for the total that has come in through him for L'Abri.) Names and addresses and the amount sent in are listed and it is exciting to read the names of those whom the Lord has touched to give. Often there are new names of people we have never heard of before, or names of some whom we have not heard from for a long time. Why had there been only seventy dollars one time during the "low time"? Why now for October was there a long list of people who had felt led to give ten dollars, five dollars, fifty, a hundred and one gift of over a thousand? . . .

My birthday this year happened to be on a weekly Day of Prayer, which is every Tuesday. Being in early November, it also was a drizzly, foggy day without any sparkle of sun or sky to be seen! But the Lord was to bring to light that day something which had bothered us all for some time, something which had been lost for just three months!!! Mary Johnson came over from Bellevue in mid-morning with a slight frown accompanying her question, "Did you have cornstarch in that order you lost?" My answer was a hopeful "Oh yes, did you find some cornstarch?" And Mary produced a carton of boxes of Maizena cornstarch. "Why Mary, where did you find these?" A conversation followed concerning the soups, and Mary left with my order sheet as she said she wanted to check something. It seemed that perhaps the mystery was going to be solved. About an hour later a happily smiling Mary came back and yes, it *was* solved, and she handed me the money for the lost soup order, minus the amount for the cornstarch. It was this way: The day before the wedding the soups had arrived at the post office in three heavy packages, too heavy to be delivered by Alice. Three boys (identity still unknown) had descended to carry them up, which they did nobly with only one small error—they delivered them to Bellevue, rather than to L'Abri and Mélèzes. Now Mary was away that week, and Mélèzes was buzzing that day, because it was August 7th. At Bellevue, without Mary there to check the order, it was taken for granted that this was *their* soup order, and the packages were put neatly on shelves. Mary said that several times later she thought the soup was holding out longer than usual, but that she never would have discovered the mistake had it not been for the carton of cornstarch which she knew she had *not* ordered. You can't imagine the relief and sheer joy we all felt over the finding of the lost soup!! Also the cash, rather than the soup, meant that we could buy that weekend a grocery order which was much more needed than the soup because it was still going to be a few days until the accounts would be finished, and the food money was gone. For some reason the Lord allowed that soup to remain "hidden" to us for three months, and

---

*A former L'Abri Worker, living at that time in Detroit and serving as L'Abri's financial secretary.

*The dedication service, a concert, then later a wedding have
"opened" our finished chapel. The remaining lumber piled
on the side of the chapel will be used to build the
bottom floor for Farel House.*

to bring it back to us in the form of money at just that moment. To at least one person it was an answer to a specific prayer *on* that Day of Prayer, which was an asked-for "sign" that the Lord was hearing. . . .

In September's closing days the dedication service, followed a few days later by a concert, then again by the first wedding there, saw the chapel a reality of answered prayer. We all sat, we who had prayed, along with some who had come in answer to prayer, listening to the messages preached from the Word of God , and sung, to His glory, ears filled with music of violin and voice, eyes filled with breathtaking beauty of that which the window framed. And since then we have been gathering there each Sunday morning for worship, and we look forward to the time when the lower room will become the scene of Farel House students studying with tape recorders, and library books within easy reach. . . .

Trudy's approaching departure* caused us all to pray for someone to fill her place in her work on the accounts and financial books and so on. It seemed that it was almost an "impossible request" to make, because such a one would need a long time of training under Trudy, and how could such a time be found? Time cannot go backwards, and that was the only solution that seemed to fit the need! But the Lord knew that *He* had been preparing the right person already for quite some time. John had been acting Treasurer of L'Abri for quite a long time and for a shorter

---

*Trudy was to marry Chuck Evans of Detroit at Christmas time.

---

time, Treasurer. He had helped Trudy with the books and had already learned quite a bit. Our minds, however, were fixed in the direction of finding a bookkeeper to work with John. Then one day Pris called me with a rather hesitant expression of ideas, then a sudden rush, as ideas tumbled out faster than the words. This was the gist of what she said, "Mother, I'm just not made for having people to cook meals for day after day, lunch and dinner, lunch and dinner, and to try to have a L'Abri conversation in the midst of the hubbub of children clamoring for things. I just get all nervous when people start to come in and I'm still cooking and that tenseness isn't just temporary, it goes on and on and I have begun to feel I'm a round peg in a square hole. I've been feeling so discouraged and then suddenly it seemed to come to both John and me that there *is* a solution. If we did *not* have people for meals all the time, John would have plenty of time to do the bookkeeping work, and he could combine that work on the books with copying tapes. He could fix up an office with tape recorders and desk for the accounts and so forth, and do both jobs at the same time, without being interrupted by the need of conversations with people, or mealtimes, etc. Then, Mother, *my* work could be the opening up of a *nursery* school. Not just a babysitting job, but a proper school which could later develop into first grade. I could take the children from nine to twelve, which would free Claudie and Linette for cooking and talking to people. And when the children go home, they could just be fed and have their naps before the one o'clock meal time. What do you think of that?" It struck me as a wonderful solution and one in which John and Pris were willing to take a lot of unglamorous work in the background, but a thing of "working together" that sounded marvelous to me. So the nursery school is now a daily affair with little ones trotting happily off in the mornings: Keith Martin, Timmy and Peter Baldwin, and Elizabeth and Becky Sandri. Soon there will be one more—the youngest child of the Johnsons who are coming to stay for six months of study at Farel House, renting a chalet in nearby Pannex for this time. . . .

In London, Ran and Sue and Margaret have been suffering a bit from the cold in the large house without heat except in one or two rooms and have been going through some difficult times of illness and so on. However, the deluge of people coming to listen to tapes, to ask questions or study the Bible has been very encouraging, and has shown that it was really the Lord's time to commence a L'Abri center in London. Franky has enjoyed his "three weekly" periods of a weekend visit at 52 Cleveland Road, and it has given him a real London home. We continue to be so very thankful for Franky's fine school. . . .

My mind has been going over our recent experiences in London and Zurich. Individuals with real burdens for their friends, earnest prayer and now a group of non-Christians coming, *not* for entertainment, *not* for an evening of relaxation with an epilogue but for serious conversation of *truth*.

For example, there is Liz, a Swiss Airline hostess, brought up in a Christian family, but one who like many young people today, had rebelled and had slipped away from the Lord. Sometimes there is a lack of reality accompanying a lack of satisfying "answers"; sometimes it is an inconsistency or a lack of love. Liz came to L'Abri once . . . twice . . . three times . . . and in these times she began to "be proud of being a Christian." As she prayed and thought about the fact that none of her friends were Christians, she began to get a burden for them. How to get started? She would invite her friends for a buffet supper at her apartment in Zurich, and on the invitation would appear a statement that there would be a lecture given following the meal: "Modern Man from Leonardo da Vinci to Carl Gustav Jung"—a lecture by Mr. Schaeffer of Huemoz followed by a time of questions. The "arty" invitations went out, and that evening in her tastefully decorated apartment . . . bookcases of bricks and boards, fat candles and Swedish glass, black and white prints of photography on one wall, a modern painting on another . . . a white fur rug, Moroccan leather stools . . . a group of frankly curious young people gathered, chatting and eating. These were not just students, but lawyers, doctors, engineers, a salesman for a hat manufacturer, a few secretaries, and Liz's younger brother and some of his friends. While eating, I informally told some of the L'Abri story to a cluster of people, while others talked to Fran. Then we arranged ourselves on the floor, chairs, daybed, and stools, and Fran started. His lecture was obviously a surprise to them all, and I could see interest coming alive on faces as people shifted and sat more and more "on the edge," listening. When the line of the history of philosophy was drawn and the present "line of despair" made clear, questions began to flow. That night something happened to me in telling the Lord that nothing was too difficult to do that this truth might be made known. I went back to the chalet to pitch in to the scrubbing and cooking with a renewed vigor. *Could* this be duplicated in other places? *Could* college bedrooms with students sitting cross-legged, artists' studios with feet perched up on tables, cabins in the woods with people stretched out before a flickering wood fire, sophisticated city businessmen, scientists, engineers gathered in a variety of living rooms—*could* people wherever they *are* reach people with whom the Lord has put *them* in contact? And *could* the results be a real turning to the Lord, and understanding new births that would affect the sweeping tide of unbelief in our day?

With much love in Him Who *is able to do anything*,

EDITH

1965

Dear Family:

There is a sequel to the mice and their devastating work! One December afternoon I snapped on kitchen lights and hurried to start the pot of soup boiling, while other parts of the dinner were being prepared. My mind, however, wasn't on the cooking. It was dealing with things "spoiled" yet usable, things no longer any good in their present pattern, yet with a whole new future ahead of them if only a new pattern could be shown. Suddenly an idea flashed into my mind which illustrated what I was thinking about and answered a problem I had about Christmas presents all at one fell swoop! I dashed upstairs to get a couple of the mouse-eaten, holey sweaters, a pair of scissors, a big wool needle, and some grey and black wool, then ran down again, dashing into Gracie's room.

"Oh, Gracie, I've got an idea! Here, look through Winnie-the-Pooh with me and let's see what pictures we can find of Eeyore and Piglet." "See? Isn't this grey shetland just perfect for Eeyore and Piglet? With a red wool mouth, tiny black dots for eyes, and I'll show you what I mean." . . .

Perching beside her, I cut out a body, ears, legs. Shapeless-looking blobs of cut-up sweater were all that these looked like, but as I looked at the picture, and the wool in my hands, I was seeing the finished product. . . . (Yes, dinner was over an hour late.) . . .

"We'll make Christmas presents for all the children of L'Abri. I'll make Piglets and Eeyores for the boys, and dolls for the little girls, with sweaters, hats, and socks that you can knit for them. For Franky and Chris I'll make black-cashmere African boys with red knit trousers and striped jerseys you can knit. Oh, they'll be fabulous!" It was just what Gracie needed, the best "occupational therapy" she could possibly have had following her accident last October.

"Remember ye not the former things, neither consider the things of old. Behold, I will do a new thing; now it shall spring forth, shall ye not know it? I will even make a way in the wilderness, and rivers in the desert" (Isaiah 43:18, 19).

A human being can take a ruined, hole-filled sweater and make it into something of an entirely different pattern which is completely desirable. The ruins could have been thrown away, in fact most people turned away in disgust, wishing they had been thrown away. The same things, in their new "shapes" or patterns, are sought after, the old ruins which brought forth distaste, forgotten entirely. . . .

The question of what L'Abri "is" is a hard one to answer. We who have lived through many of the ten years of God's unfolding His plan for the work find it hard to answer. That it is a spiritual shelter, we do know, and that the Lord sends people of His choice in answer to prayer, we are constantly reminded, lest we should fall into a "rut" of thinking that they should fall into certain definite categories.

When Monsieur Ob telephoned me one blustery winter evening and asked whether we could "board" an eleven-year-old boy whom he was tutoring, because the child has a reading problem (based on a psychological difficulty), I hesitated and then said, "Noooo—I'm afraid not. You see we really don't have time to spend with a child of that age. Why, our own Franky is away in school and I mean, a boy couldn't fit into the life here. Meals are long affairs because of the conversations, and no, I'm sorry. Anyway we are *not* a boarding house at all." But he went on to say that he felt the "atmosphere" in our home might be a help and gave many reasons why he felt we should accept Chris. Finally he said he wanted to bring him down—"just to talk with you so you may have an idea of what he is like."

Chris sat twisting his hands together in his lap and biting his lip nervously. "Because I don't like school where I am—because—and so I want to come to your school. Yes, I know I would like to come here." We carefully explained that we were not a school, and tried to tell him a little bit about L'Abri, but we couldn't discourage his eagerness to stay.

Could you say "no" to one who might never again have the opportunity to hear the clear message of the Bible if you did say "no"? We couldn't.

This happened while Jane, Betty, Minna, and Frances Kramer were in America. That meant that Coxe was sleeping in Chesalet to care for it for Jane and Betty, and so Coxe's room was free for Chris. Also I discovered to my utter amazement that Chris had been in school in Villars with the Kramer children, and they had been praying for him for weeks! Hence, I suddenly realized his coming was an answer to their prayers! Did that mean it was smooth sailing for all of us? No, as Chris took turns with the various L'Abri families for meals, his boisterousness made serious conversations difficult, and at times he was a "hindrance," "a problem," but our assurance that God had brought him to us increased, and did not diminish in spite of any "problems" that arose. He spent time with Larry feeding the chickens, with Rex as he helped over at Beau Site, with Allan as he worked outdoors, and with each of the families at mealtimes. In each of his contacts he was learning by observation as well as in conversation things about the Christian life. At night I put him to bed, as I always did Franky (and the girls when they were young) with a story. After my reading the first two nights, Chris began to ask questions about L'Abri so I started the "L'Abri Story" as a continued story, one hour each night and he had the longest version ever given of that story, with details of various people's lives as they came and then believed and went on in a life the Lord opened up to them. He heard of the beginning of the work in Italy, in Holland, in England, and many instances of answered prayer. Each night he would beg, "Oh tell more; go on tell more." When we came to the end of all that, then I began to give him a "bird's-eye view of the Bible," but as he had not ever even heard the stories of Jonah, Daniel in the lion's den, or anything, we took a long time to get through it all, and I began giving him a story at breakfast too, animated ones with gestures (sometimes observed by others who came in on the end of them!). I was carried back into the joy of teaching children once more, with just one child to teach.

The evening came when we were talking about the second coming of Christ, and he suddenly broke in, "When is He going to come? When? And what will happen to us when He does??" I explained that those born into God's family need have no fear, as the coming of Jesus will be wonderful for them. "*I* believe in God. How can I know I am in God's family?" was his eager question. Then I carefully went through four areas: "Do you believe in God's existence?" "Do you believe that you have sinned and are guilty, in need of being cleansed from sin?" "Do you believe that Jesus was born, lived, died, rose again in His body, truly in space and time and history, not a myth?" "And do you believe that Jesus died for *you* as if no one else were in the world, just the way we can talk to God in prayer as if no one else were with Him, as if He were alone with us?" I took time to make each of these "areas" clear to him with illustrations of all kinds, ending with an illustration of what it means to believe. At the end he did make a profession of faith in Christ, and prayed a very sweet, original prayer, thanking God for bringing him to Chalet les Mélèzes. He was so excited when Peter Spink gave him a New Testament and he began to take great pride in "finding" verses when John gave verses in Sunday School even though he had not yet learned to read sufficiently well to read them when he did find them!

Chris left just before Christmas, with "Trouble" under his arm. "Trouble" is the name he gave to the boy doll which he had watched me make, and Gracie knit for, with such excitement that something was actually being "*made* just for me." His parents, grandparents also, are psychiatrists and money is not a problem, but the home is a broken one, and Chris needs that which cannot be bought or "arranged for"! Do pray that now as he is in his new "special" boarding school, the Lord may keep his memory fresh as to all that he had learned about God's Word, until he may someday read it for himself. Surely the Lord brought him to L'Abri. . . .

In the midst of washing, ironing, packing to take Franky to Geneva to fly back to school for his winter term on January 18th, mail arrived which informed us that Fran's mother was ill. It was hard to be sure just what we needed to do and so a call was put through to Philadelphia to ask my friend, Margaret Walker, to visit Mrs. Schaeffer, talk to her doctor, and call us back with definite facts and advice based on "on-the-spot" knowledge. The message which came back, just a few hours after Franky was safely back in England at his school, turned our small world upside down for a time, as we were told that Mother Schaeffer needed 24-hour-a-day nursing and that I was needed immediately to take over from a neighbor who was filling in temporarily.

We had "expected" (can we ever look forward to any aspect of the future without saying, "Lord willing"???) to have Fran go to America for a short speaking trip, as he had been asked to be in Boston for ten days of lectures and discussions. Then I was to have gone to England to be with Sue and Ran, helping a little with curtain making and so on, and being there when Franky had his mid-term vacation of five days. Fran was to have met me there, and we were to have then had a month-long "English Trip." Cynthia had written that the English Trip was going to be so very full of engagements around the general London area (including Oxford, Cambridge, Bournemouth, etc.) that we could not accept anything in Ireland or Scotland this time. The schedule was *full!*

Suddenly, *both* of us were on our way to America, I to nurse his mother; he to care for any matters concerning her that needed care, the future a huge question mark!! We were on our way by the 20th, leaving all the dear, faithful L'Abri Workers in charge. . . .

For me, it has been the most "different" time of my life. At first the nursing care was a 24-hour job. Slowly Mother Schaeffer has recovered from what the doctor called a slight stroke, but it is apparent she can never live alone again. As she has chosen to return with us, rather than go into a nursing home, all her belongings have been either sold, given away, or packed into the five trunks I have been packing "in between" other things. We expect, Lord willing, to fly back to Switzerland on March 7th, taking 84-year-old Mother Schaeffer back with us to live in Mélèzes. It will mean some changing around. I shall give my upstairs rooms to her and move down into Trudy's office for my "work room." I never thought I should be the one to occupy it when Trudy and I prayed together wondering who would be the next one to type in there! Please do pray for us in this new "impossibility." After all, L'Abri was started with a 13-year-old Susan in bed with rheumatic fever, and a 2-year-old Franky still having therapy for his polio, and never has the work been without "impossibilities." The care of the elderly ones of one's family is something everyone has to face whether they at the moment are the younger ones, or the elderly ones. We change places as life goes on!! This is another place where we must pray for a "demonstration of God's existence" in asking *Him* to work out the problems of doing L'Abri work, plus this new responsibility. We also need to pray for the tremendous adjustments ahead of Mother Schaeffer as she leaves America for the first time in her life; in fact she leaves Germantown for the first time in her life to live elsewhere.

Fran has had his twelve days in Boston during which we felt some of the "fruit" of the times of prayer and struggle in our various lives was seen. There were three main lectures attended by from 350 to 400 students of MIT, Harvard, Wellesley, Radcliffe, Smith, Mount Holyoke, Barrington, etc., and there were discussion groups, personal conversations, and so on, an exhausting but thoroughly satisfying week. It is as if *suddenly* both in England and here, doors have swung open in a new degree. Fran gave approximately the same lectures in Wilmington for the Philadelphia area in three seminars and one public meeting. Debby and Udo drove from St. Louis to spend one weekend with us and the Lord gave me several "days off" from my nursing job, as a nurse who was at L'Abri for a time and who now is in Philadelphia with her intern husband, offered to stay to relieve me. During these "days off" I was able to visit my father in Wilmington for a few hours and to speak at an all-day "retreat" of Beaver College girls. As Beaver was my alma mater this was very much fun! It was a kind of "marathon" as I spoke for five hours, but the girls not only said it seemed all too short, but came back for more when they heard I was speaking at Dick Gray's church in a tea-meeting before Fran spoke to a private school group of teenagers, and we had conferences with Dorie and Judy concerning a new Christian girls' school which will be opening on Long Island soon. My "day off" today has been spent in a friend's bedroom, shut away alone to write this! And soon we shall start back to face the new "unknown."

Do you suppose any of us *ever* get to the end of being suddenly faced with something we feel is "*really* impossible this time"??? I think Satan makes sure we have temptations to "give up" in one way or another. On the other hand, I think also that the Lord allows us *opportunities* to *trust* Him, and to *pray believing*.

"Behold I am the Lord, the God of all flesh; is there anything too hard for me?" (Jeremiah 32:27).

"Ah, Lord God! behold, thou has made the heaven and the earth by thy great power and stretched out arm, and there is nothing too hard for thee" (Jeremiah 32:17).

With love in this One,

EDITH

June 18, 1965   Huemoz sur Ollon, Switzerland

Dear Family:

We were in the middle of a Workers' weekly meeting when Franky burst in the Beau Site living room door and announced in an out-of-breath voice, "The truck from Holland is here with the organ and he's trying to get down that steep part of the road. We need five men to help lift. Right away!" Jane and Larry left like a shot. . . .

We had long prayed for an organ for the chapel that would match its beauty to the loveliness outside and within. After a series of unbelievable circumstances our custom-designed Flentrop organ arrived from the workshop of its Dutch builder and was unloaded into the empty chapel.

Boxes containing 400 pipes had to be carried in and other "parts" in careful succession. There was a constant audience watching the organ assembly: Jane, Betty, Franky, Bruce, and two of the young fellows from the cerebral palsy home next door to us, in their wheelchairs. Others came and went for shorter times, to report progress to those who could not go down at all!! It was exciting to see it all slip into place, each pipe in its own spot, the unseen ones as important as the prominent front ones; the decorative woodwork cut into the patterns Betty Carlson had drawn for them—(The central design is a lamb, slain, yet standing upright, and there are other sections—a sheaf of corn, grapes, Swiss Alpine flowers, etc., all cut out in light wood matching the wood walls of the room, though the organ console itself is of darker wood. The cutout work simply covers the top portion of the pipes). A few hours of assembly work, but only possible because of a perfection of organ making which had taken months to complete in Holland, and all this as a result of years of prayer for an instrument which would be the right one for this particular spot, for the use the Lord would make of it.

The truck driver needed to stay over night, and so he had a time at L'Abri that was probably quite unique in his experience of driving loads to many parts of Europe and the Near East. Coxe translated the conversations into Dutch for him and for supper there was a Dutch-speaking table. . . .

In the midst of a cold, snowy, late spring, and a cold, foggy, rainy, early summer, came a few days of hot, sunny, sparkling weather with gorgeous full-moon nights which turned the snowy peaks into a magical blue-white—the kind of beauty which is almost painful. It was during these "perfect days" that May 14th arrived! May 13th in the afternoon Mr. Flentrop, the famous Dutch organ maker, and his wife and Mr. Jensen, the famous Dutch organist, and his wife arrived, had dinner in Les Mélèzes, and then walked through the beauty of the evening to the chapel where Mr. Flentrop showed slides and gave a talk on the history of organ making. Mr. Jensen illustrated certain portions of

*The wonderful Baroque organ designed
and constructed especially for our chapel
by Mr. Flentrop in Holland.*

the talk by playing things which let us hear the variety of pipes and stops. Our own L'Abri Family and community, as well as L'Abri guests, felt much more appreciative of what the Lord has given us in this organ after his talk. The next day was one of the busiest! Not only had the chapel to be cleaned and decorated, but all the musicians and singers had to practice, and the fellows had to carry chairs from the village schoolhouse to the chapel (since we have not nearly enough chairs for a capacity crowd). Somehow all was in readiness, and everyone in his place by 3 o'clock that afternoon: villagers and people from Villars and Chesieres as well as more distant places. Many were there for whom some of us had been praying a long time. I wish you all had been with us to hear the first strains of the organ music and all the concert that followed, as well as Fran's message on "Music and Noise"—a contrast drawn from many passages in the Scripture which brought the gospel clearly to those who heard it.

Minna played the organ for the afternoon concert. She spent two weeks in Holland learning what she needed to know about Flentrop organs. The concert thrilled us as Jane and Merrel [an American opera singer] sang, Frances Kramer played the violin, John Sandri the cello, Betty Carlson and Regina Rutland flutes, and Minna the organ. The sermon was translated sentence by sentence by Priscilla as Fran preached. Not only did it thrill us to hear what God had given us in music, but it was so satisfying to know that this sermon was being understood by all the French-speaking people there. Also, the organ maker and organist and their wives were so appreciative of the message that we could praise

God anew for the wonder of His working all the details together for so many lives at once.

The evening concert was a gift from Mr. Flentrop himself, as he had brought Mr. Jensen and was paying his fee to give us this music. Jane sang several selections, and I don't believe I've ever heard her sing so perfectly before. Mr. Jensen's playing was magnificent; the building was absolutely filled (I think every village family was represented, as well as all sorts of people from outside the village, Lausanne, Montreux, etc.). As I sat listening, and looking out of the window at the mountains, ethereal in the moonlight, my mind went back over the past ten years in praise to the Lord, thinking of the step of faith we had taken in stating that we were going to pray that our lives and this work would prove the existence of God, thinking of how we had prayed that He would send to us the people of His choice, who needed help; send the needed material provisions for the "family" and guests; and unfold His plan for the work. We never in our wildest imaginations would have dreamed that a Flentrop organ (provided for by designated funds in memory of Jane's father) would have been part of the Lord's plan in making music one area of the L'Abri work, nor would we have expected all those villagers to have been sharing an evening with the people the Lord had brought from distant places. Our feelings of wonder, awe, worship, and praise for all that God had done in answer to prayer—prayer that we might be used to demonstrate His existence overwhelmed us. He has done so much *more* than we could have dreamed! It has certainly not been a ten-year period of jumping from one peak of excitement to another, and it is easy to shrink from the great variety of struggles and hardships which have been, and will continue to be, a part of it all, but our prayer together is that we may be given strength to keep on, allowing Him to use us as He will. . . .

If you recall a bit less than a year ago, you will read the details of how the Lord led in the purchase of this house in Ealing, England, where I am now sitting by a window, overlooking the lovely walled-in garden (the wall all but hidden by masses of various colored climbing roses), and writing this letter. A year ago I was feeling hopeless as to how to find the "right place," "crying out to the Lord for His guidance," and now I marvel at the "*just* right"-ness of this big old mid-Victorian home-like house which He so clearly led me to that June day. It was a good "buy" from a business point of view, and it has the charm which grows through the years with a well-cared-for garden planted with a love for shrubs, flowers, and trees and added to by a small greenhouse with a grapevine flourishing in it. It has a huge drawing room which is just right even with scarcely any furniture in it. A few lovely pieces of furniture which which were given, plus some flower arrangements from the garden, turn it into a wonderful background for the Sunday evening service (held regularly now each Sunday at 6 P.M. if you are in London), and then for the high tea served after the service, and the discussion continuing until about ten or so. It also is a fine background for the Saturday night discussions when larger numbers come. If there are not enough chairs, the floor is quite adequate for the overflow numbers! When we are not in London, Ran and Sue use the smaller cozier living room across the hall, easier to heat in winter, for the smaller numbers coming for Saturday night supper and discussion, Sunday services and tea. But as the work grows they, too, will have to use the bigger room! Ran and Sue moved in here last October, at which time Ran began his studies at King's College in London University. He has his law degree from Cambridge and has studied at Farel House as well as being a L'Abri Worker for three years already, but now he is going to get his BD in London, while he and Sue do the L'Abri work here, with Cynthia who was the L'Abri representative before, continuing to be a Worker. Thus far the Lord has been bringing a variety of people from various nationalities and for various kinds of help here, not only on Saturdays and Sundays, but for times of personal conversation at teatime or for lunch or morning coffee, during the week. Even though the numbers are small, it is, as in the beginning of L'Abri in Huemoz, a demonstration of the Lord's plan in a definite way already, involving hard work, prayer, and sacrifice in the daily personal lives of the Workers. The work is one based on prayer for each aspect, just as it is in Huemoz, and is independent of Huemoz in that they pray that the Lord will send directly in to the London work, that which He would give for their needs here. There is a *personal* aspect in communication with the Lord in the opportunity of waiting day by day, week by week for direct replies to one's prayers, which is very precious.

I came to London directly from Huemoz, while Fran went by way of Holland, where he spoke in Amsterdam and Kampen, and also attended the inauguration service in which Dr. Hans Rookmaaker became a full Professor of Art History in the Free University of Amsterdam. Dr. Rookmaaker and his wife, Anky, are Members of L'Abri, and Fran was glad to be able to share this very special occasion with them, as well as to be there once more for lectures and times of discussion with students. He said he was amazed at how many people there are in the Dutch audiences now, who have been at L'Abri as Helpers, Farel House students, or guests. It was the 29th of May when Fran got into London, and the first English trip with 52 Cleveland Road as its base commenced, and now there is only one more weekend, and this well-prepared "trip" to Oxford, Bournemouth, London, Reigate, and Burgess Hill will be past history!

But this letter must go back and cover more space, because I last left you in March before we brought Mother Schaeffer back with us from America. March 7th—flight back, rush to get furniture and rugs to make Mother S. at home and comfortable in two rooms with balcony and a bird-feeding tray to watch at breakfast time. Other rooms and furniture

This is my new ground-floor office where I am typing this letter.
However, I write this through the night, not to be interrupted
by window conversations.

moved around, and I took up my new "headquarters" as Trudy's old bedroom/office became my office and room in which to talk to people (Mother S. settled in happily, praise God for answered prayer in that.) Easter time brought people in summer proportions, but harder to care for without summer weather! End of March "Members' meeting" brought Members from various places: Mr. Exhenry from Champéry, Rookmaakers from Holland, Woodsons from Italy, Macaulays from England, and all Members from Huemoz to be together for a nonstop time (food served in the living room), to talk over past, present, and future aspects of the work. Each person marveled over the unity among us, not only "unanimous decisions" but a growth of ideas concerning decisions that had to be made, a *growth* which came in conversation which gave evidence so often that the *same* thought had come to several simultaneously. Rather than arguments, there were developments and then decisions. . . .

One last wonderful incident from among the things the Lord has done these past months: Nicky, the Japanese Farel House student, has often spoken of the difficulty of communication in the Japanese language in Christian things, as he has learned all his knowledge of Christianity in English. "When I pray in Japanese words confuse me and I begin to see and think in Buddhist patterns. The word 'God' brings Buddhist concepts to me." This he has been struggling against, realizing he must present Christianity to others in Japanese soon. Then at Easter time, a Chinese businessman arrived from Paris. He had heard of L'Abri in Formosa from his Professor Andrews (missionary), and from a Swiss architect in France. He is from a Buddhist background, but calls himself "agnostic." Though he understands English, it became clear that communication was going to be a problem. Then Nicky and the Chinese fellow made a wonderful discovery: the Chinese had needed Japanese in his business and spoke perfect *Japanese!* From that moment on Nicky translated everything to him in Japanese: lectures, conversations, sermons, and the Lord did two things at once: gave Nicky some needed practice in communication of Christianity in his own language, and gave the Chinese fellow a possibility of understanding that which was being said! It is the Lord who brings people and brings the translators too when they are truly needed.

With love in the One to Whom *nothing* is too complicated,

EDITH

August 24, 1965   Huemoz sur Ollon, Switzerland

Dear Family:

In the fall of 1954 a family picture was taken in the living room of Chalet Bijou in Champéry. The picture was taken in October one afternoon when Susan was dressed to go to Monthey to have a blood test, because of her rheumatic fever—and when smiling Franky, aged two, was delighted with new shoes in spite of the fact that he could not yet manage more than two or three steps without falling because of paralyzed muscles following his September attack of polio. The floods and avalanches had not yet hit our village—and the edict to leave Switzerland had not yet been handed to us—so we were still in the state of feeling "settled" as the new curtains were being admired and the couch we sat on was looking splendid in its new upholstery and repaired springs. . . .

We repeatedly have discovered through the ten years of living in this realm, by prayer, that one *must* go through periods of real testing, of "low times" and "dark moments," facing real need, going through times of enforced frugality and deprivation (not pretend ones!), in order to see the reality of answered prayer; in order to know that the money is not coming in in an easily explained "expected" way, but is truly a miracle of answered prayer.

When reading in I Kings one day, the 17th chapter suddenly became strongly impressed upon my mind. The Lord had commanded the ravens to feed Elijah there by the brook, in the midst of this time of hiding. "Ravens," I thought to myself. "Ravens are birds that steal food, normally—what a miracle it was! God commanded them in His own way, and

Taken ten years after leaving Champèry, a recent family photo-graph by the hedge between Mélèzes and Beau Site. Left to right: Susan, little Margaret in Ranald's arms, myself with Franky, Udo behind, and Debby between Udo and her dad.

they did it—they brought meat and bread morning and evening—even against the natural inclination of these birds." Then I thought of the two months approaching—July and August. "Oh, Lord," I prayed, "July and August are months which on church and mission records are 'low months' for giving. They are not months that bring in money because people are away from home, or for other reasons are not *naturally* thinking in the direction of giving. Lord, I see July and August as two huge, black ravens—*not* inclined to bring us bread and meat. Please cause these two months to be the biggest months of the year thus far, rather than the smallest, in this area of material things. Please use this as a demonstration to any who are watching the work, no matter from what viewpoint or attitude, that *Thou art truly answering prayer.* Show each of us in the work, and those praying with us, and others watching—that *Thou* art able to answer in a time when it is *most un*likely." The rest of the Workers joined me in this plea.

July's story can be told. John, our Treasurer, found to his own amazement as he did the July accounts, that July was the largest month of the year thus far, and that it would be possible to pay the Workers their personal money, as well as to meet the basic needs of rent, electricity, mortgage payments, etc., and to give a larger proportion of "food money" to the housekeepers than at any time for over three months. God *did* answer—not just ten years ago; not just five years ago—not just two years ago—but last month! And now, though the story cannot yet be finished the answer is going to include the second "raven" too. Not only is it encouraging to plan meals with more leeway, and to purchase some needy personal things, and to replace some broken glasses and dishes—*but it is exciting to us who are living through these experiences to know that the Lord really is hearing and answering prayer.*

Similar stories could be told of London L'Abri, and of Milan L'Abri. "The wonderful thing about it all," said Harvard Bill, the musician, the other day, "is that you don't have to simply say that these things happened ten years ago. They *are* happening today." . . .

One bright July morning two fellows arrived before breakfast on the first bus after having traveled all the way from London's Victoria Station. One was 6'5" blond Hugh, thrilled to be back after a year in Oxford. The other was Eddie looking a bit uncertain! Seventeen-year-old Eddie would not look quite as strange to anyone in England as to the villagers of our small, Alpine village. They looked . . . and greeted the two with, "Bonjour, monsieur, madame," the greeting given to a fellow and girl. It was not as strange to them to see a "girl" walking along in bluejeans and a man's sport jacket as it was to think of that shoulder-length head of bright bold-red, curly hair belonging to a boy. The head of hair framed a sensitive face, responsive blue eyes, and a gentleness which came out in conversation about the *third* arrival who *flew* in with them and landed in the Mélèzes tree behind the chalet . . . but came down at Eddie's call to preen himself on his shoulder! Yes, Eddie had brought his jackdaw with him all the way by train (how it missed questioning by the customs' official, I can't imagine!) . . . and he sat at breakfast with the bird sharing the meal, on his shoulder. This much will simply give you one small glimpse of the variety of people the Lord is drawing to L'Abri.

One evening sometime after 9 o'clock, just as I was finishing tidying the kitchen with Gracie, after dishes had been done in quietness because everyone else had gone to a lecture, except Grandmother, Gracie, and myself—and *just* as I had sighed, "Now at last I think I can get down to my office and do a bit of correspondence,"—the doorbell rang! There stood a middle-aged man and his wife, whose "burr" soon revealed that they were Scottish, having come to L'Abri with very little idea of what it was at all. How? Well, the two nights and days spent on the train from Dundee, Scotland (made longer by taking a wrong train and ending up in another part of Switzerland) had been made on the strength of a sketchy description of L'Abri given to the wife by a girl named Elizabeth, in *Wales,* when this Scottish woman was visiting there. . . . As I hurriedly prepared soup, an omelet, and salad (the 31 people at supper had not left any leftovers!) and a pot of tea which I hoped would be strong enough to suit Scottish tastes, I wondered and prayed, "Why, Lord, did You send *these*? They really seem to have *no* idea what this is." And I struggled with the thought of going to my office once they were fed. But, "thereby entertaining angels unawares" was a phrase that went through my head, and I decided that the Lord's command of hospitality did not mean leaving weary, confused travelers alone, and I sat down with them and gave a condensed version of the L'Abri story and of the bird's-eye view of the Bible. They had had no interest in Christianity. One of only two sons had died of a burst appendix. He told of being in charge of the signal lights for trains in the harbor of Dundee. Intellectual? University students? What category would you put these people in in L'Abri? Whatever brought them in their own minds' explanations, it was soon clear that the Lord brought them. As the week went on, they were listening to tapes very earnestly. They pitched in to help in Joe and Linette's chalet to dust, clean, scrub, and they got into all sorts of conversations. They fit into the life of L'Abri, growing more and more interested day by day. Before they left they had a good talk with Fran, and they told him that they have access to a tape recorder and that they would be taking a copy of the Romans studies and of the L'Abri story home with them, because they intended to invite Dundee friends to listen with them. If the Lord takes us back to St. Andrews University, a home in nearby Dundee will be having an evening gathering of friends and neighbors, not in university circles. . . .

Andrea, a 15-year-old Italian, one of Hurvey's boys in his boys' group, was helping Nicky to set the table outdoors for the 49 people counted for lunch when suddenly I heard a melodious crash!!! And as one of the girls brought a tray with at least five soup bowls accounting for the myriad pieces of yellow china, my heart sank and I thought, "Oh dear, we soon won't have enough to serve everyone soup even in a mixture of dishes." Do you know what that dish breaking resulted in? It resulted in Andrea's having a struggle there on his bed that lunchtime which ended in his assurance of salvation! His mind worked in this direction: "What a mess I've made when I was trying to be *helpful*. But if you fail so when you try to be *good*, what hope is there for anyone?" This line of thought brought him to a seemingly clear understanding of what Christ has done for us in His death on the cross. His decision seems to be a very clear one, and he seems happy in the certainty. It has been a lesson to us as to the worthwhileness of broken dishes when the Lord turns it to good. It is in a thing like this that we learn to say, "Lord, if You have some purpose in this, don't let me hinder Thy purpose by my reactions." But learning takes time, it takes a lifetime! . . .

As years have gone on, we have felt it is necessary for a person to be a Farel House student or a Helper *before* becoming a Worker, to give us time to get to know each other. But this "rule" has not diminished the reality of Workers being given by the Lord in answer to prayer.

Larry Snyder came to Europe seeking some answers as to a purpose in life. It was in an Oslo Youth Hostel that he began a conversation with a fellow he had never seen before, and who said to Larry after a few minutes, something like this: "You sound confused. Do you know where you ought to go? There's a place called L'Abri, way up in the Alps in Switzerland. You can get your questions answered there. I've been there only for two days or so, but I have never known a place like it." Larry said that when the fellow said, "L'Abri," something responded within him, and he knew he must go there. At any rate, he searched for a job in order to earn money to pay whatever it might cost to go and worked on a construction job in Germany for a time. Late one cold, rainy night, Larry arrived on his motorcycle, eager to find out everything he could about L'Abri "right away, because I want to start studying tomorrow." He read the book manuscript* that night and the next morning commenced Farel House. As time went on, Larry became an understanding Christian, and the problems he had in philosophic areas and areas of doctrine cleared up. He not only studied hard, but was an outstandingly good help in the afternoons and evenings. After some months (at the time of Debby and Udo's wedding, to be exact), Larry was ready to take over in Udo's place. During this period as a Worker, Larry became assured that the Lord was calling him to prepare himself for Christian work and the desire to make known that which so many of his friends and family had never heard explained became a very burning one to him. So early in the summer, Larry left, heading for Covenant Seminary, after a visit home. And the Lord had prepared one to take Larry's place. That was Nicky. . . .

And so the Lord continues to bring *His* choice of Workers in answer to prayer, whether for shorter or longer periods of time. . . .

May we thank God for the *continued opportunities* to call upon Him, and for the *continued answers!!*

With love in this *One*,

EDITH

---

*My manuscript for the book *L'Abri*, which was not yet in print.

1966

February 2, 1966   Huemoz sur Ollon, Switzerland

Dear Family:

... The days seem to stretch out ahead of us and behind us like water from a well-supplied water system, almost endlessly. But when you begin seeing a whole year or a large portion of a year, looking back, or even ahead, there are mighty few portions like this in a lifetime, and two main things stand out. The *first* is the importance of fulfilling the Lord's purpose in our lifetime, for our individual lives are important in the total picture of the Lord's purpose. The *second* is the importance of realizing that as Christians we know the Lord has said that something is being done *in us* as we live. "Why should God allow me to have so much trouble?" "Why should I have such horribly frustrating and disappointing experiences, when others—" The "why" so very often is found in the very important, needful, and *real* growth inside ourselves. Our Heavenly Father sits as a refiner of silver, skimming off the impurities as heat liquifies the silver. These are *not* pretty little religious phrases and concepts, but the reality of what our lives are meant to be accomplishing as the months and years speed by, and the time for our entering the next portion of our "eternal life" gets continually closer. ... Of course, we know we can add nothing to what *He* has done for us in giving us salvation. But it is clear from the Word of God, that we have missed a lot if we haven't come to some understanding that very, very, *very* often the interruptions, the disappointments, the frustrations, the sufferings, the agonies, the longings, the unfulfilled dreams, the wasted time, the lack of visible results can be far *more* important than the successes, the efficient, smooth-flowing days. Far *more* important because of what has been going on within us or within others with whom we are linked in the agonies or frustrations.

What has all this to do with the last five months at L'Abri? ...

If you were to see *all* those who really have a share in what is going on in L'Abri, you would have to see pictures of all those who faithfully pray, and who send a share of what the Lord has given them in material things in order to provide seeds for gardens, electricity, coal, food, tape recorders, tables, chairs, and so on. Ever since the early church, the Lord has *blended* His children together to do different portions of His work so that the *total* results will be for His glory, and the salvation of men. . . .

September 23rd Fran and I left Huemoz for America, taking Franky back to England to school on our way. The rush to get ready was incredible! That busy summer, the short vacation, a speaking engagement at a missionary conference in Paris for Fran, Franky's things to prepare for another term away, and a six-week traveling and speaking trip in changing climates to prepare and pack for, plus the household to arrange for in our absence all in a space of about four days! . . .

Some have asked, "What happens to L'Abri when you are away?" The answer is that it continues! After all "L'Abri" changes from day to day and week to week according to the sort of people who come as guests and students. You can't have questions from an oriental Buddhist, unless such a one is here! You can't have eager-seeking questions on the part of an agnostic who has never heard the truth presented from an intellectual viewpoint, and who has never heard of such "reality" as answered prayer unless you have such a one here! So not only does "what happens" depend on those of us who are Workers and who are here to cook, serve, talk, listen to questions, write letters, go shopping, and preach, but "what happens" depends on the kind of people that come, and how thoroughly their hearts are prepared, and how serious their seeking is as well as what sort of personalities they are. . . .

The other household that is involved in the work, and in an increased way when we are not here, is Tzi No. John is busy with the copying and sending out of tapes, the financial accounts, and all the business matters of L'Abri. Pris has the nursery in the mornings, and cares for the reading, answering, and forwarding to us of mail she feels we should read. This is a daily task, of course. John also, along with others, gives Farel House lectures, and Pris serves guest meals a couple of times a week, as well as teaching Sunday School. . . .

This time as we went, Peasy, from St. Louis, literally arrived one-half hour before we left for our plane. We wished we could stay on to talk longer to her, but we had to leave without that wish fulfilled. Peasy was born again in L'Abri when she came back during the Christmas holidays of her junior year abroad in Florence, Italy, where she was studying art. Now, as a graduate of Smith, Peasy returned for a time in Farel House. She then lived in Beau Site and became a basic part of that household during the period when Allan was away.

Why did we go to America?

The first invitation came as a call for "help" like the "come over to Macedonia and help us" of the early days of the church. Often, when people say, "Why should you be in Switzerland? Can't Swiss Christians take care of any need here?" one feels staggered by the lack of comprehension of what the "field" for Christian work really is. The "field" is the world and the needs change from one century to another. In the 20th century, those who are being fed the 20th-century "thinking" in very large doses exist in every country and America is certainly not immune from the effects of 20th-century thinking, 20th-century philosophy as it oozes into every subject in high schools and colleges, especially English literature, or contemporary literature, and as it oozes into all the movies, plays, television broadcasts, magazines, and newspapers. Everyone is being affected even though they may not know it. As Fran's understanding of the 20th-century thinking has grown through the years of discussing with the amazing variety of people the Lord has brought him in contact with in the fields of philosophy, art, science, etc., the "answer" he has been giving, and the "apologetic" which has developed, is helpful to "intellectuals" and to those who would shy away from that word, yet who have the same basic problems. The Lord planned this place in Switzerland not for Swiss primarily, though Swiss have been helped, but for the people from many different countries who come to Switzerland and whom the Lord directed to L'Abri. *He* chose the location; we did not.

In the same way, the Members of L'Abri felt that this "call" from America was part of the Lord's plan. Just as ten years ago we were willing to remain in a mountain chalet and talk to twos and threes at a time, so in September we set forth on the American trip, finding it necessary to bow with a *willingness* that did not come easily, to give larger groups that which smaller numbers had come to the chalet to find, and to *go* where the Lord was *sending us*, rather than waiting in prayer for Him to send those of His choice *to us*.

We waved to Franky, Susan, and Margaret in the London airport praying that the Lord would keep them safely until our return—Franky in his boarding school, Sue as she waited for her next baby in the midst of busy London L'Abri work. One meal, and quite a number of handwritten letters later, we saw New York appear beneath us in mid-afternoon heat! We had left London at 1:30 P.M. London time, and now it was only 3:30 P.M. New York time. It seemed wonderful to "save" so much time or "gain" so much time. But when we were sleepily eating supper with Dorie and Judy in Smithtown, Long Island, and realized that it was long after midnight by the time we got up, it didn't seem like much of a "gain" after all!!

It would be impossible to describe the American trip as a running story without writing a booklet. Let me say that we marveled at all that the Lord did and at the evidence that *He* had taken us for a very special purpose. It was thrilling to meet face to face some who had prayed for L'Abri for years, or who had given gifts which came in times of crucial need. The dear Salisburys who gave that first thousand dollars toward buying Chalet les Mélèzes which arrived *just* in time, suddenly became real flesh-and-blood people as they attended a meeting in the Indianapolis Bible Presbyterian Church where I was speaking. They had driven a hundred miles to get there! As I saw them for the first time, I trembled at the thought, "If those two had not obeyed the Lord that night ten years ago, we would have had to leave Switzerland without placing an appeal and there would have been no L'Abri." What a tremendously important thing it is to fulfill one's place in the Lord's "blending"!!

It was a moving experience to meet people who had prayed for us, whom we had not even known *were* praying, as well as others we had corresponded with; and to meet in every part of the country those who had been born again at L'Abri. It was also a very emotional experience to meet people from every part of our past lives, members of our various past churches, or people with whom we had been coworkers as much as 28 years ago!! Somehow, the Lord tied together a lot of loose ends and gave us a glimpse of the blending of the total Church, even wider than we had had before. Then it was thrilling for me to watch the faces of young people as Fran spoke—first a lack of understanding, then a dawning of what he was saying, then a realization of what it really meant to *them*. Looking back over an auditorium with 1,800 students in it, plus professors and others, made me feel as if I were watching a crowded living room at Chalet les Mélèzes in front of the fireplace with the growing interest and understanding coming into the faces of from 20 to 50. This was the same, but simply multiplied. And I breathed a prayer, "Oh Lord, if You want to multiply the number who will be helped by these answers to their rebellions and rejection of Thee in the light of today's philosophies, may I not hinder Thee by dreaming of a quieter life, and a retreat into the woods and cliffs. May I be willing for the travel fatigue and the crowds which Jesus knew, and Thy servants have experienced many times. May a desire for a humble place not mask a desire for personal fulfillment. But, may we never seek the large 'place.' " How we must struggle for honesty at each point, as the Lord unfolds His plan for our lives.

We flew to Detroit to be at our L'Abri center there, which consists of Karl and Alida Woodson's home. They send out these Family Letters after getting them printed and have tape-listening evenings and discussions in their home, they speak at various times about L'Abri work, they receive gifts and send receipts and then send on the money to John, they send out tapes to those who want to borrow or buy them for listening to lectures, etc. We were deeply touched to see the big basement which holds Karl's table full of L'Abri papers and work, nearby Alida's ironing board and sewing machine as we saw for ourselves how central L'Abri work is for them. . . .

We stayed in St. Louis two weeks, as Fran had been asked to teach a concentrated course in Covenant Seminary. He gave 15 consecutive lectures there and had some evening meetings with University groups, medical student groups, a doctors' Christian medical banquet, etc. My time filled up with a variety of meetings with ladies and girls in a girls' school there. Interestingly enough, the ladies' meetings almost all opened up through the arrangements made by two mothers whose daughters had been helped at L'Abri. . . .

From St. Louis we flew to California, spending a weekend with the Jamisons and their church. It was the first time we had been with them since Dot became the first L'Abri Worker outside of our family ten years ago when L'Abri first started! The ties there were fantastic too, ties of prayer through the years on the part of several "Praying Family Members" and others and ties because in that area, too, some came who had been born again at L'Abri. . . .

Mr. Jamison drove us to Westmont in his air-conditioned car, a most welcome vehicle in 101-degree heat which is something we have not felt for years! And there we began five days again with Fran giving the series of lectures he gave in Wheaton.

The return to Switzerland, via London, meant that we had a meeting in 52 Cleveland Road with over 80 sitting (mostly on the floor) in the long living room, 80 from many different nationalities, as well as different periods of L'Abri "past" history. There really is no difference in the total need; the field is the world and *place* to *be* is the place where *the Lord wants you*, and us, no other.

The London visit gave us a glimpse of Franky. Franky cavorting around fireworks on Guy Fawkes night at the school celebration, Franky playing soccer on the first school team against another school, a happy, growing Franky in a school which the Lord obviously chose for him. It was a comfort to know this, in our missing him!

Back in Huemoz we found it hard to plunge into the work. Hours were needed for sharing experiences, there and here, and to "catch up" on each other's needs and fulfillments, struggles and victories.

My time in Huemoz was spent with one ear "open" for a phone call from London. You see, I had promised to go back to London to help out at the time of the birth of Sue's new baby. Day by day more things on my "list of things to do before leaving" got checked off, even to some few Christmas preparations. Finally, on December 4th, I left even without the phone call!! My promised two weeks could not be over *later* than December 18th! The Lord *timed* my going since Sue needed me at the time of her labor to care for Margaret who had fever, earache, and a bronchial cough which kept her awake most of the night while Sue was in the hospital. The long labor was finally over the second night and on December 8th, a fine big girl, Kirsteen Merritt Macaulay, joined the family to be Margaret's prayed-for baby sister. You who have had households and sick children and new babies will know that my help was needed those two weeks, as Sue came home two days after the baby's birth!

Franky and I flew home together the 18th of December. The Champéry service was to be as usual the 24th and all of Christmas had to be prepared. "Impossible," my inward reaction! but again, the lesson of

Another L'Abri tradition, the day after the Champèry service the Christmas dinner table is all set! I have just ironed the very special cloth and rushed into my Norwegian costume made for me in 1950!

sharing and blending as planned by the Lord! Priscilla stayed home to prepare Christmas supper for everyone at Les Mélèzes the evening of the 24th. Christmas morning Claudie and Allan had the students and guests at Beau Site for breakfast and stockings, leaving our immediate family at Mélèzes to share the early morning celebration. Nicky was one of our family that day, his first family Christmas celebration, and next year he will be in Japan for that date, *Deo volente* (Latin for "God willing"). . . .

It is the Lord who puts His hand on one, and then another, calling them to share, and to be blended into the work of L'Abri. It has been so in the past, is certainly so in the present, and will be so in the future as long as the work continues under the Holy Spirit's direction.

As you pray for the immediate future, there are several outstanding things to pray for: (1) The writing and publishing of Fran's book, *The God Who Is There*; (2) An English speaking trip from February 17th to March 17—in English and Scottish university circles; (3) Huemoz L'Abri during this time; (4) Jane's trip to America to sing (she and Frances still have some days open for concerts) during April; (5) Continued guidance to each one in every area of the work as to their part and portion! (6) The Holy Spirit's power upon us all.

With love in *Him* Who is *able* to blend each life together into His total pattern,

EDITH

May 25, 1966   Huemoz sur Ollon, Switzerland

Dear Family:

. . . Early February seemed to be chaotic with noise as an electric drill worked away removing the old cement from the ground floor hall and kitchen floors and "cave" wall. This was preparatory to putting new cement and asphalt squares down on the floors, and preparatory to cutting a new window in the cave which was to be transformed from a storage room, into a little "ship's cabin" bedroom with a double-decker bunk.

We have been stumbling over broken floors for a long time so we welcomed the commencement of the repair as well as the promise of more space, as the new window flooded the cave with afternoon sunlight. However, the noise and dust added strain to that week when, as usual before a trip, everything seemed piled up to do "before leaving."

The morning of February 17th found me standing at Aigle station at 7 A.M. waiting for the London train, to catch the first glimpse of Susan, little Margaret ready to jump off the steps into my arms, and Kirsty in her carry-cot. Sue had come to take my place in Chalet les Mélèzes during our time in England, a plan which was not only good for the work here but which provided an opportunity to get Margaret out of London's damp cold air into the mountain air of the Swiss Alps. Margaret had been repeatedly ill with bronchitis all winter and the effect of antibiotics and the disease had dragged her down. . . .

It was "different" to walk into 52 Cleveland Road, and not find Susan and Margaret and Kirsty there. The house was almost too quiet, that is until the telephone started ringing, and people began coming. With all the comings and goings and activity of that month, I was thankful that the children were out of it though sorry for Ran's loneliness!

It was different, in that there were myriad open doors, not just into student rooms for discussion, but invitations to speak in colleges in an official capacity, and then to have discussion and question times following. A total list would be boring but let me give a few examples of Fran's lectures: Oakhill Theological College: "Has Christianity an Answer to Humanism?"; London Bible College: "The Christian in Contemporary Culture"; King's College theological students: "A Critique of Liberalism"; International Student House: "Christianity and Eastern Thought"; Caius College, Cambridge University: "Christianity and Existentialism"; Meeting in a home in Kingston-upon-Thames (mostly university professors and their wives): "The Modern Predicament." We then traveled to St. Andrews University and met with instructors and professors as well as St. Mary's Theological College students also in St. Andrews. There were further meetings at North West Polytechnic in London, and two meetings in Bristol with largely unbelieving, humanistic students, and instructors. The topic: "Christianity and the Basic Moral and Philosophical Problems." Next was Manchester University where the topic was "Existentialism, Humanism, Christianity ... Which Works?". ....

In St. Andrews, Scotland, Fran was in the midst of intense discussion with an instructor in philosophy and one of his students. The futility of man's wisdom, or the foolishness of man's reasoning, without God, was borne home to Fran with force, as in those few hours the newest English philosophy was probed. Then, a bumpy bus ride out across the country-side finally deposited all of us (Peasy, Nettie, Fran and myself) by the side of a road in Tayport, across the harbor from Dundee and we walked hesitatingly up the sidewalk looking with fascination at the tiny cottages with their sloping roofs which could be touched as they met the low front doors even by someone as small as I am! Suddenly we saw a figure hurrying to meet us, a face crinkled up in a smile of welcome. "Aye I'm glad to see ye here" said a voice with a Scottish burr. "Come an' we'll be havin' tay right away, 'arry's waitin' fer ye." Embraces were exchanged and we introduced the girls, then walked quickly up the charmingly quaint curved street where all the houses met the sidewalks without grass interrupting the brick and stone. Harry and a sister were waiting indeed, and a table was laid in front of an open-grate coal fire, glowing red with darts of flame. We ate an abundance of sandwiches, cheese and tomato wedges with good strong Scottish tea and milk, and they chatted and asked questions eagerly. "Aye we'll niver ferget coming into yer house that night. The fine meal ye gave us, an' the story ye told us about L'Abri, jist fer us alone, aye it was fine." They laughed about 'arry going to sleep in the first lecture. "Can't remember much of it, but 'twas bout a man named Hydigger I know." Whose house are we in? Why, it is the Scottish couple who came to L'Abri, do you remember? A humble little couple whom the Lord chose to bring in an amazing fashion and now *He* has chosen to take us to see them. Not only to see them, but to have a Bible study on the 3rd chapter of John before that glowing fire. They really "saw" the emptiness of life, the senselessness of life without God, and told how their questions had never been answered, even their childhood questions of pastors they had known then, so they turned away. But now God had brought them someone who was caring to take time to answer, to explain, to read, and to pray with them. Why? Well surely *He* sees the seeking hearts. He *knows* each one. His eyes are looking for those whose hearts are inclined toward Him. God used this vivid afternoon of contrast to illustrate something very definite and real to Peasy and Nettie too. He can remember each one.

The second instance of contrast was this: The International Student House is not a religious place, but a beautiful building in the heart of one of London's loveliest parts, prepared for students from many countries to come, either for meals, rooms, or recreation. The announced meeting at which Fran was to speak on Christianity and Eastern thought was crowded. Here sat over seventy-five men and women from widely different countries: Africa, Arabia, Japan, India, Egypt, Australia, etc.;

many of them are Ph.D.'s. Some are working now on graduate studies. There were scientists, doctors, lawyers, men going in for political life, truly an intellectual group of widely different backgrounds. We watched their growing interest and heard their statements afterwards of hoping there will be another such evening. Clearly the Lord touched hearts in some measure that evening, and one wonders how many thousands of miles, how many "impossibilities" would need to be counted if one were going to speak of the "*unlikeliness*" of any number of these ever hearing the "truth." A mass of unknown faces to us, yet each one *known* to God, in a *personal* fashion. *He* had "worked things together" in their lives to bring them there at that moment.

Then by contrast come with me to a Salvation Army Hall in West Ealing one Wednesday afternoon, amid the hubbub of voices as old charwomen gathered to drink tea, sing, and chatter to each other. It is a "club" of poor, elderly women, mostly above seventy, who live (most of them) alone in one room, on very, very little money and with a very, very narrow existence. This Wednesday afternoon is the social event of the week. There were 135 of them there, and they had never been known to keep quiet while anyone spoke to them. But as I stood to speak, in an accent quite foreign to them (they speak Cockney) a hush fell over the hall. The Lord gave me the words to tell them of His existence, and what His infinity could mean to them, if they become His children. They heard of how *He* can be everywhere at once, not as the air, but as a *person*, because He is infinite. I told them of how frustrated I am by having to be in *one* place, doing *one* thing at a time. I told them of a number of places I would like to be at once, of a number of people I would like to be with at one time, each one alone but I can't. But, *He can!* And so He can be with them in their rooms alone, or with me, or in an African hut, anywhere with anyone who is His child and who is talking to Him. This is what prayer is. I then went on to tell the L'Abri story, a brief version of it, mingled with the clear picture of salvation, of how Christ's infinity meant He could *die* for each of us who would believe in Him, as if we were the only one; of how He died *personally*, not for a mass of blurred faces, but for individual people, personalities. The L'Abri story made a personal medium for all that I wanted to tell them and gave them illustrations they loved to hear. You could have heard a pin drop! And at the end, not knowing what else to do, they clapped and cheered, and asked me to please come back. Snowy, the elderly man who opened up the possibility of my going there told me later that his landlady, "And she's a hard one, she is," who had never let him tell her the gospel, had come home and sat down and wept for ten minutes, then had said, "I niver heerd anythin' like it before." "I've prayed for this afternoon and your speaking, a long time," said Snowy to me. "And I know the Spirit of God spoke through you in a special way. God has answered my prayer." Snowy is a gardener with whom Ran has had many talks and prayer.

Did the Lord plan this trip for the intellectual unbelievers? Yes He did, but He also planned it so that these elderly women, many of whom have a short time to live (they say the average number of deaths in that "club" is over 20 a year) could hear a clear message they could understand. I loved talking to them, but the main thing that struck me was *God's* love for these gnarled old faces and hands worn with work. We wouldn't have thought of *looking* for such opportunities on an English trip but when we prayed that the Lord would take us to the people of His choice, it turned out to be university circles and charwomen in London.

In our absence a kind of flu had traveled through the community, flattening first one and then another. Sue had been looking forward to shifting the burden of responsibility for Mélèzes. Everyone was expecting a report of the English trip that Sunday night but I returned so dizzy I could hardly stand up. My fever was 103°. I did something I haven't done for over 15 years . . . I went to bed with a good old-fashioned Asian flu and my fever soared to 104° and seemed to just stick there for days! I didn't even unpack. Five days of that and suddenly it was time for our Annual Members' Meeting. It was a wonderful two-day meeting this year (yes I did go down to it . . . even with laryngitis!).

It was Sunday evening after the last tray of sandwiches and cakes had gone down to the living room, when I ran upstairs to peek in at grandmother and freshen myself a bit before going down to meet people in the living room and did not go down again for a long time. I got into grandmother's room just as she commenced coughing. That coughing spell, along with vomiting a kind of froth, kept on for almost four hours and then the cough along with delirium continued for days. I went down to consult our Swiss doctor by telephone and gave some codeine as a result but that did not stay down. The next morning our English-speaking Italian doctor Gandur was able to come and he commenced antibiotic shots for bronchial pneumonia, and sedative shots. However, the delirium continued, and grandmother kept talking all night and all day long irrationally. Dr. Kennedy then offered to sit with her on Monday night to give us a few hours of sleep as it had not been possible to go to bed on Sunday night at all. . . . It all seemed "*too* much." But somehow that week and the next weeks passed without our collapsing. The Lord gave the needed strength. The doctor came almost daily. A visiting nurse came to give intravenous feedings, and various shots from time to time. The nursing needed on our part was constant. All correspondence in my office came to a standstill.

Franky returned for Easter holidays at the beginning of April expecting to go to his new school at the end of April. . . . But he came down with what seemed like a stiff case of flu Tuesday the 5th. After a week of high fever and aching arms and legs, head and back it was discovered that what he had was infectious hepatitis, contracted at school, where three boys had cases!! Poor Franky learned that his blood tests showed "astronomical figures" and that his case was the worst Doctor Gandur had ever seen. It meant bed for six weeks and then a continued diet, and rest, *not a new school* with sports and full schedule!!

Now there were *two* patients to nurse. Grandmother was gradually getting better, though the doctor still was not sure she would make it, and Franky needing careful diet and dishes washed separately upstairs, medicine given regularly and various complicated things. The nursing is important. In grandmother's case everything had to be done for her and the only safe way to leave her alone was to have a side built for the bed. Jeremy and Steve built the side along with all the other carpentry work they are doing in Farel House, Beau Site kitchen, and in making outdoor tables for Les Mélèzes summer meals. (Now she is much much better, herself again, except for a lack of balance. She cannot walk alone, and spends most of her time in a chair with a table across it.)

Easter came and went. Kirsty was baptized one Sunday. Ran and Sue had their vacation, living in Chesalet. People came and went. And through it all it was not possible for me to leave my patients at all except when John came to "sit" for some hours on Monday afternoons. Impossible? It seemed so at the time.

How does all this fit in with a loving, *personal, gentle* Heavenly Father??? I cannot tell you in detail as I do not know all the intricate workings necessary for each life affected, nor the part Satan plays in it all in trying to discourage and ruin. For instance *all* this took place as Fran was trying to write his book, *The God Who Is There,* and surely it seemed as if it was Satan-directed, trying to *destroy* the book before it would be written. On the other hand, *some* understanding is clear about *some* aspects of it all.

For instance, Franky. Suddenly we realized Franky *could* go to America with us for the time at Wheaton and in Colorado in June. "Perhaps," we began to think, "this is an answer to our prayer that Franky might have a longer time with his family, and a time to get to know something about his own country." It surely seems the right moment in his growing-up days for this very thing. We began to pray for guidance and among other things a doctor's appointment worked out with the surgeon who operated on Franky six years ago on the one day we could stop at the Pittsburgh Children's Hospital. This, and other circumstances such as a possibility of Franky's visiting his sister and 90-year-old Grandfather Seville and seeing and hearing one of his father's "American lecture times" points to the fact that the Lord is bringing out a *very* gentle reason for allowing Franky to have this severe illness. This trip can be tremendously important spiritually, as well as in other ways. The Lord does *not* allow us to suffer *needlessly. . . .*

No, it is *not* one "constant song" as far as ease of life goes, but the wonder of *His* Personalness, and His personal dealings with us, and His gentle answers to prayer are *real.* There *is a personal God* in the Universe, and one *can* have communication with Him. He *is* allowing this to be demonstrated in our midst, even as we have prayed He would.

With love in Him Who is your personal Father too, if you have come through Christ as your Saviour,

EDITH

October 20, 1966   Huemoz sur Ollon, Switzerland

Dear Family:

. . . What is the extent, geographically, of what the Lord has used L'Abri to do from this tiny Alpine village spot, an unknown village standing in fields on the side of a mountain?? Could *any* effect be made upon the world by a family setting forth simply to *pray* that God would send the people of His choice here???? and unfold a work????

Let me try to give you a tiny glimpse of how overwhelmed we are when we see the reality of what God has done and is doing. A Bulgarian postmark on the envelope caused us to know that this letter was from one of the 16 Kenya Africans who had been studying at Farel House and were now back in Bulgaria in the University. We tore open the envelope and read a report of how the 16 "boys," as he called them, are "going on." Duncan, a student, said earnestly that he could see a change in the life of each one. . . . Another letter came from Japan where Nicky is listening to tapes with a certain amount of nostalgia as he thinks of L'Abri . . . A postcard from El Salvador brought exclamations of delight from all of us who remember Mario, the El Salvadoran who was born again at L'Abri about 6 years ago now. Jose, another El Salvadoran, also an engineer who accepted Christ as his Saviour here when he was in the University of Lausanne, now lives in Lausanne with his wife and two children. . . .

L'Abri seems to be growing, with more people *coming* here all the time, and more calls coming for us to go to a scattered number of places to speak; as Fran is being asked to prepare radio programs and television programs and *The God Who Is There* is being prepared for publishing; as more are coming to the London classes and discussions, and Sue is teaching women and children's Bible classes, and Ran has more individuals to talk to all the time; as Workers of L'Abri are pressed day by day with more to do than they can ever get finished, and the work seems to be multiplying, it seems as though "private life" is fading out from any of our daily schedules. As Susan said to me on the phone, "We are up at six with the baby and I keep working steadily until nearly midnight, and then just fall into bed to sleep." Is the work growing easier? Are we over the early time of *utter dependence* upon the Lord? No. More than ever we need to pray for *His* strength made perfect in weakness, but we cannot pray to be removed from the strenuousness of the life the Lord has unfolded to us as we have asked for *His* plan. "This is not your rest" is a good verse to remember for any of us! Our rest is ahead of us. The glory of that rest is beyond any imagination we have and we are told that present suffering cannot be compared to it. . . .

Let me tell you a story. Some years ago Jane Bowman was bustling around the kitchen making a sponge cake, following my Hot Water Sponge Cake recipe with careful attention to detail! Just before putting the mixture into the tube pan to bake, she called upon me with distress in her voice, "Oh Mrs. Schaeffer *do* tell me what's wrong with this, I think *something* is but I am *sure* I followed the directions perfectly. What could be wrong?" I examined the texture of the gluey mess, tasted it, went over the recipe with her. "No—no—no—I'm sure I didn't leave out anything; I'm sure I put all that in in just the right way—Oh—wait a minute, I left out the *sugar*. Oh dear! What shall I do now? Do we have to throw it away?" "Oh no," I hastily replied, "Don't throw anything away! We have to think what it can now be turned into since it is too late to put the sugar in, as a sponge cake depends on the delicacy and order of mixing." I began to think, eggs, water, flour, baking powder—what could that add up to? "I have it," I cried. "We'll add more flour, until it is about this texture, see? And then we'll roll it out very thin like this, and we'll let it dry a few minutes, and then cut it in strips like this. And we'll have lovely homemade noodles for our chicken broth!!!" When a person who is seeking to have the Lord's plan for his life directly goes out of His will through *deliberate* disobedience, or disregard of His Word in carelessness or ignorance, that one can suddenly find that the life is a "gluey mess" instead of the feathery texture of a sponge cake. The question is, "Is it impossible to be guided by the Lord from now on? Have I forfeited the possibility of having His plan?" The first necessity is to bring the gluey mess to the Lord, for Him to look at, to confess to Him that something is wrong, and to have Him place His finger on the mistake, or sin and then to ask forgiveness with the immediate handing over of the situation to Him. With His wisdom, *He can always take us where we are* and go on from there, to unfold and direct one into a different plan than the original one. We may not be able to go on with the "sponge cake" which would have been the first plan, but the "noodles" can come out of it, and the "noodles" can be used to fulfill a very real place in the "meal," or in the overall picture of the Lord's total plan for His people, His children. History *is* significant. We cannot erase the effect of what we have done. The fact remains. There are results *in* us, and historic effects upon other lives. The pattern is different from what it "might have been." But God's forgiveness is real too. The cleansing of the blood of Christ is real. There is no point at which He cannot take us back and show us His plan from that moment on. The important thing is to *not delay*, to hurry back to Him with confession, and turn over the problem to Him, so that He can direct. . . .

The date right now is October 25th. I did *not* have an opportunity to go on writing this after commencing it and had to stay up all last night to get even this far! The staying up was interrupted by a white-faced Nick who came to my window to tell me news that let me know that Minna's baby had decided to be an October baby, rather than a November one! No news yet, except that they are keeping her at the hospital. Perhaps we won't get any news before we go!!

Yes, tomorrow morning we shall be on our way for another intensive speaking trip. The Lord has opened some amazing doors. Very briefly we shall, Lord willing, be in Berlin, San Francisco, Seattle and Tacoma, Santa Barbara, Denver, St. Louis, Detroit, and Ann Arbor. Fran will be in Buffalo for a few hours to speak between planes, then in Philadelphia, while I will be in Newburgh, New York, and in Watertown (to visit my father) and then I shall join Fran in Philadelphia. We expect to be back in L'Abri by December 17th, meantime the Workers here will carry on with Farel House *full*.

This has been a very condensed account, leaving out so very much, but perhaps you will read also "between lines" and realize why we are so overwhelmed at what the Lord is doing! It is exhausting to have "more than enough" openings in so many places, and "more than enough" people to fill the space here but when one contemplates how short life is, and how close the Second Coming of Christ might be, to make it even shorter then, we are truly *thankful* for the "more-than-enough."

With love in the *urgency* of His work in which He has placed us together,

EDITH

1967

February 3, 1967   Huemoz sur Ollon, Switzerland

Dear Family:

My intention is to write to you all at least once in two months. Being finite, we human beings find our "intentions" are hindered, interrupted, and rendered impossible by a variety of things. We are constantly being reminded that we *are* finite. Rather than causing us to feel frustrated and depressed, the evidences of our finiteness ought to emphasize the wonder of God's infinity.

Yet the reality of our finiteness is constantly illustrated! More than three months have gone by since I sat at this spot writing to you in the quiet hours of the night, *just* before leaving for Berlin, and then straight from there to America. That letter was mailed as we went off to Geneva airport. Since then we have spent six exhaustingly full weeks traveling and speaking in the States, have plunged into the busy Christmas period here at L'Abri, and Fran has returned to England to speak at two conferences even before the New Year, and has spent ten days of concentrated editorial work on his manuscript. People, of course, had been awaiting our return with questions and problems, and cooking, housekeeping, marketing, and so forth, needed to be resumed. With the "pattern interrupted" by the long time away, it seemed that getting back into my office at this typewriter was the last thing to be done each day. . . .

And so I sat down to care for the amazing pile of letters that had waited for my return (needing my personal attention). A check for $860.42 fell out of the first envelope, and the opening paragraph said this, "Oh, it is with such joy and freedom that I can transpose this little bit of money from a bank where 'moths and rust get at it' to perhaps a chip of block of stone or wood in the bracing Swiss mountain air to God's glory where there is so much activity that no moths nor rust have a chance to work and corrupt." Again—it was an answer to prayer for increased space for L'Abri, and we thanked God as we added it to the fund toward buying

113

and building—but *we* would not have chosen to have a student sacrificially empty her bank account. It is a comfort to know that the Lord has put the desire in the heart, and hearts, of those of *His* choice as we pray that space may be provided so that no one need be turned away.

I am sure that this girl, the one who gave her salary, the dear couple whose thought was of Chalet le Sapin just before the husband entered the operating room for a serious heart operation, are examples of ones who will "find" something very specific as a result, in heaven waiting for them, because of a literal willingness to let it be "lost" to them here. I'm looking forward to discovering in heaven, the full extent of His meaning as He clearly has told us that complete fulfillment of such promises is not in this life. I wonder what the results would be if all Christians truly placed their time, energy, possessions, attention, talents, desires honestly into the Lord's hands with *trust* and belief in His word to us. I wonder what we would "find" in this life, as well as in heaven?? One thing I am sure, there would be a literal fulfillment of His promises. Abraham, walking slowly up that hill with Isaac, had the kind of trust that we need as we contemplate handing over the most precious thing we have to *Him*. What is more precious than the composite total of all that makes up our "life"? It is not some airy-fairy mystical something that can be done in a dark corner without a practical effect upon our lives. When we "lose" our life willingly for His sake, *something* has been handed over that makes today, or tomorrow different. Our "security" is then in *Him*, and not in a tidy little schedule or pattern of our own.

How can a six-week trip be squashed into a few pages of typed words? How can thousands of miles of travel and thousands of people be described in a limited space of a few paragraphs? I will try to take you with me—

Berlin brought a vivid horror of realization on what the "wall" meant in the long succession of days, months, and years since the old housefronts were formed into a wall separating East Berlin from West Berlin, separating brothers and sisters, mothers and children, grandparents from younger members of the family who could care for them, separating a generation from the knowledge of freedom. A conviction grew that the "wall" is an illustration of what a lack of understanding the enmity of the enemy can mean in Biblical Christianity, as well as in such a thing as this vast number of human beings in that area of the world.

The flight to San Francisco was 27 long hours of travel or waiting in airports, losing nine hours along the way and becoming exhausted. A bright spot was celebrating my birthday with Franky and Ranald as the four of us had tea together, and I opened gifts and cards in the tearoom in London Airport's overseas building. We were met in San Francisco by Steve's mother and father.

One evening a group of L'Abri people gathered for a typical Saturday night discussion; it was even a Saturday night! A buffet supper was served, eaten in a living room, a tape recorder was there to record what took place, and Fran answered a variety of questions. What a variety of people the Lord brought! Among them were Alma, a nurse at L'Abri for a summer as a Farel House student; John, an engineer with his own company, who some years ago crossed the Alps in Hannibal's footsteps, also with an elephant! and wrote about it; Bruce and Charlotte, both artists— Bruce became a Christian at L'Abri now five years ago; and a pastor and his wife who had had Jim Hurley attend their church for a time.

In Seattle there were lectures in Seattle Pacific College, discussion groups in the University of Washington, chapel talks in Bellevue Christian School, women's meetings (where I spoke) out in the country with women coming from several churches, driving quite some distance, evening talks with girls in a dorm, others in the living room of a Christian "residence"; individuals wanting to talk with us and never enough time for all the requests! A rush came to write the foreword to my book *L'Abri* to add to the manuscript taken off by an editor for consideration; a rush to try to keep up correspondence and travel arrangements. There was a constant feeling of needing to stay longer! to fulfill the eagerness of some to ask questions. We had the joy of meeting those who had had the ministry of Debby and Udo among them last summer, especially the college-age young people of that church. What a thrill it was to meet a Cambridge University man whom we had known well in Cambridge who is now in Seattle with his fine Christian bride.

In Tacoma came chapel and discussion groups in Puget Sound University, students wanting to come to L'Abri even after the short "taste" of hearing intellectual answers, two or three interested professors also wanting "more," a meeting in Karl Straub's church, a telephone conversation with the niece of another L'Abri person, constant realization of the Lord's taking us to accomplish His purpose for the "one's and two's" as well as for larger numbers. His "efficiency" and "economy" we may be sure are perfect. He does not "waste."

Travel down to Santa Barbara took us again to San Francisco for a few hours to lunch with Bruce and Charlotte and Alma at a tiny Chinese restaurant into which we stepped after wandering slowly around considering a number of places. Menus were being regarded with some absorption when suddenly a very nice looking Chinese man stepped over to our table and exclaimed with un-oriental display of excitement, "Mrs. Schaeffer, what are you doing here?" A short confusion of memory was resolved quickly, and we greeted John, the Chinese fellow brought to L'Abri by Peter Pattison some six years ago along with other orientals. John was born again here in Huemoz on his birthday, and I had prepared a very special Chinese dinner that night in celebration, with a western birthday cake! He is living and working in San Francisco and introduced us to his Christian wife and showed us a picture of his darling two-year-old boy. Can you wonder that we are *certain* that the Lord directed our steps that afternoon? We had the next morning to ourselves, then drove to the ranch belonging to Bruce and Roger's father.

The fog closing out all view of the sea reminded me again of how simple the word "believe" is. We "believed" when we were told the view included miles of sea coast. Believing God is the same kind of belief. It is simply believing He has spoken and that what He has spoken is *true*.

At Westmont we had an incredibly busy time of lectures, chapel talks, and discussions, including a lecture in the U.C.L.A. and many personal interviews. My time included late night talks in dorms as well as some afternoon talks, plus all-day interviews. When asked how many would like to come to Farel House sometime this year, 35 students and three professors came to talk over practical details. We began to have an uneasy feeling about "space" in L'Abri for next summer.

We were driven from Santa Barbara to the Los Angeles Airport by dear Veda and Verna of Los Angeles who came to do this for us in order to have time to talk. I promise you it was a *solid* time of fast talking to get questions answered in that short time! Out of the corner of our eyes we could see the beautiful sport of surfboarding, and the tantalizing waves rolling in on the beaches but we were quickly past this tempting sight, and again in a busy airport, lugging heavy bags the interminably long passages that are a part of the modern air travel. Jets arrive too quickly, time is "saved" in that travel time is nil, but adjustment to a new set of problems and circumstances comes too quickly after leaving the one before. On Sunday we spoke in a Sunday school 25 miles away in Boulder, then at an afternoon meeting 125 miles from there, then at evening church in Colorado Springs and were driven 100 or more miles back to our Denver motel again. There were lectures in the Conservative Baptist Seminary, in the University of Denver, and to about 125 students in the University of Colorado. The time was all too short, it seemed, yet again the result was that some (both non-Christian and Christian) students want to come this summer.

Precious time was spent in St. Louis with Debby and Udo on Thanksgiving Day, after a Thanksgiving service in our old church. Days of speaking: Fran at the Seminary, at Washington University, at a Medical Society group, at a Discussion Club, and at homes where the numbers gathered increased to a group of over a hundred the final night. For me there were women's meetings, times with young people both of the school where Pris used to teach and the school where Debby now teaches, and some individual times of conversations with the growing number of young people in that area who have been saved at L'Abri. Truly the prayer and reality of commitment to the Lord on the part of these young people are much of the source of the very visible "revival"-type growing interest and eagerness among some of many age groups in St. Louis.

Bitter cold winds and snow flurries flew in Detroit and warm welcome and fellowship came in Karl and Alida's home, which is the L'Abri center in America. Within a very short time after our arrival, we needed to hurry to an evening meeting where a church was full of those from the Detroit area who wanted to hear about L'Abri as well as a lecture by Fran. A lot was squashed into a short space of time. The *growing* feeling of the limitedness of *time* continues to grow! The following morning again the time was far too short for answering phone calls, reading the mail, and trying to talk to Karl and Alida all at once, and then, it was time to be driven off to Ann Arbor for a luncheon discussion with students. Lectures, discussions with students led by Fran, one in a student "café" with beatniks edging in with interest. One vivid incident: Remember Lok, the Chinese student who came to L'Abri some years ago? He came an atheist, listened with interest, made a decision to leave an atheist. I had heard that he was teaching at Ann Arbor. Have you ever looked at the telephone directory of the professors and instructors of a big American university? It was the size of a small town's directory. I knew "Lok" was his first name. That's all I had. I sighed a bit hopelessly then turned to "C." Many Chinese names commence with "C." But to my dismay, there were many Chinese professors whose names commenced with "C." Ahhhh, here is one. L. Chen—perhaps that "L" stands for Lok. I'll try it first. The phone rang once, twice, three, four times, then a voice answered. "I am looking for someone, and you may be the wrong person. I am Mrs. Schaeffer from Switzerland, and I am looking for—" but I got no further! An excited voice cried out, *"Mrs. Schaeffer! Did you drop from the sky?"* The Lord had led me to the right name *the very first call,* and what is more, when Lok and his wife came the next day, he told us that he *never, never* answers the telephone. His wife said she cannot even get him on the phone. Hence it was amazing that he had answered. We had a good chat the next morning. Of course, the time was too short, but they do hope to come to L'Abri in a couple of years, when he has finished a thesis. Do pray for him. It is wonderful the way the oriental thread keeps running through L'Abri.

I was driven from the New York Airport to Newburgh by "Bud" and his wife who met me after my flight from Detroit. "Bud" was a very small boy when my father and mother, my sisters and I arrived in Newburgh years ago in my childhood. My father was pastor of the Westminister Church there from the time I was eight years old until I was nearly fifteen. It was a real homecoming indeed to talk to a dear group of people at Sunday School and church that Sunday morning, who knew me as a harum-scarum child who climbed their pear trees and stood on my head as much as on my feet!!! One thing struck me: There really *is* a *gap* between the generations which the new philosophies have caused, which is there even if a person has never studied philosophy.

In order to have more time with me, the church people had arranged a luncheon in the basement of the church, right after the morning service. After a bite to eat, I spoke again while the others ate and practically had to be dragged out by those who were to drive me to the railroad station in Poughkeepsie, as I simply had not finished all I wanted to share with them. A vivid incident took place in Newburgh too. The telephone rang while I was at breakfast and a man's voice said, "Do you remember a red-haired fellow in Ann Arbor with whom you talked?" I did, as this was one who wants to come to Farel House this summer and I had had quite a talk with him. "I am his father and we live in Fishkill. Are you speaking in Sunday School? I would like to drive to Newburgh and hear you. Will you explain about Farel House?" So a description of L'Abri as it is today (a condensed description) was given in that Sunday hour and a boy who plunged into doubts about the existence of God, due to his studies in the university, will be coming to L'Abri with his parents' joyful consent!

The train took me up the Hudson River to Albany and then Syracuse where my sister and brother-in-law (Elsa and Roger Van Buskirk) met me to drive me to Watertown. The purpose of this journey was to visit my father, Dr. George H. Seville. I stayed from late Sunday night to early Tuesday afternoon, again an all-too-short length of time for a visit with one's 90-year-old father, who will be 91 on March 19th! He is in quite good health, taking walks even in the snow and cold, when the walks are shoveled, and keeping up with correspondence.

Meantime Fran had left Detroit mid-morning on Sunday after his preaching. The flight stopped in Buffalo where he had just four hours between flights. A meeting had been arranged a few miles from the airport, and quite a number of professors from Houghton College, as well as other people had gathered there for a lecture and time of questions. That was the shortest visit of the whole trip, but a most worthwhile one. As in other places, it meant three things: an invitation to return, not only to Buffalo, but to Houghton; students and professors asking to come to L'Abri to study at Farel House; and requests for tapes!

Fran then arrived in Philadelphia that same Sunday night; I came from Watertown on Tuesday afternoon. We stayed in the home of Dr. and Mrs. Clouney, President of Westminster Seminary. Our days were full to overflowing. Fran had lectures and times of discussion at Westminster, interviews with a succession of people, and he preached three times on Sunday and had a college discussion group late Sunday evening at the Willow Grove Presbyterian Church. I also spoke at a number of women's meetings and at a gathering of high school and college girls, and just before leaving for the airport, I spoke in a Christian school telling the L'Abri story. Does it all sound like "flat facts"? This letter would be a mile long if I tried to be really descriptive. There is just too much. But let me tell you an incident that happened at that last meeting just a few hours before we flew back across the ocean. As children and young people flocked up to say that they "loved the story," and "thank you," one teenage boy seemed to be so deeply moved I turned from others to see what he wanted. "I have got to talk to you," he said, and I found a little office where we could have a short time alone. The story Barry spilled out and his depressed feelings concerning a lack of reality and doubt of God's existence caused me to come to a quick decision. This time was too short to help in such a deep need. In quick succession things began to happen. Mrs. Clouney drove us to the Seminary where we talked with Bill Edgar (a seminary student, born again at L'Abri, who was flying to Switzerland December 23rd) and found the number of his flight; then we drove to see the boy's father (by this time, Fran was with us) for a talk with someone who had never heard of L'Abri before was bewildering for him and difficult for us in such a short time. Then off to pack and to be driven to the airport by the whole Baldwin family. . . .

We arrived in London and stood waiting an hour for Ranald to come to meet us. It was early in the morning, and their usual alarm (the children) had overslept! Waiting there was a study in humanity, and as we were watching partings and meetings with display of emotions, praying for "humanity" as a whole, who should we suddenly see among the surging masses of strangers' faces, but Richard Ducker, Deirdre's husband! A former Farel House student, husband of a girl who was born again at Chalet Bijou back in our Champéry days!! San Francisco Chinese restaurant to London Airport—it rather overwhelmed us with what the Lord has done in these few short years in L'Abri, and we felt the Lord was speaking to *us* with a word both gentle and strong at the same time, ". . . what is that to thee? follow thou me." How does this from John 21:22 fit our case? Often we feel completely exhausted by the pace of this work, never more than at the end of an American trip. It is easy to be tempted as Peter was to look at the "Johns" and ask, "Why not a more regulated life like his for *me*? Why not a peaceful spot on a cliff, with some evenings of privacy for *me*?" Whatever it is that is tempting in other lives by comparison to our own, whatever it is that creeps into "daydreams" and tempts us to covet (and coveting is certainly not limited to material things) is spoken to when we hear Jesus speaking to Peter. Jesus was outlining Peter's difficulties ahead. Peter wanted to know whether John would suffer in the same way too. "What is that to thee? follow thou me" not only answered Peter, but answers us. There is *purpose* in what the Lord asks us to do. Sometimes we catch glimpses of that purpose. Sometimes we feel the curtain is drawn back and we marvel at the far-reaching effects, or results that we can see. Other times we need to simply *trust* His purpose and not murmur and complain about what it involves *us* in, that other people seem not to have to suffer! . . .

Back at Huemoz again, I could start another ten pages now, but I won't! Our first impression on our return was how wonderfully the Workers had carried on in our absence.

People had been received and cared for just as if we had been there. A Christmas concert had been planned by Jane and not only had L'Abri community people attended, but villagers and tourists. Yet there is something to be remembered, a long American trip means not only fatigue of a special sort for us, but more responsibility and sacrifice on the part of Workers here at Huemoz, and there *is* also disappointment on the part of some who come wanting to discuss or ask questions or have seminars with Fran himself. Hence as more and more come *here*, as well as more and more invitations come to speak elsewhere, prayerful decisions must be made.

Christmas Eve found everyone rushing to get ready to get on the bus John hired to take us to Champéry to trim the chapel, and the 18th consecutive Christmas Eve service over there for English-speaking skiers. Yes, a *bus* was needed, seating 40, in addition to a couple of cars going. Suddenly the doorbell rings, and a tired duffle-coat-clad boy cries out to me, "Mrs. Schaeffer, *I'm here!*" It is *Barry*, the boy with whom I had talked in the Christian High School in Philadelphia. "Just think, until twelve days ago, I had never heard of L'Abri. You spoke in our school just twelve days ago, and now everything worked out for me to come, and here I am." As tourists and skiers flocked in, as Fran preached in the hush of candlelight, giving the message of Christianity clearly, as Bill Edgar rejoiced that his family had agreed to come and we thought of his joy in the midst of others, as we prayed for Barry sitting there as if he couldn't believe his ears and eyes, our crowning moment of praise came when George Exhenry, the man whose salvation caused us to be put out of Champéry, the human event behind the whole beginning of L'Abri, the human "cog" in all the events therefore leading to the salvation of all who have been saved at L'Abri was called upon to pray and stood up and prayed there in the midst of his own village, a prayer in French with no uncertain tone full of fervency and certainty and courage. It seemed as if we could hardly keep from audibly saying that which was mentally being said to the Lord, "It has all been worth it, Lord. Don't let us ever *hinder* Thy plan; keep us willing for *anything* that is Thy purpose. . . .

Much love in Him Whose purposes continue to be worked out in us as we submit to Him,

EDITH

1968

September 9, 1968   Huemoz sur Ollon, Switzerland

Dear Family:

How can a Family Letter be written in the midst of packing to be done, a book manuscript to check, endless instructions to write out (menus, gardening and freezing notes, ideas about the school, the carpentry workshop, etc.), people to talk to about vitally important things? It can't, not really, but there is too much to tell you to *not* write. . . .

Time? The whole weekend was a strange and wonderful lesson in how time can be picked up and used completely differently than our expectant imaginations picture the days before us.

Satan's strongholds are being penetrated from this tiny mountaintop. No wonder a new attack has come. "Oh, Mother, I don't know whether you are ever going to get off to America or not." It was Priscilla on the phone and she was introducing the news of the new blow which reminds us of the beginning of L'Abri. She went on to tell me that she had heard a rumor that some people living in the village (not the true, original villagers, but those who have come in more recently, Swiss and other nationalities) are getting up a petition and signing it. A petition which complains about L'Abri, saying we are too big, and the young people are annoying them with noise, etc. Because we have not had enough space for all those who have arrived on our doorstep without writing ahead, some have gone to houses in the village and asked for a room. As many as 30 were staying in village homes, and these, of course, came to lectures in the evening and returned after the villagers were asleep. Perhaps this was a mistake.

Fran felt we should have a half day of prayer on Sunday about this petition to stop the growth of L'Abri, asking the Lord to give a victory over whatever Satan might be trying to do, and praying that the power of the Lord might be seen by many people. We had an early Sunday lunch and people met at the chapel again at 2:45 to start the afternoon of prayer. New prayer lists for September that had just been mimeographed and the verses selected before we knew about this new trouble were so very appropriate it seemed the Lord had given them. . . .

We do not know yet what the petition will mean, as we have not been officially told about it. I have spent some hours with John Sandri visiting some village people to ask about it. Much prayer is needed for guidance as to what the Lord would have us do. As you know, both *space* and *our strength* are limited. What has the Lord in His plan for the future? Is the number of people to be born again through L'Abri to be limited because of too little space *and* strength? It would seem to me there is *much* need of all the L'Abri Family praying together for the Lord's solution, *not* thinking up our own. The whole work started with prayer, has continued by prayer, and now we must not be frightened into hurrying up to find a solution by combining our "ideas" and coming up with a brilliant human plan.

I feel Satan overstepped himself in that the first result of the news of this petition has been a day of prayer such as we have never had before, with people being born again *during* the day, three of them, and new Christians and older ones being "revived" in a very definite way. It seems this is a very real victory over what Satan is attempting to do, but we must pray that we shall be sensitive to God's leading for the future, step by step. For a time we wondered whether we should cancel the American trip because of this petition. Pris and John have not been well, nor is Debby. It is a lot for them to face during the time we are away. We wondered whether our place might not be here. Yet, as we continue to pray, it does seem the American trip is *His* plan, and that perhaps Satan is trying to hinder it. . . .

Debby and Udo returned from seminary to a full chalet, and Debby came to the end of the summer feeling exhausted as she had been working in spite of a low fever, joint pains, and a cough which was hanging on month after month. Feeding never less than 30 people (except on one day off a week), along with nursing a baby and caring for her, is a lot for a 23-year-old mother, without the added hurdle of a nagging fever, cough, and pains. The "price" is so often not glamorous.

Satan's attempt in this battle to try to discourage and to cause us to give up and say, "Now we really have had enough," is very clear to be seen. . . .

To picture the summer with some degree of accuracy, you need to know that the Rookmaakers came to Huemoz to take care of not only one of the houses, but to help in other ways. Dr. Rookmaaker gave many lectures and was most helpful in individual conversations too. Ran and Sue were in Rhodesia visiting Ran's parents but also doing a very real "missionary work" in their many contacts and times of teaching. Cynthia took over the cooking and care of Mélèzes during the times when I had to be at the hospital with Priscilla.* Cynthia is wondering when the

---

*Priscilla was recovering from a miscarriage.

122

Dr. Hans Rookmaaker giving an art history lecture in the chapel.
This is one of his many lectures this summer.

Lord wants her back in Japan and is certain that time here is a preparation for that. An Arts Workshop took all of one week and this gave creative young people an opportunity to try out, or work out, their ideas for communicating in the 20th century. Udo spoke for a week in Austria to a group of German theological students. . . . And now? Well, now it is 8 o'clock in the morning of Tuesday, September 10th, and I have been writing all night. You see, yesterday when I put the date down, interruptions were without interruption in a straight line! Phone calls, people to see me, mail arriving, then village people to see about the petition and some talk to me in the late evening about personal problems, took my day right up to after midnight. It has been hard to stay awake, and if this letter sounds jerky, my head had jerked up from an almost asleep position at times so it is no wonder if that came through! My reward has been a most gorgeous sunrise with all shades of pinks and reds inflaming the sky and gradually tinting the snow on the glaciers, and finally fading into the yellow light of the sun itself as it hit the Mélèzes tree in line with my vision. What is left to do today? Packing! More work in the office on catching up letters! More work on the manuscript and so forth for the book! Notebooks of instructions! Phone calls, and oh, dillions of things! I am afraid some of these will spill over into the week ahead which is our week of vacation before leaving for America. We shall not be coming back to the chalet, but will sail directly from Italy. You will *know* as you read all this that *much* prayer will be needed for the work and the Workers in Huemoz during our absence, and *much* prayer will also be needed for us as we start the American speaking trip with Fran feeling so fatigued. Prayer really is a weapon, and you can use it to share in this battle. Satan is trying to stop further fruitfulness. The world is in such a terrible moment of need, it seems a terrible thing to cut back or diminish a work of the Spirit.

We may see some of you soon, and perhaps the Lord will come before that, don't let the enemy hinder His purpose being fulfilled through you.

Love in the Victor, Who can give us the victory,

EDITH

1969

Dear Family:

The New Year started on a Wednesday, our weekly day of prayer. Pris had said to me, "Mother, can you lead the prayer meeting tomorrow morning?" as with Sylvia and Gracie we had prepared the special New Year's Eve supper while the others were in Champéry. This was the twentieth consecutive year for the Christmas Eve and New Year's Eve service in the Champéry Temple Protestant. Twenty Christmases ago it had been eight-year-old Susan who had carefully lighted the candles, while four-year-old Debby watched admiringly and lit a few low ones herself. Pris, then twelve, was the organist, pumping away at the wheezy old organ while she played the familiar Christmas carols. All this filled my memory with emotion as I watched sixteen-year-old Franky lighting the candles, and then looked around at the faces of those intently watching. There was Elizabee, Pris and John's seven-year-old, swinging her feet in contented appreciation of one of her favorite hours of the year, sitting beside her Aunt Debby. There was Mr. Exhenry still living in the midst of uncomfortable pressures and loneliness brought about by his conversion over sixteen years ago. . . . Larry had slipped in after finishing the candles and somehow the reality of his rapidly deepening Christian life seemed to really glow from the inside out. Suddenly, I looked up to see Anne playing the organ with Assaf, a student, standing next to her playing the bassoon. Another twenty years? How long is a lifetime? How important is history and the effect of our choices upon history? Our eternity. The eternity of each one of us and of other individual personalities depends upon our choices; the ripples we make affect other lives. Thank God that we can consciously *ask* Him to make choices for us, as that is what His leading means. How exciting to be involved in giving the Infinite Creator the "raw material" of one's own human personality to mold into something with purpose in the beauty of His plan. How frightening to do the opposite. . . .

My answer to Pris about taking the Wednesday morning prayer meeting had been "Yes." My reading some days before had brought me to Isaiah 43, and it had seemed to me, during the roll-making and the carrot-shredding, the beating up of sponge cakes and the measuring of ingredients for chocolate sauce, that this passage was being impressed upon my mind in relation to the new year, not just for my own personal life, but for L'Abri. I felt increasingly sure that it was a special message for L'Abri as from the Lord, and thanked Him and took courage, with excitement writing a "thank you" by the date in the margin. This passage I would like to give you for your own personal reading and comfort, but also for your special times of prayer for L'Abri.

Isaiah 43:1 to Isaiah 44:8. Do read it all. However, I want to jot a few notes here from this passage. "When thou passest through the waters, I will be with thee; and through the rivers, they shall not overflow thee.". . . This is the same One who later stood up in a boat on a rough sea and commanded the waves to be still, that His disciples might have the calm waters for the next stretch of their journey. What kind of "waters" can He command? The rough waves of village petitions, illnesses, need of funds, need of more space, fears and fightings within and without are within His realm of power. He *can* make a promise to not let the "waves" of life engulf us, overflow us, drown us, because He is able to do all things. "Thus saith the Lord, which maketh a way in the sea, and a path in the mighty waters." He *did* literally make a path in the Red Sea for His children but I do believe He indicates clearly that in our present "sea" of "impossibilities" He can make a "way." One of the ways God makes Himself known to men is by working in the midst of His children's difficulties in an area where no man *could* work. No man could have turned back the Red Sea. No man could have fought the Midianites with three hundred men. God chooses to work in men's "impossible" situations to let it be *seen* that He is there. This is one of the reasons we are told to "ask," that men may see His answer as reality. "Ye are my witnesses, saith the Lord, and my servant whom I have chosen: that ye may know and believe me, and understand that I am he: before me there is no God formed, neither shall there be after me." "*Behold, I will do a new thing; now it shall spring forth; shall ye not know it? I will even make a way in the wilderness, and rivers in the desert.*"* It seemed to me that the Lord was speaking to L'Abri in this verse for 1969. I feel it is to be a year of "new things" which will provide the solution in our particular "wilderness" at this time. "This people have I formed for myself, they shall shew forth my praise." I do believe L'Abri has been formed for the Lord, that we might praise Him and cause others to praise Him. He has answered so many specific prayers in the past, I do believe He would have us "call upon Him" in a very definite way at this time, that we might show forth His praise.

*Isaiah 43:19.

My last letter was written September 9th, 1969, immediately before leaving for Italy and then the American trip. Our short vacation was not what we had hoped it would be and the "restful ocean voyage" which we had counted on to refresh us turned into a nightmare. The Italian Line employees went on strike, and after two hopeful, but tiring, days on the deserted boat, we gave up and flew across the ocean.

In Boston Christian students in Harvard, MIT, Wellesley, and Radcliffe had been wearing buttons "Schaeffer is not a Beer" which one of them had thought of having made. (Schaeffer beer is the most popular beer in the Boston area.) These buttons had started conversations starting with a question, "What is it then?" and ending with an interest in the "ideas" this Schaeffer man expounds. We were thrilled with the growth of interest during our days there. Fran spoke at Gordon Seminary and Andover Seminary, where he gave "A Critique of Liberalism" and had various discussions as well as preaching three times on Sunday. Os Guinness* spoke in a number of places, and I spoke at Tufts and Wheelock. The final lecture at Harvard found Lowell lecture hall jammed with people sitting on the floor in the aisles, and standing at the back, after all the downstairs seats were full. Os reported that one could feel almost an electric charge in the air, the interest was so keen, and at the conclusion of the lecture, "The God Who Is There," there was a burst of applause that lasted 10 minutes, although many of the audience were agnostics or atheists. The wife of a Harvard professor who is a deeply spiritual Christian, later told me she had never felt the power of the Holy Spirit so definitely in any meeting at Harvard before. Truly the Lord worked in those days. Now the numbers indicating that they want to come to L'Abri next summer from Harvard and the other colleges in the area are a bit frightening to us. Bill Wysor, who had come up from Virginia, among other things, talked and prayed about the growing need for a L'Abri in America somewhere in the future. Bill has offered to send out the Family Letter, already has the tape library, and is sending out a constant stream of tapes.

We came back from the American trip to face an almost immediate call to appear before the Council of Seven of the commune (governing council of this area). It was set for Monday morning at eleven o'clock. We called a half-day of prayer for Monday, that we might begin the day with prayer before leaving for Ollon, and that everyone here might be praying while we were talking to the men. . . . In Ollon four of us were ushered into four empty chairs, sitting in a formal row before the seven men, three on each side of the president! John (who is himself Swiss), Marc Chessex (a Christian lawyer in Montreux who has cared for L'Abri's needs of legal advice), Fran, and I sat down in the empty chairs, and first listened to the President as he said that they had nothing

---

*At present an author living in London, Os Guinness has been a student and Worker at L'Abri several times.

against us personally, but that they had to do something when they received a petition of complaint. He said he felt the small village felt threatened by so many foreigners overflowing them, and that the complaint was that young people talked as they walked through the streets after ten o'clock when there should be quiet and that they walked on the peasants' fields at times. Then he asked for an explanation of what our work was. John explained the present set-up, Mr. Chessex filled in on some points he felt should be understood, and then I spoke for a brief time of the fact that our work is based on prayer, and that people come in many amazing ways, often arriving on our doorstep having come great distances, with the question, "Is it true that a person can stay here and ask questions concerning the purpose and meaning of life?" I gave a few stories by way of illustration. Then it seemed important to tell them that we had lived in Huemoz fourteen years and that it is the only home we have. All three of our daughters have been married in the Ollon church building, each has had a baby born in the same hospitals where the children of these men are born, and our son was born in Switzerland. Hence we do not feel like "strangers" but a part of the village. Mr. Chessex told of the fact that we are not a strange "sect," but are "reformed," and we gave them copies of the tape lists and of the Twenty-Five Basic Bible Studies, and read them the letters written to Fran from the President of Senegal (written in French) concerning the books *Escape from Reason* and *The God Who Is There.*

We asked them their feeling concerning our building on the land the Lord gave us two years ago. The attitude was completely favorable. In fact, they seemed to feel strongly that we should have more adequate space for study, writing, reading and so forth, as well as for eating and sleeping. They felt that if we could keep the young people out of the village houses (an overflow has sifted into village houses to rent rooms during the summer, which has not been good as far as noise at night, etc.), it would be much better. They mentioned measuring the cubic meter space per person, and we realize that we haven't the normally required space in any of our sleeping rooms. We later heard that their reaction was favorable, and that one man remarked, "If that woman had kept on talking for fifteen more minutes, I would have been converted."

A few days later we had a call from Mr. Tchividjian from Montreux saying that one of the Council of Seven, Mr. Anex, had been in his office on a business matter and that they had talked together of the petition, etc. He said he and Mr. Anex were coming to talk to us further. When they arrived we had tea by the fire, and Udo, John, Fran, and I met with them. The men were deeply moved by the stories of what the Lord has done this past summer and realized that it would be very difficult to turn people away who came with special need. Mr. Anex left saying that he hoped we would have all the men of the council for an evening to tell them some of these things and also said he wished his daughter could come to L'Abri. Again, one of the strong opinions voiced was that we should have more space, not to have greater numbers, but to more adequately care for those who *are* here.

When the verse "Behold, I will do a *new* thing; now it shall spring forth; shall ye not know it? I will even make a way in the wilderness . . ." continued to repeat itself in my mind, one of the first things I thought of, and prayed for was "space." "Give a new building, Lord, with the foundation dug this April. Oh please give another chalet soon." The Friday after Christmas I awakened to be certain that I should telephone an architect (one whom the commune men had mentioned) and with the agreement of all the L'Abri Members here, I asked him to come and talk over a new building. He came the next morning! Our talk was largely about philosophies of life, the twentieth-century thinking, Christianity, the history of L'Abri, our problem with the village, etc. We made an arrangement for him to come again the day after New Year's Day. The second time John and I met with him, and in answer to his inquiry as to what sort of building we wanted, I sketched him the rough idea of that which was needed. Mr. Nichole is now drawing proper architect's sketches of the proposed building which he will present to the village council for consideration. When permission is given for a new building, the regulation is that the sketches have to be posted in a prominent place for a specified length of time to see whether any complaints are registered. However, if there is not an "adequate reason" to back up such a complaint, the person making the complaint is fined! Swiss law is very fair to both sides!! The architect said he hoped the foundation could be dug in April as soon as the ground is ready. I have a feeling that many of the local men will be watching to see what happens this time in answer to prayer. Because of the petition many will be involved in present developments. We are praying for the people of this area, and for the workmen who will be working on the building, that the Lord may use the result of the attack to be turned into a defeat to Satan, with people being snatched out of his kingdom who would not have been otherwise. . . .

In the first days of the New Year, a tremendous "new thing" opened up. A gift had been given a long time ago toward renting an apartment to "run away" to for rest, and also for Fran to have quiet for working on manuscripts. Mr. Chessex had been on the lookout for such a place. Suddenly, he called to say a very suitable place had been found! It can be occupied immediately, so that our ten-day vacation starting tomorrow can be spent in it. When the Lord begins to do a thing, He is so thrillingly able to *really* "work all things together" in a way man never can do. . . .

One thing for which I was very glad when our last American trip ended in London was the possibility of spending a good long evening of talk and prayer with Deirdre Ducker. You remember Deirdre became a Christian way back in our Champéry days while she was in a finishing school. That was about 18 years ago. She has a strongly atheistic Jewish father who made life miserable for her as far as having any freedom to go to church or to go on as a Christian. However, she pressed on in spite of difficulties encountered. She and her Christian husband, Richard, were, with Ranald, the first three Farel House students. Richard was an airplane pilot, flying for a small English company taking BBC photographers to the scene of their work, etc. It was while we were at Wheaton College that we received the telegram telling of Richard's death in a crash in Wales. He was alone in the plane, flying a new plane to get enough flying hours in it to meet the requirements. Deirdre is now not only a widow, but she has three little girls ages five, three, and two, and a new baby boy born after Richard's death. Do pray for her as she goes on, a day at a time, in this very hard path. She has been asked by Mr. Holdsworth, my publisher, to do sketches for my book, as she is an artist. She is also praying about doing a book in collaboration with Susan, illustrating Susan's children's version of the 25 Basic Bible Studies which she would dedicate to Richard. It is good to remember that Jesus wept at the grave of Lazarus, as well as to remember that we sorrow not as others who have no hope. Separation is not easy. . . .

A new year—"Behold, I will do a new thing. . . ." Oh, let us pray together that He may do all the new things *He* knows are important and necessary to history—our personal history this year, the history of L'Abri—without our hindering Him through selfish choices or failing to pray for each other's protection from Satan's temptations.

With love in Him Who makes all this possible by promising His strength in our weakness,

EDITH

June 11, 1969   Huemoz sur Ollon, Switzerland

Dear Family:

This is a *preface*—or a *foreword*—just to say that this is two Family Letters, this one and the one I didn't write in April. For many, many years now I have not found time to write the Family Letter except while other people slept. I have tried but never succeeded, to do it in the day time, so have written all through the night. However, my energy has not been up to par in recent months. Anyway, Fran put his foot down some weeks ago and said, "No more working all night! Not if you never get a letter written!" The result has been a five-month gap. Today I'm in our hideaway apartment alone. Trying to write under different conditions. Wind, rain, grey skies, and quiet ought to substitute for the accustomed night, but my thoughts are louder than voices or knocks on the door, and it is almost as hard to write as it would be with the usual interruptions.

Thoughts about what?

Death in the City is now out in America and will be out in England in the fall. One generation gives away the base of its culture, but keeps a general pattern of life and behavior hung in mid-air, so to speak. The next generation throws away the pattern of life and behavior. It happened in Jeremiah's time. It is happening right now. Rebellion, revolt, revolution, riots, on a small family scale, and a large university or city-wide scale. And drugs, drugs, drugs! Young people, and even children, who should have clear eyes, fresh skin, and an interest in so many things—excitement about so much—imagination and creativity at a boundless peak, are bleary-eyed, with dark circles around them or have a glassy, unresponsive stare, skin pasty-grey-white, and accompanying the "drugged look" is a lack of interest and excitement, a dulled imagination and a sapped creativity. The attitude soon becomes one of "couldn't-care-less-about-anything."

The flood of drug taking, and the flood of reasons, excuses, and arguments touches not only those who have been brought up in homes and schools where they have been given no base, but like any flood, it oozes under the doors and through the cracks into every home with its slimy river-bottom silt. If the dikes have burst you don't just protect your own house, you need to help repair the dikes and fight for the total situation. Any kind of fighting, flood or forest fire or whatever it is, involves time, energy and material possessions, money, etc. How foolish to hang onto one's neat schedule of life and energy and material possessions when the house is burning down and everything will soon be gone. I'm sure this is the picture many Christians present to God and the watching angels today. Why aren't we more *serious* about our shortness of time and *reality* of the situation? At what point has a youngster "blown his mind" so that he really can't think properly any more? How late is "too late?" . . .

One young man, a singer from Malaysia, started experimenting with drugs when he was in a pop band. "All nine of us did, just before we played. It really was the Beatles' influence . . . the Western pop influence which started it among Malaysian young people. It's not true that it isn't habit forming, and I know it because I couldn't stop when I really wanted to."

Yes, I am down here trying to write, and my mind is whirling with thoughts about the drug problem which are not impersonal thoughts about the masses, but about girls, boys who were just babies when God started L'Abri 14 years ago, but whom He saw as needing help now. These thoughts are made more clamoring because of a Members' meeting I am missing because I'm here, a meeting to discuss what to do about the new problem of a teenager's giving others gathered in his room a joint to smoke, choosing those to whom the struggle to say no is very hard indeed. Obviously, fighting for the people who come here to be helped means protecting them from being faced with the temptation right here. It is not just that people have come here for help, but that others who have other problems don't need to add this one because of curiosity to try it out. It is clear that this is a worldwide problem. One can't read with a detached interest. This isn't far away from *anyone*. It is a 20th-century flood, a very vivid and real flood which has followed the very real sequence of history having consequence. One generation of fathers and mothers, schoolteachers and professors, writers and entertainers threw away the base. "The Bible? Myths and fables, contradictions, only for children and the weak-minded, a psychological aspirin pill. God? An *un*understandable force, a 'something' far off and impersonal—no God at all. No, no God, and then, no truth, no absolute, no personal God, no personal universe, and finally, no personality at all and man is nothing." The next generation of children, pupils, students, audiences began to demonstrate in their lives the nothingness. Free? Free to live without restrictions, without stodgy limitations. Suddenly the incentive to live at all is dwindling away.

It's so exactly like watching a gigantic demonstration of Satan's whispered lie to Eve. "Eat—eat and you'll become wise like God. You'll be free from ignorance—eat." Eve ate, and Eve was separated from her communication with the only One who could have given her wisdom, answers to her questions, freedom from ignorance. "Smoke this, swallow that and you'll become free. You'll experience reality; you'll perceive. . . ." Not one person now, but millions are involved personally, and the generation to follow? Communication and even clear thought of what the questions are gradually can be cut off. Blur, fog, unreality. Where is God? Where is man? The blind leading the blind through a maze filled with fog.

What are you doing about it? What am I doing about it? Is there anything *to* do?

We called a day of prayer last Sunday. Church was a half-hour early and the first half-hour was spent in explaining the day of fasting and prayer, and in considering together some of the strong commands of the Lord to "sanctify yourselves," such as in Joshua when God commanded the children of Israel through Joshua to be sanctified so that they might see the miracle He was about to perform. There are two aspects strongly given, both in the Old and New Testament, that we are to confess sin and be cleansed by the Spirit *for* prayer, and also to be prepared spiritually for the answer to prayer. Fran preached a sermon on the conditions needed for prayer, and then we gave out prayer lists. For a period of time people stayed together and had a prayer meeting, then gradually they slipped out, and most people spent the day in the woods or fields praying.

Our day of prayer was for spiritual preparation for this summer. Members, Workers, Helpers, students, and guests all need much prayer. We who are in the work must have the "motes cast out" of our own eyes before we can pray and help others. Spiritual preparation is not just a nice, pious phrase to be considered as a part of a formal service, but it is something to be struggled for in the struggle for honesty before God. Then we need prayer for wisdom. To deal personally with each person as an individual, remembering the responsibility for other people in the "family" is not possible for a human being. The wisdom of God is needed to be able to help one "child" without harming all the other "children." Only God can work things together in the lives of each of His children without endangering all the others. We make mistakes. Much prayer is needed as all of the Workers, some of the Helpers, and the Members talk and work with individuals. . . .

About a year ago I told you of a young man from a far-off eastern country. Now Mus, for that is his real name, wants his story told—that is, he wants you to know that he is a Malaysian from a family and nation that has been Muslim for generations . . . because he wants you to pray for him specifically and for his people and nation. You will remember that he came to study in the West—came through very dangerous experiences in India and Greece and truly miraculously was brought to L'Abri. You will remember that I told of his struggle and his bowing to the God who is there . . . as he became a Christian last June. Mus has grown through the year . . . but there have been real Satanic attacks at times, and a real victory as superstitions and magic were definitely put on the fire before the Lord, and the very moving day came when Mus wanted to be baptized and join the church. That same day Charlene from South Carolina (teaching here in École du Monde) joined the church. Mus stood there . . . such a picture of "some from every tribe and nation shall be there" . . . joining the church with one from a Christian background . . . as a minority from his "tribe and nation" but as a clear picture that Satan can*not* build walls of superstition, fear, police-enforced law, threat to life—*strong* enough or *high* enough to keep *everyone inside*. . . .

In the midst of all of February's difficulties there came the day when a telegram arrived from Virginia telling of Anne Bates's death. The children in Bellevue had had prayer meetings daily, wheelchairs in a circle, or alone with a Worker or therapist.

In the afternoon of the 19th of February, Debby and I stood in front of the flower-decorated room at Bellevue. The children and Workers were gathered, dressed in their Sunday clothing. In America there would be a service in Virginia; this was the children's service. Fran would be preaching in the chapel for a memorial service for all of our International Church members, and for L'Abri, but this was especially for the children who loved Anne and had prayed so faithfully for her. What was there to say? First of all, the victory is over Satan. The final victory will be the resurrection of the body, but the victory now is in the hearts of each one whom he (Satan) is accusing before God daily. "You'll see, God.

This will cause that one and that one to stop trusting You and loving You." It was the sort of thing Satan said about Job, and we know that he is accusing the believers daily before God. Perhaps one of the most important battles and resulting victories in the lives of those who know and worked with Anne, or thought of her as mother of the home there, is the victory of *really* trusting God at this moment rather than becoming bitter or doubting. It is for this kind of victory of being able to trust, that Christ died, that among other victories, He died to give to those who would believe in Him. We read verses and talked of this, and Debby translated into French. Then we thought of Miss Bates and her joyous entrance into the presence of the Lord. The children were delighted to remember that there are two of them up there who would have been waiting for her, a wee little girl and a nine-year-old boy who also loved Anne before they suddenly went to be with the Lord. Then we thought together about the resurrection of the body. It is such a thrilling truth to think about, for any of us, but especially for anyone who is imprisoned in a body that has been spoiled by accident, disease, or birth damage. Suddenly in a twinkling of an eye, someday, these bodies will be changed to be like His resurrected body. Danny almost jumped out of his chair at the thought of moving about freely, running, walking, flying through space, for we come and go in the real universe, and it's going to be so wonderful that "eye hath not seen nor ear heard nor the heart of man imagined" all that He is now preparing for those who are His children. The wheelchairs will be discarded! So we comfort one another with the hope that is *real*.

Meantime, it would be well to remember as we think of our own lives, that Anne came to a point in her life when with Mary she prayed as to what the Lord would have them do next. This was when they were both L'Abri Workers. There were marvelous positions that opened up—good salaries, apartments offered, car, honor, travel. Supposing they had *not* taken the step of faith in buying Bellevue, had *not* lived through the sacrificial weeks and months and years of getting started with 24-hour "duty." Looking back on it from this vantage point, let's just consider Anne. She had ten years. God knew this. He led her in a way that looked to men foolish, a waste of talent and energy, far too difficult. At points there was not even enough money for food for it was a work based on prayer, even as L'Abri. But she and Mary did not give up, nor did Rosie after she came. Just think of the people who have been helped in Bellevue, who have come to be born into God's family there: patients, nurses, therapists! As for "success" in the world's eyes, the Lord has given something there too since the work has become recognized medically as being a tremendous service to Switzerland in this field. "He that loseth his life for my sake findeth it." Could you think of a better use for Anne's years? And now? The work goes on. Mary has just come back and is going on. Rosie is there and Adri, and they are continuing with courage, "showing forth His sufficiency," in the home for rehabilitation for cerebral palsy children. There are all sorts of victories. How can we tell which is the most important? . . .

My book called simply *L'Abri* is finally out in England and will soon be here. It has been five-and-a-half years since I wrote the first 20 chapters, but I am sure the Lord timed it, and knew that it needed Chapter 21 to finish it. Deirdre Ducker did the etchings for it and I can't wait for you to see her sketches as well as for you to be able to read the story all in one piece at last.

I haven't had room to tell you about the Scandinavian Conference, the first L'Abri Conference in Scandinavia arranged by Pol Madsen in Nyborg, Denmark. It was the first time we had been back in Scandinavia since canceling a trip at the time we were put out of Champéry 14 years ago! It seemed to be picking up the pieces out of the past as well as a new step into the future. It was a short, but full, conference. The L'Abri Ensemble gave a concert, Fran spoke three times a day, Os spoke two different times, Udo spoke twice, and I gave a talk on prayer, one on marriage, and then gave the L'Abri story in far too short a time so didn't get half through it. The result was that people rushed to buy books to get the rest of the story and the few copies were sold out in a few minutes (only 27 copies there). That wasn't planned, though some people accused me of stopping on purpose! Some time was fitted in later, by the way, to tell a bit more! The conference was held in a hotel right on the shore of the Baltic Sea, a beautiful location. It seemed to us that the Lord used that time to "open doors" to a good many people—students and older ones too, and that it may be the beginning of further contact in Scandinavia, to His glory. The number there was exactly 200, the number Mr. Madsen prayed would come! . . .

The drug problem has covered the earth with floods. I end as I began, with a cry for a counterflood, a flood of prayer, a flood of giving our possessions, our time, ourselves. Here, Lord, use these, use me. Do I have ten years? Five? How long would be too long to trust to His use? How much would be too much to trust to *His* use? In the final analysis we stand face to face alone before God. Our commitment must be made directly to Him, not through people. Our excuses or reasons must be given to Him, no one else. Where are the ripples? Where are the floods?—that the knowledge of the true and living God's existence and person might cover the earth?

With love in Him,

EDITH

October 13, 1969   Huemoz sur Ollon, Switzerland

Dear Family:

   . . . We awakened our first day in Holland to find that the weather was
closer to California for an October day than to usual Dutch weather. It
has been an unusually warm summer here which has continued into autumn. As the Rookmaakers drove us through the countryside, the sudden appearance of a Dutch wedding "ride" enhanced still more vividly
the beauty of the later-than-usual roses among the green grasses, sparkling canals, and warm red and yellow leaves fluttering down to form
fresh carpets on the ground. The wedding party consisted of a white-
robed and veiled bride with her formally dressed bridegroom beside her
in an open horse-drawn carriage. Before this carriage rode a young man
in black riding habit with a banner fluttering in the breeze. Behind the
carriage came 24 other young men, identically dressed, riding two by
two on beautiful horses. Can you wonder that we exclaimed over this
unusual and enthralling sight? All this, however, could not dim the
beauty of the village and countryside surrounding the "barn" we were
all being taken to see. Canals of various widths and levels, trees of vary-
ing colors and varieties, fields and meadows which could only be described as peaceful, in one word. Truly a peaceful view!

   "Here we are." We were turning in beside a 17th-century farmhouse,
white brick, lovely old leaded windows, tiled roof. "And there is the
barn." Hans Rookmaaker was pointing to the long, low building attached to the main house in the manner of American New England
barns, so that the farmer can enter the barn without going outside in
the winter time. Here was a place with fantastic possibilities. "Let us
first go into the house." The young Dutch pastor owner had felt led to
offer to Dutch L'Abri his barn to be remodeled into a weekend meeting
place and conference place for L'Abri. We first looked at the artistic
kitchen he has produced in this 17th-century farmhouse, with its murals copied from Old Danish murals, tile on a portion of the walls, a
small organ in one corner, copper and brass pans and kettles, and
spices on specially made shelves. Then we went to see his other rooms,
all remodeled in the last three years by his own hands and with his
own ideas, full of antiques and full of creativity. We sat in front of a
wonderful old stove set on tiles and drank coffee as we looked around
us. This young man lives and works here, his mother living in a small
house next door. The barn seemed a waste, and he prayed that God
would show him how to use it. Now, he and the Rookmaakers and Van
Seventers are convinced that the Lord means it to be the L'Abri of Holland. They are praying for the needed money to convert the barn into a
place to use for weekends and conferences now and perhaps later for a
permanent L'Abri. The Lord shows just a step at a time. The first step is
to make it usable.

When we walked the few steps from the kitchen door through a passageway into the barn, we found we were standing in a building larger than our chapel at Huemoz. We looked out through the wide barn door (which is to become a huge picture window) to find that the view looks first through a flower garden, then beyond that to a pasture enclosed by a fence, and then out to a field, bordered by small canals and a short river.

We walked out to look at the field, which the owner said could be used for football! Then into the old pigsty, a smaller separate building, also white brick and also with a beamed ceiling and tremendous possibilities for being made into a house eventually, for a L'Abri couple caring for the work. There is room for a dorm to be made in the "attic space" in both the barn and the pigsty. By the way, the pigs also had the beauty of curved and leaded windows!!

All this is unbelievably close to Amsterdam, with splendid public transportation, making it possible to come at various times of the day and leave as late as midnight. It is only 15 minutes by car from Amsterdam. As the Rookmaakers and others in the L'Abri circle in Holland have prayed through the years, the Lord saw this barn and waited for the right time to make it known to them.

Perhaps this is the right moment to stop for a flashback to Huemoz, that you might know how things stand right now in October. Every bed is full, and there are camp cots placed in some of the rooms as well! We thought October would be the "low" month, in the sense of fewer people. Workers planned their vacations for October, and some are now taking their vacations. Speaking trips were planned for this "low" time, a leave of absence was given to Os to visit his parents. Hence, we are less ready to cope with the numbers than in the summertime yet the numbers remain just about the same. As for the "new building," after the plans were accepted by the commune's council, a notice was placed in the newspaper, by the architect in accordance with the law, and three weeks was given for anyone having objections. An "opposition" was filed against the building by a village man owning the property behind it. This delayed things for such a long time that we didn't even hear what had been going on until a couple of weeks ago. At that time the architect came to talk with the "building committee" (John, Udo, and myself), and he told us the tale of his various conversations with the representative of the communal council and his resulting headaches about the building plans. The plans now have to be redrawn, lowering the roof, and thereby doing away with a lot of space, leaving only an attic, rather than usable dormitory space, toilets, and washrooms on the top floor. We feel that the Lord knows the use He will make of the building and that perhaps He wants us to have space for couples, and a few single rooms, and *not* space for a larger "dorm" which would add perhaps too many people as a total. We are satisfied that this is of the Lord. As to *time*, however, the new plans will have to be presented to the council, if accepted once more. The notice will again have to be put in the newspaper, and if no objection is made this time or if the council does not accept the objection, *then* we will be given the permission to "go ahead and build." The architect says that permission could not come through until December now. Please pray that the permission and the right amount of money *will* come at the same time so that as soon as the frost is out of the ground, M. Baratchi may start digging and making the foundations.

October 2nd Pris called and informed me that she had been awake most of the night as she was sure the baby was on its way, 18 days early! "Well, I had Elizabee's birthday party for the village children so that is out of the way. The baby's things are ready, the room is ready, the meal lists are caught up for all of Huemoz L'Abri and I just need to talk to Gini this morning and explain it all to her since she will be taking over the meal lists and coordinating the work until I can do it again. *Everything* is ready except me. I mean I am so tired because I had just come to the moment when I was going to *rest*. Ha! Ha! We were going to take our vacation starting in a couple of days." She wasn't too disappointed, however, because the joy swallowed up any regret for a lost preparation of rest. By four that afternoon she had turned over the meal lists, packed her suitcase, prepared the other things she wanted to have ready, had Jane Douglas there to take care of the children, and had started down the mountain to the Vevey "Hospital Samaritan," in true L'Abri tradition of working up till the last minute! John was ready for his part, and the next hours were spent in the "natural childbirth" procedure, with John reporting that "Pris is doing very well." At 9:20 Debby called me. "Mother, have you had a call from John?" "No." A giggle came in response. Then, "Well, stay by the phone, he's trying to get you." Then came the most frustrating wait for a ring that didn't come during which I nearly swallowed my tonsils in an effort to stay calm. Finally, I called the hospital, and after a long wait, got John on the hall telephone. His change had run out! Happily I had called, so I did then get the news directly from John himself, *"It's a boy!!"* This is our sixth grandchild and the first boy among them! Pris and John, however, had expected a third girl and would have been happy to have her, so had not even asked whether it was a boy or a girl, so thrilled were they to have a healthy baby. It was several minutes before they discovered it was a boy, and were greatly amused that they hadn't even thought about that part! The grand welcome had been for "the baby." His name is Gian Andrea Sandri (John Andrew, in English). You can imagine John's father's and mother's joy of a special sort when you know that John is the only male Sandri of his generation, and now there is a little boy to carry on the name. Meantime, little Gian Andrea peacefully slept, not knowing all the commotion he was causing! He is a beautiful baby (no prejudice, of course!) and looks like Elizabee and John, as far as one can tell. Thank you all for praying. It has been a very happy answer to prayer for us all, and especially for little Becky and Elizabee, whose faces I'd love to have had a picture of when they first saw him through a glass door. . . .

Moving backwards again . . . let's go to the L'Abri Ashburnham Conference in England. Sue and Ran had prepared a conference which would allow some people to come for the first weekend and stay a full week, and others who could simply come for the second weekend. A bit complicated for Birdie who was registrar, etc., at the door, but it all worked out to fit over 400 people in. People who had been there for a week wanted to stay for the second weekend, but since there was only space enough for 200 at a time, they had to leave to make way for the second two hundred. It astonished us how many of the people, especially the second weekend, had been at L'Abri . . . it was a real L'Abri reunion. The speakers were Fran giving some lectures on Epistemology which he hopes to put into a book along with Ecology; Hans Rookmaaker on Art, again taking a large group by bus to a London museum one day; Ranald, Udo, and myself. The L'Abri Ensemble, Jane Stuart Smith, Frances Kramer, and Gini Andrews gave two formal concerts, and two Sunday afternoon musical times in the chapel. There was an informal afternoon concert . . . with a tremendous variety of things . . . Ran singing and accompanying himself with a banjo-ukulele he had borrowed!; Nigel giving some readings, and the children Susan and Debby had been teaching for four days giving answers to catechism questions, singing all sorts of illustrated songs with pictures and motions, and displaying the various things they had made in their creative play . . . made of shells, branches, old plastic bottles. We were all amazed at all that could be done in four days.

After the Ashburnham conference, we had a very unusual three days. It had been twelve years since we had had a vacation with Sue. Our times together since then have always been in the midst of the work. (My dream is to one day have a complete family reunion for a week or so, alone together without the work, but that is still a dream!) Sue and Ran had arranged to have Debby and Udo take care of the work at 52 Cleveland Road, and the children, for a few days while they took us away for a three-day rest. We had a really delightful time in the historic old village of Rye, relaxing and talking together in quaint little tearooms, and wandering about looking at Elizabethan houses. Ran also drove us out into the country each day so that we could walk. It was a different sort of walking than the Swiss alpine walking, but in its own way, just as beautiful.

Sue and Ran are praying for a *farm*. Not to replace 52 Cleveland Road, but in addition to it. A farm that would have a L'Abri couple running it so that it could produce crops and have some sort of livestock. This would then be a place where people needing more time in L'Abri would have space to stay long enough to be helped. Pray for the Lord's direction, His choice of such a place to be shown "in time" to Ran and Sue, then His choice of the one, or ones whom *He* would use to provide the means to purchase such a place.

What is "in time"?? One wonders how long any of us may have. The new house in Huemoz, the barn in Holland, the help needed in the Italian L'Abri work, the farm in England, the thought and prayer about a L'Abri place in America—how long do we have to see these things become a reality, and to be used for the rescue of those who otherwise will be "lost"? I don't think that is being dramatic. We are dealing with personalities who live forever. Human beings have so much significance in the universe, that it is terrifying to think of how casual and calloused we so often are. True, we seek God's guidance. True, we are finite and cannot do more than a finite creature can do. Yet we do have responsibility, and the phrase "in time" has *some* connection with us. God clearly shows that it does, when He places in His Word the picture of the man whose barns are bursting with material possessions and he is called a "fool" by God, as he is told "this night your soul is required of you." Hence I feel strongly we should pray that what *needs* to be done, what the Lord would have us do, *may* be done "in time" and not hindered by Satan. . . .

We have all suddenly and with a great feeling of dismay, awakened to the fact that there is *not* going to be a difference between summer, autumn, winter, and spring as far as numbers of people coming to L'Abri. Yes, right now in October every bed is full and there are extra camp beds in some of the rooms. And as Darrow has mapped out November, although some are leaving, yet on November 1st, twenty-two will be arriving, and as it looks now, we will have eleven more people than beds! Unless a miracle of answered prayer either brings another available chalet, or a cancellation of some people's coming, we are going to have a problem which seems to have no solution. In the summer there are balconies to sleep on, but now not only is that impossible, but there are not enough blankets for extra cots, etc., let alone enough space for indoor eating for all these people. Perhaps you can "feel" with us the urgent need of the new building to just take care of the number of people we already have. Living room space is needed as much as sleeping space, and there simply isn't enough "living" space these days for time in between meals and lectures!

Turn down more requests? Yes. Of course, that must come. But, it isn't easy to say "no." Another Malaysian arrived with a pack on his back the other evening. Unexpected. He had hitchhiked from Malaysia, taking two months to come from the same village as the others. Another friend of Mus's who came in response to letters, now studying the Bible and asking questions. He wants to be a Helper. Do you say "no"? A Korean Airforce man, Kim, who wants to go into the ministry arrived unexpectedly, having heard about L'Abri in Germany. He is digging into studies and helping very energetically. Do you say "no"? There are black and white, European and South American, hippies and clergymen, those from Christian background and those from utterly heathen background, atheistic and false religions, Christians with great need, and the lost with great need. Swiss are discovering L'Abri since the book came out, even villagers are now coming for help.

I feel so strongly and vividly that this is the picture. I feel L'Abri is like a raft floating on a stormy sea near a great ship that is sinking. People are swimming toward the raft, hands are clasped and they are drawn on board, one by one, two, three, one again, and they are safe on board, though some slip back into the sea before making it up. Suddenly, however, there are too many hands, too many fingers grasping the edge of the raft. If *all* come up, the whole raft will sink. What to do? It is obvious that the raft needs to be enlarged!!

Udo and Debby are already in America for a time of speaking. Fran and I are leaving next week and will be in the States for 21 days. Saying "no" to the speaking invitations hurts also, as it is not just a "no" to some kind of "thing," human beings are involved, and to say "yes" might make a difference to some. But even three weeks away right now is going to be hard on the other Workers here as they carry on in our absence. . . .

The continuity and the encouragements continue. We *are* thankful. People are being helped, changed, some being born again. There are struggles in which there are visible victories. Can there be a "but" then? But we *are* finite. We cannot work without sleep. Each day's hours are limited by an exacting "tick" to 60 minutes. If one person is talked with alone for one hour, and there are 96 persons to talk to, how long would it take? How thankful we should be, and how increasingly we should thrill over our infinite, unlimited, all-wise, changeless God Who always has time for us all, one by one alone. And how thankful, too, that our quietness can come from remembering that He has a plan for us which is on the basis of our finiteness. Let us intercede for each other, and pray for ourselves, that we may not fall into a rut of living by someone else's pattern, but seek His plan moment by moment, remembering when that plan is disappointing, that "this is the will of God in Christ Jesus for you."

With love, in Him Whom we love and Who loves us,

EDITH

1970

February 21, 1970   Huemoz sur Ollon, Switzerland

Dear Family:

Not only is it four months since I wrote the last Family Letter, but my
desk and daybed are piled high with letters from you that need personal
replies. You are waiting for a "thank you" letter, or an answer to a personal problem you have asked advice about, or you have just read the
L'Abri story and you kindly wrote thanking me for writing it, or you
want to come here sometime soon, or you want us to come there. Most of
the letters asking about coming here have been answered by Fran or Bev
or Phyllis, but there are a few very personal ones to me buried in that
stack of letters "screaming" silently. . . .

So, get in a comfortable chair, or sprawl out on the floor, or tuck yourself into bed, and settle down to listen, feeling the "togetherness" of
what God is giving us in reality of our communication with Him *together*, the reality of His acting into this present moment of history in response to our asking, interceding, making our requests known. It *is*
possible to share in the wonder of His working in response to our *united*
asking as a Family, to know that we are not watching from afar His answers to someone else, but that we are involved *together* in both prayer
and answers in a manner that is *real* and *true*. . . .

There was the day that the mail brought word from the Police Department dealing with foreigners in Switzerland saying that Gini Andrews
and Claire Oleson's permits would not be renewed. They would have to
leave! Since both Gini and Claire are L'Abri Workers for as long as the
Lord would keep them here, it was indeed a "blow."

We then discovered that we were being "investigated," that is, all of
L'Abri, which struck us with uncertainty as to what might be the result
of this investigation. John and I spent hours in Lausanne, first at the Bureau des Etrangers, and then at the Department of Justice, talking and
answering questions about L'Abri. Another day, Udo and I spent hours

with the president of the commune on the same subject. How big were we going to grow? We were becoming a "threat" to the village in the sense of changing it altogether and overwhelming it with foreigners. And how about our space? We needed more space for the people we have in order to be in line with Swiss regulations. . . .

The investigation brought a plainclothes police inspector to go through all our chalets, talk to several of us, filling sheets of paper with notes, and answers to his endless questions. Then silence for weeks of haunting wondering, "What is going on?" M. Chessex, the Christian Notaire in Montreux who helps L'Abri with legal affairs, very kindly looked into matters and one day we had the cheering news that God had arranged a business matter to give M. Chessex a whole day driving with one of the top men in the Department of Justice, so he had an informal time in which to explain about L'Abri to him. All this paralleled some of the encouragements as well as discouragements of what took place when we were being "put out" of Switzerland fifteen years ago. However, weeks of uncertainty have had an effect upon each of us in different ways.

Whenever we asked anyone in official capacity whether we were going to have the permission to build the new building this spring, the answer was the same: "It is necessary now to wait until the Department of Justice makes its decision concerning L'Abri after the investigation is complete."

And as the weeks went on, darkness seemed to increase. The man who owns the land behind our piece of land for the new building declared to John he would continue to object to our having a building there. Short vacations also always need to be fitted into the work . . . but in the midst of all the difficulties plus the various illnesses, times away almost seem to need to be placed in the list of calamities!! Fran had to leave right after the Christmas services in Champéry for a time of speaking in England. When one considers what happened in England in the meeting of about 700 vicars, curates, canons, and bishops where Fran gave the principal message, and in several other meetings and seminars, the time should be listed among the wonderful things God is doing. However, his being away in the midst of all the "troubles" added to the difficulty of carrying on in Huemoz.

Additionally, there is the emotional strain of having to read letters from people wanting to come, some pleading to come, and knowing we have to say "no" to so many of them. The system now is this: Fran and I read the mail first (mail directed to us or to L'Abri). We put a remark on the envelope if there is anything we feel we need to point out about the person's request to come. Then we pass on these letters to the one who looks at the dates asked for and then at his chart which lists all the people who have been promised a place. He then notes on the letter the ruthless truth "No beds left for that date" or whatever the truth is "an opening seems possible," "perhaps a cot," or "OK." The letters then go

on to a committee of Debby and Cynthia who read them and discuss the
intensity of the need as they see it from reading, and they pray about it.
They then pass the letters on to Bev or Phyllis or Fran to answer, recom-
mending some other date if possible, saying "no" if it seems necessary,
or "yes." For all who have some part in this whole thing, there is emotional strain, often tears, and always much prayer. For everyone who is a
Worker or Helper or Member, as we meet together and discuss some of
the cases, and as we are conscious of turning people away, there is sorrow and heaviness. The worst thing of all, however, is to have to tell
people they cannot stay longer because of others coming when these individuals are themselves weeping and asking to stay on. Not only are
beds full but Farel House desks are more than full. We have only 32
desks in Farel House. Using them in two shifts, that is 64. It means putting tables and tape recorders in other places. An additional problem is
that as the change comes in the way the Lord is using L'Abri, more and
more people want to come as Farel House students. This means that if
fewer guests are accepted, and more Farel House students, the study
space and tape recorder need increases all the time. . . .

As we prayed during these past months for the need of space to be
met by God's work and guidance, for the need of decisions in government circles to be guided by God's plan for the days ahead, for the need
of material provision to be sent in answer to God's moving in the
hearts of men, and then also prayed for the individuals in our midst,
for spiritual victory as Satan battled to keep people in his kingdom, or
attacked others to cause them to stumble, it was often a temptation to
have a reversed understanding of what was the more difficult thing for
God to do.

In this area of the spiritual reality, the Lord gave us encouragement,
coming to a crescendo which touched us all with deep wonder and worship and praise, *before* other answers came. . . . Sunday, the 15th . . . come
with me up to the front of our chapel. It is packed with every chair full,
and also the floor. Jim Hurley is to preach. I am sitting next to Fran and
Dean on the front row. There are a tremendous variety of people . . . the
Nethery family of seven; the Ball family of seven; an old friend of Ran's
from Cambridge, Clive, on furlough time from Kenya; students from all
over the world. Fran rose to stand beside the table holding the bowl of
water . . . and Matt walked from the back of the room . . . his Malaysian
blouse loose and flowing, his feet bare (ice and snow outdoors, but the
bare feet which indicate respect in Malaysia) . . . his Bible held firmly in
his hand . . . a look on his face that make many of us think of Stephen.
He answered the questions most clearly, emphasizing his belief in the
Trinity and his need of a Saviour. He was baptized . . . he bowed his
head in prayer, and then he embraced Dr. Schaeffer with such a natural
movement of true joy. Tears were flowing freely among us all with *real*
emotion, joy, sober realization of the possibility of martyrdom indeed.
As Matt turned, Dean arose out of his seat and walked forward to em-

brace his brother in the Lord . . . Matt had only just learned of Dean's salvation . . . and they wept together, with a forgiveness of past friction. Something very real took place among us all that morning. Jim preached a sermon on "Who Is This Man Jesus." *Truly splendid and suited to the need of the morning.*

That evening we were grouped around the fireplace . . . David, Mary Lee's husband, came forward to be received into the church. These two came from San Mateo, California, and now wanted to be one of our congregation.

On the first of February we had a beautiful baptism service as Priscilla and John brought little Giandy (Gian Andrea) before the congregation. As they stood there making the promises to teach him and to be willing to give him to the Lord for *His* plan for his life, whether by life or by death, little Elizabee and Becky stood there with them. Truly a picture of a family responsibility, a responsibility for each other's spiritual life to "speak of the things of the Lord" together, to live together in the midst of the reality of His existence hour by hour, not just in moments of "special days," but daily. The continuity of our own family life and the continuity of this work *He* had planned for us was again made vivid that day. . . .

On February 11th, the prayer meeting in England was one of real freedom and fervency. Susan and Ranald phoned the next day. "We had a truly wonderful prayer meeting last night, for a long time, and asked the Lord for His guidance to the place of His choice, and this morning we have heard of the most amazing place. We plan to go to see it tomorrow. Do pray for us as we go." "Tomorrow" brought forth a great and transportation-crippling snow storm in England, so the trip was put off until Monday. Therefore, it was Monday evening the 16th that we heard the news.

"Guess what? The driving time from our door in Ealing, to the door of this place is exactly 45 minutes! Yet, it is in the country with a view of rolling hills. It has 21 acres, a huge house and four cottages, greenhouse, a walled-in vegetable garden, stables, marvelous trees and lawns, a rose garden, etc., etc. It has enormous oak-paneled rooms and big fireplaces with a charm and atmosphere which means it would *not* be like an institution at all. There are 18 bedrooms and six baths. The cottages are livable houses. It really is amazing."

We rejoiced over the good news and began to pray for guidance. All this came right into the "picture" the week which had been looked forward to as one of the *most* importance. February 19th we had set aside for a day of fasting and prayer. February 29th at 2:30 P.M. we were to meet with the Communal Council of Seven, and the representative of the Cantonal Department of Justice. (By "we" I mean John, M. Chessex, and Fran and myself who were to represent L'Abri.) At this time the results of the investigation were to be discussed, more questions asked, and a decision was to be made. You can imagine something of the natural fears and apprehensions, and the need to pray for the Lord's quietness and *His* choice of words for each of us as we spoke. However, the "pressure" as to the limitations which might be put on us were now lessened, as if the Lord took off part of the heaviness of the weight to allow us to breathe and relax a bit in front of the men. For now, it seemed clear that *He was showing us that we were to divide* the work of Farel House. We had on our day of prayer then, not only the urgent need to pray about the Council's decision, but the urgent need to pray that the Lord would clearly guide us in England. It was a most important day of prayer and one was conscious of a oneness of purpose, a "togetherness" with not only a large number involved here at Huemoz, but those in Italy, Holland, England, and scattered around the world in the Praying Family involved in being in the closet in secret when no one knows but God, but there is also value in togetherness, in knowing that *He hears and answers and leads* a group of people, who are one in Him, as well as one individual.

During the day of prayer, we were given news from an individual being led by the Lord. Word came that the individual was feeling led to buy the property in England, to keep their identity as a secret (not letting the left hand know what the right hand was doing), but to own the estate privately, putting it at the disposal of L'Abri for as long as L'Abri stays in existence.

It was a staggering answer to prayer. The transaction has not yet taken place, but, Lord willing, Fran will be leaving for England in a few minutes, and will be looking at this estate with the individual interested, and will spend time with Ran and Sue. The full Surveyor's report will be in tonight. (His report yesterday, February 24th, was that it is an amazing buy and that one could have looked for years and not found anything as suitable and perfect for our particular use.) Pray for the purchase, for the furnishing, for the guidance needed as to who should be the Members to work there and what Workers and Helpers should be the ones to help. How very, very much the leading of the Lord is needed that each person, each step, may be *His choice*, and *His alone*. . . .

Then the 20th dawned. It was not easy to face the actual moment as it drew near in spite of many assurances from the Lord. I had prayed whether I should say anything at all or not, being a woman among eleven men. I asked for a clear sign. I didn't expect such a clear one! The phone rang just a few minutes before we were to leave. I was in the midst of doing up my hair. It was one of the Council of Seven, "Are you coming to the meeting?" "Oh, yes, Monsieur. We shall be there on time." "I mean are *you*, Madame Schaeffer, coming yourself?" "Oh, yes Monsieur." "Then be sure to *speak*. Tell the men some of the true-life stories about your work as you did before, and bring with you some evidences." "What sort of things, Monsieur?" "Oh, letters from afar. Things they would be interested to see which would make the work more real and understandable to them." Like a flash, my mind thought of what "thing" to take. Matt had said he wished he could thank the Swiss people for letting him come to their country to find the Truth. I would ask John to call Matt. John was by then standing in the hall waiting to go. He got my message in person, he called another chalet, and I raced up to finish putting up my hair.

We seemed to have missed Matt somehow and drove on down to Ollon alone: Fran, John, and I.

At a U-shaped table, we faced the Communal Council; the Department of Justice representative sat at the head. A two-and-one-half-hour meeting commenced. They spoke, Mr. Chessex spoke, John spoke, Fran spoke, back and forth, explaining, asking questions, and out of it, understanding seemed really to come. One felt sympathy, understanding, not antagonism. One felt a desire to work out something which would meet the needs of both the village and L'Abri. In the middle of it all, a knock came at the door, and *Matt* came in!!!! He had hitchhiked down!!

The final points which you are all waiting to hear were these: L'Abri in Huemoz is to be restricted to 110 people total (counting us, but not the children of our personal families). We *are* allowed to build our new building. In fact, they want us to have it *as soon as possible* as they feel it will help us to keep our young people more in one area. We may use the rented house down in Forchet until the new building is ready for use, but they hope we will not "spread" down into small villages if there is growth or other houses to be used. They prefer us to have people up in Chesieres rather than down the hill in smaller villages. They urge us to keep the young people (and others) from talking under the windows of sleeping villagers as they go back from lectures at night.

You can't imagine the relief of the decision. Two years ago we ourselves had decided never to have more than 120 here in Huemoz so that the family atmosphere could not be lost. What a miracle of answered prayer. It could so easily have been otherwise. Then, Matt spoke, in English, but with John translating into French. It was most moving. Here stood this slender, black-haired Malaysian with his hands spread forth in delicate gestures, so earnestly and with such real feeling, thanking the Swiss, thanking the Council, thanking the villagers, that he had come out of a dark country into a place where he had found the light, that he had learned that Christ is true and Mohammed was false. It was surely a most realistic demonstration to the men of what is going on at L'Abri, and in their midst.

What is 110 people total? Oh, so few! But let us pray together now for all the needs. The Lord has surprised our "tidy" little schedule as we prayed for Huemoz's new building first, and then another L'Abri in the place of His choice. He has chosen England, it would seem clear, and He would have us continue to pray for the building here that it might be started when the ground thaws. May hearts thaw before the ground thaws and may the hardness of unbelief "thaw" too, in the very midst of building, as well as in the building after it is built. . . .

Much love in *Him* Who does exist, and Who really does want to provide Himself strong in behalf of those who seek *Him* with hearts made perfect in the blood of Christ,

EDITH

July 22, 1970   Huemoz sur Ollon, Switzerland

Dear Family:

Each Worker and Member of L'Abri goes through repeated times of feeling "It's too much—I can't stand it *any* longer. I am overwhelmed. I feel ready to collapse. I can't face one more day, I can't face one more person."

Then—there comes a letter, a telegram, a phone call, or a conversation with a person, and suddenly the overwhelming feeling is different. It's all worth it. *Every*thing is worth *this.*

It isn't that each hard thing is balanced by some exciting result. It isn't that every struggle ends in a victory. It isn't that one can see all the threads being woven together so that the total pattern becomes clear and the dark and foggy spots all disappear. It isn't that one can "time" the depressed moments with a stopwatch and know that a lift in spirits is due to arrive. No, it is anything but automatic. But, when one is in a flow of work that God is being allowed to direct, one has moments of certainty, of evidence, that *He* really is the Director. *Only God* and God alone can know what is *really* taking place day by day as this work which He started and which He is directing and carrying on is starting its 16th year. . . .

Fran, Franky, and I sailed off on the *Christopho Colombo* from Italy to America in March about 500 years after the original Christopher, and in quite a shorter length of time! Seminar 70 at Buck Hill Falls was where Fran was to speak, and boxes of paintings and sketches were with us, as Franky was to have his first art exhibit in the Edward Frisch Gallery on 3rd Avenue in New York, arranged and sponsored by Lady Edward Montagu and Mrs. James Morrison who had taken an interest in Franky's painting and sculpture. The time in New York was a combination of the art exhibit and Fran's lecturing at Columbia and preaching in Broadway Presbyterian Church, and discussions with Columbia students. Os Guinness came at the same time, and spoke in a number of colleges around New York, as well as in Bill Mahlow's church in Annapolis, in Willow Grove, and in St. Louis.

As we returned from America, we had with us for the very beautiful journey planned by the Lord, Genie, who was to be the newest member of our personal family, making it complete in a very special way. Franky and Genie became engaged in April and we had a family announcement dinner to celebrate it, and at the same time celebrated John's April birthday and Udo's March birthday which we had missed!! It was a very special family time of being alone together (a rare thing) and of welcoming Genie into our midst. Not a hard thing to do as we all love her. We telephoned Susan and Ran to include them before the evening was over.

May was the time of listening for the telephone or Udo's car on the back road. At 1:00 A.M. on the 21st, I ran up the back path to say "Goodbye, I'll be praying" to Udo and Debby as they left for the hospital, not any too soon!! At 3:50 A.M. little Samantha Abigail was born, a lovely little sister for Natasha. All went well, with the doctor commending Debby on how well she had cooperated in the natural childbirth method, and of course, Udo received all possible compliments in doing all the father is called upon to do in this which is a "together" experience with the father assisting. Seven pounds three ounces of beauty rapidly increasing now as the weeks go on!! While Debby was still in the hospital, Fran left for a time of speaking in Milan which was a most important time indeed to the Italian work, and to Dorothy and Hurvey.

It was a Thursday afternoon and I was at the Workers' meeting in Bourdonette, where we had had a good time of praying, discussing things and just being conscious of each other's existence (an important aspect of the Workers' meetings indeed, as we rarely see each other these days, each chalet being busy with its own overwhelming work). We had just finished, when Franky came running down the steep hill calling, "Come quickly, Mother! Grandmother has fallen and I think she has broken something." He had lifted her from the hall floor to the bed, covered her up, left someone with her, and then had come to get me. That was May 28th!!!

Doctor, ambulance, X-rays, hospital, telephone to Fran, two-hour operation the next morning! A leg broken in three places near the hip, some loose bone, a plate put in with seven screws and one long pin into the hip, all during a three-hour operation. Fran said he felt he should come straight back if there was a train he could get. There was, and Hurvey sadly drove him to it. Happily, he and Dot and Hurvey had had a few hours of worthwhile talking, but the cancellation of the lecture in the University of Milan was a great disappointment to them. Fran did get back after riding all night to meet me and see his mother before they rolled her into the operating room. She was still "awake" and wept with appreciation of his coming.

Then came days and days of "interrupted schedule" indeed!!! Grandmother does not speak or understand French. She is 89 years old and of course, she was confused by anesthesia, etc. At first, I stayed for more than 24 hours. This I did three times, but a schedule was worked out and many people took turns "staying with Grandmother" night and day. Franky stayed the hardest night, when she was hallucinating the most. Priscilla stayed two nights; Sylvia stayed many nights; Cynthia stayed some nights. People took turns during the days and evenings too. Kathie and Ann ran a sort of "taxi service" up and down to the hospital "changing the guard" day after day. It was a cooperation and sharing of burden which was a special thing to see. A "family life" includes babies and old age!!!

Grandmother is home now. We have rented a hospital bed and have some other equipment. Sylvia is giving much time to nursing, Veronica is giving therapy, and we have had some Farel House students who were nurses helping, and there is a schedule of people who have as part of their daily work certain hours of "responsibility for Grandmother." Of course, Fran and I are responsible during the nights and early mornings when we are home. I am expecting to move my office up to the little room which I have used as a storeroom as soon as Barry finds time to move a wall out to the end of the balcony to give three feet more length and a bit more light to the room. Then I can hear her when she calls as I am typing, rather than being two whole floors away.

In the midst of all this time, from May 28th's fall on, there was Franky's wedding to prepare for! The wedding dress had been designed by Franky and I had cut it out. But oh, when to make it??? Madame Marclay came to the rescue a few days before the "day," as she returned from a "mineral bath cure" to Champéry in time!!! Believe it or not, the actual sight of so many people sitting sewing and preparing in such a "family" sort of cooperation for a wedding, in the midst of the "Grandmother schedule" really impressed some of the boys. Yes, it was so often a boy, one after another of the 20th-century boys, who remarked to me what a fantastic thing it was to see people "sewing like that, making clothes for a wedding—" And the look in their eyes was most thoughtful. There is something very real about being creative, making bread that is necessary for food, making clothes that are important for an event. Creativity combining necessity and beauty blend together to add something far more than can be put into words. Barry's making tables and benches, shelves and cupboards and teaching others to help him; Susie's garden crew being taught their work by Tom or Susie, to produce food that is important to us as well as a beautiful thing to see when seeding and watering are finished; Birdie's knitting as she talks to people; Gini's sewing as she talks; Udo and Debby's garden and interior growing more beautiful with each year's additions; Pris and John's terrace that developed out of John's careful hard work of bringing home a large stone from each "day off hike"; Jane and Betty's raspberries and blackberries climbing over the fence loaded with food as well as beauty, and a multitude of other things. Yes, it makes a difference. And it would to *any* home, not just to L'Abri. "Family life" is a matter of doing creative things which are a blend of providing what is needed by the whole family, or some members of that family!!! This sort of thing cannot be "artificial" like some sort of cooked-up activity to amuse a child at play school. It needs to be a *real* part of life.

The wedding day dawned grey and rainy! But it was a beautiful day
for all of that, beautiful in a way that did not depend upon the weather.
The Ollon church, the one Farel had preached in to start the Reformation in this part of Switzerland, a 12th-century building, had been decorated by Tom and Rob Killam, partially the night before while we were
practicing. The early morning found Tom and Rob and a couple who
kindly drove me along with masses of daisies to the church to finish
decorating. Pat and several who spent their day off picking daisies had
gathered buckets full, so little bunches were tied to the end of each pew
as well as bouquets of them being arranged among the fern, moss, logs,
etc. which had been brought from the deep woods. This is our last family wedding, and it seemed fitting that Franky should want it where his
sisters had been married, in the Ollon church. For the first time in a long
time, the whole family was together. (Pris was not able to be present at
Susan's wedding as she and John were in America, and Sue and Ran
were not able to leave England for Debby's wedding.) As I sat on the end
of the front pew, you can perhaps imagine the emotion, the thankfulness for what the Lord has given us as a family, with Pris just behind me
with little John, then eight months old, quietly playing beside her;
Debby next with Natasha dressed as the other little girls, but not being
trusted to carry the train up the aisle with them, and tiny Samantha in
her carry-cot fast asleep. Next came Susan, who had arrived with Ran
and the children from London, although on June 6th, just exactly two
weeks before, Fiona Mary had been born in London's St. Thomas's Hospital. Now, smiling, Sue had beside her a similar carry-cot, with tiny
Fiona fast asleep! A glance to the front and I saw Fran, Franky, and Os
enter—Fran standing ready to perform the ceremony; Franky, the bridegroom, with Os as best man beside him. Then the girls were coming up
the aisle, each one brought in on the arm of one of Franky's brothers-in-
law. The dress was white pique of a special blend of threads, the high
neck was outlined with two rows of delicate eyelet embroidery threaded
with turquoise velvet ribbon. The full sleeves drew into a deep cuff
threaded with the same ribbon. A cape-train buttoned at the shoulders
and lined with turquoise gave a small outline of that color to the bride in
the straight white dress and gave a medieval look which fitted in with
the old church. Four little girls walked beautifully in spite of the floor-
length dresses (new to them) holding the train. The bride had a crown of
natural daisies in her long brown hair; daisies were the flowers in the
children's hair, the bridesmaids', and in the bouquets. Now as they
reached the front, Jane's beautiful song—"And Ruth said, 'Thy people
shall be my people, thy God my God—'" was an echo in our memory
through the years, as she sang it first for Priscilla and John now 13 years
ago, and then for Sue and Ran nine years ago, and then for Debby and
Udo six years ago!!! There was a completeness about the continuity as
she sang it before the processional. For our personal family, it was a tremendously together time, and a time of thanking God for our oneness in

*Our fourth child to declare, "With this ring I thee wed," in this
same Ollon twelfth-century church. Os Guinness, best man,
Franky, and Genie.*

Him. In a day of loss of communication, of splitting away from Christianity, of scattering, not geographically, but in ideas and philosophy, it was a tremendous moment for us.

Caramels thrown to the village children, friends to greet, all who were at L'Abri, and villagers from Huemoz and Ollon and friends from Villars too. A small family reception was provided for us by Genie's family, Mr. and Mrs. Stanley Walsh of San Mateo, California, in a restaurant in Caux. The Walshes couldn't be there, but were hosts in absentia.

Genie and Franky are back from their honeymoon now, and have their apartment on the ground floor of Mélèzes, which they are fixing up. Franky is going on with his studying of literature and art history and with his painting, sculpting, sketching, etc. In addressing them remember there are now three Mrs. Schaeffers with Grandmother here, so the new couple should be: "Mr. and Mrs. Francis A. Schaeffer V." . . .

Since the last letter, the Lord has closed the door to the first place in England in the country, and also to place number two! But a third place has turned up and has been visited several times by Sue and Ran and a person who feels led to purchase this place for L'Abri. The man I mentioned in my last letter decided against buying a place in England and has given a gift toward the new building in Huemoz instead. Now the Lord is opening up an entirely different place in England, but this time it seems that this is really "it." It is a 17th-century house with a Victorian wing, and needs lots of "fixing." It has no central heat, etc., but seems more like L'Abri than the more luxurious places! The Lord led the Members to ask Ranald and Susan if they would be willing to go to the country and commence the second L'Abri there, as He leads it to be (not trying to make a carbon copy of the first L'Abri). They felt led to say "yes." God has supplied a couple to care for the work of L'Abri at 52 Cleveland Road, in Ealing, London, which Ran and Sue will be leaving, as He led Dick and Mardi Keyes to apply after long prayer for guidance. Dick finished his seminary work this spring. Both Dick and Mardi have long been a part of the L'Abri Family. They arrived just yesterday in Huemoz!!! where they will spend some weeks or months (as the Lord leads) before going to England to commence their work there. This means their baby, due August 29th, can be born in the Samaritan Hospital in Vevey (Lord willing), and that Mardi can have some time to "catch her breath" before starting in England. The new English L'Abri then would open, Lord willing, and in God's chosen time, with Ranald and Susan, and Cynthia. All are Members and could have their own Members' meetings for the decisions before them. Cynthia will soon be marrying Korean Kim and Kim will be a Helper, and also the first Farel House student there!!! It is all very amazing to us. After all, for years we ran all of L'Abri with less than, or no more than, five Members. (Now we have seven in Huemoz and three in England, two in Italy, two in Holland, and one in America.) Surely the Lord has prepared the *time*, the *place*, and the *staff* to begin that which He sees is ahead. We wait to see! . . .

In Huemoz, the commune has let us know that they expect us to build a building, and that their only requirement before we commence is that we provide a parking lot, actually build one. Betty Carlson offered a piece of her land to make this parking lot, and at present, Monsieur Barachi of the village is supposed to be making plans and getting the practical arrangements made to go ahead and build that parking lot, which involves digging on one side, filling in on the other, and making walls. After that, as far as we know, the next step is to go ahead and start digging for the building!! The Members have decided to go only as far as our money allows, and not to go into debt.

Lord willing, we expect to have the *first* L'Abri Conference in America, for some who may not be able to get into Huemoz L'Abri. It will be held at *Covenant College, Lookout Mountain, Tennessee,* March 12 to 22, 1971. Do pray that the Lord will cause it to be a time of reaching the ones who *need* L'Abri and not to be a time of just "conference goers" having another one to go to.

Much love in *Him* Who can continue to *direct* His work when it is any size and at any point in history,

EDITH

December 1, 1970   Huemoz sur Ollon, Switzerland

Dear Family:

What do I mean, "family"? That's a good question. This really *is* written to the family. It is not a book, not an article, not a devotional pamphlet, not a perfected piece of writing, just a letter to the *family*. It started out 22 years ago being a letter to my mother and father, sisters (Janet and Elsa) and their husbands and children. Then Mother laboriously copied it and later, my sister copied it with carbons. It went into a second stage later on of being mimeographed and now it is printed. Did the family grow? At first I thought of everyone outside my personal family as people "reading over the family's shoulders." But, as L'Abri began and people were born again in Huemoz, the reality of a growing L'Abri Family began to take place. . . . So the "family" really includes all those who are deeply involved because the Lord has chosen to put us together in this special way in a work which *He* has brought forth to meet something of the 20th century need. . . .

This is what the Family Letter is all about—It is primarily for the "family involved together in something," not for observers looking on from the outside.

Our "working together" may mean we are isolated as Mother MacMullen in Nova Scotia on a chicken farm, or it may mean packaging tapes in a basement office and sending them to "names" of unseen people, like Bill and Jane Wysor are doing. . . . It may mean earning enough to live on by doing hairdressing and then working like mad to send out receipts, write letters, send out tapes, and talk to people, as well as being a "L'Abri" for those who are in that area and are homesick for L'Abri, as Claire is; or opening one's home for tape listening, and one's time for conversations and teaching, such as John and Alma Hoyte are doing. These and so many others are the ones I think of when I say, "Dear Family," with the realization that there is a need to give *something* of the picture of what is taking place in order to be fair. Fair? Well, in Deuteronomy there is a passage that clearly states that parents are to *declare* the works of the Lord unto their *children*. They are to *make known* what God has done. This element is included in keeping in contact with the *family*. The hewers of wood and carriers of the water, the ones "staying by the goods," all have a part in the total work of the family.

We are, Lord willing, going to have two days of fasting and prayer, tomorrow and next day, as L'Abri in Switzerland faces a moment of special crisis. We are going through a time when it seems a three-pronged fork is digging at the very roots of L'Abri's existence here in Huemoz, and yet a time during which the Lord has been working in lives in a most marvelous way. While the physical existence is being threatened, the spiritual reality of the work of the Holy Spirit is more evident than ever. As the number of people here is being questioned, and the space seems to be "shrinking," the arrival of the most sincerely seeking and earnestly eager "unexpected" ones seems to be increasing. Human wisdom would certainly be inadequate to come up with a solution. How thankful we are that we can take time to pray, and that we can look forward to God's answers and solutions!

While Fran and I were on our hiking holiday in October with packs on our backs, and our boots for transportation, with the freedom of stopping for the night when we felt too tired, and the satisfaction of doing 90 miles in six days, we heard of the first "prong." Pris and John told us on the phone that four men had arrived with measuring tapes; apologized for disturbing the households, but measured the exact cubic meter measure of each chalet in L'Abri. It obviously had not been their idea to do this. It became clear that it was not even the "commune" who had instigated the measuring. Someone had demanded that the measure be made to see if we exceeded the number allowed in each sleeping room by law. There is an exact measure stated in law books. This measure is enforced when new buildings are being built but there are many buildings, homes, workmen's dwellings, schools, children's pensions, etc., which have never been forced into the exact measure. The letter of the law is *not* enforced in this area. However, it is a perfect area for "complaining," and when the council is the recipient of a complaint, it has a duty to investigate. It reminds one of the king in Daniel's time who *had* to keep "the law" in throwing Daniel into the lions' den when the enemies of Daniel and of God pointed out "the law" and pointed to Daniel's morning, evening, and noontime praying. The king had to keep the law, but he was delighted when he discovered that Daniel's God was able to protect him from the lions. Remember that not only was Daniel released unharmed, but "Then king Darius wrote unto all people, nations, and languages, that dwell in all the earth; . . . I make a decree, That in every dominion of my kingdom men tremble and fear before the God of Daniel: for he is the living God, and steadfast for ever, and his kingdom that which shall not be destroyed, and his dominion shall be even unto the end. He delivereth and rescueth, and he worketh signs and wonders in heaven, and in earth, who hath delivered Daniel from the power of the lions."* Note this carefully, Daniel's being thrown to the lions resulted in the greatest evangelistic message of truth being sent out in that period of history. Did God let the non-Jews know of *His* existence in Old Testament times? Well, *all* people, all nations, all language groups heard at that time that Daniel's God *is* the living God, and that He has all power demonstrated in His protecting Daniel. What a worthwhile and fantastic result! Asking for God's will involves allowing God to unfold His will according to His perfect knowledge and plan, *not* asking *Him* to fit His will into our preconceived plan. It may seem strange when one is surrounded by lions, or in a fiery furnace, that *this* is

*Daniel 6.

His way of making Himself known to thousands of men who know Him not. One imagines freedom from difficulties, release from hindrances, an atmosphere of peace in which to work, to be the expected thing in order to "do the Lord's work." But God has used a tremendous variety of difficult situations in which to demonstrate to men of various generations that He indeed *is God*.

The immediate result of measuring the chalets was sending a letter to L'Abri from the Commune, stating that such and such number of people could be in each chalet naming the chalets and giving the number next to the name. The total number given is 62 persons. That 62 includes L'Abri Members, Workers, Helpers, students, guests, *and the babies of the Workers and Members, Helpers, students, and guests!* So *if* this is enforced literally, it means that each baby that is born will send one more person away from L'Abri, each child already in our families counts as one, and each couple wanting to come with a child is asking that their child be here in place of some seeking soul wanting to come. At present, we have in Huemoz about twenty Members, Workers, and Helpers.

Now, dear family, let me be sure you understand the immediate implication of that letter. Let me say we did not "ignore" it without seeking advice. Swiss people with authority and standing have advised us *not* to send any young people away *yet*. We would have had to send about 30 people away, and we would have had to cancel many, many, many reservations (and of course, may have to yet) immediately, affecting people signed up for this winter, spring, next summer, and fall.

There are *two possibilities* of meeting this problem:

1. We could be given a special category in which the fifteen cubic meter measure would not apply to us. Such categories do exist, as exceptions *are* made, everyone sleeping in Switzerland does not by any means have that amount of space.
2. We could have the new building built, and perhaps another chalet added, which would give us space for the number we now have or a few less, and each one would then *have* the needed cubic meter space.

One can easily imagine that God will use this to *give* more space because more space per person would very, very much help the Members, Workers, and Helpers in L'Abri by giving more privacy and less crowded conditions. Those of us here permanently have to face the crowdedness in our homes month after month and year after year. Giving more space, regulated not by our decision to demand less "sacrifice," but by regulation imposed upon us, could be a blessing. However, to care for the same number of people with more space would require the means to build, "to repair the walls" so to speak, to add to what we have now. God is *able* to multiply houses as well as food.

The phone rang again, toward the end of our vacation, bringing Udo's voice as he apologized for bothering us, but felt we ought to know that another blow had come which might need immediate attention. A letter had come from the Commune giving us the signed and sealed *permit to build*, which we had long been waiting for. The day after the arrival of the long prayed-for and awaited permit, a letter came from the police who have charge of all complaints concerning construction in the Canton, a higher council than the Commune. This letter informed us that another "opposition" had been made to our building by the same man. In other words, the man objecting had gone over the heads of the communal council to continue his opposition. Udo felt we might want to talk to someone immediately about this. *He was right!*

Conversation with a couple of people whom the Lord provided at just the right time and with just the right information showed us that one of two things could meet his new problem:

1. The opposition could prove to be not valid and therefore, the building go on.
2. There could be the possibility of another site opening up.

Again, dear family, it is important that you understand just *what* this building means. In the light of the crowdedness of L'Abri right now, and in the light of the fatigue and difficulties under which the Workers work, the new building does *not* mean more people to be added. It *does* mean that it is imperative to have it to continue the work being done *now*.

What does it consist of in the architectural plans? A first floor which will have a larger room than the present Farel House to be equipped with desks and tape recorders to take care of the total number of Farel House students during their study hours, that is, the present total!

What, you may ask, will the present Farel House be used for? Please understand that right now we have *no* place for tape listening on the part of guests except the dining rooms of the chalets. It means that housekeepers, *when* their living rooms are being used, have to wait to set the table until the last minute for a meal. Veronica nearly went out of her mind feeding 20 to 25 people in the same room, too small for even that, which was full of people listening to a tape all day all this summer. Add to that frustration, the strain of always listening to the *voice* on the tape day after day, as a background noise to housework and conversation with Helpers! Yes, the present Farel House, *plus* as much other space as possible, is needed for tape listening and for conversations and places to study, removed from the chalet dining/living rooms (*no* one has a separate living room).

The first floor will then have a Farel House, library, an office, and an entrance hall and toilets. It will also have one bedroom for four people, a laundry, and a furnace room.

The second floor will have a dining room and a living room which can be thrown into one when needed, at such times when it would be good to have the entire Huemoz family together for a meal such as Saturday night supper, or Sunday high tea, or New Year's Eve, etc. It will also have a kitchen, larger than our other chalet kitchens which can handle larger meals, as well as the normal-sized daily meals.

The third floor will have a few single and double bedrooms, two bathrooms, and toilet and washbasin rooms. There will be an attic above this floor for storage, etc.

Fastened on to this as a wing will be a two-storied separate house for the house father and mother, with their own family of children, having some privacy, yet being in the midst of things.

As soon as this building becomes a reality, the other chalets will be able to "breathe" a bit as each chalet will have fewer people, either sleeping or coming and going, or listening to tapes in the dining rooms, or using the telephones, or doing laundry, or coming in for baths, etc. The building will mean much to each Member and Worker in removing a certain amount of month-in, month-out confusion, Lord willing.

If we need to keep to the 15 cubic meter space, having this building and the chalets we now have will give us a total of about 84 people, with enough study space for a few more living in village homes where there are rooms for rent.

Within the same week another document arrived from the police. This one was in the form of a "fine" for Fran, and for Bettina. Why? Well, please listen carefully, dear family. You must know *clearly*, or you won't understand the position we are now in.

Ever since L'Abri started, there has been someone in the department of the police caring for strangers (foreigners) in the Canton who has understood L'Abri. When the first man, who understood our work and our living "by faith" without a salary, retired, the man to take his place very graciously, and with real interest, listened to the whole L'Abri story and said he was going to personally take care of the living permits of Workers and Helpers who would be staying longer than the three months allowed to tourists. He said, "You people do not work for a salary. You are benevolent aids. You are volunteers. You must *not* apply for work permits because you simply do not fit that category."

Work permits to work in Switzerland are considered not only from the viewpoint of the desirability and need of that person to be in Switzerland, but also from the viewpoint of the job meeting the minimum wage law and so on. When Birdie's permit was refused, it was because it got into the "regular channels" by mistake, and as a New Zealand fully qualified nurse and psychiatric social worker, she was classified as needing a certain salary. And in addition to that, the decision was made that Switzerland did not need such a person, so came the refusal. It was when the man who really understood L'Abri entered into the situation, that the matter was cleared up, and L'Abri continued to have Birdie as one of our Workers on the same basis as all our Workers. None of us has a work permit, and none of us would be classified as specialized in any field because we are "volunteers." We are living on the basis of prayer. We receive very little money, asking that God will use our lives and this work as a demonstration of His existence. The word "volunteer" really fits, I think, as we have volunteered to have God use us as a demonstration that He is there, that He can communicate His guidance to us, and that He can supply our needs!

When a policeman came to the office door one day in Mélèzes and asked Bettina what she was doing, she replied, without thinking, "I am Dr. Schaeffer's secretary." As a matter of fact, she was a Farel House student at that time, and working in the office as her half day of helping. However, the police jotted down her reply, and in due course, the fine came, a fine to Bettina for working without a permit, and fine to Dr. Schaeffer for "hiring" a secretary. John picked up the phone to call the man who understands. "M. is in the hospital undergoing an operation," was the reply. The "boss" was *not* inclined toward L'Abri, and in addition to that, "someone" (probably the same someone in all cases) had gone to this person, and other people too, saying very false things about L'Abri, and stirring up opposition.

Hence the word came through, "You all have to have work permits." We could not continue if we all had to have minimum wages based on our education and qualifications!! L'Abri has been a sacrificial work. God has supplied our needs but we have seen Him develop the work and accomplish all He has accomplished through this place through the years on a "shoestring."

Comfort came in the words of Isaiah 49:23b and 50:7 " . . . and thou shalt know that I am the Lord: for they shall not be ashamed that wait for me. . . . For the Lord God will help me; therefore shall I not be confounded: therefore have I set my face like a flint, and I know that I shall not be ashamed." Satan tries hard to cause each of us fear, to draw back, to be discouraged, to drop into a depression, to doubt. It is a battle. The "peace" that passes understanding, passes our *own* understanding because it is given in the midst of battle. There will be an understandable peace when we are removed from the battlefield.

The day we came back from our vacation, I ran up the back road, up the angled path leading to the field where my favorite stone for "prayer-quiet" is, and along the path to Colonel Matile's chalet. Colonel Matile is a retired Swiss army colonel whose lovely chalet and hillside garden is above us on the mountainside. Switzerland does not have generals in its army; in any other country he would have had the rank of general. He and his wife live a healthy life of gardening, skiing, mountain walking, as well as taking their place in many portions of church and government life in this area. Their daughter and her husband are missionaries in Africa, and while on furlough, their little grandchild became a close friend of Elizabee Sandri's. The deep snow this day was sparkling in the sunshine, and as I neared the chalet, I saw the most elegant snowman, complete with eyes and mouth, and only a few finishing touches to be made. The laughing, happy grandchildren of the colonel were eagerly completing their work with their father as I greeted them in running past. Once in the living room, I related our troubles, asking for advice and help. . . .

Was it just a coincidence that the colonel's son and daughter-in-law, who had been a friend of Susan's years ago when Susan and Ranald were in Beau Site, were visiting their parents at this time? It certainly was not *our* planning that brought them there. Before the next two days were over, several things had happened to show that God was working. One of the most wonderful things was that as John and I visited again the next day, drinking tea and talking with the Matiles, the colonel's son said, "Do you know I am a lawyer and will represent L'Abri in all these things? I will study the matter and help you all I can." What we discovered later is that M. Matile is not only a very fine lawyer, but he is also the Mayor of Morges, one of the youngest mayors in Switzerland, and of an important city.

M. Chessex, a Notaire in Montreux, has long been helping L'Abri with legal matters. Without his help, we could not have gotten through the years. The Chessexes have long had contact with L'Abri. Now, as a meeting approached to be held December 3rd in Lausanne, three men prepared to go to represent L'Abri and explain what L'Abri is, along with John who had to be present to answer any detailed questions. The meeting was to be with the heads of departments, the Chief of the Department of Justice, etc. . . .

And the report? The result?

A high pitch of expectancy—and a flat report—in essence, "no conclusions."

There is a tremendous need for continued prayer. We must wait to see about the possibility of L'Abri's being put in a "category" which would give a more true picture of what we are. . . .

As we have prayed for space, it seems to us that what has come in answer has been *more* people. One Saturday night I prayed and prayed concerning the space, and the answer seemed to come in a constant remembrance of the disciples saying to Jesus, "Send the multitude away," and Jesus' answer, "they need not depart: give *ye* them to eat." This has come to mind before; now it seemed an even stronger word. "But, Lord," I prayed on, "there was the boy's lunch to be multiplied. Please give as a sign, a boy with his lunch, his sacrificial gift, to be multiplied." The next day a boy came to my office asking to use the telephone for a call to his parents. In discussing his call, and praying about it ahead of time, he told of his desire to leave early in order that his bed might be free for someone else, and also said he desired to give up his long-wanted trip around the world in order that the money could be used for the new building. I was amazed! It seemed so clearly the answer to the prayer of the night before. How is the Lord going to multiply space? We don't know. But we do see something of the beginning.

The English country house, that 17th-century one which needs so many repairs, plumbing, heat, etc., will be occupied by Sue and Ran,

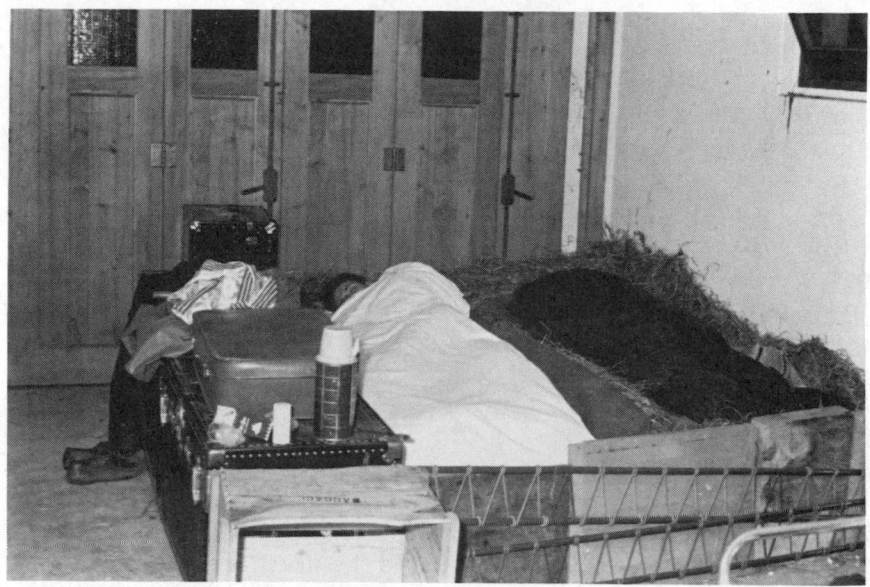

One way of creating more beds you see here! Temporary extra "beds" are made with board boxes and straw in the garage of Chalet Bethany.

Cynthia and Kim, by January 6th, Lord willing. However, it will take time for repairs and preparation. At the present time there would not be pots and pans, dishes and silver, sheets and blankets enough to start a L'Abri, let alone the plumbing, electrical repairs, etc. So please don't deluge the English L'Abri with requests to come, not yet.

At the same time as papers were being signed in England, L'Abri in Holland was being given clear leading as to the right place. A farmhouse on four acres of land with orchards and gardens, surrounded by an old moat, near the Rhine River, and about one and three-quarters hours from Amsterdam, seemed just the right place to the Rookmaakers and the others. A group of Dutch people who call themselves the "Friends of L'Abri" in Holland has gathered a certain amount of money. Then a man felt led to loan, without interest, a large sum payable in ten years. A young fellow who had a rather large amount of money felt strongly that he should use it to purchase the apple orchard (part of the land around the farm) and the apples would bring him in some needed income, while the land would be saved for L'Abri to buy at a later date, preventing someone's buying and building there. The three amounts of money put together are exactly the price of the house and land, and there will be no need to have a mortgage and no interest to pay. It all came so quickly and fitted together so amazingly, that Fran went flying off to meet with the Dutch L'Abri so that the final arrangements could be made without waiting. In just this period of time, two things happened: Hans and Joanne Van Seventer became sure that God was showing them that they should be "the couple" for this new work, and Wim and Greta Rietkirk accepted a call to a church nearby, so that they will be able to help out. Dr. Rookmaaker and Anky expect to be able to go out to the country L'Abri during the weekend, to help with conversation or lectures. The expected date of occupation is sometime in mid-February, Lord willing.

As I am writing this letter, a conference is going on in Florence, Italy. Hurvey has been working among university students, as well as being pastor of the Italian congregation of our International Church in Milan, and as well as working with young boys and a multitude of things. This conference is for Italian university students and there are over 60 of them there. Fran and Os have gone down to lecture and hold discussions. Fran's lectures are being given *in* the museums as they walk from room to room, and he gives a history of the Renaissance period of art, and what it means in the understanding of the birth of modern man.

It was about the 18th of August when Mardi, prepared by Pris and Debby, calmly announced that perhaps she was going to have a baby that day. Udo, in his Citroen (known as the *deux chevaux*—two horsepower) which has taken the trip to the *maternite* for many a mother, not only drove Dick and Mardi down the mountainside, but waited to drive Dick back up! Yes, it was only a little over an hour when Christopher made his entrance into the world and let his father go back up the hill! What a thoughtful child! Dick and Mardi had only a short time to spend in preparation for going into the work in England, so it was good that the baby came so easily and was so well.

Three people were walking along a London street on August 20th. Two were boys with shoulder-length, curly hair and long beards, dressed in garments of white resembling Indian garments. One was the wife of one of these, long, straight, beautiful brown hair, and an earnest, sweetly serious face. A young Englishman walked up to them, "Are you lost?" was his question. "No," came the reply, "But we are looking for such and such vegetarian restaurant." "I can take you there," came his reply. And so they walked along together, talking. The conversation was in a serious area concerning the meaning of life, and the fellow said, "I found Truth to be Christianity when I was in a little place in Switzerland called Huemoz." And he went on to tell about L'Abri. As the three sat down to eat and talk, they looked up a while later to discover that their guide to the restaurant had returned with a book. "Here is a book for you to read, and if you are interested in going, I have written the address of that place in Switzerland for you." The book was *The God Who Is There,* and the address of L'Abri was inside the cover. It was in October that I returned from Lausanne one day to hurry up to Mélèzes to do my next "thing" when I noticed Franky sitting on the grass talking to three long-haired people with back packs beside them. "I wonder who they might be," I thought. "We'll have to put them on the floor, if they stay."

It was Veronica and Barry Seagren who generously offered to fix up space on the library floor for the couple, and the single fellow was fitted in elsewhere. Veronica and Barry have so often had the added strain of people sleeping on the floor, with bedding that needs to be put someplace in the daytime. Repairing broken tape recorders, building shelves, cupboards, pushing out walls to change rooms and teaching fellows to do carpentry in the shop, giving very little time to prepare sermons or Bible studies, added to the work of running a house which is as overcrowded and inconvenient to run as Beau Site is not exactly what a top physicist with mathematical genius expected to be doing as he took honors at the university, nor even what he might have expected as he left Huntsville and the space program where he was working, to go to seminary and prepare for Christian work. Yet the Lord needs His children not to be just "willing" for the imaginary sacrifices of concentration camp, floods, or persecutions, but to actually *be willing* in day-by-day life for the mundane drudge of the kind of unglorious sacrifice of *not* setting up an ideal schedule time-wise, or as to the use of the house, which is a rigid unbreakable ideal. God alone is the One to set the standards, and to direct the days and weeks, one at a time!

Who are the three who were given space? A Jewish couple who were searching for meaning in life, searching for answers, expecting to find them in India where they were headed to study Yoga under holy men, and their friend from a Christian background, searching also. And now? These two dear children of Abraham in physical line stretching back through the centuries, are now also spiritual children of Abraham. With tremendously fresh excitement and eagerness, these two have asked questions, studied, listened, and on Thanksgiving evening, during the very Spirit-filled time when people were spontaneously telling of the things for which they were thankful, one on one side of the room and his wife on the other, inwardly bowed and silently accepted Christ as their Messiah. It was only afterwards that they discovered the timing of this in which they are so one. Together they went to Birdie to pray with her afterwards. Together they came to tell us after that. Such joy in heaven took place as these lost sheep of Israel came into the fold! (No, that is not poetic fancy; the Bible says so!) And such joy in L'Abri as the Lord gave us the encouragement of His promises kept—"If with all thine heart ye truly seek me, ye shall surely find me." These two are a joy to us all, and an encouragement. Soon they'll be spending their first Christmas. . . .

As we come to Christmas and the New Year, may each of us ask God to bring us to a place of honesty before His face in *really* saying, "Here I am, O God. Take me and use me," without preconceived limits and barriers.

With much love in the God of Abraham, Isaac, Jacob, of Paul, Peter, John, of history—past history, and our present history, of eternity—

EDITH

1971

May 1, 1971   Huemoz sur Ollon, Switzerland

Dear Family:

Thank God we are not limited to communication only with other limited, finite beings all thrown up into existence by a roulette wheel in a chance universe! Thank God we can not only know *about* Him, but we can know *Him* personally, and be in personal communication with Him now and forever!

For the past five months you have been praying, and we have been praying. What has happened? You remember that there was "opposition" against our building on the land L'Abri owned. A fantastic answer to prayer came, as we prayed for God's solution to this, when a doctor and his wife way off in Indiana, looked at the map of Huemoz in the front of the book, *L'Abri* and decided to come over to buy the plot of land marked "For Sale," just above the chapel. They had prayed for months and he had not taken a vacation for three years!! The very *day* they arrived to sit in our bedroom talking about this to us was the *day* we had been told it would be a good thing if we could exchange the L'Abri plot of land for that plot and ask permission to build on *that* plot instead. Their reply to this information was, "Now we know why God led us to come here at *this* time. Of course we'll buy this piece and exchange with you." In quick succession the sale went through, the land was measured and the building was found to fit with no further changes. The young lawyer (Mayor Matile of Morges) made application for us for a permit to build there and the day arrived when the good news came that we now had permission to build!!! All this, we do not believe, happened "by chance," but we do believe it was the Lord's solution for which you and we have been praying. Another piece of information came to us soon after this permit question was settled, and that was that we are faced with a decision: to build, or to cut down the numbers to 62. In other words, we are allowed to remain crowded until the building is complete, *if* we begin to build this spring. If we do not build, then we must send people away soon.

Whom would we send away if we had to send 48 people away, or even 30?? We'd have to send away some Workers, Helpers, students, and guests and we'd have to cancel many who are "signed up" for months ahead.

Before we voted on the question to take the step of faith, putting our "feet in Jordan"* to build or not to build, we listened to Debby and Udo read a letter to us that had just come that day from a European girl asking to come.

We silently wept. We prayed. We *voted* to have John take the next steps toward getting the building started as soon as possible, praying that the Lord will supply each need as we go along. He is now getting all the estimates (or "bids") in for the work, and seeing about a mortgage. Do pray with us that the Lord will continue to give us clear signs of His leading as we go along, that we may not go ahead of Him, nor lag behind.

Did just that *one* letter cause us to make such a *huge* decision? There are letters every day. Some days there are five letters asking to come; sometimes 25.

What am I trying to make clear? The fact that I do believe that there is answered prayer, and continuity taking place in such a way that we can *observe* the reality of God's work in response to our "asking," and God's work in weaving the details of lives and circumstances together to bring forth His purpose in *history* for which He brought L'Abri into existence. We have a tremendous responsibility to pray with faith believing that He is able to open locked doors, providing more space and material provision for the increasing numbers of people He is sending. . . .

By faith the work in Greatham Manor, Greatham, England, was started late in January, and Fran and I were there to be present at the dedication in February. People whom they felt they could just *not* turn away began arriving before the plumbing, wiring, repairing of floors, digging of drain pipes, painting, etc. had been more than started, and people were born again there (and still are being) before there were enough cups and saucers, silverware, sheets, and blankets, desks, and tape recorders, furniture, etc., etc. Farel House has *started* in the midst of the chaos of trying to repair and settle in, rather than after a tidy preparation of empty rooms and desks!

We planted a tree as part of the dedication time at the edge of a wide lawn overlooking rolling pasture lands. Seeds have been carefully patted in as vegetable gardens are being prepared in the walled-in garden section on another side of the house. A sudden, unplanned rush of beginning? No. One sees the wonder of answered prayer, years of prayer as to the right place, the right house, the right time for starting an En-

*Joshua 3:9–17.

glish L'Abri in the country, and God's clear answer as He showed why certain places were *not* His choice and why this place *was,* and he put it into the heart of the person of His choice to buy *this* one for L'Abri. The wonder of His clear answer as to a couple plus another Worker to take over the work in Ealing, opening the way for Ran and Sue to leave there. Tremendous continuity as Dick and Mardi were brought into L'Abri years ago, first Dick and then Mardi, and then their time of preparation together. Tremendous continuity as Susie Clark was brought to L'Abri, also from Wellesley, where she knew Mardi. Tremendous continuity as Cynthia and Kim entered the work in Greatham, Cynthia as a long–time L'Abri Member with years of experience in Huemoz as well as London, Kim to be a student, but to bring his skill in woodwork as his great contribution to making bookcases and paneling walls. Seeds in a garden for future peas, carrots, and lettuce, planted by *someone* knowing what she or he is doing; houses, lands, Workers, springing up from seeds *God* has planted and has been caring for in *years* of growth and preparation; a continuity that can be traced with enough understanding to be staggering, exciting, satisfying. Who was one of the first Farel House students to come to Greatham? Someone from Australia. Where did he hear of L'Abri? In India where he had gone to seek answers in Indian philosophy and where an Indian had introduced him to "Schaeffer's books"!!! From India he came to England to discover Greatham and to become not only one of the first Farel House students there, but one of the first converts. Chance? Another was born in Kenya and was studying oriental languages, a Buddhist with properly shaved head. He, too, became one of the first Farel House students in Greatham and one of the first to be born again. The dedication day wove an amazing number of "threads" together as people from many parts of England, many periods of L'Abri history, many different backgrounds came together, in spite of a postal strike (no announcements of the event) and grey rain. And another demonstration of continuity came when at the yearly meeting Jerram and Vicky Barrs applied to be Workers in Greatham. Jerram was a Worker in Huemoz when he met Vicky who, also a Worker, was then Fran's secretary. Since their marriage, Jerram has been a student at Covenant, and Vicky has taught French. Jerram's elderly father, for whom we have long prayed, lives along with Jerram's mother on a farm not far from Greatham. Is it a chance detail: That prayer for the right Workers, and prayer that Jerram might be a help spiritually to his father is being answered in the *location* of Greatham, as well as in the Lord's direction to this couple in this moment of their history *and* L'Abri history? Our God is a God of continuity—how exciting to be a part of that continuity and to catch glimpses of the *extent* of it all!

By faith in Holland the Members and Workers of Dutch L'Abri prayed through months and years for the right place and time to start a country L'Abri there and took the step of starting, also by faith, that the Lord would supply daily needs. Eck-en-weil is the name of the village about an hour and a quarter's drive from Amsterdam where a house stands, surrounded by apple orchards which are being pruned by L'Abri Helpers right now! If one could tell the whole story in detail, it would include many threads of circumstances and lives woven together in a way wherein there is obvious continuity. Equipment in the way of tape recorders, furniture, etc., is being prayed for, but the *work* has *begun!* And Wim and Greta Rietkirk felt led to help in Eck-en-weil full time. Nick and Minna Corneliesse are in Amsterdam where Nick is doing graduate work in the University, and they are to be Dutch L'Abri Workers in Amsterdam. . . .

Dr. Hans and his wife, Anky, Rookmaaker were two of the first people we met in Holland in 1948. They were engaged to be married at that time. In fact, since it was right after the war and rationing included things like sheets and towels, we were able to help them have a proper supply of sheets and towels, etc., as we brought them from America. Little did we dream then that there would ever be a L'Abri, let alone a Dutch L'Abri. Little did we dream that the Lord was preparing to draw us together in a work that was going to be "tiny," yet international, that was going to be an opportunity to see a reality of a demonstration of His existence as we took Him at His Word, becoming "buried grain" and seeing *Him* bring forth something fantastic in the way of a continued harvest. . . .

By faith a new step was taken during these same weeks in France. Where is there any continuity or assurance of guidance in that? It was Pris who had prayed for a long time that rather than pushing aside the possibility of caring for any more people at all in Huemoz, we might have a place over the border of Switzerland into France, just the other side of the lake. One can drive to the border in less than forty minutes, and there are villages and towns by the lake, or up on a plateau above. Several things came together all in one week this winter indicating that her prayer was being answered. Juanita, who had worked a number of years in a French mission, and had often brought French young people to L'Abri for help, had just finished three months as a Farel House student. She had a great burden for doing a L'Abri-type work with French young people. Within a very short time, a number of things had happened in quick succession. Juanita found a house with two apartments in it in a charming village right under a mountain ski resort near Evian, France, across the lake from Lausanne, and only about an hour and fifteen minutes' drive from Huemoz. There will be room for twenty to sleep over there, but it has been started with just a few. The few students over there are listening to tapes as they do Farel House studies there, are discussing and asking questions at meals, are helping in washing sheets, etc., at the village "fountain" and cleaning the house, peeling potatoes, etc. and they all come over all day Thursday for the seminar in the morning and the lecture at night, and all day Sunday. The next step before having more people over there will be the purchase of a Volkswagen bus, or something of that size, to bring more over. The work is an extension of the Huemoz work. We do not intend to exceed the number of 110 here in Huemoz, but this will give a bit more space, yet be close enough to be part of Huemoz. The time may come when the work in France will be partly in French and partly in English, just as in Holland right now some of the lectures and conversations are in Dutch and some in English . . .

What happened in America? Some of you know that among other things, we went to look at properties which were offered to L'Abri. Fran spoke in Dallas, Texas, for a series of lectures and because of the number of people coming, it was impossible to hold these in the Seminary. Over 2,000 people came each morning at 10:45 to hear such subjects as Epistemology, etc., in a series called "He is There and He is Not Silent."* Really amazing interest. . . . We, Fran and I, went on to Tulsa, Oklahoma, where we each spoke. Meantime, Os and Udo were in Harvard and other colleges, marveling at the growth in fellows who had been born again in Switzerland and are touching the lives of so many others. We spent a week in St. Louis where Fran gave the series of lectures he goes for every other year at Covenant Seminary, and then we went to California. And then we all, Debby and Udo, Fran and I, converged on Lookout Mountain, Tennessee! . . .

In California on a highway near Santa Cruz is a property which has been cared for tenderly by a man and his wife who bought it many years ago and built a chapel, open for travelers to stop in. They prayed it might be a mission to people driving past and called it "Wayside Chapel." This man built with his own hands two little houses on the property and cleared wonderful walking paths through the wooded mountainside. After reading the book *L'Abri*, they felt this might be used in the work somehow. While Fran and I, Claire Olsen, John and Alma Hoyte, and Mr. Webb, the owner, walked through these mountain paths, reminding us so much of the path through the woods from Pannex down to Aigle, it occurred to me that this would be a wonderful place for L'Abri Helpers and Workers and other L'Abri people to come for a Day of Prayer, or a day of listening to tapes, or Bible study. No need to do anything big, no need to make a huge decision to "start" a permanent work or an "American L'Abri," this property could be used as a place to get away for quiet and prayer or conversation for two or three, or twenty or thirty. I mentioned this to Claire and the Hoytes as we were walking, but after we went back to the Webbs' home, and sat in a circle to talk, Mr. Webb (without having heard what I had suggested) said he had a suggestion to make. "Let's put out a 'fleece' asking the Lord to give us a sign," he said. "Let's have you use this place for a time, for a day or a weekend, and we'll see what develops later." And so, without any cataclysmic decision, what has taken place is that, in simple fact, a lovely

*Later to be published by Tyndale House, in 1972, as a book with the same title.

"away-from-the-city" mountain place to think, study, pray, walk, within 15 minutes' drive from Claire's house in Menlo Park, is now available for L'Abri Workers and Helpers and friends to use, *and* the Webbs *and* we will pray that the Lord will really use this ground to His glory in ways we cannot yet know about! . . .

Now about the first L'Abri conference to be held in America, at Covenant College, we were interested as anyone as to what would happen and who would come. There was no formal advertising; an announcement was made in this Family Letter, and some very simple mimeographed application forms were sent out with personal letters. Everyone was curious as to who and how many would come. The lectures covered a wide variety of subjects—the total impact was one of giving an understanding of the 20th–century dilemma and the Christian answer. There were two classical concerts given by the L'Abri Ensemble and one concert in which many people took part. It really was great, and the closest thing to having a small number of people sharing an evening together that one could possibly have with 800!!

It was not perfect, but some girls and fellows will go back to very drastically difficult college-dorm situations with courage to stand against the "rapids" in the river as they struggle upstream, often alone, or with only ones and twos with them! It was not perfect, but it means that 800 did have a touch with L'Abri during those days when we are facing having to cut down in Huemoz or build, when we are excited about new space in England and Holland and France, but when in each of these places, we are talking in terms of "twenties" and not "hundreds.". . .

Three thousand cassettes were made of the lectures and carried away, so one hopes these are clear enough to reproduce the content for many people. Your questions, "When will there be another one" has no answer at present. We simply pray that the Lord will show us when.

And what happened in Huemoz during our absence? John and Pris were in charge of the work and all the Workers pitched in and cared for lectures, Bible studies, sermons on Sunday mornings, mealtime discussions, and endless details—as well as endless personal discussions, and personal counseling and help. Of course, the cooking of meals and carrying out of the physical work of gardens, chickens, carpentry, tape recorder repair, marketing and various kinds of letter writing and office work, reading of mail, etc., continued day after day. Always there are new people to be greeted and cared for and constantly there are new "situations" arising. . . .

Do all come from non-Christian backgrounds? No. Elaine came from a Christian home, but told me the other day, halfway up and halfway down the stairs as we met, "A year ago I didn't know L'Abri existed, and I had come to the conclusion that from everything I had heard, there was no intellectual base for believing Christianity to be true, and this being so, I could see no logical conclusion to life except suicide. Nothing else made sense. Amazingly, my mother brought home a copy of the book *L'Abri* just a month later, though she did not know anything about it. She just bought it in a bookstore. Reading the book changed everything. I wrote asking to come, and was accepted, and came very soon after that. Now, I'm not only a Christian, but I want to be a Worker in L'Abri. It just doesn't seem possible that all this has happened in a year's time." . . .

You, and we, prayed about L'Abri being used to speak in some way to more Swiss people. Recently, there have been unsought-for articles about L'Abri in five different Swiss papers, several of them really excellent, and one of them by Collet Muret, a leading Swiss journalist. Last week there was a one-hour radio broadcast giving a summary by a woman announcer about our work, and interviewing John, Udo, and myself, and one newcomer (we wondered what he would say), an English medical student who knew French (this was all in French. Yes, I spoke in the hearing of a radio audience in my French!) and who told where he had heard of L'Abri (on the road as he was hitchhiking in the Rhone Valley another hitchhiker told him about it) and gave his impressions of it (really interesting first impressions)—and said he was not a Christian, but he was interested in hearing more! The whole broadcast was amazingly accurate and gave people a good introduction as to what L'Abri is. Now the illustrated magazine *Illustré* sent a photographer and a reporter this week to get an article. Both were themselves interested. We don't know what the article will be like. There will be a Protestant magazine coming up next. Pray as to our need of protection from being "overrun" by people, and also for the Lord's use of these articles.

The police have come around to inspect our "police books." In other words, to see when people arrived and whether they have overstayed their time as three-month tourists in the country. Please pray for a solution for our Helpers and Workers.

We have just canceled a trip to Scotland, England, and Holland. Fran and I both came back from America utterly exhausted, and also had a virus infection which hung on and on. We don't seem to get our energy back. A three-week trip seemed just too much and the Members voted that we must cancel. I must say we felt we could not really do it, though we very much regretted it. It is harder, somehow, to cancel and to not feel a weight of responsibility, than to say "no" in the first place. Do pray as invitations come in from Japan, Australia, Africa, India, South America, and many states in the USA, Canada, etc. We feel at times, and the Members feel, as if we should stop traveling and speaking and just take care of the people who come *here*. Only the Lord can guide us in accepting and rejecting, in canceling and in making daily decision as to the use of time. This is true for L'Abri as a whole too, the pattern for us as individual Workers, and as a group must come from Him. He alone can give the continuity that is important, and He alone can see what our finite possibilities are in a lifetime.

Ten years—twenty years—thirty years—five years—ten years—fifteen years—no matter how big a "jump" you lump time into, nor how small, it comes to a kind of "count down." What *are* we meant to do? *We* are a responsible part of the present history. "Why didn't somebody do something" the future cry can be. Let God do the choosing, as we ask Him, "Show us your plan for *now.*"

With much love and prayer that we may honestly want nothing but His plan for L'Abri and for our individual lives.

EDITH

September 24, 1971 Huemoz sur Ollon, Switzerland

Dear Family:

I think the most difficult thing about writing the Family Letter is the agony of the *unwritten* stories remaining unshared within the mind, more than the work of writing. . . .

If a "family" of any kind is going to have a oneness and a growth together, there must be communication, and understanding of what is "going on" in some measure in each other's lives. The last few months have shown in a crystal-clear manner for all of us who need reassurance and encouragement that in each of the four areas in which we set forth to build the work by prayer, we have a *more vivid* demonstration than ever, that He *is* there, and *He is answering.* . . .

May 26th found me in an airplane flying off alone to Africa, a very new experience for me, as I had never been to Africa, nor had I gone alone on a speaking trip. Again there had been a unanimous decision on the part of the Members that I should accept the invitation on the part of the women of the Africa Inland Mission to speak at a conference of women missionaries in Kenya. The story of how some of them had prayed for the money for a ticket, and how God answered through using a woman thousands of miles away to send them the first gift toward this, and had then enabled them to purchase the whole ticket and send it to me, is another one of gentle listening and answering on the part of a loving Heavenly Father to His children's pleas.

It all seemed incredible that after I rushed through cooking lunch one day, Betty Carlson drove me to the doctor's for a cholera shot on the way to Villars where I was to speak to a group of American women on a tour, and then rushed down again to pack for going off to Africa. That same night a plane was flying me to Rome and thence through the night across the "map" to Kenya. Morning sun gave furnace-like heat as we stepped off in Khartoum, and the wonder of seeing white-swathed black faces above white robes gives me a memory of *something* of personality to relate to when I read newspapers about trouble in Sudan. How hard it is for finite man to be *personal* about stretches of *map* and reports of un-named thousands of people. It did not seem possible hours later to be driving through flat lands dotted with scrubby trees and to be met by my first giraffe who seemed to be giving me a personal welcome as he came close to the road to peer at our car! Nor did it seem possible that I was actually speaking to Kenyan Bible school and college students the next morning in Machakos, after spending the evening before talking with the missionaries there. I was really impressed by two things. First, that there were *no walls* around the mission grounds, the Bible school, and college, and the homes of the missionaries. One steps over a low hedge to the tiny village of African huts and the playing children on the ground in the midst of these huts. There is no fear of robbery as there would be in some American cities! My second impression was of the missionaries' willingness to live there, not on the standard of the wealthy landowners and businessmen, but with things that through the years have been added by ingenuity and hard work. The same cement houses are there that were first built, and the same metal beds, but there are improvements such as electricity from a small power plant the men have made, etc., etc. And not all stations have this much, nor do people shrink from weeks of walking, cooking outdoors, and sleeping on the ground as they travel to preach out in the bush. Also, the Bible school girls bring and cook their own food over an open fire, so that there is not a false separation in their schooldays from the life they have come from and will go back to in most cases.

The next morning I was driven via the game park to the conference place in Limuru. Even more fantastic than seeing wild ostriches and gi-raffes running in their floating fashion across the fields was seeing a waving hand and a car stopping on a "highway" the other side of Nai-robi, and finding that it was Ran's good friend from Cambridge days, Clive Boddington, who with his wife and sons had gone to see me, but had thought they had missed me! The Lord gave strength and His words for the next days of conference. That should not be accepted with a nod of the head as a kind of trite way of saying things went well. *He* gave strength to speak and surely His choice of what to say, during a time of terrific headaches and fatigue, because I had left Switzerland exhausted. Yet the excitement came in being aware of His work in answer to prayer for those days. I spoke three times a day, and I hate to say for how long each time! The final day I was driving to the missionaries' school for their own children, preparing them for college back in America or En-gland, and spoke for a long evening there. I had a wonderful trip along back roads and a visit in a tiny grass hut the next morning. It was a joy to be able to thank God for the mansions in heaven for *all* His children, and to know that although no amount of work could equalize living condi-tions in the world during anyone's lifetime, the spreading of the *truth* of the gospel *can* give people a more equalized future to look forward to forever and ever! . . .

Early in July Fran and I flew to America, first to speak in Washington, D.C., where Fran spoke to some White House press men at one private press dinner, and then to some congressmen, and I spoke to three women's meetings. We did feel that the Lord had led a Christian White House correspondent, Forrest Boyd, and his wife to pray for years preceding this time, and to ask Fran to come. It was not a "sudden" sort of thing at all and we also feel the Lord is doing a work "inside" some people in which He used this time in a special way. Right after that, we flew to Boston where Fran received an honorary Doctor of Literature degree, and a citation during the Gordon College commencement where he was the speaker. It was indeed a "flying trip," as the very same night of the commencement we were flying out from Boston Airport, after supper with my nephew, David Bragdon, his wife Jill, and my brother-in-law Ralph. Morning found us back in Switzerland, and the world seems to shrink into a matter of fatigue, vibration, take-off-and-landing noises, and mixed-up time! The constant changing of watches and the shortened time between sunset and sunrise makes one wonder about time in eternity. It's all very exciting to contemplate, and we are promised there will be *no* fatigue!

You will be waiting to find out whether we started to build the new building. *We*, too, were all waiting, and praying, and looking for news during May and the first part of June. We had had, you know, what we felt certain was guidance to have the architect draw plans and engage workmen. We were waiting for a gift to be given, or an adequate mortgage to be given. It seemed clear the space was urgently needed and that all the "signs" had led to that last sign that we could go ahead. Suddenly, many things happened in quick succession! The American dollar dropped in exchange value, the Swiss franc stayed up high, the mortgage was refused (nothing to do with us, just a general policy to avoid inflation at the present time on the part of the Swiss), the Forchet bill for chalet repairs amounting to about $5,000 came to us, and the architect when he was told that we could *not* build due to the refusal of the mortgage, sent an enormous bill for what he had already done and it seemed as if we were overwhelmed with the "impossibility" of it all. *No* building, huge bills for what seemed nothing, and yet no change in the very urgent need for more space. The very same day that the three big blows hit us, the Aigle newspaper carried a letter-article against L'Abri written and signed by the man who has been the one opposing us all along, and saying that we had not complied with the order to have fewer people, after we had been measured. This, in effect, was not true, because we had been given time in which to build or obtain more space. What to do???

We talked and prayed about it at the Workers' meeting, and called for special prayer. Then we called a Members' meeting for the Members to have special prayer and discussion of the problem. Then a special day of fasting and prayer was called on Thursday. We felt it to be a most serious time indeed, and one in which we *must not* "light our own sparks" in the darkness, but *must* put our hand in God's hand to direct us through the fog.

We had a really good prayer meeting together in the chapel on Sunday night, and a time of communion together with the Lord. Then the Members went to Chesalet after 10 o'clock for a very special Members' meeting. We prayed and talked, prayed and talked, and as we talked, we shared, each of us, our feeling of willingness to go back to "square one" as we waited to see what the Lord would have us do . . . We (especially I) had been sure that the Lord was preparing to have us build a *new* building. This Sunday evening, I expressed my willingness to fold up that "imagination" and ask the Lord to show us what His plan was to be for the next step. We were unanimous in really putting aside our own ideas and simply praying. At about 1 A.M., Fran said, "Let's begin by looking tomorrow morning at that Pension which is for sale in Chesieres." . . .

Soon after the beginning prayer meeting, I heaved a sigh, and said, "OK, I'll go up and look with you." Fran and I, Debby and 3-year-old Natasha, and little Samantha in the seat on her back, and John with 20-month-old Giandy, all got into the "two horsepower" (if you were to translate the French literally), and drove slowly up the road to Chesieres, stopping in front of Pension Gentiana. We stepped into the old, wide hall, into a big old living room with a lovely olive green tile wood stove in one corner, out into the hall again and into a big, old bedroom with a wonderful balcony looking out over the land, vegetable and flower gardens, fantastic trees, a peaked-roof summer house, a log barn, sweep of fields, pine forest beyond, and an unhindered view of mountains, mountains, mountains, and we *all* drew a deep breath of wonder! It was unanimous!! As we walked on from that moment, it was with the shared feeling, *"This* is *it!"* "This is the Lord's choice." This is L'Abri *so* much more than a new building ever could be." The certainty grew as we walked over the place, all four floors and a basement! Twenty-one bedrooms, some very tiny single rooms, some with balconies, all sorts of little cubby holes and nooks and corners. A big dining room, L–shaped with drawers full of plated silver and cupboards full of plain white dishes, glasses, and teapots. The homey room next to the dining room that has a piano with brass candleholders built into it, and a bay window corner, the big, old kitchen with its wood and coal cooking stove and astonishing side pantries, the good, new washing machine and enormous hot water boiler in the basement below, the space, the charm, the old furniture all of it "hit us" as *just right* for L'Abri. "And there it is, built 65 years ago, all furnished even with sheets and pillow cases and blankets, ready to move in. Just *think* how long it would take to build."

We went excitedly back down the hill to call the Members together in Chesalet at 2 P.M., just exactly 12 hours after we had stopped praying! We voted *unanimously not* to build a new building, to fold up the plans and pay the architect, and to buy the old chalet in Chesieres. The cost is *half* of what a new building would have been, and it is already there and furnished (though, of course, needs repairs and some additions such as another bathroom). Before the afternoon was over, John had been told "Yes" by the bank, that they would grant the needed mortgage for buying, and arrangements were made for the first step of making a "promissory payment." . . .

September 21st was the date set for meeting with the owners and Notaires. We prayed for further assurance in the supply of more money, and in a most amazing way the Lord *timed* a very large gift to reach us on the 20th, enough to reduce the mortgage by a quarter, and to keep for the purchase taxes and what is known as "expenses." It has really been such a parallel to the assurance the Lord gave us in the purchase of Les Mélèzes!

The house was left in a scrubbed and shiny condition, with crisp sheets and towels on the shelves and not a speck of dust anywhere. The key is ours, and as of September 21st, L'Abri has a house in Chesieres!!! An occasion for much thanksgiving and praise and worship of the God who works all things together in a most marvelous way when it is *His* time for things to be accomplished.

Three new couples have recently been accepted into the work in Huemoz . . . and the Lord has guided the Members in accepting them, one at a time, without knowing where any "increase" is coming from, as to caring for material needs. It is a new "stepping out" on the basis of prayer into the unknown, just as thorough as our step as a family deciding to live by prayer. *Is God able* to answer prayer? . . . Pierre Berthoud is Swiss and first came to L'Abri from the University of Lausanne way back when Debby was a student there. He came to realize the barrenness of the liberal theology he had been given by his professors, and to delight in the wonder of the truth of the Scriptures as he was truly convinced in the discussions of the weekends and the weekly studies and discussions at the Café Vieux Lausanne. Pierre went to Covenant Seminary to complete his theological studies where the teaching was Biblical and sound, and there met Danielle who had been one of the first Farel House students in L'Abri! Danielle is French by birth, but now Swiss by marriage and she and Pierre have three little ones. Amazingly enough, a house in the village that was for sale has now been offered to rent (just until April), so again the Lord opened a place.

It was early June when Grandmother Schaeffer had another stroke and was unable to get out of bed again. She had recovered well from her first stroke seven years ago and then later had various illnesses and a year ago suffered a fall and a broken leg. During these years, part of the "family experience" of those coming to L'Abri has been observing, or being involved in the care of an old person during long weeks in the hospital, growing disability, and finally five weeks of shared 24-hour care. I am sure the Lord brought Grandmother to us for her own need of a home and care, but also to teach each of us spiritual lessons we needed to learn, and to give people coming and going from L'Abri some glimpse of what "family life" means. Family life is not pictured by two glowing parents of two beautiful well-behaved children surrounded by enough affluence to give constant comfort, so healthy as to be free from all worry, so "spiritual" as to be free from argument or struggles in the area of communication! Family life includes illnesses, old age, birth and death, disappointments, disagreements, fears, worries, stumbling and falling, as well as the beautiful oneness in shared excitements and wonders. Sharing hard work, sharing fears and weaknesses, the need to care for each other "in sickness and in health" extends to more than just the unit of man and wife—it extends to the "family" including grandparents, parents and children, and to the broader family of the community.

During those weeks of Grandmother's last illness, the Lord brought people into the L'Abri Family to help in a special way. Joy, a nurse from Canada, was not only a Farel House student, but stayed on to nurse Grandmother as her special "calling" for that time. Two dear German twins, Elke and Ellen, took turns through the days along with Wendy and Virginia. It was July 11th when Grandmother died. She had not been able to speak at all for over a week though she moved her head a tiny bit and seemed to indicate she could hear us. Debby had come in evening after evening to sing hymns to her and to read the Bible just in case she could hear, and it would be a comfort. All of us were in and out of the room and there was never a time when someone was not sitting there beside her. Each day seemed as if it might be the last, as she grew weaker and weaker and did not eat or drink anything for over two weeks, except for tiny bits of sherbert or frozen orange juice or wee sips of tea Joy and I managed to get her to swallow. The reality of the human body breakdown and the abnormality of the spirit's leaving the body became a burningly real thing to each of us as we watched her struggle to keep breathing, and her heart kept beating. How completely *real* is our being made for *life* not death. Death has been ushered into the world by sin; it would not have been, otherwise. And the *victory* of Christ was the victory over death. We *shall* be raised!! As our personal family drew together during this time, it caused us each to regard life more soberly, observing that *time* does go on with measured "ticks" of the clock.

It was Sunday afternoon, July 11th. Franky had felt an urge just to sit by Grandmother for a couple of hours. Becky had come to help make Sunday tea sandwiches and had gone up for a few minutes by the bedside. Natasha had come to see Grandmother with a few flowers, and Samantha looked down from her mother's arms. Little Giandy came in too with Pris, as did Elizabee. Each one of us had been there during the afternoon, in and out again. I had just said we could serve Sunday tea for it was ready, when Elke ran down and called, "Come quickly." Fran was already there; Franky was just ahead of me, running upstairs , and we arrived just before she left. Yes, a person really does *leave*. There is no doubt that the person has gone. The difference between a person who is really *ill* and a body which has been just vacated by the person is a definite difference. It is a very stupendous reality. Fran had just taken his mother in his arms as she gasped for breath, but there is an indescribable before and after when the soul departs. I cannot imagine the feeling of one who does not believe the soul exists at such a moment nor the one who thinks there is *nowhere* to *go!!*

In Switzerland, as in all of Europe and England, there is no embalming, nor undertaker to "take over." All the care is given by loved ones. Birdie and Joy prepared Grandmother for burial and dressed her, and she remained in her bed as flowers arrived. The "box" is brought by the policeman and the one man who does sell and prepare caskets. There is nothing that is unnatural, it seems. We did have a close time as a family talking together those next two days and caring for the details. Elaine arranged the meal lists so that we did not have to feed people in Mélèzes and could be alone as a family. Priscilla and Debby came whenever possible, and Franky and Genie ate with us too. Susan flew from London to be with us and said she had not realized how very important it would be for her, as well as for us, to share this time. The funeral was the third day, Wednesday, in our chapel, and the policeman and the casket man are the ones to take the casket to the chapel and to wait outside to drive up to the cemetery. Udo, John, and Franky read passages of Scripture; Hurvey prayed; and Fran himself preached the sermon. We had a bus so that those who could not walk up could all get to the cemetery. It was a comfort to us that the "commune" agreed to sell us a family plot in the cemetery just above us between Huemoz and Chesieres, a lovely, grassy place filled with shrubs and flowers overlooking the wonderful view. The children brought their flowers while Grandmother's body was still in her bed, without shrinking from death, speaking of the resurrection and asking whether her dress would have holes in it when Jesus comes back. Yet, in spite of the reality of expectation and hope, the separation and broken communication is so final it cannot help but be a shock to anyone of any age. . . .

So many hours have gone by in the writing of this—I hate to look at the clock! Grandmother's life here has gone by, our years are going by— oh, that we may *trust* God to unfold His plan, and then to give us quietness about the seemingly "neglected" things, and the need to say *"no"* to so many kinds of requests.

With love in Him Who *is able* to help you, and us, hour by hour—

EDITH

1972

March 4, 1972   Huemoz sur Ollon, Switzerland

Dear Family, each one of you—Father in Watertown (who will be 96 this month), my sisters and brothers-in-law, nieces and nephews, children and grandchildren—and all the L'Abri Family (. . . It is a *very big* family included in the "dear family," but *not* just a mass of people! . . .):

October 10th found Fran and me on our way to San Diego, after the usual rush of getting "caught up" in office work and a variety of other things, and after turning things over to the Workers in Huemoz who more and more share the burdens of caring for the people whom the Lord sends up the mountain to our doors. September and October are usually the months when Workers take the bulk of their vacation time, and we try to plan the weeks accordingly. Our vacation was to be in November, and since we had accepted two California speaking engagements in October, we decided to say "yes" to a wonderful invitation to use a California "hideaway" for our rest. . . . We traveled from San Diego straight to Oakland, where Miss Wetherill Johnson and Miss Alverda Hertzler have their homes, and where there is the center for the work of the Bible Study Fellowship Bible classes. Fran and I were to speak for the teachers and group leaders of these classes who had been well prepared for Fran's messages by having first read *The God Who Is There* and *The Church at the End of the Twentieth Century* and taking an exam on the books!! No one who had not read the books and taken the exam was allowed to come to the conference. There is a real discipline in this work. . . .

Claire welcomed us to the little suburban house in Menlo Park where the tape library of L'Abri was residing, and where receipts for gifts were being sent out. No invitations had been sent out for the time we were to be with Claire, as the whole idea was for us to see exactly what was going on when we were *not* there. We had planned to be there for these few days before our vacation in order to pray with Claire and those who were helping in the work, and to answer questions and give advice. However, the Lord in His perfect knowledge and in His power to "time" things had brought us at a very special time.

You remember that in March the Lord had taken us to California and had opened the way for us to visit Mr. and Mrs. Webb in their little house on a property near Santa Cruz. Mr. Webb had written to us in Switzerland, saying he felt that God was leading him to give his 21–acre wooded hillside land with the two little houses and a chapel he had built with his own hands there, to L'Abri. No one realized that these scattered days of fellowship with the Webbs were times of being with Mr. Webb before he died and were to be an introduction to a new location for the American home of L'Abri. One day, when Donald Drew was in California and was speaking to a L'Abri group in the chapel on the Webbs' property, Mr. Webb slipped away to be absent from his body and present with the Lord. We did not know when we accepted the dates in November that we would be in Menlo Park *just* at the time when one of Mrs. Webb's family had persuaded her to go to live with them in Iowa, and when papers arrived to be signed by Fran and me representing L'Abri, accepting the property for L'Abri.

It was as if we were watching a play, as events took place. We signed the papers and on Sunday, a service which had already been planned in the chapel on the property turned into a most amazing dedication service. .... For Fran and myself, it was an additional wonder because of having so recently taken part in the dedication of Greatham L'Abri in the English countryside, and Eck-en-weil L'Abri in the Dutch countryside. All three dedications took place in less than the space of one year. Surely not because of the plan of any one of us. The Lord is a fantastic Director of a work.

November in Huemoz found a change taking place. Larry and Nancy were moving into Les Sapins to make it their home, open to about fourteen Farel House students and guests, while Debby and Udo were moving into Gentiana, feeling a bit overwhelmed by the carpentry work, restoring woodwork and beams in the dining room, making a Farel House study room, as well as fixing up the fourth floor for their family area, and the bedrooms on the other floors for Farel House students. The students living up there (Gentiana is in Chesieres, about a 20-minute walk uphill from Huemoz) have breakfast and do their Farel House study in the house, eat lunch there, and usually supper too, but do have some meals in Huemoz, and do get put on the "work list" in Huemoz chalets as well as coming to church, lectures, and prayer meetings in Huemoz. Students living and studying in the French L'Abri come to Huemoz just two days a week, so they are more a separate unit than those in Gentiana. However, Gentiana does supply a smaller family unit, as well as make it possible for other chalets in Huemoz to have fewer beds. As you remember, we were told we must have fewer people in each chalet. Gentiana has made it possible to do this without reducing the total number. . . .

Fran is working on his book on Genesis which will come out by Inter-Varsity Press, Lord willing, in July. It is called *Genesis in Space and Time.* . . .

So many people write letters to us wanting to come to L'Abri, to sell homes, furniture, leave all, and "join the community." Let me say, and all the Members, Workers, and Helpers of L'Abri will join to swell the sound of my voice with theirs, L'Abri is *not* a rosy glow of excitement and perfection, not even for one day—nor will your life be if you honestly ask the Lord to lead you into *His* will day by day. "Washing feet"— "visiting prisons and sick"—"giving cups of cold water" are not glamorous things to be using your time! What is L'Abri? An imperfect collection of people living in some measure on the basis of prayer, having reality in some measure of asking the Lord to direct their time and work hour by hour. . . . One Saturday night just before Christmas, in the middle of when Ann Sizer and I were serving supper, and peering into the oven to see if the dessert was burning, Kathie Cross came to the door looking silent and stunned, trying to tell us something in the midst of all the chaos. "My mother just died. I have to go home to Philadelphia." Our times are in *His* hands. How true it is that we can plan an hour, a day, a week, a month, and suddenly one phone call three minutes long, over mountains and sea, a voice, speaking sentences or broken words, can change the future. Kathie was an only child. Her father died years ago. She was needed as quickly as possible to care for all the practical arrangements. What sort of "protection" can we expect in which to have our enormous moments of emotion, of realization, of understanding deep things, or gaining a new perspective, or of looking deep into our own relationship with the Lord, and our own preparedness for "upheavals and unexpected news"? So often I have said we cannot have a package labeled, "quiet, privacy, and respect for this special section of time," handed to us in each moment when we feel the need of it.

Christmas comes in December. A trite statement? Perhaps. Was Jesus born on December 25? No one knows the exact date. One thing I do want to say—in L'Abri we attempt to live in the light of Jesus' birth, life, death, and resurrection 365 days of the year. Also, as L'Abri is a collection of *homes*, open homes, our homes are open 364 days of the year. No, I didn't make a mistake, I did type 364. We have felt that it is very important to have family times—"days off"—each week, a day during which a family can be alone. Because of the work, it is necessary to have these weekly "days off" staggered through the week so that when one family is off, another can receive the people who come. Why should families have time alone? The answer is simple—it takes *time* to *be* a family. It takes time to find reality of love, communication, and oneness, and to have it be a *growing* thing. We made a mistake in the beginning, Fran and I, as we did not take a "day off"—and we later rectified that mistake in regularly taking a day together once a week. Our L'Abri families do this. It is impossible to "share family life" if the family is *never* alone together to grow in their togetherness so that there is something to share.

We have felt that one day a year we should *all* be alone as families; that is, each chalet and L'Abri home should for one day be shut to the swarm of people coming to the doors. On this one day, we do not have a gathering of all of us together, but are quiet in our own chalets or houses, having our "togetherness" for an uninterrupted number of hours. Christmas is the day we have in this way—a day for families to be together and children to feel that togetherness in a planned-for and pre-pared-for beauty of sharing and thinking of each other. Does that mean *no* person except our personal families is in L'Abri on Christmas? No, each chalet has some people who have been with us for some weeks or months, or has invited lonely persons or old friends. But as letters *pour* in from people wanting to "spend Christmas at L'Abri in a Christian atmosphere" the answer has to be "No." We do *not* have a day for some sort of conference, nor do we have a "holiday ski camp." Some places are prepared for this sort of thing and have a burden to prepare such a peri-od of time. But L'Abri is *not*, and we have not felt led of the Lord to use this day in that way. It is a day when the cooks and mothers in L'Abri can sit quietly (at least to some degree) rather than rush around to serve, and then eat in the kitchen! It takes work, but we feel it is worth it for the children, as well as others, to have the memory of a day set apart in which to be together in a special way. . . .

John and Fran had left each week to travel by train to Monte Carlo. After much prayer and consideration, the Members of L'Abri had said "yes" to a request by the Trans-World Radio Station in Monte Carlo for Dr. Schaeffer to give a half–hour broadcast each Monday night. This broadcast, an informal time of talking and answering some question asked by John, follows in general the material in *The God Who Is There* and *Escape from Reason.* The first broadcasts were made in Monte Carlo early in December. Now they are being made in Huemoz as John and Fran work together late at night when other things are done and the village is quiet and dark. Fran walks down the back road to John's tiny one-room chalet office building!! And with a turkish towel as a back-ground and a folded up blanket on which to put the equipment, the "sound" seems to turn out very well. A proper piece of equipment was bought and given by a woman who felt led to do this, and in this infor-mal setting, the broadcast is prepared. It started to be put on the air Janu-ary 3rd, and is now being heard each Monday from 11:30 to 12:00 midnight all over Europe, behind the Iron Curtain, in the Near East, and North Africa. This is really a powerful station. The radio station knows that L'Abri does not ask for money, but prays for it and as we are praying that the Lord will show His will concerning this, we need to not just take it for granted, but really *pray.* The people at the Trans-World Radio Sta-tion feel strongly that there is a need for meeting the intellectual questions, and they have undertaken to put this on the air for at least six months of trial. It is amazing to us that among other people listening, our own scattered L'Abri Family are gathering around radios in Holland, England, and other places and inviting friends to listen. Do pray that people struggling with 20th–century thought and intellectual questions may tune in and be helped and the Lord will meet the expenses for the radio station. . . .

Right here let me say that "space" is a problem in getting office work done, as the little office by the front door of Mélèzes is simply too tiny for three or four people to work in and we have no other "offices." Kathie is taking her work down the road to her home, but that puts her where she cannot refer to files, nor be reached by phone. The phone is, of course, a constant interruption, as are people coming to the front door, but these also are "people," as are the people on the other end of the letters!!! So the problem is not an easy one to solve. Another "space" problem is space in the chapel. Our Sunday morning services are now being attended by some Americans or English (and people of other nationalities) who are residents of Geneva, Monthey, or other Swiss cities because of being in business here. Also, people are coming to stay in nearby hotels to attend lectures or church services, and these, plus the families renting nearby chalets, and the people living in our L'Abri chalets *more* than fill the chapel in January. What will happen in the summer? The Lord can give a solution to these problems of space, but I do feel we must be specific in prayer, asking His solution. . . .

It cannot be said too often, *we live in the eleventh chapter of Hebrews when we attempt to live by faith.* Read it. There are answers to prayer which change circumstances. There are direct answers to requests. There are also the instances of trust and faith which defeat Satan with a tremendous victory when circumstances continue *without* change, yet the individual loves God and trusts Him without wavering. Would there ever have been any martyrs otherwise? To love God and trust Him to the death means certainly loving Him and trusting Him in the midst of the tiny "deaths" of problems and troubles too. How else can we demonstrate to the angels and demons, as well as to other men, and to our dear Heavenly Father, that we *truly* love and trust Him? People talk about the reality of His hearing and answering us, but what about reality in the other direction? The reality of our showing forth something which proves we trust *Him?* One day, Jesus is coming back again. After that day, we will have perfect bodies, no struggles, no sorrow, no tears, complete fulfillment for all eternity. We are given much in the way of promise concerning the future. We are really warned that it is important to show forth our love of God *now* because the opportunity of that reality will not continue. There is a battle now. The battle will not always continue. It is impossible to have a victory after the battle is over.

Let us all think about it and talk to the Lord about it. Yes, we are meant to have some reality in which to show forth to others answers to prayer in which we can say, "He is there and He has heard me," but we are also meant to take the opportunity to show the scoffing demons that we love Him when things are *not* easy. Our time is limited in which to have both.

In January the Members' and Workers' Seminars were started. Every other Thursday evening when Fran is home, we have a warm, cozy-by-the-fire time in Chesalet. Almost everyone brings knitting, sewing, leather work, or some sort of creative thing to do with their hands. John polishes brass! Fran gives a short lecture, or a reading of some part of the consensus upon which we work, and then questions are discussed. Discussion is in theological areas, home life, various subjects, etc. It is not a business meeting. These seminars mean that Fran has less time with students, but as Members and Workers are the ones who are daily with students and guests, it is important that we have more time together. . . .

February was a month of many goings and comings! Birdie went to help in the Dutch L'Abri in Eck-en-weil while Hans and Joanne were in America. Os and Jenny went to speak in another country. Jane went to Rome for a time of singing and speaking in Christian business women's groups and in a church. Betty went with her. They both reported very special things that the Lord had opened up in the meetings, and in individual lives during that time. The Lausanne class in the Café Vieux Lausanne has started again, and Os and Udo take turns leading discussion and teaching there weekly. Fran and Udo went to Helsinki at the end of the month for a week of meetings in Helsinki University. Over 900 came to meetings with Fran lecturing and Udo answering questions until 2 A.M. each day. Fran gave one lecture at the Theological Faculty entitled "A Critique of Liberal Theology." Response seemed really enthusiastic, but in all these goings and comings and lectures and conversations, only the Lord knows the results, and the fulfillment of what *He* planned. Udo gave one lecture in Helsinki to a group of law students on the Biblical view of law and interest ran high, although only three out of 25 were Christians. One can only pray for the "seed" scattered in so many places, that the Lord will send water and sun to continue growth! . . .

A young man, who has been in and out of prison since his early teens, in a South American country, had lost his job in a Villars hotel and was wandering down the street one chilly day looking for a ride to another place. Several times in this wandering, he sat down and looked around and each time he realized he was looking at the same house, "a very beeg houze" he thought. Finally, it was dark and he wondered where he could sleep since no "ride" had stopped for him. Looking up, he saw the same "beeg houze." "I will sleep here. Surely they have a leetle corner in this beeg houze." So he knocked. It was Udo who opened the door, a little startled at the announcement "I will sleep here." But Udo simply replied, "Come in." He was given a bed in the room where chairs were being caned, and day by day Udo talked with him. He couldn't understand tapes too well at first—partly because of language, partly because of a fuzziness of mind due to the effects of years in drugs. But little by little things became more clear, like the lifting of a fog. He told me the other day that it was New Year's Eve after the Champéry service, during the time the chapel was full of people eating the special dinner that he asked God, "Please make me know if You are there," and that he became sure of God's existence. As we had music and then midnight communion, he came to an understanding, he "saw" with intellectual understanding, the truth of the existence of the triune God, and the way to come to Him through the work of Jesus on the cross. He is a new creature through Christ, a tiny babe in Christ, but really *born!!* He has felt an amazement at what God has done for him in bringing him out of all that which has so destroyed his friends. My amazement is again the *timing*. Do you know it was *November* that he knocked on the door of Gentiana? It was *November* that Udo and Debby moved in. The living God deals so personally with His children; He cares about putting Udo on the other side of the door in time for this young man's knock!!! Please pray for him as his Farel House time comes to a close and space must be made for others. . . .

Then there was Noriko from Japan, a Ph.D. student in history at Syracuse University who had been introduced to Christianity by my niece and nephew, Lucinda and Jeremy, at their home. Her interest developed into a desire to come to L'Abri. A very bright person, a cultured Buddhist and scholar, Noriko's background could not be more different from J's!! . . . From the other side of the world literally. How deeply moved many of us were that Sunday evening when Noriko stood before the fireplace in the chapel in the midst of our prayer meeting to be baptized and to openly declare her acceptance of the second Person of the Trinity as her Saviour and Lord. She faces much opposition as she goes back to a Buddhist family, and to teach in a Japanese university.

Fran's new books are: *The Church Before the Watching World*, InterVarsity Press in both America and England; *True Spirituality*, by Tyndale House Publishers in the U.S., and by Hodder and Stoughton in England. Expected in July—*Genesis in Space and Time*, InterVarsity in the U.S., and later Hodder and Stoughton in England; *He Is There and He Is Not Silent*, Tyndale House in the U.S., and Hodder and Stoughton in England in September; *The 25 Basic Bible Studies*, by Tyndale House in U.S.

Do pray about all these new books that the Lord will use them in His own way. We have so many letters come to us about what the books have meant in lives. Most recently, letters have come telling what *Hidden Art* is doing in lives and in changing homes. Some have been born again in reading it, and so many have taken courage to even leave their jobs to make a home for their children, one that is really creative and fun. I do pray that this book may bring about a *practical* revolution in day-by-day living, and make homes too much fun to leave! It is amazing what a wide range of people can be touched by books, even in an age when TV is supposed to be diminishing reading!

Seventeen years! So much has taken place in this tiny spot the Lord chose for His work.

With love to you all, and prayer that the Lord will open your eyes to His plan for you, and give you patience and determination to keep on letting Him do His work through you—in His place for you wherever that might be: doctor, lawyer, baker, butcher, farmer, artist, housewife, engineer, pastor, teacher, bricklayer, architect, landscape gardener, nutritionist, biologist, businessman; *His* place, the place no other person could fill.

EDITH

June 23, 1972   Huemoz sur Ollon, Switzerland

Dear Family:

This past month has been a strange one for me. A month ago tonight, I was in Clinique Mont Choisi in Lausanne, waiting for what was supposed to be a small operation to remove the cyst which was diagnosed from a swelling at my jawbone. Blissfully unconscious under anesthesia, I was unaware that I was having a major operation to have a fibrous tumor removed. A *très delicate* operation it turned out to be, with the facial nerve involved (because of the location of the tumor). The days of waiting for the laboratory report were ones of quite excruciating pain. My dear visitors scarcely knew me, as I looked a bit more like a prizefighter "the day after" than like my usual self! The enormous swelling and bruises went away after some days. The report came back negative as to cancer or tuberculosis, but that there had been a very deep infection which had come from the wisdom tooth area. This means that I have had this infection for over ten months and accounts for some of the fatigue of this past period! What I am left with now, a month after the operation, is more fatigue, plus a partially paralyzed lower lip and a "dent" where scar tissue is drawing a bit of my cheek into my jawbone. The incision was inside, but it was a long one, and I guess it is not surprising that there is still some pain as well as the frustration and discomfort of a lip that will not "work" properly for speaking and eating!! I feel a greater appreciation than I ever had of the importance of each tiny branch of nerves which govern the movement of muscles. What a fantastic illustration the Lord has given us as He calls the entire number of people who are believers, all who have ever believed, *the body of Christ.* Not only can the hand not do the work of the foot, but each individual nerve branch has its own work. When each tiny part is fulfilling its purpose, it may seem to be unnoticed. But the whole body is affected when one tiny part stops working. A sobering thought. We are surrounded by a "cloud

*In the middle of all else going on, Fran answers questions hour
after hour. Each person is important to him.*

of witnesses" but also surrounded by a host of people whom we are "affecting" when we are not fulfilling our "tiny" part.

It has been important for me this past month to realize that my "tiny
part" is something which I am to be doing in the midst of what *is* going
on! It is not what I imagine I should like to be doing "if only I didn't
have this hindrance"! It is what I am supposed to be doing *because* of this
"hindrance"! That is easier to say than to do, or to feel. . . .

Guest-listening tape sessions are now cared for by Pierre Berthoud and
Larry Snyder who not only select the tapes and organize the details of
setting them up, but who also pray with those who take turns with them
monitoring these sessions. The tape monitoring is *not* an easy task. The
"guests" consist of people from a wide variety of backgrounds. Some are
those who have "wandered" in to L'Abri on their way to India or Morocco; some are those on drugs, fresh from some "commune"; some are
Christian tourists who want to "experience L'Abri" and are staying in a
hotel nearby; some are Christians with many doubts and questions; others are atheists or are deep in some mystical cult. It is not easy for the
monitor of the tape to keep a balance of time for listening to the tape (on
Basic Philosophical Problems and The Christian Answers, or Os's on
Eastern Thought or something quite different) and time for asking questions and having discussion. Often the most difficult person to "handle"
is the Christian who has a lack of sensitivity and compassion for very
lost people in the room, and who insists on arguing or even just discuss-

ing some unhelpful theological point, quite selfishly and thoughtlessly. After all, some of the "lost" are on their way to a cliff and will be dashed to the rocks below unless some deep, basic question finds an answer that will stop the headlong rush to destruction. Some of the most wonderful realities of changed lives have had their beginning in these tape-listening sessions. It is anything but a "time filler" for taking care of guests!!

As for *"meal lists"*: the identical lists hanging on some wall in each chalet each day do *not* get there by magic. A Worker works hours to place the combination for each meal of 110 or more people in groupings at eleven L'Abri homes involved in having people for meals. Yes, it is a bit like the old-fashioned children's game of "fruit basket," as people scatter for meals in various chalets, never in quite the same combination twice. This is for conversation purposes! But it also means that people observe and become a part of a variety of homes: homes of single people, homes of married couples married only one or two years, of people married eight, thirteen, or thirty-six years!! For some young people, L'Abri homes are the first really happy homes they have ever seen. Some have never been in anything but a broken home, for their own and their friends' parents are all divorced. You can't imagine what the opportunity of eating, doing dishes, helping to peel potatoes, being a part of conversation and family prayers in such a variety of homes does, which any amount of lecturing and "talking about home life" could *never* do. The meal lists contain not only the lists of chalets and names of those *eating* in them, but information as to what is going on that day, *and* where each Farel House student is *working*, whether in the gardens under Veronica's direction; in the carpentry shop under Barry's direction; cleaning Jane's chicken house; helping in office work; cutting grass, weeding, painting, window washing, cleaning toilets, scrubbing floors, or helping with meal preparation or jam making or sewing, in whichever chalet the student is being assigned to. Priscilla is sort of the "executive organizer-in-chief," if we had titles, which we don't!!! As much as it is humanly possible, Pris keeps the various households in mind, gets about 35 phone calls a day (with troubles, complaints, distresses, panics, in areas of leaking roof, broken washing machine, a meal that has had only half the people turn up, a person that has had no Helper turn up for the day, sudden illness and the need to cancel serving a meal, a sick child, what doctor? and how to get to him?, a villager's complaint, or a villager's delight in having help with haying, someone wanting one of our young people to help in an emergency of some sort, a chalet for sale, a newspaper wanting an interview). You can't imagine the number of phone calls Pris gets, nor the variety, in any one day!!! . . .

One Worker stayed up half the night the other night talking to a new girl who had heard about L'Abri in her travels, and then started to talk to some man in Geneva who kept her as a kind of prisoner throughout some days. He was drunk most of the time and kept her locked in a room. She *really* was in a confused state in a number of ways when she got here. After a long time of talking, the Worker just felt she needed a hot bath and to be tucked into bed and made to feel at home. Things have become clear to her in these last days, and she has accepted Christ as her Saviour. It surely makes all the work worthwhile when you live through seeing a change like that take place in a person. . . .

Chalet Gentiana, a large, old chalet, or small, old hotel, has four floors. Udo and Debby and Natasha, four, and Samantha, two, sleep on the top floor. Breakfast finds them four floors down, on the ground floor, having the first meal of the day with sixteen students, Helpers, and guests who live there. The people living there start the day conscious of the fact that they are sharing the home of Debby and Udo and Natasha and Samantha. Since everyone studies right in the house, at one of the eight Farel House student desks with tape recorders, or in some other spot to listen to a tape together, no one leaves the house except to go down to Huemoz for lectures in the evening, the seminar Thursday morning, or on Debby and Udo's day off when they are not serving a dinner in the evening. It means everyone living and studying there is also working there, which has the advantage that they are all thrown together and really get to know each other, and the disadvantage that if there are difficult personalities, there is no possibility of working out a difficulty in relationships by having people work elsewhere. Things just *have* to be worked out in the combination of people who are there at any one time. . . . The evening meal is eaten together in the dining room, with candlelight, of course. On Friday night they have a book-reading time after supper when Udo reads aloud something like *Three Men in a Boat,* or some other amusing or particularly entertaining book. Since reading aloud was one of our family customs, it pleases me to know it is being carried on in Gentiana regularly. Franky and Genie always go up for that!

Gentiana has had several people knock on the front door without really knowing what the house was. You remember my telling you of the young man from South America in the last letter? There is a sequel to that story. He finished his time at L'Abri and then found a job in Ollon helping a farmer whose home had burned down, and who had been "butted" in the stomach by the horn of a cow. He came happily up for church services and Bible study, and then felt it was time for him to travel home. However, he told us as he reappeared a couple of weeks later with two fellows in tow, "I was standing on zee street corner in Madrid reading my Bible, and zees fellow come up to me and I said, 'No, I don't do zee drugs anymore. I am a Christian,' and I started to tell him sings and zen I sink, I will take him to L'Abri. God gave zee money to me. I will pay him zee train." Off went this boy with Alberto to the railroad station, and as he stood in line, he made a most fantastic discovery. Standing in the ticket line in front of him was Michel, "Michel, *my old friend* that I had taken drugs with for so long; Michel I had prayed for him. Michel an Algerian, what ees he doing here? I said to him, 'Michel, Michel, eet is me!' "

You would have had to see this young man when he first arrived, clouded eyes, face closed in, sallow, spoiled by drugs, and then see him now—glowing brown eyes, bright clear smile, a lean, tanned healthy look, dark curls cut and shiny, bursting with excitement in the super enthusiasm of a happy Latin who is also a "new creature in Christ Jesus." Michel (so he told me later) could not believe what he saw! "It can't be you. What has happened to you? You are not on drugs! I thought you would die, you were taking more than any of us. How can you look like this? *What* has happened?"

Let me tell you in Michel's words, as he talked to me a few nights later in Mélèzes' dining room. "I wanted to find out what had changed him. He said to me he would pay my way to Switzerland. *He* could pay. I could not believe it. He said I had to find out truth as he had. He said he had found out all about God, and that he is a believer and that is what has changed him. Oh, Madame, I was on my way to Finland, but he persuaded me to come here first. Even on the way, I could not believe what a change in him. It was cold on the train, and he saw someone shivering. He, my friend, took off his coat and put it around the cold Spanish one. He paid my ticket and Alberto's ticket." Yes, so this one came back, excited to the stage of jumping two feet off the floor as he talked, so certain that God had led him to these two men as he had prayed for guidance. Michel says he will return; he went to Finland where he faces some danger, to do a very honorable thing. However, the Lord in His own gentle, wonderful way of planning, had a Finnish Farel House student be present in Huemoz at that time, so that he could give Michel addresses of Christians who would help him while he is in Helsinki. As for Alberto, he is still in Chalet Gentiana, eagerly reading and studying, really asking questions, but sometimes putting aside the "seeking" to take off to a bar with another fellow who has alcoholic problems. Don't ever forget the "sacrifice of answered prayer"! When we pray for the ones of God's choice, it does not mean it is all an easy, exciting thing to care for them after they come! But being allowed to have a few small glimpses "behind scenes" to watch God weaving threads of lives is always exciting. Please pray for this one as he is in his own country as he hopes he may marry a girl whom he met at L'Abri who also came from a drug background and is now "free in the Lord's freedom." He needs prayer as Satan sets his traps quite subtly at times. Pray also for Alberto in Gentiana, and for Michel wherever he is. A South American, a Spaniard, and Algerian! Tribes and nations are integrated in heaven, but also in the Lord's workings in this life.

There is another story springing literally from Gentiana's doorstep. There was a girl, who had come from one of the worst kind of 20th-century commune situations and was wandering by a fatalistic "schedule" of asking for a coin of another country (after first giving all her money away), then going to that country. In Greece, she was given a Swiss coin, came to Geneva, stood on a street corner saying she would go wherever a ride took her. In the car of a Villars hotel owner, she let it be known that she was going wherever he would take her. As he drove through Chesieres, he drew up in front of Gentiana and said, "Knock at that door, I think they'll give you a bed for the night." It was supper time. Debby opened the door and in reply to the question, "Can I crash here for the night" invited her in to a candle-lit flower-decorated supper table and to listen to the tape of the L'Abri story. It was not an easy three months to have the waterfall of stories of evil living on the basis of an evil philosophy pour out mealtime after mealtime. It is not easy to have a helpful discussion when at one end of the table there is a really "far out" 20th-century person, scattered along the side there are very square conventional church people, a rather "scattery" teenage type telling jokes, and some serious ones wanting to find an "answer to life." Don't ever think of L'Abri as a "method." Time after time there is a feeling of "failure and tears" as well as victory and rejoicing over discussions and meals. The hardest thing on each of those who cook and serve meals is to feel that suddenly one is serving a "restaurant" instead of having an open home where people are appreciating the opportunity to have conversation with "the family." . . .

Now comes another of those glimpses of the Great Weaver as He works on a pattern. In Huemoz, many who had come to love this girl were especially praying for her. In Gentiana, Debby and Udo were praying with the hurting aching feeling that comes as a person leaves to walk along the old path away from God. In London, she was going to the American Express to arrange her travel, or pick up a letter. In Ealing, Fran and I were spending a few hours on our way back from Mexico, just before going out to Greatham for the formation of a new congregation of the International Church.

This girl saw a bluejeaned, shirt-slightly-too-big, long-haired girl looking sad and a bit uncertain as she stood in the American Express. She started a conversation with this person—"Bobbie is my name"—and before she knew it, she was telling Bobbie, who had come to Europe to throw herself away, perhaps even to suicide (after a series of really ghastly 20th–century experiences), all about L'Abri and Christianity. "I'll take you out to the London L'Abri to meet the Schaeffers now." When, pray tell, are we ever at the London L'Abri? A few hours, often months apart!!! The Gentiana telephone rang in Chesieres, Switzerland, then her voice out of the blue, "What is the address of the London L'Abri?" A couple of hours later, just as Fran and I were finishing a radio interview in the little sitting room, the doorbell of 52 Cleveland Road rang, and I heard voices in the hall speaking to Dick Keyes. A door opened, and suddenly I was hugging her. "But how did you get here?" Time was short. I had been away and was not sure what her decision had been. I felt impelled to talk about the wonders of being in the Lord's family, of the certainty of our future as being His people, the coming of Jesus, the creativity, fulfillment, and wonder of all that I believe is ahead in our new bodies after the resurrection. I prayed with the two girls. We all had lunch together and then off we went to Greatham!! But not before I told the girls we'd be praying for them and told Bobbie I hoped she'd visit L'Abri in Greatham before starting her European wandering.

It was the next day as Dick brought a carload out for the installation of Ranald as pastor and Jerram as elder of the new congregation, and to receive the charter members, that he told us she had bowed before the living God and accepted Christ as her Saviour and asked for baptism. A victory of answered prayer. Rejoicing in Huemoz, Ealing, Greatham! And on a plane she was flying rapidly into untold pressures and yawning open traps of Satan's as he would try to hinder her from going on as a Christian. (Do pray for her before you go on reading, right now.) In the carload was Bobbie. Yes, she had decided to "look into it." We had a two-hour talk together during which, with tears streaming down her face, Bobbie told me her story. One of the most heartbreaking ones I've heard yet. I prayed for her, and we have prayed for her. In a few days, I had news from Susan that she was staying on as a Farel House student. Then later came the wonderful news that Bobbie had become a Christian!!!

Then, this last weekend, as I went up to Huemoz to break my "recovery time" with some time there, seeing how far my tiny package of energy would stretch!!! I "happened" to look out the back kitchen door and who did I see coming down the steps but *"Bobbie,* how did you get here?" "I'm staying at the village house, Ruchets' and this is my roommate." There was a quick recounting of the wonder of God's gentleness. As Bobbie has no home to which to return, she felt a desperation which almost took her away from her thought to come to Huemoz before returning to America. Then, she put aside the "temptation" to turn aside, and came. No room in L'Abri so she ended up at Ruchets' on the back road, to find the Lord had placed her with a roommate whose Christian parents, when telephoned long distance, replied, "Yes, of course you may bring Bobbie home with you and she can have a room in our home and go to college here." Thank God for such parents! And thank God for *His* personal, loving care for details as His children seek His plan, and His path, in their faltering first steps as "babes." . . .

I had called Les Sapins for fresh news in the middle of the Workers' evening discussion meeting when problems and ideas are shared and prayed over. Larry talked for a few minutes "Did you know we had fixed up the old sun porch on the first floor into a guest tape-listening room? We're trying to decorate it now. Four Helpers are helping Pierre translate tapes into French. We have a number of Helpers living with us. As for me, I guess you know that I take charge of guest tape programs three days a week and go down to monitor the Huemoz Farel House twice a week." At Beau Site Veronica has turned the sun porch into a room for sewing and weaving. She has her loom out there and the sewing machine too. There has been a rug woven on the loom already. . . made out of strips of old clothing. Then, of course, she is in charge of the vegetable gardens, not only at Beau Site, but down in the field. The branch of the Evangelical Library is still in Beau Site, and we are working on recataloguing the books right now. At Mélèzes, Gracie has just set the tables for lunch, and looked after her little bird, and then she took little Jessica to see the bird, and Jessica jumped up and down! We had five sleeping on the floor here last night. Two in the dining room, two in the kitchen, and one in the office. Gracie got out all the blankets and pillows and sheets and made up the beds on the floor after she had put away the silverware. . . .

Os, Franky, and Jane are now arranging an "arts week" in which those who are in Huemoz L'Abri right now may display their creative works in some way in the chapel. There will be lectures and a concert, too, using just those who are a part of Huemoz L'Abri, or are students or guests here now. It is not an international week in the sense of bringing together the people with creative talents in other branches of L'Abri. . . .

Only in heaven—in eternity—in our new bodies are we going to have time to find out the total blend of what has happened in a month, a year, a lifetime, as God has woven our lives together with others in our own moment of history. So, don't stop painting your pictures, writing your music, cooking your meals, planting your gardens, writing your letters, reading to your children, sweeping your floors, selling your houses (or fish!!), studying your lessons, don't stop doing the "unimportant things" if they are the Lord's plan for you now. *He is making the blend.* The thread does not tell the weaver where to put it; the clay does not tell the potter how to mold it; the paint does not tell the artist to use a brush or a spatula.

With love in Him Whom we can *trust* to love us and use us in the only way we "fit" into it all—

EDITH

September 30, 1972　　　　　　　　　　Huemoz sur Ollon, Switzerland

Dear Family:

It is impossible to write to you right now! It is impossible because we are going to leave early the morning of October 3rd for a speaking trip which will take us around the world. You can imagine my large piece of cardboard which I prepared with a page torn from the calendar in the center. *September,* it announces with a nice clear number of days topped by the picture of a village tower and clock! Around this calendar I have made a list of things-to-be-done before leaving. The list is in five colors and a variety of types of printing and handwriting, trying to impress myself with the importance of getting to *work* day by day. Most of the "days" are canceled off now with turquoise felt pen marks. Many of the items of work are canceled off too. The arts week is over. Lectures have been given. Two-page letters and prayer list for October have been prepared. Marketing has been done and menus for two months ahead have been prepared. The dentist appointment is over. Flights have been arranged. What remains for the two-and-a-half days left?

Well, today I am supposed to be speaking in Chateau d'Oex to a group of women from Dallas, Texas. It has been arranged for months. Also, I have on my chart the Family Letter to write, a foreword to write for Betty Carlson's new book, a farewell tea to attend for Donald Drew, a dress to finish making, a portion of our travel to rearrange by phone with the travel bureau, the menus to make for this weekend and to finish for the two months ahead, letters to get "caught up" before leaving, new mail to read, Giandy's birthday party Monday, legal papers to sign for promissory payment for "the house" also on Monday, people in special "need" to talk to, and endless little things plus interruptions.

Last night my husband walked into my office and said, "Edith, I have an offer to make you. I think I am more caught up on work than you are, so I'll go to Chateau D'Oex and speak in your place while *you write the Family Letter*." After the amazement wore off and my reaction of "Oh, no, I couldn't let you do that. You have enough as it is. I *must* do it," I thought seriously of the fact that this would really make the Family Letter a possibility instead of a "stay up all night to write" or a "hoped to get it done but failed" sort of thing!! I have faithfully promised Fran that *as* he is there speaking, I will write to *you*. . . .

How am I? I am much better than when I last wrote you. I went on feeling more and more exhausted, more and more as though each small thing I did was like walking up a steep hill in a blinding snowstorm. I felt faint and nauseated several times a day. I thought old age had arrived and this was what it was like, so how could I possibly go on? People said encouraging things like "You look awful, so white—" and I thought, "If they only *knew*." It wasn't just that I had pain in my face and annoyance with my lip. It was deep exhaustion such as *you* (so many of you) warned me was coming some day!! August 1st Fran was to speak in Cincinnati, Ohio, to the Christian Booksellers' Convention to introduce his new books now out. I waved goodbye to him at the Aigle station. Two days later, I went into the hospital for a small gynecological operation. The doctor solemnly told me the day after the D and C, "You *must* have six months' rest." Fran phoned me from London a couple of days later and there in the hospital bed I heard Fran say, "You looked so white and grey and wan as the train pulled out and you stood waving that I determined to stop everything and take you away for two weeks of real rest in the sun. As soon as I get back we'll prepare to go." I began to say, "It can't be done; there is too much—" but it became so obvious to me that something was needed that I just said, "Oh thank you!" Debby spent a day at a travel bureau trying to find beds in a hotel, having chosen the Island of Elba as *the place*.

So it was that only a day after coming out of the hospital, I had somehow thrown the necessary clothing and a bathing suit into a suitcase and had dragged myself off to the Aigle station once more to take the early morning train to Genoa. It was a hot day in Italy, and with several train changes and a late boat (ferry) we wondered whether we had made a mistake in letting Debby choose "Elba" as the right place for a rest. However, after just a few days of lying in the hot sun, sleeping long unbroken hours, swimming a half mile at a stretch in the marvelously clean water and rock-bordered bay, reading books aloud to Fran, eating without cooking or doing dishes—writing *not* even a postcard—I was astonished at the *change* in feeling. Suddenly, I began to remember what I normally had felt like all my life. Suddenly, I began to have *some* energy, and ideas began to flow again. By the time two weeks was over, not only had my color changed from grey-white to a red-brown, and my muscles tightened up from swimming, but I felt for the first time in over a year, like my "old self."

In answer to "How are you?"—Thank you for praying for me. I do feel Fran was guided to do what was a drastic thing—to take me off in the middle of the busy month of August in L'Abri to *really* rest. And I know the Lord used that time both physically and spiritually to give both of us the "full stop" we needed for refreshment and restoration! Perhaps it was too short, but it was much more effective than any "halfway" sort of rest for a longer time. The brown has mostly faded now; long hours of work have brought tiredness again, but *not* the same as before. We both still feel much better, in spite of minor "aches and pains!!" . . .

The letters we are getting from many parts of the world are showing how the *Lord* is following up people in answer to prayer. We must be faithful to intercede for those who are our responsibility before the Lord. "God forbid that I should sin against the Lord in ceasing to pray for you,"* should be something we remember is a needful prayer. We are in *danger* of sinning against the Lord if we neglect to do that for others which He gave us to do, namely to *pray* faithfully for them. But whether those for whom we pray are in prison, concentration camp, hospital, an adverse home situation, a difficult working situation, a desert or a jungle, in war or in too affluent a circumstance, there is *nothing* that can separate them from the love of God, or from some very *real* and *specific* answer to prayer as we intercede for them. . . . There is no place that cuts us off from joining with others in the oneness of being together in prayer. Sitting in a high cell or working at a hotel desk in Japan, milking cows in Wisconsin, working in a hospital in Palestine, or sitting under a cedar tree on a cliff in Oregon or near San Francisco, we can really experience a togetherness in prayer. . . . Governments may frown upon gatherings of Christians, but they can never wipe out the oneness of the Holy Spirit, nor the oneness of being *together* in the presence of the Lord

*1 Samuel 12:23.

in prayer. Astounding isn't it, when you think about it. No worldly organization can give what the Lord's plan for "integrating" his *real* family has made possible through the centuries. The loneliness of a child in this "gathering" of people, can*not* be the same as the loneliness of someone "outside." . . .

Night before last, I went down to say goodnight to Gracie after midnight, and glanced in the kitchen to see a boy reading *The God Who Is There* as he lay in his "bed" on the floor, one elbow on the spot where someone had been standing washing dishes some hours before! Last night I learned something of the background of his coming. He came to find a friend who had given this address for letters. No one who ever came to L'Abri knew less than this fellow. As he met Franky and then Bruce in the hall, the only question he was asked was whether he was hungry and that if he had finished his supper before coming, would he like some tea and ice cream? "It blew my mind. What was this? I hadn't even heard English spoken for three weeks and suddenly I was in a dining room with candlelight and flowers and all these people eating ice cream and talking in English. It took a long time before I had the courage to ask, 'What is this place, and what are people doing here?' " It took some time before he discovered that it had something to do with Christianity, which he had discarded. *He* was just looking up a friend! Now forty hours and many discussions later, having read most of the L'Abri story by this time, he knows much more, but perhaps he doesn't yet know that God has brought him here in answer to whose prayers? You see, he doesn't yet know whether God exists or not. But, he is staying on for a time. There are some people we are so *sure* have been "brought" by the Lord, that not only do we "move over and make room" but we are encouraged to keep on, in spite of discouragement or tiredness. . . .

The arts week was better than any of us expected, and people were very excited about all the really "new" lectures and things they learned. By the way, it was *not* announced so that people could come especially to it. We did not want anyone extra to come as we simply do not have the space. As it was, the chapel was very crowded throughout it all. . . .

Wednesday night Jane sang as a final portion of the concert, the last part of Brunhilde's aria in the final act of Wagner's "The Ring of the Nibelung." I am not sure I can put into words what happened that night. It has been sixteen years that we have known Jane. Twelve years ago Jane left opera to become not only a L'Abri Worker, but left opera to do whatever the Lord would have her do. She especially did *not* want to simply "change applause" as she called it. She felt it was important to be willing to stop singing if that was what the Lord wanted. As singing to her meant a hundred-piece orchestra, fantastic costumes, "props" of all sorts including in this portion of Wagner, a horse, the stage in "flames," and smoke, and a "reality" of what was being sung about for the audience to see and feel, she found it hard to even sing simple hymns at first, especially when the acoustics of our little, low-ceilinged living room in Mélèzes was the only "church." As time has gone on, Jane added to her L'Abri work of housework, gardening (which she commenced whole-heartedly in Mélèzes), serving meals, and being hostess in Chesalet, the Bellevue hymn-sings for the patients next door, music in the chapel services and lectures on music history, as well as the tours of the L'Abri Ensemble. However, one thing Jane did *not* do through all these years, and that was to go back to singing anything of Wagner's. She sang Brunhilde the *last* time she sang in opera. She sold her costumes as a final "turning away" and the money was given toward building the chapel.

Wednesday night of the arts week was a very special night. After 12 years, Jane was going to sing this half-hour aria from Wagner's "The Ring of the Nibelung," and she was going to do it in just a simple dress without any of the fire and smoke, without a horse or any props, and with a piano in place of a 100-piece orchestra. . . .

Before going on, let me say, *no one can be the Holy Spirit for anyone else.* Everyone has *some* kind of sacrifice to live through, and there are some whose temptation to doing something really forbidden in God's law is much stronger than others, so that person's struggle is in a different area. For some people, the turning away from a "good thing " is just as painful and agonizing as some other people having to turn away from a "bad thing."

Fran and I sat in the back of the chapel. The place was crowded with the floor full on every side. Students and professors, old and young, long-haired and "square," Christians and non-Christians, those who have been at L'Abri a long time and newcomers, music experts and some who may not know one note from another, all kinds of people, hushed and expectant. Finally Jane stood and related what she was going to sing to the full lecture she had given in the morning, telling what the story was all about, and also what needed to be "imagined" as far as orchestra and supporting cast, flames and smoke, etc. She also said that it would be an emotional thing for her to do since she had last sung it 12 years ago to a full opera house, and then had left opera forever. The pianist plunged into the opening bars as if the piano were a dozen instruments in one. Then Jane began, and went on and on and on and everything was forgotten in the power of her magnificent voice and the skill with which she could interpret the part, alone and without anything but the simple chapel and its crowd of awestruck people listening rather breathlessly to her. What took place in the listeners? Different things surely in different people. Some were thrilled and satisfied with the sheer beauty. Some were startled and amazed at the unexpected power. We who have known Jane for 16 years, but who have never heard her sing opera, suddenly felt as if we were seeing and hearing Jane for the first time. I realized that one really doesn't *know* a person when one has not had the communication of that person's particular kind of creativity. There is a dimension which simply is lost in the communication of the *person* if the communication is limited to only a fraction of the possibilities that exist. I am sure I was not the only one who felt that night, "Now I know Jane in a different way," and who wept at the depth of what Jane had walked away from. It was not just leaving opera, it was putting aside a medium of expression, of creativity.

Later conversations related the obvious sacrifice of putting that expression aside to the person who must sacrifice in other areas: not being "fulfilled" in some basic portion of their lives, whether it be an amputated leg, a paralyzed portion of the body, a blind eye, or an unfulfilled desire to "mother" a child one has never been given. There are those who long for marriage (a good thing) but who have not been fulfilled because no person has been "found." There are those who are homosexual, whose agony is unfulfillable in the framework of the Biblical teaching, yet whose turning away from the wrong thing brings no more agony from lack of expression than does the willing turning away of others from the "good thing" *given* unto the Lord, as He has led. It is so easy to think one's own difficult "thing" is in a different category of agony than anyone else's.

All this and much more swept through me as I heard that voice and thought of "what could have been through 12 years" and what has been. And then when the standing ovation and deafening clapping ended, and I got through the press of people up to Jane, words didn't come, but Jane managed to whisper, "It's all been worth it. I'm glad I left opera, but do you think *He'll* let me sing again some day?" I *do*. I think the music that is ahead of us will include the entire *range* of possibility of voice and instrument being used to its fullest expression. The "wrong" things will be righted as people will have blind eyes restored, amputated legs back in place again, paralyzed parts made perfect, and imbalances and psychological ills healed. There is so much ahead of us, beyond our imagination, as eye hath not seen nor the heart of man imagined the glory of what God is preparing for those whom He loves. We don't need to be fearful of not being able to sing, paint, sculpt, communicate in a vast number of ways, be creative to the full extent of what God made us in His image to be! His creation is to be *restored*, and we are a *part* of His creation. Nor do we need to worry that we are *wasting* anything He leads us to put aside, or to use only partially. He is able to make our place in history significant in carrying out His plan which includes the "whole" of what we *are* to do, *and* to be willing not to do. . . .

À bientot! A good French expression that seems more compact than "see you soon!" With much love to all you "ones" in Him Who is able to care for us personally, and as individuals,

EDITH

1973

February 10, 1973   Chesieres, Switzerland

Dearest Family:

Once again I am going to write a very quick quickie, instead of a really long Family Letter. It will be quite a while before we get down to a "normal life" if, in fact, anyone can define what "normal life" is composed of! Meantime, you need to have *some* idea of what has been taking place since you had a hastily written Family Letter just before we left for the speaking trip which took us around the world. . . .

February 14, this year, Udo and Debby, Natasha, and Samantha will be leaving for the U.S., as Udo is to speak to a lawyers' conference in the Los Angeles area. We and Birdie, Os, Hurvey, Ranald, Hans Rookmaaker, Claire, Jane S., Betty C., Jim and Sandy, Franky and Genie, will be making our separate ways from different geographical points to Covenant College in Lookout Mountain, Tennessee, to take part in the second L'Abri Conference to be held in America. It will be a very full time of lectures by all of us, discussion times, concerts, sermons, prayer time, etc., as for ten days people will be together from all over the States and Canada, and from various times of L'Abri's history, for a "reunion" time.

There are two urgent prayer needs to be noted right here. First, the whole permit question has been reopened. Switzerland work permits for foreigners are getting more and more difficult, just in general, that is. Inflation is being fought in various ways. There is very imminent possibility that we will be cut in the number of Workers we can have here, which will again mean the possibility of having to cut the number of people who can come to Swiss L'Abri. Prayer is needed urgently for this. We need to be sensitive to the Lord's plan, as well as to pray believing He is able to do all things. In the Canton of Vaud, for instance, there are 3,000 foreigners applying to continue to live here, that includes very wealthy influential foreigners, and out of 3,000 only 400 permits will be given.

So you see it is *not* a thing directed against L'Abri. Second, as you may know the American dollar has plunged, so that at the present time the exchange means we have only about 3/4ths of what we used to have as the dollar becomes francs. Please pray that it will be clear to everyone who is watching L'Abri that *God does the arithmetic*, and that as we pray for the material needs, *He* is able to touch people to send the amounts needed *as* exchange changes. We truly pray that He will supply the needs, and this is a special time, I believe, to demonstrate the reality of His sending *people* in the right numbers, giving us *Workers* in the right numbers, and *money* in the right amounts, in spite of governments changing the money exchange and the permit possibilities!!! *His* power is not regulated by government regulations, and this is a time to pray for a special victory in areas *not* within our own possibilities of controlling.

Right now we are having the deepest snow of the winter thus far. It is coming down like a blizzard and is already very deep. All the landscape is covered in drifts and mounts of white, trees are so laden that only a few dark lines trace a pattern in the white, and windy gusts of snow make almost a white wall in the middle of steadily falling flakes. L'Abri is full, yet we are leaving at 6 tomorrow morning, and others are going soon. Barry and Veronica are in England, helping in the work in Greatham while Veronica awaits her turn to be in the hospital for an operation. John is busier than ever with the finances to care for as the C.P.A. accounts are examined in February, and in *addition* to doing all that late-night work, and caring for the chalets for a variety of families arriving to be near L'Abri, John had food poisoning (we can be very glad he didn't die from it) with violent pain. Dr. Gandur at first thought it might be the prevalent intestinal flu, and prescribed over the phone for that. But, after thinking about it awhile, the doctor got into his car and drove down as he felt it might be poisoning. It turned out to be that and the proper shots did work! It was probably mushroom pizza John had had in a restaurant! This paragraph is simply to try to give you a picture of the fact that such things as L'Abri children having flu one after another, Veronica and Barry being away, Juanita of French L'Abri needing a rest in a quiet spot in England because of great fatigue, are some of the daily "hindrances" which make the work like an obstacle race.

In the midst of hindrances, sicknesses, fatigue, impossible succession of work which threatens to bury us like snowdrifts, news of the dropping dollar cutting the money, news of the ever more restrictive government rulings, there have been shining moments when we have seen something of what God is doing. Just a minute ago a break in the clouds brought a stop to the snow, and almost like magic an apricot-pink color flooded a spot in the sky. There the flaming color streaked the white snow with glory and gave a breathtaking light in the midst of the monotone of white and dark trees. It was a perfect illustration of the things we have been "seeing" in the midst of difficulties. Take the last two Sundays for instance—one Sunday we had nine stand up to make a profession of faith, some to be baptized and to join the Huemoz congregation of the International Church. One of these was an Indian girl from a Hindu background, brought up in Rhodesia, another was a Swiss man married to an American girl, another was an American black and his wife, another was a middle–aged American couple who had been in Thought Control and other mystical types of things—such different backgrounds, such fantastic stories each one had of how the Lord brought them to L'Abri and then to Himself. There was a "remarriage" of a couple who had been only married in a civil wedding before they became Christians and wanted now a Christian wedding. A week later four more were baptized and joined the church. Does this just "happen"? It mean *hours* of time people have been talking to Os and Jenny, Debby and Udo, Birdie, Gini, Gay, Sandy and Jim, Elaine, Barbara, Ann, Kathie, Larry and Nancy, Vic, Pris and John, Franky and Genie, Jane and Betty, Karen, Bob and a host of others. One cannot trace all the threads that are woven together to bring about the results which are suddenly visible. Many of the threads are not visible, but are needed! And the hidden washing of floors, toilets, stairs, scrubbing potatoes, drying dishes, making beds, marketing for food, writing lectures, paying rents and electricity, writing letters, practicing the organ, singing solos, praying for short moments or long hours, all the "hidden" parts of the "whole" are part of it all. . . .

The day after our Family Christmas Fran insisted, "Edith, today you are to start the book, you simply can't wait any longer." And he was right for had I put it off a week the deadline would never have been met. So it was that on December 27th I began to write and without a single day off, working about 18 hours out of the 24, in 30 days the nearly 400 pages of a new book were finished! It is to be called, *Everybody Can Know* by Francis and Edith Schaeffer. I have written it, but it is based on the work we did together 20 years ago on Luke, and also is a weaving together of Fran's philosophic answers to 20th–century questions, and many illustrations of "things to do" which make various teachings more clear. It has been written to read to people of all ages, that they might *know* something of God's truth, and be able to talk together about it. It is written to be read aloud in a family, or to be read aloud by a single person to friends, children living nearby, to people in a hospital ward, a prison, a retirement home, or any grouping of people who are together. Naturally it may be read silently by individuals, but it is especially written to share with others. People will need to be prepared to look for dried beans and peas, old silver to polish, candles to light, blindfolds to tie over people's eyes, cloth to wrap a person in, a curtain to tear, a jigsaw puzzle to put together, an album of Handel's Messiah to listen to at various points! All these things will be used to make points clear, and also to involve the family together in what is being taught. We are praying that the book will make it possible for ten–year–olds and people of many ages, to be prepared to meet the situation in the world today without being drawn into deep waters by that which is like a treacherous undertow dragging people out into a sea of despair and blackness. It is written really for my own grandchildren, as well as for the children of all L'Abri families, and then for the wider circle of families who will be able to use it.

During those thirty days I was really shut up to the Lord, away from people, and had an amazing time really "living" in Luke and other parts of the Bible. The strength to write was an answer to many people's prayer for me, I'm sure. It was an agony as of labor pains and childbirth followed by most exhilarating wonder as various fresh understanding came, and ideas flowed. Fran read it chapter by chapter and checked it as I went along. One week as I wrote, Fran went to Basel with Udo, to teach in the German theological school there. L'Abri, of course, continued full force, but my only contact was by phone! At nine P.M. on January 25th I finished the book! By ten P.M. Debby had arrived to help me pack everything in our little hideaway apartment because after four years there, and after 18 years in Chalet Les Mélèzes, we had come to the moment of *moving*! It seems incredible, but the Lord had used the apartment literally up to the last moment, as a place in which to write (it has also been used for rest, for recuperation after operations, for a family place). Now in recent weeks the Lord gave us a succession of clear answers to prayer, and signs, which gave us all assurance that we were being led to move into a home of our own. Mélèzes began as our home, open to any whom the Lord would send. However, at some time in the past years, the balance has changed, a line was crossed, and Mélèzes ceased really to be a shared home. As the numbers of people coming to the door to inquire, or to ask to stay increased, the hall became a kind of youth hostel or entrance to a pension in atmosphere at times. One could not walk through without being asked dozens of questions, or without having a picture snapped! "Housekeeping" became a kind of farce, as the number sharing came to mean that no one really felt responsible, including myself much of the time. Several things became clear— that Mélèzes *could* be broken into two apartments, with the center floor as a kind of "arrival center," and still be Mélèzes with a better arrangement than had developed. It seemed this would fulfill what the new building would have given, the portion that Gentiana could not provide. It also became clear that as Fran and I grow older, we would need a *home* again, a more gracious place in which to receive people to talk to when we have guests, but also a home in which to receive our own children and grandchildren. I so often have said that one cannot "share" a family when there is not enough time spent in *being* a *family*, and I feel that a yearly family reunion is *not* enough time for me as a mother and grandmother to spend in being a mother and grandmother! It seems the time has come to readjust the use of time. *Not* that I would say the last 18 years of L'Abri have been "too much" but that just as the Lord did lead in all that has happened, and just as He has taken us on many speaking trips and led us to write books and to work 18 hours a day so much of the time, so now we do believe He is leading us to have a change of pace if you would call it that, and a change of *place*. It has been many years since we have had a bedroom that was not also Fran's office, so that the bed has always been his desk. It has been 18 years since we have had a dining room that was not *always* shared with guests, and my husband's need of quiet has meant he has eaten in the bedroom much of the time, too. Enough of all this—I must tell you that the Lord has given us a *house* which is *space*. It is an old chalet built in 1906, designed by the same architect as Gentiana, and built so that the land joins that of Gentiana in Chesieres. The barn belonging to Franky and Genie also touches the land of this house. It is as if 67 years ago the Lord built Gentiana, the barn, and Chalet le Chardonnet for the use it is to have now! We feel the view, the sweep of empty field behind us, the closeness to the grocery stores and autobus, the closeness to Huemoz, yet the possibility of being a little apart from it, the space to have an office for Fran, much storage space, a grandchildren's play room, a dining room, balcony with space for dining and wonderful noonday sun all has been "designed," not just by an earthly architect for the last 67 years of use, but by the Lord for what He has planned for the next years of our lives. We feel as if this is our last move on earth!* Though, of course, only the Lord knows what is ahead in any of our lives. It was a doctor's house before, and the ground floor was where he had his offices and X–ray rooms, etc. Now the ground floor is being prepared to be an apartment for Franky and Genie. We will "spread out" over the other floors, Fran being so very quiet in his office on the top floor. We will have plenty of exercise going up and down stairs, good for the heart! It is like an old rambling farmhouse if compared to American houses. It is to take the place of the apartment and of our living in Mélèzes. We have given up the apartment, and Mélèzes is to be lived in by single Workers and students. . . .

So the book was finished at 9 P.M. on January 25th. Debby and I packed half the night, and the movers arrived at 7:45 A.M. along with John and Fran; and we spent the 26th of January moving from the apartment to our new home! As we finally drove up the mountain just ahead of the moving van, it seemed as if the Lord had wrapped His gift for us up in a glorious sparkling sunshine and blue sky. I had been in the deep fog most of the time in Veytaux, and to drive up on one of the most brilliantly clear days the winter has had was a tremendous experience and seemed like a gift-wrapping on a stupendous scale. We entered rooms into which the sun was pouring, and it is difficult to describe the feeling but it seemed as if something of every house we had ever lived in had been combined to make us feel at "home" for we felt as if we had *come home*, instead of having *left* home. We slept in Chardonnet from that night on, although it took the next week to "pack" Mélèzes and the fol-

---

*We were subsequently to share three more houses in Rochester, Minnesota.

lowing Friday we had the movers come to help in the impossible task of leaving a house after 18 years of a most amazing growth in it as a family, from one stage to another. The date of moving from Mélèzes was February 2nd, and on February 5th Michael Hughes, my editor, came to read the manuscript of the new book. He was our first houseguest. Lord willing, my book is to come out in England by November 8th and almost simultaneously in America from Tyndale House.

You can picture something of the piles of boxes of books, cooking utensils, clothing, sheets and bedding, and all that makes up a collection of 18 years of living, and you can picture the unpacking that has been going on, in between L'Abri lectures as Fran has gone down the hill to preach and discuss, etc. Now we are busily packing for the trip to America as we leave at 6 A.M. tomorrow morning, and this is being written while I should be preparing the two of us some supper!!! . . .

October and November for Fran and me meant a two-month period away from Huemoz in a speaking trip that took us around the world. For the Workers and Members here, there was a two-month period of carrying on with all the struggles and joys of seeing people come as the Lord had brought them to seek the fulfillment of needs, the answers to questions, the healing of one or another kind of brokenness, or to study and discover fresh understanding of things that had been "fuzzy" or "hazy" before.

Of course, it is impossible to cover in one tiny paragraph what went on in Huemoz in October, November, and early December. And, of course, it is impossible to cover what took place in the voyage which took us to speak in the States at Princeton; L'Abri reunion in New York; Geneva College, Pennsylvania; Los Gatos, California where a L'Abri conference was held; in Hawaii where Fran lectured at the University of Hawaii; Japan in Tokyo, Osaka, Yokohama, with as many as three lectures a day; Hong Kong, in both the University of Hong Kong, and the Chinese University in the New Territories as well as other lectures; Singapore with a series of lectures in a hotel room, and other scattered lectures; Kuala Lampur and a series of lectures in the University lecture hall each evening for Fran, other lectures for both of us in the day times; and Bombay for evening lectures in a church. I could write pages about the impressions of the countries, the new friends we made in each place, our love of the Orient, the deep need of India. Yes, pages would need to be written to tell of the things we saw, heard, and felt which will cause us to never be quite the same again. Pages also would have to be written to tell of the people who seemed deeply moved by the lectures, the ones who were changed, the old friends we saw, and the amazing numbers who had read the books. Pages could be written about the translations of Fran's books into these languages, and of the Japanese translation of *He Is There and He Is Not Silent* coming out only three months after it came out in English. Pages could be written about the L'Abri Family members (people who have been born again at

L'Abri or who have lived and worked with us) whom we saw in *every* single place we went.

In a matter of just hours now, we will be leaving and Fran is saying, "You must pack."

What is ahead? Not one of us can know the immediate answer to that. The Second Coming we can be sure of! What is between today and that—none of us can know. Please do pray that all God means L'Abri to do, however long the time is, may not be *hindered*.

Much love in Him Who can *answer* as we pray for each other,

EDITH

September 1, 1973   Chesieres, Switzerland

Dear Family:

Fran and I just came up from the garden a few minutes ago with a big basket overflowing with peas, another one with beans, an armful of let-tuce, and a pan of spinach. It seems such a short time ago, mid–June, when he was shaking the topsoil off the squares of turf dug up by a suc-cession of Farel House students in the field. It seems such a short time ago when a pocketful of seeds was planted in rows in the prepared soil. The tremendous "increase," the multiplying by more than "a hundred-fold," was a sharp illustration to us of the importance of digging, fertil-izing, weeding, planting, watering, if one wants to harvest. . . .

All that however is a day-to-day, week-by-week preparation for un-derstanding what the Bible is making known to us in the various ways God refers to seeds and plants. Yes, we are to plant seed which is God's Word but we are also ourselves to be as seed when *we* are told we are to be like a grain of wheat that falls into the ground and dies and brings forth a hundredfold, etc. In all the L'Abri branches among Workers, there is a growing understanding of some small measure of what this remaining planted means. . . . The "harvest" of "new plants" . . . or the number of new births that have been taking place have caused each of us to pick our own lettuce, peas, beans, and spinach with constant thanks for the double meaning God has stressed we are to constantly remember. We are to be involved in the gardening of which we are told . . . some plant, some water, but God brings the increase. *He does the statistics* . . . He is the One who stands as a Shepherd counting one by one as the lambs enter, but also who counts the harvest. It is rather staggering to think that to be what *He* would have us to be, and to do what *He* would have us to do, we need to share the planting and weeding and water-ing. . . . in the "field" He gives us to care for—*but* we also need to remain "in the ground," dead to self. . . . so that the place where *He* has planted us may be a place of harvest in His own time. *Not easy* to remember . . .

that we are the farmers, but also our lives are to be the harvest.

It has been over six months since I last wrote a Family Letter, but during that six months we have had a constant harvest of people, or a constant maternity ward of new births. Sunday by Sunday people have stood at the front of the chapel to make a public profession of faith in baptism. Day after day we have heard, "so-and-so became convinced that God *does* exist, that the Bible *is* true, and has accepted Christ as his or her Saviour." The rejoicing is a shared thing because the people are known not to just one, but many of the Workers, and not just one person, but several have been involved in the garden of *people*, one by one. A harvest means a very different thing when you have had a part in the gardening. . . .

As I speak of "Members' meetings" it makes me realize that you don't know who the new Members are! I wrote in February, and immediately left for Lookout Mountain, Tennessee, where we had the L'Abri Conference. We all felt it was something very special. Ranald and Susan were there, Ran's first time in America and Sue's first time for 18 years. Udo and Debby, Jane Stuart Smith, Frances Kramer, Dr. Rookmaaker, Os Guinness, Franky and Genie, Birdie, Hurvey, Claire, Betty Carlson, Jim and Sandy, and Fran and myself. Not only were we able to speak to well over a thousand people who were cared for very efficiently by those who managed the housing and food, but we were able among us to talk to a good many personally. *Not* having to cook and do housework, etc., freed us all for conversations in a way that does not take place at L'Abri. We felt that it was an amazingly "personal time" with so many people. Also, we did see a special reality of our working together, and of our lectures "fitting together" in a way that only the Lord could have brought about. It was helpful for each of us to be able to sit and listen to the other lectures as that, too, helped us in a togetherness of thought, and helped each of us to benefit from what the Lord had given others in the way of fresh understanding. As for results, one after another, people did come to an understanding and belief, so that there were new births taking place quietly all through the time. There were exciting moments for each of us, such as the time when a dear Jewish girl listened as I outlined to her the central teaching of the Old and New Testament and how they fit together, and then came to be *sure* that Jesus was the Messiah and accepted Him as her Saviour. The people who were coming back looking for familiar faces and warm welcome were not disappointed as they found others whom they had known at L'Abri, or found the ones in whose home they had been born again!!! Discussion groups met after the evening lectures, and these half dozen groups asked questions and listened to answers until midnight or much later. In spite of floods and tremendous rainstorms, with the airport closed for some days and certain highways blocked, the people continued to pour in.

Immediately after the conference, we returned home for Easter, our personal family reunion, and then the three-day Members' meeting which is held annually to discuss, pray, and come to certain decisions concerning the L'Abri work in all its branches, the books, speaking engagements, L'Abri conference, and various matters that need to be brought to the attention of us all. This year the annual Members' meeting was held in our new home, Chalet le Chardonnet. It was very special to have space for all the Members in the living room and to have a dining room to set properly for all of us to sit together at the same table for meals, and to have a "children's" room and places for babies to be put to sleep. We began to realize the possibilities of this new big, old chalet as a place to be host and hostess to a variety of groupings of people.

The house seems like an old "homestead" that we have returned to rather than a new place, and it is suitable for so many kinds of use at the same time. The Members really appreciated it this year as they sat and listened to reports and had discussions as Ann Sizer and Joseph helped in the kitchen to prepare and serve the special meals and refreshments to give energy and keep us going for long hours. We marveled at the report from Italy as Hurvey and Dorothy told us of all the recent "fruit" after so many years of building a foundation in the work there . . . Ranald and Sue reported about the work in England . . . both Ealing and Greatham. Their report of the expected arrival of Clive and Daphne Boddington and their children is now past history as the Boddingtons have been in a trailer, living near the stable which is being turned into a house for them. They are the new L'Abri Workers in Greatham, brought by the Lord from Africa where for some years Clive has been Chaplain in the Nairobi University. Clive was a classmate of Ranald's in Cambridge and the way the Lord brought Clive into oneness with us, through the books and through his coming back as a Farel House student to Huemoz a couple of years ago, and then brought him and his wife to a certainty of His leading into the work at Greatham is a long story . . . and the thing to marvel about is once again the *continuity* and preparation covering not weeks and months, but years. The Lord is patient in His weaving . . . it is like a handwoven tapestry, compared to a machine-made one!

Vic meets people at the Mélèzes door, but more than that, he finds out as much as is possible about who they are, what they feel they have come for, and, through prayer and the sensitivity the Lord has given him, makes a decision as to how serious each individual's need is. He has discovered that the most amazing cases of people being sent by the Lord are often the ones who come with very little idea of what L'Abri is, from a kibbutz, or an ashram, or having met someone on a train, plane, or bus who told them there was a place where you could find truth, or ask questions, or discuss seriously. No one can possibly know how many there have been this summer who have been "drawn out of the mire" and who have had their feet really placed on *the rock* as they have come in these amazing ways here. (We can't know because we don't keep statistics, and because people are known to only a few of the Workers. Each one is talked to personally, but not by everybody!) Yes, Mélèzes has Kathie's apartment where our own used to be, with two students staying there as her guests, and six or eight at a time for meals, and sometimes the attic used for extra ones to sleep. The middle floor still has Gracie's room and balcony with her canaries, etc., and Vic's room, and the dining room floor and kitchen floor with people sleeping in sleeping bags for a night or two apiece. The bottom floor is Ann Sizer's home, and Barbara, who cooks for the many guest meals on the middle floor, has her bedroom down there too. Mélèzes is being used to the "hilt." The Lord doesn't discard, but uses in different ways the things He has provided along the way. . . .

In October, Fran is to be speaking in Sweden at Lund University along with Udo, and later in October he and John will be speaking in Paris. In November, Udo and Fran will be in German-speaking Switzerland, about an hour from Zurich, with Fritz and Ina Rohr giving lectures to young pastors and theological students. This is a result of years of prayer and of the books now coming out in German and stirring up interest. But except for these commitments, and a commitment to go to India in November 1975, we are simply not sure what the Lord would have us do about speaking. We realize that the Lord has jolted us out of a pattern, but what comes next is *not* known. . . .

In speaking of L'Abri Workers one would need pages to go to each house and report what is going on there. We have been going to Gentiana through the last few days, as our drains have been stopped up and no toilets could be used here or water run down the drains in washbasins! There is Debby cooking away, serving breakfast in the garden to her student family and her own family, though the new baby is about to arrive any day now! L'Abri work does not stop for births, weddings, illnesses! Pris has her mornings filled with nursery school still, so she sees the L'Abri children in an intimate way and keeps in touch with the Workers this way as well as in her time leading Workers' meetings and helping John in their work of "coordinating." However, she can be occupied in helping someone in the midst of a nervous breakdown as she stirs the stew for supper of 25 people soon to come, or she can be in the midst of marital trouble as she stops to fish Giandi out of some new escapade such as throwing all the shampoo into the bathtub, or hanging dangerously from a high branch of the tree. The L'Abri work in each household goes on in the midst of no carefully protected situation for *any* stage of life. Each stage has the things one might feel "impossible" to have interrupted, but other people's problems cannot be kept to tidy little "hours.". . .

Before our annual day of fasting and prayer on July 30th, we had on July 14th a special day of prayer for Malaysia as Mus and Verena went back to visit Mus's family and others for the first time in seven years. God has answered prayer, and Mus is back in Basel after amazing experiences.

On June 17th, Francis August Schaeffer the Sixth was born! This is the second Francis August Schaeffer to be born in Switzerland. Amazing how the generations follow one another! Now there are three generations of F.A. Schaeffers living under one roof, though the little one has not yet started to help his father and grandfather garden, chop wood, and cut the grass!! The swift passage of time, the following of one generation after another, has made us feel very certain that our new book, *Everybody Can Know,* is important for our own children's children as well as our L'Abri Family's children. So many have asked, "What shall we teach our children?" *Everybody Can Know* is meant to meet a need of *families* gathering together to read and discuss, and to *act* on their belief together. . . .

Without battle, there cannot be victory. Without sadness, there cannot be comfort. Without tribulation, there cannot be patience!!! The wonderful "inside" things have been going on in all of us as we are in the midst of growing as well as in the people who come from "afar" to find that there *is* a God, and that He is in three Persons and that they can be born into His family and have communication with Him and from Him.

With much love in Him Who is able to give you the needed thing in this moment of your need,

EDITH

December 29, 1973

Chesieres, Switzerland

Dear Family:

. . . A year ago I was at this same typewriter at this time, writing *Everybody Can Know* down in our apartment, while everyone at L'Abri was preparing for the New Year's service at Champéry and the communion service held each year from eleven P.M. until midnight December 31st. What tremendous changes have come in this year! The little apartment hideaway we had for over four years is now someone else's home. We have moved into Chalet le Chardonnet. And the book *Everybody Can Know* is in bookstores all over England and is already being read aloud in a good many family gatherings.

Peek into this chalet the night of the 29th. In the living room you would find Fran and Barry constituting a session meeting of our little International Church. Udo and Christian are also Session Members, but Udo was leading the Saturday night discussion and Christian was in America with his wife, Sandy. The Session was meeting with Zempi, the Japanese boy who had asked to be examined for baptism and joining our church. One Japanese boy who heard about L'Abri as he traveled by ship from Japan to Russia is Makoto and he became a Christian a few weeks ago, stepping out of the darkness of a Buddhist background into the light of true truth, accepting the second Person of the Trinity as his Saviour. Bob Jono, our American Japanese Worker, had spent many hours slowly and patiently answering questions and teaching both of these fellows. Now the taller, thinner, quieter Zempi has become a born-again person in the Lord's family too. How did he come? Well, it was a little over a year ago when Fran and I were in Japan that Zempi's friend heard Fran lecture. He wanted to come to L'Abri himself, but due to responsibilities at home, he could not come. He had long had a burden for his atheistic friend, Zempi, who had turned from believing in Buddhism (his family religion) but had nothing to take its place. "You go to L'Abri in Switzerland and study to find truth, and I will help to pay your voyage there." A beautiful sacrifice! But months of going on in the same job, continuing the "daily grind" is not a very glamorous sacrifice! Now, the answer to this man's prayer for his friend has taken place half the world away, and when they meet again in Japan, one can imagine the months of uneventful work will seem as nothing in the light of the meeting of *brothers*. . . . No longer friends with two separate philosophies or sets of answers to argue, but brothers in one family!

Yes, Saturday night you would have found a long and quiet discussion and answering of questions as Barry and Fran talked to Zempi and they had tea together. As the tea was served, the doorbell rang and there were these two girls in tears, saying, "We are on our way to try to buy some drugs. Will you stop us please?" You can imagine my mind's response: "But the Family Letter, and I promised also to put Jessica to bed—" However, I said, "Come in." A short time of conversation and then it is time for Verena to go to the Saturday night discussion. In the moments I disappeared to put Jessica to bed with a story and prayer, Verena had persuaded the girls to go to the Saturday night discussion but her little two-seater car would only take one person at a time, and there was another woman to be taken first. Yes, a brief time alone and the girls had disappeared. Yes, off to look for a pharmacy for certain combinations of pills they thought they could buy innocently. Verena appeared back and no girls were in sight. We prayed together, and again the doorbell bringing the information, "Drug store was closed." Yes, a tug of war in two directions at once! Looking on from the outside, we almost feel it is theatrical: asking for help, pushing it away, all at the same time. Running away to get drugs, running back when the door is closed. Is it worth the time? Do you ask this question? I would say that this is where I feel we are not to judge. We must take seriously the pleas for help, unless the Lord makes it very clear otherwise. He alone can see into hearts and know when things are desperate. We need to be willing to be available, and to be interrupted!!! . . .

Tick tock, tick tock—Debby and Udo gave me a battery clock for our bathroom by which to time my morning exercises. It, and the grandfather's clock ticking with the same rhythm, remind us of the relentless passing of time. Time used one way cannot be taken back, washed off, and reused! A minute goes by; an hour goes by; a day goes by; a week goes by; a month goes by; a year goes by. Life is limited. These last hours of 1973 I have chosen to spend with you. The buses have left for Champéry. I cannot remake my decision. The buses will arrive; people will walk, have tea in various tearooms, look up at the towering Dents Du Midi, think back over the year, talk to Fran or John and Pris, Udo and Debby, or our grandchildren and ask questions perhaps about past years. But this I am *not* to do this year because the time for this letter was used up on Saturday and Sunday with other things. Literally, I am to spend the end of the year with you, here alone looking down on the white fog covering the valley and out at the peaks.

Why such detail on small bits of small days? Because I am struggling to put into words the fact that life is not only made up of huge sweeping events which are heralded by trumpets and flags, but by a series of interruptions, of irritating hindrances, of mosquito bites and broken cups, of spilled water on crisp, clean tables set for Christmas dinner, and of little children crying about cut fingers. It is how one meets the little things that matters. It is stopping to give comfort and a band-aid, stopping to get a dishtowel cheerfully to wipe up the spills; and it is stopping to listen to desperate troubles rather than protecting oneself to do something "more important" that counts. You could follow around in the chalets today and in each place I am sure it would be the detailed, small bits which would capture your attention, and you might leave saying, "Why, nothing is happening here of any importance." You might think, "Everything is being interrupted. Why don't they arrange things more efficiently and push away the interruptions?" Big, organized companies would. L'Abri is a demonstration of how, when the living God works, He works with a situation like Gideon's. Remember Gideon with his 300 men selected by the Lord's way of choosing? Thirty-one thousand seven hundred men sent away; 300 kept to fight the Lord's battle, with lamps, trumpets, pitchers. What an inefficient way of meeting an enemy numbering into the thousands upon thousands. But you see the whole point of it was that men might know that God is *God indeed.* If you have a smooth, efficient machinery, it is too easy to trust the smooth, efficient machinery, or to admire the smooth, efficient machinery. We are meant to demonstrate that God exists, and that *He is God* indeed, and that He is able to do the impossible. I believe that is why so very many times when we place our minutes, hours, days, and weeks into God's hands, He lets it be seen that *we* are *not* doing "it." He *is* doing the impossible as we have asked Him to. Paul made it clear in II Corinthians 11 that all the results of his life were not coming forth from any smoothly efficiently run "bed of roses." Anytime you feel sorry for yourself, read that 11th chapter "in perils of waters, in perils of robbers, thrice shipwrecked, in weariness, painfulness, in hunger and thirst . . . " The promises given, and the examples cited do not give us any place to feel "cheated" of perfection in this life. The perfection is ahead. The rest is ahead. The re-wards are ahead. At present, we are in a battle, one that has a continuity with Paul's time in an unbroken line.

The oil crisis and upheaval in the world has affected L'Abri. Our heat has always been "turned down" because of the need of economizing, but it is a little lower now. We had three Sundays when Switzerland was silent of any noises of motors, no cars being driven. It was beautiful to experience walking down empty roads to church, but it was sad that some people from a distance could not come. Dr. Rookmaaker wrote and said we would talk later about whether we should go to speak in Dutch L'Abri in the light of the shortages affecting travel. In England, Greatham L'Abri is without heat except for fireplaces, and the shops are not only open only three days a week, but often are open with candle-light replacing electricity. People have so long thought that "progress" has meant constantly growing affluence, constantly increasing efficien-cy of machine and modern inventions, without stopping to realize that it is a limited universe which God has created, and that they can deplete some of the resources and find themselves going "backwards" in a vari-ety of ways. The peace conference was held in Geneva and we were told by Geneva people that two regiments of the Swiss army were out to pro-tect Geneva during that time, and machine guns were stationed at the airport for defense "in case." "Peace, peace," we are told people shall cry "when there is no peace." What a description of a peace conference which needs to be protected by an army!!! But many do not see what there is to see. He has promised to lead us "to the end" because I believe it is harder to keep on as life goes on than it is earlier. Our admonition to each other should be as this new year starts, "Remember we are to *endure to the end.*"

Last year, the Workers came to a new conclusion about Christmas. With L'Abri being open the entire year around, it seemed there should be a few days when Workers could have a time in their homes (not need-ing to go away to be alone) with their children, or with other Workers. We always do say that you need to *be* a family, to share a family life. There needs to be time to grow in personal relationships if those rela-tionships are to be extended to other people. The decision was made that for four or five days, L'Abri would be "closed," that is to say, Farel House students would not be there for study; there would be no guests; no guest tapes, lectures, guest meals, etc., and people could have a peri-od of time to either walk, sled, or go Christmas shopping, to make cook-ies, wash curtains, bring holly and pine into the houses, paint or sew or make out of wood some surprises for each other, or prepare special meals to eat together. Single Workers are able to have other Workers in as guests, or join together with a family which invites them for Christ-mas. Families with small children can plan their days around the chil-dren. It is during this period of days that Fran and I have a Helpers' Tea one evening, and a Workers' Tea another afternoon. Of course, on the

24th of December, the same thing has happened now for 25 years! This year we had our 25th Champéry Candlelight Service at 5 P.M. in the Champéry chapel where we first had the service when our own girls were ages four, eight, and twelve! An amazing continuity! In this age of "splits" in families, in groups of so many kinds, in friendships, we cannot be too careful to have times to give real "understanding" the opportunity to develop. Warm memories help our understanding of each other.

The fact that L'Abri is closed for Christmas is made known to people who come in the period of the year which makes it necessary for them to go away for a few days and come back again. We try not to have it be a sudden shock to anyone. However, there are always exceptions. This "Christmas Story" combines a lot of things at once. It seems to me the combination of things in this story speaks to us of the fact that God is still answering our prayer that L'Abri may be a demonstration of His existence.

Two years ago, Canadian Susan set forth to "bum around Europe" in the twentieth-century fashion of the young who are dissatisfied with simply doing things because they have been accepted as the acceptable manner of living by their families. Susan was "seeking" in this particular fashion of seeking in the midst of drugs, Eastern religions and something of the occult, and found in Austria a "kindred spirit" in Bridget, who shared her manner of life and ideas. The moment came, however, when Susan became more serious about her search, and these two, long-brown-haired, fresh-faced girls who look as though they should have been always running across daisy fields or swooping down sun-drenched ski fields with a base for being expectant of joy, bid each other goodbye, never expecting to see each other again. Susan was determined to stop drugs, to get rid of the hazy hindrance to thinking, and to search for truth in Morocco, or India, among those who "meditate." Bridget continued to live as she had been until cold and hunger drove her back to her home area in the midwestern part of the United States where she could find more to eat, warmth for her physical frame, while continuing to be with others of the "same mind," also basing their lives on the nothingness of an impersonal, meaningless universe.

On her way to Morocco, Susan found to her dismay one day in a youth hostel in Corfu that her wallet had been stolen. All her cash and some important papers were gone, though she still had some travel checks in another place. Three or four days of delay were necessary because of this theft, and it was *just* during those three or four days in Corfu that Susan got into a conversation with a girl about "spiritual" communities. The girl casually remarked, "I know a spiritual community in Switzerland that gives out good vibes!" and the address was exchanged along with more conversation.

Now Susan's expectancy of what she might find at L'Abri revolved around Eastern meditation and related things! You can imagine her shocked horror and revulsion when she discovered in the first days that it was *Christian*. Her first thought was to get out, and fast! But one day led to another and as she listened, discussed, saw and heard, it was not long before she had had her eyes and ears of understanding opened. She began to *really* see and hear, and in a very short time, to believe and to be born again. Obviously, the Lord who had brought her to L'Abri so amazingly and "impossibly" had also prepared her. Hers was a sincere and honest search. She was one of those who "seek with all their hearts" to whom the promise is made, "ye shall surely find me." How can I say that? Because of what has happened. We can't tell except by results or "fruits." Only God can see the hearts. All right, you can imagine what Susan did as she became a Christian and started to study at Farel House. She wrote a twelve-page letter to Bridget in Greece, and then other letters to Bridget as she went back to the States. These letters were an annoyance at first to Bridget, but not to be forgotten. When Susan's three months as a Farel House student were up, she returned to Canada to talk to her brothers, sisters, mother, and friends. Her brother Jeff became an understanding Christian, then her brother Rob, her mother, her sisters, four friends! The corn of wheat grew in a special way during the next months, with very green sprouts indeed! Or you can think of this new thread being woven into the fabric of God's design, with a riot of colored threads coming forth in the pattern at that point!

A year later, Susan was on her way back to Switzerland with her brother, Jeff, to try to study more at Farel House. Farel House was crowded, a waiting time was needed *just* when Peter and Mary needed someone to help as their third child was on its way. Susan fitted in their time of need, until the place in Farel House opened for her. All through the year, as you very well can be sure, Susan had been praying for Bridget.

Now, to follow Bridget's "thread" for a while under a magnifying glass! Having turned away from Susan's pesky letters about this place, L'Abri in Greece, and again in the States, the remembrance of Susan's intelligence kept recurring. Perhaps? The thought was pushed aside, the same drug life was continued, the occult got a deeper hold on her. Reality, unreality swims murkily along in dusky water in such a combination. There was a moment of making a decision *not* to listen to Susan, *not* to go to L'Abri and then as days blurred into weeks, Bridget found herself pregnant and pushed away from home on her way to an unknown future, as she traveled without real reason to England. Sometime later in England, now with wee baby Jessica in her arms, Bridget concluded there were only two possible avenues to follow. What is life? A wee, helpless baby growing into a wrinkled, helpless, stumbling old person. Why bother? To kill the baby and then herself might be the kindest thing to do. Or to walk away and leave the baby in a hotel room and dash her own life into silent darkness, would that be better? One or the other seemed the only choices offered to a logical mind in a meaningless universe. The occult was frightening her more all the time. The needs of this tiny baby in her arms which she seemed to have no way of fulfilling frightened her as much. To end life for both? To walk away? Which should it be? Then suddenly, she thought of L'Abri again, and Susan's caring, and Susan, and decided to go to L'Abri. Suddenly? Prayer for a year is not a very "sudden" kind of experience. Is it worth it to keep on interceding? Importunate prayer—is it dull and unrewarding? Prayer for a year, for five years, for ten years, for fifteen years—when is it too long to pray for a person who is deep in your heart, a burden to your emotions, often in your mind? There is a battle that is real. One does not have to be in the occult to be fought for by Satan. We are warned in Ephesians 6:11–18, that we are to put on the whole armor of God in this fight so that we can withstand the wiles of the devil. We are told we are not fighting against flesh and blood but against very real rulers of the darkness of this world, Satan and his armies. Read it. See that we are to pray "*always* with all prayer and supplication in the Spirit, *with all perseverance* and supplication for all saints." Yes, we are to pray with perseverance for each other, for our dear ones who are *not* yet born into the Lord's family, but also for each other who *are* His children, but who are also in danger in this battle of Satan against God.

Suddenly Bridget found herself at Huemoz at the very same time that Susan had found an "opening" to study in Farel House, and the two girls were back together again, as fellow students. The baby was being carried to lectures and church services and Bible study and meals in the various chalets, and Bridget was asking questions, thinking, studying, and understanding, and just before Christmas she, herself, became a baby in the Lord's family, a lamb in the Shepherd's flock. You see, she was one of the "lost" that Jesus came to find. She was one of the ones that the first Christmas was all about. Jesus so clearly taught that He came to seek and to save the *lost*, and to cause blind eyes to see. The "good" ones who *feel* so righteous in their outward keeping of certain standards are the ones like the Pharisees of Jesus' time, about whom Jesus remarked that He had come that they which "see might be blind." The proud *un*seeking hearts without honesty, so sure of their own goodness, are the ones in the most dangerous position. To know one is "lost" in some small measure of understanding is the beginning of being found.

Let me tell you about Christmas at L'Abri in 1973. Bridget with Jessica on her lap, Susan and her brother Jeff, and Charles the organist who had arrived a brief time before, sat discussing what they could do for Christmas. Some had gone to ski camps, some to visit friends, others to be together in a pension. Bridget had a room in a village house which rents rooms, and they decided they might be able to fix a spaghetti dinner there together on one burner. Priscilla heard about this and offered her oven and suggested that the chapel would be a place where they could eat in front of a fireplace and sing as the organist gave them superb accompaniment. The plans grew, and pennies were counted. Some of the rest of our L'Abri Family here heard about it, and quietly, some gifts were made: a turkey, some money, and Ann Pelican offered the use of her apartment. Ann's apartment happens to be the Mélèzes living room with the stone fireplace, and the kitchen across the hall, in fact the *very* room and fireplace where we had our *first* Christmas as L'Abri started 19 years ago. Others heard about the plans and asked to be included. "I didn't know where to go, could I share it too?" One evening at the local pub, while eating supper, Charlie, Jeff, Susan, and Bridget noticed a Canadian pair of backpacks identified by Canadian flags. "Wonder who is here in the café from Canada?" Two dejected-looking young people sat there eating a supper, "Are you from Canada?" They had come, hoping to "drop in for Christmas" on L'Abri and had found it closed for a few days. So, the invitation was given, "Join us . . . "

Christmas day! The marketing had been done, greens had been placed around, the turkey had been stuffed and placed in the oven, tables had been set, the Champéry service was a memory of yesterday, and in all the L'Abri chalets the "families" were gathering to read Luke 2, to open gifts, to observe their own diverse little customs, and to serve the special surprises they had prepared so lovingly for those gathered in their own houses. In the living room of Mélèzes, one could imagine the walls and stones remembering Christmases past, as 18 people gathered to bow their heads and thank God for the food. It had literally been provided in answer to prayer, and there had been exactly enough money to the penny to provide the fulfilling and beautiful dinner that was to be shared. Seventeen adults each expressed the fact that it was the first Christmas being spent among Christians. A few of them were spending their first Christmas as members of the Lord's family, their first Christmas as believers. They marveled together at how the Lord had provided them with a place, the food, even gifts to open, and finally, a place to sing, as Charles played carols for them. "It was the most exciting and best Christmas," one after another reported. Little Jessica was loved and enjoyed as she was the 18th member of the family put together in Mélèzes for that one special day. You can imagine what a comfort it was to all the rest of us to know that these who had no place were given a place, yet you can also imagine how impossible it would have been to add that many, plus 40 others who had gone away, to the family gatherings!! . . .

May 1974 be a very special year of deepening in personal knowledge and closeness to the Lord, and of making *known* to our children, and other people's children—no matter what age, the things it is so important to *know* in this our *one* life before standing before the Creator of the Universe.

With much love in Him Who is *able* to keep us from falling, in a time when Satan's wiles are designed to trip us into a state of despair,

EDITH

1974

June 29, 1974   Chesieres, Switzerland

Dear Family:

You can't imagine how many times my weekly lists of "Things to Do" have included capital letters announcing to me "WRITE THE FAMILY LETTER." Had it been written some other month, some other week, it would have been a different letter. Amazing how true it is that communication, whether it be a phone call, a conversation, a letter, or a book, is affected by what we personally have just lived through, or have suddenly come to "see." We *say* in our conversation, we communicate in our writing, something that we are full of, something that is going to affect other people. If what has colored our own feeling and understanding is what is a part of the unfolding plan of God for us, the blending effect will be something very *real*, and not just an artificial tinkling of words.

Fran and I have been away for a two–week vacation, but as we came home, we felt a bit discouraged about still feeling tired, and yet needing to plunge into all that was waiting for us, letters from people needing answers, and people wanting conversation in the midst of their needs, announced by either the telephone or the doorbell! If you think *we* are always "bright and shining" in an eagerness to talk to people, you should have been in the kitchen last night, to observe me frying and folding 20 Chinese omelets (egg foo yung with bean sprouts and chopped new onions) while Ann was frying the Chinese rice with smoked tuna, and while the chicken and cabbage with pineapple had its cornstarch thickening added in between seconds. A steamy rush—to prepare a Chinese dinner for twenty people having Friday night dinner with us. Fran, the host, had brought out the soup dishes simply because he felt he couldn't face answering questions, and was staying out to watch us cook, loath to return. Yet when each person had his Hong

Kong turquoise bowls and wooden chopsticks and Fran was in his place, and Ann and I in ours, the conversation did not drag. . . .

It was the first day of July when the telephone rang and Pris wept out to me the tragic news she had just received from Marry Meester Berg. Hans, Marry's husband, had left early in the morning for a long drive to work. Marry and the children were with her sister in a summer cabin in the woods for a little vacation time. Hans had been with them for the weekend. It was a rainy, slippery day on the road. A truck made a wrong turning movement, and a second later had plunged into the driver's side of Hans's car, instantly crushing Hans's body and Hans was absent from the body and present with the Lord in less time than one could tell about it.

Marry was our second Dutch Worker living with us in Mélèzes in the very early days of L'Abri. She has been so close to us through the years as a friend and almost a daughter, and she and Hans have also been members of our local congregation of the International Church, as they lived in Switzerland for a number of years. For the last year, their home has been back in Holland to be within driving distance of the special school-home where their handicapped little Steven spends five days a week. Steven is deaf as well as unable to walk or talk or use his hands properly. This dear little six-year-old is a very handicapped cerebral palsy child and has needed hours of therapy and special care since birth. Because of his very special needs, Hans and Marry have very constantly talked about the second coming of Christ, and the new earth to little Jaapjan who is two years older than Steven and has had many questions as to when his little brother will be able to walk and talk. "Steven will walk on the new earth, when Jesus comes back again and everything will be made all right." The vividness of the coming fulfillment of the promises God has given us in His Word for the future are at present a help to both eight-year-old Jaapjan and to Marry. However, the hours and days and months stretch out, one at a time, and it will not be easy for Marry. She needs the prayers of the L'Abri Family as well as of her own family. We are meant to care for each other, sharing grief as well as joy. God has told us that when we have sorrow, we will have comfort, *His* comfort, and that with that comfort, we are to comfort others. Jesus wept at the tomb of Lazarus with a hatred of death, the enemy, but the only way He could defeat death was with His own death. He could raise Lazarus, but Lazarus would die again. The only complete victory giving eternal life and placing death behind us forever was by the death of the eternally alive Second Person of the Trinity. The solution was costly. Our more minimal help to each other must cost something too. *Real* help to each other in a time of need takes a toll out of our personal ease and uses up time we would have used in other ways.

In January, Fran and I were in England visiting and helping in Greatham and Ealing for a brief ten days or so. We stayed with Ran and Sue in their part of the house, so had the unusual privilege of experiencing their family life and hectic fitting in of the "big house" life at the same time. Margaret and Kirsty's scrambles to get hair brushed, school books and special projects gathered together, breakfast finished, and then off to school for the whole day, followed by Fiona and little Ranald's finishing up their breakfasts in time to welcome little Benjy for the morning is something to be seen, not described! Benjy's mother is a L'Abri Worker in Greatham, so our Susan takes him for the morning and Benjy's mother takes both boys for another part of the day. As both were then about 18 months old, it was a sidelight of L'Abri to be experienced as you think of the various ones who are doing "conjuring tricks" as they replace all the books toddlers have carefully removed before going to answer a phone, to talk to a new person just arrived, or to fill up the washing machine with the sixth load of wash for the day. Laundry in each of the L'Abri homes is titanic with the "sharing" of houses and the regular family day in and day out. It was special to attend Sunday tea and hear Margaret play so well on the recorder and hear Ran read aloud. Later I was asked to read a chapter of *Everybody Can Know* to them myself, which was fun. Fran and I were very impressed with the way the stables were turning into a very nice house for Clive and Daphne Boddington and their three boys, as they are now L'Abri Workers there. It was something to be seen and heard, as we watched five or more painting window sills and frames, walls and doorways, while someone else hammered away on a bit of carpentry work—all listening to music and humming as a tape recorder played away. We were taken all through the various rooms of the big house, and shown the new kitchen in the old 17th–century part of the house, and given a description of how "someday that old courtyard will be the scene of a remodeling into a house for Jerram and Vicki." Changes of all sorts in the house, three couples working together, Jill and Susan W. carrying on with an amazing schedule of daylight to midnight kind of hours, not only cooking and doing endless gardening, housecleaning (showing students what to do next, etc.), but also talking to people with deep needs far into the night hours at times. In the week we were there, we couldn't get to the end of being shown what had been done or was going to be done, not to the end of the stories of lives being changed, or in deep, deep need. There are a number of younger teenage people being helped at Greatham, so that the variety is pretty amazing. One brought a horse with her to add to the farm there! The Greatham and also Ealing L'Abri have more people who have been deep in drugs, or are still having problems in this area, than anywhere else, or so it seems. However, in each branch of L'Abri, the "problems" differ from month to month or year to year. One thing—there is no lack of variety in the problems to be faced! It may be exhausting but it is not boring!

In Ealing we stayed with Ros Kramer in her lovely little apartment, and it seemed like old times for me to go into London with Cynthia, although London was rather weird with lanterns in the department stores, and no lights in the windows or on the streets—an eerie ghost town overnight, so to speak, caused one to feel that the things so taken for granted can after all be very temporary. Changes ahead of us can be fearful unless we take each step in the assurance that we *do* have an unchanging God in whose hand we are. . . .

In early May Fran and Franky flew off to Houston where they were speaking at a conference and where Franky had an art show. I went on a sunny Sunday to Birdie's little Chalet le Nid, appropriately "the Nest" for my first Sunday dinner in another chalet than our own. Franky and Fran had already left and Pris and I had not gone yet so I was invited after church, even as many strangers are invited to one or another chalet *if* there are extra open places. There were ten there for dinner sitting at an attractively set wood table in the garden, looking over the Rhone Valley and on to the Dents du Midi. Birdie pointed out her vegetable garden which flourishes at the side of her house, and also the two plots she shares with other people, as Os and Jenny have a garden there and so does Vic. Pris and I then went off by train to Berchtesgaden, Germany, to speak to a conference of military wives, 350 leaders of the Protestant women of the chapel coming from the various military centers all over Europe. We had never realized before that there are over 350,000 military men and families in Europe. There is a tremendous need among them that we never knew much about, and I must say we knew that the Lord had taken us for those days of intensive speaking and personal conversation. It was the first time Priscilla had been away from Huemoz L'Abri (except for short vacations) for 12 years! She had not only not spoken or done anything elsewhere, but had not even gone to a "meeting" elsewhere. Also, it was the first time Pris and I had ever done anything together like that, and it was a great treat, perhaps once in a lifetime! The eager and hungry attention was deeply moving, and we only wished there had been more books in the book room as the one hundred copies of *Everybody Can Know* and the one hundred copies of *L'Abri* that were there were literally sold in a few minutes, and many were disappointed. Some are so isolated in Turkey, Morocco, Iceland, etc., that they long for books, which are hard to get. Again, it is a question of being finite. Invitations have come from a number of army posts now, but it is impossible to be in L'Abri and travel like that frequently. It was good for Pris and myself, however, to be made aware of both the need of prayer for this whole section of people, and to realize that the Lord's children are so very scattered! . . .

The latest thing the newspapers in Switzerland are talking about is the new "push" the anti-foreign minority is making to get rid of more foreigners in Switzerland. Their goal is to get 300,000 foreigners put out of Switzerland in a certain length of time—a year or two. To counterbalance that, it has been rumored that the government is going to put a stop to giving special "permits" so that hospital workers, hotel staff, theologians helping in Christian work, etc., etc. would no longer be exempt from being given sudden notice to leave. The Lord has cared for the couples in L'Abri through giving these exemptions as "theologians." Others of us have our Permit C which gives us the same rights as citizens. And, of course, John and Priscilla and Pierre and Danielle are Swiss. Humanly looking at it, anyone who does not have a Permit C, or is not a Swiss citizen, is in danger of being on the "list" to be put out. . . . It must not be taken for granted that the freedom of living or doing things in a variety of countries is going to continue. . . .

And letters! Hundreds of letters come from people who are being affected by the books. So many have been born again reading them, all the way from a prisoner in for "life sentence" in Australia, to a psychiatrist in the Midwest who was a reader of Tillich before, but who was convinced of the true truth of the Word of God in reading *The God Who Is There* and *He Is There and Is Not Silent.* Letters come from people helped by reading Udo's books, Betty's, Fran's, mine, from amazingly widely separated parts of the world: South Africa, India, Hong Kong, Canada, South America, New Zealand, and the ends of the earth. And letters need answers whether they ask questions, or want to come to L'Abri. . . .

Is there something wrong with Christianity when one faces violent separation by sudden death, harsh news of fresh cancer breaking out, fearful possibilities of being put out of countries, lesser yet difficult moments of broken legs, horses eating the rooftop of one's small car (yes, Larry Snyder's car top was eaten by a horse this month while they were on vacation!), need to leave a life work to face an entirely new thing, weariness beyond description at times—yet no "let up" in sight? Is this the "green pastures and still waters" of Psalm 23? What is wrong? . . .

We need to comfort one another by reminding each other that Jesus is coming back, and maybe it will be today. But we need also to urge each other *not* to "nig out," but to endure to the end. We are surrounded by all the "witnesses" who have gone on before; the ones who have gone on last week, as well as centuries ago, who are interested in our enduring, as are the angels too. One day, we'll all have peace and comfort and *endless time,* to discuss all that happened, and to praise our loving, living God for the way He brought each one of us through fire and water to our mansions and very special green pastures.

With much love in Him in Whom we have assurance of the future,

EDITH

P.S. You will notice that my father, Dr. George H. Seville, is no longer listed as Treasurer Emeritus. This is not because he is not living and well, at the age of 98 and 4 months!!!! But that a few people send checks for L'Abri to him, not realizing that he is not handling business now. Therefore, his name will be removed, although he is still living in Watertown, New York, with my sister, and is very keenly a praying family member of L'Abri, sitting in his rocking chair each morning, going over the prayer list item by item very carefully.

November 26, 1974   Chesieres, Switzerland

Dear Family:

Some weeks ago we had in our living room a Swiss woman, formerly a missionary nurse in Africa, a leading man in a certain African country who was studying in Switzerland, an Egyptian man of some prominence in his country, and a little Swiss man who used to be a street cleaner, but had had a breakdown. The Egyptian needed to know the truth of the Triune God, Creator, and Saviour whom the Bible sets forth. The man from Africa needed to know what this God, his Father and Saviour, wanted him to do about returning to possible martyrdom. As I sat pouring tea for these two men, and the others, somehow on that couch those two sat as representatives of the seriousness of our own decisions hour by hour. To say "yes" to a phone call in the midst of an already-too-busy-day had given some hesitation. "Yes, do come. Yes, of course we will pray with the man from Africa and talk to him." But now the other things to be done—cooking, writing, ironing, washing the bathtub—seemed ridiculous as the man related the torture and killing of 110 of his friends which had taken place a week before on the basis of their staying true to the teaching of the Bible rather than bowing to the heathen initiation rites. Not a pastor, but a well-educated leader, this man had given a very thorough Bible study to show that we are to be true to the Lord, even to death. To sing these words, and to solemnly say them in church or in prayer, is another thing from having friends killed on the basis of carrying them out. And the Egyptian? If he comes to believe that the God of the Bible is the true God, what would happen???? But if not—???? . . .

Someone from India studied at L'Abri for a month this summer and has obtained the news, back in his own part of India, letting us know by letter that about 5,000 to 6,000 Lisu are at this moment being persecuted in the north of India where they fled some years ago when Communists entered their hill country southwest of China. The Lisu had become Christians through the China Inland Mission missionaries. For years we have prayed for these people, and how special that their definite needs now come to us through one whom God brought to Switzerland to L'Abri.

The network of need, the continuity of God's threads through history, and through geographic space, the pattern from the early church on, of changed lives, scattering believers from Jerusalem, Judea to the uttermost parts of the world; the succession of persecutions, the number of martyrs, yet the continuing aliveness of the message; the fact that the Bible has not been stamped out any more than the last believer has been stamped out should really *shake* us in our own pinpoint moment of history. We *must* not kill the reality of the wonder of what we have been given by acting as though we had merely joined a club, or decided upon a political party. We *are* the people of the *living God,* and He is our Director. *Dare* we tell each other what to do, or glide along lethargically in a rut, without *praying* positively for the Lord's plan to be unfolded and yet before that, for *honesty* in wanting to do it, even if it turns our present little securities upside down? We must pray actively against the devil also, as we are told he is seeking whom he may devour, and he is accusing the "brethren" (the family of God) daily. How dare we feel capable of planning our own lives, but even more the lives of others? It is *so* easy to slip into a laxness of prayer, and to take things for granted. . . .

November 3rd was my 60th birthday, and that number seems to have no relationship to me. Has it to anyone, I wonder? Time does not "feel" like time as it slides by. The counting of years "since—" comes always as a shock. Fran and I will have been married 40 years this summer. L'Abri has just had its 20th Thanksgiving service, which means that by June, L'Abri will be 20 years old. God has not, nor will He now, hand out a blueprint for the future of our individual lives, or our work. My father, who helped as being treasurer and the one to send out the Family Letters at the beginning of L'Abri, will be entering his 100th year when he becomes 99 March 19th. He does not "feel" the reality of a hundred years.

The happy thought is that God really does take care of the future. He has the whole of eternity as a reality to Him as He guides us in the present. Who else can we trust? This is the One who tells us to "take no thought for the morrow," but to put first the kingdom of God. He knows about the possible depression, the rise in food prices, the quirks of the weather, the state of our health, the threatening illnesses. "Take no thought—" "In nothing be anxious, in everything by prayer and supplication with thanksgiving let your requests be made known unto God,"* was written with God's *knowledge* of the very things which make you, or me, "anxious" today! Therefore, today is the opportunity we have to carry out His solution to the anxiety. And if the anxiety doesn't go away? We keep praying, while we are typing, peeling potatoes, using the adding machine, or sawing wood. Don't stop praying. . . .

If you are discouraged by some coming to L'Abri with a kind of vague, romantic idea of coming to the place they have read about, remember the Norwegian girl who was skiing in Zermatt two years ago and who fell into a crevasse, head down, with her skis catching on two sides of an ice wall. Hanging there unconscious for a period, she came to, to find her clothing was frozen to one wall holding her there, and that all she could see was a frightening, blue, icy light. It was hours before her friend could get a rescue squad there, and before they could gingerly work their way down, cut her loose, and bring her up. A saved life in an extraordinarily impossible circumstance! The friend found her way to L'Abri that year in an amazing way. Now this year, the girl who hung between physical life and death for hours is here, "hanging between

*Philippians 4:6

life and death" as she struggles with the problems of certainty of the truth of what she is being taught, and willingness to bow. Then there is a German girl who had been one of the many "wanderers" in Europe. She had become a part of a strange "commune" in Switzerland where a fellow who inherited a lot of money bought a house and filled it with young people "experimenting" in making films and "doing drugs," with wild ideas of living in a blimp, going around the world in a boat, and experimenting with LSD in the process. This girl was hitching rides with a friend, expecting to go to Amsterdam, when she got a ride with a couple of L'Abri people on their way to do "Migros shopping" (supermarket for food). Sitting outside the supermarket with one fellow from L'Abri, while the other shopped, she heard about L'Abri for a very short time. Not immediately, but a few hours later, she decided to drop in at this place to see what it was like. That has been nearly three weeks ago, and she is still at Bethany where Cristel can talk to her in German to help her understand some of that which is an entirely new thing to her. It may take a long time, but we pray the way will open for her to continue to be here.

Think of the impossibility of F. and D. coming here from another African country. These two were Christians in a church where a number of people had been killed for their faith. A warning was given them that there was to be further persecution and their lives were particularly a target, so they escaped to Kenya. However, in Kenya there are too many from their country, and an edict declaring that they must be sent back meant that these two would probably go back to their death. It would take far too much time to relate all the complicated "network" that brought phone calls from America to us, and letters from Fran to the Swiss Consulate in Nairobi, and the entrance of F. and D. into our midst for three months. They must go elsewhere afterwards, and we need to pray for the right country to open up but their lives have been spared for something the Lord has yet for them to do. It is clear that our God is able to do most complicated things to bring the "people of His choice" as we pray for Him to do that here. "L'Abri" means "The Shelter" in French, as you know, and God is the One who reminds us often that it *is* a "shelter" in many ways for a variety of people who need a shelter spiritually, emotionally, physically, or intellectually. There are many kinds of "storms" in 1974!! . . . Enid is on her way back to her own part of India. This dear Indian girl, with her great variety of lovely saris, has been a part of L'Abri since July . . . cooking Indian food for a number of chalets' special meals, and warming the hearts of many of us with her bright smile and understanding brown eyes. Enid is a Christian who has been a youth leader in her own country, writing articles, and speaking at gatherings. She also has done a work among villages with a practical combination of teaching Bible, and teaching some skill in crafts to help people earn enough for food. She also has taught how to cook a greater variety of things in order to help people have better nutrition. Hers is a practical work among children too, with which India swarms, as they wander homeless and often foodless, around the streets of all the cities. An Indian doctor, Sheila, was also here as a student at Farel House and has gone back determined to teach university students that which she has learned at L'Abri. Along with Kumar, who was here studying for six months and is now back in India, (and others) . . . it means that God has operated a kind of "airlift" in His own way to do something in India which is *His* plan there, and in which He meant us to have a small part. Enid has been studying Hindu and Eastern thought and putting it together with what she has learned here to try to prepare to make Christianity more clear, and to try to really answer the questions which come from the Eastern "mentality." Enid prepared a "farewell" meal in Ann Pelican's dining/living room in Mélèzes, and she had a dozen or so there, with me, too, as a guest in the room where L'Abri all started!!! Her idea was to have all the girls in saris, so she shared hers, and dressed each one up, including Gracie, in a proper sari. We ate with our fingers and felt almost as if *we* had been the ones whisked to another land! There is no doubt that in addition to what the Lord has prepared these various ones to do in India as a result of their being at L'Abri, He also means us to *notice* the need in that country, and to pray for the individuals, as well as the great general need.

When we pray for "God's plan to be unfolded"—how encouraging to really *take notice* of the miracle of what He has done, and is doing. Think of the fact that Mrs. Rookmaaker has been burdened for India for the last few years and has gathered enough money to build an orphanage and help very much in the work among children in India, going herself several times. This is not a part of the L'Abri world, but we are glad for it, and share in it in prayer. Think also of the fact that Bob Jono, the American Japanese Worker who was so helpful here in L'Abri, went to India for several months to work with Kumar among young people, and to visit ashrams and talk directly to the gurus. Bob has now left India and we have letters from him from Bangkok, where he is staying with the Morton family (Mr. Morton is a Pepsi-Cola representative, and both he and his wife are Christians and have been at L'Abri for a period). The Mortons offered a room in their home for someone to come from L'Abri and talk to students in Bangkok. At the moment, Bob is doing this . . . and has been amazed at the people the Lord has taken him there to be with. This is something *no human committee* could do.

The Swiss vote went through *against* putting all the foreigners out and *for* keeping them in, so for the moment there will be no *new* problems about permits, although permits are no easier to get than they have been. This, too, is something to say "thank you" for. . . .

The Ashburnham Conference in September was the first one in England in five years. It was wonderful to be driven along English country roads by Ran and his brother, John, with time to talk, as others from Greatham hitchhiked or came by train, and others from widely scattered parts of the British Isles converged on Ashburnham, near Battle, near Hastings! Sue brought the four children by train, feeling it was easier to load the car up with all the suitcases and paraphernalia.

The speakers were Barry Seagren from Huemoz L'Abri, Jerram Barrs from Greatham, Dick Keyes from Ealing, Dr. Rookmaaker from Holland, Os Guinness, Fran, and myself. Susan and Jill and Sue Whitehead cared for the younger children with Bible stories and projects, as well as much finger painting, games, and comforting crying ones! Ranald, Clive, and Daphne took care of the organization details and projects for older children, which included boating on the little lake, games, and walks, as well as Bible studies and songs. It was a time of reunion, as so many were there from different "years" of L'Abri, and it was a cause for saying "thank you" to be reminded of those who had become Christians at the last conference, like John Baslington. The messages fit together without being planned that way, which gives us such a sense of the Lord's planning things.

The following Monday, Fran and I flew to America where we visited Nancy and Boyd Anderson who are in a hard period of time, as Nancy has had all sorts of treatments for cancer and is having one hard thing after another. Then we were in Macon, Georgia, for the Presbyterian Church in America General Assembly where Fran's messages were helpful in fortifying the stand on the Word of God in practical beginnings of a new denomination. From there, we went to Syracuse to stop with Jeremy and Lucinda Jackson (my niece) as a new project is bringing us together in a special closeness for the unfolding of something God clearly is leading us to do. Jeremy is a history professor in Syracuse University, formerly in Cambridge with Ranald, and a L'Abri Worker in the early days of L'Abri, for two years. A whirl of a ride to Watertown to visit dear Father who is praying that Jesus will come back before he "goes another way" and who is still a faithful part of the L'Abri Family, and my sister Elsa and husband. And while there, a sudden change of plans to fly out the next day, as a call came from Gordon Seminary asking us to come there for just a day. . . .

In the light of the truth of the whole Bible, the shortness of life, the reality of God's being the One to plan His pattern and shift us and place us in *His* timing for the total purpose, we need to be careful not to waste precious time in *not* trusting. It seems to me that part of trusting *Him* is to be constant in our interest in each other, and in praying for each other whether we stay where we are, or are shifted.

You should know that Fran is working on *The Rise and Decline of Western Thought and Culture,** tracing history, art, music, science, philosophy, theology, political thought, etc., from the fall of the Romans until the present time. As we have been together, it has been a time of feeling that God lifted us up (almost literally) and dropped us into a period of forced

*This marked the beginning of work on the book and film *How Shall We Then Live?*

study, research, writing, praying, and walking together. We have been able to have late night walks by a quiet lake to talk and pray, as well as uninterrupted work. It has been what many people have suggested we needed, a kind of "sabbatical," in spite of its being hard work. One stage is behind us now and the manuscript will be in the hands of researchers for the next weeks. In February and March we will be gone for two months— away, yet not too far for me to be here once a week. My part is being Fran's wife to be with him in all this, but when he is needing the hours of solitary concentration then I am writing.* So the Lord has given me this opening too, along with the possibility of having the therapy I need for my back—a pool nearby to swim in a half-hour a day of non-stop backstroke! God is a God of details, and there is so much more to tell as to how He has woven in the details which only *He* could do. More detail in another letter soon!!

And right now? In a few *hours* we leave for speaking again, this time in St. Louis at Covenant Seminary and Washington, D.C., where Fran will speak to Southern Baptist leaders of Evangelism from 50 states and will also have some meetings with press men and government men. I am being taken to speak to a number of women's groups in Washington. In McLean, Virginia, it is the Christian Women's Club's Christmas luncheon. There will be small Bible classes, one after another of various wives—such as press media wives, congressional wives, etc. Then we go to Philadelphia for two days to be with Dr. MacRae, an old friend, and his seminary, Biblical School of Theology, and then a L'Abri reunion in Philadelphia, and one lecture at Westminster Seminary. Then, Lord wiling, we fly home to be back the 17th of December. . . .

We have had two days of fasting and prayer, one in October for guidance and unity and a closeness of understanding among us as we seek the Lord's will and one in November for the need of material things. The Lord *has* provided through all the years, and none of us have been in "want," not one has starved. But the coming or not coming of funds is guidance, as well as a need for a call to prayer. The Lord has told us not to be anxious, but to *pray,* and if there is no *need* to pray, one never knows either urgency or the relief of an answer. There is nothing that binds people together more than a common *need.* Whether a tiny family, or a big family, troubles or needs draw people together. Perhaps November's needs were an answer to October's prayer for oneness!! . . .

Isaiah knew what our fears are like, because he experienced the same, with a strong solution for his own moment of life, and for us: "For the Lord God will help me: therefore shall I not be confounded: therefore I have set my face like a flint, and I *know* that I shall *not be ashamed*" (Isaiah 50:7).

With love in Him—

EDITH

*This was the first work on *What Is a Family?*

1975

Dear Family:

I am writing this in Montreux near the lake where grey fog shrouds the buildings with mystery, and cuts the lake off a few meters away from the shore, with ghostly looking trees making a background for the lake gulls swooping around in and out of the mist. One would never know there were mountains on the other side of the lake, nor a blue sky somewhere above us. As for warm sun, that would seem to have departed for warmer climes thousands of miles away. It is damp and penetratingly chilly. Brrr. Yet a phone call to Huemoz has brought us the *fact* that up there, just 35 minutes by car away from here, a brilliant February sun is blazing away, and people are happily sitting outside on balconies for lunch and remarking on how the snowdrops and early wee yellow flowers are decorating the grass. Veronica has said that she is having lettuce from her garden, and Janine says her "rampon" (a tiny green plant to eat raw in salads) is growing by leaps and bounds. If you drove on up the mountain to Chesieres, five more minutes above Huemoz, you would find our garden still covered with snow and our "rampon" unable to put out shoots yet. If you then took the mountain train from Villars on up to Bretayes—a twenty-minute ride to the ski fields, you'd see people whizzing down the slopes and remember that it really is winter (although more snow is needed for really good skiing).

But there are more than tantalizing "upsets" in weather to be used as illustrations to us of our limitations; the fog here and the sun so dazzling above, to be reached by driving through the ceiling of fog, should comfort us over and over again as it pictures so vividly the reality of the Lord's presence being "there," so close to us, even when one or another kind of "fog" of depression, sadness, pain, or irritation *seems* to be separating us from feeling the reality of His being there. Often we need to go some distance, even a very short distance, to get into the warmth of His

227

presence. Happily each of us has access to the "transportation" because as we read the Bible, and talk to Him, we discover that the mist is thinning out, at least for the moment. "Thy mercy, O Lord, is in the heavens; and thy faithfulness reacheth unto the clouds. For with thee is the fountain of life: in *thy* light shall we *see* light" (Psalm 36:5,9). "Forsake me not, O Lord: O my God, be not far from me" (Psalm 38:21).

The Bible is the place we need to go to find the Lord's presence, and any of us who are not sure what 1975 holds for us, even though our "agenda's" pages already have things written in for the months ahead, a schedule already filling up, need to comfort ourselves in reading over and over again the fact that the Lord God is the One who will light our candle in the darkness. The One who gave the pillar of fire in the wilderness to lead the way for the Israelites is quite able to split the fog for each one of us. . . .

We look back . . . each one of us, and we see some tiny part of the whole, a tiny part to marvel about and to thank Him for. We look at each other and marvel at what God has done with "each other," because we each can be amazed (knowing ourselves) at what He has done with the very "impossible *me*" . . . but some of us know each other well enough to marvel at His power in each other as well. The L'Abri reunion in Philadelphia was a time of that kind of marveling. A "Mélèzes High Tea" had been beautifully prepared by Bob Beck, Judy Little, Ann Sizer, and others . . . and Eric's house, with Peter and Becky Foster (who were at Greatham L'Abri) as host and hostess, was the most beautifully welcoming place . . . with every window in the white frame house lighted with a candle . . . candles on the sandwich-filled table, candles on the table holding the teapots and cups and saucers, plates and napkins . . . a fire in the fireplace. It couldn't have been lovelier! We would have needed hours and hours to be reminded of all the "miracles" that had taken place in lives . . . and it seemed almost every year of L'Abri was represented. All too soon, the hours had sped past, and what had been so looked forward to became a memory. Thank God for memory! Speaking of memories . . . Arlene wanted to introduce us to her father and mother, and her father said to Fran, "Schaeffer . . . Schaeffer . . . you wouldn't by any chance have been in troop 38?" Fran's memory went back to his Boy Scout troop in Philadelphia which indeed had been Troop 38 and the two men discovered that they had known each other all those years ago. Arlene's father! Any of you who know the sheer wonder of what the Lord did in bringing Arlene to L'Abri in the first place, and all He has done for her since, will be amazed to think of her father and Fran being in the same scout troop. It makes the whole world seem like a small neighborhood. Fran wasn't a Christian when he was a boy in the scout troop. There wasn't anyone to answer his questions or to explain true truth to him. It's all rather sobering when you think of the "what ifs . . . " that come to one's thoughts. What if Francis Schaeffer had not decided that it would be more honest to read the Bible before throwing it away and declaring himself to be a confirmed agnostic back when he was 18 years old? What if he had not thrown himself upon God, accepting as true truth that which he felt gave all the answers to his questions as he made the discovery of what the Bible taught, all alone, with no one to talk it over with, without knowing there was anyone else who had discovered what he had discovered? "What if . . ." One could go through the years asking this question in retrospect, and through the lives of each of those who have come to be truly "saved" in one or another of the L'Abri branches. What if L'Abri had "disappeared" before Juan came up the hill, or Jane S. Smith, or Bill, or Peter, or Bob, or Ros . . . or so many others? The courage to "keep on" as long as it is time to "keep on" must be prayed for day by day by each one of us. . . .

The L'Abri Ensemble has traveled around having an amazing number of "reunion" evenings along with their concerts, and even they couldn't tell you all the "threads" the Lord wove together in their November tour, but there'd be no L'Abri Ensemble if Jane hadn't been born again now 19 years ago, and if Betty hadn't been born again in Champéry.

There is going to be a *first* Canadian L'Abri Conference in Calgary, Canada in 1975—May 3–11. What kind of preparation has been made for that conference? As far as I can remember, that preparation started when the Lord brought the first G.I. from the American Army in Germany to L'Abri, back in 1955. The army gave three-day passes to the G.I.'s at that time, and I won't forget the day when a tall boy with curly blond hair and big blue eyes happily brought his chugging motor to a stop in the gravel in front of Chalet les Mélèzes. "I heard that you have a place where people can come, and I've come," he said as he got out with a pleased grin. It was teenaged Bill McColley doing his stint in the army before finishing high school and having a hard time in the barracks as taunts were slung at him when he read his Bible or tried to pray. A haunting fear that Christianity was after all only for people who were too uneducated to know it couldn't be true wouldn't stay pushed away!! The reaction that first time? "Boy, it's been great! I couldn't understand a thing Mr. Schaeffer was talking about, but I sure am proud to be a Christian. I know now it isn't just for simple uneducated people." I've often thought of that statement and have realized that whether a person has philosophic questions or not, it can be helpful to know that the answers are *there*. In Calgary, Alberta, near Bill was another pastor who had spent months at L'Abri, Bob Ball, who was a Farel House student with his whole family living in Huemoz for months. Bob and Bill began to talk and pray together. . . .

After Christmas break, people began arriving again, until very, very soon L'Abri was *full*. Hotels and pensions in Switzerland complain that the English, American, French, Italian (and some other countries) tourists are *not* coming because the Swiss franc is so high in relationship to their currencies. Of course, you are reading about this in all your papers and news magazines. The strange thing is, however, that we have *no* fewer people coming to L'Abri. And the Mlles. Chaudets, and M. et Mme. Ruchet, and Pensione Les Fugeres have no fewer people because people coming to L'Abri are filling them!! Also, all the Workers have been reporting that they have very serious and interested people— that is, people with real needs, real questions, and a desire to discuss and study. This is very encouraging and makes all the difficulties more than worthwhile—and brings into focus something of the fact that things are taking place inside people that are going to have eternal importance. . . .

The "world" would like to say that it is an "impossible " time to "live by faith" with the American dollar strangely dropping in value all the time, with "depression" always around the corner. "How can you go on?" is a question thrown out of the air with an underlining Satan would like to give it. How easy is it going to be for Christians to "keep on" just the week before Jesus comes back, I wonder? We're called to "keep on" over and over again. . . "Impossible," Peter's heart and intellect both cried out within him. "It is impossible, Jesus, what you have asked me to do. I can't—I can't—I can't—I'm drowning!" Peter, we know, looked down at the waves and began to sink. However, what he had asked Jesus was, *"If it be Thou*, bid me to come . . . " We declare we want to do the will of the Lord, that we want His plan. "If it be Thou, unfold Your plan." And all He has said to any of us is, "Come . . . " He hasn't said it will look easy. He hasn't promised it will look smooth. He hasn't said He will give a blueprint of how it will all work out. . . . Peter's waves stayed the same, and they were *not* stable, or secure to walk on!!!

Jesus says to us, "Come. . . Come, if you want My will . . . " But the admonition is strong and important—to keep our eyes on *Him*, not on other people's advice or counsel; not on the circumstances, but really on the Lord Himself. Only from Him comes whatever we need to stay on top, and not to drown.

From 1955 February to 1975 February it has been the same, one stormy set of waves after another—*impossible* to walk on, unless we hear His unutterably sweet, strong voice saying, "Come," with the promise of His help. At those times, we can walk, and not sink. And when we begin to sink? "Immediately Jesus stretched forth his hand and caught him, saying O thou of little faith, wherefore didst thou doubt?"

With much love in the One Who is the God of diversity as well as the God of unity, our Eternal God and Father, Guide, Counselor, Who is able to call us, "Come . . . " and to hold us up in all He asks us to do,

EDITH

July 4, 1975   Huemoz sur Ollon, Switzerland

Dear Family:

American Independence Day is July 4th as you very well know, and Swiss Independence Day is August 1st. In the early years of our being in Switzerland, on through the first years of L'Abri, we used to celebrate both these days with some fireworks and ice cream ending hot sunny days with the warm dark night lighted up with bursts of stars, and conversation over dishes of homemade ice cream, as we sat out in front of Les Mélèzes. Today, not only is everyone too busy to remember what day it is, but the constant rain and fog, cold weather with fresh snow on the mountains, makes it hard to remember what month it is. The February Family Letter started with a description of our snowy autumn and foggy February, so I won't go into a long detailed account of the thus-far *un*summer, nor of the disappointment of people who came for short periods and never saw the mountains in all their beauty during parts of May and June. The whole year seems a bit like a fallen-apart jigsaw puzzle, and it becomes necessary to look at the calendar and not out of the window to remember what season it is. The children are now out of school. Exams were taken during the last few days, and so the summer vacation is beginning. It will end August 23rd or so, therefore you can imagine how all ages of people long for a burst of summer weather. How much the sun is missed! . . .

This July we are having two days of fasting and prayer, July 7th and July 30th, first because there is much need of prayer, secondly so that the Workers who will be away for the period including the 30th can be praying here on the 7th and others who will not be here for the early date, can be "holding the fort" on the 30th.

It takes special arranging ahead of time, to prepare for a day of fasting and prayer at any one of the L'Abri branches. The essential work must be done early before we meet at 9:30 for our time of preparation together in the chapel, during which one considers some prayer preparation from the Word of God, and also we together look back over some of the things we have prayed for through the years, having the advantage now of seeing some of the amazing results ten and twenty years later, which wouldn't have been dreamt of then. One chalet (in Huemoz) is chosen as the place for a pot of soup, bread and apples, or some simple food, having been prepared the day before, to be put out midday for anyone who feels ill without some food, or is not a Christian and does not want to take part in the day of prayer; they can find sufficient food, being asked *not* to use this as time of conversation. We feel people should be allowed to have quietness, without anyone else's voice, or ideas, to penetrate during this possible time of being alone with the Lord. It is a day of freedom to be with *Him*, unless He shows it should be otherwise. Parents of small children, people caring for sick persons, someone caring for an old person cannot neglect the ones in their care that day, or the "fasting unto the Lord" becomes a farce, and not a help to prayer. . . .

God's promises are there. If we *really* fast from time to time this way (different from our everyday schedule, a special giving of the time to Him in giving it to others in need) "then shall thy darkness be as the noon day: And the Lord shall guide thee continually" (Isaiah 58:10).

My own operation in Pittsburgh, Pennsylvania, in June was a sudden surprise! As you know my knee has been needing some kind of help ever since July of 1973; and Dr. Ferguson, who is a top orthopedic specialist who operated on Franky many years ago, kindly gave me an appointment for a consultation in Pittsburgh, where the Lord had arranged to have Fran and me staying with our friends the Todds. He took one short look at my knee, and said, "Into the hospital *tomorrow*, and I'll operate to remove a torn cartilage the *next* day." I simply *had* to recognize that it was amazing that he was willing to give the time in the midst of a full schedule and *cared* that my knee needed immediate attention.

The Lord knew that our time with the Todds was going to be invaluable to them and to us. The Lord knew that Fran needed an extra week to be there to work on his manuscript with Jim Sire, and He alone prepared a place for that to be possible. All our schedule had said ahead of time was that Fran had promised to speak to the combined General Assemblies of three Presbyterian denominations, and that probably I would *not* be there at all. I feel this is part of what is meant by "Before they call I will answer, and while they are yet speaking I will hear. . . ." Even as we understand only "in part" we can make our requests only "in part" on the background of what we do know. . . .

At the Members' meeting in the spring, some changes took place in the work of various Members here in Huemoz. As we sat discussing and praying together in Chesalet, and as we talked around the beautifully set table Veronica prepared for the meals (a cloth in dark shades of purple with lovely white daisies in small glass bowls forming a line down the center, interspersed by twisted white candles) various ones declared their willingness to put aside other work to spend *more* time with the people coming to L'Abri for help. Barry loves the work in "the shop," making beautiful things of wood for the various chalets, but he has now put this aside entirely to talk to people, and to "set up" courses of study for those coming to Farel House. Priscilla and John are taking more meals of 22 to 25 people stuffed in their kitchen and little living room, not just to feed them, but for conversation. Priscilla has stopped nursery school in order to have more meals and talk to more people. John also is "talking" with people in between his essential work in the financial books, the legal things, and the renting of chalets or apartments of people coming, etc. At the Members' meeting the new Members elected were: Juanita of French L'Abri, Mardi (Dick's wife) of Ealing L'Abri, Vicki (Jerram's wife) of Greatham L'Abri, and Greta (Wim's wife) of

Dutch L'Abri. In case you don't know, the Members are like the "Board" ... Dick Keyes reported to us the things going on in L'Abri, and in the International Church, Presbyterian, which is another congregation of our little denomination, in Ealing. Just as in Huemoz and Greatham, the little congregation that is permanently living in the area is a bit overwhelmed at times by the number of people coming to L'Abri for help. Yet—a church is *meant* to be a shelter for the lost, seeking lambs and is not meant to be a cozy family just enjoying each other without a welcome for strangers. This is the problem of any church that is fulfilling what the old hymn says to do, "bring the wandering ones to Jesus" ... if people are *truly* "bringing them in" ... then there will always be a flood of new faces to bewilder the "regulars." The balance of "feeling at home"—of "caring for the community"— and of "opening doors to the lost"—is an important balance to work at. And it takes prayer and work for a lifetime, and then into the next generations' lifetimes. At Huemoz when the most recent baptisms took place, Udo, who was preaching, asked the congregation of church members to stand and welcome them. This helped the members to feel their oneness and to express a togetherness openly. With the little chapel stuffed full and the outside balcony also full, naturally the "visitors" so to speak, were *far* in the majority. Never mind—the minority ought to *love* to welcome the majority. What a fantastic thing if the minority of believers could one day welcome the whole majority of the world's unbelievers to simply *listen*— just once! Not "cozy" but our command—to go into all the world and preach the gospel. What if they came to listen???

Hans Rookmaaker, Anky, and Wim reported various aspects of what is going on in the Dutch L'Abri. Henk is a Worker now, and so is Edith, who does all the cooking in the "big house." Wim and Greta live in an apartment in the big house, remodeled recently. The Rookmaakers live in the four room "workmen's house" under the roof of the drying barn, until they recently found a home to buy near Eck-en-weil, after selling their Amsterdam home. This means they will be near L'Abri where Anky does the financial books, etc., helping in the work regularly, and Hans commutes to the Free University where he is a professor of art history, and gives much time to leading discussions and talking to individuals at L'Abri too. Henk has given up most of his university teaching to devote his time to L'Abri. Wim preaches for the Sunday church services (as well as a multitude of other things, including the work of the apple and pear orchards which are a part of Dutch L'Abri property) ... and soon, Lord willing, there will be a chapel on the property for these services, and for conferences, and so on. Nick and Minna (formerly L'Abri Workers) live quite a distance away now, as Nick is pastor of two churches. A very wonderful decision was made by some of the men of Nick's churches, to build a chapel for Dutch L'Abri. No special permission is required to build—if the building is *inside* existing walls, or under an existing roof. An architect became interested and designed a chapel to fit *under* the roof of the drying barn, and men of the church are going to contribute not only money for materials, but time to do the building themselves. As villagers like to come to the services, this will make far more space available, Lord willing, when it is finished.

What else is going on in the wider circle? There are Christian professors teaching in a variety of colleges and universities . . . who have been at L'Abri to study and are teaching in a very different way. There are those who write that their law businesses, their teaching, their way of treating people as doctors, are entirely different because of reading the books, and understanding "the questions" as well as "the answers." There are people opening their own homes to people in need, whether for short periods of time, or in adopting a variety of children—such as a dear family near Chicago who have children of a variety of nationalities listening to *Everybody Can Know* read aloud, but also listening to sermons and lectures from L'Abri on tape. There are seminary students preparing for a wide variety of futures, as only the Lord knows, who have been born again at L'Abri. You'd be amazed at how many there are in Covenant, Westminster, Trinity, Gordon, Dallas, who have been led to go on to study, after lives have undergone a change only God could accomplish from the inside out! (Inside each person I mean.) One of the earliest portions of the "outer circle" of L'Abri was the springing forth of the work of Bellevue, the home and rehabilitation center for cerebral palsy children which God chose to have Anne and Mary and Rosemary commence next door to Mélèzes. For years this medical work, entirely separate in organization, has been intertwined in L'Abri . . . with nurses and therapists, being helped in L'Abri, and with Jane's Sunday music hour in Bellevue, Pris's and others Sunday school classes for the children, and L'Abri Workers holding church service for Bellevue. The International Church Reformé Presbyterian is also separate, yet very intertwined, in Ealing, Greatham, and Huemoz as well as Italy.

The radio broadcasts have been a part of the outer circle of L'Abri. As Fran discussed with John asking questions (John also setting up the recorder and the purple turkish towel as a backdrop for absorbing sound etc. . . . all in his little one-room *mazot*, a tiny chalet, where his office is) it was a quiet midnight use of time, in between the chimes of the village clock . . . just half an hour. Walking back up the quiet back road it was impossible for either Fran or John to know that these broadcasts would be used to spread out into homes, first from Monte Carlo as the Christian station there beamed it all over Europe and North Africa and behind the Iron Curtain, then from stations in Ecuador, in the United States, in Canada, in the Far East. God's thrust "out"! Pierre has been helping in the Reformed Seminary in southern France, lecturing from time to time, even as Udo and Fran have gone from time to time to lecture in the Bible–believing seminary in Basel. . . . the Lord's ripples being pushed out.

It would take a book to write, even what we have seen thus far, of the Lord's amazing leading in the preparation this last year of the thirteen half-hour TV films to speak out to the chaotic lost dark world.

When did God begin to prepare this project? Back in the summer of 1930 an 18-year-old boy read his Bible in order to satisfy his honest curiosity before throwing it away. He had heard liberal preaching in a Presbyterian Church as the only Christianity he knew existed, and it had "no answers" to his questions about life and purpose. He had come to a decision to be open in his agnosticism and get rid of church going, and his Bible, but decided to read the Bible once before throwing it away. During the reading, over a period of months this boy became a born-again Christian, by finding answers that really answered his questions in the Bible itself, and by accepting the Lamb of God as his Saviour. No human being had explained any of it to him, and he thought he had made a unique discovery that no one knew about! One lonely summer night, the boy walked down Germantown Avenue to hear strains of music coming from a tent. He walked in, sat on a bench with his feet on sawdust, and heard verbalized in a human voice that which he thought no one else knew about. That night, Francis Schaeffer, who had already been born again, had *heard* the gospel for the first time verbalized by Anthony Zeoli!

God knew then in the summer of 1930 that in the summer of 1974 the sons of these two people would be meeting in the Swiss Alps! He brought Billy Zeoli, son of Anthony Zeoli, not yet born in 1930, and Franky Schaeffer, the youngest child of Francis Schaeffer, together for a long conversation and time of growing conviction that God meant them to *do* something that might break through the barriers the world has put up through the usual media and the majority of religions and philosophies so that truth is not even considered.

One year ago this month an outline began, and during the year the Lord has amazingly "filled it in," using His children in hours of terrifically hard work, but making it clear that He is the *only* one who could have fit so many pieces together. Franky was named "producer" last summer for a film project, with his father doing the narrating and first writing a book which would then be also adapted for the film. The subject matter consists of the rise and decline of Western thought and culture, covering the time from the fall of the Roman Empire, through the Middle Ages, up to our present time, speaking of history, art, music, science, philosophy, theology, and government. It is an offensive attack against humanism, showing the decline of man without God. It can't be summed up in a sentence! It will take a total of over two years for the final product to be "cut" but each "thread" would take pages to follow through. Time after time, incident after incident, a magnifying glass is being placed on the "weaving of God" and we see something of the intricacy of His work. It is not just one person, it is a grouping of people

God is putting together. The researchers include Hans Rookmaaker in art, Jane Stuart Smith in musicology, Jeremy Jackson in history, John Baslington in general research, and many others in science, law, and so on. . . . Thus this announcement can be made: Gospel Films, Billy Zeoli, president, Wendy Collins, vice president in charge of production, is expecting to release a film for use on TV, in colleges, churches, conferences, seminaries, study groups, military communities, in conjunction with a book which will have far more detail than the film, to be used in further study, or along with the film for a semester's course. Franky Schaeffer is the producer of the film, John Gonser the director, Francis Schaeffer the narrator and author of the book, which will come out under Fleming Revell Publishing Company in America, with Hodder and Stoughton in England. Both the film and the book are expected to be used in many countries. Dutch television has already accepted it and is kindly helping in a number of ways to provide materials needed, etc. . . .

Fran was reading, back in February when the going was particularly hard, Ezekiel 33:1–11 and it seemed God spoke to him in that passage. Read it all. Listen to a bit of it here, ". . . if thou dost NOT speak to warn the wicked from his way, . . .his blood will I require at thine hand. . . . Therefore . . . speak saying, If our transgressions and our sins be upon us, and we pine away in them, *how should we then live?"*

Then we come to Jeremiah 1:4–9, be sure to read it all, too. "Say not I am a child: for thou shalt go to all that I shall send thee, and whatsoever I command thee thou shalt speak. *Be not afraid of their faces:* for I am with thee to deliver thee, saith the Lord. *Then* the Lord put forth his hand, and touched my mouth. And the Lord said unto me, Behold, I have put my words into thy mouth." . . .

Whose face are we afraid of? A sneering lip? A scornful look? An angry frown? A doubting eyebrow? For L'Abri Workers, Helpers, Members, praying family members, those who help in other ways but are bound together with us in this "inner circle," the word comes to us, one by one, "Be not afraid . . . for I am with thee to deliver thee . . . "

With much love in Him in Whom we look to the future, behind a fog, hidden in a mist, with confidence that He will not forsake us, but will keep His promises.

EDITH

1976

<u>February 23, 1976</u>   Hueinoz sur Ollon, Switzerland

Dear Family:

. . . This is one of those February days one dreams about, but for Fran
and myself, not one we have been able to take advantage of except "out
of the corner of our eyes." Fran has just been driven to the airport and is
on his way to Washington to speak, but also to deliver his manuscript
which Mary has been getting up at 5 A.M. to type, and Anne Wells and
Betty Carlson have been proofreading to get it ready on time. If we were
talking on the balcony, it would get chilly as the sun set, and we would
need to look for a sweater or coat so that we could keep on talking as the
mountains grew rosy with the Alpine rouge, and sky flamed apricot
with an afterglow. I'm sorry it has been so long—in between letters, I
mean.

Former medical doctor, Jennifer Bryant Robison, just wrote saying
that it would be 20 years on the 14th of March since she had become a
Christian at L'Abri. Twenty years! Now she was asking whether her son
could come for a short time before he goes to Oxford University.
Jennifer had been an Oxford graduate such a short time before she came
to L'Abri. It is exciting to see L'Abri become part of the "relay of truth"
to the next generation in this way.

At the present, Chalet les Mélèzes is divided into "two homes," with
Anne Wells having the top floor where she serves meals, and talks to
people, with Phil "heading the table" most of the time. Libby lives all
the way downstairs, but cares for the two floors as her home, serving
meals in the dining room, Sunday tea, and occasional tape-listening
groups in the living room. Gracie still lives in her usual room on the
middle floor, and Betsy lives in the room next to Gracie, although she
works in Bethany. As always, Mélèzes is the place where everyone getting off the bus automatically comes up the steps and knocks at the door!
It is the "arrival spot" in spite of no sign pointing the way! For a long

time now, Phil has been the one who meets the newcomers, listens to them, talks to them, discusses with them, prays for guidance about them, and then makes decisions as to who can have the next open beds and who needs to wait longer in a pension or village farm house, for another opening. John Macaulay (Ranald's brother) helped Phil all last summer and fall, and it was great having him here. Right now, Phil is alone in his enormously heavy task and needs our prayers. Libby takes over on his day off, and of course, there are others who are helping with office work, as Phil also answers letters of people applying to come here and "heads the table" at Chalet les Sapins when Larry and Nancy are away. "I head my own table," said Libby, "as well as cook and serve. It gets to be a bit of a hassle getting conversations started at times, that is, in interesting areas, and so I bring an article with me to the table, or something from *Newsweek* or *Time,* and read it and use that as the beginning of a discussion. It really works well." Several people have remarked to me, since we have been back this time, that they really enjoy Libby's Family Prayers at the end of the meal as she reads the Bible and prays. It's kind of amazing to look back through the years and remember that this same Libby was a dear little Jewish girl in Debby's French classes which she taught in St. Louis. The pattern is the Lord's. His weaving is always amazing because "His thoughts are higher than our thoughts"!

Lots of spontaneous things take place—like the "coffee evening" at the chapel the other night, organized by Richard who lives at Bourdonette and is a pianist from Canada. A long table was fixed with candlelight, cookies and coffee were served, cushions and the rug were placed in front of the fireplace, and the evening was spent in listening to Lloyd's piano music, poetry reading, guitars, David's singing, and discussion, in an opportunity for people to talk to each other. . . .

"Hi, Pris! I'm phoning to find out what is going on in various chalets, to let the Family Letter readers catch up a bit!" "Well, of course, Giandy's long illness has kept me in the chalet for weeks. It's sort of history repeating itself, isn't it? His breaking his leg summer before last and being in traction so long, and now this pneumonia that took so long to diagnose, and the anemia that was discovered when he had the relapse of pneumonia. Just think, it's been seven weeks! And we still have to be so careful to see that he doesn't overdo, and that he eats as he has to. I've been so scared." But meals have gone on of course. The day they took Giandy to the hospital for X-rays of his lung and discovered the fluid in one, it was Becky (12 years old now) who cooked the meal for the people, and "hosted" the table too. In fact, Becky cooked three meals during that time. History goes on! It is never easy, never a show-piece.

John and Pris are going to work in the English L'Abri in Greatham for ten or twelve days this summer in order to observe and "feel" the work there. Juan comes up from Milan to lecture here regularly, which is a two-way thing too. Everyone appreciates his lectures, and it is a "bridge" to Milan as well. . . .

Chesalet continues to overflow with people and music, hymn sings and conversations as meals are served and people discuss or ask questions in Betty and Jane's home. Jane has been doing lectures on Shakespeare and music that he influenced, and Betty has been writing a new book, which she put aside to help check Fran's manuscript with Anne Wells this past week.

We were squeezed into Greatham's living room church service one Sunday during our filming time in England and were deeply moved by the variety of people who are coming from the area, as well as those in L'Abri. It was a literal picture of the early church with "some from Caesar's household" sitting next to some in the place of "slaves" or "the other end of the scale." Integration is surely a wider thing than most people think of and the oneness in Christ is meant to be demonstrated by the friendship and love among church people who are thrown together from every walk in life, as well as "from every tribe and nation." There was a "pottery class" announced that day, the teacher being Ken Cope who has a room in that old house of endless rooms, for his kiln and wheel, etc., and who not only makes pottery, but teaches others in the church and at L'Abri. Now today, I have a wedding announcement on my desk that came while we were away, announcing Boopie's and Ken's wedding on January 31st in Greatham. Trumpets should blow! I remember cutting carrots with dear Boopie years ago in Chalet les Mélèzes soon after she arrived, having found out about L'Abri on a train. You've seen Boopie's picture on the cover of Sylvester Jacobs's photographic book *Portrait of a Shelter.* Jerram and Ranald have written a book together and are working it over again now, and Dick Keyes is working on a book to be called *Identity.* The most beautiful things happening in all of L'Abri are the things that cannot be seen, the things happening inside people, inside each of us. . . .

Alfredo, born in Colombia, South America, in a family prominent in the government, was educated in England, and had been for five years a talented and well-accepted actor in England. Paloma is a girl born in a titled English family, having degrees in both architecture and philosophy, and had for some years been Alfredo's friend. Neither successes, accomplishments, nor discussions produced satisfactory answers to the basic questions of life for Alfredo. He was given some of Fran's books in England and in reading, began to desire "more of the same." Upon arriving at L'Abri, it was French L'Abri that had open places for these two, and it was there that they became part of Farel House, listened to tapes, read books, asked questions and discussed. Juanita said that it was during a conversation with an unbelieving philosophy professor that she realized Alfredo had become a Christian, as he was giving the answers from the Christian viewpoint! Barry spoke of how great these two were, with their interesting questions and Alfredo's talent in reading aloud during long evenings at French L'Abri, holding everyone fascinated with his expressive reading. However, their "eyes of understanding" were opened at different times, and while Alfredo became a Christian here, it was not until some months later that Paloma became a Christian after attending services and discussions at Ealing and after talking with Dick Keyes. Alfredo went to visit relatives in Russia, and when coming back to England, he not only got into the full swing of things in Ealing, but also acted in two plays put on by *Upstream*, a very fine Christian drama society doing some outstanding things. Now on February 21st, a beautiful wedding took place in St. Julian's Retreat Center in Sussex in a lovely chapel by a lake. Dick Keyes was the presiding pastor who married Alfredo and Paloma, surrounded by the guests from Ealing Church, as well as actors, family, and Karen representing French L'Abri and Nigel as a tie into the past of L'Abri, etc. There is no end of the repeated surprises as we continue to pray for "the people of the Lord's choice" to be brought here, and for the "Workers of the Lord's choice" to care for their needs.

One girl, Joy, an American, was picked up by Ranald on a country road as she was hitchhiking there in England. Conversation about the basic things led Ranald to invite her to L'Abri in Greatham. After some time there, she came to Swiss L'Abri and ended up in French L'Abri where she asked questions until she became satisfied that they had been answered and became a Christian. Who is responsible for her salvation? Can't you see something of the "blend" God uses, just in this one person's experiences? There was Ranald who picked her up and was faithful in talking about serious things. There were people at Greatham, Huemoz, and Thollon who were patient in answering questions. There were people praying for her specifically, and people praying for all who have come to L'Abri seeking answers. There were those who shared their material goods with L'Abri as they felt God wanted them to, and those who scrubbed floors and wrote letters, made up the meal lists, and made endless pots of tea, those who copied tapes or led guest tape sessions, those who repaired tape recorders or helped set up a study program. It is the "blend" of those who are willing not to be "bright and shining stars" but just to do anything the Lord unfolds for them to do and the *whole* blend is responsible for the results. . . .

Starting at the end of August, Fran and I have lived very different lives, or have worked very differently from any other period of our lives. It has been in many ways the most difficult period of our lives thus far! We have been introduced to what it means to "shoot" a documentary film, traveling by car from town to town, country to country, sleeping in a variety of places for one-night "stands," often getting up for "dawn shots" and staying up for "night shots," and being involved in the grouping of a "crew" all involved in the same thing for a period of time. It is all-consuming in time, energy, and concentration, and does not leave room for correspondence or dipping in to other areas of life. For Fran "pasting up" the next day's lines from the script, studying them, packing and unpacking, constantly washing his hair before breakfast to keep the continuity of looks for cutting together various parts of any one episode, taken of course in different places at different times, caring for a deluge of physical difficulties, actual speaking for the camera in a tremendous variety of places (top of scaffolding, on the ledge of a dam, walking through a field of cows, in museums, churches, on an empty beach, etc., etc.), the long hours of waiting, the retakes, took more than a "normal day" compared even to L'Abri work. For each member of the crew there were tremendously long lists of things that needed to be cared for each day, including putting all equipment on an elevator to take it up to a room to be safe overnight, driving the equipment truck across national "borders" where long hours of waiting to go through customs and be checked used up precious sleeping hours. If anyone thinks it is a glamorous work, do be disabused of that idea! It is more like joining a traveling circus and pitching a tent in a different place every few days. I've never been in a traveling circus, but now I think I have some idea of what it is like! There were not only "attacks" on Fran's health, but tremendously diverse "attacks" came to hinder the filming. Fran said to me he felt that he had never felt the presence of evil in his personal form so thoroughly as during this time. We were sure that Satan was furiously attempting to destroy what was being made. Yet from August to February, filming in France, Italy, Switzerland, Holland, Belgium, Germany, England, and America, we also had a succession of marvelously answered prayers in the areas of permissions, weather, props, customs, safety of travel, "near accidents" which were averted, protection from theft, no shots "pulled" because of health, shut doors which suddenly opened, and so on. Time after time we felt we were being reassured and then again re-reassured that this whole project is the Lord's and that we are simply following His plan. As in any section of life, being assured that one is in the Lord's will does *not* mean letting up in prayer. In fact, much more prayer is needed as one continues in the Lord's guidance in the midst of warfare. As we do that which is a thrust against Satan, we need to do it surrounded by prayer, and praying ourselves. The battle is real, and not a mock battle! For Fran this has been a time of fresh understanding of Paul's shipwrecked journey and of stark reality of what it means to call for "His strength made perfect in weakness." The literal possibility of God's strength made perfect in recognized weakness became practical day by day.

In my last Family Letter I told you briefly how the film came about. For the content of what is in "the lines," and for a description of the visual the best thing for you to do is to *see* it for yourself. There will be Seminars in the States, Lord willing, three days long each, to show 10 episodes with discussion times in between and Dr. Schaeffer giving it as a lecture in person. There will be time for questions. It will be like a series of illustrated lectures with questions afterwards, but in this new form.

Pray that *How Shall We Then Live?* may not be just the title of the series, nor even that which will be recognized by some as coming from Ezekiel

33, but pray that it will be an honest question asked by many honest seekers and that they may find the answer.

Do pray also that this series will be a blast of the trumpet needed to stir up Christians before it is too late to do anything.

The editing of the film is now under way, but some "pick up" filming needs to be taken to finish that portion, hopefully by the end of March. L'Abri Workers and Members have very patiently and lovingly, as well as with great conviction as to the importance of doing this task, taken on more pressures and responsibilities here in the Swiss portion of the work. Special pressure has been upon John and Pris. Thankfully, however, it is the Lord who knows who has done what, and what the combination is that produces any amount of the "Gideon's band's shout."* An enemy is to be defeated, and a warning is to be given to release his prisoners. Obedience to the Lord's part in it for us, each one individually, is the only thing we need to be concerned about. In that sense, we are all a "crew" working together to produce something under the direction of God Himself. . . .

Most amazingly my father, Dr. George H. Seville, will be 100 (one hundred) years old on March 19th, having then lived from 1876 to 1976!!! All our birthdays seem less serious compared to that! So cheer up, you who are reaching 30, 40, 50, 60, 70!!!

The L'Abri Annual Members' Meeting will be April 8th to 10th. The manuscript, which Fran just delivered in Washington, is the one which goes with the film, a more detailed, documented covering of the material for study as well as for reading. It will be a good reference book with index, chronological index, and bibliography. Revell Company expects to have this out simultaneously with the premiere of the film.

With love in the One who *sees* the next steps ahead around the bend in the road!

EDITH

July 6, 1976   Huemoz sur Ollon, Switzerland

Dear Family:

This is our *41st* wedding anniversary! What an amazing number of years! Since Switzerland is having Mexican weather (hot, no rain, grass drying up in the valley so that a drive to Geneva looks like a drive through the driest hottest parts of Italy during the summertime), today is very like that hot July 6th when we were married in Germantown, Philadelphia, 41 years ago. We are having a Family Tea with our chil-

---

* Judges 7:20.

dren and grandchildren who are able to come, at four o'clock this afternoon, in a Villars hotel, Lord willing. Of course Sue and Ran and their four children are busy with an overflowing L'Abri in Greatham, and with the "end of school" sports days and plays in Margaret, Kirsty, and Fiona's schools. Naturally there is no possibility of *their* being here. Also Natasha,* now eight years old, has ventured out on her own and yesterday traveled to England by plane alone, to be met by Ran and taken to Greatham where she will spend a week or ten days with her cousins. So *she* isn't here. "However" suddenly this morning another two who were planning to be at the Tea Party had a conflicting "engagement" turn up!!! Something which could *not* be put aside, be assured. It seems that perhaps our wedding anniversary date is from now on to also be the date of Debby and Udo's fourth child's birthday, and our thirteenth grandchild's birthday!! At five this morning Debby began having contractions which seemed to be serious ones, so by about 9:30 A.M. Samantha and Naomi came over to be with us, and to play with Francis and Jessica. I carried their "party clothing" on hangers, and bathing suits, etc., in a plastic bag, after taking Debby a rose from our garden to take with her, and spending a little time there, being thankful that all this happened while we were still *here* and not off on a speaking trip. Fran and I waved Debby and Udo off as she settled herself with pillows as comfortably as possible and Udo edged his VW bus out into the road and started off down the mountainside for Vevey's Samaritan Hospital where so many of our grandchildren have been born. Dr. Mean has brought many L'Abri children into the world. Today he will have to change Debby's three o'clock appointment at his office, to another hour of appointment in the hospital. With a "family doctor" kind of interest rare in today's world, it is wonderful to have someone with an interest that is personal and not just mechanical, and who will greet the baby as a person, not one more collection of molecules! . . .

July 7: Yesterday afternoon at three o'clock Hannah Emily Middelmann was born, weighing about seven pounds. Mother and daughter are happy and well, as is father Udo. The *timing* was quite astonishing. Three o'clock was the time of Debby's doctor's appointment! So he was delivering the baby while other patients waited for him to get back from the hospital, but they didn't have to have their appointments canceled!! Also everything was over, and Debby comfortably back in her bed, so that Udo could leave, drive up the mountainside again and join us all for our anniversary tea. It made a most unusual 41st wedding anniversary celebration indeed, and a very lively day for the sisters of the new baby to remember as we had time to talk about it together. Incidentally, it was a special answer to prayer as the baby was "due" on July 17th, and we had prayed that it would come before Fran and I had to leave for America, so that we could be with the children while Debby was in the

* Debby and Udo's daughter.

hospital, and visit her, and so forth, before leaving. There are times when the Lord answers with detailed "special touches" which comfort us with increased understanding of His personal care for us. What about the afflictions? They are a part of what He has warned us we will have in this life, and His grace is given for the enduring of the afflictions, sufficient for the immediate hard thing. But the times when He answers in breathtaking detail are sufficient to give us promise of what the future will be like when Jesus comes back and we begin to have the glories of the millennium unfolded to us. Our dear lovely God of details is planning untold wonders for each of us. Courage! May we endure to the end, and not listen to Satan's ugly whispered lies about God.

I wish the whole L'Abri Family could have gathered together from all places East and West on July 4th. Since America's 200th birthday seemed an occasion worthy of notice, Veronica (Barry's wife who is English!) decided we should have a Sunday High-Tea-Picnic-Supper, with everyone invited to join in. Each chalet prepared food, an old-fashioned American menu of baked beans, potato salad, homemade rolls, pickles, radishes and lettuce, hot dogs, chocolate brownies, iced tea, and marshmallows to roast over the same fires over which the hot dogs would be roasted. Franky was appointed to purchase fireworks from some store which had already put in a supply for the Swiss First of August, and to prepare a wooden frame, etc., for the display. All these preparations were made ahead of time. Sunday morning people were gathered together in the chapel as usual spilling over onto the balcony, outside the door, under the windows, etc. The people *did* come from widely scattered areas!

Barry preached a splendid sermon, one of his series on Galatians. The choir sang beautifully, but more than the singing was beautiful as you looked at the faces filled with the beauty of believing the words and singing *to* the *Lord*, not just to *people*. Jane sang two numbers, one of Bach's and one of Handel's, and the tiny children stood up and craned their necks to see her as they swayed in time with the liveliness of Handel's rhythm. During the sermon Barry stopped as he was speaking of the oneness in Christ of Jews and Gentiles, males and females, slaves and masters, and said that we had three people to come up to the front, two to be baptized, and one to join the church. As Dr. Schaeffer came up to ask the very serious questions of these three, it was an intense time of rethinking the reality of the meaning of the questions and answers, not just for these three, but each Christian for himself or herself. . . .

The communion service was held at four o'clock. Our communion services are held the first Sunday afternoon of every month as the most convenient and feasible time to have the congregation together, as well as the visitors. We sit "in the round" with the table in front of the fireplace, and the chairs arranged in a different way than the morning church service, to give a more intimate togetherness as the loaf of bread is broken and carried around for each one to break off a piece, and the juice of the grape is later passed around in little glasses. There always seems to be someone taking communion for the first time, entering into the reality of being a part of the "family" of the Lord who are looking back to His death, and forward to His coming again, and to His one day "eating and drinking with us" at that marvelous moment of the marriage supper of the Lamb. Some from every tribe and nation and kindred and people will be *there*, and the tiny piece of the fabric which is here at L'Abri is so much a cross section of people from many nations and language groups and backgrounds, so that already some of the thrill of the way those who are seeking find *Him*, sweeps over us during a communion service, when someone lets it be known that a decision has been made, by breaking off a piece from the loaf for the first time!

After the communion everyone swarmed around not only the road in front of the chapel, but climbed up the sharp incline to the tilted grassy field L'Abri owns opposite the chapel. Three circles of stone outlined three wood fires built and lit to prepare for cooking hot dogs. Two long tables were covered with cloths and adorned with twists of red, white, and blue crepe paper, while the flag Natasha had laboriously crayoned was tacked up on the outside wall behind the tables. Huge trays of rolls, large bowls of potato salad, big pans of baked beans, nicely arranged carrot sticks and raw cauliflower and cucumbers "appeared out of nowhere," platters of chocolate brownies were placed by pitchers of iced tea, and the tables began to "groan"! A group of people sat on the bank and began to sing hymns, while others stood in clusters talking, and others wandered around the field selecting places to spread their blankets to sit on for the meal. Bellevue children were there in their wheelchairs, and Jane arranged her chair, for her reading, next to one of the wheelchairs and Gracie sat down next to her. A girl who had just arrived from Texas presented Fran with a straw Texas hat and yellow rose. As the hat sank down over his eyes about twenty cameras clicked! Paper soon stuffed the too-large-size and made it wearable, so that Fran went around the rest of the evening looking like a Texan with Swiss mountain-climbing pants! The chalets had brought enough food for their own people, plus quite a few more. It was good that everyone had "overestimated" the amount, because in the end there were more than 220 people fed. When the last hot dogs had been cooked, and plates of food eaten, and when the last child had discovered the last marshmallow to roast over the glowing coals, Barry put out the fires with water, and we all gathered on the bank above the chapel to listen to Jane read to us from Christopher Columbus's Diary, and to hear how much he had spoken of how he felt God was taking him to make a journey of discovery. After Jane's reading and talk, Patricia (from Washington, D.C.) sang, unaccompanied except by the evening bird songs. As she sang so freely and beautifully in the time of the setting sun, the littlest children, Francis and Naomi, slid down the bank and climbed up to slide down again in sheer joy, without spoiling the spontaneity of the program. Somehow 220 people became a family enjoying a 4th of July evening together with individual differences in the way of enjoying the time, but with a oneness that could be felt.

Then Franky asked us to go up to the top of the field, and seat ourselves in another "arena-like" arrangement, above the place where he had fixed fireworks, pinwheels tacked on a wooden frame and on some apple tree branches, Roman candles placed in empty apple juice bottles, "fountains" placed in little rows to be lit in succession. While it was slowly growing dark, Franky gave an impromptu talk, including the day's news about the Israeli rescue of the hijacked people, and other miscellaneous subjects, then suddenly it became dark enough and Franky began lighting fireworks in succession. "Ooooohs" and "aaaahs" and "isn't it lovely," "OOOh how beautiful" came from children and adults alike. Barry followed around with a pail of water putting everything in safe condition. There was a relaxation and a oneness that night in a cross section of people celebrating America's 200th birthday in the Swiss Alps together, which may not have had its counterpart in any of the much more elaborate celebrations going on in other parts of the world. 200 years! How few really. How many more years will there be for America, for any country, before Jesus comes back? Generations add up so quickly.

A day is like a thousand years—a thousand years is like a day. What does that mean, really? Certainly *something* hinting at a perspective from God's view of history, which makes each minute more important, and the long times of waiting shortened. The result of thinking in this direction for a time should be our getting up from the grass, brushing off our hands, and saying, "Come on let's get on with it while there is time." We mustn't lose the sense of urgency. . . .

Swedish Staffan has been translating *He Is There and He Is Not Silent* into Swedish lately. He already has translated *The God Who Is There* and it is now on the market in Sweden. Staffan has been a student, a Helper, and a Worker at L'Abri in the past, and his wife Lisa has finished her student time, too. Just recently an application came from them to come back into the work, and after an exchange of letters, pointing out the "insecurity" as far as permits go, it became clear that they should come for as long as the Lord would have them here. So with their trusting the Lord for His plan, and we as Members also trusting the Lord to show us together, they will come soon. As this is a "continued story" you'll have to wait for the next installment to find out what happens in this part of the story, as well as in other things!!!! When writing true accounts, it is possible to go back over the past, but not to project imagination into the future. All any of us can know about the future is that Jesus is coming back—or that we may die before He comes! Otherwise we cannot know whether we will be sitting in a hijacked plane, or in a hospital ward. It is a good thing to be careful about saying, "Lord willing, thus or so." Lord willing, Staffan and Lisa are coming from Sweden soon! And incidentally, we have been having many more Norwegian and Swedish people here recently, as well as a few from Denmark and Finland who "drop in" as the Lord brings them. . . .

One of Veronica's beautifully prepared evening meals of the three-day Members meeting found us without Udo, as he was at Mélèzes, serving communion in the middle of the Passover Seder meal which Libby and Jill had prepared. Jill had come to L'Abri through going into Franky's candle shop a couple of years ago and listening to classical music as she sat reading for a while. Then a conversation led to talking about philosophical things and a base for life, and ended with her deciding to go to a Saturday night discussion. It would be a very long story to tell you about how the Lord brought Jill and the French boy who now is her husband into our lives in amazing ways, such as on a rainy "day-off" when we were hiking in Gstaad, the time of her "new birth," the time of their both being baptized and joining our church, the time of their wedding. Jill and Libby shared with each other their Jewish background, and decided to write (after careful research) a Seder service which would be in accord with the Scripture, and yet would give them a full and beautiful connection with that important time of the Passover celebration as they had had it before. Cooking had been going on for a number of days (in between Libby's feeding of many L'Abri meals) and traditional dishes were ready to place on the long, decorated table stretching the length of the Mélèzes dining room. With mimeographed sheets giving the service and the songs, people sat around that table, taking part in the reading, and the eating and singing. Of course all the Jewish people at L'Abri were invited, but Libby and Jill had wished that someone would be there who could sing in Hebrew! Udo was there as Associate Pastor to give communion, but singing in Hebrew is not one of his talents.

A Jewish girl who had become a "fulfilled Jew," a "spiritual child of Abraham" or a Christian, a short time before, had heard about L'Abri in New England, and was on her way to find it. "This will be the first time I have been away from home for Seder and I am going to feel *so* strange. I wonder? Mrs. Schaeffer wrote a book *Christianity Is Jewish.* I wonder whether they might have a Seder." Thus went this girl's thoughts, and coming up the winding road from Ollon to Huemoz she prayed that God would give her this gift, the celebration of Seder at L'Abri. Now we have *never* had a Seder service at L'Abri. This was Jill and Libby's unique contribution. The girl came up the steps to Mélèzes and as the door was flung open and she stepped in, the full flurry of preparation was soon recognized: the food, the table setting, the paper sheets of the "service" ready to be handed out, the lamb bone, the bitter herbs, it was all there. "What an answer to prayer," was her response. Have you guessed the final sentence? Yes, she had learned the Hebrew songs years before and could well sing the one they wanted sung, accompanied by Jill's husband.

When Udo came to the Members' dinner, halfway through, I tried to sit still for a while, but didn't succeed! I excused myself and ran up the incline through a mist, across the road, up Mélèzes' steep steps, and got in, breathless but eager to sit down beside Libby and take part in the ending of the meal and service. "Next year in Jerusalem"—Oh, that Jews really were looking for the return of Jesus, the second coming of the Messiah who one day *will* be King in Jerusalem! . . .

We must finish the Members' report with just a few lines. There were reports of the L'Abri Ensemble trips and results, given by Jane. There were reports of the books, radio broadcasts, translations of books, and of the film. There were many discussions, and much knitting, embroidery, sewing, letter writing (at odd moments) polishing of brass and copper pots and even some of John's accounts got done, during our three days of being in Chesalet and Bourdonette, and *new Members* were elected. Veronica and Nancy, as new Members, joined the rest so that now there are: John and Priscilla Sandri, Francis and Edith Schaeffer, Ranald and Susan Macaulay, Udo and Debby Middelmann, Jane Stuart Smith, Hans and Anky Rookmaaker, Barry and Veronica Seagren, Wim and Greta Rietkirk, Dick and Mardi Keyes, Jerram and Vicki Barrs, Larry and Nancy Snyder. There was much discussion of the Bible as well as theology and new dangers facing Christians today. And we stopped often for prayer. So, in all, L'Abri Members' meetings are not much like formal "Board Meetings." If you would look in at times you'd be amazed at the firm business being transacted in the midst of informal and just plain open communication. The ideas are not preconceived and brought to be voted upon, but formulate in our minds *as* we discuss and "think out loud" together, and pray for guidance.

There are so many "beginnings" of "new years" at L'Abri it seems. There is the Members' meeting which is a beginning. There is the beginning of the school year which comes late in August in Switzerland, with three to start school this year (Katie Snyder, Samantha Middelmann, and Jessica Schaeffer).

The chapel was filled at our beginning meeting together to prepare for the Day of Prayer. It was another of those hot, sunny, clear days so that people could scatter and find private spots to walk and pray, or sit and pray with Bibles, prayer lists, empty paper and pencils to write in names of people to pray for and special requests. For many it was the first day of fasting and prayer they had ever had, the first day of having six or seven unbroken hours of time to spend communicating with the Lord. For others of us it was the arrival of a long-awaited special day. We started with an answered prayer to say "thank you" for. Bob Jono had just arrived back from California and his mother whom he had visited (seriously ill with cancer) had been "born again" on Friday Bob said. What a joyous piece of news!

I led the morning meeting, spending some time on Jonah and various other passages. It is so great to realize that even when "going in the opposite direction" from the Lord's will, and even as far "down" as in the insides of a great fish, it is still possible to "call upon God," and to have an answer, and a new beginning. God is so patient with His children, and so ready to forgive and unfold a new plan, though it is often a case of of our having to be "noodles" instead of "sponge cake" because of having spoiled His first plan by our willful changing of the "ingredients" of His plan. I read two old prayer lists, the one for 1956, and the one for 1965, to remind us of what we were asking for then. Back in '56 we were praying for more cups and saucers, among other things, because we were having "19 people to feed at once"!!! And in '65 we were praying for a freighter to be found for Larry Snyder to cross the ocean, on which he could earn his passage, so that he could go and start Covenant Seminary that autumn. Years pass and the Lord gives continuity, and here is Larry with Nancy in Chalet les Sapins with Matthew going to school with Giandy each day, Katie eagerly waiting to start school with the other two little girls, and Seth thinking up new dangerous things to do as he looks at you with his big innocent blue eyes, all of twenty months old now. Eleven years ago as we prayed for that "next step" the Lord had already the knowledge of where it would lead. So comforting to have such a Father. We try to pray for *all* the people who have been at L'Abri in the past years each Annual Day of Prayer. That is, we pray that the Lord will bring names into our minds, and refresh our memories.

For so many years I have prayed for Mario in San Salvador on these days of prayer. It has been at least sixteen years since Mario came here while he was studying on a scholarship from El Salvador. You remember his story from *L'Abri.* A couple of Sundays ago, after a marvelous service with a fine sermon and wonderful music, I stood up to peer around a bit and noticed a dark-haired man and his dark-haired tiny wife, both nodding their heads, and "Why, *Mario.*" "Yes," said Debby stooping to pick up the children's crayons. "Yes, it's Mario after *all* these years." What a reunion! Mario whose oldest daughter was named Linette so that he could have some memory of L'Abri in his family permanently!!! Mario who was so excited about his fresh discoveries in the Bible that he forgot the passage of time, and pounded on our door to wake us at 3 A.M. with a discovery in Ezekiel! We hadn't heard anything for so long, and here he was with his vivid wife who was sharing his excitement in the "homecoming." . . .

Pray for the film. At last the filming is finished, Lord willing, and the editing is going on now. We feel certain with all the ups and downs and difficulties that the *Lord* is the One who is directing and bringing forth something which is His plan in all this. No one could have foreseen the combination of things. The book is at the press! Those who have read and checked feel it is "great," "superb" and that with the study guide it can be marvelously used for a long time. It should be out in November. *How Should We Then Live?* Pray for the Lord Himself to open the *doors* to the places of His choice for this film. The seminars will be in February and March, Lord willing! It has been a long hard work for many people. You can't imagine the relief I personally felt when just two weeks ago the last filming was finished in this house. As for Fran, he is a bit numb. People have an unrealistic romantic idea of what it means to be "used by the Lord." If you say, "Here, use this typewriter or this car or this washing machine" you should expect some wear and tear! "Lord use me, here am I, use me," needs to be said, sung, prayed with the realization that there is a *cost* involved. He alone is able to know what the cost will be, and He alone is altogether *worthy* of any sacrifice you, or any one of us, or I make. If we do what we do for *Him,* unto *Him,* then His understanding is all that is important. Pray that this film may be used in the midst of the "battle of the 20th century" to His glory, making His name known.

I almost feel as if I were writing you a solemn "last words" kind of epistle!!! It is the early morning of the 13th as I finish and the hot dry weather has turned into a kind of monsoon rain which has leaked into my little office with a driving force. Grey day. Puddles. And only hours to put together a week's work. It all makes me feel sort of dramatically urgent in my closing. "Goodbye, lots of love" seems too everydayish somehow. The Lord's final kind of greeting to us all, as He left, seems more appropriate. "Watch, and again I say watch." We do need to admonish each other not to let time be wasted with ridiculously letting "a speck in our eyes" take up all our time and energy, when there is the need to be unhindered in "seeing, hearing, and *doing* His will till He comes."

I like John's word in Revelation "your brother in tribulation," so I think I will say with much reality, "your sister in affliction." We share much, knowing that in all our affliction *He* is afflicted and understands.

Lovingly,

EDITH

December 3, 1976   Chesieres, Switzerland

Dear Family:

Nothing could be more different or a greater contrast than the view from our windows today, and the view when I wrote my last letter of July 6th. Yesterday morning it was raining in Huemoz, but it has already started to snow here. In the afternoon the rain changed to snow in Huemoz, and it continued here. Jan called from Nicole's "barn" where they live, to say that the snow was over a foot deep this morning early, and I told her that here it is well over two feet deep and still coming down hard and fast. Snow is such a silent transformer of the landscape. No matter how many times one sees the transformation work of snow, the first deep snow of the winter is always an astonishment! Our big wooden outdoor table has an exact oblong of white on it, over two feet high now, with the benches having identical sharply squared corners of deep white cushions of snow. The new little pine trees, which form a hedge at the front wall, are simply a row of pyramids with white points sticking up in the solid white slope, pointing to the strange wall which is two feet higher than before, hiding the sidewalk from view so that we see heads shrouded in scarves or hoods slowly floating by without legs! Tree branches are bent with their burden of white, and the field has strange mounds in it, but no bushes can be distinguished from any other humps and the fences are merely dark dots marching through the drifts. Naturally "Whiter than snow" comes to mind. "Though your sins be as scarlet, they shall be as white as snow"* is illustrated pretty titanically with all this overabundance of snow. However, it also makes one think of being covered, "covered with the righteousness of Christ," covered in robes of white, and so on. The efficient covering that has taken place so quickly and silently is comforting when thought of in that context. How lovely of the Lord to give us illustrations which are repeated so often throughout the years. What a contrast today is to that July day when the brownness of grass and bush gave evidence of the drought and too intense heat. "While the earth remaineth, seedtime and harvest, and cold and heat, and summer and winter, and day and night shall not cease" (Genesis 8:22). . . .

A week ago we were having Thanksgiving in L'Abri. Each chalet had a capacity meal. L'Abri is full, and there are people who have been waiting more than six weeks to get "in." People are staying in Mlle. Chaudet's pension, in the apartment of the Bratchi's, at Blackburn's near the cemetery, at Mme. Ruchet's, at Bonson's farm, and some short-time guests are in hotels. For Thanksgiving dinner we felt that no one should be left out, so each chalet arranged for as many as they could have sitting down at tables. However, as we have so many nationalities among our people, there needed to be some explaining as to what all this turkey dinner and pumpkin pies was about! Priscilla and John had all French guests so they could have conversation in French and the children giggled as they told me about their "American Thanksgiving Dinner." As we sat down at our table with my carefully made "harvest centerpiece," we had Australians, Canadians, English, Scottish as well as some Americans. We had just finished the prayer before the meal, when an Australian fellow staring a bit puzzled at the arrangement flowing forth from a basket cornucopia with a tiny pumpkin, a huge cabbage, potatoes, onions, a rutabaga, green and red peppers, carrots, broccoli, gourds from Nancy's garden with sprays of rose hips and another kind of red berry finishing it off, "Could you explain to me what all this means?" I realized then how odd it might seem that the usual flower arrangement had

*Isaiah 1:18.

been replaced with vegetables (mostly from our own garden) and hurried to tell a short history of the Pilgrim's first Thanksgiving. Our own thankfulness came from the "crop" of *people* the Lord has sent this year, and especially as we heard each one around the table tell where he or she had come from and how they had come to L'Abri. . . .

December 8th. Days are flying by, and this is really not a good time for you to be receiving the Family Letter in the midst of all your holiday mail, as well as all *you* have to do. I'll try to just give you the "essentials" of what is going on right *now*.

Tonight at the chapel there will be a presentation of Dickens's *Christmas Carol* with various ones taking part. Ev and Jan Bauman have been working with Jane on it. Ev and Jan are an American couple who have lived in Caracas, Venezuela, for over thirty years and have been clearly "woven into the work" of L'Abri in an amazing way. We have already had a classical concert in candlelight, and there will be the carol sing with Scripture reading, as well as the Champéry Service on December 24th. Christmas is coming close now. L'Abri is officially "closed" for a week, during which the families are meant to have time alone together, and single Workers also can have similar families of their friends for these days. . . .

Pris is very well right now, and having nursery school again several mornings a week, as well as taking "meals." If you know how tiny her house is, and that Pris and John serve in the kitchen where only eight or nine can sit at the table, you can imagine the "squash" as she often has served 28 recently, sitting on the stairs, on the floor of the tiny living room, as well as crowding into the kitchen. But the reports are good as to how Pris is "coping" with it, and how the people enjoy it. Elizabee is now 15 and is in the midst of the very serious time of Swiss school, with Becky at 13 not too far behind, so having quiet for doing homework presents a "hurdle" as well as time and quiet for piano and violin practice. John is approaching the end-of-the-year accounts which is a complicated time for the treasurer of any organization—and L'Abri has no easy set of figures what with all the currency exchanges, etc., as well as having Swiss taxes and insurances to care for all the Workers, American reports to fill out, mortgages, rents, medical insurance, and so on and on. No wonder John stops to carefully run his daily miles, or swim his weekly lengths up at the Villars public pool, or to play his cello, "in between." The Lord really has answered prayer year by year in the material area for L'Abri, and this year too, but caring for the accounts is just as exacting and careful as it would be for a business company and the Swiss Fiduciare (Public Accountant) goes over it all just as carefully. Legally L'Abri has several foundations, the American, the Swiss, the Dutch, the English, and it all takes "paper work" which is part of living in today's world. . . .

At this point I went to the phone and called Greatham to say, "Happy Birthday" to Kirsty who is 11 today!! It was great to hear her excited "thank you for calling" and to be told about her birthday party with four school friends for lunch and then swimming in the public pool nearby, and that three of the little girls will be staying overnight. As Sue's children, three of them, sleep in the same room in bunk beds, this means that the two younger ones have had "cots" put up for them in Mommy and Daddy's room to give up their beds for Kirsty's friends. Eleven years ago tonight I was in Ealing, taking care of Margaret, while her little sister Kirsty was being born. What a chunk of life eleven years is! We can't "put off" taking care of each other because each other is always getting older, and the things we "could have done" are no longer needed, or appropriate, or desired. It is good to do the things in the "now," the present, which will adequately supply each other's needs, and let the "each others" who matter to us know we really care about them, as well as fulfilling something important at the time it is needed. It is OK to *save* time, and money, and energy in some measure, but it is far more important to *spend* time and money and energy in "doing unto the least of these" the things that they need, (and the things we can do for the Lord at the same time) in the *now*, which we can never do again. Babies all too soon are eleven years old, and ten-year-olds are just that quickly twenty-one, and the mid-energy years soon become retirement age so that someone who longed to ski or dive or sail a rough sea, suddenly couldn't do it even if someone said, "*Now*, you can have the money to do that." These are facts important for us as parents, brothers and sisters, children, aunts and uncles, nieces and nephews, grandparents to think about as well as thinking about caring for the needs of people in far-off countries. One does not cancel out the other. . . .

Static? That word does not belong to any work of the Lord, nor any of His plans. True that God raises up either works or people for one period of history, and then does another thing at another time—but His plans are communicated as His children call upon Him and wait for Him. The "static" quality is not that of the Infinite, Unlimited Creator. As my husband often says, the Holy Spirit is not fifty years behind in His knowledge of what the battle is, and what the present need is.

Fran and I moved into Chalet le Chardonnet feeling that we would perhaps really enjoy a nice quiet "rut" of working in the garden, talking to whom the Lord sends to us (of course cooking for them too), helping in a category a bit removed, even as grandparents are a bit removed from the responsibility of children! But—the Lord did *not* take us out of Mélèzes to be a "bit removed" from the center of things, from the chaos, from the battle, from the heat of the day. We see now that He had another reason. It was to lead us into a tougher spot, not a soft rut.

The past two years of working on the research, the manuscript, the filming, are now behind Fran, and my involvement in all that, plus writing *Christianity Is Jewish* and *What Is a Family?*, are also behind me. We face a new year, and a very new first months of that year. What comes after these next months, only God knows. But He does know. He is the living God, the Creator of the Universe—nothing He has told us is too hard for Him, and His thoughts are far above our thoughts. It is not surprising that His plans are beyond our imaginations.

This book, *How Should We Then Live?*, and the ten-episode film of history, philosophy, art, music, law, government, and theology took years of preparation! God's preparation of people. That Franky had the idea, the vision of doing such a thing with what had been given before to comparatively small numbers of people, was not an "accident" either.

How limited we all are when we pray—"Lord show me Your plan for me," "Lord show him Your plan for him." So often we fence in our requests with small fences. . . .

In essence this film "pushes out the walls in a most extraordinary way." When I finished the book *L'Abri* with a description of the dialogue Fran had with Bishop Pike, and the television programs which followed, I said, "the walls of Mélèzes' living room suddenly flattened out and 3,000,000 people came in for a short period to hear the conversation during those three days." That was now eight years ago. I quoted from Deuteronomy 3:24 and Joshua 4:22–24 to close the book. It seems that what is taking place now flows naturally on. We do pray that ". . . all the people of the earth might know the hand of the Lord, that it is mighty: that ye might fear the Lord your God forever."

And I now want to give you a message that Fran dictated and asked me to insert in this letter, as his four "hopes" for the use of this project:

1. That thousands might be saved through this film and book that would not normally be interested in Christianity.
2. That Christians would realize that the Lordship of Christ after we are Christians covers the whole spectrum of our thought and our lives.
3. That if God would grant this to us, our culture might be turned around and there might be reformation in the church.
4. That if the culture is not turned around, the Christians would be prepared for the harder days which are ahead and that they would realize that soft days are over.

Fran also says he wants you to know how he looks at the project:

"As I see it, the whole project is a unity composed of four parts:

1. The book, already released by Revell Company.
2. The study guide for the book, also already released by Revell Company.
3. The ten-episode film version of *How Should We Then Live?*, put out by Gospel Films.
4. The study aids for the film version, also to be put out by Gospel Films."

. . . My father will be, Lord willing, having his 101st birthday on March 19th at which time we will be in the film seminar at Fort Worth and he will be in Watertown, New York, so you see there will be a lot of frustrations as to being "so near, and yet so far."

Fran just came back from a Workers' meeting at Chalet les Sapins and it is midnight. Rain is drumming on the roof, rain on top of snow, bad roads, and disappointing mixture. The house was empty when Fran and John got there and the reason was soon discovered. Little five-year-old Katie's "grumbling appendix" had suddenly given her acute pain, so Larry and Nancy had taken her off to the hospital for an emergency operation! Larry and Nancy came back toward the middle of the meeting, but you can imagine it was, and will be, a difficult evening for them. It is never easy to leave a child at the hospital. So with prayer for many other things, for the cassette program, for guidance in other matters, for many of you whose lives and needs mean much to us, was prayer for Katie and her parents.

And so the L'Abri Family goes on—thankful for our Heavenly Father who sent His Son to enable us to be a part of *His* family. May He guide you and each of us into His plan for 1977 that we might not be a raveled thread.

It is now December 10th, Katie was operated on last night, and the surgeon discovered that it was *not* appendicitis, but that she had an abscess in the abdominal cavity which was the result of infection elsewhere in her body. They took out her appendix while they were there and drained the abscess. She is having antibiotics intravenously and extensive blood tests are being taken to find the source of the infection. They think it might be in her lungs, or some strange disease of the intestines. Please do pray for Katie, as well as for wisdom for doctors and nurses, and for Larry and Nancy throughout all this. John and I, on our way for Christmas grocery shopping, inched down the slippery hill in a wild snowstorm, passing Nancy on her way to the hospital to visit Katie. The Lord had brought us at just the right moment, because Nancy was frightened by the extremely slippery road. How perfect is the Lord's timing—once again He had sent comfort just when it was needed as John stayed in front of Nancy to help if needed. We step into the path of the New Year which may have its slippery patches with the assurance that *He* goes before us, as an Eagle flies under her young, to catch us when needed upon His "feathery back." "Unto Him Who is able to keep you from falling . . . "

With love,

EDITH

1977

May 1, 1977   L'Abri, Switzerland

Dear Family:

There have been lovely mayflowers in the brilliant green of new spring grass; daffodils have bloomed even at this altitude, and the tree branches brushing my window do have pale green buds tightly folded over a promise of leaves to come, *but* today the fog shrouds the houses nearby as well as the mountains in the distance, and snow is falling thick and fast to add a whiteness to the fog as well as to cover all the green and to bend down the tulip buds and any flowers that were already out! Thick fog, unseasonal snow, icy cold temperature, the need to pull out some warm clothes to wear to church—and it is the first day of May! Disappointed expectations are so vividly being illustrated today by the weather as I try to get down to writing to you, dear family, to tell you the recent ups and downs, the victories and the blows we have been experiencing in the *battle*. The reality of the battle in the heavenlies is consistently illustrated through life. But there are times of intensity which seem to plunge us into a serious recognition of reality and to shake us up so that we cease to be blinded by the day-by-day tasks which are apt to lull us into a feeling of having "plenty of time" ahead to use in any old way— as well as plenty of time to do the more important things "tomorrow." It takes sudden changes to shake us into a more realistic perspective. We have had a strong succession of such changes in L'Abri recently, which you need to hear about in order to be really "with us" in the family of L'Abri.

That is as far as I got without interruption! Then as May 3, 4, 5, and half of 6 were the days of the Annual Members' meeting, I did not get back to you until this evening. We had a most unusual beginning this year, sad, solemn, deeply moving in a variety of ways as we saw all of life, as well as L'Abri's history and future, in a strikingly sharp perspective. We began the meeting in the Huemoz village church!—the first time in our history that we have met as Members there! We began the meeting with a memorial service to which Workers and some others close to Dr. Hans Rookmaaker also came. Basically it was a memorial service for the Members because two L'Abri Members* had left "the church at war" to join the "church victorious" in heaven, through death very close in time to each other. These are the first deaths we have had among Members, and we have been, and are, struck with the speed with which a lifetime passes, and the limitation of "finishing" the work one thinks of doing in one's plan or imagination. Our present life is not open-ended! There is that reason, among others, of asking the Lord to unfold His plan hour by hour, and of asking for His strength in our weakness to accomplish in any one hour, or day, or week, or year, all that He has for us to do. We are not meant to feel frantic, but we are meant to trust in the Lord and lean not on our own understanding as we face the present, willing to be *given* His strength to press on, rather than to just give up, feeling that after all our health and strength are so *completely* inadequate we can't fight on *any* longer.

The L'Abri chapel is a charred mess, filled with holes in the roof and one wall totally destroyed, a burned and blackened organ which needs to go back to Holland for lengthy rebuilding, a piano which is zeroed and only trash, burned chairs, destroyed couches at the back, etc. Strange indeed that three of the shocking "happenings" came together at that memorial service so vividly. There we sat conscious of titanic changes that would never have been imagined at the time I wrote my last Family Letter. I spoke of the New Year ahead and of the "unknown" it contained, but these first four months have brought about shocks that were like earthquake shocks, continually being added to by a new tremor.

Fran led the service, commencing by telling a little history of each of the two men. It was hard for him to use the past tense concerning his friend Hans Rookmaaker, who was ten years younger than Fran and had been a friend and coworker for so many years. Tears flowed unashamedly. Jesus wept at the tomb of Lazarus, *with* all of us who weep as we "stand at a tomb" of a loved one. Death is a shock at any time of life, even at 101 as Father was when he died. Bodies are made to house the spirit. We are whole people, body and spirit, and thank God that Jesus died so that we may look forward to being "whole people" in all eternity. Fran read us Scripture passages, we had a time of general prayer, and we felt not only a oneness in our sorrow, but a continuity of history as we met in that building which stretches back through pastors and people to "threads woven" in the Lord's family we can only glimpse in bits and pieces. Who will take Hans Rookmaaker's place? No one. No one can take another person's place. We go on with an empty chair, remembering his "position," referring to his opinions, ideas, convictions, in

* Dr. Hans Rookmaaker and my father, Dr. George Seville.

our discussions as Members. There are his tapes and books which remain. But no one will fill his place. Others need to pray that there may be prepared and raised up some to carry on in the same spirit and the same direction, which he did. We walked out soberly, sadly, in stark reality of what life and death mean and how true it is that we must say "Lord willing" about what we expect to do tomorrow and tomorrow and tomorrow! And we made our way up the steep bit of hill to meet in Chalet le Chesalet, Betty and Jane's chalet where we have met for so many years. A sudden stroke suffered by her mother had taken Jane back home. We met with a view of the burned chapel across the fields, and put on our minutes the memorial service as the first item, then went on to business, and reports from the various branches, and all the things before us. The Lord's work goes on, and although Satan tries to hinder there is an on-going which is victory, and is also proof that God is stronger, that "He that is in you is stronger than he that is in the world." . . .

Interruptions make up so *much* of L'Abri life for *each* Worker, Member, Helper. Interruptions have to be put aside at times when one is certain God has led in writing or packing to leave for a journey or rushing off to make a train or plane, but interruptions have been a central part of the story of L'Abri, and continue to be. We need constantly to pray, "Lord, please make me sensitive to *Your* interruptions and help me to recognize where the *one* place at a time is to be through this day, and what one thing at a time is my work this minute, this hour. Protect me from the wrong interruptions and give me courage to say "No" at the right time, but help me not to be dogmatic in sticking to the schedule I am carefully writing for today." There is no push-button method of finding the Lord's will for the use of our time, and we can miss what He wants us to do by being too efficient and regulated, as well as by letting ourselves be interrupted too easily.

Perhaps you won't believe it, but as I sat here at the typewriter, I heard Fran's voice in the kitchen. Who could he be talking to? It was Sunday morning early and I thought he was still asleep. I was here writing in a warm wool nightgown, so I ran downstairs as I was and called out, "Are you talking to anyone?" expecting him to say "Franky" but as I stepped into the kitchen I saw Fran serving tea to a well-dressed man. "This is Mr. J., an international lawyer who just stopped between planes and came to ask a few questions." A rather astounding scene—Fran in his pajamas had thought to surprise me by fixing breakfast, and as he passed through the hall saw a man standing hesitatingly at the front door. When he opened the door he discovered that Mr. J had been looking for "answers" and had been helped by some of our books. As he had come from Iran, and would soon be on his way back to America, he had no time to stay for church, but had driven all the way from Geneva hoping he might have a short conversation. It seemed incredible that as I was in the midst of writing to you all about "interruptions" Fran was being interrupted both in preparing breakfast and in dressing, and we both were a bit late for church. Yet both of us were convinced that this was no "chance interruption." Our whole day went on in the same rather amazing fashion. . . .

Since last I wrote, the traditional Christmas Eve five o'clock service in Champéry marked our 28th year of having these services, and our 29th Christmas in Switzerland as a family! Quite an amazing continuity. You see, the Christmas Eve service is much older than L'Abri as we had it from our first Christmas in Champéry in 1949. (Our very first Christmas was in Lausanne in 1948.) To use the same logs with holes in them as we used for candlesticks the first year, to see the grandchildren lighting the candles and singing in the candlelight, to greet new people and old friends, and to go up the hill to visit the Marclays, is all a part of that season of continuity, marking the continuity that God has given us all, dating back to the first lamb which was born and then died, looking forward to the time when the Lamb of God would come. New Year's Eve the Workers have decided not to repeat the service in Champéry, so meals are in individual chalets, and we gathered in the chapel at 10:30 to have the communion service ending at midnight. It is a wonderful way to end a year and usher in the new year—looking back with thanksgiving and prayer, looking ahead with aspirations for doing the Lord's will and dreams of what it might include, yet looking into really hidden events. We sang, prayed, listened to Scripture, and took communion, and when the midnight bells began to ring for their fifteen minutes, the windows were suddenly opened, letting in the chill air, and the bell sounds which let us know that all the bells of Switzerland were ringing in unison whether we could hear them all or not. Alone with the Lord that night, together, yet each alone, we face the new year in communion with the only One who knows us truly, and knows what is ahead of us. He therefore alone can give us what we need in strength and preparation to do, or bear, what He knows we face.

We got home at about one o'clock to pack for our departure the next morning at a very early hour. "It sounds impossible to me, Fran." "No, Edith, I am certain we need to be in Dutch L'Abri for the dedication of the new chapel on January 1st, and there is no other way to be there." How important it was to be there at that time we were not to know right then, but we *were* glad to be there to see the marvelously artistic building which Nick and Minna's church people had built in the barn, a building with four-hundred-year-old tiles on the floor (taken from old Dutch kitchens), beautiful dark wood beams, rough white plastered walls, panels of reeds in between the ceiling beams, a white fireplace of rough, split bricks, and a front of windows with a garden on the other side—dark earth waiting for spring flowers. We sat on the front row with Hans and Anky Rookmaaker. Minna led their choir in some lovely carols of a variety that made a special mix indeed, geographically and historically. Nick preached and led the service with presence and dignity as well as with a special fire. Wim preached also, giving a splendid message in his bilingual manner, a sentence in Dutch and one in English. Fran brought greetings from Switzerland and the other branches of L'Abri, and thanked the church for what they had worked so hard to give for over two years. Only 22 families had not only paid for this building, but had built it with their own hands. While the men were building, the women were making a special artwork in a long piece of applique which covers the back wall. It was quite a sharply defined moment for us of seeing years of L'Abri life and work brought together almost like a pageant before our eyes. Of all the people, the ones we had known the longest were Hans and Anky Rookmaaker. It was the summer of 1948 that we first met them, and Hans was still a student, although he had a newspaper column as an art critic. We helped to get sheets and pillowcases, etc., for their first home, as they were only engaged then, and as the wedding time approached in Holland, there were not enough "rationing stamps" to purchase sufficient household linens to get started. And when L'Abri started, they, with their own three children by that time, came to spend a couple of weeks with us in Mélèzes. Then Hans started L'Abri in Holland in a very small way by having discussion groups in their own home in Leiden where, by that time, he was teaching in the art history department. Later when he became head of the art history department in the Free University in Amsterdam, the L'Abri discussion group moved along with him.

The time came when the Lord led the Rookmaakers from Amsterdam, and several possibilities turned up, but as we all prayed together, gradually the Eck-en-weil house became the place in everyone's mind. Not only did the Lord provide the house, but a student at the university, who had become a Christian in L'Abri, felt that the Lord led him to buy the apple and pear orchards surrounding the house, so that L'Abri could have that land, the trees, and bring forth crops to sell. As time went on, Hans became not only Dr. Rookmaaker, but Professor Rookmaaker, and he not only gave important lectures in colleges, churches and in art museums, but he helped many young Christian artists to have a balanced view of art, and encouraged many artists to keep on. His book *Modern Art and the Death of a Culture* is a classic in that field, and his book on jazz as well as his writing on the covers of records give understanding in the history of jazz. He had three more books underway, and it seemed that his help in the area of Christianity and culture was needed for a long time more. There we sat that day at the dedication of the chapel, and the grace of the building, the beauty of the music, the blend of Christianity and culture bound up in that whole day seemed a tribute to what Rookmaaker had been striving for for a long time—a kind of climax moment in his history. We went on together to be with all the people who were staying for the lunch and after general conversation and some general discussion, we went to be with Hans and Anky in their new home fairly near L'Abri, that we had never visited before. The afternoon was spent in a very long and relaxed conversation about many subjects, and exchange of ideas and thoughts, hopes and fears for the future of the world, as well as about some concrete things such as the film, *L'Abri*, the Dutch TV's use of the new film which Hans was looking forward to, and his own next speaking engagements. It was a long and uninterrupted conversation which ended in a very real time of prayer together. The next day, as Hans drove us to the airport after an evening dinner together eating oriental food with the L'Abri Workers, was the last time we were ever to see Hans on this earth until Jesus comes back again.

"Last moments together" so often are unannounced. The last moment I saw Mother's face was on the New York wharf as our boat moved slowly away; the last time I saw Father was after hugging his frail little body, as he stood at the doorway waving goodbye. There will be a "last time" which will usher in the "first time"—the last time we will have these bodies will be the split moment before Jesus comes back, and then we will feel our new bodies for the first time. Then, no more death and separation for us. No longer will "time" be sand coming to an end in the glass.

Rookmaaker was to go to America the next day to speak in Boston and New York. He was to come home very tired and plunge into his work at home again in the university and L'Abri and the week before his death, he was to talk a whole Sunday afternoon with the last person who would be making a decision with him, the last one he would lead to salvation in person, a girl who is now a "new creature in Christ Jesus." . . .

A "first" can never be matched with the excitement, hopes, and fears, breathlessness of wondering how it all turned out. For me personally to sit in San Francisco (at the end of January) and see that film (*How Should We Then Live?*) after all the months of being in the midst of its conception and making; praying in the background and working in hidden ways "around the edges" day after day, week after week, in and out of cars and hotels, living in suitcases and going through customs, to finally see the results of what had reached the completed film was indescribable! However, I wasn't the only one who sat in excitement during those episodes, surrounded by Fran and Franky and various ones who had worked together in the crew. The general feeling that ran through those auditoriums was one of amazement at all that had been put together and of the titanic strength with which facts were being illustrated. The first two days of the San Francisco Seminar people were divided into two auditoriums, one in Oakland and one in San Jose. Fran took the question-and-answer periods in one auditorium one day and the other the next, and Franky took the place of answering questions and leading these discussion periods in the other, alternately. The final day, everyone was together at Oakland and the final count was 5,600 that day. Fran led pastors in a time of discussion in the Peninsula Bible Church and Franky spoke on "Art Forms and the Christian's World View" in one auditorium while I spoke on the Family in another auditorium. Jim Buchfuehrer and Wendy Collins, both of whom worked faithfully and hard on the preparation of the seminars, introduced the films and told about the format of the day's schedule and so on. We worked as a "team" with much joy throughout the weeks with the same general format in each city. Billy Zeoli joined us in various cities. The last evening was the eve of Fran's 65th birthday, so Billy, without any forethought, suddenly led the whole 5,600 voices in a burst of singing "Happy Birthday to You" to "Dr. Schaeffer." As it was his third birthday during his working on some stage of this film, it seemed a rather fantastic celebration, being greeted by that many enthusiastic people who had just watched the results of that work. In this Seminar, as in all the other eighteen, there was a mixture of people made up of all ages and all kinds of backgrounds. There were many people who had been at L'Abri. There were friends and families of those who had been at L'Abri, often people whom they were for the first time able to bring to something "Christian." There were people who had read Fran's or my books, or Os Guinness's, or Hans Rookmaaker's, or Udo Middelmann's, or Betty Carlson's, or Gini Andrews', or Donald Drew's, and who had not been able to come to Europe, but felt a part of L'Abri through these books. There were many who had been born again through reading *The God Who Is There*, and there were many who had already read and studied *How Should We Then Live?* in preparation for the Seminars. There were pastors, and Bible teachers, and many involved in the work of Bible Study Fellowship classes, as well as scores of people seeking for truth.

Finiteness is never so blatantly illustrated as in a situation where there are too many people and only one right hand, one pair of eyes, one neck to turn in one direction at one time. Frustration.

We flew out to Portland next, and although they did not know it was Fran's birthday, there were lovely red roses and a nicely wrapped gift book of views of Oregon waiting for us on the hotel table. Tickets for the Portland Seminar had been sold out since before Christmas and the Civic Auditorium was jammed full. It is hard to think of all those who could not get in, but we are thankful to hear of the hundreds of churches and schools which are already showing the film now, on Sunday nights, or for three-day retreats, or making it a part of the curriculum for credit. . . .

The very next morning we flew out early to Chicago. Many of you were praying for snowbound Chicago, that the Seminar would not be canceled. God did answer. The weather suddenly changed, and the three days of the Seminar were the warmest three days they had had for weeks. Here at L'Abri they had a day of fasting and prayer for the "impossible weather" during which, as you well know, schools and all sorts of businesses were closed. You mustn't think each seminar followed the other as a kind of automatic thing as time went on. Problems of a diverse variety faced us all in each one, and having union men sell tickets, and run the projectors, etc., brought more problems than just the need to pay for that. Film can be easily destroyed if it gets a bit crooked in the speed of running through, so there were some "hidden moments" of near disaster, such as when Heinz F., the expert in filmmaking who had done much of the cutting of this series, heard a noise which he recognized with his sensitive ears as pending trouble, and dashed from a row near the front to speedily get up to the projection room and see that the film was rewound and started over again before it got torn. In Chicago, as in each place, the preparation or "ground work" for the Seminars was done by people who will get their reward in heaven. . . .

We packed the morning after the third day to fly off to Indianapolis to start the same night on another three-day Seminar. Once again the Lord had answered prayer for weather, and the warmer weather lasted *just* until the Seminar's three days were over, when a snowstorm commenced again. Many people had come from St. Louis, as well as other places, to Indianapolis, so driving conditions were important.

We packed once again and flew out the next morning to Seattle. When Jim went to get auditoriums, they could not be arranged in order to make travel easy, as auditoriums must be taken when they are free!! We had plenty of time to "feel the size of America" and to look down on so much unused ground. It is an incredible experience to fly low over Montana and the Dakotas. What a lot of land the Lord made in the world! If nothing had spoiled His creation, if blights had not changed things, how fertile would it all have been, I wonder? We arrived in Seattle to find that they had not even unpacked the advertising folders at all because the tickets had all sold before any advertising was sent out. An announcement on the radio from the Kings Garden station informed enough people so that many, many more were turned away. They told us that the fire department had finally allowed them to sell 300 tickets for people to sit behind the screen and see the film blurred and backwards, but, of course, to hear and ask questions and when those tickets were put on sale at eight in the morning, the line formed at 6 A.M. and by 8:20 the tickets were all gone. The 3,075 seats of the opera house were filled, with 300 on the stage besides. . . .

After the Seattle Seminar, we went straight to the airport to fly, night flight, to Chicago. That was our all-night flying period! But it wasn't a "chance meeting" which took place on that plane when a member of Congress recognized Fran and began a conversation which ended in his taking the new book and reading it all the rest of the night. His wife goes to Joanne Kemp's "Schaeffer class" in Washington, D.C. We transferred in Chicago to fly to Toronto where there were to be two one-night Seminars because there were too many people to get in for one. . . . Gospel Films very kindly arranged to have a little plane fly us over on Sunday with my father in Watertown (where he lived with my sister). It was the only way we could have gotten to Watertown, and it was the last time I shall see my father on this earth, until Jesus comes back. I want to thank the Lord for that comfort, and thank Gospel Films, too.

It was during that last conversation that Father asked me, "Edith, do you think all the theological differences will be made clear in heaven?

On the platform at the How Should We Then Live? *Seminar
in Boston, three generations of Francis Schaeffers—father, son,
and grandson! Really a special picture.*

Will God let us know just what was right so that we will see?" "Oh yes,
Father. I do think so," I shouted. "Oh I am sure He will show us clearly."
"That's good," said Father, shaking his head with satisfaction. "I don't
think it would be very heavenly otherwise." Nearly 101 at that moment,
sitting in his chair, still praying for the ones he had taught through the
years at seminary; still remembering some from China days!!

It seemed rather fitting to be in Father's birthplace of Pittsburgh for
the next Seminar, which had been well prepared by Jack Todd, and was
another place where the auditorium was packed. Among people from all
sorts of our own past history in life, there were some there from Grove
City where Fran and I went after seminary days in his first pastorate.
Amazing that this film is being used to speak to people we could never
gather together and talk to—people we haven't seen for years, but
would like to talk to again, as well as totally new people.

Boston was our next flight, and there were many "near disasters"
there: pouring rain, the late arrival of Billy Zeoli and Buster (who was to
run one projector), and a lot of small hindrances. Tremont Temple was
the place of the Seminar, with overflow in Park Street Church, but the
"overflow" was as full as the original place. There the unique thing of
trying to have two going at once meant that Fran, Franky, and I ran from
one church through the rain to the other. Fran gave the final lecture in
Tremont Temple, and Episode 10 was shown in Park Street (with the

same content) and Franky finished the evening there. It was one of the most frustrating places for us as the time seemed so very short to see people from years and years ago of L'Abri's history.

Early in the morning, we flew out through the Grand Canyon to Los Angeles where the Anaheim Convention Center was the place where the Seminar was held. There we had the joy of being able to see face to face the men involved in the long hours of cutting, putting in the music, etc., the detailed, tedious work that was so important to the kind of finished product it turned out to be. "Cogs" in a machine? No, people, personal to God and important to this moment of history in His plan. Los Angeles' count was 6,600 and people stood in line a couple of hours waiting for tickets. Six thousand, six hundred blurs? No, individuals; people asking questions; people getting answers; people going out into the night determined to *do* something about the mess the country is in; people resolving to pray more for the Lord's direction. . . .

Whish! and we were in San Diego, though Fran had to stop in Chicago for a day first to be at a committee meeting, and I went to San Diego to work on my "proofs" for *A Way of Seeing*, coming back for the last time with my editor Dick Baltzell. Genie and Franky and the children were there with me, so I wasn't lonely, though I only got a short look at the wonderful zoo with them due to work on the book "calling" louder than the animals. I did have a lunch period, however, with two cousins I had not seen since childhood, so the Lord used the time in each place to "reunite" us with people He wanted us to be with personally, as well as in speaking. . . .

When we arrived in our hotel in Grand Rapids (where we flew after San Diego), we had a phone call from Billy Zeoli and he told Fran of the call that had come from Priscilla from Switzerland, telling us that Hans Rookmaaker had just had a heart attack and had died with no warning! We waited up until 1 A.M. Grand Rapids time to wait for morning in Holland, and I called Anky Rookmaaker. We could not believe the news! The shock was numbing. Franky kept walking back to our room from his to say, "I can't believe it. He was so alive. He is really young. He is the only one who is doing what he has been doing for Christianity and culture. He helped me as a young artist, from the time I was twelve and started painting." We, too, were stunned, and it seemed unreal. When I got Anky, she told us that he had given the Saturday night lecture at Dutch L'Abri as usual and had led the discussion afterwards. Sunday, he had gone to church at L'Abri Chapel, and then had not felt like eating, so was lying down on the couch all afternoon. About eight o'clock, he spoke to her, and then suddenly said, "Oh, I don't feel well" and clutched at his chest and he was gone! Gone! Out of communication with anyone on earth. Absent from the body, and present with the Lord, as suddenly as that. We found from our children that L'Abri would be sending representatives from the other branches. John had *just* had a very unexpected operation a short time before. He had torn a tendon in his leg and had had an emergency operation to splice the tendon with a piece of his calf. He went to the funeral in his cast, and Udo went in pain, because he had just torn the cartilage in his knee and decided to fly straight on to Texas for a needed operation which would be done, after examination of course, by George, a Christian orthopedic specialist in Fort Worth who does a lot of "football knees." Jerram went from England. Wim preached the funeral sermon, but each of the men brought a word from the rest of the L'Abri people whom they represented. And the Free University had a representative there to bring something from the University in appreciation of Hans's life, etc. At times it seemed that life couldn't just keep going on with Hans having died, but the space ahead of us, no matter how long or short, is the time that is imperative to be used. Satan tries to divert us in a variety of ways, and it seems to me that one way is to make us feel: "What's the use anyway?" The Lord's strength in our weakness is needed during the time of shock whether physical or emotional. It is a minute at a time we need to live.

The Grand Rapids Civic Auditorium had been sold out far ahead of time and the seats that could see the film were all full, over 4,000. It was a joy to us to have the film be such a satisfying success for the men who had taken the financial risks and to have it speak in a sharp, vivid visual manner, as well as in its verbalized content, right there where the Grand Rapids businessmen and lawyers, legislators, and so on were gathered.

We arrived in Fort Worth feeling a gathering kind of weariness, but very conscious of the wonder of what God was doing in the partial way we could see it. None of us know what results really are. There are lots of surprises ahead in heaven. It was good to be with Linny in Fort Worth as she was Fran's assistant all through the filming, and it was a time again of sharing the results together in a special way. Questions were good there and the discussions could have gone on much longer, as really was true everywhere. Wendy quietly stopped them, so that Fran would not be completely worn out. Udo arrived the day we did and entered the hospital straight from the airport. Franky and the doctor went to be with Udo as he checked in, and Fran and I, of course, went to see him then. The next day I was able to get from my lecture over to the hospital in time to be with Udo for part of the time he was coming out of anesthesia. I had gone in the morning before he was operated on, and as I prayed with him, the nurse came in to wheel out his bed, and stood behind me. When I finished, she said, "Oh, Mrs. Schaeffer, it was wonderful to be a part of this time. Udo and Debby were in Seattle, where I come from, the summer our church had Udo as the assistant pastor." Amazing that she was to be his nurse in Fort Worth, Texas! She was not the only one who was coming to the Seminars and who had read the books among the medical people who surrounded Udo. The Lord had prepared the way in a very special fashion. However, mingled with concern about John's leg as he recuperated in Switzerland, and Udo's operation (the knee was locked badly and it was very necessary), and Hans Rookmaaker's death, we had a deep set of emotions as a background for talking to people about their problems, whether in lectures or in question-and-answer times. Life took on a more serious look and the intensely important use of it seemed uppermost in thoughts and feelings.

Houston was the place we were to get our next "shock" from a phone call. It was as if Satan were trying to divert us from whatever we might be doing, and we were very conscious of the "battle" continuing, which we had felt ever since the beginning of this project. Actually, a fine Christian lawyer, Tom Berry, who has been at L'Abri several times, was in the act of helping us with our wills, and he had just read them to us and we were in the act of signing them, when the phone rang and I was given the news of my father's death. You see, our whole family was to be together in Dallas for the *first* time since we left in 1954, and of course, the first time of our sons-in-law and daughter-in-law and grandchildren to ever be together in America. It was an important thing for them to be together for a Seminar and to be together in America, but we had not known the full reason God was bringing us together there. We were to have our children with us for Father's funeral. What timing! Speaking of battle, it seems to me that this was a victory for the Lord. All the children would have liked to see Grandfather, but it was Susan's eleven-year-old Kirsty who for years had prayed that she could see her great-grandfather before he died. It was the longing of her heart. As I prayed for the provision for the whole family to be at that Seminar, it didn't really occur to me that Kirsty might visit Grandfather. Mary Crowley, whom the Lord used to make it possible for the children to come to the Seminar, also was *wonderfully* lead by the Lord for this combination of reasons she *could not possibly have known*. Ran and Sue got to Watertown just five minutes after Father had been taken to the hospital with a stroke. However, as Susan spent about four hours with him (and the children stayed for about an hour), Sue said Kirsty was deeply satisfied to be able to say, "I love you, Grandfather," and to kiss him and hold his hand, even though he could no longer say very much. He did say, "Susan" and "hospital" so Susan felt satisfied that he was understanding something of her praying with him, and holding his hand and just being there. It has been a great satisfaction for Sue to spend what were almost his last hours of consciousness with her grandfather, after so many years of not being there.

Such a mélange—life and death, operations and decisions to be made, little children to consider, and a funeral to plan by telephone! And yet the Houston Seminar to go on without a break!! I so often have said there are no neat little packages of time given to us, "time for a funeral," "time for tears and aloneness," "time to push everyone aside and be sad." Life is a mélange, and the mix is tears and laughter, work and illness, and the decisions in the midst of it all are not protected from interruptions. Interruptions such as I talked about earlier, and interruptions of a more severely shocking kind, are not separated from the rest of life. We go on. Houston Auditorium was filled—people were deeply involved; questions were very real. The cross section of people were there, as in every other place, and for those who had been preparing for months, the time of the Seminar was a long-waited-for reality toward which they had been working.

Dallas was the final Seminar and corresponded a lot with San Francisco, the first. We went to Dallas to find that the coordinator had had as his secretary for this final Seminar preparation, Tricia, who had been Franky's secretary in Switzerland for the beginning of the whole project two-and-three-quarter years before. All kinds of people had come to Dallas from all over the place, including our own children. Libby was there from California L'Abri, and Anita. Dallas was again a place of reunion, and it was a place that with all our children and grandchildren sitting on the floor at the front, reminded us of nothing other than our own chapel services on Sundays as every bit of floor space is used. After three tremendous days in every way, the response was real and special, and people seemed deeply moved not only by the impact of what was being said, but by a desire to do something personal about it with some reality of cost. After it was over and we left to pack at the hotel, John stayed on for a long time, answering questions of about 150 fellows who had very serious desire to go deeply into things for a longer time. "Who can we talk to about these things?" was the question at the end which made John feel that really L'Abri has responsibility before God to be more help in America, whether through conferences or seminars or what he did not know, but he felt burdened by a need he had not felt in the same way before. We went back to our hotel, not just to pack, but to arrange for the next day. Father's funeral was to be in Wilmington, Delaware, where he was to be buried beside Mother. I was not able to fly to America for Mother's funeral; at that time there was no such money available, so for me, it seemed a kind of double funeral, the first time I would see Mother's grave. A dear couple who had been born again through the books, and had been at L'Abri, offered their home for us to stay in, along with my sister Elsa and her husband who would be coming. Other friends of theirs offered places in their homes, so we were to have a real "homestead" kind of time with no actual home there at all for our family. The Lord gave us a new set of "relatives" in a very real way. However, Wendy had called to say that there were *no* places (except two) on any commercial flight. It was a time filled with students getting out of college for spring breaks. As I sat dejectedly praying for help, the phone rang and in literally 20 minutes, our new friends from Houston, finding out that there was no way to go to the funeral, arranged with a friend of theirs to have six of us, along with Debby's baby, go in a private plane as a gift. Not only was it a miracle of provision to get Debby, Priscilla, Franky, and Ran (who was going to preach the funeral sermon, as Sue felt she had had her time with Grandfather) and ourselves to Wilmington in time, *but* there were storms stopping flights back in Houston, and also in other directions, so that the course we were taking was about the *only* open course in the skies at that time. It could not be coincidence.

What a battle was going on, however, because just as we were rejoicing over this marvelous provision for our funeral, and rejoicing over the generous offer from the Reformed Presbyterian Church in Wilmington to use their building, the phone rang again, and it was nearly midnight. It was Priscilla, "We've just had a call from Switzerland, and Barry told John the chapel has been burning since sometime in the middle of the night. It was discovered by a man driving down the mountain from Villars, and he honked his horn until he had the village awake. The flames were leaping up into the air, but Barry got everyone to concentrate on saving the central beam, with the fire extinguishers our people brought from all their chalets, so when the village firemen got there, some of it had already stopped from spreading, and our people were carrying out the tape recorders and books from Farel House downstairs. It started in the cupboards on the balcony at the back of the church. That wall is completely gone." Our beloved chapel! Blackened and unusable, burning exactly, time-wise, the same time that Fran had been giving his final message in Dallas with a different kind of fire, the fire of the Holy Spirit we have so often prayed for: "give tongues of fire to preach Your Word, O God." It seemed so clear that Satan was fighting back.

We heard more details, of course, later on, but our deep hurts inside were like slashes of knives in several places at once: death, death, operations, fire. We thought of Job. The battle goes on. The fire started, it was discovered, in a vacuum cleaner bag. The fireplace had been cleaned out Saturday night by a boy who had the reputation of being *very*, very careful, but someone had told him to finish up with a vacuum cleaner. He put the pail of ashes back in the fireplace to await being taken out until early morning, but the vacuum bag had some still smoldering ashes in it. He felt he saw a bit of smoke, so he soaked the bag with water, then put it away in the cupboard. Through the night that smoldering turned into tiny flames, and then big flames, in the way fires have of spreading. Dolly Johnson's thirty-year collection of music (57 boxes of sacred sheet music, plus a lot of sheet music from the collection of Marilyn of the Chicago Symphony, who has frequently been to L'Abri) was in the next wooden cupboard to the vacuum cleaner. The invaluable collection, worth so much financially to Dolly, but even more in the real value, turned into ashes early in the fire as that whole wall burned to charcoal.

The whole chapel is black; the roof has holes; the organ is blackened and when the Flentrop man came from Holland to examine it, he said seventeen pipes are completely melted and destroyed, and it will take them two years to rebuild the whole thing, and get it back to us, saving the wood and design as much as possible. The piano and hymn books, chairs, and the soft couch, chairs where mothers sat with the children, are in sad rags and tatters, with so much gone. We didn't see it, of course, until we returned, and the actual standing together in that building when Franky drove us there was a time of shock and of seeing the temporariness of the "familiar" things of life. The beautiful things that have come forth from the fire began to come forth right away. The way the Workers and Members and Helpers and students worked together that night was wonderful. Also, the coming of the village pastor soon after 3 A.M. while the fire was still raging, to offer the use of the village church for L'Abri Sunday services, was also beautiful. The feeling in the village has not changed overnight, but there is a more friendly attitude on the part of many people. Eternal results have already taken place. Of course, one cannot say that the fire brought three people into the family of God and not realize that there was much searching, studying, considering and a coming close of those three people before, but in actual fact, it was the result of the fire that one girl became a Christian right after the fire was out, and two others as a result of the fire. The attitude of the Workers, and the working together of it all, that instead of weeping and wailing and blaming people, the Workers were having a cup of something hot to drink and muffins at 5 o'clock in the morning, with a prayer meeting spontaneously starting while Barry called Dallas to give John the news and to ask what to do about the insurance, etc. Barry did a great job of speaking French as he had to deal with the police, and the various Swiss men whom he had to talk to not only during the fire, but in all the legalities and complications that followed. The first church service took place in the village church with what everyone has described as one of the most wonderful services they ever attended. The prayer was spontaneous and real; Jane (who had called the fire company and had called Janine and other chalets at 3 A.M. after Betty looked out and saw the chapel in flames) sang and the music was very special, although our own organ which was dear to Jane's heart had burned, and Dolly's music was all gone. The offering was put aside for the rebuilding, and that will be the first amount in the "fund." Already other amounts have been given, with a five thousand franc gift anonymously given the week after that in an envelope in the offering.

Twenty-two years ago, Priscilla made a chart with a thermometer on it to help us all see visually how the money was coming in as we prayed for the Lord to send us what we needed to buy Chalet les Mélèzes. Now twenty-two years later, Priscilla and John's daughter, 15-year-old Elizabeth, has made a beautiful chart to record the money as it gathers for the rebuilding of the chapel. Somehow we do believe that the "latter house" will be even more beautiful than the "former house" and we pray that the Lord will fill it with special peace. At present there is red tape concerning the insurance, and permission to extend the wall a bit, etc. Do pray that the Lord may clearly guide in all this. Haggai 2:3–9 has been a special comfort to me these past days.

As I started this, I think you must have guessed that I am finishing it with only a few hours to go before we leave (for more speaking engagements), and no packing done yet, nor any other sensible preparations. I do want you to know in this last paragraph before I have to stop, that there is much more to tell you. For instance, in the Members' meeting we came to a good decision to have more time in the future during the yearly meeting to discuss the Bible and ideas and to keep more together in the realm of our thinking and understanding, rather than to spend so much time on details of business. We also after much discussion and prayer came to a recognition of how it might be possible to do something more to help in America. Hence the decision was made to have Franky (and Jim Buchfuehrer with whom he will be working) arrange another series of Seminars which will have not only Fran and myself and Franky speaking and answering questions in question periods, but also at least three other L'Abri Members, so that the impact will be more like being here. This seems to be the way, and the decision was taken for one series next year which you will be hearing more about later. We, and all of those who are a part of the L'Abri Family need to be praying about this and advertising, etc., as none of us have time to give to such a thing, yet it seemed a thing of compassion to fill some of the many requests for speaking. Many, many requests are being turned down, but these Seminars will give an opportunity for doing something that can be a provision for some of the need for a wider hearing of what people are hungry to hear as they ask for L'Abri speakers.

With very much love in the Lord Who is able to do all things, and Who loves us and cares for us in the midst of the battle. Never forget that He loved Peter as much as John, although Peter was going to be martyred early in life, and John was going to live to an old age and write Revelation. Both had "finished their work," even as we pray He may enable us to do. Let us pray for each other in these diverse needs we all face,

EDITH

October 17, 1977

Chesieres, Switzerland

Dear Family:

Our Monday morning prayer preparation meeting this morning was held in the strange atmosphere of the Huemoz village schoolhouse assembly room. It is a drab little room with a rather too-high stage-type platform, and no windows except one at the back. Bedraggled streamers and dingy tinsel from last Christmas still hang from the ceiling in uneven loops, and there is nothing to take away from the stiffness of rows of schoolroom chairs, and the starkness of naked light bulbs. As I spoke of seeing the gorgeous beauty of clear mountains and brilliant blue skies with the yellows and reds of autumn colors mingled with dark pines in the warmth of an Indian summer October sun—the heads of people could *not* turn and look to see what I was talking about, as they can in our chapel with its once whole wall of windows overlooking that magnificent view. We all had to remember what we had seen before we came in!! Next Monday morning we will, Lord willing, begin our day of fasting and prayer, with a meeting of Bible study and preparation in that same schoolroom. It will point up our need to pray for the rebuilding of the chapel.

The work has commenced on the chapel. We had a very real answer to prayer as permission was finally given by the Council of Seven in the commune to extend the back wall as far as the railing of the balcony had been on that end. It does mean we will have two more rows of seats, a little help for the rainy days, as well as for giving more people the possibility of being inside the building, while others sit out on the balcony on the window side. The left of the chapel is at present piled high with mounds of charred and burned wood. Quite an amazing sight! The right side, of course, is close to the chalet next door. The roof has already had all the tiles removed and has been extended to include the new portion. The work is progressing well, and this glorious weather we have had for five days now is a definite help. The organ has gone off to Holland on a truck, and we pray that work will be started on restoration of that lovely instrument. Meantime we meet in the village church for our Sunday church service, and in the village school hall for lectures, Saturday night discussion, and our Monday mornings. It would have seemed almost unbelievable if someone had told us some years ago that we would be using these buildings. We were refused permission not too many years ago to allow a group of people, many of them Swiss, to come and gather in the village church so that they could hear about L'Abri. They were people from a Christian conference for children's work, coming for just an afternoon. What a miracle it has been to have *both* the school hall *and* the village church opened for us now. For any of you who wonder how it works on Sunday, we do have to have our services later than usual, to not get there and disturb their service. We have flowers left over from their services, which give the building a prepared look. Also of course we use their organ, although we bring our hymn books. Many of ours were burned in the fire, so we haven't all that we had before, just the small Christian praise books, and the Psalms. After church then we are responsible to have it cleaned up. People take turns. This week it was Priscilla and Becky who were busy with brooms and mops and dust cloths by the time half the people were out. It is important to leave it in "tip top shape" immediately. All of us have appreciated worshiping in this old building, with the lovely soft shades in the paintings around the deep windows, depicting the Lamb slain but standing victorious, a dove at another window, and so on, in shades of beige, cream, brown, rust. Thinking of how many generations of families have worshiped here, or have been married, baptized, and had their funerals here, there is a continuity felt with Christians of past times.

We have called another day of prayer and fasting for October 24th because all of us feel the need of taking more time for prayer. We really do believe that prayer changes history, that things are different because of taking God literally when He tells us to call upon Him. Psalm 50:14, 15 can be relied upon specifically as we act upon these commands. "And call upon me in the day of trouble: I will deliver thee, and thou shalt glorify me." The result of prayer is to be something that will relieve something that is a "trouble" in some definite way in the lives of the Lord's people, but it is also to be a result which will glorify God, in us, through us, in a variety of ways. As Jehoshaphat in II Chronicles 20 called upon God, he set himself to proclaim a fast throughout all Judah. And the reality took place of the people literally coming together with their whole families including their little children, to spend time praying as they fasted not only from food, but from their ordinary work and times of conversation. It is imperative that from time to time we, living in the midst of the 20th century's speeding away from the absolute base for law or morality, for group action or individual decision, stop to make clear to ourselves that as children of the Lord, we have not only an Absolute, but we have access to Him. But at times we need to *stop* and take a whole day, or take sections of time, day or night, and have concentrated times with Him, shutting ourselves away from the regular normal "good things" to take seriously the portions of His Word that take for granted that we *will* have periods of prayer that are arranged for, set aside, put *first* before anything else at that particular time, at some cost to our schedule, time, and energy. . . .

We are told to pray always "with all prayer and supplication in the Spirit." This prayer is to be perseverance, and you can't persevere in just one minute; the very word means a succession of times. Each one who lectures, preaches, leads a Saturday night discussion needs prayer for "utterance" but so does each one who daily wants to speak what the Lord wants him or her to say to the person of the "Lord's choice."

All this will not happen without *someone* praying. Satan does not only battle in the area of trying to hinder the "utterances" of each of us as we long to speak truth in this moment of history, but he battles in the areas of health, spoiled crops, frost, broken furniture or washing machines and stoves and refrigerators. Discouragements and the feeling of "It is all impossible" come at us from many directions.

Who has prayed for L'Abri since 1955? There are some still continuing, but a number of the faithful ones in the praying family of L'Abri are now in heaven, and no longer kneel, or sit in rocking chairs with Bibles open, and looseleaf notebooks open, praying for at least 45 minutes a day. October is the month of my mother's birthday, and she has been in heaven a good many years now, but would be 103 this month. It caused me to remember that Mrs. MacMullen who lived on a chicken farm in Nova Scotia had promised to pray in mother's place, one hour a day for L'Abri, in detail, but now Mrs. MacMullen is also in heaven. Helen

Creenan, a worker in the county clerk's office in a Pennsylvania town, was one of the original praying family, who prayed every day and took days of fasting and prayer when she prayed in early morning, then all through her lunch hour, and again in the evening, even on working days. She now is in heaven. Dr. Byram (a woman missionary doctor, who spent a long time in a prison in Manchuria but who was miraculously released in answer to prayer) used to pray for years, 45 minutes a day for L'Abri with a looseleaf notebook full of her requests, and who took one full week a year to pray in addition to the daily time, is also with many others in heaven who used to be in the midst of "the battle" as really prayer warriors. There are others, most recently my father and Hans Rookmaaker. . . .

We need to pray that some will feel called upon to resolve, or vow to the Lord to pray *in place* of one who is no longer here to pray. However, we each need to increase our own time of prayer. How? By replacing something else we are doing with prayer. By stopping for five minutes each time the clock strikes the hour to pray. By praying as we walk, alone or with someone, eyes can be open but the time can be used in conversation with the Lord rather than with a person. By getting up earlier, or by consciously stopping some small pieces of "wasted time" and gathering them up, so to speak, to use that time for prayer. There is a "cost" to prayer. One thing must be said, one cannot pray without taking time. A rushing into God's presence to shout a request, with *never* taking time to spend talking it over carefully with Him, and thanking Him for all He is and all He does for us, would be like trying to have a human relationship develop with just a few shouted commands as the only form of communication. Of course we can take one second to whisper, "Help me Lord," and He hears, but we need to look back over our last months and check up on ourselves as to whether we have been serious enough about prayer. Certainly L'Abri cannot continue without prayer *growing*, even as the work grows.

The last Family Letter, written in May, was finished just before we began packing to leave for a brief time speaking. Fran was with the committee in Chicago (concerning the Bible), and I spoke in Kalamazoo, Michigan, to a conference of "Winning Women," then we both went to Toronto for a conference of Canadian pastors and Christian workers, where we both spoke. I must say we were both at the "bottom" as far as exhaustion goes. Only the Lord's strength, given for the immediate times of speaking, made it possible at all. We had the kind of exhaustion one feels after running a physical race and dropping on the soil with a dry mouth and slightly nauseated feeling. It continued! We were on a boat going to Southampton which gave a four-day period of rest, interspersed with having serious talks with the Jewish couple who shared our table. Then we plunged into a time at Greatham L'Abri, which gave us joy in being able to discuss, have some lectures, time of eating with students there, and quiet times of talking. . . .

*One Sunday dinner is over, and a young
photographer snaps Fran as another
unseen person waits on the other side
of the table to ask, "Just one more
question please."*

Susan just wrote to tell me of their last day of fasting and prayer, when her whole day was used in the urgent need to "fast from prayer" in order to meet the need of a family torn by the immediate circumstance of one parent's alcoholism. There are the times of the "visiting in prison," "giving a cup of cold water," "caring for the sick," which is our giving to the Lord Himself, which involves getting dirty, frustrated, tired, in marketing, cooking, making beds, washing feet, literally for others in addition to our own family, or the people we had thought were going to be our "task" for the day. The *additions* to *any* day, that are unexpected additions to the use of our time, so *often* seem to "spoil a spiritual pursuit," whether that is a day of prayer, or a scheduled day in the regular work. When to let the time be totally swept into another use? and when not to? are questions only the Lord can give the answer to. . . .

We came home in that same exhausted condition, wondering what was wrong with us, but others were sure it was an accumulation from all you read about in the last letter, the Seminars, the shocks of death and fire and so on, and insufficient rest. Our children were urging a long break, and rest, as were other dear L'Abri Workers. What took place was, as we look back on it, not our wise decision, but the thoughtfulness and decision of Udo and Debby and others as we agreed to rent the house they had found, as a "hideaway" instead of going away to any "sea and sand" kind of location for a vacation. Thus it was that through an amazing weaving together of circumstances *not* any brilliant plan on our parts, we found ourselves living through some weeks of rather dragging our feet along the quay of the lake at Montreaux, and gradually taking longer walks interspersed by sitting in our funny little white-plastered rooms, reading aloud to each other, or planting a garden in the square of ground we share with other people. What began to come forth right away was a series of talking to people, meeting them for tea by the lake in a hotel garden, so that we did have connections with the work. As time went on Fran took the Saturday night discussions, I prepared (with Mary Jane's or Linny's help) Sunday dinner for from 20 to 28 people, with Fran leading the dinnertime discussion until at times six in the evening. Monday mornings I took the "day of prayer lecture" and we each had some "appointments" with a variety of people coming for help. However, the other section of the week gradually changed from our walking and reading, to our starting working on new projects. I began writing the book on *Affliction*, which was finished, only by God's strength given to me in my weakness, on October 4th, and read by Dick Baltzell on October 5th and 6th, and worked over with him, by me, in the midst of a dillion interruptions, including the cooking of Chinese meals and so on.

Fran started work on a new film which will follow along as a sequence to *How Should We Then Live?* which Franky's new company (formed with Jim Buchfuehrer, who worked closely with Franky on the first film) will be, Lord willing, bringing out in 1979. As we look back over these past months we realize that the Lord chose this spot, behind a glass factory, with the breaking of glass as our music at times, but with a hidden-away-in-a-totally-different-country kind of a feeling, as the spot *He* meant us to have for a new period of creativity, not too far away from L'Abri, yet without a telephone, and far enough to work for uninterrupted hours. It is all quite astonishing as so often in life when one looks back over the "road" and sees how the curves and turns were hidden, and yet how our Guide helped us to know where to put our feet down "next." It is always just one step at a time we are meant to be concerned about. "Sufficient unto the day is the evil thereof" is the Lord's way of telling us that we shouldn't shoulder the heavy burdens of the frightening possibilities of what "tomorrow" and the tomorrows might bring forth. There is enough difficulty of today, and it is today's difficulties He will give us strength for. Just one day at a time. No more. . . .

The first part of the new film will deal with the inhumanness, or the dehumanization of people which is rapidly progressing—as seen not only in the diverse kinds of violence and disregard of individuals as having any significance, but also in the rising crescendo of elimination of lives in abortion, infanticide, and euthanasia. Dr. C. Everett Koop, Surgeon-in-Chief of the Philadelphia Children's Hospital,* is coworking with Franky and Fran on this. The second half of the film will be on

*Now Surgeon General of the United States.

the importance of the Bible as a base upon which to live, and to have as an absolute in striving for a change in all that is taking place. . . .

As you look in the little old kitchen at Chalet Tzi No with its wooden table and benches with room to squeeze in ten people in a tight squeeze, you wonder how they fit in as many as 28 for meals often these days— another table brought in from the outside seats six and fills the kitchen. Other people sit on the stairs with a plate in their laps. Some are in the tiny living room, and maybe a couple more in Becky's bedroom perched on her bed. The atmosphere is cozy, warm, and very special. The family is almost the same in ages as we were when L'Abri started. Elizabeth is now sixteen (Priscilla was seventeen when L'Abri began) and Becky is fourteen, Giandy is eight. It staggers us that our grandchildren are our children's ages and that L'Abri has lived through one entire generation of time!! If you shake your head and say, "It isn't what it used to be," true, there is more variety in the diverse chalets, but as far as our family goes, it is becoming a repeat one generation later. Priscilla is our eldest daughter, and Elizabeth our eldest granddaughter. When people come having read the L'Abri story and expect us to all have stopped growing older twenty years ago, they are finding what happens in a generation of time! We thank God for the part in conversation and discussion the *next* generation is having. When I say "little living room" actually the room is about 10 by 12 feet, and the space is taken up by one wall being covered with bookshelves built to the ceiling, a daybed along one wall, a piano taking the other wall and half the room, a music stand ready for John's cello playing as Elizabeth plays the piano, so the room usually is called a music room. In this tiny place much music comes forth, and a great deal of discussion. The scene changes in the mornings when Priscilla has the small L'Abri children of the Workers' families for nursery school. You who know anything about the number of dishes to be washed, and the mess to be cleaned up after children, must realize how many clean-up periods go on each day. Tzi No has no hot water in the sink, it needs to be heated on the stove for dishwashing, but that is Priscilla's private rebellion against the affluent age of the 20th century!! . . . .

Other changes *inside* our house (not so drastic as land stolen by a man building an apartment next to us and much happier) have been the moving in of Gail and Mary Jane. Mary Jane will be my helper and secretary when time is available (soon we both hope) and she has just recently become a L'Abri Worker. Mary Jane is a Canadian girl who was looking for more answers when she wandered into a Roman Catholic Church in Toronto and found *L'Abri* on the book rack. The priest asked her if she would like it, and when she said she hadn't the money, he said, "Just take it and read it, and pray for me." I would love to know who that priest is. She came, as so many others, expecting to stay a short time, and has been a student, a helper to me for a long time, now a Worker, and will soon be doing the secretarial work in Linny's place. The apartment downstairs (since Franky and Genie moved out) has been divided into two little homes, sharing a kitchen and bathroom, and Gail will be living in half and Mary Jane half. Gail was a Worker in French L'Abri for quite a long time, but has been Fran's secretary now for over a year. Amazing the way the Lord prepares people and fits them in in His own way. Gail's father as a naval man has had appointments which have given Gail a diversity of background, in Japan, in Russia and various parts of the world with one section of time in a Swiss boarding school near Lausanne, the same one I told about in *L'Abri*. When she was there she knew nothing about L'Abri. It is often astonishing how close people have been to L'Abri years before they are finally brought here.

Bob, a Japanese American, often has people coming to Bethany with children, or with some other special set of "differentness" not too easy to cope with. Bob cooks the meals, and has his own vegetable garden and, although of course with the help of students and guests in his chalet, has no special helper this summer. There was one period of time when he had two Cambodian young people. The boy, still in his teens, had seen his family killed, and all of his friends brutally tortured and killed. Nightmares occur . . . how long? How could such scenes be forgotten? He told of how the Cambodians now "in charge" have systematically killed first everyone with a university degree, then those with college education, then high school graduates, on down until, when he escaped, the "eighth grade graduates" were being eliminated by being buried up to their necks in soil, then stabbed through the skull. At least a million have died, but who can count them. The cruelty of man to man, of human being to human being, of person to person, is shattering to hear about, but we need to stop being romantic about it. This dear boy has an amazing story of escape, but he tells it without a smile. Life is too shatteringly serious. He heard of true Christianity through a Korean man who was a Christian, and who gave him help in Thailand, and then whom this boy helped in turn, to care for 50 refugee children in a house, until they could be taken to homes elsewhere. We are not allowed in L'Abri to be in any kind of an "ivory tower" no matter what people conjure up in their imaginations about this mountain spot. While these Cambodians were at Bob's chalet, and while someone else from Japan was with us, the Japanese translation, beautifully "out" now in a lovely edition, reached us. Bob had done the pictures for the cover of that edition; dear Noriko, who became a Christian at L'Abri, was baptized in our old chapel, and married a man who became a Christian in Syracuse while he was getting his Ph.D. at the university there, translated the book *L'Abri* into Japanese. Word Publishers in Japan have published it. . . .

Now I must rush to finish this. Fran will be going to Holland soon to be on a program on TV November 3rd when he will be presenting Anky Rookmaaker with a book, the Dutch translation of *How Should We Then Live?*, with all kinds of Dutch dignitaries present. The program will be live and filmed in a museum. Many will be speaking during the two hours, which will introduce the commencement of the ten-episode film series, *How Should We Then Live?*, on Dutch television, starting November 8th, Lord willing. Pray that Dutch L'Abri will be prepared by the Lord to be the help it may be to any who are helped by the film, and seek further conversation.

Fran will return on the 3rd, and I will be leaving for the States, Lord willing, on the 5th, to speak on TV and radio, and also to give some lectures that will be taped for the tape program for cassettes. Revell is bringing me to America to answer questions on TV and make known the books they feel are important, *What Is a Family?*, and *A Way of Seeing* which has been out for four months now, and is being quite astonishingly used to help people. . . .

"Faithful is he that calleth you, who also will *do* it. Brethren pray for us." (I Thess. 5:24, 25). Not a dichotomy, not contradictory. Yes, He is faithful who has called us. He will *do* it and will give us strength in our weakness and courage to go on. *But*—"brethren pray for us"—has meaning moment by moment. We are meant to intercede for each other. Not casually but as a basic responsibility. Who will pray?

With very much love in a time when we need each other's love, and in a time when God should have our love and trust in the midst of the battle,

EDITH

1978

Dear Family:

. . . Yesterday the village of Huemoz and people from the surrounding area were stunned and shocked as they crowded into the village
church. It was Wednesday, the proper three days after a death for the
funeral. On Sunday, during the village church service, in a chalet not far
from the church, a single shot had broken the quiet of the morning.
Birdie heard it in her little chalet nearby, but thought it must be the
practice which so often takes place at the shooting range, as Swiss men
who are all a part of the army practice some Sundays. But no volley of
shots followed. As L'Abri people gathered for our time to use the village
church for a service after theirs finished, the few village people who had
been in church scattered to their homes. The ten-year-old Turrel boy
had been visiting Giandy at Tzi No while his mother was in church, and
ran and skipped home before his mother, calling "Papa" as he entered
the chalet, but assumed his father was in the toilet. The 16-year-old
brother had come in just before, but assumed his father was taking a
walk, so did no more than call "Papa" just in case he might be there.
It was the mother, the wife, Madame Turrel, who came in from the
church service and searched the chalet for her husband and found the
dead body of Monsieur Turrel slumped over his desk in his tiny office,
shot with his own gun. Finality is never so clearly felt as in the human
act which separates the soul from the body so rapidly. People do so
many rash and destructive things in moments of despair and despon-
dency and great frustration, but suicide severs so frighteningly rapidly
the continuity of life here in the land of the living, and the family
life. The severing does not affect only the person who now is absent
from the body, but affects the little ten-year-old son, the sixteen-year-
old son, the twenty-one-year-old daughter, and the wife; the old parents
living in the chalet in the bend of the road from the chapel to whom all

L'Abri has smiled and waved after church services, and also affects all the village, the fellow workers at the railroad station, and a far-reaching number of people. People do *not* "live unto themselves" nor do they "die unto themselves." The effect on other people may not be wanted, but it takes place. None of us can separate our lives from the effect our lives have on an ever widening circle of people.

And so yesterday a Swiss village funeral took place, with so many men in the church, and outside who could not get in, as well as the women, the immediate family, the whole village, and some of us who have so long been a part of this village, although basically taken up with the people the Lord sends to us from distant spots in the world. These were all the people we had known for many years, and many of you have known, as you have been at L'Abri, or as you have read the Family Letter. Picture all the village there with tears, fears, twisted faces, tightened lips, thinking each his or her own thoughts. The schoolteacher who used to teach Debby, back from his post in Africa, the Dubis and the Ruchets, and Jane, Bob Jono, Veronica and Barry, John, Priscilla, Debby and I, and other L'Abri people and the Chaudet sisters looking so white and worried. You who have been here can picture it. How often we have for years gone away from funerals—sad at the emptiness of the message.

Priscilla and I stood in the crowded center aisle and squeezed each other's hands with relief and thankfulness as the pastor, a retired pastor from Vevey with a bald head and a fringe of white hair began to speak in a firm voice with strong words directly from the Word of God. He read from Isaiah 25, from John where Lazarus had died and Jesus wept, and I Corinthians 15:6. He spoke of the resurrection as his central message, and of the need of believing in Jesus, and of truth. He said that there is no one that can throw stones, as we each know our own weaknesses. He spoke of M. Turrel's illnesses, his recent open-heart operation, his time all of January in the hospital with asthma, and his despair about the future, and told how the human frame is weak and can "crack," but the bulk of the message was on the forgiveness of the Lord in Christ, and the resurrection, and he urged everyone in the village to read I Cor. 15. Never would we have chosen this manner of gathering the entire village, nor can we dare to say that God chose to do it this way. However, certainly it is a time to say that God can turn what Satan means for evil, to bring forth something to His glory. The village heard the gospel preached on the 12th of April 1978 under circumstances during which surely ears should have been opened, and minds should have been considering the importance of being certain of having a base for life, and the wonder of the resurrection, the hope of the Word of God. "I am the resurrection and the life, he that believeth in me, though he were dead yet shall he live . . . "* That gathering of so very mortal, helpless, weak, finite, limited, human beings in their shared shock pointed up vividly the fantastic change that is ahead of us when our ears shall hear the

* John 11:25.

trumpet with startling response of joy, and our eyes shall see each other as we are changed. "In a moment, in the twinkling of an eye, at the last trump: for the trumpet shall sound, and the dead shall be raised incorruptible, and we shall be changed.". . .*

"Mmmmm," sighed the little blond mother of the two identically dressed little blond blue-eyed three- and five-year-old girls. "It is so wonderful being here, the only trouble is the time is going to go by so quickly. You can't imagine how wonderful it is for us to be in such a beautiful place where there is no danger. To be able to walk with the children along the paths and through fields and woods, and to be able to sit quietly on the grass or a rock and eat a picnic is something they have never known. It is a thing of wonder to us to be able to go out without a machine gun!" "But," I replied with a kind of gasp of shocked incredulity. "How do you manage? How could you carry such a gun?" "I just don't go out for walks at all, or take the children out, unless my husband goes with us. There isn't any freedom to do such things." I was talking with the Rhodesian family who came to L'Abri to study for a couple of months. The "cost" of coming was great and I am not just talking about air fares and so on, but the husband had to resign his job in computer programming without knowing what might open up upon his return, and they had to use up savings to do this. However, after reading *L'Abri* and other books of Fran's and mine and others here at L'Abri, they felt they needed a time of study in Farel House in the midst of a variety of "peace" to prepare for whatever the Lord might lead them to do, and whatever might be ahead for them in today's Rhodesia. "The day before we left," the mother said as she went on, "we were having our Bible study group, and suddenly a young fellow burst in and told of how he and his friend had been two alone against 60 guerillas. Bullets had whistled around his head, his friend had been mown down by his side, but somehow he had escaped and come back alive, terribly shaken, to come in just at that point in our class. This is not an uncommon happening. All our children have the terrible trauma of saying goodbye to their daddies, over and over again, then waiting for news. You see the men have to fight a certain number of weeks as guerrilla attacks never cease to come, and then work a certain number of weeks. It seems to us it is worse than a war where the fathers or brothers go until it is over." . . .

Somehow L'Abri has, through the years, been a tiny cross section of what is going on in the world. Conversations here make newspaper headlines come alive with flesh-and-blood reality. Personality emerges out of what is too easily read as something happening to impersonal masses. The problem facing each one of us as Workers and Members in L'Abri has always the same base as we face one person after another. We are *finite* and *limited*. In our finiteness and limitation we can give only finite and limited help and then urge individuals to turn to the One who

*1 Corinthians 15:52.

is infinite and unlimited and who in His wisdom can unfold His path to individuals in the midst of this point of history, even as He has in past points of history. . . .

We have been having not only a sprinkling of people among us from a *great* variety of trouble *spots*, so that they are in essence refugees, seeking shelter for a period of time, and asking for advice, but we also have had quite a number of refugees from *situations* which are ugly and a result of 20th-century living on the basis of "no absolutes," "no truth," "everything is relative," in day-by-day life.

Most personal stories cannot be told. People need their privacy protected, and we need to just say, "Pray for the many people we have among us now and who have recently come and gone, who are facing 'impossible' situations, and need the Lord's strength in their weakness, as well as His guidance."

The word "refugee" applies to quite a number of people coming these days. However, pick up any week's *Time* or *Newsweek* and discover how much of the world is in the midst of violence of terrorist origin, or because of guerrillas or the schemes of people thirsting for power at one level or another, and it is no wonder that some of the people affected by these things find their way to L'Abri in Switzerland, Holland, or England.

What kind of "days" are we living in? Is it the time of the "end"? We cannot predict the time when Jesus will return. He told us not to. The knowledge of that time is in the possession of our Heavenly Father. Surely however it is a time when "the very elect" seem to be fooled. There are so many warped and twisted ideas put forth on every side. There are the blatant denials of all that the Word of God teaches, with false teaching coming at the level of the new rise of "goddesses" as women have started a movement to go back to the old pagan Greek religions, and are having gatherings like one in the Santa Cruz University just recently. But there are also the dangers of Christians looking for more dramatic happenings and excitements, bypassing the day-by-day faithful hours of prayer and not only reading and studying the Word of God, but of attempting by His help to *do* it in undramatic unexciting areas. Part of the tribulation is as undramatic as measles, broken dishes, burned toast or eggs, spilled tea staining new tablecloths, or broken legs, or unappreciative people taking everything one does for granted or with downright barbed criticism. The "enduring to the end" that makes up the Christian life, is not talking about "enduring" a string of exciting entertainments or people rising from the dead. All the "bewares" of the book of Jude and other places in the Bible are meant to help us to keep our balance as we walk today's tightrope doing what the Lord has given us to do, and not rushing off to something either "easier" or "more exciting." Beware of false prophets, and of Satan clothing himself as an angel of light. . . .

Our tiny bedroom in Mélèzes is where we sit to talk to a variety of people. One day a photographer snapped this photo of me while I talked with someone sitting in the rocking chair in front of me.

We were approaching our yearly Members' meeting, and we all strongly felt that the only absolutely essential preparation we could have would be a Day of Fasting and Prayer. There is nothing that substitutes for that in any "crisis" time in our personal lives, or in any time when we need special help or guidance in our group lives. . . .

Thursday, May 4th, was the day chosen, and the first answer we had (as has been the case at times before) was a perfectly gorgeous sunny day with warmth and marvelous view of all that God has created that surrounds us here. We have had snow since, and are shrouded in fog and rain at the present, but that day was perfect for walking or sitting and praying outdoors. The opening meeting was held in the Huemoz schoolhouse, perhaps our last time in there, as our chapel is *ready* (chairs missing but we can use it starting this week)! It was the Swiss holiday celebrating the Ascension. We hadn't chosen Ascension Day purposely, but it was a special time to be having a Day of Prayer. Everyone scattered with their prayer lists and Bibles and climbed up, or walked along paths, sat on stones or benches, out of sight of each other. Fran and I walked together up back paths, taking turns reading the verses aloud, and praying aloud. We ask everyone to go alone, or to at least not talk together but pray together if husbands and wives or friends pray by two by two. It is so important to have an unhindered communication with the Lord. There are other times to communicate horizontally. Ascension Day is the day the Swiss men shoot, practicing at the usual place in Huemoz, hence there is not perfect freedom to walk wherever anyone might want to, but there is need to keep in mind the dangerous paths on the other

A photo was taken of Fran a few minutes later by that same photographer. Notice Great Uncle George Paden's pocket watch on the wall under the ivy.

side of Chalet Bethany which come in range of the shooting. Such a serious day, yet kept only as a holiday to give men time to keep prepared for war. I couldn't help but think of the need of our "practicing" to be constantly prepared for the attacks of the enemy. Ephesians 6:11 you remember is "Put on the whole armor of God, that ye may be able to stand against the wiles of the devil," and verse 18 follows right along in the battle preparations with, "Praying always with all prayer and supplication in the Spirit, and watching thereunto with all perseverance and supplication for all saints." So in a way the sound of the gun shots was not after all a very bad accompaniment for a day of battling in prayer. Everyone came back to the closing meeting, during which Fran led a time of prayer. It seemed to us all that it was one of the best days of prayer we had had. Unless you have actually taken a day like this, with five or six unbroken hours of prayer, interspersed with reading some portions of the Bible, you can't understand the reality of refreshment which takes place, in addition to the results. . . .

The yearly Members' meeting started with a whole morning of prayer. Everything is put aside as we pray together for some hours, but when reports are being given or discussion is taking place, there is also knitting, embroidery, mending, and even the signing of letters or adding up of accounts. The reports are always a tiny condensation of what has taken place in a year's time. Juan had come from Italy to report on the work there, which is turning into mainly a local church work. The congregation is mostly Italian, the services are in Italian. . . . Dick Keyes told us of the work in Ealing where the church continues to grow . . . Dick and Mardi, after much prayer, became certain that they are to be in the residential L'Abri at Greatham. . . . There is the possibility of L'Abri starting a branch on the East Coast, in New England, if that is what the Lord would have Dick and Mardi involved in after a year's preparation at Greatham. . . . Another thing that happened during this year is the drastic fall of the dollar . . . so that it is a staggering piece of arithmetic to multiply the dollar by what it *used* to be . . . at 4.32 Swiss francs for one dollar, and now it hovers between 1.80 and 1.90!!!. . . . Jane reported that the new book she and Betty have been working on is *A Gift of Music*. . . . Udo's *Pro-Existence* is still as up to date in subject matter and content as ever, and many people write to say so. Udo told us of his time in Fergus Falls, Minnesota, and in Walnut Creek, California. He gave lectures before the showing of each episode of the ten-episode film and then had times for questions afterwards. It was astonishing in such a small town as Fergus Falls to have 1,200 people out the first night of the five-day Seminar.

Fran and I were in Washington, D.C., in March, along with Franky, for a seminar which sprang from Joanne Kemp's class of congressmen's wives which studies our books, chapter by chapter. This seminar was by invitation and was for these women to invite others. Senators, congressmen, State Department people, industrialists, and their wives and other Washington people made up the 200 who came for a two-day Seminar, with discussion after the films given by Fran, and at mealtimes. The films were introduced by Jack Kemp, and Franky told about the next project which is in the process of being made. It was an extremely warm time of very real and honest questions, excitement about answers, and spontaneous discussion. During that time Fran also had a luncheon for discussion with some senators and congressmen, hosted by Congressman Don Bonkers and Congressman Jack Kemp. Do pray about the Lord's own continuing of results. I also spoke at a women's meeting there one other morning. . . .

When I wrote the last letter, I told about finishing the book *Affliction*; now Lord willing, it will be coming out in August. It seems that just about the time it comes out, I will be in the hospital having an operation. My gynecologist just discovered that I need to have a cyst removed. It is to take place in Samaritan Hospital in Vevey, a very familiar place as it is the birthplace of many of our grandchildren, and also other babies of the L'Abri Family. The time is to be either the 31st of July, or the 2nd of August (as the 1st of August is the national Swiss holiday!). Strangely enough that is *just* the time when, Lord willing, the filming of the new film, *Whatever Happened to the Human Race?* is to commence, and Fran will probably be flying out to America at that time. When we pray for the Lord's *timing*, and for His unfolding His plan, we need to accept the dates that would not be exactly our choosing on a calendar!!! Is there an element of Satan's attack in here, of trying to make a "barb" concerning what I have said in *Affliction,* and of trying to make the beginning work on the film harder for Fran? Perhaps, but there is also the promised "sufficient grace," and His strength made perfect in *weakness* so that countervictory is not just a vague possibility but something we are given to expect. The doctor says I will be needing to be eight days in the hospital, and then will need three weeks of *rest!*

In writing about the filming first let me say that Fran completed his work on the manuscript, as did the researchers, and Ranald in his particular contribution to assembling the last two episodes, and Franky's part. At present the movie script is finished and ready for the work to commence. The book manuscript is in the hands of Jim Sires, who is editing it. All this has taken place since the last writing of a Family Letter! And sentences like this, one following another, cannot possibly hint at all the work each person has put into this. At the present moment, Franky, Jim, and the cameraman Allan, are traveling and "blocking" in preparation to the time of filming. Lord willing, the filming will occupy the months of August until December. But who of us can see around the "next bend" in life, so my report of what takes place during these next months will have to be after the months are over. . . .

Franky's visions for these films is that of presenting the "content" that is given in discussions here at L'Abri to a far wider section of the world, entering places it would never otherwise be heard. The use of the film has been a help to L'Abri Workers in speaking or discussing in various places. Barry Seagren led the discussions after the showings of the film in Geneva University auditorium during the Sunday nights it was shown there. Ranald has been there to answer questions and speak as the film was introduced in London, and Ranald and Jerram will be helping with various Seminars there, to say nothing of the additional help the film is to Bob Jono in Japan. Of course there is a blending, as the Lord has brought forth both these "works" at this particular stage in history to send forth the light of truth in an ever increasingly dark world. It is a marvel to me to see the "flattening out of the walls" of our chalets to let literally millions peer over the shoulders of the small numbers sitting at our tables, so that they may "see" and "hear" with eyes and ears of understanding.

But—don't get confused, L'Abri has not become a work for the children of India and Kenya rather than what it used to be, that is Anky Rookmaaker's special calling in addition to L'Abri; nor has L'Abri become a company to put out tapes and to make films, that is Franky and Jim's special calling; nor has L'Abri become a publishing house, that is the calling of the various publishers who are, or have been, publishing the books written by L'Abri Workers. . . .

Now it is time to close the letter with a description of the dedication of the chapel! We all were very aware as we sat on the floor that the new chairs were needed. We are *using all the old chairs*, sandpapered, and cleaned up except for the ones that were completely demolished! Fifty new ones had to be bought, just very ordinary wooden chairs with metal tube-type legs, and the price John tells us is far more than double the old ones and the shock John had was transmitted to us as we heard it is 300 dollars for fifty chairs. At the dedication we were very aware that the organ was not present, and that there were yet no curtains, or awnings but we were "home" and happy to look out of those wonderful windows of clear glass to see the view of God's architecture had not changed. The Dents du Midi and all the other mountains, the Rhone valley below and all the slopes came alive in shades of fresh green, topped with the still white covering of snow. It was like moving into a home that is not yet furnished completely, but yet *home!* As the balcony had been painted and the paint was not yet dry, people could not sit out there, so in the end people were standing around the door, and on the grass. The loud speaker system was not yet working, so those outside couldn't hear much. In spite of all these "flaws" it was a tremendously moving time. . . . You see, no one knew exactly when the chapel would be ready enough to start meeting in. The combination of what took place that morning was an astonishing demonstration of the wonder of the Lord's planning. One girl became a Christian (after, of course, a period of time of having her questions answered and of discussions and study here) after the night of fire-fighting because of the marvel to her of the attitudes and actions of the Workers that night. She was struck by the reality of the truth of Christianity as she saw them praying at five in the morning while they were having hot chocolate at Barry and Veronica's. . . .

You know of course, as well as I, that a book couldn't cover the stories of that combination of people the Lord brought that day, Sunday, May 28th. They were there from all over the world. One fellow is a person who was put into a Buddhist monastery in his country Sri Lanka when he was four years old and was a monk when he was six years old, then later became a priest. The way he got to L'Abri is *one* of the most miraculous stories of God's bringing prepared and seeking hearts that we have ever known, and we have known a good number of them. In his travels he left his guru to come to Switzerland, and in Basel developed a terrible pain in his stomach. He arrived in the hospital as an emergency kidney stone case. After the operation he talked with some Christians, who hearing his questions (he had gotten a Bible at some point in past months and had been reading it) told him he ought to go to L'Abri. He thought he would come for a day or two and is now in Mélèzes for at least a month. . . .

In spite of the shrieking headlines and horror pictures of violence and cruelty of person to person—let us take heart and continue to *pray* for the lost world and for the seeking ones, and in the same time as praying, to be ready to go where the Lord wants us to go and do what He wants us to do, whether that place is a hospital, an airplane, a neighbor's home, our own backyard, or halfway around the world. Let us consciously let the Lord be God in each other's lives, and pray for each other's leading, believing He does have a diversity of plans for His children, and that for each of us there can be changes ahead. Pray for each individual Worker, each branch of L'Abri, but also for the "ripples" that are going forth into such wide circles through the dropping of such pebbles as the books, seminars, films, and tapes. Finally, pray for the Lord's leading and timing and location for a L'Abri Conference during 1978. The Members feel it is time for another such conference. Do pray for guidance concerning this, as well as for the other wide circles rippling forth. Jane tells us there will be another L'Abri Ensemble tour this autumn, Lord willing.

With very much love in the God to Whom nothing is impossible,

EDITH

November 12, 1978   Rochester, Minnesota

Dear Family:

It has been one month since we arrived in Minnesota for the first time in our lives, one month since we were met at the airport by Dr. Victor Wahby and also Dr. Morlock from Mayo, one month since Fran entered St. Mary's Hospital for a checkup, one month out of 1978 that was not planned by anyone that wrote a schedule for this year, one totally unexpected month of our lives as individuals, as a couple, as a family, and as a L'Abri Family, one month of change, change in perspective more than change in geographic location.

The change has been as great this month as Alice in Wonderland's change as she fell through the rabbit hole, or walked through the looking glass. A huge jolt in life, uprooting and transplanting, sudden illness, war, famine, earthquake, or accident brings with it a certain measure of unreality, but also an adjusting to *true* reality, that of a fallen world and of our really living in the period of history before all the abnormal things of the spoiled creation have been restored. Our expectations at times are too expectant of being able to go on undisturbed personally by the abnormal universe. We know that the victory Christ suffered to bring about is marvelous, but we are not as keenly aware of the sharp contrast between this being true and unchangeable for us as children of the living God, and the lostness of those who have no Heavenly Father and no large family to care, until we live in the midst of the sudden shattering of our "normal" schedule or situation and recognize what the unchangeable structure and base means to us. We have the unchangeable God as our Father. Our communication with Him is constant. He has given us horizontal communication with our family, whether the personal family, or the larger family of those who are the Lord's children, and who love Him as well as loving the rest of "the family." How lost are the lost when disaster of some variety strikes! Living through some understanding of what this loneliness would be by contrast makes the imperative to make truth known stronger than ever before.

What has happened in this past month of titanic change in our lives?

Five weeks ago Fran finished his part in the film *Whatever Happened to the Human Race?*, so that everything he had to do and say in that film was completed. Franky, Jim, and the film crew had filmed with Dr. Koop, and with Fran, in the United States, Israel, Austria, and Switzerland. The *timing* of the Lord is something we look back on with awe. Rather than the film taking longer than the schedule, it finished a bit earlier than schedule because a scene in Greece had to be replanned to do elsewhere, due to a cancellation of permission by the government. *Had that cancellation not taken place,* the timing would have been "off" by a week. It was at the last period of filming, during that last week, that Fran's weight loss became noticeable, and Dr. Gandur found he had an enlarged spleen! The phone calls to Dr. Wahby in Mayo had a background of an exchange of correspondence which had taken place over *months* of time. Years before that, Dr. Wahby had read Fran's books (*The God Who Is There* and others) in Egypt and had heard him speak in Switzerland. Months before that Len Rogers had introduced Fran by letter to Dr. Wahby. It was *not* "by chance" that Dr. Wahby answered his beeper in St. Mary's Hospital the night Udo and Debby, Franky and Genie, Prisca and John, urged me to call Mayo Clinic, and not "by chance" that he made a decisive recommendation. "Come early next week, by Tuesday if possible." Sunday night we said goodbye to the film crew as three were on their way back to their homes in Israel, another on his way to England, and two back to California. The ending of a block of time in a shared piece of work always brings a sadness as well as the shock of how quickly history takes the place of present!!! Many phone calls and arrangements, with the help of Len Rogers (who lives in Nyon as International Director of Youth for Christ), had prepared the way for us to get to Zurich by Monday night (hastily packing suitcases for what we expected to be a week's "checkup" at Mayo Clinic, plus a conference in Holland). Fran's passport had run out, and a lot of the phone calls were to get arrangements made for getting a new one quickly on Tuesday morning as the American Consulate was closed Saturday, Sunday, and Monday. Tuesday morning at about 6 A.M. Len Rogers jogged around the blocks from the hotel to the Consulate just to be sure of how to drive there quickly, because we needed to be there on the dot when it opened at 9 A.M. and then take the new passport and zip out to the airport to make the plane in time. In Chicago we had a three-hour wait. We then flew on to

Rochester, Minnesota, with some curiosity to see what Minnesota would be like, as well as a kind of gnawing uncertainty as to what the "tests" might reveal.

At the little airport we were met with what seemed like a warm welcoming committee! There was Dr. Wahby and another doctor who used to be head of a department in Mayo Clinic (41 years but now retired) Dr. Morlock, Mary, an anesthetist in St. Mary's Hospital, and then off to one side Avis Dieseth from Fergus Falls (where Udo had led a Seminar along with the film) who had come to be sure we had a hotel room and were cared for. Dr. Wahby took us to our hotel (room had been reserved for us by Billy Zeoli), and we found that the arrangement was that Fran was to be entered into the hospital the next day so that tests could be done more conveniently and quickly. That sounded sensible, but brought with it a little more of that apprehension of what might be ahead.

As we prayed together that night in the hotel room, it was with the expectation of probably being a little late for the speaking engagement Fran had in Holland, but still thinking in the direction of going to Holland before going home for "normal L'Abri life."

By the next night our prayer time together was after Fran had had some of the first tests, EKG, blood tests, and so on, and after Dr. Wahby had seen the glands in Fran's neck and stated firmly, "tomorrow morning we'll have you upstairs to take one of those glands out and have a biopsy." How strong the reality was at that moment of excruciating uncertainty as to what the report would be in the morning, of *having* the eternal God as our Father, the Infinite Personal God who could stay in the hospital room and also go to the hotel with me. This same God could hear and answer prayer, as well as comfort, and could prepare the way ahead, knowing what preparations were necessary. We are fulfilling His commands when we make our needs known, and spread our cause out specifically before Him. It is not a dichotomy to ask—"ask that the Father may be glorified in the Son," and to recognize that there is a battle going on in which Satan is trying to get us to stop loving and trusting God, in which our need is to pour out our complete trust "no matter what."

I went back to the hotel to spend most of the night awake and praying. Small comforts had already been given, the pleasant room in the hospital with its three white walls and one dark blue wall, the lovely small panes of glass and brown woodwork and a print of a Dutch painting on the wall with cheerful blue and white curtains. It was a comfort to know that Fran had a phone by his bed and that he could dial at any time of the day or night, and I could dial him. These and other "cups of tea" had been supplied by the Lord, not by chance, we felt strongly. We prayed together by telephone before he went to sleep that night, and in the morning as he came down from the surgery to tell me the news as we held hands and looked together at the sunshine pouring through yellow leaves, it was on that same telephone that he talked directly to each of our four children to tell them personally what he had told me, "The gland is malignant, and the lymph system is involved." It was so good Fran himself could tell each one and also encourage them by his own attitude as well as words.

Strange the sharpness of that word "malignancy" or the word "cancer"—the words themselves are like the sudden change in music which speaks of disaster ahead in the story the music is telling. Yet really, as Debby remarked and each of us has echoed in different ways, we are *always* living on the edge of disaster, changes, shock, or attack. After all we are in a battle—the battle of the centuries between Satan and God, and the "peace and affluence to enjoy that peace" are always a false separation from the reality of the raging battle. Somehow our perspective gets sadly out of line when things go along too smoothly and comfortably and when all the "shocks" are someone else's shocks that filter through to us a bit blurred. Not only is our understanding of what the "fall" actually consists of blurred, but our understanding of the absolute marvel of what God has done for us in making victory certain and complete is dimmed when we can rush on without interruption in our scheduled days.

Whatever is ahead, we have been living a very important period of our lives during this past month. On that same telephone by his bed, Fran talked to Birdie in her bed in the Samaritan Hospital in Vevey where she was waiting for an operation. What a wonderful connection! Not just of voices over the sea and land, but of understanding in such a moment in her life and Fran's.

Birdie has something very similar to what Fran has with painful and difficult days ahead. To be given "connection" at such a time was a specificness of communication that surpasses anything known by anyone except two children of the same Heavenly Father.

On Friday the 13th of October Franky and Debby had arrived and were in the hospital room, rather than on the other end of the phone. We were able to wait together for the report and diagnosis to be given on Tuesday. The CAT scan test and the bone marrow test were made on Friday, and Fran was allowed to go to the hotel on Saturday to await the time of the doctor's appointment. Sunday we had one of the most precious family times we have ever had with the four of us having a two-hour time of sharing things from the Bible and our thoughts in the midst of that sharpness of perspective which is separated from time and space and is a gift in the midst of a time of being pulled away from the normal (and good) daily work of life. We felt we were in a different "time period" isolated from the things that distract. How very real and exciting is the certain teaching in the Bible concerning the Second Coming of Christ and all that is ahead we felt in a fresh way as Fran read the last three chapters of Revelation to us. How reassuring are the Psalms as we considered together answers to prayer and the history of comfort through my last few years recorded beside some of the Psalm verses, and then read together Psalm 71 and prayed in the context of verses 17-20. . Debby brought us something from Peter, and Franky reported a sermon on affliction and we had a time of very fervent prayer together. How does one pray in such a time? "Don't let any one of us stop trusting You Lord, please may we be *real* in our love for You, and in our wanting to be in Your will, and in our victory over whatever Satan would be trying to do to us now. Please Lord give us present victory in the heavenly battle. *This* is the time that counts for Your glory Lord—don't let us flub it." These urgent requests have to take place in the land of the living!!! We need to realize that there is danger in *wasting* precious time in simply agonizing, rather than using well our opportunity to feel and see things in a perspective that is closer to heaven's perspective. Then can't we ask to be made well? Of course that is a freedom given us, and we can be relieved that accepting God's Word as true gives freedom that is beyond finite understanding, freedom to bow before God's will, and yet to ask with fervent faith, "Please God give time, give strength to show forth *Your* strength to this generation, and Thy power to the ones who need to know about You now." We are not asked to give up and stop making requests, the opposite is true.

While we waited for Tuesday, Franky had Heinz bring his father some of the rough footage of the film, and Fran was filled with rejoicing and tearful thanksgiving for the beauty of what is there. Answered prayer for the filming is already visible in the rough state of unedited film. We thanked God over and over again for His *timing*. It was so clearly His timing that this very important work had been completed and can now go on into the editing. How we marveled at the strength given the midst of the disease already present, to say those strong words on the top of Mt. Sinai where Moses stood, and at the Sea of Galilee near where Jesus stood in His resurrected body. How we thanked God for strength given so clearly day by day to each one involved in that filming, each with their own weaknesses or personal difficulties. "It is well done, and a gorgeous series of shots" was a song in Fran's heart, as well as in all of ours as we considered all this in the time of waiting for Tuesday's diagnosis. It somehow brought all of life into focus—the importance of doing things well for the Lord, in spite of the hard things in each day's work, and our waiting for His Second Coming.

Tuesday October 17th brought the second wave of shock when Dr. Petitt spent an hour and a quarter with Fran and me, to carefully and frankly explain that Fran has lymphoma, a malignancy of the lymph glands, treatable only by chemotherapy; he said it is in many of the lymph glands and has entered the bone marrow about 30% invasion. That is *not* bone cancer, but a blood system malignancy that responds to chemotherapy but cannot be treated with radiation or cobalt. Dr. Petitt's suggested program was six months of 21-day cycles, with the formula COPA being injected by intravenous drip followed by five days of pills, and then about sixteen days of "rest" from the medicine. We had prayed for clear guidance as to what to do about the treatment, when it was suggested, whether to return to Switzerland, go somewhere else in the United States where friends had offered us rooms in their home, or to stay right here in Rochester at Mayo Clinic. Before we left Dr. Petitt's office Fran said, "You are my doctor, we shall stay here and follow your plan under your supervision." It means having checkups in between the chemo, and having the doctor's advice who is following the case right through. It also meant being able to start the treatment without delay.

Things unfolded in quick succession after that decision. The Lord opened up a little apartment in the form of a "town house," three floors in one of about twelve such houses stuck together like a child's blocks. Avis and Bob had seen it from the outside, then Debby and I went to look at several possibilities, and this seemed "right" though a bit dingy and dark that day. A dear friend made it available to us and also insisted we get it painted and fixed up. You can't imagine the "instant interior decorating" which took place (hours of working and walking miles through stores, etc.) but in three days, Debby and I were able to get a real "home" complete with ivy, philodendron, and other green plants, pots and pans and dishes, etc., and the beds made up with sheets, so that Fran could "move in" to a home, rather than be some other place, "marking time." I can't say too strongly what a difference it has made to both of us, and to the whole family. For any "patient" the surroundings make such a difference, and the feeling of a "beginning" rather than an ending, or a marking time, has been given us as we water plants, make our own bread or muffins, extract the juice from fresh Minnesota apples or carrots and celery, and sit and talk to the people the Lord has already sent into this house. There is an inner surge of wonder and even excitement in recognizing that the Lord *has done*, and *is doing* something very special in the midst of this sudden change and uprooting and transplanting. It is not a "chance happening," and words concerning Joseph's time in Egypt "you meant it for my harm but God has used it for good"* keep running through my head. We have been given loving people here in Minnesota to help in many ways.

Debby slept here the first night we were here. Susan had come from England while we were still in the hotel, and the second Sunday we had another family service there, as special as the first one, with Susan, Debby, Fran and myself and Chuck† making it like the beginning of L'Abri with one person entering into the family at a time. Franky had left to go back to Switzerland on Saturday and had mysteriously disappeared for the afternoon Friday. At the end of the afternoon he called his father to see something in his room, and of all amazing things he had produced eight works of art, four paintings and four wonderful drawings, to give us "home" instead of unfamiliar things on our walls. Noth-

---

*Genesis 45:1–15.
†An assistant to Billy Zeoli who was sent to help us.

ing could have been a more loving gift to Fran. Franky had not painted since starting his film making four years ago, and it was a fantastic thing that had taken shape in that hotel room, far more than just eight beautiful art works to put on our walls. The vividness of creativity released at that period of time was an exciting demonstration in living practically the thing Luther pointed out when he said, "If Jesus were coming back tomorrow, I would plant a tree today." We are to live on the edge of time with today as the day Jesus might come back, but with today's creativity and care for each other as urgently important as it would be if we knew we had a long time to prepare for right here. The smell of Franky's paint lingered behind as he left, and the paintings dried out that weekend before we moved. As Debby left for Switzerland, Susan stayed on to help in the first weeks in this house.

The first chemo treatment took place while we were still in the hotel, and Debby and Franky were there to discover through those first 24 hours that instead of the expected nausea and "flu symptoms" we had been warned about there was no nausea at all, just long sleep and a desire for several small meals during that 24 hours. Then after the five days of treatment, up and down periods of extreme fatigue and stomach pain, etc. We have tried (Susan, and now Priscilla and I) to make healthy food—a pint of fresh apple juice through the morning, and a pint of carrot, celery, and other vegetable juice in the afternoon and evening. We sprout alfalfa sprouts to add to salads and are following a balanced diet gathered from the big pile of books people have been sending us and telephoning us about. We are not being extreme, but are observing what we feel to be a sensible amount of attention to having plenty of vegetables, etc. It would seem to us that the use of the medicine, and of the right kind of food, a walk in fresh air each day, and as much relaxation and restful surrounding as is possible, is *not* canceling out the central importance of prayer for Fran. We have been overwhelmed and amazed at the thousands of people praying daily in prayer groups, churches, as individuals, and so on, for Fran's being restored to the place of continuing to speak to "this generation" for a time longer. Letters, telegrams, phone calls, pour in to let us know of prayer taking place and we know God is answering and that things are *not* the same as they would be without the prayer. That, however, does not blot out the fact that at this point of history this particular chemotherapy has been discovered. We can't sort it out in our finiteness and limitedness. Thank God, we aren't asked to chart it. We can have the comfort He has given us of a measure of knowledge, and still pray for His work which is above all the "natural" means we have at hand.

To close this portion of the "reactions and result," let me say that the first checkup in the middle of the first 21 days brought happy news. Dr. Petitt was surprised and pleased that Fran's platelet count was a high normal and that his hemoglobin had increased from 11.9 to 12.4, also that the glands in his neck and underarms had gone down, and that the abdomen was soft and very decreased in size, with the tumor slightly diminished. Now he has had his second chemotherapy, once more with no nausea at all, and with thus far about the same kind of reactions as the first time. On the 14th he goes for his next blood tests and checkup.

I would say that we are encouraged. Fran was openly facing that it could be that he would *not* get well, and be approaching death as well as the fact that he could be given a long measure of time to continue in the work the Lord has for him to do. At this moment, if you were on the other end of the telephone, I would say to you, My feeling is one of expectancy; I do not feel this is the end, but that it is the beginning of some kind of a new chapter. Both Fran and I feel it is not an accident that we are in Rochester at this particular moment in history and we feel that God is right now doing things that needed this combination of factors to bring forth.

The letters and messages that are coming to us are an overwhelming thing. It is as if we were having a glimpse behind a curtain as to what results God has given, hitherto hidden from us. We feel as if we are observing a harvest. Love expressed, spiritual results in people's lives, growth in the Lord that is very real is being made known to us in ways we feel we would never have had if this cancer had not come as it did. We feel the times we have already had with each of our four children (Priscilla came for two days while Susan was here, and then Susan left and Priscilla is helping until I get back from speaking in Cambridge, England) is something we never would have had in any other circumstance. Our L'Abri work has been of such an all-consuming nature through the years, that except for the family reunion, and Christmas, we never have much time to be together and in those times we are *all* together so that this period has been more like going back in history to having our children in their growing years. It is a gift.

As for the wider family of L'Abri even in separation geographically, there is closeness that is precious, even as is the special closeness right now of our grandchildren and those whom our children married. It can't be put into words properly, but rather than a gloomy time, this has been a time rich in relationships. A time of sweeping away cluttering things to have some basic things "seen" rather than lost. We have heard from people who have not written to us for years, people from all the years of L'Abri, but before that from our former churches, and old seminary friends. We have heard from people we have never met who have been saved from darkness through the books or film series. We have heard from people in high places and low places, people who say their lives have been changed from the books and films, whose family lives have been changed. It is all so much that we find ourselves weeping over the mail. . . .

The people we are being brought in touch with whom we would never have talked otherwise are quite amazing. This started in the hospital as Fran talked a little bit about the "problem of being" to the surgeon as he was cutting out the gland in his neck, and prayed with two of the nurses after talking to them about Christianity, and in the Mayo Clinic as he met a woman on the elevator who had been helped by his books and prayed with her in this time when her mother is dying. It has continued in many ways—phone calls and prayer on the phone with a great variety of people and some who have come to this house.

What I am saying is that we both feel that God does have some very special series of things ahead in our lives, and the lives of our family, and of L'Abri work, as well as the books, films, and Seminars, which *includes* our being here for some preparation, or for some immediate reason. What I am saying is that I do not think it is a "mistake" any more than I think Joseph's being in Egypt to prepare for a famine ahead was a mistake. There is no doubt that there is a famine ahead, a spiritual famine, and that we have something to say and to do. Whether the "period of time" I am talking about is six months or six years it is still a period. We don't need assurance of a long time to be aware of the importance of time, nor even of the excitement of time. Don't you see? Time is important to use for what God is planning for us to do in whatever geographic spot we are in, even if it is the last six-hour period before the bomb falls!!! Eternity will point up the importance with an emphasis, which will not be measurable, I believe. Who can know what is the most important piece of time to be used??? As to what has been happening here, Dr. Victor Wahby gave a reception for my birthday, November 3rd, with a gathering of Mayo doctors and their wives and a few other people in Rochester, and some out-of-town people. It turned into a "Saturday night in the chapel" kind of discussion and Fran answered questions with his usual sharp interest and involvement in people's need of answers. There is a kind of atmosphere of excitement in this little house (the living room can't really hold more than six or seven people graciously) that is not the feeling of being thrust into a desert place, but having been placed where God has some people He wants us to talk to. . . .

Jane is in America needing a hip operation. As she and Betty have prayed for guidance, and we too have been praying, it seemed that the Lord gave me access to the possibility of setting up an appointment for Jane here at Mayo so that she could come here where they have done more of those operations than anywhere else, even though it originated in England. It is not "chance" that the Lord sent us as forerunners, or in a place to do this for Jane. Lord willing, she will have her examinations starting November 21st.

The new L'Abri property at Southborough, Massachusetts, has been purchased. The person who bought it for L'Abri wishes to remain anonymous but all the circumstances surrounding the finding of the house, the impossibilities, and yet the answers to prayer which Mardi and Dick had in making arrangements and in the context of opposition and a town council meeting are similar to, and just as wonderful as, the way the Lord gave us Mélèzes and afterwards our permits to stay in Switzerland, back in 1955. As Mardi exclaimed excitedly, "It's just like the L'Abri story—I mean—oh dear, it *is* a continuation of the L'Abri story, isn't it?" It is an old New England house (1812 is the date of the main part of the house) just as correct for that area of the world as a chalet is for Switzerland. Mardi and Dick are continuing at Greatham until spring. Pray for the Lord's perfect timing for the commencing of the work in Southborough, and for certainty as to the couple who will go with them. We need to be very sure of the Lord's plan. We can trust Him to unfold that plan. Our concern as individuals, and in our grouping in L'Abri as Members and Workers, is to be *sensitive* to His leading, and not to make rigid plans ourselves, which we resist having changed by Him. . . .

Fran's diagnosis of a malignancy, Jane's need to be out of the work for this urgent operation, and Betty's need of an operation on her hands, Birdie's illness and operation and need of loving visits and care from Veronica, Nancy, and Claudine . . . and a great many individual physical hardships and difficulties recently . . . all bring about an urgent need to *pray for* the L'Abri Workers as a *whole*. There are people seeking answers, finding them and being brought to a decision to accept Christ as Saviour . . . day by day and through the weeks . . . as well as people arguing and being "difficult." There are the moments of it *all* being "too much" . . . or of the next knock on the door being "the last straw" . . . and prayer is very urgently needed. In England the work is always overbusy . . . with so many coming, always some in the deepest of needs, and outside speaking engagements as Ranald and Jerram and Dick, as well as the girls, feel strongly that they have a responsibility for England as a whole in some way. While thinking of England . . . there is a special piece of news after years of prayer and waiting upon the Lord. Cynthia and Kim have been clearly led into the church work, growing out of the amazing fact that God has gathered a number of Koreans together in Wimbledon (yes, where the tennis is played!) to start a little Korean church. Cynthia was a Worker and Member of L'Abri for years, and Kim was a Worker too before they left the work as he started his studies at the London Bible College. Cynthia and Kim also have adopted two little Korean children who need a loving home. . . .

Not only are the books and the films a help to countless people in a variety of places (the film series is being put into Japanese, German, Spanish, and soon other languages) but the films and the books, as well as the taped lectures are a help in each of our L'Abri branches. The Dutch L'Abri has a special machine where their students watch the film in a video form, with the Dutch subtitles, and then have discussion about them. Wim and Greta have moved with their children into the big house, to make it an open home so that it is more like Greatham in its setup now.

Anky Rookmaaker has a full life with her part in L'Abri as the Dutch treasurer and in living so close and being a part of the work but also in her marvelous work for the children of India and Kenya in her orphanages there. Receiving money from Dutch church people for these orphans, and the wonderful plan of keeping the children until they are well educated (20) so that they can hold jobs and not slip back into despair and poverty, is such a "complete" care. Pray for her as it does not get easier to be without dear Hans who has been in heaven for over a year and a half now.

So I come to the end of my first Family Letter written from Rochester! Where will the next one be written?

Early tomorrow morning I will leave for Greatham L'Abri for a day before speaking in Cambridge. I'll be back here before Thanksgiving, at which time Priscilla will return to her little family and tremendous work—not that she won't have been doing a tremendous work here!!

Fran's next chemo treatment will begin on November 30th, the following one on December 21st and, Lord willing, we hope to go home for Christmas, to reassure the grandchildren who have been so worried about "Av" (the Hebrew word for father which is what they call Fran). We would of course be back here in time to get ready for the next treatment on January 11th.

With much love in the One in Whom we are One Family, Whose we are, and Whom we serve with trust and love and excitement and expectancy, because He really *is* coming back some day,

EDITH

P.S. Since Edith wrote the above I now have the results from the second set of treatments. The first set of treatments was 75 percent strength, this time it was 100 percent. Naturally we were concerned as to the results and just today (Nov. 15) we have the results. We are overwhelmed with thankfulness. The physical examination yesterday was encouraging in every way—and the results of the full blood tests which came today are equally positive.

Of course, the battle goes on into the future but we are deeply moved with thanksgiving before the Lord for the large steps of progress as shown by the tests. We do want to thank all of you who are praying. Lets keep on together.

With love in the Lamb,

FRANCIS

1979

Dear Family:

October is the month that the Canadian geese fly in beautiful V formation swooping into Rochester, Minnesota, above the Mayo Clinic buildings and down to the little lake area where they settle in to waddling around in the park, or floating on the little lake for the winter months. Although it was not too many years ago that Dr. Charles Mayo bought the first geese and put them in Rochester, now the thousands of geese which come to winter there have become a landmark and a symbol of the town. The small lake is warmed by water that pours in from an electric plant, and it seems the geese have spread the word to their friends and relations that they don't need to fly the extra miles to a warmer climate! The surrounding farms are invaded for their corn during the winter, although residents go with little bags of feed to feed the geese as one of their interesting things to do. Then when March begins, as if the geese could read a calendar, the beautiful V formations swoop out over the town again heading for their other homes, honking a farewell!

Strangely enough we arrived in Rochester about the same time as the geese in October, and we flew out again in March just as the flocks of geese were taking off, following their individual leaders. Our parallel five-and-a-half months there had a different purpose, and our leaving time marked far more than the end of a winter of calendar time. Our period in Rochester, to be near Mayo Clinic, was a different kind of a "winter" than merely ice and snow, low temperatures and wind chill factors. It was, as you know, the sudden "winter" of cancer, a "wind chill factor" that made us shiver indeed. As you remember from the last Family Letter, the first full report we had on October 17th presented a chilling picture indeed. Lymphoma was present throughout the body, the gathering of nodes behind the intestines formed a mass (which I called a tumor) the size of an American football, the bone marrow test showed 30% invasion by cancer cells in the bone marrow. The last Family Letter was written November 12th, after two chemotherapy treatments had been given, and after we had established ourselves with a program of balanced diet, fresh homegrown sprouts, vegetable and fresh fruit juices, vitamins and daily exercises, in the lovely surroundings of our little "town house" so much a "home" and so lovingly provided by Gospel Films and Billy Zeoli. You remember I told you of how we had word from literally thousands who were regularly praying for Fran, in groups, alone, as churches, as Bible classes, as friends, as family, as fellow Workers in L'Abri, and so on. I thanked God in my last letter, and I would thank Him again now, that one does not need to "weigh and measure" the "credit" that needs to be given to good medicine and careful doctors, advances in scientific research and discoveries, wholesome and balanced food giving proper nutrition, the addition of vitamins, sufficient regular exercise, the atmosphere of an attractive homelike place to live with "caring people" whether family or friends helping and encouraging, the "ongoing" daily work of doing (within the framework of the limitations) what the Lord has for each "today," and direct intervention of God in answer to prayer. . . .

I do want to write more about prayer, but this is a Family Letter, not a book. In this letter I have a report to give you which was given to us just before we "flew out with the geese." Before giving the report there is one more thing I feel it is important to say, and that is "thank you for praying." It seems to me that each one of us who prays for something we have agreed together to pray for must feel truly alone with God when we pray, as if we were the only one responsible for asking. This is an aspect of our significance as people created in the image of God. When it is time to say "thank you" *to the Lord* for an answer we are aware of, or for many answers we are suddenly aware of as woven threads in a fabric, the "thank you" must come from *each* of us, as if we were the *only* one who remembered to say thank you. We must not take for granted that all of the others will be thanking God, and that our small voice wouldn't count for anything. So, as I thank you for so faithfully praying with us, and for us, these past months, I'd also ask you to join and cause a crescendo of thanksgiving to be heard by the Lord. Then we must take courage, and go on. Answered prayer is usually followed by a new wave of difficulty of one kind or another, we continue in a battle. We have been carefully warned of this fact by the Word of God. We need to pray on.

Seven chemotherapy treatments had been given, twenty-one days apart, and just before the eighth one was due Dr. Petitt wanted extensive tests taken. These tests were done on March 16th and 17th, and consisted of really complete blood and urine tests, as well as the more painful bone marrow test, and the CAT scan which would look into what had taken place "inside" where the malignancy had spread so thoroughly. It was right after the L'Abri Conference in Lookout Mountain, Tennessee, and Priscilla had returned from that with her father, so was here with us, along with Mary Jane (the L'Abri Worker who is my secretary) so there were four of us waiting and praying together as the time approached for "The Report."

On March 19th as Fran and I sat in the waiting room on the fifteenth floor, West, of the Mayo building, we saw others he had seen when he was waiting for his bone marrow test, and other tests—they too were now waiting for news. We were very, *very* conscious of the fact that it is selfish and unkind to forget that whatever one's "news" turns out to be, there are others whose news is *just* as major a moment dividing a period of past history from future "history." Fran and I prayed together, softly, and he prayed for all the others waiting for news, as well as for our own. . . .

As we sat there waiting we remembered our time back in October when as a family we had started to pray in the context of Psalm 71:17–20. Look it up again! Our prayer was that God would give Fran a time of being "quickened again" that he might show forth God's power to this generation, and God's strength to the ones that "are to come"—children, and children's children! There is a plea for guidance wrapped up in that request. And whatever the Lord answers, in the midst of the answer we need to be careful to glorify Him to the best of our ability—frail though that ability be!

Suddenly "Dr. Francis Schaeffer" was called, along with two or three other names, and we got up to move toward the right hall which would take us to the doctor's office. I slowly went along on crutches trying to stand as straight as possible, my bursitis in my right knee needing a time of not putting weight on it, and crutches being more effective than a cane! Humbling hobbling!!!!! Oh well, there is no way to find out how other people have to live within limitations, than by having a variety of limitations, to live through.

Dr. Petitt sat at his desk and waved two pieces of paper happily, "I have a fabulous report for you!" he said. Our response was one of restrained exuberance and then we turned to the details. We were shown the bone marrow report which was compared with the one taken in October. All the details were given in scientific language, but the sentence which stood out was, "No Lymphoma present." The CAT scan showed that the "watermelon" (as Dr. Petitt called the large mass that had been there in back of the intestines) was no longer there. "If I were looking at your present CAT scan without knowing your history, I would think it to be that of a perfectly normal situation." The blood tests were all normal (hemoglobin slightly low, but in normal range, everything else excellent), liver normal, spleen normal, etc., etc., through the tests. The conclusion was, "We'll just put the poison back in our pockets in case it is ever needed again. No chemotherapy now." So Fran was discharged, but with of course an appointment for "checkups" regularly.

"Good news" was our word to each one waiting. Fran called each child of ours, and of course told Priscilla face to face. It is almost as hard to believe good news, as to believe shocking news. Tears express joy as well as expressing sorrow.

How wonderful it is to give you this good news. The Lord has answered prayer, there has been a victory over whatever Satan was trying to accomplish in hindering something the Lord is preparing to do. "Offer unto God thanksgiving; and pay thy vows unto the most High: And call upon me in the day of trouble: I will deliver thee, and thou shalt glorify me" (Psalm 50:14, 15). It would be wrong to *not* rejoice, and it would be wrong to not thank God with fervent thanks. It would be wrong not to glorify God in the midst of rejoicing. We need to be careful not to fall into the place of people who ate the fish and bread and yet who turned away from the One who had met their immediate need. It is easy to do because new needs, new "impossibilities" arise so quickly. . . .

When Fran was asked to say something for the radio concerning this news, he felt strongly the need to point out that it is *not* a demonstration of greater faith when an answer like this comes. Many whose faith is just as great as any of ours who have been praying for this "longer time to make Your Truth known to this generation" for Fran, have been praying for someone just as precious in the sight of the Lord, just as dear a child of His, and have been praying with as great or greater a measure of faith and their answer has been an opposite one. It is to be remembered here that the early church prayed for Stephen as he was being stoned and he died. The early church prayed for Paul in similar dangerous moments, and he lived. The need to really remember this in our emotions, thoughts, actions, spoken words, as we are together in this moment of history is very important. *Balance* is something we need to think about, or we are too easily thrown off the tightrope we walk in our Christian lives. A spirit of pride, or a spirit of criticism can creep into our attitudes unnoticed, unless we consciously ask the Lord's help to lean against it. . . .

What did take place between October and March 25th when we flew out of Rochester? What else did the Lord weave into the period of time during which the seemingly "basic" purpose was "being treated for cancer"?

First of all we had a home in America for the first time in 30 years, and the feeling of being at home, and in a very real community (in spite of never having been in Minnesota before) was very special indeed. People were extremely kind to us, and as quite a number had read our books and felt like old friends, we had what amounted to many old friends all offering to take me grocery shopping, to go to the airport to meet someone coming to be with us, to take me Christmas shopping, to drive us to the Mayo Clinic etc., etc. We experienced the friendliness of Minnesota mailmen, storekeepers, taxi drivers, nurses, and Mayo Clinic doctors and personnel as well as so many other townspeople we met. It was a refreshing glimpse of an America we thought had almost disappeared! Secondly, our children were able to spend time with us, helping in practical ways, but also having time to have conversation and to experience a togetherness that is not possible in the ordinary swiftly moving days of life's schedule.

Fran had numerous discussions with people who came to see him from various parts of the States. He wasn't well enough for too much of this, yet it is quite amazing how many were fitted into that period of time, as people came to Mayo Clinic, or came especially to see him. Then he agreed to an evening discussion with medical students after they first watched the science episode of the series *How Should We Then Live?* That night was an especially bad one for him physically, and he felt so dizzy he thought he couldn't start speaking; however, once the questions began, instead of stopping early, he went on for the full time. The second such gathering was a noontime meeting of chaplains from the hospitals connected with Mayo Clinic. The discussion was extremely worthwhile, and once again Fran was conscious of being given energy enough to carry on. A third such meeting took place in the auditorium of the Methodist Hospital, where doctors from Mayo Clinic, and other staff members, gathered to see the science film, and then to ask questions. This carried on through a lunch period when some stayed to discuss longer.

Then Dr. Charles Kennedy and the Zumbro Valley Medical Society and the Rochester Ministerial Association undertook to rent the entire series of *How Should We Then Live?*, and to hire the local John Marshall High School Auditorium for five consecutive Sunday nights. They had no idea how many would come and felt it might be about 300 or so. Fran was to answer questions after the showing of two episodes of the series, each Sunday night. To everyone's amazement about 1,600 turned up every single Sunday night in spite of "the coldest night of the winter," "TV competition," "blizzards and driving warnings," and so on. We prayed that Fran might be able to go each one of the five weeks and the Lord answered! He sat on the platform in a metal armchair and answered questions as people lined up behind three microphones placed at different points through the auditorium. The first week questions came from younger people, medical students or other students, but as time went on the questions came from a cross section of ages: doctors, lawyers, engineers, pastors, musicians, artists, businessmen, women of various ages as well as men of various ages. The response was one of sincerity and honesty in seeking answers and in discussing, and many, many expressed regret that the time had to come to an end. Wendy Collins came one night and announced the Minneapolis Seminar for the new film which will be, Lord willing, October 1st and 2nd. Many, many people took cards to fill in asking for information as they want to come to that too. It would seem that the Lord has opened up something there in Rochester which has not been "contained in five months" but which is to affect the future in some way. We have found an enthusiasm for having a L'Abri Conference there in the future. Naturally others of the L'Abri Family who are in Minnesota are happy about this, and praying with us for the Lord's clear direction as to what His plan is, for which all this seems to have been a preparation. We know of some churches and also schools which hope to have the film series now, as a result of this five-week period. Also quite a number of the doctors want to have further time of discussion with Fran, when he is back there for further tests.

During the earlier part of our time in Rochester I spoke several times. Then while Priscilla stayed with her father, I fulfilled a previous engagement to speak in Cambridge, England (Michael and Sylvia Diamond had made the arrangements long before) where Ranald came to "shepherd" me during a very busy time of nine speaking engagements in a week. Among other places, I spoke at Great St. Mary's The University Church, at Holy Trinity Church, at St. Andrews the Less, and at Ridley Theological College. It was an amazing time that only the Lord could have prepared, and that which was the most astonishing to Ranald and Susan and myself was that it took place just 20 years from the time when Fran and I had first come to Cambridge, and Fran had spoken to a gathering of about 20 young students in Mike Cassidy's room, among whom were Ranald, Jeremy Jackson, Hugh Searle, Clive Boddington, who have been a part of L'Abri at one time or another. Yet, 20 years ago we could never have imagined such a series of open doors as met me in November. Now since that time the film series *How Should We Then Live?* has been shown in Cambridge and has been very well received. Ranald went to answer questions. To finish off my time in Rochester, I also went off to speak in Birmingham, Alabama, one weekend. Soon after that however, my bursitis became so severe that I needed a cortisone shot and had to really put *no* weight at all on that right leg. At the same time an "extreme exhaustion" overtook me and my situation at the present time is one of needing to "rest" (that includes the exercise of swimming laps, a half mile or so each day I can get to a pool), and recover for the schedule of Seminars next autumn. . . .

It would not be a complete picture of the five–month time to forget to mention phone calls, and a deluge of letters, all of which we tried to answer. I wrote "two-page letters" which some dear person always typed and mimeographed for me. . . . This is help beyond measure!!! An "exceedingly abundantly more" kind of thing, which the Lord so often gives His children, but which involves other of His children "giving as unto *Him*." . . A Scandinavian Conference has been reported to us by Udo and Staffan and Lisa. The attendance at *Kristen Infor 80–Talet* (Christian in the 80's) exceeded every expectation. We do thank God for the weekend and for all of you who came from far and near. Yes, there were those from both Norway and Finland such as Riita whom we met back at Swiss L'Abri and coming alone all the way from Rauma in Finland. We know that the conference became an encouragement and a help not only to Riita but to many who for long have been fighting out in the cold on their own. . . . In the whole of L'Abri we are in the midst of, and looking forward to a variety of changes. Lord willing, in May Dick and Mardi and their three boys, Barry and Veronica and their two little girls and one boy, will be making their way to Southborough to start their lives in the house given to L'Abri, and to pray for the day-by-day needs to be met and the day-to-day unfolding of what the Lord would have them do there. Naturally their leaving will bring about great changes in both Greatham and Huemoz. As Dick and Mardi leave Greatham, Richard Winter and his wife and children will come into the work and live in the converted stables which has been Dick and Mardi's home. . . . John and Ann Smith have come back into the work of L'Abri. After finishing at Westminster Seminary John and Ann and little Martin Luther returned to Huemoz to eagerly plunge into the work, taking over the responsibility of Chalet Bethany almost as if they had never gone away. However, a sudden message came to them from John's home in Texas, and they hurried to go to John's dear father, who was dying of cancer. Mr. Smith had gone to be with the Lord before John and Ann arrived. There is never a time when death is not a shock, even when it is expected. The change of being absent from the body and present with the Lord is a tremendous change . . . Jane, Betty, and Gracie had gone to America for the L'Abri Ensemble concert at the conference and for Jane's lectures there . . . Amazingly enough, within hours of the news concerning the death of John's father, we had word through Rosie (whom Jane had phoned) that Jane's mother had died in the hospital just a few hours before . . . What a hope we do have, as we sorrow, but not as the world sorrows . . . our hope is that when the resurrection takes place, we will have new and perfect bodies with health and energy not dimmed by the present abnormal universe.

Life is such a strange mixture at times of huge crisis and big changes—it is still necessary to prepare meals, eat, bathe, think of and care for business details, care for bills and money matters, dust the furniture, and put out the garbage. And then the "future" becomes present, and the "present" becomes history so rapidly! Wounds that still feel "raw" to us are hidden by bandages from other people; yet we feel somehow that they ought to be noticed. . . .

Lisby Sandri has a serious jaw and teeth problem arising from a "straightening" job long ago when her teeth were straightened in a mistaken way. She faces a probable surgery which would be done by Dr. Howard Sather in Rochester (if that decision is made final). Dr. Sather is tops in this field in the world, and amazingly enough, Elizabeth's specialist in Lausanne knows him and has been in consultation with him. The Sathers are a fine Christian family and it is Mary Lou Sather who is helping with our correspondence. Amazing how the Lord weaves the threads together in Huemoz, in Rochester, in England, in Holland, and throughout the world as He cares for His children and hears their prayer. We do have a personal God who cares for us as persons. We have individual attacks by Satan too and a great diversity of hard things. I am so glad the Lord helped me to write the book *Affliction* which has been such a great help to me, and to us, as well as to others. Bill and Jane Wysor (you know Bill is the one who sends you who live in America and Canada this letter) told us of how they read together the book *Affliction* during his painful as well as frustrating time in the hospital for over three weeks. The strange disease giving him a high fever and pain in his neck and head, along with extreme weakness in his legs (unable to walk), has never been diagnosed, in spite of a terrific variety of tests of every kind given in the Medical Center in Charlottesville, Virginia. Pray for him as he is home now, and gradually getting better. . . .

The new book and film *Whatever Happened to the Human Race?* are almost finished. The book had its final proofreading as Mary Jane and Priscilla and Fran checked it in Rochester. During his early days there in October, Dick Baltzell, the editor, had come to work with him. Fran finished his part in the actual filming in October just 36 hours before we were on our way to Mayo Clinic, as you probably know. Franky has gone on with the rest of the filming and the editing. It is exciting to hear of how it has all shaped up. There are five episodes of exactly 50 minutes each on abortion, infanticide, euthanasia, apologetics for the existence of true truth, and the final episode on the Bible itself, filmed in Israel. In April Franky will be in London (Lord willing) to work with the London Philharmonic Orchestra, to be directed by a special director from Chicago Tim Simonec, who works with composition (his own) as well as classical music especially directed as he watches the film for which he is preparing the music. This is costly but important as music is so integral a part of a film.

We are leaving in just a few minutes now, literally, to fly to Florida, where Fran will preach on the Resurrection for the Easter sunrise service in the stadium in Key Biscayne. After a rest down there, we will be going to Rochester for some more blood tests for Fran, for a time with doctors and others who want to go on with discussion (after the other Seminars) and also a two-day meeting with the coordinators from each of the 20 cities where the new film will be introduced. Lord willing, Dr. Koop and Francis Schaeffer will be answering questions at these Seminars, and during the two days Franky will give a lecture, and I will give a lecture on affliction. Susan has written a short book (about 60 pages) for teenagers, *How to Be Your Own Selfish Pig*, which will be important to go with this film series (which we pray will be shown in high schools across the States, as well as in many other places). . . .

Yes, we in L'Abri are still in the battle, and the Lord does call upon us to be good soldiers in the precise field where we are. Until we come to the moment of final change, the hardships do not obliterate what God has for us to do, and it remains true that the ones of us who are shut away in a hospital bed, or behind the four walls of an Iranian prison or a tiny house in a field, still may be having the most strategic part to contribute in the battle in the heavenlies as Satan continues to strike with fury and as that fury grows rather than diminishes as time speeds on toward the future moment when Jesus will return in great power and glory.

With love in the Lamb, so long looked forward to as the coming Messiah, and so long looked back to as our Saviour and Lord, Who died, was buried, and arose again the third day giving us a *hope* that cannot be destroyed,

EDITH

September 1, 1979   Chesieres, Switzerland

Dear Family:

This is an in between or "special message" Family Letter written at a time when there is no time to write!! It is a time when there is no time to write, *but* a very great need for communication with each of you, so that you may know some of the things that have been going on in L'Abri as well as in some of our individual lives, and in the preparation for the film seminars in America and other countries. I have put our Swiss address on the letterhead because this is after all a L'Abri Family Letter, and that is our home in L'Abri. However, I am actually writing this in Rochester, Minnesota, in the "little brown house" where we are for a few days for Fran's checkup and other preparation for the weeks of travel ahead. . . .

When the news swiftly traveled to many friends that Fran had lymphoma, one of the people who prayed and did all he could to help and to show his love and concern was Bill Wysor, who for many years, with his wife, Jane, has been sending out this Family Letter. In the spring we heard of a strange illness Bill had, and called him in the hospital in Charlotte, and rejoiced to be able to pray with him and Jane on the phone, as well as to hear how much the book *Affliction* was meaning to them both as Jane was reading it aloud to him day by day in that difficult time. Bill recovered from that undiagnosed disease, but in July had a massive heart attack (soon after their 32nd wedding anniversary) and was taken to the hospital in a coma from which he never recovered. It was July 24th when I talked to Jane Wysor and found out that Bill's coma was deeper and deeper, but that the doctors had said he had "stabilized" and might live a year in that condition. The condition? One of massive brain damage, deep coma, and slow loss of weight, etc., with no recognition or response of any degree. Jane and I prayed together over the phone, and asked the Lord to please either restore him to health, or to take him to heaven quickly. "You know the doctors say there is nothing that will cause him to die unless he has another heart attack or pneumonia. They expect him to live at least a year in this condition." I went from the phone back to our Workers' Meeting to report as to what was going on. It was just about that time, Thursday evening, July 24th, that Bill went to be with the Lord, absent from his body which had become a kind of prison at that time, and home with the Lord. Bill was just 55 years old, the same young age that Hans Rookmaaker was when he had his heart attack which took him away from his family and L'Abri work in Holland about two years ago.

I have talked to Jane Wysor again today and she said, "I just can't get over that big answer to prayer that we had when the Lord so shortened the time of Bill's being in that condition and took him. There was no reason the doctors could find and they didn't expect it. It really was a miracle." The mystery of the Lord's hearing and answering prayer is one that has great diversity. Anyone who thinks that "answers" must only be miracles of healing and of immediate freedom from all troubles doesn't even begin to understand the perspective of seeing life as it flows into eternity all in one piece. The present history is a tremendously important part of the "whole"; the battle in the heavenlies involves us and our lives and deaths and responses to the Lord. Victory for the glory of the Lord is not just a waving of flags as we sing hymns. Victories are won in hospital emergency rooms and in the midst of dull drudgery as well as in the midst of fear and pain, disappointments, and at times, excitements. . . .

On July 30th we had our 25th Annual Day of Fasting and Prayer. Thankfully we don't need to measure our individual contribution, but we do need to realize there would be a "hole in the fabric" if we pulled back and didn't pray, or do the piece of work the Lord has for us to do. We aren't puppets!

We had a good day weather-wise, and were able to pray outdoors after the morning time together reviewing some of the prayer lists from past years that we might not forget what the Lord has done, with thanksgiving. Fran and I prayed together sitting on a rug out in the field by a rock, amazed at how quickly five hours go by in reading verses from the prayer list, and remembering people who had been at L'Abri in past years, praying that no one would be forgotten, that someone among L'Abri Workers and the whole praying family would remember people who have come and gone, so that *everyone* who had ever been at L'Abri would be prayed for personally that day. . . .

The new film and book, *Whatever Happened to the Human Race?*, is causing Satan to sharpen his darts and to sling them fast and furiously. There are fantastic openings for this film and for Seminars in England, Sweden, and Australia as well as the 20 so soon to start here in America. Ranald will be showing the film to some prominent people in England in preparation for the wider Seminars there. The first group includes some members of Parliament. Staffan will be doing the same sort of thing in October in Sweden, and Udo is to be showing it to some in France, and so on. The possibilities of people being brought to the conviction that God is truly *there*, and that the Bible is *true*, and the probabilities of many, many coming to a conviction that the lamb in the Old Testament indeed pointed forward to Jesus, the Lamb of God, and then accepting Him as Saviour as well as the fact that many, many will come to an understanding for the first time of the need of taking a strong position for the preciousness of life, are together making Satan fight very hard. We realized this, along with realizing that not only would the arrangements and all that is to do directly with the film be "attacked," but that L'Abri had entered into a very special period of need. So we called another Day of Fasting and Prayer in mid-August, just two weeks after the Annual Day of Prayer. I wish all of you could have joined us for that day. We pleaded for His strength in our weakness, and for His direction in the work of L'Abri, His will to be made known to us as individuals and then as Workers and Members in all the decisions before us. We also prayed for each of the 20 cities where the Seminars are to be held. We prayed for all the people who had ever been to L'Abri, and their families and friends. We prayed for the auditoriums to be cleansed and prepared, and for the presence of the Lord to fill each place. We prayed for the preparation and strength needed by each one taking part, as well as for "eyes of understanding and ears of understanding to be opened" for each one attending. I wish you could have been at the closing meeting to pray with the lawyer from Texas who prayed for each Supreme Court Justice by name, and to pray with the dear woman who thanked God her daughter had not had an abortion and had kept her baby, and for the one who prayed with tears as she could not go back and live her life over again as the abortions she had had were unchangeable. . . .

I'll try to condense another part of this summer's report in this paragraph. Lisby came to Rochester, Minnesota, to overlap our time here four months ago and get started on her *long* "ordeal." We were thankful that the little brown house was still being rented and was furnished with all that was provided last October here. Lisby had then "Nony" and "Av's" (our grandchildren's names for us) home to live in while she went through the preparation time, then the recovery time, after her operation. Priscilla came over to be with Lisby before the operation (a reconstruction of teeth and jaw, needed because of an orthodontic mistake in a straightening job done when she was a little girl. Lisby is 18 this summer). As it was a 13-hour operation, and as Lisby's jaw was wired shut for eight weeks, both she and Priscilla were very glad that they could be together in our little house during that time. In the end, it was necessary for Lisby to be here for four months. (She and Prisca have just returned to Switzerland.) During that time John, along with Becky and Giandi, came to Rochester so that the family could be together for a six-week period. . . .

Oh yes, Chalet le Chesalet also was a place where we missed our Workers. Jane and Betty had to be away for a great deal of the summer, first to prepare for Jane's operation, and then to have both Jane's and Betty's operations right here in Rochester too at Methodist Hospital. Amazing that Priscilla and Lisby were able to visit Jane and Betty every day in the hospital. The timing of the Lord, and His putting so many of us here in Rochester in quick succession has been tremendously interesting to watch. Jane got along very well with her hip operation, which turned out to be a partial hip replacement instead of a complete one, and with her loss of weight, and the skillful surgery, she is making a good recovery. She has been swimming a lot which is good for her general health, too. . . .

August 27th was another beautiful, sunny day, just as had been July 30th, and the mid-August day of prayer. In between, there had been rain and snow coming down as far as Bretaye! While they were praying there, we were spending the whole day at the Mayo Clinic here, first with Fran's tests and then with his time with Dr. Petitt. In the late afternoon, Lisby had her checkup and we all met together for a farewell tea, as she and Prisca were to leave the next day. Fran's tests brought forth a series of good results. However, there was a jarring note of needing to be watchful and to have further tests in mid-October. The most difficult new "blow" was that while we were in Massachusetts (where we stopped our way to Rochester), Fran developed shingles. The blisters spread and developed with the usual pain inside following the nerve, and the day of the tests, Dr. Petitt said we should stay in the little house and not travel until the last possible moment, to give the shingles time to recover. It was a blow to all of us to hear about the shingles. It just seemed another portion of Satan's attack, and almost "the last straw." They talked together about who might come and help so that I could get this letter written, Fran cared for, the groceries bought, dishes washed, phone answered, housework done, etc., and off flew—Debby!!! Wednesday Debby got up early to make ice cream for the congregational dinner and helped Udo to get started on the rest of the menu he agreed to cook for the 40 people who were expected. Udo's part was to stay there and care for the children, the L'Abri work, preach on Sunday, perform a marriage ceremony, and do such a diversity of tasks that it would make a letter in itself. So Debby arrived here before Prisca had returned to Switzerland. There had been a secret that no one knew anything about, which suddenly had to be announced to us. Debby was eight weeks pregnant, and on Thursday there were faint signs that she might be having a miscarriage. With Dr. Kennedy's kind help, a gynecologist was alerted, and on Friday Debby and I entered the Methodist Hospital emergency room at about 5 P.M. She did lose the baby that night, and the next morning had a D and C and was in the hospital until Sunday afternoon. So often when one thinks "*this* is impossible, *this* is all we can take," then something *more* happens. Satan throws the darts in this abnormal world since the fall, but God is able to weave together the events in amazing ways which give us assurance that He has heard our cry for help. . . .

The day is now turning into late afternoon. Franky has called from this side of the ocean, having arrived for preliminary work before the first Seminar. We have just one day left to gather up the "pieces" and to leave. Our feelings somewhat resemble that of a first grader approaching the first day of school with fears and tremblings. The "unknown" in some ways is every day, yet it is also at crisis times of starting something new, something beyond our strength. As we start this new step of our lives, this next four-month period, each L'Abri branch also starts its next four months. They will be with us in so many ways, and among other things, they will have the film to see also. It is powerful, and truly beautiful in the artistic results, as well as its content and message. In a way, we are coming to the fourth "impossible block of time": the first was the filming time itself, the second the discovery that it had all been done with Fran's cancer racing along, the third the block of time for chemotherapy, and now facing 20 cities and all that the travel and speaking and Satan's ideas of hindrances will combine to bring forth day by day.

For each of you, and for us, I feel like ending with "Now unto Him who is able to keep you from falling . . . " Only *He* can keep us from falling— spiritually, intellectually, emotionally, physically—by giving His protection and His strength. Let's commit each other to His care, not once, but time after time, hour after hour, moment after moment during these next months.

Fran joins me in sending love to you,

EDITH

October 16, 1979   Rochester, Minnesota

Dear all of you in the Family:

I haven't had time to write even postcards to our dearest 13 grandchildren nor birthday cards with the notes that are in my head, nor get well notes to the sick members of the family, nor letters to tell the running story of our last weeks to our own four plus four children—let alone letters to all the L'Abri Workers, or the wider L'Abri Family—to say nothing of answering letters that catch up to us from time to time! *Now* we are back in our little Minnesota home for a "break" and Susan is here to give her time and energy to take care of us—soooo—I can have time to write this much of a letter to let you all hear a tiny bit of what has been going on. Both Fran and I will use it so that we can write short handwritten notes to be in contact with you. He will be having

Fran as serious and intense as ever continues to talk to individuals at the Seminars for Whatever Happened to the Human Race? *Cancer and chemotherapy treatments have not stopped him from keeping on with a fire in his bones.*

his checkup tomorrow at Mayo Clinic, so we can add the results before sending this off.

First—thank you for your faithful prayer for us, and for all the Seminar crew, and for the Seminars as you have followed us along through the first ten cities. . . .

What effect have the first ten Seminars had on us? I think both Fran and I would say that as we are involved in thinking, praying, listening, looking, as well as in talking to individuals and to the whole audience, we ourselves are learning more day by day, and are coming to realize how very important education in all that is going on, is and how titanic the matter of *timing* is in this education. Things are so swiftly changing that our having this film and Seminar series, this book and study guide prepared for use now, really is a matter of being "almost too late," or "*just* in the nick of time." . . . We all feel it will soon be too late to stir up people to really do something in our country to check the tidal wave of public opinion and public apathy. The combination of a lethargy that chokes out enthusiasm of being involved in *any* kind of controversy, and the false teaching that is being accepted without examination is frightening. An alarming number of people are brainwashed into thinking that unborn babies are not people, and that imperfect babies ought not to be allowed to live, and that the "quality of life" of an old person is a questionable thing. People are being prepared to accept the fact that human beings can take the place of God in rearranging the population to include only those whom it will be convenient or profitable to have around!!! The longer Fran and I have to hear what people have *not* known before about what is going on, or to hear questions from confused Christians, the more we are convinced that *God timed* the writing, the actual filming, and the editing of this film, and now the having of these Seminars in America, and the introduction of this film simultaneously to key people in England, Australia, New Zealand, and Singapore and in Norway, Sweden, and Denmark. . . . Fran keeps saying, "I know we must keep on, and that these Seminars are more important than we realized. I have a fire in my bones." As for me, I feel like Paul Revere and can imagine myself surging from door to door blowing a trumpet warning and crying, "Can't you understand we are in *real* danger? Wake up and listen!" We are so thankful, we share this urgency with all our family and L'Abri Workers and L'Abri Family. . . .

Now it is 4 P.M. October 17th, and we have just come home from seeing Dr. Petitt at Mayo Clinic. The blood reports were back from this morning, and everything was in good normal range, showing that the bone marrow is working very well without hindrance. The liver and kidneys also were good, and Dr. Petitt was pleased, to say nothing of how pleased we were! However, there is a matter needing attention, and prayer, in that lymph nodes are enlarged in Fran's neck and may need some medication which would only be a matter of pills that would not interfere with his schedule. This medication may not be needed, and Dr. Petitt wants a further check on Monday (to examine the spleen) because both of us have intestinal flu today and that may make a difference. So once more I'll repeat, don't let up on praying and let us continue the battle the Lord has put us in together!

With much love in the Lamb,

EDITH

December 13, 1979   Chesieres, Switzerland

Dear, dear Family:

I'm writing this in the superlative—dear, dear family because I have just been seeing so many of you in 20 different cities as you crowded up to give me a hug or shake my hand or whisper something of what has been happening in your life since last we saw you in L'Abri. . . . How thankful I am for you!!!! . . .

I pray it will be a special Christmas for each of you. The world is in a chaotic condition and clouds are swirling in dark formations above us all, with shrill winds and high, cold waves threatening all of our little "boats." The Iranian crisis, the Cambodian situation, the new threats of violence, the twisted ideas of people concerning life and death and meaning, the surge of changed "ethics" well described in God's Word (Isaiah 5:20, 21 "Woe to those who call evil good and good evil, who put darkness for light and light for darkness, who put bitter for sweet and sweet for bitter. Woe to those who are wise in their own eyes and clever in their own sight.") have added to the education in our Seminars to give all of us a basic feeling of "how can you say, 'Merry Christmas' or 'Happy New Year', or even 'Happy Birthday'???" . . . We *can* have a reality of a "special Christmas" without feeling guilty, and we can have a joy and even a rejoicing that in our storm-tossed boat among the wild waves and salty spray, we have the Lord in the boat with us. It is not too dramatic to say that as we start the 1980's we start it with His undiminished power in the boat with us, with His ability to pilot us still offered to us in this moment of history. . . .

We are sure you have all been faithful in prayer day by day during the months of the 20 Seminars. We have so much to be thankful for. God has protected us in travel. No one missed a lecture or a discussion time or anything they had to do in the Seminars. Each one taking part was right there on the platform on time, in place after place. We were conscious of the "impossibility" of going on as each of us experienced fatigue, and often the current virus would hit us, one after another, yet the reality of the Lord's strength being given to us one after another also was evident as the lectures and discussions took place.

Let me quote you a paragraph from a letter from Fran to a Texas law professor, a friend of his.

I'm so glad you found *Whatever Happened to the Human Race?* helpful. Two things about the Seminars:

1. Edith and I have never seen such meetings that ended with such intensity, etc.

2. The numbers were low and it became increasingly clear this was a specific indication of the general apathy among 'Evangelical' Christians, but even more serious an attitude among the leaders to keep people away from the Seminars so that their own acceptance by the surrounding culture would not be disturbed. Increasingly I feel that if we let this time and issue go, that the time may be passed for any real changes for the country, society, or law. . . . Edith sends her warm greetings with mine.

Francis

I would say to you that we often remarked to each other that we had never in all our 45 years of marriage and taking part in conferences, camps, and meetings together as well as in L'Abri, been involved in meetings that were so enthusiastically responded to by the entire audience, nor in which people expressed and indicated in a variety of ways that they meant to go forth and *do* something about. . . . We have often pointed out during Monday days of prayer and fasting that sometimes our "fasting" needs to be the care of our patients if we are nurses, or rushing out in the night if we are doctors and so on. Sometimes it is the most *un*spiritual thing we can do, *to* fast and pray, if we are neglecting someone God means us to help, who is in need. The need to *do* something in this moment of history about abortion of precious human beings who have potential that only God can know about, and the killing of newborn babies who have defects, who need love and care, and have immediate purpose in their own families, and the killing of older people whose life is deemed not valuable enough to preserve, are things that belong to the civilizations we have always thought of as heathen, and in need of being taught what value human life has, and who God is who enables us to be compassionate and full of the love He describes as suffering long, and being kind, love that never fails no matter what the circumstances. The verses which need to be lived *now* in the midst of *today's* real issues, are: Isaiah 58:6, 7—"Is not this the kind of fasting I have chosen: to loose the chains of injustice and untie the cords of the yoke, to set the oppressed free and break every yoke? Is it not to share your food with the hungry and to provide the poor wanderer with shelter—when you see the naked to clothe him, and not to turn away from your own flesh and blood?" Combine this with James 2:15, 16, 17: "Suppose a brother or sister is without clothes and daily food. If one of you says to him, 'Go, I wish you well; keep warm and well fed,' but does nothing about his physical needs, what good is it? In the same way, faith by itself, if it is not accompanied by action, is dead."

Responses in every city and at every session indicated that the films would be used in churches, schools, conferences, retreats, women's meetings, pastors' meetings, colleges, for some government people, for doctors and medical students, nurses, and other hospital personnel. At one Seminar there were 300 medical students and 150 doctors present as well as nurses, one State Supreme Court judge from Alabama, and many lawyers. The impact of the questions was a double impact at times. The questions themselves revealed a higher incidence of infanticide going on in our hospitals as babies with congenital defects are allowed to starve to death with a sign "do not feed by mouth" placed on their cribs than Dr. Koop realized was the case when he wrote that portion for the book, *Whatever Happened to the Human Race?*. In other words, things are much more extreme, or worse, than we thought they were when the Seminars started. We each have been becoming educated along with the audience! . . .

We have finished the 20-city seminars and are back in Rochester for Fran's tests at the Mayo Clinic. Saturday, the 15th, we will meet with the L'Abri Conference Committee to talk about the conference which will be held in June. Then, Lord willing, we will fly back to Switzerland on the 16th, to arrive just four months from the day we left!! You can imagine how anxious we are to be back in that living room I have looked at 20 times in the film!!!! . . .

We got the news that Staffan's and Lisa's, Ann Brown's, and Gail's permits were renewed on Thanksgiving Day, so that was *very* special. Mary Jane's was renewed a few days prior to that, and we are still awaiting news regarding John's and Ann's permits. All the permits received were for a year!!

That was extremely exciting news for Fran and me as we had not heard it before, and we have been praying for the seemingly impossible need of these permits. It is wonderful to know that the Lord has answered those prayers, enabling these Workers to continue in the Swiss L'Abri work at this time.

Gail and Mary Jane each have an apartment on the bottom floor of our chalet, with a shared kitchen and bathroom. Gail is Fran's secretary, but in addition to the many letters and other kinds of secretarial help, she serves meals to L'Abri guests and Farel House students in her home, and talks to individuals, helping them as well as working in the garden during the summertime, and filling in where there is need in other parts of L'Abri. Mary Jane helps me in many ways that can't be enumerated and also serves meals, etc., in her home. This means that they have been caring for the house in our absence, and Mary Jane has prepared the "tea" for "my" Thursday morning Bible class which Linny taught for quite a long time, and now Debby has been teaching. . . .

As David and Judy were leaving the work of French L'Abri to go to be near Greatham and as the house was going to need expensive repairs, and a new van was needed for traveling back and forth to Huemoz, it seemed that the Lord was guiding the Members to close French L'Abri at least for this time, and wait for His further leading. Remember that L'Abri does count on a constant leading from the Lord and we have always said we believe a work should not be perpetuated without constant re-examining. It is quite possible that the Lord would raise up a work for a length of *time*, as well as for a geographic location.

David and Judy left for England September 15th with a very dramatic departure having to redo their boxes to send via train at the last moment, making a mad drive to Aigle, flying through red lights, getting stopped at customs because a bank had been robbed, and arriving with 30 seconds to spare as a Swiss train was six minutes late!!! Perhaps it was best this way as goodbyes were not going to be easy. . . .

Life in the ground floor of Les Mélèzes is much the same as at last writing, that is to say, it changes each day as new people arrive. It's at once frightening and fascinating to get to know so many from such diverse backgrounds and Greg needs your prayers as he continues in this part of the work.

December 3rd was the first day called to pray concerning the need of cutting food money and so on, that we may be shown clearly by the Lord that He can lead us as definitely at this stage of history as He did 25 years ago, and all through those 25 years. The work at Southborough has *just* begun, the amazing giving of permits in Switzerland has *just* taken place, astounding doors are opening in Scandinavia as well as for the conference in America and in other places, Bob Jono as L'Abri's representative or missionary for a short term in Thailand has been put in charge of 30,000 families to see that they have cooking utensils, food, etc. We are entering the 80's we have all talked about for so long. We haven't ideas at all really as to how long the Lord is going to keep doors open, nor when *we* will be the "hostages" in some situations. *Now* is the time to pray with more seriousness and commitment and "listening" for His direction to us as individuals wherever we are, as well as for L'Abri.

Susan sends us a vivid picture of Greatham that I want to share with you:

December 5, 1979   Manor House, Greatham, Liss, Hants, England

Nine years ago on January 6th, England was in the frozen grip of cold winter. Ponds were frozen over and the countryside was dark and bleak by 3 o'clock in the afternoon. That was the day that our family arrived at "The Manor" for the beginning of L'Abri here. Light streamed out through only one window, as most of the electric fittings had been torn out at the time of sale. The house was cold, dirty, and completely void of furniture. The Manor is a large rambling house, built at different periods of history. There are attics, cellars, a courtyard. There was a floor that hadn't been used for 60 years. There were many shed-like rooms that had had hay stored in them. Horses had just vacated the stable block, although half of the "stable" had a fallen-in roof. The large trees and beautiful lawns were lost in the cold, dark shadows. The Macaulays, our family, consisted of Ranald, Susan, Margaret (eight and one-half years), Kirsteen (just five), and Fiona Mary (eight months old). Kim and Cynthia had come to help for one-half a year. They had a fire going in the kitchen. Soon Kim was helping us set up the children's beds, get light bulbs in, while Cynthia prepared a supper. There were about twelve of us for supper, enjoying a cooked turkey a thoughtful friend had provided. The task before us seemed amazing. We were to start with putting in electricity, drains, everything. Meanwhile, we had a group of people who had come to help us. This meant a L'Abri family right away. We had about fifteen for breakfast, lunch, and supper, and no physical aids for living! Before another two weeks had passed, a white face appeared one night at the kitchen window. When welcomed in, the face belonged to a boy who had tried Buddhism. His head was shaved, but his question was one that has since been repeated almost daily, "Is this L'Abri?" Within the month, several students were valiantly the pioneers of this branch of L'Abri. They ignored the dust, noise, and confusion every morning in order to study. As there was no heat, they climbed into sleeping bags, put on hats and gloves before listening to tapes! We also accepted a single mother with her four-year-old boy and baby, and soon the house was humming. At that time, right until tonight, there was a reality which has been a main factor. Unless the Lord builds the house, we labor in vain. And so, the cry, day by day must be: "Lord, *You* build the house!" Through the years, the ordinary, gritty work has been mixed in with the beautiful work of the Lord's building *His* work in people's lives. And the whole time, not a day has passed that we have not thanked the Lord for this beautiful home provided so wonderfully.

It is again dark, winter, and fairly cold. Nine years later, the garden is again still and vacant. But should a nocturnal visitor arrive and stroll about, he would be surprised at changes visible even before entering the house. Light streams from all the floors as rooms are occupied all over the house. The stables are now a home, and light shines out, welcoming a group of students for their supper. A fruitful orchard now supplies lovely fruit instead of nettles and briars. Large vegetable gardens look bumpy with beets, turnips, and cabbages. But come in! Let's hope that the hall has been swept this afternoon so that the shining wood floors will greet you warmly! I don't want to concentrate on the house, even though I'd love to show you the new kitchen (six years old) and drillions of other nooks and crannies. Enough to say that after nine years of elbow grease on the part of many, plus financial gifts as supplied by the Lord, the house can now house up to 35 students (crowded) plus Workers (ten) plus our eleven children (of Workers' families). We are still working on the property, but the Lord has already supplied more than we could ask or imagine. This is not a "commune" but the Lord has given each family a home.

Jerram and Vicki Barrs came after we had been here only eight months. They have shared in the work at each stage. It has been special indeed that the Lord supplied the balance of teaching and practical concern and friendship amongst the Workers year by year. Jerram and Vicki lived at first in an apartment in the main house. Two-and-a-half years ago they moved into a home on the property called "The Old Schoolhouse." They now have three sons, Peter (seven), Paul (six), and Philip (three). A couple who met each other while here as students, Rob and Nancy Turvey, are now living in the apartment in the Manor with their lovely baby, Fiona who is six months old. They contribute their work to the whole: serving meals, gardening, talking to students, seeing to the cassette tapes, and doing the bookkeeping for our branch (Rob is an accountant—fantastic!!).

The main house with its large family is quite a handful! We are thankful to the Lord for the sharing of this load by Sue McNabb and Jeremy Watson. Sue cares for all the applications, letters, and bookings. She also takes over the house most afternoons. She cooks, sees to the afternoon work, is hospitable to visitors, etc. Jeremy is also a Worker and his special task is the building project. At present this is translating a gift of money into a lecture room in a big old shed. This has meant putting on a roof, bricklaying, etc.

I must tell you that now Ranald and I have a little boy aged seven years, Ranald John. As Margaret is now nearly 18, our family has grown up a lot!

Now to meet the new family working here. In the stables live Richard and Jane Winter, with their three flaxen-haired children, Joanna (seven years), Matthew (five years), and Rebecca (two years). Richard is a doctor who, with Jane, had prayed a lot about joining us here in this work. It was a special provision of the Lord when they joined us this September. Already they are settled as a part of the whole here, and their contribution is appreciated every day. . . .

We are grateful that the Lord allows us to enjoy this place. We are grateful for the strength of the truth in Scripture which is sure and certain. This is a Light worth sharing with any who come up to the lighted windows of this home, walking in out of a cold and dark century.

Susan Schaeffer Macaulay

From the Pen of Francis Schaeffer

December 15th.

I am sure many of you have been waiting to hear how I am physically. Before the Seminars began, I had an examination at Mayo Clinic on August 27th. This included a CAT scan. It showed that some of the lymph nodes were enlarged again. The doctor told me that we would have to conclude that the extreme remission I had had last May was not a "cure" and we would have to keep observing how things would go. In the middle of the Seminars I had further tests on October 17th, and the nodes were enlarged further. Thus I was given a mild chemotherapy to take by mouth. My blood mechanism has tolerated this well. Now at the end of the Seminars, December 11th, further tests show increased nodes, and thus chemotherapy by mouth is being increased. I will get blood tests in Switzerland every two weeks to be sent back to Mayo, to see how I am tolerating the increased dosage. Assuming this goes well, I will continue this dosage until June when we will be in Rochester for the L'Abri Conference and then we will see where we are. I would be glad for your continued prayer.

FAS

With everyone busy at Christmastime, and with mails as slow as they are, I don't know when you will get this. It is now after midnight and we leave here at 8:30 in the morning, so I must get to the packing. Fran is already asleep. He feels better since Dr. Kennedy gave him some medicine to take retained water out of his system, but it has been a long and busy day, with conversations with several doctors and the committee meeting. Now so soon we will be in Switzerland, Lord willing, and you and we will soon after that be entering into 1980. May the Lord show us together just what He would have us do in the year ahead. Wish you could start it with us in the chapel with communion at midnight—but we can be together in reality as we are with the Lord in whatever geographic spot, starting the New Year and New Decade consciously with Him.

With very much love from a year older me, to a year older you!!!!

EDITH

1980

June 21, 1980   Rochester, Minnesota

Dear Family:

It has been *six months* since I wrote the last letter!!! That is shocking to me, and I hope it won't happen again, but the last six months have been so crammed full with a diversity of things, and so much of it has been spent in "living in a suitcase" that I have not had an "unbroken stretch of time" to quietly communicate with the L'Abri Family with this letter. I don't have time right now either, as the L'Abri Conference in John Marshall High School is still in full swing. I am not there in the midst of it as I have been the last six days because I feel dizzy and my throat hurts—exhaustion mixed with some virus, probably, which releases me to at least begin to "talk" quietly with you-*all*, instead of having discussions with various *ones* at the conference today. You see the advantage is that I can "talk on paper" with my mouth shut!!!

Los Gatos, California, June 29th—

That is as far as I got with my communication, in spite of all my sincere intentions! Now not only has the Rochester L'Abri Conference become a part of history, but the California L'Abri Conference is a thing of the past too. . . . However, before telling you about the two conferences, or about various things that have taken place during the last six months, I must plunge into the immediate present to tell you the tragedies that have touched the L'Abri Family so deeply that all else is dimmed and misty for the moment.

First, during the Rochester L'Abri Conference word came to Dick Keyes that his brother's little six-year-old girl had been suddenly struck with a very terrible type of leukemia, so although she was immediately flown to the Philadelphia Children's Hospital, she was bleeding internally and paralyzed on one side and unable to talk by the time she got into the hospital. Also during the Rochester L'Abri Conference dear little one-year-old Sarah Snyder was with us, being wheeled about in her carriage until the moment came for her to go for X-rays and tests to see what sort of tumor she had on the end of her spine. When Sarah entered St. Mary's Hospital for her operation it was found that she had a fever so surgery was put off a few days. On Tuesday in the first 20 minutes of the operation her heart stopped, and although they were able to resuscitate it, they waited two more days to go on with the operation. It was the Thursday that our California Conference started that Sarah was operated on the second time. The report on Thursday was that all had gone well, and it seemed that progress would be all right. However, Nancy and Larry went through some agonizing changes of despair and hope in the next hours when Sarah went into a coma, came out of it again, seemed to be sleeping normally so that when they went home to get some sleep on Saturday afternoon, it was with lighter hearts. Yesterday evening they were called back to the hospital because she had taken a turn for the worse. Nancy's call to Mary Lou gave the message, "She's slipping." At 9:30, a half-hour later she had left her tiny body. It was Mary Lou Sather who called immediately so that the announcement was made right at the end of Fran's Saturday night discussion at the California Conference. It did *not* seem possible. The questions *"How?," "Why?,"* the "Oh, no, it can't be true!" simply have to spill out of shocked mouths in response to the *sting* of death. Slipping out of reach is so horrible a chasm to be confronted with, a chasm that puts distance between the one who was there a moment before, and now?? Ah, but that is where we can feel the first warmth of comfort—it is *not* a question mark with little Sarah. We *know* she has gone somewhere where she is marvelously well cared for by the One who said, "Suffer the little children to come unto me, for of such is the Kingdom of Heaven." She has gone from the hospital, from her little body that was experiencing pain, *to* a place that will be perfect, but will become more complete one day when her wee body is raised from the dead, along with so many others who have died in history, at that very *sure* moment in the future, when Jesus will return. The resurrection will have more of a personal meaning and importance to us all than ever before. . . .

The L'Abri Conference in John Marshall High School in Rochester, Minnesota, was prepared for by a Conference Committee made up of many people who took different responsibilities as they were led by the chairman, Dr. Charles Kennedy of Mayo Clinic. Really, the L'Abri Members who took part in the Conference were the guests, who took over the lectures and concerts after all the preparations were efficiently made by the Committee. John Marshall High School was a wonderful place to hold such a conference. The grounds blossom in the summertime with green lawns, bushes and trees and marvelous flower gardens, all planted and cared for by the horticultural classes of the high school. The total number who came totaled 1,987, just a few less than 2,000, from 47 out of the 50 states, from many parts of Canada, and a few from New Zealand and Venezuela. They were of all ages and diverse backgrounds. There were people from almost every year of L'Abri's 25 years of existence, as well as many who had never been at L'Abri. They stayed in hotels, motels, camping grounds, private homes, and some in sleeping bags in a school gymnasium (with privileges of taking showers offered by a nearby Roman Catholic Church gymnasium). Lectures were in the auditorium, or in the gymnasium. At many times films (of both Schaeffer film series) were shown in one place when a lecture was in another place. Questions poured forth and in the last evenings, six discussions took place in different rooms simultaneously.

The L'Abri Ensemble gave two concerts and also an informal concert was given made up of various ones in the conference. Never have we had so many Members at a Conference! It would take pages to tell you of individuals who made known what kind of "lifesaver"—"fantastic help"—"encouragement"—"eye-opener"—"education"—"straightening out of confusion"—the Conference turned out to be. The "food" was a great diversity which met a great diversity of needs. The stress on the fact of needing to be aware that we live in a broken and fallen world, a world that is abnormal and was plunged into the opposite of what God created when He created all things perfect . . . when the choice of Eve and Adam brought effects that continue . . . was a stress that is too often forgotten by Christians. Many people felt a relief in understanding "the battle" better, and renewed hope in the wonderful day which *is* coming when restoration will take place, and the victory will be complete.

The L'Abri Conference on the California L'Abri property was prepared for by Libby and Lloyd Davies and Diane Gothrup, the Workers in Los Gatos, and others who came on weekends and helped to prepare the grounds, plant flowers and grass, carpet the chapel, wash windows, prepare mountains of food, and so on. There were 250 or more there, and they filled the chapel, spilled out on the grass where a loudspeaker carried the lectures, and into the little houses. Jerram, Udo and Debby, and Francis and Edith were the lecturers, and it was a full four days with discussions in smaller groups lasting until late in the evenings. . . .

At the end of February we had to fly back to Mayo Clinic for a checkup which revealed that the lymphoma had taken a surge ahead again, glands had increased over Fran's body and some enlarged in his chest and caused water on the lungs. The good news of an excellently strong heart (shown by a new cardiac test) meant that chemotherapy could safely be started again. There was an almost immediate response, in fact, Fran's breathing was so improved that within two days he was speaking to a large gathering of Presbyterian ministers in Pittsburgh, and soon after that, we were in Washington, D.C., at a dinner hosted by Congressmen Jack Kemp and Don Bonkers and Senator Armstrong, where two episodes of the film were shown (on abortion and euthanasia) and Fran led a very excellent discussion. In fact, throughout the chemotherapy series, he has continued to "keep his schedule." Before the end of March, we were headed back to Switzerland for some time in

L'Abri work, a Family Reunion, and then the English Seminars of *Whatever Happened to the Human Race?*. By that time, Fran was having his third series of chemotherapy in the Royal Free Hospital in London. . . . The combination of recognizing the Lord's provision, yet not ignoring the thoughtfulness and loving care of human beings whom He uses to provide such important things, is a combination we always need to be aware of. We thank God for answered prayer, but we thank *people* also, the people who have shared energy, time, and their material goods.

Dr. Koop also shared the platform for lectures and answered questions at the English Seminars and was very pleased not only with the response at the Seminars, but also with some of the meetings he had with medical doctors along the way.

For two brief weeks we were back home in Switzerland. "Brief weeks" are shortened by packing— unpacking—trying to catch up on reading mail and answering at least some of it—washing clothing— nonstop phone calls—Fran's nonstop dictating of letters—trying to leave instructions for planting gardens and cutting grass—and then trying to fit in the "really important once-in-a-lifetime things" like a family farewell luncheon for Franky and Genie and the children who are moving to the East Coast of America (a big change for all of us), and Mary Jane and Greg's wedding with a reception afterwards which Debby had prepared in the Gentiana dining room. . . .

I must also tell of our other wedding, as amazingly, both Mary Jane (who has helped me) and Gail (who is Fran's secretary) became engaged within a couple of weeks of each other and their weddings were also fairly close in time. Mary Jane made both their wedding dresses, very different in style, both beautiful! Gail's and Jim's marriage took place miles away from Huemoz, however, in Rochester, the first day of the conference, held in Covenant Church in Rochester. Gail's mother and father, brother and some other relatives, and Jim's family from Canada, came to Rochester which was about halfway between Washington, D.C., and Canada!! Udo performed both wedding ceremonies and preached the sermons! You might call him a traveling pastor!

During the L'Abri Conference, Fran had another chemotherapy injection. The next one will be in July. It has become increasingly clear to us that "checkups" need to be regular, and it would seem that Mayo Clinic is "our place" for physical help at this point in our history. There has been a parallel of spiritual help going along during the past year and eight months!!! You remember the story of what has taken place in Rochester in Fran's Seminars last winter, as well as the way the Lord used John and Pris's time in the little house as a kind of "L'Abri time" too.

"If," we thought, "L'Abri were to sell the land in California, and exchange that for two houses in Rochester" so that the office work which took place in California could continue (the L'Abri business headquarters moving, in other words), then when we (Fran and I) came to Rochester for medical reasons, at the same time we could be helping in the L'Abri work, and be working with our Workers. We would go from L'Abri Switzerland to L'Abri in Rochester rather than being "away." Both places would be our L'Abri work. The houses in Rochester would not be for Farel House "live-in" students, as in Holland, Greatham, and Huemoz-Chesieres, but rather would be open for tape listening and help needed so much by some of the international patients, as well as doctors, nurses, therapists, etc., and the IBM people or anyone else in town. People interested in "helping" could help fold and stuff envelopes, and do other work connected with the sending out of Family Letters and tapes, etc. These "thoughts" expressed to each other and shared with Members took shape in house-hunting during our days before the Conference, and then with the Members during the Conference itself. . . . Anyway, we *did* find two houses next door to each other. Truly, houses next to each other do not usually become available at the same time. . . . We do *not* believe that God gave Francis Schaeffer cancer so that he and L'Abri could have a new kind of ministry at a place where the "world" seems to come for physical help. But we do believe that out of all the places we could have gone for Fran's physical help, God did direct us to Rochester. We have no idea of what is ahead in the next ten years. The Lord may come back in a shorter time than that (we hope so, and pray for it). All we can say now is that the Members of L'Abri voted after hearing the details of the story of the steps that took place bringing us to the two little (or medium and small) houses, voted unanimously to sell the California property, and to move the work and the Workers to Rochester, Lord willing. . . .

In the din of the clashing voices, among the ugliness of the world's violence, in the struggle of staying above the floods, in the midst of the abnormal world may we be given eyes to see, ears to hear, sensitivity to feel, to smell the beauty of the rare bits of what seem like glimpses of perfection of sight, sound, texture, and fragrance.

With love in the Creator, for Whom it is worth struggling to go on and endure to the end,

EDITH

P.S. Since Mrs. Schaeffer ended her letter in the middle of the night there is more news to add before we take the letter to the printer tomorrow. Although we did not know it until some time later, Dick Keyes's niece, Lisa, died on Saturday, June 29th, the same day as Sarah Snyder. The funerals for these two dear little girls were both held on July 2. Udo preached a strong sermon at Sarah's funeral in St. Louis which was deeply appreciated by the Snyder's relatives as well as all the others who were there. He stressed the Fall and the abnormality of both life and death; families torn apart by death really are separated until Christ's return. Dick attended Lisa's funeral while Veronica flew to St. Louis to be with the Snyders. . . .

Warmly,   Libby

November 16, 1980   Switzerland

Dear Family:

What an amazingly full year and yet what a rapidly passing year it has been, 1980. For each of you in the widely scattered L'Abri Family and for each Member and Worker and Helper in each one of the branches. . . .

Perhaps Fran and I are feeling this more keenly than ever in this rather strange time we are having right now. We are "hidden away" doing a work. Fran is revising all his first books, to be put into four volumes: i.e., several combined in each volume. Ran and Jeremy Jackson have done editorial work, and also Udo has done some and Fran takes what they have done, goes over it, along with the manuscript of the original, and makes his own additions, considering their remarks which are extremely helpful. It is a long, tedious, difficult, and at times unpleasant job involving hours and hours of concentration. Meantime, in another room, cluttered with all the letters, papers, documents, magazines, guest books, old family letters, diplomas, birth certificates, endless things from a *lifetime*, I sit, surrounded by "life," strangely, almost mystically, all spread out on a floor and some tables! It gives a rather weird feeling I must admit, like looking through the wrong end of a telescope. Things seem small! And I feel as if I need to put a period when I *hope* to put just a comma. I am writing a biography of Fran and myself, but God willing, it is to be more of what the title says it is, *The Tapestry*. God, I believe, in my imagined picture of history, is weaving a tapestry but the individuals, the "threads" of which I am one and so are you, also affect the pattern in their choices. My prayer is simply that the magnifying glass be put on one portion of "The Tapestry" small enough to handle, starting with our ancestors, to see how amazing it is that any of us exist and that what has happened has happened. It is God who is astonishing, to be worshiped and glorified. His works are fantastic. As I read the Psalms, I ask, "Who can proclaim the mighty acts of the Lord or fully declare his praise?"* and then pray that this book may tell something of the wonder of His works in this tiny, tiny portion of the enormous tapestry covering all history through all time and space of which we are a part.

Fran feels his work is worthwhile because of the opportunity to bring things up to date, and to add such things as an appendix on apologetics in *The God Who Is There*, but this feeling goes up and down as the work is tedious and of course he has the handicap of "health."

You'll want to know how he is. His September checkup in Dr. Petitt's office gave good news of the cancer seeming to be in check and of the possibility of going on with chemotherapy by mouth, a "course" every month. . . . But he has had now two series of infections, the elbow, and this month a urinary infection which went into his groin and genitals

---

*Psalms 106:2.

which the doctor (Petitt) says is due to the chemotherapy cutting down white cells. However, Fran's blood tests this month were excellent, and he is at present on chemotherapy again. The infection is much better, pain almost gone, and as for the "glands" in his neck, they have almost disappeared. Please keep praying for him, as it is a battle between the cancer, the chemotherapy, and the lowered resistance to germs. He is taking vitamins very faithfully, supplied by Mary Crowley in Texas. Lord willing, we expect to be in Rochester again for a checkup, and to be at L'Abri there, from December 29th to January 18th or perhaps a few days more if needed.

The September trip was also to take us to Franky's home, where although the new baby was expected "any moment," Franky had all the crew and equipment set up to do a new film with his father. He felt that it gave a series of ten episodes of discussion which would be similar to an informal Saturday night discussion quietly by the fireplace. Franky and Jeremy Jackson were involved in it and during the last portion I was involved for some conversation.

Dear Genie quietly had "contractions" all one day, then went to the hospital about 11 P.M. that night, and on September 17th at 9 A.M. John Lewis Schaeffer arrived tipping the scales at ten pounds and four ounces! We did get to have a glimpse of him through the glass, with excited Jessica and Francis as they saw their new brother early in the afternoon. He looked darling, with dark brown hair and rosy cheeks, opening one eye to look at the world!

Within a short time we were back at the house: with Franky having a banana and a glass of milk the filming went on!!! Life, as I have told you all so many times, does not have portions of time packaged neatly and marked, "for birth of a baby," "for a wedding," or even "for properly saying goodbye." Franky was deep in urgent next steps, finishing the work that needed to be done on the end of the film, while we were rushing to pack and get off to the airport and all too soon that thing called "Distance" stretched itself between us all, and we were flying the ocean! . . .

We expected to have some days in Greatham to be "home" with the grandchildren and Sue and Ran and to be at L'Abri there. *But*, Kirsty had chickenpox, and others were about to have it, and Dr. Petitt had said that Fran (because of his lymphoma) should *not* be exposed to the chickenpox virus, as it could be dangerous. An amazing provision came from the Lord at the last minute, as they had a day of prayer at Greatham for "a house for the Schaeffers" and Liz Fiske met a L'Abri girl on the streets of Liss one day, heard about this, and said, "Oh mother and dad have rented a house in Liss, are away for three weeks, and would love to have the Schaeffers there." So it was that Sue and others from Greatham scurried around and put "provisions" in this home that had been opened to us and welcomed us away from Greatham! Thank you to the Fiske family! It is wonderful to see the succession of answers to prayer, in the midst of the really hard times. Fran was to have a period of extremely painful infection as his elbow swelled up with infection and pain during that time in England. However, he was able to keep each engagement and the *How Should We Then Live?* film and seminars continued. Susan took my place for the last one in Edinburgh, as Debby was having a very terrible time of pain (following a sudden miscarriage) in Vevey Hospital, and as Udo was speaking in Australia Fran sent me, as his gift to Debby, in her time of needing family nursing care, which is different from just professional nursing!! Susan did a fine job giving "my speech" (her own of course) on Fragmented Families, or something close to the title. Ran enjoyed having her work with him in a Seminar, and she also took good care of her dad.

Fran came back from Edinburgh just in time to get ready to be grandfather and the pastor preaching at Becky and Rodman's wedding. I wish all the L'Abri Family could have been "little birds on the window sill" to hear Jane sing "Ruth" at the first wedding of the *next* generation. She had sung in that same church for the wedding of each of our four children. Becky was as young and fresh in her Laura Ashley cotton as the petals making the garland in her hair, and her rosebud bouquet! Giandy reminded me of Franky carrying the ring for his sisters, as he brought the rings solemnly up, and found it almost impossible to get them off the pillow at the proper moment! The sermon was a gift to Becky and Rodman from "Av" (Fran's name to his grandchildren) and all about the responsibility of passing on the flag. It will be heard again, thanks to tape, by all the rest of the family who missed it, at our reunion, Lord willing. Another milestone! Rodman has been accepted as a L'Abri Worker, is in charge of tapes at present, and also will help at the "Mélèzes front door" which means talking to people. Becky is studying a variety of things including English literature but is also, of course, involved in L'Abri. . . . preparing meals and talking to people.

The wedding reception gave us all an opportunity at last to hear the three generation quartet as Grandfather Sandri (who is now in his 80's) and Tante Titi (his sister) and John Sandri and Becky played us a Mozart quartet. Mr. Sandri plays first violin, Becky second violin, Tante Titi the viola, and John his cello. It was truly beautiful to listen to and very moving to watch. We also could meet Rodman's parents from Columbia, South Carolina, and one of his brothers and his wife. . . .

Now—Merry Christmas!—and may God guide you clearly even as we pray He may guide L'Abri, as 1980 comes to an end and we approach 1981. There is a great deal to fight for—and to fight against—and a great deal to be done. We who have survived the "blasts" of this year must *keep on!* We have survived for a *reason* and we can't give up!

Let us commit each other unto Him Who is *able* to keep us from falling.

Love,

EDITH

1981

Very dear Family:

. . . My mind is full of those of you who have written to me personally, and whom I have not answered, so the letter rushes into a communication to "very dear" friends who deserve a personal reply, but who will have to discover why it hasn't been written, as the reasons will be unfolded in this letter. Writing a Family Letter is akin to speaking to a gathering of individuals, all in the same auditorium, looking like a "mass" or a "crowd" unless you look straight into the faces of family and friends, one at a time, your eyes moving around from face to face, longing to be able to sit and talk alone with one after another, but having to sigh, and settle for talking to the "one and one" while they are quietly sitting together, unable to really make it a two-way conversation. Frustrating, but better than silence. . . .

It is the eve of the beginning of a L'Abri Conference in Urbana, Illinois, and we are still in Rochester. A Rochester L'Abri Workers' meeting is going on in the next room and I am "absent" from my place there, and "present" with you, dear family. To write a Family Letter, or to write a book, seems to necessitate my *not* talking to the people who are in my own house, or in whatever branch of L'Abri I am part of. This has been one of the most frustrating periods of feeling the limitations of finiteness that I have lived through, since during the last months, in fact ever since writing the last Family Letter, I have been writing *The Tapestry*, a 600-page book which will be published by Word Publishing House, and is, Lord willing, to be in bookstores by November 1st. While struggling with the thought of not wanting to write a biography about Fran and myself and our lives and work, the thought emerged, "Why not write a book that weaves something of history together with glimpses of people's lives and the glimpses of God's plan, recognized in often short flashes of understanding, along with glimpses of crucial choices made

---

329

which changed the direction of life for one—then for thousands of other people affected by that one?" . . . .

It has been an amazing experience of seeing some things "come together" in a way we would not have recognized had I not written the things I "discovered" as well as "remembered." We have gone back in history to our ancestors and I have found sheer wonder at the mystery of "being." How did any of us come to "be," anyway? It is so much more than an account of continuity to be marveled at in the perspective of looking back over so many years. It is an encouragement to be reminded that God is God indeed and that He does have a pattern, not a deterministic one, but a marvel that only He can understand of the effect of choice, the choice of one person after another, yet the reality of His weaving steadily, the wonder that the loom has not been demolished. There is a meaning to history, and the pattern is continuing, history is going somewhere! . . .

Although my writing kept me from being able to attend the yearly Members' meeting this year (the *first* time I have not attended every meeting, or at least have been involved in cooking meals for the meetings for the past 26 years), it was a time that made me happy indeed, as reports came from one after another, that it was the best yearly meeting that anyone could remember. It was a time of real communication, not only with the Lord in *long* times of prayer, but with each other. Each Member felt refreshed and the word "revival" in its deep sense, not the superficial one, could be applied to that which could not be described, but which was a reality in various individuals, and also in the renewed and truly felt *oneness* which not only took place but which is continuing as Members and Workers are plunging into the work at the present time. Individual Members had had a hard year, and each branch had had its times of puffing uphill. There has been fatigue, illnesses, accidents, death, lack of funds at times, fears, and struggles with depression and disappointment. In the midst of it all each Member and Worker had had to meet a diversity of *other* people's needs in the midst of their own needs. In a very real way, the picture of L'Abri is the picture of taking an amount of food meant for *twenty* plates, and dividing it into smaller amounts, adding a touch of parsley and some leaves and candles on the table to distract attention from the amount of food, to serve *thirty* people! . . .

Tonight as I write this, Udo is flying the ocean to come to the L'Abri Conference in Urbana, Illinois, to speak. Ranald and Richard have already arrived in Urbana from Greatham. In Greatham Jerram was not able to come, because of Vicky's back. With two slipped discs, Vicky has been lying on her back for some time already, but her condition hasn't improved, and we need to pray for wisdom as to what doctor she should see. Surgery has been mentioned and it is the wisdom that God alone can give that is needed, as to which doctor would be the one to give the best advice and wisdom as to what decisions to make. As Ranald and

Richard are here, and Jerram needing to give time to Vicky's and the children's care, Susan and the others will be having their hands full with the work of "running" L'Abri in Greatham. . . .

Last Sunday while Fran was preaching the baccalaureate sermon in Covenant Seminary, I was speaking in the evening to people gathered from all nineteen churches in the town of Worthington, Minnesota. It was a mind-blowing experience for me to fly across green fields, dark brown ploughed soil, small towns with church spires, farms with their small grouping of barns and silos around their houses (with Avis, Diane, and the pilot and his wife who had just read *L'Abri* for the first time, and wanted to hear the talk that evening). To "drop down" in a town of 10,649 people, and to find a welcome that was like a "homecoming" instead of a meeting of new people I had never met before was one of the most astonishing experiences I have ever had. There was a reception at Judge Crippen's home where among others I met dear old Peter Stam, in his nineties now, living in a home in that town, as his daughter lives nearby. A lovely looking, slim young woman, who played the piano as her daughters eleven and ten played cello and violin during the banquet, told me eagerly that she had been waiting to meet one of us for a long time. "In college I had lost my faith entirely when someone gave me *The God Who Is There*, and in the middle of that book, suddenly all the lights came on!! It made sense, and I found true truth and believed. I have read all your husband's books at least eight times, and almost know them by heart. You can't imagine what a help they have been to me in my own life, and in my teaching." She went on to say she had read my books too, and also had listened to the tapes from L'Abri. Person after person came to me with the same sort of story, and the Judge and his lovely wife, Nancy, told of what the books had meant in their lives. Judge Crippen is standing firm in the issues of life today and has a far-reaching influence. As I spoke in the evening to a packed church, 850 there, it gave me such a feeling of seeing something of the fruitfulness of scattered seed. What a fantastic multiplication takes place in communication among finite human beings because of language being able to be put into writing, and then further increased by printing presses! We should marvel at the difference this has made in God's Word being spread from generation to generation, and country to country. . . .

As once again it is after 1 A.M., and this time bags are packed and standing by the front door ready to be taken to the airport with us at 7 A.M., I mustn't write too much longer. A short talk is better than continued silence.

Swiss L'Abri has had a time of new beginnings, with the Workers and Members closer together than ever before, new lectures coming forth, and a warmer reception to guests and students coming to study as they are received into the chalets immediately as long as there are free beds. Four Members rotate the chairing of the Workers' and Members' regular meetings, and very enthusiastic reports have warmed our hearts as to the close working together. A day of "spring cleaning" seemed to be far more than one of cleaning attics and gardens! And days of prayer are warm and real. The beds have been full, and an amazingly wide variety of people have been coming, including one Spanish-speaking one from Mexico, and a Polish fellow who needs everything translated by Debby into French for him, and so on. Gardens are being dug and planted with conversations being carried on more like "the old days" right out in the midst of the work, and seven new chickens have been purchased by Jane and Betty, while Debby and Udo have twenty chickens. . . .

As the summer rush commences in England, Holland, Southborough, Switzerland, and also Rochester, and phones ring off the hooks, and people ring doorbells, and ask to talk to someone, listen to a tape, or stay to study for some weeks, please pray for the people of the Lord's choice to go to the branch of His choice! We need to pray to the One Who *is* able to supply our needs according to His riches in glory, and we need to bow before Him, each of us in the L'Abri Family, asking Him *what* part He would have us do. There is some part each of us has which no one else can fill. Surely His admonition to us to pray for each other is essential in whatever part of the battle is ours.

With very much love in Him in Whom we are one family,

EDITH

May 26—P.S. A L'Abri conference is an overwhelmingly real reunion. The L'Abri Conference in Urbana was meant to be a "regional" conference and it was planned and prepared by Greg Pritchard, who had studied at Greatham, and others in Urbana who worked hard for months ahead, selflessly, to prepare for it. In the end, *they* were surprised that between 650 and 700 people came from all over the States and Canada and Australia—a great many of them were leaders. Udo, Ranald, Richard Winter, Dick Keyes, Barry Seagren, Fran, and I each gave lectures in the auditorium and also led smaller groups in workshops or in late evening discussions. Dallas Graham, a New Zealander who wrote and sang the four songs in *Whatever Happened to the Human Race?* played the piano and sang for an hour one evening, giving some of his new compositions as well as the ones in the film. The film *Whatever Happened to the Human Race?* was shown, one episode each midday, and two were shown the final day. Of course, many questions came from the film showings. Fran gave the same lecture he had given to the Christian lawyers' conference in South Bend a couple of weeks before—"The Christian, Government, and Civil Disobedience" . . . a powerful message—you'll want that and the other tapes made of all the lectures at this conference.

September 3, 1981   Huemoz, Switzerland

Dear Family:

We began our 27th year of L'Abri in June. Days of rain, and some chill mists that were snow as "far down" the mountains as below Bretaye, brought a request to our lips for a "clear day, please, for the 27th annual day of fasting and prayer on July 30." The day dawned and kept on with blue sky, warm bright sunshine, crystal clear air giving a view of details on the mountainsides and the valley below, as well as of the fresh snow on the peaks. There is something very special in our Annual Day of Fasting and Prayer each July 30th. On that Annual Day of Prayer, we can be sure that not only are people faithfully praying all day in Huemoz–Chesieres (scattered over the fields and paths walking, or sitting on rocks, or leaning against a tree in the woods), but are also praying in Greatham, in quiet spots on the grass or walking along English country roads, and in Holland in the orchards or along the canals of Eck-en-wiel L'Abri and on around the world. . . .

In spite of sounding like a "stuck record" I want to repeat here that which has struck me so forcefully day after day as I read daily newspapers, *Newsweek,* or see headlines of the *Wall Street Journal* among other papers on every Swiss newsstand. Isaiah 59 could have been written by God for us right now as we read of all that is going on in Iran, or various parts of Africa, or Ireland, or the reports of bombs placed under an American car in Germany, or planes shooting at each other "by accident," or pompous statements set forth by world leaders speaking lies that have such a thin covering, the nakedness shows through with startling clarity. Isaiah describes it so well because God is speaking, and His description of the human situation is more accurate than the most brilliant commentators of the affairs of the world. Isaiah 59:7–10 and 14–16a:

> Their feet rush into sin, they are swift to shed innocent blood. Their thoughts are evil thoughts, ruin and destruction mark their ways. The way of peace they do not know; there is no justice in their paths. They have turned them into crooked roads; no one who walks in them will know peace. So justice is far from us, and righteousness does not reach us. We look for light, but all is darkness, for brightness, but we walk in deep shadows. Like the blind we grope along the wall, feeling our way like men without eyes . . . We look for justice, but find none, for deliverance, but it is far away. . . . So justice is driven back, and righteousness stands at a distance; truth has stumbled in the streets, honesty cannot enter. Truth is nowhere to be found, and whoever shuns evil becomes a prey. The Lord looked and was displeased, that there was no justice. He saw that there was no one, and he was appalled that there was no one to intercede.

If God lets us know that lack of intercession in the midst of problems, attacks of one kind and another appalls Him, He has certainly gone on in the New Testament to continue to say to us loudly and clearly that *prayer makes a difference*, and the reverse is true, lack of prayer, lack of "constantly praying for each other" also makes a difference in each other's personal lives and work, as well as in the results of our lives and work in other people's lives. The "ripples" are *different*.

I feel very much like the grandmother of L'Abri as I write this urging not simply a togetherness on the Mondays of prayer, and on days of fasting and prayer but urging myself, as well as each one reading this, to not be lulled asleep by thinking that all we can do is to "keep up" with what is the present darkness, or to help us have a "map" of the crooked paths, but that in addition to keeping up with the progress of the deep shadows of 1981's last three months, that we take God literally in portioning out time and energy to *act* upon what He says will make a difference. We each have three more months in 1981 to do whatever the Lord has for us to do and as people who are helping by prayer, by time, energy, material possessions, or whatever. We each have three more months in 1981 to be creative in living as a demonstration of Him in *whose image we are made*, as well as to *battle* in the midst of the war we are involved in, both on earth, and in our part in the heavenly battle. . . .

Look through Udo's eyes as he takes Polish Eva "Migros shopping" with him to get the groceries for Gentiana. Eva stands weeping, tears flow unhindered as she looks at the unbelievable amounts of food, fresh fruit and vegetables, canned goods, flour, sugar, nuts, raisins, meat, chickens, fish, all waiting to be exchanged for only money!! "You can't imagine, Udo, what the empty stores of Poland look like. I haven't seen food like that, not anywhere, not for so long, not since I was in Switzerland last time." Udo could "see" Poland far better than through the news articles, as well as understanding something of the struggle within Eva as she faced the choice to go back into all the deprivation in her home. Eva is a Christian because of coming to L'Abri some years ago, but she came to L'Abri because a Polish orchestra conductor who could have at one time "escaped to the West" and gone on with his music, chose to stay in, where he was given menial labor to do, so that he could continue to translate (some of the L'Abri books among others) things that would help his people have "eyes of understanding of the truth." This dear man, Mr. Prower, has died early of a heart attack before he could come to L'Abri, because of the unreasonable hard menial labor he as a musician and a professor of literature had to spend his days doing. But I am sure he has discovered already there with the Lord, what a fantastic harvest of results his choice has had. The measure of results is not one we can find until we get to the heavenly city, or the new heavens and new earth. Eva has already returned to where that supermarket overflowing with food is just a memory, but where the promises of God for the heavenly city and its endless supply throughout all eternity is close not only in memory, but ready to be read and re-read in that unchangeable Book, the Bible. Thank God for the continuity of His Word from generation to generation. . . .

Fran and I returned late in June to be greeted with a beautifully clean house which Mike and Gail and Jim, and Gracie, had labored to prepare, full of flowers as a surprise. The vegetable garden had been planted by Gail and Jim, and the grass cut, the flower beds weeded with help from Helpers and students. Jet lag or no, it seemed to me that an *immediate* hot dog roast was needed to say "thank you" to all who had so wonderfully prepared the place to give us a feeling of being home, and being ready for a rare entrance into "normal life" of L'Abri. That very day we had a quick and complete hot dog roast, with Naomi (Debby and Udo's eight-year-old) visiting, and Hannah promised she would be "next." That time ended with strawberry shortcake and coffee served on our very old dining table on the balcony. We were so excited with this "first" and pictured a weekly time like that! Ah, but human promises and expectations have hindrances, and another such time *never* came! Hannah did not get her "turn." She was sick the one day I thought it could be done, so we didn't have it and since then, not one day has "turned out" to be right for such an event!

Yes, we have had our Sunday dinners with from 28 to 32 fitted in like pieces of a jigsaw puzzle. Yes, with Mike's faithful help in making the rolls and ice cream, the sponge cakes, and the roast chicken, we *did* manage not only the four-course meal served with candles and flowers, but Fran did answer questions and have a time of discussion until 5 P.M. or later. Those Sunday dinners introduced us personally to some of the ones who had just "arrived at the front door," as well as to Farel House students, and some of our own grandchildren, or church members sprinkled in. It was when people told a little about themselves that we were reminded of the absolute miracle of answered prayer as you and we pray "Bring the ones of your choice, Lord" and the Lord brings people from *"impossible* circumstances." We need to be reminded of this, and we *were*, Sunday by Sunday. . . .

I feel it is important for all of us, myself first of all, to pray for the children of the world in a new way. So many of them are starving for physical food, and so many of them are being fed "poison" in a variety of forms, whether in chemical form, or philosophical form. Lies are being "dished out" as well as drugs, and it is time we tried to do something in the area of education in one form or another, *early* enough before the fifteen* die! I don't pretend to have an answer, but we need to recognize what is taking place in the lives of so many who have been robbed of any childhood at all.

Twelve is not too young to understand what the "questions" are, nor is eleven or ten, in some cases. While some adults are always pushing

*One of the young people then at L'Abri had had fifteen of his friends die of overdoses.

the basic questions away, some children are really struggling over them. It doesn't have to be children of just one basic "culture" or "philosophic" set of parents. Take Mike, for instance. Mike Sugimoto, a L'Abri Worker who has been here over two years now, is an American from a Buddhist Japanese-American family. He was very young when he began to listen to the words of rock music, the words which so aptly put the questions as to whether there is any base for life, any absolute upon which to base morals. By the time Mike was 12, he was struggling in his own mind with the questions as to meaning and purpose, and recognizing that Buddhism didn't give him answers. He listened to the music so thoroughly that he understood what it was saying and pondered in his own mind the really basic philosophic questions. Then a school friend invited him when he was about 14 to go to the Christian Church where the young people's group was led by a couple of Japanese college students. He was given a thorough teaching of the Christian base that night: creation, the fall, redemption, in a manner which he recognized answered the questions he had, and he believed it to be true. He didn't see ahead that night into the next months and years. In a couple of years he was given *The God Who Is There* and *Escape from Reason* to read, and he would be in college before the Seminar for *How Should We Then Live?* would come to Anaheim, when he began to think of coming to L'Abri to learn more. But, note please that very serious search can take place at just the age so many children are being given the very worst kind of "ignoring" or a shove in the wrong direction, by parents who are "lost" themselves, or who live in a kind of "rut" they have gotten into without thinking of any questions about life, let alone about any possible answers. . . .

We have had a normal schedule for our few weeks of being "home" before having to leave again—with many exceptions thrown in. Fran has taken every Saturday night discussion the whole summer, except for the days we were in Germany when he spoke in Bremen and answered questions after the showing of the film *How Should We Then Live?* which has been dubbed in in German. Fran said it has been very well done, and he enjoyed hearing himself speak German!!! Do pray for its further use. Then we were in Heidelberg, along with Mary Jane and Greg Grooms, where *Whatever Happened to the Human Race?* was shown at The Patrick Henry Village Chapel, with Chaplain L.T.C. Perkins organizing a five-evening series, along with a Sunday morning time tied in. This means many officers, including generals, as well as enlisted men and women and dependents have been involved in seeing, hearing, and asking questions this past week.

Fran has also given four lectures here in our chapel this summer, as well as having many individual conversations, and some "groups" that have come to a hotel nearby for an afternoon discussion. However, much of his time and energy has gone into writing *A Christian Manifesto*, which is to come out, Lord willing, this November with Crossway

Books. Franky and Jim expect to be bringing out a law film, *The Second American Revolution*, also fairly soon, so that there will be much material for considering as well as for education in areas of law and government that we all need at this moment of history when we have to remember past history to keep a balance in the midst of present history!!!

Fran and I feel so "disconnected" when we are traveling around, that this ten weeks of being here has been important in continuity. Fran has even rowed a rented boat for an hour on Lac Leman on three of our days off! The "day off" is important to each L'Abri Worker, and to each family, in keeping a continuity of life. Vacations are similarly important for refreshment, for giving a chance to stimulate thinking, for giving time to be quiet with the Lord. It is a relief to pray, to talk to the Creator of the universe while swimming in salt or fresh water He has made, while looking at birds, or stars, and reflecting on the marvel of *His* diverse creative ideas. . . .

When people want to "see" L'Abri, really the most important things to be "seen" can*not* be seen! The important things are going on in the brains or heads of Members, Workers, Helpers, as well as students and guests and those who are interceding for us all, miles away. We are all meant to be *not static* but growing, and that growth is inside heads and hearts, inside the whole person, although glimpses are meant to "shine through." Another thing that can't be "seen" is the weakness we each have, and we each feel, and the exchange that takes place, time after time, of God's strength to do a particular task, get through an impossible day, say the words that are helpful in a situation we feel we can't meet. Really, the basically important realities that are "earthshaking" in the victories in the heavenly battle are hidden things taking place inside. . . .

Let me say that Fran and I expect, Lord willing, to leave September 10th (today is now September 6th) for a variety of things, among which he will speak in San Antonio for Bible Study Fellowship, and in Detroit, and I will speak in Louisville, then both of us will have a short rest, and after that be in Rochester L'Abri with Libby and Lloyd and Diane from October 1st to 19th (a time full of various engagements already, plus a checkup for Fran at Mayo Clinic)—another bracket—Fran has had ups and downs of sleeplessness, or sleepiness, extreme fatigue, etc., with his chemotherapy, but on the whole, has accomplished an astonishing amount of work, especially writing *A Christian Manifesto*, these months. Also, later, Lord willing, we will be back in America again in January and February for other engagements, in various parts of the country.

Then please note for prayer that, Lord willing, Ranald and Udo and some others will be going to Australia for a L'Abri Conference in May (at the beginning of their autumn). Also, June 12th to 19th there will be another full L'Abri Conference with many of us taking part, and some interesting new areas of discussion, including Medical Ethics, in Rochester, Minnesota, Lord willing. These conferences need time for you to prepare to come, hence the *"preview"* of time! . . .

. . . A fine fellow was the last to leave after Sunday dinner today, and he said he wanted to say how very much he appreciated all the influence we had had on his life. "We are Russian immigrants in the Argentine and it was there, in the Argentine, that your books [the L'Abri books] first influenced my life. For so many years I have wanted to come here and now in these last three days, I feel freed to go on with my Christian life, *and* my music composition and performing. I have never seen the breadth and depth of Christianity before. Thank you." This fellow is at present studying Renaissance music in Neuchatel and will later be going back to UCLA. It has been years since he wanted to tell us this!

A letter arrived yesterday from Singapore from a girl who read *L'Abri* seven years ago, then some of the other books. This Chinese girl works in the investment banking department of the Development Bank of Singapore, and says it is an answer to prayer that her bank is sending her to London for two banking seminars, with a week in between during which she and another Chinese girl from Singapore would like to come to Switzerland to L'Abri. Her excitement over the way the Lord has opened the way for her to come is something we could know *nothing* about unless she had told us!

There *is* something to do about the conditions in the world that distress us. We can take courage, encourage each other, ask for God's strength to keep on, and *pray.*

With very much love to you who have been praying and helping so often when we do not know it, but are only aware of a sudden breeze, or a surge of new strength. Thank you—

EDITH

1982

January 9, 1982   Huemoz, Switzerland

Dear Family:

... Do family members always agree on every little thing? Does the word "family" give an immediate picture of a mutual admiration party, with everyone saying "Yes, that's right," and not shades of differences of opinion, no original thinking, no fresh creativity, no development, no growth, no increasing understanding, nothing to continue discussing and learning??? A good family situation is one in which each member from the new baby to the old great grandfather has something to contribute to the other members in their moment of life. The whole of creation is diverse. The excitement of God's infinite creation is its diversity and the wonder of being made in His image (even though limited by finiteness). . . .

It was September 3rd when I wrote the last Family Letter. A third of a year has gone by! For Fran and myself, September took us to Texas for the dedication services of Bible Study Fellowship as they entered their new headquarters in San Antonio, Texas. I felt God gave Fran a powerful message at a time when he was too fatigued physically to give such a message; also, it seemed so clear that "threads" were being woven in a central way for not only Miss Johnson and Miss Hertzler and others there, but for Anne Wells as she came from Houston to be with us. September also gave us a short, but restful, vacation walking on a lovely broad Charleston, S.C., beach, watching birds and ducks rather than people, as well as taking me to speak at a women's conference in Louisville, Kentucky, and another in Lynchburg, Virginia, while Fran spoke in Detroit. We had a "normal stretch of time" in Rochester in October while I worked with editor Jan Dennis on my next book (called *Lifelines* which is on the Ten Commandments) and Fran worked with him on *A Christian Manifesto*. We also had our regular Monday night discussion times with as many as 80 crowding in to ask questions, drink tea and be served little things to nibble on! We also spent time in Washington, D.C., in October where Fran was the banquet speaker for CREED, a new organization formed to really inform people, and *do* something for Christians being persecuted in Russia, and other Iron Curtain countries. Senator Jepson and Congressman Jack Kemp hosted this official beginning. Dr. Gordon is the president. Fran's book, *A Christian Manifesto*, arrived in Washington just in time to be given to congressmen, senators, and others at the banquet and copies were to be given later by Jack Kemp and Robert Pettinger to a wide number of men in the government. My book, *The Tapestry*, had also just come out, arriving in Rochester, Lynchburg, and Washington as the first three places in the United States. Somehow that *timing* of the books impressed us as *timing* only God could have brought about. . . .

As we returned to Switzerland, urgent intercession occupied the minds of all of us during the "Polish Trip." It was just a few days before martial law was declared that Udo went to Bavaria to speak in John Walker's mission.* John Walker had asked for two L'Abri people to volunteer to drive an eight-ton truck of food into Poland. So Rodman Miller (a L'Abri Worker and Becky's husband) and Greg Laughry,† a Helper at L'Abri, offered to go. You can imagine the urgent prayer on the part of not only Becky, but so many of us as we anxiously waited for word. They were our representatives—a part of us—involved in a dangerous mission, and we had responsibility.

During Sunday morning church service, December 13th, the fellows made their report to us. It was strikingly real to all of us that both fellows were certain that they had seen God work miracles to keep them from accident or other harm. Time after time they had passed wrecks of cars and trucks, time after time they came to impossible situations driving through blinding blizzards when road signs were obliterated and even the road itself could not be seen. A steep hill was hard enough to negotiate when suddenly they realized a truck had jackknifed almost across the road. A snow plough was in front of them, and had it stopped, they would have crashed into it, but it went around the wrecked truck and they followed closely on its tracks. An "uncharted road" through alien countries in blinding blizzards is something like all of life itself, as we follow where the Lord leads, with no knowledge of what is ahead! For Rodman and Greg the trip was an astonishing impossibility in so many ways, during which they were conscious of the Lord's specific care. They had been stopped at the Czech border for six hours when entering, and waiting there were strongly "hit" by the difference in the "East" and "West." They felt they had suddenly come under a dark grey cloud, as Rodman expressed it. Not only are empty shops dismal to look at, but there seemed a bleakness about everything, and a "fear" that could be

---

*An American missionary based in Bavaria.
†Later to be Lisby Sandri's husband and Rodman's brother-in-law!

felt as definitely as the icy air. During that wait, they had a long time to observe the barbed wire at the border, the searchlights searching for anyone crossing, the armed soldiers and guards. It was a long distance physically and psychologically and philosophically from the border between the United States and Canada!!!! Citizens are not forcibly kept in in the countries we know so well in the West. To find roads, towns, turnings to one town or another, and finally a street address, coming to first Eva and her church group, and then the other assembly of Christians where the food was being distributed, was an amazing piece of "guidance" *not* from all the little pencil marks!! Certainly God was taking care of the boys as we all prayed. I don't think Rodman and Greg will ever forget the sharp contrasts and the great thankfulness of people for what many have considered small necessities of life!! The encouragement came on both sides of the Iron Curtain! As Ellis had prayed at prayer meeting here, when they were driving there, for safety in case they were going down a steep hill in a blizzard, and discovered that the "timing" of that prayer was probably very close to the time when they were behind the snow plough—it was not only Ellis who was encouraged! . . .

In our finiteness we can't do everything in the midst of a needy world—but the Lord does show us a diversity of the use of our time, and helps us to know when to say "Yes," even if we can't drive an eight-on truck! It was Monday, December 14th, that we had our beautiful Christmas carol service. Dolly Johnson had been having practices at Gentiana with a collection of Farel House students, Workers at L'Abri, children and parents, young people and middle-aged. The Scripture lessons were read by a variety of people in between the carols sung by the congregation, or the special selections sung by the choir. Matt Snyder is tall enough now, at 11, to stand at the lectern, but when Naomi, eight, read her passage, she pulled a chair over herself, climbed up on it, and leaned over the lectern to read by the light of a candle! The chapel had been decorated with pine branches and a tree, with over 100 candles in the old logs we had made in Champéry 33 years ago! The red bows on the trees and branches were made from cloth from Mary Jane's scrap box! Into that evening of glowing faces came a chilling announcement as icy as the air many people have felt throughout the world during this unusually cold winter. Udo announced to us the sudden takeover of Poland by martial law! The *timing* of that dangerous truck trip just a few days before amazed not only Rodman and Greg who had the people's faces so vividly in mind, but all of us. Our God is the Creator and is all powerful. He is able to "slip through barriers" to remind His children of this during the worst afflictions. Be reminded of this! Udo ended that service with a moving prayer for Poland, and for all of us who are in the Lord's family in a darkening world. . . .

Prisca continues with her nursery school full tilt, as well as her working on lectures on the history of rock music and the understanding of the blackness of today's young people who have no hope. She gave lectures in England which are being asked for by pastors who need help in understanding young people. John is faced with the year-end accounts and CPA reports, etc., as well as his great diversity of help in all of L'Abri. Lisby is in the University of Lausanne starting a new phase of her own life, and being "salt and light" in that area of Lausanne that has so much a place in our hearts. Giandy along with school and hockey, faces a problem of having a new kind of tooth brace (for him) with wires outside. . . .

Jane and Betty are in America, have been since November, and are writing a new book as well as doing some concerts. Chesalet awaits their return, though it has helped Anita and others as a vacation spot in their absence.

Upstairs in Chalet les Sapins Rodman and Becky have their home, blossoming forth more and more as Becky is making slipcovers, curtains, etc., as well as serving lovely meals as a background for conversations, when they have "people" from L'Abri. Rodman is a Worker, though Becky is considered not at this time, as she works three days a week in a Chesieres store and does a certain amount of study as well as creative work. They've been married almost a year and a third now! They expect to help at the conference in Rochester. Larry and Nancy also have been hard hit by the "bugs" that come and go. It has not been an easy winter. Good news is that Matthew's eye examination was better than expected and he will not have to wear glasses, very good news for a hockey player. Added to L'Abri students, one of the Villars hockey team players is frequently at Larry's tape session, or Bible study, and he and his wife come for high tea there along with L'Abri students. . . .

Any other news must now wait for another letter! This is a "basic letter" for a fresh recognition on all of our parts (I speak to myself, too!!!) of the need of "awe" in the face of what the Lord has done, and of the need of willingness to continue to keep on keeping on.

With much love to over a quarter of a century of family!—from a grandmother, mother, sister, aunt, cousin—name of

EDITH

April 20, 1982   Huemoz, Switzerland

Dear Family:

. . . It is with tears that I sit down to write a "memorial" Family Letter concerning the one who really was the first member of the L'Abri Family, outside of our own personal family. Only God knew that when I took a tray of supper upstairs in Chalet Bijou, Champéry, to 14-year-old Priscilla, 10-year-old Susan, and 6-year-old Debby, and found them with their ears on the bedroom floor trying to hear what was going on in the living room, the decision being made down there was a decision that was going to affect the lives of every one of our family—the yet unborn Franky and all the ones our children would one day marry, and their children—! Only God knew that Georges Exhenry's firm decision to accept Christ as his Saviour and Lord was going to bring forth L'Abri and thereby affect tens of thousands of people. As I brought the children their supper, my thoughts were only on caring for all the needs "around the edges" so as to not interrupt the wonder of what seemed to be taking place in the understanding of Georges' mind and heart. As I took a tray into the living room with supper for Fran and Georges, my prayer was that this would be an unhurried and healthy "birth." Future results? Had a blueprint dropped into the room outlining the events ahead, it would have been extremely disconcerting to the decision being made. Had either Fran or Georges any inkling of the fact that his salvation would mean our being put out of the canton four years later, or had the children and I been "shown" that bit of future that was even then being "swung open" silently, like a door on oiled hinges, could we have kept our minds, emotions, energies, or prayers concentrated on the immediate needs of that moment???? One step at a time, one hour at a time, one day at a time is all any of us are equipped in our finiteness to care for. Thank God He knows, but thank God He does not tell us more than we need to know "for the size of us" emotionally, psychologically, physically, mentally, spiritually. He does not put on us a heavier burden than the human frame is able to bear, with His strength in our weakness to help us bear even that measure.

You need to re-read *L'Abri*, or read *The Tapestry*, to remind yourself of the fact that it was over 30 years ago now that Georges Exhenry sat down beside Fran on the little train winding up the mountain to Champéry from Monthey and asked, "What is the difference between the doctrine Catholic and the doctrine Protestant?" The answers brought a great curiosity and then hunger for reading the Bible, and discovering for himself what is in there. After study and frequent times of conversation, that evening came when Georges became a believer, leaving the darkness of his agnosticism for the light of truth. That was back in 1951.

It was the 26th of February 1982 that Debby telephoned us in America to let us know of Georges Exhenry's sudden going to be with the Lord. He had just gone to the post office to get mail and newspapers, had spoken to people along the way, then stepped into his store and slumped down to his knees. As he was being taken to the hospital in the ambulance and during his brief time in the hospital before he was suddenly "absent from the body," he spoke of two things: first, that he was ready to go and at peace with the Lord, and second, "Don't take my body into the [Catholic] church. Respect my wishes, please."

About thirty-one years have passed since that day in Chalet Bijou which ushered Georges into the Lord's family. What did Georges "get"

out of being a Christian? Within three years we were put out of that chalet, and the village and commune, so for Georges, no longer did our
church services exist Sunday by Sunday, no longer was there a chalet to
drop in for a cup of tea and Bible study and prayer with fellow believers.
For Georges there was the trauma of realizing that we were "in trouble"
affecting our lives and work because of his salvation. He entered a period of loneliness, as no one in his family wanted to hear about the Bible
or his belief, and his talking to his children was also always alone. Yes,
there were always our Christmas services back in Champéry, and in the
early years there were the times when Georges came to the yearly Members' meetings of L'Abri, as well as occasional other events, but the re-
buffs and opposition continued, and a life of "walking the trails alone"
is what one would honestly have to admit was what Georges "got" out
of being a Christian. . . .

About nine years ago Georges said to Fran, "I have thought of a way to
speak, yes, I think so." From time to time Fran would say to me, or think
to himself, "I wonder what Georges meant. I haven't seen any
change." . . .

The first news Debby had came from a phone call from the wife of a
cousin of Georges. She spoke of a letter Georges had left for his family
telling of "his will" for the funeral. His body was not to be taken into
the church, but to be simply taken to the grave, with a civil service, and,
if they wished to, the accompaniment of his comrades in the village
band, of which he had been a member. He wished a service later in the
International Church in Huemoz (in which he was a charter member!). . . The full text of that letter all of us were to know later, but Debby
and Fran and I, in tears, became amazed at hearing that much, as we recognized that Georges, who had been silent, had spoken firmly and clearly in his death. How clearly we were yet to hear.

Debby assured us that she was putting in three newspapers (the
Valasian paper Champéry people read, the Vaudoise paper read by many
who knew Georges, and the Lausanne paper read by many others) the
expression of sympathy that Swiss friends, and of course family, place in
the newspaper at the time of death. As you will read in the reproduction
of this on the front or back of this Family Letter, please look up the Scripture verses Debby chose, and discover what a strong testimony was given,
as clear as the single note of a trumpet, speaking to Georges' family,
friends, and fellow citizens. Debby also sent flowers from L'Abri and the
International Church, from our family and from Franky.

The interment was February 27th. But it was during our Members'
meeting, in the living room of Chalet le Chardonnet on March 1st that
Debby and Prisca told us the story of that amazing day in Champéry.
Georges means a lot to each member of L'Abri, in moments of considering the history, each one realizes that, humanly looking at it, there
would have been no L'Abri had Georges not become a Christian, lived a
changed life, and let it be known. As 22 out of the 25 of us were present

that day, we were lifted out of the moment and given a view of "life" that people seldom have a chance to see. . . .

As our Members listened intently that March day, Debby and Prisca took us to that spot on the Champéry main street with an incredible account. The day was a sparkling, crystal-clear one with the sun pouring over the chalets, the cemetery, the people's faces, as well as the fields and the peaks of the Dents du Midi and the other snow-topped mountains. "Looking out over the fields and up the mountains at that spot in Champéry, it seemed as if nothing had changed during the 27 years." Priscilla had not been back there at all during the 27 years since we had been put out, simply feeling she couldn't face seeing it all as it was too painful. "The street was jammed with people, crowded, and it looked like the scene of some brilliant filmmaker. There were all the people we had known when we lived there as children—the man with no legs in his wheelchair, children's faces we recognized as people now in their thirties and forties. Middle-aged people, grown older. Here they all were, Champéry, our old home village, crowding the street to honor Georges Exhenry at this strange funeral after his sudden death." The Exhenry's Electric Store, Clothing Store (sports and ski equipment), and the kiosk where the daily papers and magazines, etc., were sold, are directly across the street from the Catholic church and cemetery. The fence of the church and cemetery property was covered with flower wreaths, etc., and those of our family and L'Abri were among them. The church doors were shut. No bells were being rung! The village had never seen a civil service for one of its most prominent citizens. Georges had not only been head of the electric company, president of the ski club, president also of the Sports Center and its committee, but had figured largely in the governing bodies of the village and the canton as well. Georges had studied to become a lawyer, but had to leave the university when his father died in order to take over the work of the electric company and to help in the leadership of the "commune"—an area wider than simply the village.

A cousin of the family came up to Prisca and Debby to whisper that Georges' request was being followed. A man of the village, from whom we had rented Chalet Bijou, came up to strongly say to the girls that Georges really had had courage and had been faithful to the end, a man of conviction and someone you could always trust. The girls stood there, uncertain as to whether it would be kinder to not go to speak to anyone of the immediate family, not at all sure as to whether there would be animosity and a feeling that the silent bells and the closed church door and the strangeness of this occasion were, after all, the fault of our family! The door of the house opened, and down the steep stone steps, worn through many years, down the steps Georges had walked so few days before, the men of the family came, carrying the pitifully small casket, shaped (as Swiss caskets are) close to the size of the body; carrying the silent body of Georges, from which he himself was now absent! Into the silence came the burst of the Champéry village band music. The band marched down the street, accompanied the casket into the cemetery, playing all the time. These were comrades of Georges'. He had been a musician in this band. In the midst of the music came a hymn of Luther's, the girls said, which seemed to them a special tribute to Georges' clear stand for salvation through faith in Christ alone. At the grave several men stood to speak in tribute to Georges. Two of them seemed overcome by grief, and their tears spoke for them! M. Berra gave a summary of Georges' life, and his importance in that whole area, and of the high esteem in which he was held as a leader, with wisdom in many areas—a man of the mountains from a family that goes back 400 years in the same geographic spot, a man that understood community needs and who had always been faithful and trustworthy. This man from the valley spoke clearly of the fact that Georges did not have the same church as the rest of the community, but that he had a strong faith and that his wishes were being carried out that day. He went on to say that Georges always served others, which was a "hymn better than a song"!

Debby, Udo, and Priscilla that day felt amazed that in his death, Georges had, in a very real way, spoken to an assembled village in a way he could not do through the thirty years. But that day was *not* the end of Georges' speaking.

Within a very few short hours Debby was to receive a letter which answered the questions in her mind, and Prisca's, as to how the family might feel about what had been put in the newspaper, and the flowers, and their presence at the funeral. This letter was postmarked "Champéry" and was written by Georges' daughter, Marlene, and signed by his son, Claude, and the rest of the family: Bernard, Liliane, Francine and his wife. It was a lovely, warm letter. First, it spoke of the shock of the brusque and unexpected heart attack and sudden death of Georges, when it seemed to them their father (husband, brother), still had so much to do in life. Then it went on to say that the family had very carefully carried out the wishes of Georges which he had expressed in a letter. This letter had been written March 26, 1973, and had been kept on top of a pile of documents and letters on Georges' desk. The family knew it was to be read when he died, and often someone slipped it under the pile, not wanting to think of his death. But always, Georges looked for it and placed it carefully on top. One can be sure he often prayed about the reading of this letter and the effect its content would have upon his dear family. He did that which he felt was his preparation for speaking at a time when that word would be listened to intently.

She said that a Xeroxed copy of Georges' letter to the family was enclosed for us, as they felt we would want to have the message Georges left them. (We were deeply moved by their kindness and openness in doing this for us. After nearly thirty years of silence, this was a marvelous reality of answered prayer.)

The letter from the family went on to say that in accordance with Georges' desire, which, of course, they respected, the service in Champéry was outside and not in the church, and only with the band and a civil ceremony. Also, since Georges had asked for a service to be held in Huemoz, in our chapel, the chapel of The International Church Presbyterian Reformé, that whenever it would be convenient, they would like us to have that service for Georges. Could they please attend this service, and would we let them know? The letter contained warm thanks for the comfort of the notice put in the various newspapers, with the verses, and for the flowers.

Debby answered that letter, and as she and Priscilla were telling the Members all this, the next step was to take place the very next day in our chapel. The chosen day was March 4th, in the middle of our Members' meeting, so that all the Members of L'Abri could be present, and a reception was to be held immediately after the service, in Chalet le Chesalet. All the family and friends who might attend from Champéry were invited to the reception.

It all had an air of "impossibility" about it as we stood in front of the chapel. I had made three flower arrangements out of the yellow chrysanthemums and pine branches that Priscilla had gotten, and the daffodils Mike had bought, and they were in front of the pulpit. A hymn in French had been mimeographed, and now the Members were seated and waiting to see who would come from Champéry. Surprisingly, the cars started to arrive and park, and Debby, Prisca, and I went up to hug, kiss on two cheeks, and express sympathy to Marlene, to Georges' sister, to the son, Claude, and his wife, and others of the family. Again, it seemed unreal, how astonished Georges would have been. I kept wishing he could come. (I wonder if he is seeing, I thought. I wonder if he is rejoicing already about this?) "That," Debby whispered as we stood outside still, "is the man who gave the speech at the grave. He is an official in the canton. And the one standing next to him is the bank president. And that man is one of the other leaders of the sports center, and there is—" Yes, they came. People came who had never been in a Protestant church. Georges had spoken in death in a way we could not have ever imagined! Nor could Georges have ever imagined about 30 Champéry people sitting in the chapel in Huemoz!!! listening to what Georges had believed.

His letter to his family had started with a simple declaration—"The hour is approaching when I will have to give an account, perhaps in a week, in a month, in a day, or in ten years—I know not when." It went on to say that they had been aware for a long time that he had left the Roman Catholic Church and that he feared what he was going to ask might be difficult for them to carry out, and to accept.

First, he wanted them to know that he had found the path to eternal life. It had been made clear to him in the Word of God that Christ has procured for us, each one who hears His call, entrance to heaven. He wanted to be buried with a civil service, and only the village band playing. He wanted them not to take his body into the Catholic church in Champéry at his death. He wanted a service held in the "English International at Huemoz when it is convenient." He hoped they would not have difficulty in accepting this. He then asked to be forgiven for anything he might have done to hurt them, and asked that they each go on in the path of their individual capabilities and aspirations. However, he urged that they, as brothers and sisters together, study the great mystery of God and His Son, that they might have the security that is freely given. And then he closed with the single word, *Adieu*. Adieu may be very carelessly said as a casual goodbye, but it literally means "to God" and is a serious commitment into the hands of God, when spoken that seriously. As Georges signed that brief letter, folded it up, and placed it in the envelope to be read nine years later, you may be certain that he did so with utmost seriousness, and with prayer.

Now here we were: our family, the Members of L'Abri, the Swiss members of our church, Georges' family and friends from Champéry, sitting in the Huemoz chapel of L'Abri, which would never have been there (humanly looking at it), had it not been for Georges' salvation and the subsequent events flowing from that. No wonder it seemed like a dream we might awaken from!

Fran gave a message, telling of how he had first met Georges on the train and of the questions then. Telling also of how Georges had been one of the first Members of L'Abri, and also one of the first Elders of our little church. He also told of the content of the Gospel that Georges believed. Priscilla stood beside her father and translated, as she had done in the "old days." It came easily to her, although it has been a long time since she had done translation simultaneously into French that way, publicly. Udo gave a message in French. Ranald read a message he had written that Debby had translated into French for him. John prayed at the end after the hymn and special music and then John gave the invitation to the reception to all who would like to come.

And they came. Everyone came! It was an incredible feeling to sit in the living room of Chalet le Chesalet and have it full of Champéry people and sit by Georges' sister, having Prisca and Debby talking to his son and daughter and others of the village. "Talking?" About what? That is the marvel. Very real questions were spilling out. "How was it Georges had been so calm, so certain of peace on his way to the hospital?" "What was the difference in what Georges believed?" "What is published in French, of your books, that we may read what Georges studied in English?" As tea was being sipped, L'Abri Members, and the Jean-Richards and other French-speaking Swiss members of our congregation talked with Georges' family and others of his Champéry friends and "officials" of that canton, something was taking place which Georges had not been able to do in his lifetime.

A "chance happening?" It seems clear to me that Georges' faithfulness in prayer, and in making a decision to write that letter and to keep it very prominently "on top of the pile" to be read, was something which God had honored and had used. We should each take heart as we pray or agonize over our families or friends who are at present turning their backs on the truth of God's Word in one way or another. Take heart— keep praying, and whatever it is we are given to do, big or little, silently or with trumpet blare, we should *not* put off. Faithfulness in prayer is after all commanded: "devote yourselves to prayer . . ." remembering that God is faithful.

That afternoon an arrangement was made for us to go over to Champéry some days later. The time came when Debby and Udo and little Hannah, Fran, and I were driving along in Udo's car. It was March 1982, 27 years after March 1955!!! Soon we had been joined by Georges' wife, whom I embraced, kissing on two cheeks, and others of the family, as we walked across the street down into the cemetery and stood by the grave of Georges, covered with flowers from Easter, next to Marc Defagos' grave, his first cousin and old friend. Life! If there is no God, what value is there to life? The sun was again on the peaks, the birds flew overhead, a plane droned by, and Georges' wife squeezed my hand and tried to silence a sob, as tears dripped down not only her face, but ours also. "Weep with those who weep" is not an academic sentence with no active reality! There is something to weep about. Fran prayed, Debby translated, and if "ears of understanding" were hearing, it was made clear that we were not praying for Georges, only thanking God for the truth of the hope and assurance given in His Word that those who die in Christ, believing in Him whom God the Father sent to die for us, are safely with Him, awaiting the resurrection that is ahead.

We crossed the street, over to the open door, and for the first time in our lives, since arriving in Champéry in 1949, *we* walked up the worn stone steps, up to the home above the stores and into the dining/living room, where the table was set for tea and a pot of tea and coffee was being placed carefully beside the cake and cookies. We were sipping tea from Georges' teacups, being served by his wife, his sister, two of his daughters, his daughter-in-law, a cousin, as we sat at Georges Exhenry's table for the first time!! Could it really be happening? I so remembered Georges' sad face as he had once said to me, "If only they would listen." What was the conversation about? Not trivialities! We were all very conscious that the cemetery and Georges' grave at the far end were in plain sight of the front windows . . . Georges' Bibles were brought to the table, and in the midst of it all were the books we had brought to them, several of the French translation of the basic Bible studies and *Escape from Reason, He Is There and He Is Not Silent* (in French) and *Everybody Can Know* which in French is called the "Gospel of Luke for Everyone." Our conversation continued through the time when the train was to leave as our attention was on the content of what was being asked, and the answers, rather than *time*. And what were the questions? Mainly the questions revolved around "What are the differences between the Protestant Gospel — your beliefs, Georges' beliefs? —" and "Where has Georges gone?" Georges' wife has been reading his Bible, but can't find understanding. . . .

We lingered over tea. Questions continued. Fran answered some and Debby translated. Debby also answered. There was an intenseness as in a moment of a storm when the lightning makes the landscape more real than in daylight. "Ideas" can be spotlighted in that way too. The books were inscribed. We promised to be available for another visit. And the afternoon that had been "prepared for 27 years" was over!

It was the daughter-in-law who drove us down to the valley and across to Ollon where Udo was to pick us up. Debby sat in the front seat talking to her. We were moved by the fact that she had found the Gospel of Luke among her husband's things recently, saved from the time Prisca and Sue had given them out to the children's class so long ago, as well as by the fact that she intends to read the book *Everybody Can Know* out loud to her mother-in-law, Georges' wife, and see if this will help her to understand what she is searching for in her sorrow. You see, suddenly, Georges is out of reach. . . .

The books are being widely used, and letters pour in as to how people are being helped as they read. The Lord has surely "multiplied" the teaching taking place in L'Abri in the books. . . .

Thankfully, we can commit each other to the care of our unchanging God, our Heavenly Father Who is eternal, His Son, Jesus Christ, Who is the same yesterday, today, and forever, and the Holy Spirit Who is our constant Comforter in every need of comfort.

With much love,

EDITH

December 28, 1982   L'Abri, Switzerland

Dear Family:

Somehow I think an hourglass with the sand running in a steady stream through the tiny opening from the top glass to the bottom is a more realistic way of being reminded of the passage of time than a clock is. Perhaps I should have an hourglass to carry around with me when I'm speaking, or at least to put on a table in the living room when I'm in conversation that needs to be limited to an hour! I've never heard of a "yearglass" with sand going slowly through for a year, but if we had one, there wouldn't be much sand left to go through. What have we done with 1982, another year of each of our lives which is now history? . . .

Now this Christmas Georges Exhenry has joined Mme. Fleischmann in heaven. Debby had visited the Exhenry family before the service—

a sad visit to a sad family approaching their first Christmas without Georges—but without Georges' son, too, who had a tragic accident while he was laying out a new hiking trail. He slipped and fell down a torrent far below to instant death. This son was the one who would have taken Georges' place in the family business, the leading of the sports center, and other Champéry activities. The need of the people of this village for "light" in the midst of so much darkness was impressed upon Debby, and Fran too, as they visited the cemetery and saw so many familiar names of people among whom we had lived. . . .

It was the first time Fran had preached in Champéry's Christmas Eve Service for five years. He gave a message that meant a great deal to him—tracing throughout the Bible all the reasons why we should "adore Christ the Lord." "Oh come let us adore Him . . . " came to each of us with fresh impetus. How serious and deep is our adoration and worship? How easy it becomes to repeat words and take the sheer wonder of all God has done for us as something simply to sing about or to say, or even to pray about, without sufficient awe, reverence, and adoration. May we adore Him truly in the midst of this next year's battles.

So often the "fear" of the Lord is never contemplated. The fear we should have means reverence, respect, adoration, awe, but if it were not for what Christ has done for us, that fear would need to be terror. The Lord is mighty indeed. How trivial can human beings be in thinking they can do anything they like against His command and simply laugh in His face? I have just been reading in Ezekiel and then in Revelation the description of the Lord as He came to Ezekiel*, and centuries later to John. Are we realistic enough ever to "fall on our faces"? . . .

December 21st we had our Annual Workers' Christmas Tea, our gift to the Workers in Swiss L'Abri, at the Parc Hotel. Why a hotel when I could make better food to serve? Because of the wonderful curved windows looking out on the slopes with pine trees and ski lift, and the deep chairs and linen-covered coffee tables, and space—space—space! You see, all our chalets are small, and for our usual student meals and Workers' meetings we are squashed together with no room to walk around. It is a treat to be able to walk around and talk together, having several conversations at one time because of space! The very feeling of space is relaxing. Monday the 20th, we had had a horrible muddy, rain-drenched scene! Disconsolate skiers were wandering around Villars, piling into tearooms with dripping ski suits! But in the middle of the night, that storm of thunder and rain shifted and silently, the snow began to fall. By morning, when each family opened its shutters, the scene had been transformed as if by magic! Instead of soggy, dripping roofs and trees, muddy puddles and ugliness on every side, the ground was white—every twig was outlined in fresh

---

* Ezekiel 1:25–2:1.

snow, fences and car tops and piles of old leaves—everything had become a thing of beauty!

We appreciated the beauty as Jim and Gail's little Jimmy crawled around on the carpet, and we remembered last year's tea with John Lewis (Franky and Genie's youngest) just about the same age then!

Prisca and John came with hair fluffy and clean, having just spent two hours at "Lavay les Bains" (ten minutes from Ollon)—a pool of natural hot water, part of it outdoors, natural hot springs used from Roman times, where one may float in steamy water, with snow floating down! Jane and Betty have used this as helpful therapy for Jane's hip pains and Betty's arthritis, and recently Becky and Rodman discovered it on a "day off" as a relaxing and amazing experience.

We were in the height of enjoying our rare opportunity to talk to each other, being served, sitting or standing quietly, instead of rushing, serving, and meeting new people, when Udo said to Debby, "I think it is time I went down to Aigle to pick up Samantha and Giandy after school. They could then get here in time for some of this." We had saved canapés and pâtisseries for the schoolchildren as they came in at different times—Katie and Seth Snyder, Hannah and Naomi Middelmann. So, off Udo went, a bit unhappily as he didn't like to miss our precious two-and-half hours of consecutive time, but feeling that the children needed to be included.

A few minutes later Debby was called to the phone and came back in some agitation to whisper to John, "Udo has had an accident. Our car is totaled—it slid 70 meters on ice. No one is seriously hurt, but can you go?" So off went Debby, John, and Rodman to see what they could do, and our Christmas tea party continued, but with a change of conversation as you can imagine.

The accident had occurred almost directly in front of our chalet, not far from Gentiana. Ice had formed on the bridge. Sudden cold had made treacherous patches on the road, and no salt had yet been put on. The car in front of Udo braked suddenly, and Udo began to skid. He successfully steered around that car, but could not pull over as the sliding continued. An oncoming car paid no attention to his honking the horn and blinking his lights, and ploughed right into the portion of the car just in front of the driver's seat. Udo was well strapped in, so although he broke his glasses, he was all right. The woman in the other car had not strapped her seat belt, so her knee needed a "pin" in it and she was taken off to the Lausanne hospital. In passing I would say, let's all fasten our seat belts!! As with all accidents, it was accidental and frustrating to think about. The ice was like glass there, but by the time one got to the Garage Moderne at the foot of Chesieres, the road was dry and safe right down to the valley. Just that quickly in *time*, and just that agonizingly in a hairline of *space*, life is exchanged for death. . . .

The fifth of December was a Sunday following a period of miserable weather—fogs that cut out all the view, nearby chalets as well as distant peaks. Earlier in November there had been sunshine and unseasonably warm weather and those foggy days brought rain, not snow. But on the Friday before, snow began to paint the scene white. When the German journalist walked from his hotel in Villars to sit at the Gentiana dinner table that evening, he walked through softly falling flakes which brought with them the kind of atmosphere that only those first snows can bring; that mountain village hush of excitement that covers everything else that has been going on. Gentiana dinner table with students asking questions, lingering over coffee and dessert, was the first glimpse of L'Abri this man had. Udo talked with him for hours afterwards. Saturday morning when the interview with Fran for the German news magazine *Der Spiegel* began at ten o'clock, the snow was still falling and the dips and hollows as well as fences and compost heaps were becoming interesting shapes. Fran and the reporter sat that day in front of our fireplace, having a discussion that seemed to be very real and not superficial. It was only interrupted by Mike and me as we set a table in front of the fire and served lunch for the four of us. At 5 P.M. the reporter left saying, "I'll be back in time to go down with you to the chapel for the discussion tonight, the Saturday night discussion you told me about." He kept his word, and also came in time to drive to the chapel for the church service the next morning, with Udo preaching, the time of informal prayer, congregational singing, and the babies trotting around at the front, all the same as usual. Mr. Hess, the journalist, sat with us near the front and took occasional notes, talking to a number of people afterwards, and then joining us for Sunday dinner.

We had 25 people for lunch that day and the menu was our usual one, as was the long discussion time, with questions flowing freely. Yet, as I stood at the doorway hesitating a few moments before serving something, I had a feeling of watching something that had been "choreographed," not by a human artist, but by the only One who can bring people together in certain moments of time and geographical space to do something He alone knows is being accomplished. Fran asked people, "Where did you first hear of L'Abri?" "Where do you come from?" "Why have you come to L'Abri?" There were many diverse stories, and then it was the journalist's turn. "My name," said he, "is Ernest Hess, and I heard about L'Abri for the first time when I read *Newsweek* a few weeks ago. I then purchased a copy of *The Christian Manifesto* and read it and wanted to come and talk to this man myself. The book seemed to present a different man than the *Newsweek* report. I have been a journalist writing for the German news magazine *Der Spiegel* for 20 years. My wife is also a journalist." After he told his story, he took pictures of some of what was going on, taking several of Mike as he told who he was.

The conversation was fascinating that Sunday, and went on until after 5:30—and all through it, I kept going out into the kitchen and saying to Mike or Jim, as we took out dishes, or served the next course, "I can't believe my eyes as I see who the Lord has brought together today!" . . .

Sunday, January 2, 1983

A new week, a new month, a new year since I started this letter! We had our annual New Year's Eve communion service with Fran leading it this time once more. As the bells began to ring in the New Year, ringing out the last few moments of the old year, we were drinking "the cup" and Fran prayed. It was special timing—a private moment with the Lord as we remembered His death and looked forward to eternity— just as 1982 became 1983. God alone knows what is ahead of us as individuals, L'Abri as a whole, and the world situation. We began the year with a day of fasting and prayer the first day of the year. It is never "convenient" to have a day of fasting and prayer and always work that seems imperative to be finished has to be put aside, always something has to be *not* done, in order to have the time for prayer. . . .

While we were away in October, Ellis, Jane, and Betty and others were conducting an arts week here in Swiss L'Abri about which we hear many good reports. Ellis also went to Poland to speak and to Sweden to lecture and be with Staffan and Lisa and to Holland for a time. So, you see, all those who are "at home" are not at home all the time! The same is true in England, as, for instance, Richard Winter, who could not come to do the miniconferences, had a number of important speaking engagements in England. As he shows *Whatever Happened to the Human Race?* and answers questions, many times in medical circles, Ranald tells us Dr. Winter is bringing about a noticeable change in the attitude of the British Medical Association toward abortion. None of us really see the whole picture, nor can we know what is the most important thing "each other" is doing. Only God knows whether the conversation at the table, in the kitchen while peeling potatoes, the girl or fellow needing a quiet, personal time at a chalet dining room table, or the letter being written to a desperate person is more important than any large audience we have ever spoken to. *But* the reverse is also true. "Little" is important so often, but that does not prove "little" is always more important than "big."

A L'Abri Conference, a full nine-day one with many of the Members there as speakers and discussors, is to be held in Atlanta, Georgia, June 17th to 25th. Now my private prayer (I'll tell you confidentially) is that many of the L'Abri Workers can come to that conference. I would like to see all of L'Abri Workers there. Why? To be in on the new lectures; to listen to discussions themselves; to hear the questions; to observe the cross section of people and to meet them; to talk to individuals in need; to "mingle" and to "feel" the reality of importance expressed by people, in order to know what is going on while they are "back there" slogging away! And to learn. You know, when Fran developed his ideas and gave them in answer to questions from such a cross section of people during those early years of L'Abri, I was so bogged down with work in the kitchen and other housework such as sewing, caring for Franky, etc., that I did not hear what he was saying. It was a period when I got "behind," so to speak, very much "behind" in the development of the ideas.

It was when I went on the speaking trip to Harvard, Wheaton, and West-mont in the "sixties" that I sat through all Fran's lectures avidly taking notes and having the ideas "click into place" in my own understanding, I could then go on with fresh development in my own way. There is a need of *that* kind of "keeping together" among the Workers of L'Abri.

For some 1982 has been the last year of their lives. For some the first year! For some the last and the first! It was Sunday evening teatime, a few short weeks ago, when Debby ran over to tell us that word had come that Udo's uncle had suddenly been taken ill and was dying with cancer in a hospital in Brussels. He had shown resistance to conversation con-cerning truth, or Christianity, in the past yet perhaps now would be the time to go. An overnight train ride brought Udo to the bedside to talk for two very rare days out of a lifetime. The end became the beginning. The last year became the first year with the Lord. Understanding, and bowing, seemed very real, "tell the others . . . " gave an indication of deep recognition of the marvel and importance of truth. We thanked God for once more letting us realize just how marvelous is *His* plan of salvation—that if anyone calls upon the name of the Lord, believing, that one will be saved. Thank God for letting us know about the thief on the cross whose time was so short yet long enough.

1982 has been a year of many births in L'Abri. You could "walk" into stories, but many would take time. The stories might come out at a din-ner table, or during a Thanksgiving service, or alone with a Worker while peeling potatoes, or over a cup of tea during a time of conversa-tion. There have been amazing conversions. Conversion is a good word—but birth is the word Jesus used. "You must be born again" is an urgent fact Jesus made clear to Nicodemus, and that birth is a beginning of another category of new year. May 1983 be a truly new year for many who need to be born this year.

May it also be a new year in the sense of each of us who need "reviv-ing" in our wholeness of life—being refreshed by turning to the Lord for moment-by-moment help.

With much love in Him Who has seen all the new years of history begin!

EDITH

1983

June 4–25, 1983   Fergus Falls, Minnesota, and Atlanta, Georgia

Dear Family:

. . . At present we are all hearing and talking about the mountains that have roared down in mud, stone, rock, tree, and water slides into so many homes and in one case, filling up two lakes in Utah! We are astounded at the floods caused by rains, by heat melting the more-than-usual snowfall, by earthquakes, by hailstorms, tornadoes and thunderstorms, by avalanches, by fires in buildings and in airplanes, by all the work of a lifetime (whatever is tied up in a property and a house), disappearing in a moment's time. Has it not always been so? Yes, but the concentration seems to be greater than usual in remembered time.

Where is a safe place to go? Imagine some having left a big city to go to a "safe, wild place" and moving exactly into the path of a mudslide!! It could easily happen to any of us. *What is the safe place to bring up a family?* Or to retire to when one is getting older? The answer is that for each one of us who is a child of the living God, for our own choices that will affect us and then affect other people, there is only *one safe place to be for our own life and for the life of each member of our families,* and for "the Work" we are responsible for, and that *one place is the place where the Lord would have us be at this particular moment in history.* History has meaning. We are not living simply to stay alive in the most pleasant place we can think of. It is not wrong to be in a pleasant place, but there are a combination of reasons for our being where we are meant to be this week, this month, the rest of this year, and moment by moment. Choice is involved, and God's sovereignty is involved, but *purpose* is part of what our lives are all about. Our agony of wondering where we should be needs to recognize one of the most important ingredients that exist—*motive.* What is our motive? . . .

Read Matthew 24 again and reflect on the fact that we are told to keep on being faithful, not to search for a safe place when things get difficult!

Then, when you turn to Philippians and we are being told that we are to eagerly await the return of the Lord (in chapter 3), chapter 4 goes on to recognize that we might be worried, or anxious about a variety of things even in the midst of this eager expectancy. And so we have the words: "The Lord is near. Be not anxious about anything, but in everything, by prayer and petition, with thanksgiving, present your requests to God. And the peace of God which transcends all understanding will guard your hearts and your minds in Christ Jesus" (Philippians 4:4–7). . . .

Whether you are clearing mud out of your living room, or sitting in the hospital beside the bed of your loved one; whether your crops have been ruined by hail or your business spoiled by the direct attack of some enemy force in one or another kind of battle, you and I continually need to realize our only "escape" into safety and security is through asking for the strength to keep on fighting. Ephesians 6:10–20 calls us into direct action. Read it. Putting on the full armor of God is an active act; "standing your ground" is a vigorous thing—actively standing against something that is designed to make you fall. . . .

Someday, the last disaster will take place and Jesus will return. The resurrection will take place and perfection will be unfolded. Until then, any "signs" which may seem to us to be described in Luke 21 as indicating that the return of Jesus might be near are only to spur us on to taking our stand more firmly, wielding the Sword more effectively as we battle against Satan's attempts to frighten us and stop people from hearing truth. . . .

As I write today, we are in Fergus Falls, Minnesota, where the weather is clear and cool, with winds blowing the new green leaves, and bending the slender birches, as well as making the wonderful purple blossoms of the lilac bushes sway in their own form of ballet! We have never walked in such quiet countryside, with rolling fields, red barns and white silos in the distance, and bird songs accompanying us all along the way. A two-day conference brought us to Fergus Falls, and as we both spoke and led discussion times, interspersed by the films, *The Second American Revolution,* and the last two episodes of *Reclaiming the World* (a discussion film which will bring you Fran's answers to questions as he and Franky talked together—ten episodes). This was a Lutheran group, the Lutheran Brethren School and Seminary having invited us. Bob and Avis Dieseth (who were in L'Abri several times and have been close to the work for some years) had prayed that this conference would one day take place. So actually, the conference was itself an answer to prayer. Then the people who came let us know something of what the books and films have meant in their lives in helping them to understand things that had not been clear to them before. Of course, one cannot shake hands with over 1,000 people, nor have personal conversations with many. *Finiteness* is always a frustration at conferences!!

There was one dear man who had been telephoning all over the States to find 30 copies of *How Should We Then Live?*, and when he called

Rochester L'Abri, he found out about *this* conference, and drove 357 miles from North Dakota with his car full of people in order to hear as much as possible in two days, as well as to tell us his own background of drugs and alcohol and lostness, then the amazing discovery of Franky's films and our books, and the "opening of understanding" that resulted in *his* salvation, changed life, and teaching now of 30 others in a class on *How Should We Then Live?*! A vanload of 14 people drove all the way from Montana, over 500 miles, with the same eagerness. It all made us feel very humble, and full of amazement as to how the Lord scatters the seed to distant places. People who need the kind of answers L'Abri books, films, conferences, seminars and discussion give, are brought to one or another branch of L'Abri, but also are sometimes simply given a book to which they respond, and which makes them cry out, "Oh, I see—I really *do* see!" "I didn't know that Christianity made so much sense."

We came to the United States first to speak at the Evangelical Publishers' Annual Seminar in Minneapolis. These are publishers of Christian magazines and papers. I spoke on "The Effect of Humanism on the Family"; Fran's topic as the banquet speaker was "Names and Issues."

When we left Minneapolis, Fran went to Chicago for a day of discussion "off the record" with a widely different grouping of leaders from Evangelical "bodies" and I went off on my own to speak at a college commencement. I spoke at Malone College in Canton, Ohio, which is an Evangelical Quaker college 91 years old. Canton is a small town with a great deal of character, and the amazing number of people I met there who tied in in some way with some portion of our past lives was a totally unexpected "reunion." I was given an honorary LL.D. and a citation on the basis of having written ten books, and also for the L'Abri work. How great it is to know that "honors" will be given to a set of people, many of whom are in prison or concentration camps—honors which the Lord is preparing, and which will be given back to Him, with love and praise one future day! . . .

Udo went in the opposite direction from Switzerland when we went to the States. Udo went to Poland, and we have just received a most welcome letter from him, written after he got back home to Debby and the children—Natasha, Samantha, Naomi, and Hannah. We can't have the pleasure of hearing him tell the details of his time in Poland, but this letter will open your eyes as it has ours. . . .

Gentiana
1885 Chesieres
Switzerland   May 16, 1983

Dear Mother and Dad,

Greetings and love to the two of you.

I came back from Poland sobered and encouraged. It was a time I would not want to have missed. The external situation was parallel to Germany in 1948 and into the early fifties, except no craters and bombed houses. But threadbare dress, shabby housing, long queues, people walking for miles to work, poor roads, no paint on the houses, dirty trains, and nothing to do other than work and live with your family. No tearooms, churches to visit, museums. Then in stark contrast the little explosions of human-ness, man against the system, against the materialist ideology; gardens, flowers, sheep taken in a line to eat the grass along the road, geese and goslings. And the love, neighborly love; an egg given, cake for the guests each day, constant visiting and talking, much and strong coffee, tea, sandwiches.

And in these particular open assemblies, people coming to the Lord: alcoholics, old Marxists, poor people and many minors—younger and older children, with joy. We are so spoiled and fail to see the true human realities, not just potentialities. Our distraction by things and variety steal the attention due the central, the human, and the spiritual. We met in a tent, plastic sheeting on grass against the cold and moisture, for two hour services, two sermons, the broken bread and the cup of Christ's testament. Before the tent came, believers would meet, 74 of them and more, in a room the size of your dining room, standing for the service the whole time.

We must pray—their awareness of being in the midst of God's history is so wonderful. This time will pass and the Lord shall return. The mayor of the town built to be a materialist statement of ideal human settlement against all religion gave his agreement to allow the sale of Bibles—we went and for a three-day evangelistic conference in the "palace of culture," used that temple of the new man and festival hall of the socialist achievements. This may well be due to the view that Protestants work also against the RC and thus against some of the ties with Solidarity, which is largely seen by them as a secular arm of the RC church.

I spent time with ——— and ———, and talked to the sister of ——— for two hours (a used and misused 20th-century girl, smoking, drinking, and sleeping . . .). I met spies, one asking me about his loyalty to Solidarity, and which ——— jumped in and forbade the man to ask me. "We talk about Jesus Christ, and only in Him do you find real freedom and a basis for life." I had been carefully looking out, but had been caught off guard at that question raised in English. Later, I saw the tape recorder!

One night a truckload of food, medicine, and shoes arrived from England, enough for two weeks in summer camps there and in Warsaw. But in the midst of all, the joy of the Lord, the human closeness and joy in the simple wonder of being human—against which no ideology can work. Then—the frustration of the West dealing with the communists, thus prolonging their dream and illusion. . . .

I would not have wanted to have missed that.

Much love,
Udo

. . . You will notice by the dates in this letter that my resolution to write you all more frequently has not been carried out!

I'm writing this part of the letter in Atlanta at Colonel and Mrs. Fain's kitchen table, writing after Fran has gone off to London with Susan for his part in the "demonstration against abortion at Hyde Park"—and while I am remaining here for the end of our L'Abri conference, and our special day together with the Workers and Members of L'Abri who came to the conference. There were about thirty or more of us all together, with tremendous thanks to those who had sent special gifts for Workers to come.

It has been a most important time for L'Abri as well as for those who have taken part in preparation for the conference, and who came to "listen," take notes, ask questions, pray and be blended with each other.

This letter has been and is being written under the difficult situation of "bits and pieces," not being written at any one time, but in scattered times. . . .

June 29, 1983 . . . In a Farmhouse in Westchester County, New York

I feel like Alice, having dropped through the rabbit's hole, to have an unexpected adventure! After hours of talking in New York "off the record" to various people the Lord sent me (so I believe) to talk to, I suddenly find that I have been provided with a small room, a desk and typewriter, and a "piece" of time—hopefully *just* long enough to finish this letter before once more doing up my suitcases and leaving for Kennedy Airport!! Lord willing, I will be flying through the night from New York to Geneva, and Fran will later be flying from London and meet me in Geneva for the next step of what we have to do! . . .

The L'Abri Conference Committee in Atlanta had been working for 14 months, praying together, dividing the various aspects of preparation, choosing a place for the conference, choosing hotels nearby, and working out all the logistics. Everything seemed in readiness. Then, during the vacation time Fran and I were having in a log cabin on a Minnesota lake, a "deluge" of difficulties descended. First, Fran had one abscess after another. A course of penicillin for the first abscessed tooth did not prevent a second one on another tooth from forming. Sleepless nights and pain, etc., plus the penicillin doses put off the period of chemotherapy, and just as this siege seemed almost over, the phone rang and Hal Simpson told us the news that plunged us into a time of struggle. The headmaster of the school which had been prepared for the conference had said that if Dr. Schaeffer did not cancel his speaking at a memorial service in Atlanta for 14 babies who had lived through abortions, in a certain clinic, then died hours later (death certificates issued, etc.), L'Abri could not use the school property for the conference. Nine days were left before the conference. The Committee looked for two days for another place, and during that time did not come up with anything! We were involved in many phone calls. Another day went by and we wavered. We began to rationalize as to how many people would be hurt if the conference had no place to go. It was the age-old temptation to think of the weighing of the good of many people over and against the basic principle involved. How many times in a lifetime do we *all* face this kind of temptation to rationalize "just for a brief moment" just for *one* thing we can rectify a bit later??? It was during these hours that Franky called his dad, and again I would say this is what the Bible is talking about when it speaks of one of us helping another, either by a dash of ice water, *or* a tug of the arm. We need to *alert* each other of the "trap" Satan may have placed before our feet to shove us into some kind of compromise. It was for us a night of prayer, recognition of what was involved as we put aside *every* consideration except the basic principle involved, and a time of calling Ranald (the secretary of the Trustees of L'Abri) and of his calling the other trustees to "vote." My husband had cast his strong "vote" or decision that he *would* speak at the rally, or memorial service. He had promised to speak three months before. We would *trust* God as we prayed to open a path in the Red Sea, as far as the L'Abri Conference was concerned.

Ranald's call after some hours was with a unanimous decision from the Trustees, "Yes, take that stand publicly against abortion, and we will pray about the conference. Let us ask God to open up His place for us."

It was an impossibility! After 14 months of work, it was an impossibility to find and prepare a place in *five* days! *But God did the impossible!*

Now when God works, when God answers prayer, when God opens the Red Sea, or opens a door in a solid wall, it does not mean *ease* for those of us involved in the "work," whatever that work is. . . .

Five days before people were to start pouring in to register at the L'Abri Conference, five days before speakers would be standing to give lectures, and lunches would be served after the morning session, five days before an eight-day conference would begin, *another school was found*. The headmaster, staff and parents of this other school (Mount Vernon Christian Academy) became excited about the prospect, and the Committee met for a prayer meeting and a time of thanksgiving together, and a time of portioning out the work to be done. They said there had never been such a good spirit of cooperation since they had started to prepare months before. The headmaster, teachers, mothers of students, and others connected with the school all began to take hours and hours to put things in order (as the term had just ended). A green-and-yellow-striped tent was found to rent, tables and chairs were rented to put in the rented tent, and mothers put geraniums on the tables. Surrounded by trees, this tent with the sides rolled up gave us the feeling of being in a camp in the woods. A round gymnasium surrounded by a circle of rooms and a kind of covered walkway became the auditorium. The fire marshal gave a special and amazing permission to put 1,000 chairs on the floor, speaker systems were hooked up, chairs rented, caterers found who agreed to do the meals, etc., etc. It all cost a lot more money because of the last minute needs to rent the tent, etc., but by the opening hour, there stood Dr. Schaeffer announcing all I have told you as, "A miracle, and I do *not* use the word lightly." Fran and I felt we were seeing a new beginning, a new series of battles and building of what the Lord has for all of us ahead, and a new lesson learned as to the subtlety of Satan's traps we *all* need to watch out for and warn each other about. Watch out! Don't rationalize, compromise, or give in to accommodation!!

Eight hundred people were registered before that first day was over.

Some people could only come for a part of the conference, but about a thousand were there as a complete count. There were all the L'Abri speakers sharing a diverse series of lectures. Workshops were held in different places by speakers, and also by some of the Workers. In total, there were about 30 L'Abri Members and Workers there to experience the conference themselves, as well as talk to people who came. There obviously were all kinds of needs, and also victories in a variety of struggles. It was a joy to have Genie and others of the family.

The memorial service was outdoors, downtown, attended by a wide cross section of people. Fran gave a strong message. The service was shared by co-belligerents including a Catholic bishop and pastors of a number of churches, both black and white. The march was orderly, and police protected, a silent march, with banners, but no talking and noise. Rodman and Greg, with Rodman's sister-in-law, had walkie-talkies with them and both in the cars we drove to the "happening," and as we were marching in the front row (Fran and I), they acted as our special "guards." However, the L'Abri Conference continued according to schedule. They were in the midst of lectures. On the Action News on channel 5 that night, there were a few moments of Fran's speech and views of the crowds and banners, and of the thousands marching, and of the other people on the platform leading the service. It was said on the news that on Father's Day there would be an opposition march! What a strange celebration of Father's Day—urging freedom to abort the next generation of children!!!

After the last lecture of the conference, Wim's, there was a closing time of prayer and various people came up to the microphones where they had come to ask questions. This time they lined up to pray—one after another—very deep and real prayer, as we were to scatter all over the United States and back to the various branches of L'Abri. Just before that time, Susan called from Greatham and I got the report from Susan and Fran. It seemed scarcely possible that they had flown out just the night before; had been at the conference all day, then flown to London overnight, simply showered and had an omelet, and then had gone straight to Hyde Park.

They were moved to tears as well as amazement as they watched the buses arrive from Wales, Ireland, Cornwall, and many parts of England, as they saw a large delegation of Greek Orthodox with banners, another large group of nuns, Salvation Army people, people from the Church of England, and many other churches, Christian groups of all varieties. In they poured, over 50,000. "Mother," said Susan, "England has *never* had so many come out to march over a moral issue. It was history in the making." A few years ago when Franky's film *Whatever Happened to the Human Race?* came out, Dr. Koop found almost no doctors who would stand with him on the platform for our film seminars. The film has now been shown all over Britain with Ranald, Dick Winter, and Jerram answering questions, etc. At that rally in Hyde Park Dr. John Stott gave a Bible study on the fact that a person is a human being at conception, a member of Parliament spoke, a girl who had spina bifida told of how glad she was to be alive, Mother Teresa of India, who is in a hospital in Rome, sent a message, Fran gave a strong message that included the basics of truth concerning God, and Dr. Malcolm Muggeridge spoke. When the people formed into a parade (ten across), it was so long that it took three hours to pass any one given spot along the route. Fran and Susan and the Macaulay children—Margaret, Kirsty, and Ranald John—led the parade. After no sleep and his speech and the hot, hot sun, Fran and Sue dropped out halfway along from Hyde Park to Trafalgar Square, as a car was driving along to pick them up, but the others kept on to the end. However, the media might minimize this, be sure to *know* that it was a tremendously encouraging event! Over 50,000 taking great chunks of *time* and energy to fight the terrible taking of the lives of the next generation of British citizens. Let us keep on keeping on, to *do* something in our own geographic areas.

Southborough has so many wanting to come, they are praying that a house may be built, or two houses—on the land that can be added from the farm next door.

In Huemoz there is the possibility of Bellevue's being given to L'Abri with space for about five wheelchair people to be able to be visitors or students at L'Abri because of the elevator and other equipment there. This would also give a new dimension for people to have "space" for larger meals together, lectures, discussions, etc., as "short term" people.

In England, there is building of space for married couples and single Workers going on.

Dutch L'Abri also faces changes and need of guidance and prayer, as does Rochester and Sweden. . . .

When you see my new film that Franky made in Rochester with real people asking the real questions, remember that this is not artificial or contrived, but a part of life recorded on film, as serious and honest answers to people's questions were recorded. Finiteness can only be "multiplied" by books, tapes (and there is a full set from the conference), or films. Happily all communication does not have to be face to face to be real.

With very much love in the Lord Who has given us communication in His written Word until we can be in *His* presence—face to face!

EDITH

1984

February 20, 1984   Rochester, Minnesota

Dearest L'Abri Family:

I am using the superlative because this is a very special Family Letter.
I expect it to be my last Family Letter that is written by me alone. For 36
years now I have written a "Family Letter"—first to my own mother,
father, and sisters to keep them in close touch with all that was taking
place in our lives in Switzerland (to be copied by them and sent to other
friends), and then to what became a wider family who were desirous of
keeping in close touch with interest and prayer.

Why my "last"? First of all, because now that L'Abri has rapidly growing work in scattered branches, it seems that the Family Letter needs to
be a gathering of "warm personal letters," or "reports," or "news articles" as to what is going on in L'Abri in Sweden, Switzerland, (Huemoz
and Gryon), America (Southborough and Rochester), Holland, and
Greatham. Also, we all need to hear what God is doing in the various
L'Abri conferences in various countries, through the films, books, tapes,
and wider areas of diverse new "thrusts" the Lord is giving to L'Abri.
For instance, how could I really report to you what is taking place in the
new experimental school and preparation of the curriculum in
Greatham to be used in the USA and England and other places? How
could I keep you in touch with what Udo will be writing and discovering as he travels in the Orient, Africa, and South America and prepares a
strong answer and lectures in giving a philosophical base for feeding
the hungry that is *not* tainted with Marxism, which so many Evangeli-
cals are falling into? How could I keep up with all that is going on in
Bellevue as it is being prepared for the next step of L'Abri in Huemoz
including the possibility of a few Farel House students who will come in
wheelchairs? How could I let you know of Susan's book on education or
of Debby's expectation for Gryon or of the new property and plans for

building in Southborough or of Wim's and Greta's plans as God leads them in the new portion of L'Abri work in Holland? I do think the time has come for a "newspaper" of a warm, personal sort, to be written by L'Abri Workers and Members in plural, not by me, alone. . . .

September and October Fran and I spent in much traveling and speaking, with a portion of time spent in having a short vacation, another portion in the work in Rochester. There was a "Miniconference" in Wheaton, Illinois, at which we both spoke, and so did Os Guinness. Fran gave an excellent sermon at the banquet celebrating an anniversary of Good News Publishers and after that we parted for a few days as I spoke on some TV and radio programs and gave some interviews in and around Chicago, speaking at Trinity Seminary, etc., accompanied by the head of Promotion for Thomas Nelson Publishers, as *Common Sense Christian Living* was being introduced to the public. From Chicago, I went on to Grand Rapids, Michigan, for a Winning Women's Conference where I was the speaker and literally left the platform for the airport after the closing service on Sunday to fly to Philadelphia. That flight was a special gift of Nancy DeMoss's—a quiet interlude of looking down at the fantastic pattern of autumn's blended colors of oranges, reds, and yellows, thanking God for His marvelous creation. The Alpha Pregnancy Center banquet, where I spoke in Philadelphia, was a flight into memory as I reviewed not only our first years of togetherness there, in the city of Fran's birth where we met when I was 17 and he 20, but also remembered that it was in Tenth Presbyterian Church we listened to Dr. Machen speak passionately for the truth of God's Word and the need to fight for the purity of the church. It was also in Philadelphia that we first met Dr. Koop, before L'Abri began, just before the deluge of "preparations" were to hit us!!! . . .

It was many years later that Dr. Koop was to come to speak in L'Abri about abortion and infanticide and euthanasia in the Huemoz chapel, and that night in conversation with Franky into the wee hours of morning the film was to be a "seed" in their minds, so to be planted in Fran's. You will remember that when Franky tore down to see his dad the next morning, we were in a state of exhaustion, an "impossible" time to start a new project. Impossible??? God brought forth through hard work and a series of frustrations on the part of all working together on it the film *Whatever Happened to the Human Race?* That film was to be used all over the world to change the thinking and actions of many people, and to give life where there would have been death to specific human beings, some of them now three and four years old. It was in Philadelphia (so I reminded people that night) that the filming began in Children's Hospital and in Philadelphia that the first seminar was held—in the midst of a period of chemotherapy for Fran. Impossible?? Yes, it has all been "impossible," but God has brought forth amazing victories through not simply days and weeks and months, but years and years. All of L'Abri has been "impossible."

At the banquet that night I found it hard not to weep in memory of all that has taken place in the battle from our days of resolving to never mix "poison" with the milk of the Word of God, from Fran's college days as we listened to Machen (and prayed alone and together) to the years of battle when at times the fire has been excruciatingly hot, and the scars very, very real in our work on both sides of the ocean. . . .

I flew from Philadelphia to Boston in time to meet Fran there as he came from Minnesota. We then had four rare days with Franky and Genie, Jessica, Francis, and John Lewis. One of those days was my 69th birthday—one of the loveliest of my life. Franky took me to Boston to walk around charming old streets that reminded me so much of sections of London, during which we had lunch, shopped for their gift to me, and had a satisfying conversation. In the evening we had a birthday supper with the children, complete with cake and the happy birthday song, and balloons that were tied to a flower arrangement. It was a "shiny day." I find it important to treasure the shiny days of life and the glowing half days, or one-hour periods of time, or even five special minutes. A fence should be put around such times in our memories to protect them from being blurred by the next storms that hit!! It is important not to forget what the Lord has given along the way. Tables in the wilderness, a time of being fed in the presence of enemies with delicate food set before us in special atmosphere—these are not to be forgotten when the next afflictions burst upon us! As I opened cards and letters from my other grandchildren, children, and friends, surrounded by the warmth of family, I am glad there was freedom to "richly enjoy" what the Lord had given for *that* day, without being apprehensive of what might be "around the corner."

We flew off to Switzerland on the Boston-Zurich-Geneva flight, feeling contented to be going back to a period of *normal life*. We were tired, and looking forward to walking along the lake on a "day off," soon, we hoped. We remarked to each other how at home we felt, after 36 years in Switzerland, to be going back. It was a joy to see Udo's face as we wheeled our cart out through the green gates in the Geneva airport, and to have a time of "catching up" on news as we drove along and stopped for a breakfast of eggs and croissants and tea along the way. "Home again" brings with it a time of list making, and my list included the menu and work for Thanksgiving Dinner and the outlining of what needed to be done before Christmas. "When should I write the invitations to Workers for the Annual Workers' Tea?" I wondered. And should I have my usual Chinese Dinner for Helpers? I asked myself. Or "shall I do something else this year?" I planned my decorations, not only for the chalet, but for the poster lists I enjoy making, which "put my life together," so to speak, after a long trip away.

But—those Christmas lists were never to be made, nor was I ever again to have a family Christmas dinner at Chardonnet, or a church children's Christmas party in Chalet Chardonnet, nor an "after Champéry dinner" on Christmas Eve, nor any of the other things that were going to be on the lists.

There were no trumpets; there was no introductory background music at all to announce an enormous change in life. I made my usual stuffing with its whole wheat bread rubbed into crumbs, celery, and onion cut in fine bits, blanched almonds added, Bell's poultry seasoning, salt and pepper and butter. One more year I stuffed the Thanksgiving turkey and got it into the oven late the night before to cook it slowly so that it would be tender and juicy. The Grandmother Seville's pumpkin chiffon pies were to be made the next day. I was feeling warm and pleased that our guests would include our Swiss church members, the Fretz family and M. and Madame Jean-Richard. "It will be their first American Thanksgiving, and then they can go down to the chapel service with us." "How good to be home again, how cozy to be chopping onions in my own kitchen." The feeling was one of continuity and permanence. "After Thanksgiving we can settle down to a schedule of *normal life* with a proper day off each week and time to get caught up on correspondence." We can get unpacked. You see, I had forgotten to tell you that immediately after getting back from America, Fran and I had had to go to Germany to speak in a conference in Worms at the American Military Headquarters there. Nancy Snyder and Cynthia Reynolds went along with us to help with discussions and workshops. Fran had been extremely fatigued during the train trip and had spent his time when not speaking in our rooms at the officers' quarters there. He felt "awful," but he spoke with power. "We need to get back and start that period of normal life," we thought. So you see, Thanksgiving had come before we could get properly settled in.

Larry Snyder called for Fran in his car Thanksgiving morning. It was he who had arranged that Fran would speak at the American Embassy Service in Berne for Thanksgiving morning. The drive is about an hour and a half. Fran gave a fine message with strength. He was wearing his good suit, which that morning fit him perfectly. He went to the bedroom to rest before the five o'clock dinnertime.

I had bought three ears of corn in Minnesota when Bob and Avis had taken us for a drive in May. One ear was a dark purple, another had a variety of colors among the grains, and the third was a dark rust orange. Three dried ears of corn with the husks pulled back to show the grain— really perfect for reminding one of the Pilgrims and their Thanksgiving. My table decorations had a straw cornucopia, onions with shiny beige skins, carrots, turnips, eggplant, nuts. The corn and various other vegetables made a long, thin centerpiece, with the corn, dark purple grapes, and ivy along with tiny branches of red berries blended in with brass candlesticks with two rusty candles and two deep purple ones to match the corn. My *last* centerpiece in that room! I didn't *know* it was the last, but I did feel it was the most satisfying one I had made. It was Minnesota and Switzerland twisted together in an amazing way, with no realization of any significance.

The meal also seemed to turn out with perfection in the tenderness and flavor of the turkey, the fluffiness of the mashed potatoes, the bright color of the vegetables and cranberry sauce, the just-rightness of the homemade rolls, and the better-than-ever texture of the pumpkin chiffon pie accompanied by the satisfying flavor of the European Migros Coffee. "What a meal!" "What a lovely time of communication!" Fran had come down to sit at the head of the table even though he did not feel like eating. It was his last time at the head of that table. Yes, I did serve 24 on Sunday with a leftover turkey meal, but that day I was sitting at the head, jumping up to serve and also jumping up to run upstairs and see if Fran needed me. He was very sick by Sunday.

Thanksgiving night at the chapel all the L'Abri Workers, Members, and Helpers, the guests and Farel House students, our own church members, and various people from their homes nearby gathered in front of a roaring fire to have a memorable Thanksgiving Service. Fran was in his place sitting on the stone fireplace. Everything looked permanent and familiar, following the continuity of years of Thanksgiving services. As one after another asked for a hymn and told something of what they were thankful for, we were all conscious of the presence of the Lord in our midst. The reality of the power of the Spirit among us that night was very evident. We felt it was the most wonderful Thanksgiving service we had ever had, and we have had many good ones. Barry thanked God for old friends, and for the joy of having had years of working with the two men who sat on either side of him that night (Udo on one side, Larry on the other). It was so special to have Barry with us again after his and Veronica's time in Southborough. (They and the children are happily entrenched in the work in Greatham at present where their help is very much needed.) Among the many expressions of thankfulness which could only be appreciated in depth by those who knew the "whole story" of various one's lives, I spoke of being thankful for Captain Alms's decision as he put first what he felt would be for the Lord's glory in his decision. You remember that I told of Captain Alms's salvation in my last Family Letter, as he accepted the Lord as his Saviour in Lausanne Hospital with Fran, some months ago. Now his lung cancer was progressing to a place where there seemed little time left. Fran felt a real urge to visit him in his chalet before Thanksgiving. As an intimate talk was had between the two men, Carl Alms came to a decision that he had had so little time to serve the Lord in the short time he had been a Christian, and that he had thought of a choice he could make to give witness to the Lord he loved. "I have decided *not* to go to Bethesda Hospital in Washington, D.C., for my last weeks, and to therefore *not* have my burial in Arlington Cemetery with full military honors. I want to be buried here in Champéry, near Georges Exhenry, and to have you take my service, that you might give a message to the Champéry people." . . .

With the last hymns still ringing in our ears, warm hugs from people I had not seen for a long time, Fran was standing at the door shivering—a chill had suddenly hit him like the blast of a sudden wind!! That night alternating high fever and terrible sweats, and bed-shaking chills kept me busy taking off wet pajamas, changing sheets, putting Fran in another bed with hot water bottles and sips of hot tea until the shaking stopped; making a fresh bed, and repeating the process. The fever climbed and dropped—and all I could think of that I had ever read about like this was malaria. But, of course, that was *not* it! After six days of this sort of succession of days and nights, with many blood tests and blood cultures being taken by Dr. Gandur, Dr. Gandur felt Fran should go to the Aigle Hospital, and days and nights went on at Aigle Hospital with *no* explanation of the apparent infection, and with an enlarging abdomen which indicated an enlarging liver, etc. Cultures showed nothing, although the lab was full of them! And X-rays did not reveal what was wrong or give a clue as to the solution. The head of the hospital made a strong suggestion, "Your husband must either be taken to the University of Lausanne Hospital, or to Mayo Clinic where he has records and Dr. Petitt to follow his case. It is too complicated for us." Fran was getting worse daily.

So Debby and I were given the doctor's office in which to make phone calls, trying to arrange for transportation for a man so ill as to need stretchers and ambulance, and who could not, by that time, even walk. How to get from Aigle to St. Mary's Hospital in Rochester, Minnesota?? We prayed and phoned. Swissair had seats. The doctor took a length of time convincing the Swissair doctor that this was not a contagious disease, and that the travel was both essential and possible. Tickets were arranged for the New York flight. We sat and looked at each other and prayed. How would we get a man who could not sit up, and who was growing worse, from New York to Rochester?

After praying, I took a deep sigh and then called Mary Crowley in Texas. I explained as well as I could (but how can such a situation really be put into words?). Later, Mary told me she knew by my voice that it was really a matter of life and death and she said, "I got busy." Not knowing the outcome of what she was busy *doing*, Debby and I prayed more. . . .

The hours that followed are a bit of a blur. Susan, Priscilla, Debby, took turns caring for their dad's needs. I went up the mountain to the chalet to pack two suitcases. Just what period of time was I packing *for*? What would be ahead of us? To try to choose all that *might* be needed to put into Fran's suitcase, and then into mine, in the brief time that there was, seemed something like pulling things out during a time of flood or fire—"What to save?"

The doorbell rang as I packed, and it was a telegram from Mary Crowley "Nancy DeMoss's plane and crew will meet you in New York;

an ambulance will meet Swissair, Paul Tiffen is arranging that. Praying for you, Mary." A heavy lump melted inside me somewhere, and I felt an assurance that God had blended people and events and had brought forth a solution to that particular "impossible" of the travel! One day we will see—all of us—what astounding importance each one's part has had in the victories over Satan's insidious "schemes." Had it not been for these two women who prayed and worked together to get that plane to the right place at the right time, and for Swissair's Paul Tiffen who arranged the ambulance, the careful pilots, the ambulance on the other end, the bed ready at St. Mary's Hospital, Dr. Petitt's meeting us, and so on and on, there would be a different story to tell. Who else had a part? Every single person who prayed throughout that time had a part in the historic "happenings," hour by hour. We need to remember that the death of Christ opened the way for communication with God the Father that would bring about results in history.

The ambulance left Aigle Hospital at 11 A.M. at the other end (by Swiss time), the ambulance brought us from the Rochester Airport to St. Mary's Hospital at 4 A.M. For Fran, that trip is remembered only in bits and pieces as a nightmare. And for Debby and myself, the fears and difficulties were strangely balanced by evidence of the Lord's care in the smoothness of how it all went. That night Debby and I were not given much hope by the young doctor who talked to us. Fran was dehydrated to the extent of two liters of liquid, lips swollen, tongue dry and cracked, breath short, needing oxygen. Debby stayed in the "visitors' room" and I stayed right beside Fran. Neither of us slept much, but kept consulting each other as to how things were going. Blood cultures, X-rays, and other tests, including CAT scans were taken. His liver was three times its normal size and there was water on his lungs. Intravenous antibiotics seemed to help whatever the infection was by bringing down fever, and the chemotherapy that was given in the next few days was a new and very much stronger combination of drugs, because it had been established that his lymphoma had changed from "small cell" to "large cell," a more aggressive and difficult form of lymphoma. All this had happened in such a short time! Thanksgiving had been such an amazingly "normal" day!

The stronger chemotherapy was given for five days, and Fran's response was good. There was no nausea, and he was able to eat well even during the intravenous administration of platinum and the other drugs. Then—BANG!! As with Job, another blow came from another source! Suddenly, bleeding began, a real hemorrhage. After trying to determine where the bleeding was coming from, it was decided that it was from the colon. Several ideas were to be put forth over the next couple of hours as to some way of stopping that bleeding, but after five blood transfusions, the surgeon, Dr. Peter Mucha, along with the other doctors, decided that surgery was the *only* way to stop Fran from bleeding to death. This was the second time he nearly died!! It seemed almost that he was too weak to stand major surgery. As Fran was taken into intensive care late that night to be prepared for surgery in the morning, you can imagine that we were assured we needed to be faithful in prayer during those next hours—for the doctor's skill and wisdom in all the choices ahead, and for God's strength to be given to Fran for all the aspects of his weakness; and for all the uncomfortable "procedures" to be borne that night, to be as comfortable as possible. If you had peeked into the hospital hall that night, you would have seen Rodman, Prisca, and me emptying Fran's room on that floor for leukemia and lymphoma patients, so that his belongings would be ready to go into another room sometime the next day on a surgical patients' floor.

Meantime, Fran was being comforted by a special touch of the Lord's "weaving" lives again. The bleakness of the intensive care unit had been softened for him by the nurse welcoming him with "I am glad to be taking care of you, Dr. Schaeffer. I have read your books. I am a Christian, and thank you for your help to me." It was a gentle provision of the Lord in the midst of a fearsome moment. We have had so many instances of the Lord's closeness and specific help during these last three months of difficulty. . . .

It was indeed a major surgery—half Fran's colon was removed as an abscess and an ulcer were found. However, the amazing thing is that he recovered extremely well from the surgery. Of course, it was not what we had expected to be happy about on Christmas!! My lists in Switzerland were not going to include trimming a Christmas tree for Fran's hospital room, nor having a *cup of tea* with him as *our* "shared Christmas dinner together"!!! But one of our joys on Christmas was the good progress of the healing of that long incision and of Fran's walking down the hall as one of us pushed his "I.V." Priscilla had come to help at that time, to be with me and her dad, and the added treat Prisca had was to find that Becky and Rodman were able to come from Georgia, so that Becky's first Christmas away from Huemoz was spent with her mother and grandparents in Rochester, Minnesota!! True, she and her husband, Rodman, were helping me to get to the hospital in that 30 degrees below zero weather (90 degrees below with the wind-chill factor). True, each one of us had the joys mingled with the sorrow of Fran, Daddy, Av having a severe illness, but nevertheless, the joys were there too. Fran and I had "stockings" hung on the doorknob of his closet next to the tree L. G. Parkhurst had bought for him, bright with a string of lights, standing on the desk. We remembered our first Christmas together the first year we were married and in seminary, and our tiny tree was standing on a dictionary! In spite of the strangeness of the surroundings, and Fran's only food by mouth being a tiny bit of tea and red jello (and I kept him company), we enjoyed our gifts, appreciated our children and grandchildren, thanked God for the gift of eternal life, and had some amazing openings to talk to some nurses and doctors about the *truth* of a created universe and its Creator. The lumpy, bumpy stockings, the stuffed ani-

Fran and I together in the L'Abri house on Fifteenth Avenue. We rejoice in the success of the operation and good response to new chemotherapy.

mals Debby had put in the top, the gifts Becky and Prisca and others had brought, wrapped and stuffed into old, familiar stockings. It is so important not to waste what is precious by spending all one's time and emotion on fretting or complaining over what one does *not* have. This isn't a "Pollyanna" formula, but there are precious things that are seen more clearly against darkness—like stars, or a new moon, or the first streaks of dawn!

That was a special Christmas, though not scheduled by us! Fran, who had almost died twice, was still alive; we were still together as a couple and as a family, and although the battle continued, we had seen victory in certain "turning back of specific assaults." . . .

It was January 2nd when he came home to 219 15th Avenue S.W., one of the L'Abri houses, with day-by-day walks progressing outdoors, as well as climbing stairs indoors and eating well. Progress toward recovery, so we thought. By midmonth, it was time for chemotherapy again and the difficulty of finding veins to use both for getting blood for tests, and for intravenous injections of the chemotherapy, combined to make it another time in the hospital. The Hickman catheter was put into him at that time. If you don't know what this is, just let me say we didn't either. Now it is a daily part of our lives. Fran was glad to find that the same surgeon, Dr. Mucha, would be putting in this surgically placed tube, as he feels confidence in this man's work. The process consists of placing a tube subcutaneously *under the skin for a few inches,* then the tube plunges into a main vein, and on into the area of the atrium. The place where the tube emerges in the left or right side of the chest needs sterile care daily. This arrangement gives access without needing to punch arms and hands, full of needle pricks, in order to draw blood or put antibiotics, chemotherapy, or any kind of intravenous feeding into veins. This daily (twice a day) sterile care of "the site," and "Heparin flush" is my new work, my opportunity to be a nurse!

This second time of chemotherapy demonstrated once again that Fran indeed is among the 30 percent of people with large-cell lymphoma who respond to this combination of strong chemicals. Not only does he not become nauseated, but the CAT scan and other tests have shown that the liver is back to its normal size and that the battle against the bad cells is gaining victory. When his colon operation was taking place, the surgeon took a piece of his liver to send to the lab to be compared with the biopsy taken earlier. An amazing confirmation of the success of the chemotherapy. The liver had been riddled with the large cell lymphoma, now not a cell showed up, and the liver is working normally again. All this was encouraging, and as Fran came home and we added our time together doing his "sterile care" to our time of reading together, we realized that the sharing of such a diversity of things in life has value in deepening a relationship. . . .

As one looks back over 52 years since meeting, one realizes that it is not perfection that is being looked at, nor does disappointment and a long list of adversities or troubles wipe out a relationship. The history of true continuity in a fallen and abnormal world includes many results of the fall to be shared in helping each other in fantastically different circumstances. . . .

At the moment of this writing (today is February 26th), the disappointment of being back in the hospital and of having to face the removal of that Hickman catheter, with a second surgical process of putting a new one in on the right side of his chest, is now a part of history. There are only three days left of the necessary 14 days of the two antibiotics— and the third period of five days of chemotherapy is over—with good success again. Coming out of the hospital is not only "in sight"—it will take place, Lord willing, in three days!

There is a whole new portion of this painting to be painted in now. I will take up another brush and begin to help you see more clearly what has been, and is, taking place in "the battle." Can I see into the heavenlies and *see* what is going on? No, of course not. I don't mean to be pretending to be so knowledgeable. Only God sees the whole picture. But we are given so many hints and glimpses—not only in Job, but in other parts of His Word.

Peter, in I Peter 5:8,9, gives us God's strong warning which is not to be simply read abstractly as having some spiritual meaning, but no practical meaning, but which is to be a part of our daily lives as a "danger" signal. "Be sober, be vigilant, because your adversary the devil walks about like a roaring lion, seeking whom he may devour. Resist him, steadfast in the faith, knowing that the same sufferings are experienced by your brotherhood in the world." In Ephesians we are given some more explanation of what resisting consists of— showing us clearly that resisting that adversary and his "wiles" or "schemes" is an active work.

Ephesians 6:10,11–16,18 . . . "Finally my brethren, be strong in the Lord and in the power of His might. Put on the whole armor of God, that you may be able to stand against the wiles of the devil . . . above all taking the shield of faith with which you will be able to quench all the fiery darts of the wicked one. . . . and the sword of the Spirit which is the word of God, praying always with all prayer and supplication in the Spirit, being watchful to the end . . . and for me that utterance may be given me . . . "

The strong warning against the devil is against a *person* who has schemes and designs to spoil God's Word and work—even as shown in the Garden of Eden, and in Job—and throughout Scripture. Satan's fierce battle against God, we are clearly told, will continue until Christ comes back again. He has not yet been thrown down. Revelation 12:10 has not yet taken place! The "accuser of our brethren" is still accusing, and is still trying to destroy God's truth and substitute his lies, in any way he can possibly accomplish that task.

Is all affliction Satan's attempt to separate God's children from showing trust and love to God? No, as I had time to write in my book *Affliction*, there are many aspects of affliction. *But* Satan does indeed attack and does try to destroy God's truth. He attacks from within and without the church. . . .

Just before this onslaught of illness, Fran and I stood in Worms, Germany (where we were to speak to our military people). We stood before Martin Luther's monument and wept with thankfulness for his courage and for his willingness to stand alone. We thanked God that Martin Luther was willing to point out the wrong teaching and to refute it, as well as to teach the positive teaching of salvation by faith alone. He was willing to point out details of what was wrong, and destructive of truth, as well as to preach what was right.

That night as Fran sat answering questions after a day of conference, questions came about abortion from people who had been taught very wrong ideas within the church, blurring the issue of how wrong killing is and how precious a human life is as made in the image of God. But also questions came from our military men and women in Germany, really defending the kind of freedoms we believe in, so near the Berlin wall and all it has stood for, asking questions that made us want to cry. We felt like crying with shame for the Christian leaders and teachers within the church who have taken a stand that is helpful to the enemies and has brought confusion and pain to those who are sacrificing in a very specific day-by-day way as they are willing to try to prevent war and defend their countries by being in the military. We were especially saddened by their difficulty in meeting their children's questions—children who have a hard time because of taunts at school and on the streets as the violent epitaphs are thrown in their faces by "peace marchers." . . .

Humanly it seemed impossible that Fran could do the needed work on his book in time for it to be finished for the Seminars. Yet, prayer has been answered. With Lane Dennis's hard work as editor, and Fran's work at his desk during the time he was home from the hospital, and his work on the bedside table tray-affair across his hospital bed, the manuscript got finished and is now rolling off the presses!!

Humanly it seemed impossible that Fran could attempt to go to one Seminar, yet right now, the doctors have said they feel he may try— "play it by ear" is the word. We are praying fervently that there will be a victory in these Seminars, and that Fran will be able to sit on the platforms and answer questions, but harder yet, to do the necessary travel in one way or another (as provisions are made). *Lord willing*, he will get out of the hospital on February 29th (thankful for the extra day this year), and Jerry Falwell's plane will touch down with motors running at the Rochester airport to let us have time to "jump in" and be flown to the first Seminar in Lynchburg. We are *praying for God's victory* in all this. Fran agrees with me that we are in a particularly hot battle, and that Satan wanted to silence him, but that God has more for him to say. . . .

Thirty-six years ago I hid after Fran's last sermon in our St. Louis church, weeping and not wanting to let anyone see my tears! I wept because I felt our leaving for the unknown in Europe might end Fran's talents in the area of preaching and teaching, and caring one by one for individuals' questions and needs would forever be laid aside!!!! Little did I have any idea of what the years were going to bring forth. In spite of the tears and the uncertainty as to what might lie ahead in the way of work, I was *certain* that we had made the right decision, given the sequence of events in his 1947 trip throughout Europe, the report brought back, and the heavy burden that was increasing as we talked and prayed together about "doing something" in Europe. You'll have to re-read that portion of *The Tapestry* to refresh your mind as to what happened then.

We arrived in St. Mary's Hospital on December 7, 1983, just about 36 years after that time of decision in St. Louis. As I have told you, the possibility of Fran's dying that first 24 hours was only matched by that same possibility twice after that!! It was December 8th, less than 24 hours later, that Franky urged me to go and get some sleep, "I'll stay with Dad tonight; don't worry; I'll stay right beside him all night—ready to give him chips of ice, to turn him and to do whatever he needs. You have been up so many nights already in Aigle. Go now; get some sleep." Mary Jane (Grooms—who, with Greg, are Workers here in Rochester L'Abri) and Anne Brown (ditto) had come over to bring some boxes of juice, cookies, and nuts, etc., for us all to refresh ourselves and said, "Come on. We'll walk you home a little longer way around for some fresh air."

Debby and Anne walked ahead of Mary Jane and me, and we breathed deeply in spite of the cold, remarking on the beauty of the softly falling snow and the misty moon, a blurred, round light behind the snow clouds. As we walked up the hill, a long block, Debby suddenly exclaimed, "There is a house *for sale—look*." Right on the corner, surrounded by a fence and trees outlined with snow, stood a delightful house with blue-grey shingles, which looked so romantic in the silently falling snow that I remarked, "Now, if this were a Grace Livingston Hill story, that would be exactly the right place, and we would be living there happily ever after!" As I looked at the "For Sale" sign, I remarked, "Why, that is K & K, the same company from which we bought our L'Abri houses, and Marilyn Stewart is the one person I could so easily talk to." I went on then to tell the girls that not too long before we had left the hospital, Fran had pleaded with me, "Please, Edith, look for a house. I can't ever make that same dash across the ocean in this kind of crisis. We need to live nearby." "This house is one block from L'Abri," I said to the girls as we looked, "and one block from the hospital. How amazing." We walked around the corner looking at the many trees in the garden and wondering what it would be like in spring. You see, my response to Fran had been quick and definite in the form of a promise, "Yes, I will, dear, be sure of that."

I was looking, with a resolution forming in my mind. I would see about that house as soon as possible. It had only been 24 hours since we had arrived at the emergency door of St. Mary's. I had no idea of how "things would go," so to speak, but as I fell asleep that night, with every bone aching and my head swirling, my prayer for help revolved around willingness to do anything the Lord would show as "next," thankful to know that the Lord is able to show us where to put our feet next, in spite of thick fog ahead.

I talked with a doctor who looked a bit troubled, as I said I was looking into a house nearby, and said to me, "Don't make a decision in an emotional moment. It is too early to know what is going to happen." My reply to her (and to him when another doctor said the same sort of thing) was my reply to myself: "Do you wait in order to be 'safe'? in order to protect yourself? before doing that which seems important in order to give the help needed at the moment?" I feel *now* is the time Fran needs incentive and encouragement to fight for his life, when it would be easy to give up. *Now* cannot be put off. Now is the moment to say, in action as well as words, "I am ready, dear, to walk away from our beloved Alps and all the familiar continuity of life with our family around us in Switzerland, in order to make a home for you near here for this next section of life. *Now* is what marriage vows are all about: 'for better or worse, in sickness or in health.' We aren't parted yet, and right *now* I am looking for a house. In fact, I am telephoning about one we saw already!!!"

There are a number of moments in life when you have an opportunity to tell another beloved human being, in your relationship—or to tell the Lord in your relationship with *Him,* that there is reality in your love and commitment— and this is a demonstration of that reality—*now.* Waiting to be "safe" misses the whole opportunity. I am not talking about being rash and foolish in a careless way, but such moments arrive that will never be the same again. I felt strongly that that second week of December was such a time for me in my firm and strong conviction—"I'll phone about that house. I'll do what Fran has asked for and reassure him we'll go on together whatever—."

Within a week I had not only seen that house on the corner inside and out, but had signed a preliminary intent to buy, making my first big business venture in putting down a thousand dollars to seal that intent. It seemed to me, and seems more so all the time, that the Lord knew as thoroughly in 1920 when the house was being built in an orchard, that the chalet on the side of the road from Ollon to Villars would be the beginning of L'Abri, but that later, He would bring us to be a part of the Rochester branch of L'Abri twenty-nine years after sending us the needed thousand dollars to help us *know* He had answered prayer and was giving us guidance to promise to buy Mélèzes, surrounded by Mélèzes trees, He would make it clear we were to step into another chapter of life, *still in L'Abri,* with my putting a thousand dollars on *that* house! Don't you *see?* God who prepares daily for us and is preparing a permanent place for us in eternity, also prepares a succession of places for us during a lifetime. This house with its fireplaces and 23 varieties of trees for us to watch in the spring, seems designed for another chapter of life in L'Abri. It is an exciting next chapter. . . .

Today is the 27th of February 1984. Two historic things have been taking place during the same day. *It is moving day!!!* Greg, Randy, Rob, Dennis, are making trips with a U-Haul truck after packing it with boxes and furniture (our bedroom, dining room, living room things that we have had for six years here since we first came in October 1978 to discover Fran's cancer) into our new home one block away! L'Abri has as a part of the work three houses on 15th Avenue. Now—as of today—there is a *fourth house involved*—our new home, and we are now Members in residence of Rochester L'Abri.

Today is also the day of a surprise word from the doctors. Fran has made such remarkable progress in recovery that he is to "go home." You can imagine how hard Avis Dieseth and I worked to "pack" last night and to move this morning in order to get the bedroom "set up," curtains up, and at least the bedroom in readiness for Fran's homecoming at noon.

Somewhere in the middle of the Atlantic Ocean a large "container" is crossing the ocean with all the earthly belongings and memories of 49 years of married life, and some childhood things of years before that!

Packed in so many square meters of space, enclosed by metal sides and sealed with lead are letters, manuscripts, books, kitchen utensils, linens, paintings, photographs, handwork, clocks, blankets and quilts, an old sled, two shutters from Chalet les Mélèzes, and a big rock Fran lugged home from a hike one day years ago with a fossil in it! . . . Amazing to see the things that won't be going to heaven but that hold the memories of a lifetime . . . a "family homestead" squashed into boxes and wrapped in papers . . . and stuffed into a container . . . as it all moves down the mountain road, piled high with the blizzard snows (biggest blizzard in years!) . . . yet safely making it to the valley . . . one day, God willing, to move behind a truck up past St. Mary's Hospital in Rochester, Minnesota!!!

It was Franky who jolted me into an abrupt state of reality when he said, "You'll have to be thinking of when you are going to pack up Chalet Chardonnet and put it up for sale." And I quickly, with a bit of panic, replied, "Oh, not yet—that decision doesn't have to be made yet." I had very unrealistically put aside all thought of "leaving one place" in order to be "going to another"! I had been living "one day at a time," so I thought, but had also been avoiding that practical necessity. Franky's reply might have been a jolt, but was completely right: "You made that decision when you stood in the hall of the hospital, Mother." Yes, I had, even though I hadn't let myself spell it out. We could not decide to live in America, in Rochester, in that particular house, without *also* leaving Switzerland and selling our big chalet and that lovely property in Chesieres. Fran had come home from the hospital in January. "Edith, you'll have to go soon and pack up; empty the chalet, and make decisions as to what to bring, put it up for sale, and so on." . . .

January 30th was Fran's 72nd birthday. "This one was a hard one to get to, Daddy. You put up a good fight," said Prisca on her card to him. It was quietly celebrated with just Debby and myself, Avis and Diane to help him open gifts, enjoy the tulips from Mary and the tree from Billy and the cards and letters from grandchildren and children, and the two stuffed dogs from friends in California with collars labeled "goodness" and "mercy." Candlelight and a silver teapot of hot tea gave a glow— and a new year of life began. At the same time (because of the time difference) it was early morning in Champéry—the morning of Tuesday, January 31st. It was right then that Captain Carl Alms was walking through the valley of the shadow of death—and continued until he was absent from the body—that body so precious to the Lord that He died in order that the resurrection might be possible for the bodies of believers. That Tuesday morning Carl was present with the Lord— and his hope became fulfillment. . . .

The 4th of February was the day chosen for me to fly my lonely flight back to Switzerland, with Diane caring for Fran's needs of food, etc., and Amy Smalley caring for Fran's "Hickman site care" each morning and Anne doing the heparin flushes at night. My part was to get our "life" packed up as quickly as possible! The funeral was taking place as I flew the ocean, praying for Udo as he preached, for Dave in his part of the service, for Marge Alms in her shock of being left (death is a shock no matter how long the illness) . . . and for the people of God's choice to come from Champéry village to that funeral. . . . Udo preached in two languages, giving a paragraph in English and repeating it in French. It was a splendid message and gave the gospel in great clarity. Fran sent a message to be read, which Udo also translated. Dave gave the military portion of the service, with "taps," the ceremony of the American flag, and all. He had the amazingly rare privilege of being allowed to wear his uniform to conduct that service in the Champéry cemetery (it is against Swiss law to wear a military uniform of any country while in Switzerland, but special permission was given). God answered Captain Alms's prayers to have his funeral service be a clear witness.

I arrived in Switzerland February 5th. The next days were sad and at the same time filled with moments of pure joy and rare family togetherness. Susan came from Greatham to help me pack and sort, and sort and keep or give away, and sort to discover "treasures." John started by sorting all Fran's office and storeroom, tying up dozens of piles of papers and manuscripts. Debby came over to help hour after hour, and although Prisca had nursery school to teach daily, and some L'Abri meals to cook for, she too took hours to come and sit on the floor sorting old letters and papers. "Oh, listen," one of the girls would call out, "listen to this letter Susan wrote to Grandmother and Grandfather Seville in 1955 on the day the money was paid for Chalet les Mélèzes." "Listen to this paper Franky wrote when he was only nine. I had forgotten he wrote so well. He was a genius." When, I asked myself, would one ever *plan* for hours of searching through old letters and papers, reliving history through the eyes of children, remembering events and thoughts long forgotten? . . . That week included my one two-hour time with "everyone"—Workers, Members, Helpers, students, and guests—as I talked my heart out for two hours by the fireplace in the chapel, and it included a very special Sunday service in the chapel. . . .

As the movers were packing our things, some things were taken down to Huemoz so the Mélèzes living room will be very like it was when we were there. The red barrel chair and stool, the red couch will again be by the fireplace where Fran sat and led discussions starting 29 years ago now. . . .

As we prayed in the chapel that Sunday, February 12th, we prayed for each person facing changes in L'Abri, and for the growing, developing, diverse work. Richard and Jane Winter and their family will move into the apartment and work in "the big house" there in Greatham as Sue and Ran leave for Huemoz. . . .

One of the gifts of the Lord that day was my having a family dinner with all the Sandris, Middelmanns, and Ran and Sue! Through the years I have served Sunday dinner to many, but not to my family. This day we went to Montreux and ate "out"! It was a rare time indeed and a special gift to each of us of a priceless memory. The Lord seemed to "tie up the years" in a ribbon as we "ran into" the Wildermuths—the people who had been our next-door neighbors in 1948 in La Rosiaz when we *first* arrived. Mr. Wildermuth exclaimed when he saw Prisca, Susan, and Debby, "But I remember your getting out of a taxi, three little girls in navy-blue-and-white-striped dresses! You were then—??? Yes, three, seven, and eleven years old, my my." This was a dramatically perfect touch but certainly not planned by us!!!

Monday, the brown-paper-wrapped furniture and boxes disappeared into the container and went off down the mountainside. Debby hurried to light candles and to make a blazing fire in the empty living room. The children stopped after school for tea, Madame Jean-Richard came to say goodbye, and so did Bea Fretz, so one last "tea" was served in that empty room, and we prayed together, remembering all the Bible classes, teas, Sunday dinners and endless discussions, to say nothing of Members' meetings held in that room. . . .

It was Valentine's Day, February 14, 1984, just exactly 29 years from the day Fran and Priscilla came back from the *gendarmerie* in Champéry to Chalet Bijou to spread before us the edict handed them. "Monsieur and Madame Schaeffer, Priscilla, Susan, and Debby must leave Champéry and all of Switzerland by midnight, the night of March 31st." Reason given, "You have had a religious influence on the village of Champéry." I flew out over mountains and land, oceans and lakes, back to Rochester, Minnesota, to begin our "new chapter" of L'Abri life, just exactly 29 years after that day when we were being "thrust out" of Champéry! Back there in 1955 on February 14th, we knew absolutely *nothing* of what was ahead of us. We did not know there would be such a thing as L'Abri, let alone all the branches that exist now. We did not dream of books, films, conferences, L'Abri Ensemble concerts, tapes, records, lectures in such diverse areas as philosophy, art, music, literature, economics, education, and a philosophic base for helping to feed the hungry. We did not dream of such a thing as Ran and Sue's educational program opening up, nor of the first years of Bellevue, let alone what is ahead of L'Abri now. We had no idea then of our children's developing lives blended with us in the work, let alone of our sons-in-law, and of our grandchildren.

February 14, 1984, did not *look* dramatic. I went off alone on a plane full of complete strangers. I was bone exhausted, and my face developed a growing pain on the left side as it swelled (as if with mumps), because of a blocked salivary gland! As I fell asleep, I would dream of waking up in Chardonnet on a sunny morning and sudden tears would come when I wakened and realized I would never sleep in that chalet again, and that I was on a plane rapidly moving away from my "familiar life," as well as home. No, the drama was not accompanied by any "glamour" that day as I arrived to find Fran in the hospital, and left the airport for the seventh floor of St. Mary's, with the future as unknown as it had been 29 years ago. But there was a "bubble" inside my insides, a bubble of excitement in knowing that our God is *able to do the impossible*. We must never underestimate His power and His plan.

I am finishing this letter in the early sunlight of March 1st—nine days after beginning to write. I am finishing it in our new home, our "latter house" which is a lovely one chosen by God! In a few hours, Lord willing, Fran and I will be flying out to Lynchburg, Virginia, to begin a Seminar tour for the premiere of Franky's film and Fran's new book and Franky's new book, etc. Yes, you are reading an account that is true—not a fairy story. Fran came out of the hospital a day early, that is, the day before yesterday, at 12 noon!! The doctors are really amazed at his progress. Prayer has been answered in a very clear manner. When we were told a few days ago that Jerry Falwell's plane would touch down with motors running for us to quickly board and be off at 12:45, March 1st, we were not really sure whether Fran could possibly be strong enough to go. Now, in these past 36 hours, he is ready to start and we will go on, a day at a time, to ask that Satan's attempts to stop these Seminars will be pushed back completely with a crescendo of results in lives.

The suitcases are packed for the Seminar tour . . . there is Fran's, mine, and then the one with all the equipment for the daily sterile care of the Hickman catheter. There is the doctor's letter explaining that suitcase (in case of need) . . . and everything seems to be in order.

Our moving in? Well, with Fran "tucked in" to the bedroom where curtains from Chardonnet and our familiar blue bedspread from our chalet made it *home* (brought over in my suitcase), the Helpers buzzed around getting things in order. The first night here a buffet was served in the kitchen, and nine sat on the family room floor to eat. It has become L'Abri from day one and we await this next chapter of life with interest and curiosity.

Pray earnestly that *nothing* will hinder the fulfillment of God's purpose in each of our lives—yours and ours—as we are blended in this moment of history, for that which could not take place at any other period, but is crucial *now.*

With very much love in *Him* Who is able to take that which the enemy means for our harm and work it out for our good, and for the fulfillment of *His* purposes,

EDITH

July 17, 1984   Rochester, Minnesota

Very dear L'Abri Family:
Here I am, back again. Yes, I know I said I had written my last Family Letter, *but* an outcry reached my ears from many of you, and officially

from the *Trustees* of L'Abri! I was asked to "please keep on writing the Family Letter." And the long and short of it is, I *am* keeping on, . . . so, hello again!

The last Family Letter was written February 20th, which is now almost exactly five months ago and it is also now almost exactly two months since Fran died on May 15th. That last letter I wrote was actually the last letter that Fran read. You remember that it ended with his being "tucked in" to the bedroom which had "familiar curtains from Chardonnet at the windows" (brought over in my suitcase after I had rushed back to pack up the whole of Chalet le Chardonnet in a few days) and just before we were to go on the Seminar tour after *another* unexpected time in the hospital ending within hours of my finishing the Family Letter.

That five months contained the last three months Fran and I would ever have together on this earth—at least until the resurrection—and the last Seminar tour we would go on together, as well as the last L'Abri Conference we would share. It contained the making of decisive decisions which will affect the next block of my life, as well as affecting our family and L'Abri. When I asked you for prayer at the end of the last letter, I do believe that you *did* pray, and the Lord *has* been answering: for the Seminars and next step of Franky's work and books; for L'Abri, as each branch faces growth and changes; for strength in my own weakness to keep on and not to let Satan hinder whatever the Lord has in His purpose for me, and for *each* of *us*, in *this* historic moment, in *this* combination of circumstances.

Have you ever thought that God's great gift to us is *time*—time *forever*? When we are forgiven of our sin and cleansed from our guilt on the basis of Christ's death for us—Christ's paying our penalty—we are given *ever*lasting life—a gift of *time*—a fantastic gift of time together with Him, and with all those who have come into the family of the living God. As we grow to feel more and more in life the limitations of 24 hours and the limitations of a seven-day week, and the limitations of a month and the fact that there are only 12 months in a year through which to distribute the demands being made upon our time, we should *marvel* at the gift God has promised us, and because of which we have an unshakable *hope* and a bubble within of delight—we are heading for *forever*! Even in the moment of separation by oceans and mountains, by water and land, and in the moment of separation by absence from the body we are still heading for forever together!

I'm going to start with the present, rather than with the period of five months ago. At present, I am in the Pink Room at Greatham looking out at the lawn which so recently had an enormous white canvas tent on it. The tent was the center of artistic activity as the Greatham church members decorated it with fantastic charm and originality and then, later, the scene of a most unusual wedding reception, with 200 adults present and 100 children under 14 years of age!!

We have just celebrated the wedding of Margaret Macaulay, Susan and Ranald's eldest daughter, to Douglas Curry, a young Canadian from Calgary, Alberta. Fiona and Kirsty were bridesmaids in lovely pale peach silk taffeta dresses, along with two tiny girls dressed in identical dresses of the same silk. They followed Margaret as she came up the aisle on her father's arm, dressed in Susan's wedding dress, as lovely as it had been in that Ollon church 23 years ago, and wearing her Grandmother Macaulay's Brussels lace veil worn in South Africa more than 50 years ago.

As the wedding guests had finished eating their fill of the wonderful array of fresh vegetables to be dipped in a variety of special dips, and had added cheeses, pâté, crackers, etc., to their plates and finishing off with a variety of cakes and berry tarts, English wedding cake with tea or coffee or cold punch, they sat in the tent on rows of chairs or benches, gathering to hear the telegrams and special music. Dallas Graham sang some of his songs and called upon Margaret to come and sing with him "She's a Star"—which was a surprise to Margaret and all of us. She performed so naturally and easily with her veil over her arm. All the music was a special combination of talent and diversity. The bridegroom, Doug Curry, sang an old song with his sister, Joanne, as they played their stringed instruments together, "I Never See Maggie Alone." Dallas brought the house down as he announced that the "fastest man on keys in the west" would next play "Slippery Mac," at which Ranald knelt to play the bass of a boogie-woogie, and Dallas took the top keys.

Let me say here that at Christmastime Kirsteen Macaulay, 18-year-old younger sister of Margaret, wrote a piece of music which was a lovely composition. Three weeks ago now, Margaret and Kirsteen sat down together at a piano and wrote words for this music, bringing forth a song which expressed what they were feeling at the time. Now at the reception came a request for the two sisters to sing their composition. I wish I could flash a color picture on this page and put it to an accompanying soundtrack, as Kirsteen in her beautiful bridesmaid's dress and Margaret in her wedding dress and veil caught over her arm, came up to the platform to perform. Kirsteen sat at the piano, Margaret took a microphone in her hand as naturally as if they had always burst forth into a deeply emotional song with great calmness!! They sang the following:

*Sister and Friend**

When I see your face full of goodbyes,
There are tears in your eyes,
I'm glad we can cry.
Plays and days full of crazy fun,
These are memories we hold
That will never grow cold.

    CHORUS
    Sister and friend

*Words and Music Copyright 1984 by Kirsteen Macaulay, used by permission.

Though the oceans roll between us
Though the mountains rise before us
I love you.
Sister and friend
You will never have to fear
I will always be near
'Cause I love you.
Yellow nursery with old bunk beds
Clothes on the floor—jumbled musical scores,
Couldn't keep our room straight though I tried.
Braids were to pull—one on each side.

CHORUS

Making sand castles on a Cornish beach
Watching waves come in—our hair in the wind,
Teach me to dance and I'll teach you to sing,
Run along scratchy rocks—a race we'll both win.

CHORUS

As Margaret and Doug will be leaving in the next few months to begin missionary work in Nepal, there will be very real oceans rolling between these two sisters! Kirsteen expects to be living with me in Rochester as she has enrolled in the junior college there. Sue and Ran will soon be leaving with the rest of the family to be in Chalet les Mélèzes in the Huemoz branch of L'Abri. But "the oceans rolling between us" and "the mountains rising before us" is not only *literal* for family members, but in a variety of ways for *all* of the L'Abri Family. As changes come in various branches, and as miles separate some of us who were next door to each other before, we need to express our love for each other *more* carefully, and pray for each other *more* faithfully.

As Fran has gone to heaven, we are separated from him by more than oceans and hills, and we do not need to pray for him, as the Lord cares for all the needs there beyond our understanding now, and for us who remain here, the Lord is always very perfectly near because of His infinity. I don't know of all the emotions and thoughts going through hearts and minds among the large gathering in the tent that day, but I do know that many felt keenly the reality of our togetherness during those hours, and our special rejoicing in sharing the blend of joy and sadness together. Many individuals have come to Susan since that wedding day and said "I have *never* ever been in such a wedding reception and wedding! The whole time was like—like—heaven." You see, it was a togetherness of so many people who had been brought out of darkness into light, out of the mire to have their feet set on The Rock.

Then came goodbyes—Doug's father, Joe Curry, soon to be back in Calgary, Canada, where he is a well-known IVF leader; his brother, Don Curry, and wife Nancy, now on their way to their little, one-room, mud

*Gracie who prayed, "God let me stop here
forever," lived in Mélèzes all through our
years there. She is now in a nice nursing
home Pris found for her in Leysin.*

house in the Pakistan desert heat, leaving behind not only the joyous festivities, but all sight of green grass and trees and colorful crisp vegetables! Doug's sister Joanne had come from her three years of teaching missionary children in Nepal on her way back to Canada. Other missionaries from various parts of India and Nepal were there too. So—the goodbyes were not only among people from different parts of England who had not seen each other for a long time, and were together so briefly, but among those who would indeed be separated soon by vast oceans.

Now it is three days later and Priscilla has just called to tell us the kitchen in Chalet les Mélèzes is being energetically painted, inside and outside of the cupboards, a bright white, and she is working away to sort out all of Gracie's collection of things in cupboards and drawers gathered during her 20 years in her room. Gracie is now in a lovely Swiss home in Leysin, which the Lord gave in answer to prayer, with a balcony overlooking a breathtaking view. The Protestant Sisters caring for this home have read our books in German, as well as some in French, and have prayed for L'Abri and been glad for it. Gracie will get care there, including nursing care, which could not be provided in L'Abri—and it is only an hour's drive away and is at the same altitude.

Greg Laughry,* who has been a Huemoz Helper for some time, is also uncertain as to where his next step is. Will it be London Bible School, or another place of study? We are not chessmen being moved about by God. We do have choice—real choice. God made us in His image with choice. It is part of who we are. Our choices affect our own history and other people's history. We need to pray for each other with fervency that we are helped in our choices by the Lord, and not hindered by Satan's vile schemes.

Another move back into L'Abri has been made by a familiar former Worker, now a Worker again. Donald Drew has applied for a permit to live in Switzerland, and his permit has come along farther than anyone else's has so far. Please pray for clarity of the Lord's direction to L'Abri in this. If he is in Switzerland, he would be a great help in lecturing and leading mealtime discussions, etc. Otherwise, he will be in the work in Greatham and possibly a "visiting professor" at the same time to Swiss L'Abri for part of each year.

Jane and Betty, Larry and Nancy, Priscilla and John, Ellis and Mary, all live in their same chalets with a variety of changes in their work. As for Rene and Anagret, a Swiss couple who are wonderfully fitted for the work in Bellevue among handicapped people, etc., they are living in Bethany, and the second apartment there is being rented by the Swiss couple who are taking over the work of Alice and Marionette in the post office. . . .

In Rochester, as you already know, I moved into a house which I *thought* was being bought for Fran *and me* to live in—but Fran moved to his heavenly home being prepared, as promised, by the Lord, as I am living there without him. However, Julie Cooper (Australian), a L'Abri Worker formerly in Switzerland, has moved into the bottom-floor apartment in my house and is my secretary and secretary in Rochester L'Abri. By September 4th, Kirsteen will also have moved into this house so that granddaughter and grandmother will be sharing a life, a home, and adventures in music as well as in L'Abri, and her study in Rochester Junior College, along with Julie who will bring her varied knowledge and experience from Australia to keep us international! . . .

If you were able to attend any one of the series of Seminars for the film, *The Great Evangelical Disaster,* for Franky's strong lecture, for Fran's answering questions with Franky holding the microphone as he sat beside his father, for whatever luncheon at each place that I spoke, you then attended one of the *last* presentations together of the things we had prayed Fran would be given strength to do. I am certain that God gave a specific miracle of answered prayer when He gave Fran strength and time to finish this book in the hospital and to get out of the hospital just two days before leaving for that "tour." He *did* complete that block of work being given, that precise block of time and the Lord's strength to

*Greg was later to become the husband of Lisby Sandri, and my grandson-in-law!

finish the task. It is not simply that Fran himself felt the *content* of what he had to say during that time was crucially important, but I believe that the Lord made clear to us that *He*, the Lord, considered it important enough to give Fran the extra time on earth to complete these Seminars. Fran and I took the evening sessions, and although he felt increasingly miserable, he answered questions and continued to give much of that which gave him such a strong desire to put forth the new film, the contents of his own book *The Great Evangelical Disaster*, and Franky's book brought out at the same time, *Bad News for Modern Man*. The urgency Fran felt can be understood even more now—as he truly had a very short time in which to "blow the watchman's trumpet." Do read again Ezekiel 33, verses 1–11. It was this passage that Fran read when beginning to write the script for *How Should We Then Live?* and which seemed to him a command from the Lord to keep on when the going seemed hard to keep on warning the Lord's people as well as the world of the necessity of examining whether or not they are putting into practice what the Lord gives as essential in His message to people. See Ezekiel 33:30–32.

After the Conference, Fran did not feel well enough to take all the trip in one day, so stopped in Atlanta at the home of the Nims for a rest. He needed to be met with a wheelchair, and he was not able to be out of bed. As we returned to Rochester two days later, he was almost unable to get to the Clinic for tests and had to be taken by stretcher and ambulance back into the hospital within two days. We had come home to find that the container with our furniture and lifetime of books and belongings had arrived *during* our absence, and that Mike Sugimoto who had come from Switzerland to help (before going back to university), was in the midst of unpacking boxes and arranging things in the house. It was not an easy thing, as you may imagine, for me to turn my back on all that and spend the next weeks nonstop in the hospital with Fran.

Although it was not "easy," it was without any question in my mind the thing I was meant to do with my time, and the place I needed to be. We had a period of time to live through *together*. Pain and discomfort need to be shared. One person may be the well one, and one the ill one, but both are involved, which, after all, is what the oneness of marriage—the "for better, for worse, in sickness and in health" are all about. In spite of being two separate persons, there is a reality of sharing life together which the modern "scream for rights" or "scream for independence" knows nothing about! Families share joys and difficulties, sorrows and refreshing times together. Families consist of man and wife, of sisters and brothers, of children and parents, of cousins, of aunts and uncles, of grandparents and grandchildren. As I walked out of Fran's room one day and down the hall of the hospital to get something, I overheard a nurse talking to a man very ill with cancer. "But do you have *no* one who knows you are here? If you have only an ex-wife, does *she* know or care if you are here?" Being independent is one thing in people's shouting for "liberation" with shrill voices. It is another, when people are alone in a hospital with some form of final illness, whether it be cancer or some other thing.

The next period of time was a pretty miserable one, but we had times of comfort in being together, and it was so important for me to be there to make a variety of decisions. Easter Sunday the doctors gathered in a room nearby to tell me that I should call the children. They felt the time would not be long. Franky came right away with Francis for a couple of days during which there was real communication. Debby came from Switzerland soon after Easter and stayed on with me to help in talking over various decisions that needed to be made, and to take turns with me as we did not leave him alone. We came to a very certain decision that as Fran was asking to go home, we should prepare the family room, looking out into the garden with a hospital bed and all the needed things to care for Fran, arrange for nurses, and take him home as soon as possible. Greg and Mary Jane, Mike, Debby, Anne Brown, and Julie all rushed around in preparation. Geraniums were placed outside the windows, a bird feeder was set up to attract birds, and squirrel food placed where the squirrels could be seen from the bed. The room was fixed up with things from every period of Fran's life—not to look junky, but tastefully arranged with familiar things to make him feel the history of our family life. By phone we had talked this over with Priscilla, Susan, and Franky, and we were all agreed that it was the thing to do. The doctors' and nurses' attitude was, "I wish other people would surround people of their families who are that ill, with beauty and familiar sights and sounds." The air was filled with his favorite music— Schubert's Quintette, Bach, Beethoven, Chopin, Handel's *Messiah*, etc. He remarked often the first few days, "I am so thankful for the beauty of that green grass, the flowers, the tiny leaves coming on the trees. Look at the birds and squirrels! I am so glad I can see life like that." It was *such* a change from the sterility of hospital walls!

Susan came soon after we had brought Fran home, and the three of us stayed with him, either together, or taking turns. The last three days we simply did not leave at all. We are so very glad to have had him ask us to pray, and to be able to fulfill that request immediately, even as we are glad we were with him to respond to the Sunday service on TV given by Jim Kennedy, as he nodded in agreement to the strong message against Marxism. We were glad we could hear and remember his admonition, "Keep on . . . keep *on* . . . from strength to strength." He was with us at home from May 5th to May 15th. We read Daily Light aloud after midnight on May 15th. (Read May 15th's Daily Light for morning and evening if you want to see how amazingly helpful it was.) It was 4 A.M. precisely that a soft last breath was taken . . . and he was absent. That absence was so sharp and so precise! Absent. Now I only observed the absence. I can vouch for the absence being precisely at 4 A.M. As for his presence with the Lord, I had to turn to my *Bible* to know that. I only know that a person is present with the Lord because the *Bible* tells us so. I did not have a mystical experience. I want to tell you here and now that the *inerrant* Bible became more important to me than ever before. I want to tell you very seriously and solemnly—the Bible is more precious than ever to me. My husband fought for truth and fought for the truth of the inspiration of the Bible—the inerrancy of the Bible—all the 52 years that I knew him. But never have I been more impressed with the wonder of having a trustworthy message from God, an unshakable word from God than right then! I did not have to have, nor pretend to have, some mystical experience to prove that Fran had left to go somewhere, that he had gone *to* the prepared place for him, and that he was indeed OK. I could know that by turning to my precious Bible, and to his precious Bible (and we each have had several), and read again that absent from the body is present with the Lord—and that it is far better. It is far better for the one who is thus present, but not for those left behind. God knows all about the pain of separation and is preparing that separation will be over forever one future day. I also know that because the Bible tells me so. I feel very sorry for the people who have to be "hoping without any assurance" . . . because they *don't know* what portion of the Bible is myth and what portion might possibly be trusted. What fear must clutch their hearts as the face of their loved one suddenly turns to wax after the last breath announces the absence!! Sad, sad pastors, described in the book of Jude as "clouds without water" . . . nothing there to refresh themselves, let alone anyone else . . . nothing but things that are not absolute; things that change with the changing winds of theological fashion.

As arrangements were being made, and family began arriving, we had some rare moments together. It is strange, but true, that God gives gifts of togetherness that are rare in a lifetime, and cannot be arranged—not ever. The ordinary interruptions of life seem to fade away temporarily when there is an extreme crisis or circumstance, and one's perspective is sharpened, and appreciation of each other is not only more real, but even more relaxed. After all, life is short, as we discussed together earlier. *Time* together is a gift to be used and appreciated.

Although letters have been written to each individual who sent money that our children and grandchildren might come to be together at their father and grandfather's funeral, and that they might surround me to be a comfort and a joy to me, I want to say here, "Thank you, and thank you again . . . and may the Lord supply *your* needs according to His riches in glory . . ." I so very much appreciated that gift of my family at that time of my life!

Telegrams, letters, flowers, plants, memorial trees to plant, began pouring in. Each expression of love and appreciation from Fran's life and work was appreciated. We had a wonderful letter from President Reagan speaking of helpful correspondence he had had from Fran, and other very specific things. There was a cable from Sir Bernard Brain of the English Parliament speaking of Fran's voice being the most influential in the pro-life question in Great Britain. There were so many tele-grams and letters I wanted to *show* Fran . . . so many articles and bits in papers I wanted to read to him! The cutoff in communication is strange to get used to. In adding "thank you's" to the letters of thanks which I hope have reached each one, I need to also give a thank you to Rochester people who so wonderfully brought casseroles of food and salads and special bread and cakes, etc., to feed the 23 of us gathered there. All the family came with the exception of Margaret in the midst of her exams, etc., in University of England, and Lisby and Giandi also detained by school responsibilities, so that made 21 of us (without Fran). And then we added Lucinda, my niece, and the baby. It was such a help to have food provided, but also such a warm-cared-for feeling to have such an "early-America" situation of neighborliness take place.

I do hope that each of you who were able to come to the funeral, or to our house the evening before, will realize the frustration it was not to be able to spend time with you personally after you had come from such *distances.* It was frustrating to catch a glimpse of old friends and to know they would soon be miles away and not be able to be with them! Howev-er, I am sure you did understand. There were over 800 at the funeral which was held in the very auditorium where Fran first answered ques-tions after the showing of *How Should We Then Live?* five-and-a-half years ago. This auditorium was also the place where the two L'Abri Confer-ences were held—i.e., John Marshall High School Auditorium in Rochester.

Ranald led the service; John gave a history of his first coming to L'A-bri and of what his father-in-law, Francis Schaeffer, meant to him in in-troducing him to Christianity now 29 years ago. Thankfulness for that period of history crowded into our minds as John so vividly described his arrival on the old yellow postal bus. How much God has done through L'Abri, those who have gone forth from there—the books, films, tapes, concerts, and conferences during those years. Tears of sor-row mingled with tears of deep amazement for what God has done. Udo then gave an excellent message, starting with the abnormality of death following the fall, and of the assurance of the unchanging solution God has given so clearly through the centuries. The music was that "Alle-luia" sung by the Trinity Church choir, which had been sung for Fran on Easter Sunday afternoon in the hall of the hospital outside Fran's room. He had remarked on how beautiful it was and had truly appreciat-ed it then. It was good to know that it was something he would have liked to have sung again for everyone. Ranald spoke then.

I had chosen to have family members—my own sons-in-law, and son, Franky, take part in giving the messages at the funeral. Franky's part was the showing of the fifth episode of *Whatever Happened to the Human Race?*. After all, it was Franky who directed that episode in Galilee and at the Garden Tomb, starting at the top of Mt. Sinai and going on through the Abraham scene, etc. I have always loved it and have thanked God for it. I so remember the deep thankfulness Fran had when he said to me "Franky has enabled me to preach the Gospel more clearly in this fifth episode of the film than I have ever been able to do in my lifetime. It is so complete. I am thankful it can go on speaking." I know Fran never thought of the opportunity to speak to the people at his own funeral, although I know Franky considered that possibility as he directed the last sunset scene. It was wonderful to have Fran speaking so very seriously and clearly for all of us who were there.

Now . . . here we sat at the funeral, and I was *so* thankful that the doctors and nurses who had cared for Fran as he became increasingly ill during those last days (and could not discuss with them as he would have wanted to do) could see and hear him give that which he longed to be able to say to them, one by one. Later, when I had the nurses for "brunch" at our house to say "thank you" and to have them watch the final memorial program from Jim Kennedy's church at Coral Ridge in Ft. Lauderdale, Fran was speaking again as they gave his long sermon titled, "The Christian Manifesto"—videotaped when he preached in their church two years ago. Thank God for *His Word,* the Bible, preserved through the centuries. And thank God that at this point of history, films (as well as books, of course, and tapes) multiply what an individual can do with a vital message, and also prolong the time that content can be used with force. Incidentally, tapes are made of the funeral for those who were not able to come for one reason or another.

Lynn in Rochester had arranged for church bells to be rung for fifteen minutes at the close of the service so we walked out to the sound of bells. Fran was buried in Oakwood Cemetery there in Rochester where some weeks before he had requested to be buried, as he had asked me where I intended to live, and I very definitely said it would be right there in Rochester. I believe the Lord has wonderfully led me, and has prepared a house for me there, even as He has prepared a place for Fran in heaven. Franky had helped me choose a piece of land, a portion of grass with a tree on it midst old stones, speaking of history. It really is a quiet, grassy, tree-filled cemetery, and one Fran would have enjoyed walking around, reading stones of people who settled in Rochester in 1849, etc. Our service at the grave was a private one, with family, closest friends, pallbearers and their wives. Thank God for the Resurrection! Thank God it is not a myth, it is true—a promise given by the Creator of life who is able to resurrect the bodies He created in the first place. Tears flow freely—Jesus wept, too. But we comfort one another with the hope of resurrection, when the enemy, death, will be destroyed forever! Meantime, we are meant to go on and to *go on going on*—from "strength to strength." "Till He comes . . ."

Life! Life consists of so many repeated actions and jobs—nothing dramatic. It is "What is it all about?" that troubles many people, and if the "other base," the naturalist world view is right (that we are all a product of chance, that we are "a result of a succession of improbable accidents"), then there is no way to find meaning. L'Abri Workers have the base God gives us—which gives meaning and makes it imperative to make that truth known—but it isn't done with some airy-fairy ethereal floating above the humdrum work that has to be done while we move through from beginning to end of our years on earth. Just once in a while the sheer wonder comes into focus—such as Margaret's wedding and the reception—or at the memorial service at Huemoz—or in Rochester—or in Boston—or in London—when suddenly you look around and see "the harvest" of all the days and weeks and years of keeping on with each hour's *work.*

Udo has already been in Bolivia, Peru, and Kenya, and will be going to many countries to be well acquainted with the conditions in these countries for the starving people who need help. He will be teaching young workers (in Gryon, along with L'Abri students), helping to give a "world view," a "base" for doing such work. So many people who go out to so-called third-world countries, dewy-eyed and naive, from our Christian colleges, plunge immediately into sympathizing with socialism and Marxism, without seeing the horror of what has been clearly demonstrated by Afghanistan, and the treatment of real Christians in Soviet Russia, Siberian concentration camps, mental hospitals where drugs are administered, prisons, etc. Christians in this country are *so* easily sold a "bill of goods" in utter ignorance. Why? Because they read the propaganda of the leftist media. You need to hear Udo's lecture (on tape) from the L'Abri Conference in Knoxville, and also read Franky's book, *Bad News for Modern Man,* and Fran's *Great Evangelical Disaster.* It was a joy to Fran before he died to know that Udo would be studying these things and lecturing and writing on how third-world people could be given help in being *creative* with the raw materials that God has put in the world, and *produce* wealth, as well as being fed by others who have creatively produced enough to share.

In this new time of L'Abri, which Fran had hoped he could continue to have a part in, and *did* have a part in, in his new book before he died, in addition to "Child-Life," Ranald is also to be going to England for *two months* out of every year helping a project called "CARE" (which stands for Christian Action, Research, and Education).

Too much? No, too short a time to live. We each need to do as much as possible in the time we have left in *the battle!* This next generation coming along in *each* of the L'Abri branches is *important.* As I look out here (where I am writing) at the Greatham children racing around, sleeping in tents some nights, swinging on the big spruce tree—the Barrs' boys, the Seagren children, the Winters' children, and the Macaulays', I think of Huemoz with Giandy and his tennis, Matt and his hockey, and all the others coming along at different stages of life. I realize how very *soon* they will be the ones influencing our society. The handing of the torch; the relay of *truth* is titanically important to the *next* generation. Discussion starts at home. To teach "students" is of no value, unless one's own children have their questions answered as time goes on. Marxism—the black cloud over the world—needs to be understood by the new generation. Soviet supremacy is over 60 years old now in Russia and I am 69. I've lived with it all my life in the world's scene, but my youngest grandchildren have a different stage of history. They have come into history when the plans laid by Lenin are far more wide-sweeping in results, just as being in the world when abortion will be taught to them as a way of birth control not only by secular teachers, but even by Christian ethics teachers in certain places. The thought of L'Abri children, or of your own children, of what "Child-Life" can do for education, or of how we may better prepare our children for the onslaught of our enemy, is not simply an incidental sideline, but is *central*. We are meant to be "doers" of the Word, not simply "tellers," and part of being "doers" is what we are *living daily* that will be consistent and helpful to the next generation.

July 26—Greatham

Now I am half packed and need to go in a very few hours to Heathrow Airport and then on to Switzerland. Last night was another of those amazing times of seeing people all in one place—who brought back memories of years—some I had not seen for 24 years! It was the Memorial Service for Francis Schaeffer, held at All Souls Church, led by Ranald, with Jerram Barrs giving a sermon that was both strong and deeply moving; Os Guinness, reviewing his years at L'Abri, and not only what Fran has meant to so many people, but to him personally. It was a vivid reliving of history for me, and a fresh recognition of the wonder of how God has used one man who, though far from perfect, certainly had a singleness of purpose in defending truth and caring for people with great compassion. Steve Turner gave his review of how Fran's teaching in the area of the arts and culture, his recognition of the art of the Beatles, and understanding of the theater and poetry, etc., had released him, Steve, to be free to be a Christian and to write his poetry as well as helping so many others in the arts. Then Raymond Johnson spoke of what the film and book, *Whatever Happened to the Human Race?* and the speech at Hyde Park, and the March for Life to Trafalgar, etc., had meant to the Pro-life Movement in England. The people there came from every period of L'Abri history, and the tea and my shaking hands with people was heartwarming, even though exhausting physically. We'll have the energy in heaven to "catch up" with each other. As Sue and Ran pack to go to Chalet les Mélèzes, and as we review the years behind us and look to the next step, it is indeed the opening of a new chapter.

I want to end with the reassurance to each of us as to the marvel of our Heavenly Father's love and care for us and His diversity of meeting our needs. July 6th was our 49th wedding anniversary and I was dreading that day, as I felt it would be a sad time of shutting the door to weep in loneliness. The gentleness and creativity of the Lord's answering prayer and meeting my need was overwhelming to me. As Kirsteen, who is coming to live with me and go to Rochester College, is a pianist and composer, I had been praying for the right piano. I also felt strongly that the Lord would have me have concerts for various invited people, along with discussion. Shortly before our wedding anniversary, Mary Crowley had talked to me and said she wanted me to look for a second-hand Steinway at a certain price. It seemed a totally impossible task without perhaps a long, long time of research and even then!!! She wanted this to be a gift to L'Abri for our house, in memory of Francis Schaeffer. I let this be known, and only a day later, Mary Jane and Greg had their piano tuned, and in talking to the tuner, asked him if he knew of a second-hand Steinway for sale. His reply was that *he* had one. Mary Lou Sather, at the same time, saw an ad in the Mayo paper for a Steinway and phoned the number given. She had a long talk about its history and arranged to go to see it. It was the *same* piano! The day before our anniversary, a quartet of people whom *only the Lord could have put together* were on their way driving 25 miles out into the country to *see* that piano. There was Mary Lou, Janet Woods (the organist at Covenant Church), David Kemmer (an expert piano technician, much in demand all through the Midwest and South), and myself. Not one of us really had *time* to use that way. Our discovery was like finding hidden treasure. Each person according to the amount of experience as pianists, and David as an expert on all details concerning condition, etc., of the piano, myself with only an amateur's appreciation of the beauty of sound, felt enthralled with the perfection of this Steinway baby grand (i.e., 5 feet, 1 inch) as to "voice" and condition in every way, which was *being built* in 1935 at the time Fran and I were being married!!!! The price was *exactly* what Mary had named, and the next day (the 6th of July!) at noon, it was being carried into our living room where it looked as if it had been made for that particular spot! I feel *so* certain that the "voice" of this piano has been added by the Lord to that room to make up for Fran's missing voice! I am sure that there are to be concerts which will make the room come alive in a special way. I feel great thankfulness to the *Creator* of people in *His* image in order that they might make pianos, compose the music, perform and appreciate music. I feel in *awe* for the precise and gentle care of such a *Father*—Whom I know was also giving Fran special joy on that day of our anniversary in heaven. Childish of me? No, I don't think so. I was able to go out to the cemetery and put a fresh basket of yellow daisies and white chrysanthemums on Fran's grave with special love for the Lord, Whose we are and Whom we serve with increasing trust.

With very much love in the Lamb Who cares for His lambs with different kinds of supplies in different moments of need,

EDITH

December 18, 1984   Rochester, Minnesota

Dear, dear L'Abri Family:

For each of us another Christmas is approaching. How many have you had in your lifetime? We also know that as it has been all our lives, the new year will begin a *week* after Christmas! It *always* happens that way but somehow, I'm not ready for a new year, a new date. It has been seven months since Fran left his body and went to heaven to be in the presence of the Lord, but the year was 1984, and to have to begin living in 1985 seems like moving into another room a bit farther away. However, the reality of life and eternity, too, is that one day follows another with continuity that is unbroken. Time flows with minutes always touching each other. Time is continuing in heaven where Fran, Hans Rookmaaker, Georges Exhenry, Anne Bates, Captain Alms, Sarah Snyder, and others of our loved ones are. That flow of time will connect with that exact moment which will come in a succession of moments—the moment of Christ's return. Time doesn't get torn in bits, not really. It is our *use* of time that makes it seem fragmented, our use of time to fall into some slough of despond, or into some dungeon of Satan's castle of despair! We fragment time and spoil the reality of the comfort and hope we have been given to have when we frantically push away reality that has been explained clearly to us by God in His Word. He knows us so well and understands our need of constant reminders of the swift approach, not only of new days and new years, but of that new life ahead of us which is connected with our life now. . . .

So many of God's children act as if they had no way that is different from the humanistic psychologist's way of finding out anything. So many of God's people say words that they don't *act* upon and don't base their emotions upon. How often do we—you and I—insult our eternal, all-wise, perfect, understanding Father by saying aloud, or in a whisper, "I wish I had—someone to talk to. I wish I had someone's advice and help." Well, we do. We have the Creator to Whom we can talk and Whose advice we can ask about everything. "Ask" is what He tells us, and when we worry about things, fuss about things, and spend no time asking, we are in danger of really acting as if God did not exist—and could therefore not be called upon at all!!! Our desire, as well as excitement in approaching a new year, and a new day, and a new hour, should be that we need to take the immediate opportunity, the present moment to *act* upon what we say we believe. We may not have many of those minutes left to live in the reality of hope. We may suddenly be ashamed because there is no going backwards and reliving.

Right at that minute, this typewriter went "berserk." It began to race through lines and lines of dashes without stopping, and then the keys locked! My night hours had to be turned into writing letters by hand, wrapping some Christmas presents, and then calling for a repair person in the morning! Did I pray? Yes, I did, thinking that maybe the devil was trying to make me deny my thoughts within seconds of expressing them. The repair person—a woman skilled in searching out trouble spots in typewriters—discovered a tiny pin out of place, a fine spring not working. Her statement was, "After working on this for nearly two hours, I am not sure, but I think maybe the original making of this IBM in Switzerland was a time of the fellow dipping into the wrong bin for a pin. He must have picked up the wrong size. Call me again if it doesn't work."

Perhaps that story is needed by *all* of us at the beginning of this year! Think for a moment. If indeed a workman dipped into the wrong bin for a tiny hidden part of a typewriter, which wrong piece would suddenly make that typewriter stop working properly many months later in a distant place thousands of miles away, *just* at a time when 24 hours were to be "eaten up" when they were badly needed, think what an effect that man's tiny action had on certain events in history! After she did all she could do and I had said goodbye and begun to type, *again* things went wrong. And now five *more* hours have passed by! Is this letter being "plagued"? Or am I being given a vivid lesson to pass on to you? Do you, do I, feel at times our little piece of life is so "hidden in history" that it wouldn't matter whether we dipped into the "right bin" or the "wrong bin" in our choices in small areas? Are we in danger of saying or thinking or feeling, "It doesn't matter a bit what I do or fail to do. I'm inconsequential, and my small choices make no difference."???? Let's remember that what we do right now will have an effect in a future moment of time, in a distant place, when someone will be affected by what we did or neglected to do properly! . . .

The last Family Letter was finished in Greatham L'Abri in England. After that, I spent time in Gryon and Huemoz. Although, of course, I wept for Fran at times and missed him at many turns of the road, yet I had very new possibilities. I have never stayed with any of my children in their homes in Switzerland in all these years, as I always was needed in our own chalet caring for my own home, husband, and those who came to us. Now this summer I stayed a few days with Prisca and John and Giandy—a special treat of being able to hear the village bell ring with the hours of the night, a sound I had not had in midnight hours since we left Chalet les Mélèzes. I was also able to really *be* a part of the Sandri family's days, not only in the chalet but going to see Giandy play in a tennis tournament in Geneva. It was a new chapter in life for me. Then I was able to stay with Debby and Udo and the four girls in Chalet Montaux in Gryon and hear the cowbells as we used to hear them in Champéry. Eating with them and their L'Abri students in the sunshine of the garden transported me into memories of not only Champéry, but brought back memories of so many hikes with Fran, as the view there is so like the views of our mountain walks. My busy years in L'Abri have not held time to be in my children's and grandchildren's chalets enough to share day-by-day breakfast, lunch, and dinner succession, and this was a gentle gift from the Lord.

My time in Switzerland also included being able to be in Chalet les Mélèzes during some of the first hours after Sue and Ran and their children arrived to live in our old home, the first L'Abri house. It carried me back through the years to have tea and refreshments served in the old living room and to discuss with five musicians, brought by Bish, who had given a wonderful classic concert in the chapel. Our discussion that night with the musicians, Sue and Ran, Prisca and myself, a missionary family, some other students, and Kirsty and Fiona serving us tea with cheese and crackers so *very* much reminded me of our early years in that same living room. Actually, it had been 12 years since I had sat and discussed that way in that room. . . .

There were Monday morning times when I talked in the chapel, sitting in my old place on the fireplace; Sunday services and a Church meeting at Simone's home in Bex one Sunday afternoon, giving time to talk to each other as a congregation. There were special times with Birdie, and a concert in Saanan with Yehudi Menuhin (all of the family and Birdie and John Jackson went together). There was a Workers' tea for me at Larry's and Nancy's, and Josianne André's wedding in Lausanne that Ran and I went to. There was a shopping day in Lausanne with Debby, and an amazing time of talking to an Italian professor of psychology (translated by his filmmaker son) in their summer chalet in Villars. This professor, formerly of Rome University with his own clinique on Cyprus, became interested through Dr. Gandur's giving him Fran's books. I wished Fran could have been the one talking, but I knew that he would have been so glad that Dr. Gandur had given his books to this man and that the conversation had been so full. The next day the professor's wife came to Debby's Bible class (which is in French in Bea Fretz's home). When they come back to Villars, Lord willing, she expects to continue in that class. She obviously liked it.

There was a time of visiting Mlle. Chaudet in her chalet, and Alice and Marinette in their apartment above the post office. It doesn't seem possible that they will soon be retiring. Priscilla was with me, and we remembered together our years of being in Huemoz and walking along those familiar roads since 1955. There were brief conversations on trains and buses with Swiss people whom I wouldn't have been meeting otherwise. . . .

We had our family reunion in August. It was our 14th annual reunion. Fran was missing, but he is as much a part of the family as ever, simply joining other parts of the family where we will all be one day reunited. Becky and Rodman were there, looking forward to the birth of their first baby in December, to be Prisca's and John's first grandchild and our first great-grandchild! Now that piece of time has gone by, and on December 14th at 6:20 A.M. Kimberly Anne, 7 lbs. 9 oz., was born in Athens, Georgia (where Rodman is a student in the university getting his Master's

This was our first family reunion after Fran joined the reunion of past generations in heaven.

degree in newspaper management). Everything went well and they are very excited about this baby's arrival into their arms, her beauty and sweetness. We'll be waiting to welcome her to the next family reunion. So we are now a four-generation family!

You remember that I told you in the last letter that Kirsty Macaulay, one of my granddaughters, was coming to live with me and go to the community college here. She began school at that point (in September when I had returned to Rochester) and we enjoyed sharing this home and our lives. One day, a crew of five from Dutch television came from Holland to work for two-and-one-half days with me for a program. They had me sit and discuss, answer questions, prepare a recipe, talking as I mixed flour and grated lemon peel to make Lemon Creme Scones, answer questions about the importance of serving food, and having mealtime conversations in a family. They had me walk in the woods and up a road, etc., etc. Also, they filmed Kirsty at school playing volleyball and then at the piano with my sitting beside her, and our talking to each other. The big question was, "What about the age gap?" Really, it isn't age that matters; it is personality, ideas, creativity, imagination, originality, listening to each other, and learning new things from each other. That series of things should be taking place all through life across many "age gaps"!!! They also took time filming a family with their children—my Christian lawyer, Peter Sandburg, and his wife, Cindy, and children. If you are in Holland, you may see it!

I also told you last time about the Steinway piano. Our first concert took place in September, and we had about 36 people for a special dinner and a classical trio playing chamber music. We were all delighted with the way the room lends itself to concerts. It seems the Lord planned the design of that living room back in the 1920s, using an architect who surely had a genius for proportions and balance. The next concert-dinner (dinner first, then the concert), I gave in honor of Dr. Petitt, to thank him for his care of Fran through the five-and-a-half years. Also, it was to thank the other doctors who had treated Fran with dignity and care. There were 36 people at this, too, (or maybe 38). The chrysanthemums and white candles, the food and conversation, all went smoothly and beautifully. . . .

Ran had come to the U.S. in November to participate in a conference in California. This L'Abri Conference at Arrowhead Springs in San Bernardino was a full L'Abri Conference which took place as a direct result of the conference in Knoxville where Fran took part for his last time on a platform. Ran and I went on to Washington, D.C., from the California Conference. Ran then returned with me to Rochester to talk with the Workers, and to visit Kirsty. He also went out to Fran's grave with me, where we stood in the snow and prayed. I am always thankful to go to the place where his precious body is, knowing full well that *he* is not there—he is away from his body until the resurrection. Yet the body is precious to the Lord, as He died and rose again so that our *bodies* might be raised to allow us to be in the same bodies, changed like His precious body, to live forever!! He created the bodies in the first place, and He never meant them to be dead.

Udo came on Friday of that same week in time to go to the Chinese Christian Fellowship with me where I spoke (and each sentence was translated into Mandarin as I spoke), and Udo answered questions (also translated into Mandarin). . . .

This next February 14th it will be 30 years since we were told to get out of Champéry—and out of all of Switzerland. Do celebrate that day!!! Celebrate it by thanking God for all *He* has done in answer to prayer in thousands of lives throughout those 30 years. Celebrate it by praying for L'Abri *now*—for each branch and for each Worker, and for all the children of L'Abri families and for the *content* of people's discussions and lectures, and for sensitivity to the importance of the issues of today, and for eyes of understanding to be always open to the dangers of Satan's subtle lies coming so often from the lips of "angels of light." We are not immune to his camouflage of critical and dangerous ideas. Ideas change the world. Ideas can destroy and undermine, even as Marxism crept in as "the answer" to the world's problems of hunger back in 1918 and on from then, and fooled so many idealistic people to the destruction of millions, and to the destruction of freedom in so much of the world.

Of the many examples from each branch this one comes from Lisa on December 4th: "Staffan lectured at a seminar on bioethics in Gothenburg. He was able to speak strongly on the basis of human life in contrast to the cynicism and dangerous idealism expressed by politicians and some of the leading medical researchers in Sweden. Staffan was invited to this seminar by some young Christian doctors who really stand for Truth—and need support. . . ." As Susan wrote from Huemoz, she began with this:

It has been a deep joy after the sorrow of my dad's death and the inevitable insecurity of change, to move back to Les Mélèzes after 24 years. This has meant seeing the Mélèzes living room returned to the former atmosphere when L'Abri started. Dad and Mother gave us the sea painting for over the fireplace and the bookshelves that were in the room, made out of the packing boxes that brought our things in 1948.

Last year this December, I sat by Dad's bed in Aigle hospital. He held my hand quietly, and as the trains ran past, we knew our human lives were ebbing. He talked to me about the *next* generation of Christians. He talked as one on the eve of that great, last journey, that strange moment when you realize your children will live to see the next chapter that for you is closing. Well, the Lord granted Dad the writing of his book for all of us; *The Great Evangelical Disaster* is essential. I now understand, after reading it, the pain in that afternoon! Will the Christian church make it through to the *next* generation, or not? Are we selling our birthright for a mess of pottage? Dad lay quietly and there was the pain of wondering, 'Has our generation of Christians gone too far in accommodating the worldly spirit?'

Our prayer is this: that this little mountain outpost will continue to shine with truth and love—the truth and love of *The God Who Is There*. Perfect? No, oh no! We are really rather pathetic, which is why we need your prayers, all of us. 'Unless the *Lord* build this house, we labor in vain.' . . .

I would say here what Fran so often said, "The Holy Spirit does not get behind times. He helps us to fight *today's* battles, not those of 50 years ago. We need to stay close to the Lord to be ready to fight what needs fighting today." I feel very strongly that the Lord has kept L'Abri as a whole, through individual Members and Workers and their individual study and perceptiveness, "up to date" with world issues and world needs.

I'll go on a bit here and report what Udo has given me. Udo is lecturing, writing articles, and preparing a book in this area. He is dealing with the ideas in the minds of Christians concerning the issues of world hunger and economic development. He stresses the polarization between the secularists and the Christian left, which has been so vocal, but not Biblical, confusing the issues without providing help. Both sides seem to forget the influence of ideas on living situations, and the effect of false religions in people's lives: Where hunger and disasters are so often produced by a faulty and inaccurate view of God's creation, and denying the Fall and its effects.

I am finishing this now on December 20th—well, it's about 1 A.M. so it is the 21st—and in just five-and-one-half hours I'll be on my way to the airport to go "home" for Christmas. Just ten days left in this year now! And what a very drastic year it has been. A year ago, Fran had his major operation, with Dr. Mucha removing half of his colon. Priscilla was here, and Rodman and Becky—and the weather was the coldest on record! This year, as Christmas approaches, Rodman and Becky are in the warm clime of Georgia and their first baby will be eleven days old on Christmas, and Priscilla will be knitting away for her grandchild.

The greatest continuity for each one of us personally, as well as for the work, is our unchanging, dependable, faithful, loving Lord, our Heavenly Father Who never leaves us nor forsakes us. As we step into another year, it is not with any guarantee of things being easier this year than last, nor of any perfection being just around the corner, unless Christ's second coming is to be tomorrow!!!!

For you and for me, the best greeting we can give each other as we step in 1985 is, "Remember, 'He will never leave you nor forsake you.' " What a promise to cling to when the winds blow! A promise from One Who is able to keep promises!!

With love *in* the faithful Shepherd *from* one of His sheep!

EDITH

1985

Dear scattered Family of L'Abri:

How consistent are we?

On what do we base our security?

Does our immediate action, and before that our basic reaction, spring from the base we set forth to live upon?

How realistically do we live in the light of the ongoing, never-ending battle during which day by day the devil has new ways of upsetting us with his wiles and schemes?

How does our fear become changed to quietness?

Fears come in many forms: fear of not having enough money, or not having enough to eat, or not having a house to live in, of not having a job, or not having physical strength sufficient to *do* the necessary things day by day, fear of failure to meet some human standard, fear of scorn by other human beings, fear of fires, floods, earthquakes, famines, and fear of accident or some dread disease. Fear of having too much to do and too short a time and too little strength to do it can be matched by fear of having too little to do, and not enough completed projects to be satisfied with one's accomplishments.

Fear of not knowing or being able to find the Lord's leading, can be matched by fear of taking what seems to be a "rash step" to *do* what the Lord is leading you to do. Fear of the Lord's *not* answering prayer can be so very suddenly turned into strong fear when His answer comes—that is the fear of all that His answer involves.

Indeed, this thing of fear and uncertainty is not simple. Our Shepherd, our Guide, our Counselor, our Leader, our Protector, can be *in* the boat with us and we can still cry out in fear, and even make decisions based on that fear, turning away from Him without analyzing it, instead of actively trusting Him, and looking only to Him to give us a solution in the face of sudden danger, sudden fear. We are in danger of being guilty of the same feelings the disciples had when the storm rocked the boat, the storm which had suddenly come up while Jesus was there asleep, in the same boat with them.

I know I am in that danger, and I think I can speak for all of us!

"And his disciples came to him, and awoke him, saying, Lord, save us: we perish. And he saith unto them, Why are ye fearful, O ye of little faith? Then he arose, and rebuked the winds and the sea; and there was a great calm" (Matthew 8:25,26).

What was wrong with what the disciples *said*? On the face of it, they were calling to the right Person, the Lord, for help. However, we *know* their attitude did not please the Lord. We know they could not have had the faith that He tells us is not only important, but necessary.

What kind of faith is required? Hebrew 11:6 gives a clear explanation "But without faith it is impossible to please him; for he that cometh to God must believe that he is, and that he is a rewarder of them that diligently seek him."

I Timothy 2:8 speaks of God's desire that people pray everywhere . . . "lifting up holy hands, without wrath and doubting." People that doubt are compared with winds that blow first in one direction and then another.

How, from those five words—"Lord, save us: we perish"—could Jesus possibly have replied, "Why are ye fearful, o ye of little faith?"

Of course, the answer is obvious. We can't fool God with our words. He knows our attitudes, our thoughts, our emotions, our feelings. God knows our fears and doubts. He knows precisely what is behind our words. We may pray with very right-sounding *words* for God's direction and help, while we are mentally working out solutions to our problems using our own ideas of how to be "safe."

We know what was in the disciples' minds that day because Jesus' reply makes it clear that they were fearful to the degree of *not* trusting Him. He makes it clear that they had little faith bound up in their request of Him to save them. They did not have expectancy of help coming.

Also, when they exclaimed with a sharp question after Jesus had calmed the waves, "What manner of man is this?" they revealed very clearly that they had *not* come to Him believing that He was the Creator God and that nothing was too hard for Him. They didn't know that He would diligently reward them for coming to Him.

Does consistency then mean we will never have fears?? A thousand times no! Uncertainty as to decisions and choices, a variety of fears, depending on what our weaknesses are and what our strengths are, *hit* us from without, and gnaw at us from within.

It is *what we do* about our fears and uncertainties that we need constantly to examine and reexamine. We are strongly warned not to "go to Egypt for help," we are told *never* to go to fortune tellers or people that foretell the future—"beware of those that peep and mutter" is a very clear picture of someone looking into a crystal ball!!! Of *that* we are to be afraid!! Isaiah is told not to go into a confederacy with a certain people, "neither fear ye their fear, nor be afraid. Sanctify the Lord of hosts himself and let him be your fear, and let him be your dread. And he shall be for you a sanctuary" (Isaiah 8:13,14).

Fear of the Lord is a very different thing. He *is* our hiding place, our sanctuary in which we may be protected and released from other fears. Over and over again we may run *to* Him asking that our faith be constantly increased, remembering that the present "thing" is only temporary!

"*Now I know* that the Lord saveth his anointed; he will hear him from his holy heaven with the saving strength of his right hand. Some trust in chariots, and some in horses: but we will remember the name of the Lord our God. . . . Save, Lord, let the King hear us when we call" (Psalm 20:6,7,9).

When James in chapter 2, verse 17, says, "Even so faith, if it hath not works is dead, being alone," he is speaking of works based on faith. He has just spoken of not turning people away who need food or clothing—who come to the door, but supplying physical things, material things. In other words, sharing what *is* there to share. This is *not* speaking of having no property, but speaking clearly of believing that *God will supply* my needs in answer to prayer, so that I then can divide what I have at the present time, believing that God will give more to be shared tomorrow.

This is July 4th—*thirty years ago* it was July 4, 1955!!! In two days on July 6th our golden wedding anniversary takes place. Yes, Fran is in heaven and has been there for one year and seven weeks, but I want you to look at something. We were married on July 6, 1935—L'Abri was just getting started in Huemoz July 6, 1955—This means, and I am speaking to the next generation, we had been married just 20 years when L'Abri began. I was 39 (my birthday is not until November) and Fran was 41. When we made the decision—the choice, the agreement—together to "live by faith"—when we defined that choice as a desire to "show forth the existence of God by our lives and our work," we were young and our children were ages 17, 13, 9, and not quite 3.

It was not "safe" by the world's standards to do what we made a decision to do. It would not have been considered practical or prudent! . . . Fran thought we were taking a step that would insure our never being heard of again. He *really* thought, and so did I, that we would be talking to one's and two's, and perhaps to a half dozen or a dozen people in that old chalet, and that a trickle of ideas that he felt were terribly important would seep out through the people that the Lord would bring, but that it would be so minimal that results would *not* be seen. We prayed that it would, however, make a difference.

We would take hands off and step out of the driver's seat, and let the Lord "drive"; and have a large enough area of reality in which to live by prayer alone that the watching world could observe that it was only God who could have "sent the fire," so to speak. We resolved that we would attempt in some practical forms to live with a willingness to face "the hosts of the Midianites with all their weapons, with only the lamps, pitchers and trumpets in our hands." We were small enough to be a Daniel, a Joseph in prison, a Gideon with only three hundred men to face thousands. We were weak enough only to be able to do what God would give us the strength to do.

We had no way of being able to turn a page to see what would happen! If we had "waited to see what would happen" *before* taking a step that was unsafe, nothing ever would have happened. . . . Our feeling of assurance was that the Lord's guidance always comes in the midst of situations which make *taking that guidance a thing that is difficult.* The constant, *constant* succession of the Lord's clear direction needing to be *acted* upon *before* the next step is shown, or before the next solution is given, is something Fran always called, "getting your feet *wet* in Jordan." Now— what did he mean? Do you remember that when the priests came to the edge of the Jordan River (chapter 3 of Joshua) ready to have God fulfill His promise that the waters would roll back, it was not until their feet were wet because they had started to cross by stepping into the edge of the river expectantly that the waters of Jordan parted and "stood in a heap"? God said they must step in first. My husband always spoke of that historic happening when we would come to a place of decision like that—a great diversity of situations—but each with a moment of taking a "step of faith" . . . that is, a step during which one's "feet," so to speak, became "wet." Waiting to be "safe" and having everything dry first is *not*, so Fran always said, what we are meant to do.

Let me bring you up to date for a moment. When Fran asked me to buy a house near St. Mary's Hospital and move from Switzerland, if I had "waited to be safe," all the things that happened this past year would *never* have happened. The chalet has not yet been sold. Or it might have been safer to wait and see whether Fran would live! That would mean he would *never* have known that I was willing to move for his sake. Also, it would mean he probably would *not* have had the incentive to work on his book in the hospital, nor to pray for, and fight for, life to do the 12 Seminars. Later, we would not have had a home for him to come to for his last days; he would not have heard his favorite old records, nor his clocks, nor would he have had a place as a family to *be* during those so-important days surrounding that time. . . .

Had I not decided within a few hours to go ahead and fulfill Fran's request, and chosen to buy this house when I did, not only would the last weeks of his life have been different, and the family's togetherness here been different, *but* the Steinway piano 281261 would never have arrived last July 6th!

That piano has been the "spark" that brought forth leading for what I believe is one of the most important books I have ever written. *Forever Music* would never have been written and I am as sure as I am of the unfolding of any portion of our lives that I have written about, that this book is what the Lord has prepared me to write during the years Fran and I have been together.

Not only did God lead me to buy this house so that I would be shown that this book was my next work, but He brought me here to have this house be a part of the Rochester branch of L'Abri, so that we could have high teas and concerts here for a cross section of people, and so that there would be a place for Bo Bush to have a one-man sculpture show along with concerts. This actual house, this particular garden with its trees (all hidden in snow and ice when I saw it and signed papers), has had a use, and will still have uses which were *not known by me* in making the choice. How often must we (I mean me too) be told that God does not give us a "blueprint" to encourage us? . . . we need to check up on ourselves as to whether we are taking our opportunities to demonstrate our trust, as well as to demonstrate His existence . . . *In time.* . . .

"Bring the people of your choice, please Lord" is a prayer that was being answered as Franky began making films, first, *How Should We Then Live?* and then *Whatever Happened to the Human Race?*, *The Second American Revolution* and others brought people to Seminars held in cities all over the States and later in other countries. But the *answering* of that prayer meant long, tough hours of working, traveling, getting up at all hours, all "in time." "It's almost too late to do anything about abortion," said Dr. Koop when that film began to be prepared, but it was made "in time" to give life to many who would never have lived! . . .

Several L'Abri conferences were held in Australia recently and Udo, Wim, Dick Keyes, Donald Drew, and Barry Seagren were the speakers. Response has been one of people declaring that they have never had such teaching before. "I didn't ever hear about a 'world view' being important and had never been taught what a difference that would make in absolutely everything I do. Oh, I want to go on reading books and listening to tapes and I hope L'Abri comes back here again, or that I can go to one of the branches." . . .

The *timing* of acting on whatever it is God is guiding us to do is crucial. To "wait and see" in certain moments of life is to not only be too late to do anything at all, but to miss the next step of God's leading dependent on having taken the step He placed before us. "Wet feet" have to come first!!!

In the Huemoz branch Susan tells me that all the chalets are full, and three families have rented chalets "outside" in order to be there studying. She said that at present less than half are Americans. Others are from South Africa, Australia, European countries, and other parts of the world. It is a very international mixture at present. That lets us know a tiny bit of who the Lord is sending—but so little, really! Gryon, too, has had the ones the Lord has brought back from past years as well as new people. The door must be there, and someone on the other side to open it! In *time.* . . .

I remember many years ago we had had 60 "reservations" for the month of August in Huemoz, and on one day 30 of those were supposed to arrive, but *not* one of them did! But 29 other people did, "unexpectedly"! Is that an orderly way to arrange things? I though at the time it was *very* orderly, God's order.

Here in Rochester right now we are being shown some of the reasons for our houses being so close to Mayo Clinic and St. Mary's Hospital and Methodist Hospital. It is very clear that part of our geographic location is to be a "door" close enough to be found and knocked upon by people in distress. . . .

A phone call came to Mary Jane from a nurse she did not know at St. Mary's Hospital saying, "I have a patient 50 years old—a man who has just been told that he has only six months to live. It is a serious heart condition; he is shattered. Could someone from L'Abri come and visit him?" Greg went later that same day. Why are we in Rochester? Which phone call is important to answer? Which bump, or knock at the door?

Jim Ingram, Greg Grooms, and Mike Sugimoto are giving lectures. Those attending the lectures come not only from among students who are residents here for a length of time, but from Minneapolis, Iowa, and places in Wisconsin. Some drove this Monday night over 75 miles to come. Discussions go on until late—midnight this Monday. The fact that a farmer, a carpenter, a graphic artist, a doctor, a nurse, a lawyer, an interior designer (of large hotels, etc.), a pilot, a home schooling mother/ teacher, a laboratory technician at the hospital, a surgeon, a piano technician, a singer, a medical student, listen, discuss, think, read, come back and continue coming, along with many other people of different professions, means that in many different places *something different is being done, or* some of the same things are being done differently. . . .

What God tells us heaven will be full of is not narrow as to *kinds* of people and backgrounds. The *way* is narrow, in that it is through The Lamb, and has never changed. We are spiritual children of Abraham because we come through the same Lamb that he looked forward to as he brought the lamb in sacrifice, looking forward to the Messiah. But as for *kinds* of people, the description is *wide*. "Some from every tribe, and nation, and kindred and people will be *there*." A diversity of people all there through the same Lamb. . . .

May this letter make *His faithfulness known*, in some small way!! May He be "our glory and strength" as we call out to Him, "You are my Father, my God, the Rock, my Saviour" (Psalm 89:26).

Just yesterday, July 10, 1985, those of us in the Rochester branch of L'Abri had a vivid observation of the extent of the Lord's bringing people of His choice to L'Abri, *and* of His taking them to diverse parts of the world to use them as "salt and light." Invitations had gone out to those in the area who have been interested in L'Abri here in the past, to come for a buffet supper, and for a lecture and discussion. They came, and kept coming. It had not been a general announcement and about 65 had been expected, but we found the food disappeared and were fearful there was not enough. Our rough estimate was that about 85 or more had arrived. In the midst of a hot spell with thunderstorms, the Lord gave us an idyllic evening as people wandered about the lawn, sat on the deck, ate their sandwiches and vegetable "dips" and drank lemonade to the sound of tinkling ice, a murmur of voices, and children's shrieks of laughter. The lecture took place outdoors as the sunset gave a rosy background through the leafy canopy of trees.

Vishal Mangalwadi (or, as he was known to us in Swiss L'Abri during his six months of study at Gentiana some years ago, "Kumar"), and his wife, Ruth, are Indian and have been doing a work for years now in his own country, as God has led him in answer to his prayer for a balanced meeting of the needs of his country based on *truth*, not on compromise. As he spoke to us in the cool of the day, the dusk deepening into dark, we could almost imagine that we had been transported to India. As Vishal made a clear declaration that the basis of India's poverty consisted of its oppression by a government which is a part of the kingdom of darkness, an enemy of the kingdom of light, he drew a vivid contrast of these two realities of the supernatural universe. His work is making the truth of God's existence known, and helping Indians understand how to come to Him through Christ, how to step out of the kingdom of darkness into the kingdom of light, and also is a work which fights the results of that kingdom of darkness—the poverty which results from an oppression by a government ruling "in darkness." His "Association for Comprehensive Rural Assistance" assists lower-caste Hindu farmers near Chatarpur, India, to get fair prices for their grain, and to reduce the price they must pay for fertilizer and irrigation into something by which they may make a profit, instead of being constantly ground down into deeper poverty. He is *against* liberation theology and all the ideas connected with the Marxist trend, and openly links the poverty to heavy government power. The idea is not to overthrow, but to limit that power which keeps the poor poor and gives no place for advancement coupled with making plain the Biblical teaching of the dignity and value of all human beings. What Vishal and Ruth have learned at L'Abri, they are putting into action, into practice in a way which is making an enormous difference. This is just one small example of the diversity of results we are now beginning to see. . . .

Thirty years have passed since the first decisions were made based on answered prayer and practical unfolding, which led to seemingly "rash" or "unsafe" or "imprudent" choices and actions. But as we walk into this next chapter of the work in each one of the branches, in the lives and work of each one of the wider family let us listen to Him speaking in the first chapter of Joshua: "Moses my servant is dead; now therefore arise, go over this Jordan, thou, and all this people, unto the land which I do give to them, even to the children of Israel. Every place that the sole of your foot shall tread upon, that have I given unto you, as I said to Moses

... There shall not any man be able to stand before thee all the days of thy life; as I was with Moses, so I will be with thee: I will not fail thee, nor forsake thee. Be strong and of a good courage ..."

As we step out into the next chapter, let us be strong and of good courage and remember that we are not to deviate because of any "man standing before us ..." We are to have a faithful leader, God Himself, who will always be with us. May famines, pestilences, rumors of war, fire, floods, earthquakes, and what is worse, Satan's thrusts through false teaching and counterfeit *not stop our walk in the path as the Lord is leading us toward His final goal* in the finishing of what He had begun!!

With very much love in our *Leader,*

EDITH

November 30, 1985 Rochester, Minnesota

Dear Family:

... In preparation for writing this, I have just read the July 4th Family Letter. It is a shock that such a long time has passed by. However, my re-reading that letter was a great help to me, and the *content* is that which I still need and I am sure you do too. In fact, it is a good letter to copy for anyone who wants to know what L'Abri is all about. Also, the Scripture in it is what we need as we approach a new year. For each of us personally, and for L'Abri as a whole (in each branch and in the decisions to be made by Members when they meet together in early March), we need to really *trust* the Lord and ask for a renewed measure of trust as we declare again: "Some trust in chariots and some in horses, but we trust in the name of the Lord our God" (Psalm 20:7).

That trust is attacked over and over again as we continue to live and work in an abnormal world, in a history that continues to be one lived in a stream of afflictions until the final victory takes place and the enemy, "death," is destroyed. There are many interruptions to planned schedules and to our expectations as to where we will *be* geographically, in health, in strength and energy, and the "what" as well as the "where" and "how" of our work. Sudden changes come, and the very suddenness is a shock to us, filling us with sudden feelings of dismay. That reaction of dismay is one that needs to be dealt with, and we need to read, and re-read, the verbalized help God has meant to have passed down from generation to generation.

The words that Moses spoke into the ears of all the congregation of Israel were the words of this song (Deuteronomy 32:3,4, 10–12):

Because I will publish the name of the Lord: ascribe ye greatness unto our God.

He is the Rock, his work is perfect: for all his ways are judgment: a God of truth and without iniquity, just and right is he. . . .

He found him in a desert land, and in the waste howling wilderness; he led him about, he instructed him, he kept him as the apple of his eye. As an eagle stirreth up her nest, fluttereth over her young, spreadeth abroad her wings, taketh them, beareth them on her wings: so the Lord alone did lead him, and there was no strange god with him.

This is our God who speaks to us as Moses spoke to Joshua with God's words of promise . . . "And the Lord, he it is that doth go before thee; he will be with thee, he will not fail thee, neither forsake thee: fear not, neither be dismayed" (Deuteronomy 31:8).

This reality of God's dependability, this need of living with trust in Him, this constant reminding of *what* He has done in the past, is what is to be passed on to the next generation of children and the next and the next!! "Gather the people together, men, and women, and children, and thy stranger that is within thy gates, that they may *hear*, and that they may learn, and fear the Lord your God, and observe to do all the words of this law: And that their children, which have not known any thing, may hear, and learn to fear the Lord your God, as long as ye live in the land whither ye go over Jordan to possess it" (Deuteronomy 31:12–13).

Why are we to tell each other not to be dismayed? What is it our *children* are to hear from us? It all springs from God's unswerving commands and promises through eons of history as He spoke to His people based on *truth*, the truth of His existence and of His accepting us as His children through Christ. As His children, as His people, we are under His command.

"Have I not commanded thee? Be strong and of a good courage; be not afraid, neither be thou dismayed: for the Lord thy God is with thee whithersoever thou goest" (Joshua 1:9).

To keep on being dismayed and afraid (without a change) is to disobey the Lord, and to act as if *He* were *not* with us "whithersoever" we go!!!! Without a change? I put that in parentheses because of course we do not ever go on without fluctuations. We will not be perfect until Christ returns to change us in a twinkling of an eye . . . which means we will not be perfect in our trust either. We will have ups and downs. *But*—we are not meant to stay down. We are meant to get out our Bibles and read Deuteronomy, Joshua, Psalms, Isaiah . . . and remember that the Lord will indeed go with us in this time of history.

Last week Jim Ingram went to New York with me to help me not only in the travel, but in the next steps to be taken in preparation for my book, *Forever Music*, and for the concert which will be the "debut" of that book, introducing it to the music world. The art work for the first announcement of the concert needed to be shown to the Manager of the Guarneri Quartet for his approval, and the book cover and that announcement also needed to be shown the vice president and others at Steinway. There were people to talk to such as Caroline Rossi Copeland, director of The Lambs theater at 44th Street, and Franz Mohr, the master technician at Steinway, and Daniel Majeske, the concertmaster of the Cleveland Orchestra and his son, Stephen, also a violinist in the Cleveland Orchestra. We had a schedule of some of these appointments, and the Lord opened far more than was on the schedule so that it was hard to have time for Josephine Carpenter and me to go over the "list" to be invited, and other details. Time after time as I have been in New York, first to do research for this book, then to begin preparations for the concert to present the book to a new audience, I have been astounded at the many unexpected developments and encouragements which could *not* have been planned. It has reminded me of the beginning days of L'Abri, with assurances and confirmations of making the "right choices" as answers to prayer have come.

We came back on Friday, later than expected because of a baggage-man's mistake. (He had *not* put the baggage in the trunk of the taxi, although he had taken a tip for it! And the fact was not noticed until we were at La Guardia.) This caused us to have to take a double trip to the airport! After all the exciting openings that had come, this seemed like a very minor "down" and we used our time well, discussing various things concerning L'Abri in general and the Rochester branch in particular. A schedule was also drawn up for the next few days. Jim would be taking little Jimmy and Gail to see *Peter and the Wolf* the next afternoon. I had a work list and menu to think about for the big High Tea and concert at my house scheduled for 6:30 P.M. Sunday night. Jim said he could come and talk to people at the tea, and then go home and put the boys to bed while Gail would come to the concert.

But the minor "down" of a double trip to the airport was nothing compared to the sudden *drastic* change in Jim's schedule. It was only a half-hour after arriving home that Jim came up to this house, looking terribly serious. "May I speak to you for a moment?" What came forth was the account of a tragic accident. Jim's best friend from high school who, with his wife and children visited Jim and Gail from Canada last summer, had called him a half-hour after Jim's return from New York. Almost incoherent, the best friend had sobbingly poured out his grief and shock! Just hours before the call, his wife (a visiting nurse) had been driving home when another car swerved into her lane on a snowy road and had hit her car head-on. The two ladies in the other car had not been hurt. Jim's friend's wife had been instantly killed!!

This friend had been like another son to Jim's parents, and as a brother to Jim. The flight was arranged immediately, and by six the next morning, Jim was on his way to a small Canadian town not too far from Toronto.

What has God said to us, *His* children? He has made tremendously clear the fact that we can*not* know *what* tomorrow will bring, and that in speaking of our projected "schedule" we *must* say, "Lord willing, I shall do thus and so." We have been warned that we do *not* know what tomorrow will bring; we do *not* know what is around the corner of the bend in the road.

Whether it is the sudden crash of two cars and the death of that young mother, or the slower invasion of cancer into Francis Schaeffer's lymph glands and his death after six years of battle and very productive work in the midst of that battle, other lives are affected by any such happenings. Not only were Jimmy, David, and Gail's expectations changed to disappointment by Jim's need to fly off, but the church in Rochester of which John Smith is pastor missed Jim, and the L'Abri staff here missed Jim in all the diversity of the work here in L'Abri from writing receipts and thank-you letters to lecturing and talking with students, caring for the business details, and many things in the preparation for the Christmas High Tea and concert. There is a widening ripple of effect when any *one* of us has a sudden change in "plans," "schedule," so that we are in another place—another city, or hospital, or—heaven!

Veronica Seagren's sudden need of an operation, followed by the encouraging news that the doctors felt the cancer had been contained in a tumor and that it had been removed without affecting other organs, was a sudden change that affected Barry and the children, every other Worker in Greatham L'Abri and also the rest of us in all the other branches . . . and many friends of Veronica and Barry's who prayed earnestly and waited for further news. Some needed to take up her work, and try to "fill the gap," as well as to pray for her and minister to her needs. . . .

Switzerland, January 6, 1986

Between the last paragraph and this, my own pilgrimage has brought me through geographic space from Rochester, Minnesota, to Switzerland, and through *time*, from December 1985 to January 1986!

I've been doing a lot of thinking about *space* and *time* recently. Both separate us from each other, but space can be bridged by communication. Letters, phone calls, telegrams, packages, messages transmitted in one way or another put us into close touch. Travel by air, water, or land bring us face to face again. *Time* is a different thing. We can*not* travel back to a former time when we and our families were at another stage in life—all of us younger, all of us having a different outlook or expectation. Going back to the same place is *not* going back to the combination of people and happenings "as they were then." A family grows. Who would want to keep a dear baby from walking and talking? Who would try to keep a child from learning to read, or stop him or her from growing taller? Who really would want to stop the generations from following one another? People never feel *ready* to be grandparents, or great-uncles, nor to be great-grandparents. *Time* seems to go by more swiftly than the scenery from a train window. We may weep for a "replay" of one period or another; we may long to turn the "reel" as if for a film, and relive some hour, but we *know* within us that all of history has taken place during the intervening time, and to "relive" would take *all* the people involved in any historic moment being snatched out of the present!!!! It may be a subject for a novel, or a film, but I am sure no one would want to leave heaven for any "replay," nor really would any of us benefit from being "stalled." God has made so very clear to us that the *present* is important, and that there is an exciting future. When we begin to experience "forever" with perfection being a part of that forever *forever*, we'll be glad, I'm sure, for the rapidity of the passage of time, no matter how much we enjoyed one period or another. There is nothing but "better" in the *future* future!! And history is important and today is history in the making.

So here I am geographically in the same place again as I was 30 years ago. L'Abri had its first New Year's Eve celebration as 1955 turned into 1956. I was here again this year as 1985 turned into 1986. Chalet les Mélèzes has not changed all that much. Fire blazes in the same fireplace; the same painting is above it; some of the furniture is there. But Susan, who sat on that same fireplace wrapped in blankets because of her rheumatic fever during that period of being a 14-year-old, is now there as not only a mother of teenagers, but the grandmother of her missionary daughter Margaret's baby, Gordon, who is off in Nepal! Distances felt in both time and space! Communication eagerly looked for from "afar"!! The pilgrimage of each of the L'Abri Workers is "pressing on" in the midst of present conditions in various parts of the world's geography, each one doing something no one else could be doing, and which couldn't be done under any other condition at any other time. To me, the idea of a tapestry is not simply a "title," but a reality of life and history which cannot be analyzed and mathematically figured out, but which can be observed as we look back over periods of time. . . .

I have never been in Swedish L'Abri but I imagine walking in and out sniffing the fresh sea air, and nibbling Swedish biscuits with tea, as I contemplate the wonder of all that the Lord has done, and is doing, in the lives of these "pilgrims" and through their lives, since they first found their way (at different times in the past) to the little cluster of chalets on the side of a mountain in an obscure village in Switzerland where God chose to make His truth clear to a number of people!

Never forget that L'Abri began in the context of one family being thrust out from where they *were* "planting seed," to get rid of any danger of a harvest coming forth! In a "nutshell," that is a summary of the beginning of L'Abri. No one could have dreamed up a story of the last 30 years, nor of what is going on today. The reality is more "impossible" than fiction. What we as "pilgrims setting forth from Champéry" were praying for was the reality of God's existence to be demonstrated. What God answered with through the years has convinced many people that indeed He does exist and is the Creator, and has spoken in space and time and history, and that "to be a pilgrim" of His is a purpose worth choices which seem "risky" over and over again. Are L'Abri *Workers* the only ones who count as "the harvest" from that planting which God continued, so that there was a multiplied crop? Of course not. There are so many who have become "strangers and pilgrims" and are scattered geographically and scattered also as to what kinds of things they are doing, each one unique in filling a job, or a place that is significant in the midst of "the Battle." We couldn't possibly follow each one who came up the Swiss mountainside in answer to prayer, let alone to all the other branches and conferences, etc., even if we knew about each one!! But as I do remember Staffan's first time in Huemoz and remember our prayer in the car coming back from Migros grocery shopping, it is a bit overwhelming to think of what his book translations, and now his own writing, is doing in Sweden, along with Lisa, and the conferences, etc.

That same kind of overwhelming recognition of an amazing outpouring of answers to prayer during the history of the last 30 years came to me when I was in Holland at the end of September. As I walked through that marvelous old house in Utrecht I thought back through the years. It was in 1948 that we were first in Holland as a family, but this "new" L'Abri house in the heart of old Utrecht gives a thrilling view of what people were seeing 650 years ago!! The bells of the old cathedral, heard as well as seen, the hump of the bridge under which runs the constant flow of the canal, the one statue that survived the Reformation, mossy bricks, a wonderful grassy bank running along the canals, various old houses with distinct roofs and windows, all can be seen from the window of the bedroom on the second floor. Greta and Wim and a faithful group of hardworking Helpers have made a really beautiful place of the old house, with study rooms (complete with cassette tapes and cassette machines), a room for lectures and discussions opening out to the garden (which was a junkheap when they bought the old place that had been a store for years). Now Greta has made it a restored "secret garden" with lawn and flowers tucked in between buildings. I really was impressed with this L'Abri house in the old city where students may drop in from the university to study tapes, or to have lectures and discussions. Before seeing the house, I had spent that Sunday morning at the church service in the chapel at Eck-en-weil and had had lunch and a good talk with Greta, Wim, and Henk.

Yes, it was many years ago when Wim first weeded the garden at the side of Chalet les Mélèzes and met Greta who had come from Germany. It was long ago when their "pilgrimage" merged and they went on together. Dutch L'Abri has seen *many* changes and gone through various periods of history since Hans and Anky Rookmaaker had us in their home in Leiden with students eating supper as they asked questions and Fran and Hans answered them. But all this was known to our Heavenly

Father when we were asking for guidance as to what to do when we left Champéry!!! Our setting forth on *that* pilgrimage was also to have an historic effect in Holland. "Blessed are those whose strength is in you, who have set their hearts on pilgrimage. ... They go from strength to strength till each appears before God in Zion" (Psalm 84:5,7).

Fran's book, *The Christian Manifesto*, was translated into Dutch and had just come out, and the Evangelical wing of Dutch TV had asked me to come and speak at a meeting introducing it, and also to speak at a concert in The Hague with a fine pianist, Daniel Wayenberg, to speak about my new book, *Forever Music*. It was very fine to have Wim and Udo at the one-day conference at Dutch E.O. Television with me, as well as to visit L'Abri later. ...

Years ago now as Ellis Potter came over from Gentiana to help me make muffins or chop walnuts in the kitchen of Chardonnet, our conversation and prayer included many requests for that time, and for the future, but never would I have thought of the old round kitchen table itself one day sitting in the family room of The Old Orchard in Rochester, Minnesota, nor of Ellis needing prayer for *his* times in Poland!

In July Ellis was given a visa again, on the basis of an invitation from MONAR, the drug rehabilitation work in Poland. Ellis spoke in camps and churches and did private counseling and had discussions with Christians and also non-Christians in many places. Doors open, and people are on the other side of those doors! As we go on as "pilgrims" we need to be sensitive to being where the Lord would have us be. As for Mary,* her entrance into Poland has come on the basis of her background and skills as an occupational therapist. Mary was in Poland three weeks during the summer visiting parents' groups of handicapped children in Warsaw, Poznan, Kosalin, and Gdansk, where she spoke with parents, doctors, and therapists. Mary also spoke at a children's camp where there were 34 physically handicapped children among the 110 at the camp. Most of the disabled children had never been exposed to the gospel before and several of them accepted Christ as Saviour during the camp time.

Where does "preparation" end ... and "the work" begin?? I would say that for each of us, whether there is a language to be learned, or new skills to be learned, whether there is experience to be gained, or "tribulation" to be lived through because of the "patience," it is in the process of "producing." I would say that *if* I have learned anything during my years of being a pilgrim, it is that "preparation" *never* ends, but that at each stage of the journey "the work" *is* taking place. *Never* discount the past or the present, in peering around a bend, or over a hill, at "the future." ...

Vishal Mangalwadi and his wife, Ruth, have asked Udo, Anky, and Ranald and Sue to come to India for what will be the first L'Abri Conference in the Third World. Plans are being discussed to have it in Landour

*Ellis's wife.

near Mussoorie around September or October 1987. In fact, Vishal spoke both in the Dutch L'Abri and in Huemoz shortly before Christmas, giving his exciting and imaginative practical ideas as to a way of dealing with poverty there in India.

Ideas need to be discussed, taught, passed on; teaching needs verbalization in writing and with one's voice—whether in the kitchen, along paths in the mountains as people walk together by fields and gullies, or along the sea or the Mississippi River! But prayer, which is the other "constant" base of L'Abri, is a matter of communicating with the Living God at any *time* and in any *space*. This is a communication which cannot be cut off except by ourselves. We have never come to the end of the need of prayer. Yes, L'Abri is continuing. Any one day's stories could take pages to recount.

I'd like to tie up this letter with two "ribbons" from Colossians 4:6,2: "Let your speech be alway with grace, seasoned with salt, that ye may know how ye ought to answer every man" (vs. 6), and "Continue in prayer, and watch in the same with thanksgiving" (vs. 2).

With very much love and prayer for the new year, a year of constant prayer and well-salted discussion,

EDITH

1986

July 5, 1986   Rochester, Minnesota

Dearest Family:

July 30th was our first day of fasting and prayer in Chalet les Mélèzes. I'm talking about 1955. Whoever took part in that first day, those of us gathered in the living room on the ground floor of Mélèzes, and those in America, the Praying Family (about 26 people initially) who had promised to pray at least a half-hour every day, and as much of each Monday as possible, and then a full day of fasting and prayer whenever it would be called—all these people are now 31 years older than they were July 30, 1955!!!! . . .

L'Abri set forth 31 years ago to try to show forth the existence of God, by attempting (in our weakness and our proneness to imperfection in all areas) to live by faith, as well as by attempting to give careful answers to honest questions as to the reality of the existence of God.

Those who are going on now in the same "stream" of life are 31 years older than they were then, and some were not born yet. It is a practical demonstration of the relay of truth—the relay of the practical possibility of trusting the unchanging God to "reward those who earnestly seek Him." In any one moment of history it is those who are taking seriously their part of keeping an unbroken line of those living by faith, who are showing the existence of God to "this generation," as the generations follow one another. It all has to be done "in time."

Why am I so taken with the idea of doing what we are being given to do "in time"? It is because of two funerals that I have just attended. One near Philadelphia, and one in Dallas.

June 11th found me hurrying along through the Minneapolis airport to find the departure gate for Philadelphia. An unbelievable piece of news had changed my careful schedule for the week. The suddenness of death is always unbelievable, but especially when a healthy young senior in college is bursting with life one moment, and brain dead the next! After a normal Sunday evening at home, David DeMoss was driving a friend home in his convertible when a freak accident took place, instantly injuring his friend and giving David fatal injuries. How fragile is life; how true and important is the Lord's admonition to each of us through James—James 4:13–15—"Now listen you who say, 'today or tomorrow we will go to this or that city, spend a year there, carry on business and make money.' Why you do not even know what will happen tomorrow. What is your life? You are a mist that appears for a little while and then vanishes. Instead you ought to say, 'If it is the Lord's will we will live and do this or that.' " Although I have been taught from childhood always to say "D.V." or "Lord willing," the fragility of the thread of life always comes as a fresh shock. That, of course, is because death is an enemy, and Jesus says it is the *last* enemy that will be destroyed. The frail aspect of life only has come because of "the fall"—it is not what God made in the first place. . . .

David DeMoss was so alive with his keen sense of humor and seemingly unlimited ideas, a person who kept his friends and family laughing, or surprised, while at the same time he was very concerned about making truth known and doing kindnesses and thoughtful things for other people. "Why?" Some are sure to ask. Why? This is the reason I wrote my book, *Affliction*. It would take all 250 pages to properly search through the Bible. I would say this to me—and to you—no one knows how long, or how short, a time it takes to affect history, to change history. Not one of us know *which* choice we are to make, or should make, is the most important choice we will *ever* make, and will affect the piece of history we are meant to affect in our lifetime. It is quite possible that David affected history as much in his 22 years as others have in 50 or 75 years. Our "battle" is in the midst of an ongoing battle. The book of Job makes this clear to us. Victory in the "heavenly battle" can bring joy and glory to God, and cause angels to rejoice, whether fought on the battlefield of a hospital bed, a Siberian camp, a prison, or by one of us suddenly dying, or sitting beside a loved one we do *not* want to be separated from. The battle can be fought in actively warring against evil, or in inwardly trusting God, and loving Him while the effects of Lucifer's rebellion are filling us with grief, or pain.

Two-and-a-half years ago, in the Aigle Hospital in Switzerland, a phone conversation was taking place. Mary Crowley was saying, "Nancy DeMoss and I have been talking together and if you can bring Fran by Swissair to New York's airport, we will share the expense of flying him in Nancy's plane to Rochester to St. Mary's Hospital."

Choice? Decision? "In time"? In time to affect history.

Other people were involved. Mary Crowley called Swissair's Paul Tiffen in the New York airport, and he kindly made arrangements for an ambulance to meet the plane. Our children and the L'Abri Family prayed earnestly for detailed guidance and strength and wisdom in choices all along the way. Debby came along to help in that very difficult trip. *Each* choice mattered.

But as I thought about all this during these last two weeks, I realized that one of the crucial "in time" choices was the choice to go together and provide that plane. The arrival through snow and ice that December 8th day was "in time." Fran lived through the night. He lived five months more—because of decisions made "in time."

Can we possibly trace history this way? Yes, in bits and pieces we can. We don't have a complete picture ever, but we can trace enough to have a feel of the awesome importance of choices affecting history. Had Fran died in Aigle, *The Great Evangelical Disaster* would not have been finished. Had he died in Aigle, he would not have asked me to buy a house in Rochester. Had I not bought a house in Rochester, he would not have been surrounded by this "home" during his last days. But also, Mary Crowley would not have had the strong idea to tell me that day two years ago to go look for a Steinway piano (she called it being nudged by God to do so). Had I not had that Steinway piano arrive two years ago this July 6th, I would not have thought of writing *Forever Music*. Had I not written the book, I would not have met the people at Steinway, included Franz Mohr's life story, nor had the concert at Alice Tully Hall to introduce it.

Mary Crowley has had a battle with cancer this past year herself. But Mary felt convinced that it was a good thing to have the concert with Guarneri Quartet members and John Van Buskirk at the piano, and both encouraged me and helped financially. When the evening came for the concert we were very aware that all the combined prayer of all of you, the hard work of sending out invitations to the New York music world, people in Washington, D.C., in government circles, people from the Broadway theater circles, etc., etc., and the attention to detail (such as flowers and ficus trees and food for the reception), had *not* been done in vain. The concert was a tremendous success, with a special atmosphere indeed, marvelous music and an enthusiastic and responsive audience. Franky introduced the evening, and me; Bob introduced the new book and presented me with roses and the first copy of the book from Thomas Nelson, and I simply said: "For 31 years we have lived in a chalet on the side of an Alpine mountain with an open door. People have been free to come in, sit by a roaring fire, and ask the deep questions of life: meaning, purpose, origins—with a cup of tea to sip and a conversation continuing for hours. I have had a dream. I have wanted to drop that Swiss chalet into the heart of Lincoln Center for one evening. The music is the warmth of the fire. This book is the conversation, to take home and have, as you read, alone."

Sitting at the front was Mary Crowley. After 34 radium treatments, she had *come*! She had donned a lovely long pink, sparkling dress and was smiling her pleasure over the victory! She had requested lots of flowers. "*Who* made the flowers?" she had said to me. "Well, He made them to *look* at, *not to eat*! So *please,* have lots of flowers! How can they look at them if they aren't there?" Her pleasure in the greatness of the music and the satisfying sight of the flowers was complete. God's creation to hear and to observe! Beauty!! Now she is seeing more perfect beauty. . . .

I want you *and* me to concentrate on this fact. Mary had a two-year period to make some choices which brought about my writing the book, doing the concert, and completing that portion of a project which will have a "harvest" *later.* And she *did* do it "in time."

You see, after I came home from the memorial service and reception in Bryn Mawr, both weeping with, and rejoicing with, the dear family—mother, brothers, and sisters of David as he had gone to be with *his* father as well as his Heavenly Father, I was to hear of Mary's being back in the hospital.

It isn't that *this* was Mary's *only* piece of work in the past two years. Of course, she had many, many, *many* things she was doing. However, the precision of this piece of history is so *vivid,* that it illustrates to us enough to help us to *pray, pray, and pray* again, that we will make *our* choices and decisions *in time.* The Lord is the only One who knows *how much time* each of us has for whatever it is He wants us to complete.

Mary died on June 18th. A little less than two years before she had had the assurance that the piano's being a "must"! Absent from the body is to be immediately present with the Lord. In His presence is fullness of joy. Fullness of joy is a complete joy that we have not yet experienced. As I flew to Dallas, thinking, praying, going over the past two years, is it any wonder my mind filled with instances of people through centuries, the Lord's people, doing things "in time"?? . . . There is a "forever" that has a new beginning, but in the continuity of history of which we are now in the midst, we can observe some of the sheer wonder of how things fit together.

When you hear the two words *patchwork quilts,* what comes into your mind's eye? Do you think of your grandmother's quilts handed down for generations? Did you go to the recent "quilt show" in New York and marvel over intricate designs? Do you know that Shirley Heibert's mother-in-law in a small Canadian town sits making tiny stitches, evening after evening, to produce one more beautiful quilt? . . . Do you have materials and patterns to put patch against patch, stitch after stitch . . . to gradually form a "whole" wonderful art work? That "whole" can be appreciated long, long before it is finished—in the making, each patch is interesting, unique, beautiful, a contrast in color or because of originality and diversity—and gradually each patch begins to fit into its place in the whole. . . . There is a mind that has been "seeing" the whole from the beginning of the faithful attention to the tiny bits and pieces. Shapes, sizes, colors, textures need the diversity of each other to produce the beauty and completeness of the whole.

No illustration fits perfectly, of course, but I have been having multitudinous *glimpses* these past months. In and out of New York, in Steinway's basement or signing books, sitting on the floor with Josephine going over names and addresses . . . talking with Caroline at The Lambs or with Orville or Richard . . . watching Franz Mohr and Richard Probst carefully check Horowitz's piano as it has its legs removed and is carefully wrapped in green padded covers, . . . sitting signing books in the hall at the L'Abri Conference in Austin, . . . then sitting signing in Calvary Book Store on 57th St. West, as people, people, people walked by, some pushing the door in . . . It seems I have been aware of "patches" in an *enormous patchwork quilt!!!*

The concert April 27th at Alice Tully Hall would make a colorful intricate "patch"! How could you embroider John Van Buskirk at the piano blending, soaring, fitting in so perfectly with Arnold Steinhardt, John Dalley, and David Soyer at their instruments? The applause expressed appreciation, audible thanks, and the desire for more. That applause was a strong vote for "forever" to be real in relationship to music. The opposite of "forever music" is "forever silence." What an applause for the creatures God made in His image, creatures capable of making instruments, of composing music, of performing that music and with ears to *hear* and to *be* a sensitive audience with capability to respond with applause saying, "More . . . more."

But another "patch" would have to be added for the audience . . . in fact each person there would be a "story patch." How did they get there? Where did each one come from philosophically as well as physically? . . . "Did you see Os and Jenny and Ann Brown and Suzie Barber?" . . . "Why, Cynthia came from London . . . and she's there with those Korean musicians from New York." . . . "There are Bob and Avis talking to the Prentices who flew in from Hawaii . . . and Dr. Petitt from Mayo Clinic and his daughter." . . . "Susan Macaulay just followed Mary Crowley out to say goodbye to her, as the reception is too much." . . . "Linney Dey is here from the Boston area . . . but her mother, Barbara, is here too." . . . "Is Franz Mohr here?" "No, he has to be in Moscow tuning and voicing Horowitz's piano . . . but that is his wife, Elizabeth, and his daughter who came from Gordon College for the concert." . . . "Oh Prisca, did you know that Betty Schlichter came from Philadelphia—and sat right in front of me?"

There were people from the Cleveland Orchestra talking to musicians from the New York Philharmonic; advertising men from Broadway talking to someone who is a writer for the Letterman show. There was a doctor from Long Island talking to a researcher from the Rockefeller Institute. There was a Houston couple talking to Washington, D.C., friends, and so many lawyers discovering each other. There were writers and economists asking, "Who in the world is this woman—and what is this book about?" But the book was under each of their arms. . . . Patches? Too many colors, too much embroidery! A confusing blur of conversations ... but examine one more carefully, under a magnifying glass.

I turned to make my way up an aisle at intermission and two fine-looking black couples approached me. I recognized one couple, and the man broke into a smile saying, "The last time I saw you, you were drying your hair on a balcony in Italy, on the island of Elba." "Oh, Mr. and Mrs. English," I exclaimed. "That was *so* long ago—years and years—how amazing. I'm so glad you could come up from Washington for this concert." "Yes, and we brought our friends too." A lifetime? A small piece of time? The significance of people? Does God *care* about people? My feeling at that point was one of great thankfulness for the personalness of our personal God. I had such a vivid memory of that afternoon, drying my hair before dressing for dinner and getting into an important conversation at dinner with this couple, praying through the years and keeping the address, keeping in touch.... Emily Remler with her father was the next surprise in that crowded aisle. A needle in a haystack? The whole of New York? How could it be that *one* person would matter that much! But, you see, God is personal as well as infinite.

I was sitting in the Calvary Baptist Book Store on West 57th Street, signing books. Suddenly, a very familiar person leaned over the table, her brown eyes smiling into mine, "Do you remember a little girl at Chalet les Mélèzes, 26 years ago or more? Debra?" I burst into tears and jumped up to go around the table to hug her. "Oh, Debra! Debby has prayed for you *every* day all these years! How completely wonderful. Where are you now?" This was someone for whom we have longed—a 12-year-old schoolmate of Debby's from Ecole Beau Soleil. The reason I am telling you this in a bit of detail is that *you must* keep on praying for whomever *you* are praying! Don't give up. We have spent hours together since then. Debra has read *Forever Music* already and says, "I have savoured every word. It is so succinct. You write so beautifully." Debra is a writer of novels and poetry, daughter of the writer I talked to toward the end of the first chapter in *Christianity Is Jewish*. She is one of the ones for whom I wrote that book! The most exciting thing *always* is the sheer wonder and awe of recognizing His gentle "finding" of people ... lost like a "needle in a haystack" ... *time* ... and *space* ... separate us from people we pray will be found, but the *One* to whom we pray knows where the ones we are praying for are! ...

A map in the shape of South Africa is stitched on to the next patch. Ranald, Wim and Ellis need to be embroidered on that map as they went in response to requests for L'Abri Conferences there. This "happening" was not without danger. Not only did they report exciting response but also the feeling that they would have had so much more to do had it been possible to stay longer, but we have received a very enthusiastic letter from a South African fellow telling us how very much that conference, and the men's lectures as well as the books, have meant to him and many others. He pleaded for a "return" time, and expressed a desire to go to one of the L'Abri branches for study. . . .

Perhaps some patches should be made with question marks, each question mark could be portraying an "opportunity to pray with trust for the Lord's solution." Picture Molle, Sweden in one. A tiny view of the village with a house Staffan and Lisa have had to leave because the lease for renting it is up and the people don't want to rent any longer. There needs to be a "door" . . . with Lisa and Staffan on the other side of it . . . to open when people knock!

Another question mark might simply circle the word "Where?" with a tiny question mark inside it. "Where" is a word needing trust, utter dependence upon the Lord, and a certainty that He *will* answer prayer for guidance and answer the prayer with a solution. Several Workers may move into another part of the work. Pray for the "right doors." . . .

Go back to another patch stitched in where the *Forever Music* patches are and you will find a Japanese garden pictured. There you will see Noriko Shimada, whose name some of you will recognize. Noriko is a Japanese mother of three children now. When she was a girl some years ago, she came to L'Abri after completing her Ph.D. in Syracuse University. She studied, asked questions, and became a convinced believer and was baptized in the chapel. She sadly broke her engagement because her fiancé was a Buddhist . . . but the story has a happy chapter when her husband, also getting his Ph.D. at Syracuse, became a convinced believer with Jeremy and Lucinda Jackson. They came to L'Abri as part of their honeymoon when Fran and I were working on writing projects. She is the one who translated the L'Abri book into a beautiful Japanese book. Now? Well, Horowitz (the great 82-year-old pianist) decided to accept some engagements to play in Japan. Horowitz does *not* go anywhere to play without Franz Mohr, which means that Franz not only has been able to give some top Japanese musicians copies of the book *Forever Music*, but also we gave him Noriko's address and phone number and he has taken them the book. The Cleveland Orchestra later went to Japan and one day Daniel and Stephen Majeske gave an amazing concert in a Japanese church with the surprise discovery of a huge poster announcing this as a "Forever Music" concert! Who designs patches in history?? . . .

I phoned Southborough and talked to Darby Zink who, with her husband, works in L'Abri there with Dick and Mardi Keyes and Susan McNabb. A short time ago Darby had to be taken to the emergency room at the hospital. She felt she was being well cared for and sent David back to give his evening lecture at L'Abri. Although it was Friday, three orthodox Muslims had come to hear this lecture. After the lecture, they rushed out the door. Quickly they spread their rugs outdoors for their Friday time of prayer. This orthodox duty accomplished, the three came back inside and stayed very late for the discussion! The prayer "please send the people of your choice, Lord" is answered in diverse ways!! . . .

I'm speaking to the L'Abri Praying Family, don't get discouraged; don't give up. We need to keep on—from strength to strength—*in time*, our piece of time.

How do you describe L'Abri? How do I describe L'Abri? "Tiny" . . . "A tiny work." "Small . . . materially weak . . . very few resources, humanly looking at it." "Oh, but the sheer *wonder* is the reality of an answer to our basic prayer. What was our basic prayer as Fran and I set forth to cut ourselves loose from the "security" of a mission board and said we were going to be directly under the Lord's direction and would ask Him to supply our needs? That basic resolve, that basic prayer was expressed in these words: *"Oh, Lord, please make Thy existence known through our lives and our work.* Please show people *You* are there; *You* exist."

Remember Gideon? He came from a poor family. His own place was "least in my father's house." When God told him He was going to use him to save Israel, he was *really* fearful, and pleaded for "signs" as a matter of reassurance. Re-read Judges 6 and 7 and remind yourself how *patient* God was with his asking for repeated signs. Yes . . . the fleece was wet and the ground dry . . . but . . . "Please, God, do it again in the opposite way!" But please do read again the *reason* given—"The people are too many . . . lest Israel vaunt themselves against me saying . . . *my own hand* has saved me . . ." Too many . . . 32,000 . . . too many . . . 10,000 . . . Then came the tiny 300. Three hundred men with such unlikely equipment following the Lord's direction and not turning back, and not trying to be "safe" by the current standards . . . not being clever by an statistical likelihoods of "success or failure" that would have been estimated by the standards of that time . . . pitchers, lamps, horns!!! Why? That men might know that *God* had delivered the Midianites into their hands. That men might know that *God exists* and that nothing is impossible to *Him*!!

David faces Goliath with a sling and small round stones—same result—so that people could *know* that the God of Israel exists!

Elijah standing before the prophets of Baal, and before Israel at that time said "Lord God of Abraham, Isaac and of Israel, let it be known this day that thou art God in Israel and that I am thy servant, and that I have done all these things at thy word." "Then the fire fell." Result? People fell on their faces and cried out, "The Lord of Israel, *He* is God."

Paul—in II Corinthians 12:3-10—is pleading for relief from that thorn in his flesh. We have so often come to the Lord in the same kind of situation. The answer to prayer is *His* sufficient grace *in* our weakness— *His* strength to go on. Why? Really, it is the same reason given . . . it is that people might know that what is being done isn't because of tremendous strength and ease of taking the next step, but an opportunity to make completely clear to some watching "men" . . . (i.e., people of this moment of history) . . . that indeed God exists—there is no other explanation of the "how" of what has taken place.

L'Abri has constantly been given the opportunity of being a "Gideon," a "David," an "Elijah," a "Paul in chains or with a thorn" . . . time and again it has been *observable* that the power is of God and *not* of us, which in turn speaks to any who really are searching, that *He exists.* The repeated opportunities to *trust* are repeated times of *needing to trust* because we have *no* solution other than His providing His solution to present needs.

With very much love in *Him* Who is able to change the picture as we bring *Him* our needs,

EDITH

AFTERWORD

"Is that all?" "Is that the end?" "Isn't there any more?" "What happened next?" "I want to *see* for myself."

Have you ever been homesick? Homesickness for a *place*, or homesickness for a *person* carries with it—homesickness for a *time*. We want to "go back" and find the lilac bushes as they were, the trees the same, the vegetable garden and flower beds as they were when we first thrilled over the rosebuds or the first violets. We want to find people there—as they were—cooking, singing, blowing on a fire in the fireplace, bringing in a steaming pot of tea and a white folded napkin covering a fragrant basket of hot muffins or orange rolls. We want to go back to *time*, as it was, *people* that have not grown older, *places* that have not changed. We want to roll back the film and have a replay! . . . a replay of some bits of life.

Reading these old letters has accomplished that in a measure, but only in a measure. We can't go to Dutch L'Abri and find Hans Rookmaaker there ready to lecture to us, or answer our questions on art history, or discuss modern art. We can't go back to Bellevue and find Anne Bates there and listen to Jane playing her small instrument to accompany her leading the children in singing Sunday afternoon. We can't see the organ in its original polished wood with Dolly playing her collection of music . . . one at a time on it! Why not? Hans Rookmaaker is in heaven, not in Holland. Anne Bates is in heaven and Bellevue is no longer the rehabilitation center, so Sunday afternoons are different . . . and the organ, although restored, has a properly beautiful and appropriate paint to cover up the wood spoiled by the fire, and Dolly's music became ashes . . . that is, the printed pages did!!

Life is not a piece of theater. A production may last on Broadway for years, and grandchildren may see *Mousetrap* in much the same form

A page turns to a new chapter of life ... different ... but full of
as many or more new and creative possibilities as ever!

as their grandparents— *but* life is not like that. It is fresh every day. A new day has not been lived before. You and I are not living a replay, we are not walking a path we have walked before. We are different this year than last year . . . the trees and bushes have grown and changed, a house has been torn down . . . or the physical "house" or bodies of people we used to discuss with have been "torn down" by death, and we cannot have that longed-for conversation or advice.

Ah, but—change is not the end. There is a continuity, a flow of continuity like a flowing stream. We come to Joshua and find God saying to him, "Moses my servant is dead; now therefore arise, go over this Jordan. . . ." The command is to go on to the next chapter of history, which has a connection to the past, and into the future.

Whether it is my personal life, the life of L'Abri, or your life, the God of Abraham, Isaac, and Jacob, says to us today . . . "Be strong and of a good courage; be not afraid, neither be thou dismayed: for the Lord thy God is with thee withersoever thou goest." *He*—our Father in Heaven— is our continuity. He never changes, and He is always there. . . . The present is not isolated from the past . . . nor from the future. The story of His people continues!

With love,

EDITH